Series on China–ASEAN Relations

ISSN: 2529-8135 (Print)
ISSN: 2529-8143 (Online)

Description

China–ASEAN Relations: Cooperation and Development is an annual publication. This annal focuses on the latest trends in China and ASEAN relations. The book chapters are contributed by Chinese scholars from China–ASEAN Research Institute of Guangxi University and China–ASEAN Collaborative Innovation Center for Regional Development.

This annal introduces readers to the issues, debates and literatures related to China–ASEAN cooperation, achievements and problems in the areas of politics, economy, diplomacy, security, defense, maritime and culture. It also explores the relations and cooperation between China and ASEAN countries in the realms of politics, economics, diplomacy, society and culture.

China–ASEAN Relations

Cooperation and Development

Volume 2

SERIES ON CHINA–ASEAN RELATIONS

China–ASEAN Relations
Cooperation and Development

Volume 2

Editor

LIANG Ying

Guangxi University, China

中国社会科学出版社
CHINA SOCIAL SCIENCES PRESS

World Scientific

NEW JERSEY • LONDON • SINGAPORE • BEIJING • SHANGHAI • HONG KONG • TAIPEI • CHENNAI • TOKYO

Published by

World Scientific Publishing Co. Pte. Ltd.
5 Toh Tuck Link, Singapore 596224
USA office: 27 Warren Street, Suite 401-402, Hackensack, NJ 07601
UK office: 57 Shelton Street, Covent Garden, London WC2H 9HE

China-ASEAN Relations (v. 2)
ISBN 978-981-120-293-3

British Library Cataloguing-in-Publication Data
A catalogue record for this book is available from the British Library.

Sponsored by B & R Book Program

《中国-东盟合作发展报告》2015–2016
Originally published in Chinese by China Social Sciences Press

For any available supplementary material, please visit
https://www.worldscientific.com/worldscibooks/10.1142/11348#t=suppl

Desk Editors: Aanand Jayaraman/Lixi Dong

Typeset by Stallion Press
Email: enquiries@stallionpress.com

Printed in Singapore

Editorial Committee

Preface

Seeking development and win–win outcomes amidst cooperation is a long-term consensus between China and the member States of ASEAN (Association of Southeast Asian Nations); it is also the inevitable choice for China and ASEAN countries for seeking self-development within the new domestic and international situation. In 2015, the ASEAN Community was established and the construction of the Belt and the Road, put forward by China, was initiated; China released the *Vision and Actions on Jointly Building the Silk Road Economic Belt and the 21st Century Maritime Silk Road*, and the economy entered the new normal, bringing new opportunities and challenges to the development of China–ASEAN cooperation.

As the important region for promoting the Belt and Road Initiative, ASEAN is crucial to smoothly pushing forward China's opening up and cooperation in the new period. In 2015, China continued to practice the foreign policy of bringing harmony, security and prosperity to its neighboring countries and features amity, sincerity, mutual benefit and inclusiveness towards those countries; China's political and diplomatic relations with ASEAN countries have generally been stable; although there was interference involving the issue of the South China Sea, bilateral political cooperation has been still further developed and deepened. In the severe international economic situation, a new development was achieved in China–ASEAN economic and trade cooperation, the two sides signed the agreement on upgrading the China–ASEAN Free Trade Area (CAFTA) and the status of economic and trade partner was consolidated. China won the bidding for the Jakarta–Bandung High-speed Railway Project in Indonesia, while the construction of the China–Laos and the China–Thailand high-speed railways indicates that China–ASEAN cooperation has reached a new level. However, bilateral cooperation has also faced a number of challenges involving institutional differences, the issue of the South China Sea and trade demarcation caused by the TPP; China–ASEAN cooperation should be promoted by enhancing mutual political trust while consolidating economic foundation.

It is necessary to fully follow the progress in China–ASEAN cooperation in various fields, sum up the experience, discover the drawbacks and judge the trends; for the people from various sectors of society, this is the foundation for pushing forward practical China–ASEAN cooperation; for the scholars engaged in China–ASEAN research, this is conducive to increasing the social value of academic research. As an emerging institution focusing on China–ASEAN research, the China–ASEAN Research Institute of Guangxi University has been actively carrying out external research cooperation while vigorously building its scientific research team and increasing its scientific research strength. In 2015, the *Progress and Review of China–ASEAN Cooperation (Annual Report)*, a major special research project carried out by the China–ASEAN Research Institute of Guangxi University and the China–ASEAN Collaborative Innovation Center for Regional Development, was implemented in the second year. At the same time, the China–ASEAN Research Institute of Guangxi University and the China–ASEAN Collaborative Innovation Center for Regional Development initiated the emergency project "The Belt and the Road Plan and Analysis of ASEAN Countries' Interest Appeal" and took one year to go deep into various countries to carry out an in-depth survey, from the perspective of social cognition, on the basic perception and attitude of ASEAN's political, academic and business circles and people within other classes regarding the Belt and the Road Initiative, thus gaining all-round understanding and research achievements. These efforts are fully reflected in this book.

With attention to and anticipation from the people from various sectors of society, the *Annual Report on the Development of China–ASEAN Cooperation (2015–2016)* will certainly be published. We hope that this report on the development of cooperation can stand the test of peers and time. The journey ahead is long, we will stay true to the mission and carry out relentless explorations!

Liang Ying
August 16, 2016

About the Editor

Liang Ying is a Professor, doctoral supervisor, currently Vice-chairman of the Education, Scientific, Cultural and Health Committee of the 12th People's Congress of the Guangxi Zhuang Autonomous Region, Director of the China–ASEAN Research Institute of Guangxi University, Vice-chairman of the Guangxi Federation of Social Sciences, the person in charge of the Group of Key Disciplines under the 211 Project — the Group of Disciplines Concerning Research on China–ASEAN Economics, Trade Cooperation and Development. He is mainly engaged in research on history, administration science, China–ASEAN issues and Party building. He has published 11 works, including *Research on the Path and Form for China's State Formation during the Early Stage*. He has published more than 40 papers in authoritative and important journals, including *Historiography Quarterly*, *Collected Papers of History Studies*, *People's Daily*, *Guangming Daily*, and the *Asia-Pacific Economic Review*.

About the Contributors

Fan Zuojun is a Doctor of Economics, second-grade professor, doctoral supervisor at the Business School of Guangxi University, Vice-president of Guangxi University, Executive Deputy Director of the China–ASEAN Research Institute, Director of the Institute of Southeast Asian Studies. The person selected for the National Talents Project, state-level young expert with outstanding contributions, the leader of Innovation Team under the Cheung Kong Scholars and Innovation Team Development Program initiated by the Ministry of Education, the person selected for the New Century Excellent Talents Support Program under the Ministry of Education, Bagui Scholar of the Guangxi Zhuang Autonomous Region. He has published nearly 80 papers in a number of journals, including the *Economic Research Journal* and *Management World*.

Lu Jianren is a Doctor of Economics, chief research fellow at the China–ASEAN Research Institute of Guangxi University, research fellow at the National Institute of International Strategy, the Chinese Academy of Social Sciences. He has been engaged in research on the issues concerning the Asian-Pacific, East Asian and Southeast Asian economy and ASEAN for a long time. He has published a number of works, including *Asian-Pacific Economy in the 1990s*, *Asia-Pacific Economic Cooperation and China*, *ASEAN's Today and Tomorrow*, and many academic papers. Currently, he has been appointed as the Chinese expert and famous person at the Expert and Famous Person

Team of ASEAN Regional Forum (ARF) by the Ministry of Foreign Affairs of China and a member of the East Asia Business Council by China Council for the Promotion of International Trade.

Yue Guining is a Professor, master supervisor at the Thailand Institute of the China–ASEAN Research Institute of Guangxi University, the Business School of Guangxi University; he is mainly engaged in research on international finance. He has published such works as *The Practice of the Financial System and Monetary Policy in ASEAN Countries*, *An Analysis of Thailand's Investment Environment*, and more than 30 papers in China.

Qin Jianwen is a Doctor of Management, professor, doctoral supervisor at the Business School of Guangxi University, Director of the Audit Office of Guangxi University, research fellow at the Research Center for the China–ASEAN Fiscal and Financial Policy at the China–ASEAN Research Institute, a member of the Expert Consultative Committee of the Nanning Municipal Government. He is mainly engaged in research on financial institutions, the financial market and the development of the Beibu Gulf. He has published more than 30 papers in such important journals as *Studies of International Finance*.

Li Hong is a Doctor of Management, Director of the Institute of International Relations at the China–ASEAN Research Institute of Guangxi University, professor, doctoral supervisor at the Business School of Guangxi University. He is mainly engaged in research on geo-economics. He has published such works as *China–ASEAN Cooperation: From 20 to 30?*, *An Economic Analysis of International Cultural Cooperation — Take the China–ASEAN Region as an Example*, and more than 60 papers at home and abroad.

Wang Yuzhu is a Doctor of Economics, research fellow, doctoral supervisor at the National Institute of International Strategy at the Chinese Academy of Social Sciences, visiting research fellow at the China–ASEAN Research Institute of Guangxi University. He is mainly engaged in research on the issues concerning Asia-Pacific regional cooperation, ASEAN and China–ASEAN relations. He has published such works as *ASEAN in 40 Years*, and many academic papers at home and abroad.

Liu Yaping is a Doctor of Science (Ecology), professor, doctoral supervisor at the Business School of Guangxi University. She is mainly engaged in research on the issues concerning tourist economy, ecological economy and ASEAN. She has published more than 60 relevant academic papers in such journals as SSCI, CSSCI, and four works, including *Ecological Culture and the Sustainable Development of Tourism*, *Analysis and Research Report on Investment in Cambodia*.

Huang Ai'lian is a Doctor of Law, Director of the Myanmar Institute at the China–ASEAN Research Institute of Guangxi University, professor, master supervisor at the Business School of Guangxi University. She is mainly engaged in research on China–ASEAN cooperation on tourism and Myanmar issues. She has published such works as *Analysis Report on Myanmar's Investment Environment*; *Restrictions and Breakthroughs: Tourism Cooperation in the Beibu Gulf Region*, and more than 50 papers in domestic and foreign journals.

Jin Dan is a Doctor of Economics, associate research fellow at the China–ASEAN Research Institute of Guangxi University, Director of the Vietnam Institute, master supervisor. She is mainly engaged in research on the issues concerning ASEAN economy and Vietnam. She has published such works as *Social Capital and Regional Economic Growth*, and a number of papers in very important national journals.

Sheng Yuxue is a Doctor of Economics, assistant research fellow at the China–ASEAN Research Institute of Guangxi University. He is mainly engaged in research on spatial economy and regional economic cooperation. He has published many relevant academic papers in such journals as SSCI, CSSCI.

Contents

Introduction

This book is an achievement of research carried out by the China–ASEAN Research Institute of Guangxi University and the China–ASEAN Collaborative Innovation Center for Regional Development. The book is divided into six parts: Part 1 is a general report, the "Review of China–ASEAN Cooperation in 2015 and the Outlook on the Future", which presents relevant achievements and issues in China–ASEAN cooperation in the political, economic, diplomatic, security, military, marine and cultural fields, and the outlook for the trend in cooperation for 2016. Part 2 provides individual reports on the cooperation between China and the ASEAN countries in 2015, including brief comments on the political, economic, diplomatic, social and cultural fields of these countries and an analysis of important events in these countries, an evaluation and analysis of the cooperation between China and ASEAN countries in various fields in 2015 and the outlook for bilateral cooperation in 2016. Part 3 is a special report on China–ASEAN cooperation in 2015, covering ASEAN's understanding of and response to the Belt and the Road Initiative, the implementation of the Belt and Road Initiative within the ASEAN countries, China–ASEAN cooperation in the economic, trade, financial and ecological environmental fields, the China–ASEAN Exposition and Guangxi–ASEAN cooperation. Part 4 is the evaluation and analysis of hot issues concerning Southeast Asia in 2015, covering the South China Sea arbitration case initiated by the Philippines, the construction of the ASEAN Community, Myanmar's elections, the Bangkok explosion and

Vietnam's accession to the TPP. Part 5 is the research and a brief comment on ASEAN countries. Part 6 is the chronicle of events involving China–ASEAN cooperation in 2015. With rich content, 20 statistical tables in the Appendix cover the overview of the latest developments in ASEAN's economy, the data concerning China–ASEAN economic, trade and investment cooperation and the trade between China's provinces (autonomous regions) and ASEAN.

Part 1
General Report

Chapter 1

Review of China–ASEAN Cooperation in 2015 and the Outlook on the Future

Research Group*

I. The Political and Diplomatic Fields

In 2015, the political and diplomatic relations between China and the ASEAN countries were generally stable. Although there was some disturbance

*The composition and work division of the Research Group are shown below: the group leader: Lu Jianren, chief researcher at the China–ASEAN Research Institute of Guangxi University, responsible for designing the research subject, examining and revising the chapters; the political and diplomatic fields: Gu Qiang, Deputy Director, associate professor at the Vietnam Research Institute of the China–ASEAN Research Institute of Guangxi University; the economic field: Sheng Yuxue, doctor of economics at the China–ASEAN Research Institute of Guangxi University; Sun Shuo, doctor of economics at the China–ASEAN Research Institute of Guangxi University; the security, military, maritime cooperation fields: Lu Wanguo, research assistant at the Institute of International Relations of the China–ASEAN Research Institute of Guangxi University; Li Hong, Director, professor, doctoral supervisor at the Institute of International Relations of the China–ASEAN Research Institute of Guangxi University; the cultural field: Pan Chunjian, Director, professor at the Institute of National Culture (Luoyue) of the China–ASEAN Research Institute of Guangxi University; Lan Xiangyun, Deputy Director, research assistant at the Institute of National Culture (Luoyue) of the China–ASEAN Research Institute of Guangxi University; the outlook for future cooperation: Liu Wen, researcher at the Brunei Research Institute of the China–ASEAN Research Institute of Guangxi University.

stemming from the South China Sea issue, the political cooperation between the two sides was still further expanded and intensified. This is mainly reflected in the following three aspects:

1. There were frequent high-level reciprocal visits for enhancing strategic mutual trust

In 2015, high-level reciprocal visits frequently occurred between China and ASEAN countries, and these visits featured diplomacy at the levels of the head of state, government, parliament, political party and local levels. Frequent exchanges enhanced the strategic mutual trust between the two sides, laid a solid political foundation for friendly cooperation between them and brought more strategic mutual trust.

In April 2016, Chinese President Xi Jinping attended, on invitation, the activity of commemorating the 60th Anniversary of the Asian–African Conference — the Bandung Conference — and the 10th Anniversary of the New Asian–African Strategic Partnership in Indonesia, and met with the President of Indonesia Joko Widodo and the President of Myanmar Thein Sein. During the period November 5–7, Chinese President Xi Jinping paid a state visit to Vietnam and Singapore. It was Chinese President Xi Jinping's first visit to Vietnam since he was elected the General Secretary of the Communist Party of China and also was the first state visit to Vietnam by a top Chinese leader in nearly 9 years; therefore, this visit was of great significance. During his visit to Singapore, Chinese President Xi Jinping had a historic meeting with Taiwan leader Ma Ying-jeou, which also demonstrated the trust between the leaders of Mainland China and Taiwan in Singapore. On November 17, Chinese President Xi Jinping arrived at Manila, the Philippines to attend the 23rd APEC Informal Leaders' Meeting, during which he had a short talk with the President of the Philippines Benigno Aquino III and met with the the Prime Minister of Malaysia Perdana Menteri. In November 2015, Chinese Premier Li Keqiang visited Malaysia and attended the 18th China–ASEAN (10+1) Leaders' Meeting, the 18th ASEAN, China, Japan and South Korea (10+3) Leaders' Meeting and the 10th East Asia Summit in Kuala Lumpur, Malaysia, during which he met with the Prime Minister of Laos, Thongsing Thammavong. Meanwhile, a number of leaders of the ASEAN countries paid friendly visits to China, which yielded fruitful results. In March 2015, the President of Indonesia Joko Widodo visited China, the two sides agreed to strengthen the comprehensive strategic partnership between their two countries, and developed the *Future Five-Year Action Plan for the Comprehensive Strategic Partnership between China and Indonesia*; the two leaders also signed eight agreements concerning cooperation on the construction of infrastructures, aviation and aerospace development and maritime search and rescue, including the memorandum involving the construction of the high-speed railroad from Jakarta, the Capital of Indonesia, to Bandung. In April 2015, Nguyễn Phú Trọng, the General Secretary of the Communist Party of Vietnam, visited China, which was the first meeting between the top leaders of the Communist Party of China and the Communist Party of Vietnam after the fierce maritime conflict between China and Vietnam in 2014; bilateral relations had been put on the right track. In June, Aung San Suu Kyi, the Leader of the National League for Democracy in Myanmar, visited China, laying a foundation for the healthy development of Sino-Myanmar Relations after the National League for Democracy came to power. On September 3, the activity of commemorating the 70th Anniversary of the Victory of the Chinese People's Resistance Against Japanese Aggression and the World Anti-fascist War was held in Beijing; the President of Laos, Choummaly Sayasone, the President of Myanmar, Thein Sein, the President of Vietnam, Trương Tấn Sang, the King of Cambodia, Norodom Sihamoni, and the Deputy Prime Minister and Defense Minister of Thailand, Prawit Wongsuwan, visited China and attended relevant activities; Cambodia sent a representative team to participate in the military parade.

2. Border issues were properly resolved to stabilize the general situation

In 2015, China and Myanmar properly dealt with border issues; China and Vietnam resolved the issues left over regarding the land border; China and Vietnam, Malaysia and Indonesia reached a new consensus on the South China Sea issue. These measures safeguarded the stability of China–ASEAN relations and were conducive to promoting the cooperation between the two sides.

In March 2015, tens of thousands of Burmese citizens crossed the border to enter Yunnan, China, in order to flee the war, shells fell into China and caused civilian casualties in China, thus exerting an impact on Sino-Myanmar relations. After this incident, both the Chinese Government and the Myanmar Government downplayed the conflict on this incident as much as possible, so as not to affect the general situation of Sino-Myanmar relations.

On April 22, 2015, Chinese President Xi Jinping held talks with the President of Myanmar Thein Sein in Jakarta, in which Xi Jinping emphasized that China supported the efforts to politically resolve the issue in northern Myanmar through peace talks, and hoped that a new wave of progress could be made in Myanmar's peace process as soon as possible. Thein Sein stated that the Myanmar Government was committed to safeguarding the peace, stability and the safety of the personnel in northern Myanmar, and would intensify reconstruction in this region while promoting political dialogue.[1] On April 27, Chinese President Xi Jinping met with the delegation of the Union Solidarity and Development Party led by Thura U Shwe Mann, the Speaker of the Assembly of the Union of Myanmar and the House of Representatives, and stressed that the two sides should treat Sino-Myanmar relations from strategic and long-term perspectives in order to maintain the peace and tranquility on the border between China and Myanmar and take actions that would be beneficial to the development of China and Myanmar and the well-being of the people in both countries.[2] With the efforts of both countries, the border issue between China and Myanmar gradually subsided.

In November 2015, during Chinese President Xi Jinping's visit to Vietnam, the Chinese Government and the Government of Vietnam signed the *China–Vietnam Treaty Concerning Navigation in the Free Navigation Area at Beilun Estuary* and the *China–Vietnam Treaty Concerning Cooperative Protection and Development of the Detian Waterfall Tourism Resources.* Both the Beilun Estuary and the Detian Waterfall are very sensitive areas and were covered by several rounds of negotiations held by the China and Vietnam Joint Commission on Land Boundary Demarcation, but this issue was

[1]Tian Fan, Meng Na, Chinese President Xi Jinping met with the President of Myanmar Thein Sein, Xinhuanet. http://news.xinhuanet.com/politics/2015-04/22/c_1115057776.htm.

[2]Tan Jingjing, Xi Jinping met with Thura U Shwe Mann, Chairman of the Union Solidarity and Development Party, http://www.gov.cn/xinwen/2015-04/27/content_2853499.htm.

not resolved for a long time. After nearly 7 years of negotiations, the two countries ultimately reached a consensus and signed treaties. The signing of the above two documents indicated that the land border issues left over regarding the border between the two countries were resolved in a more comprehensive and thorough way, making the border areas a bridge to help the two countries deepen their cooperation and pave the way for further cooperation on the border areas. During Chinese President Xi Jinping's visit to Vietnam, China and Vietnam signed the *Exchange Agreement between the Guangxi Zhuang Autonomous Region Committee of the Communist Party of China and the Quảng Ninh Provincial Committee of the Communist Party of Vietnam Concerning the Establishment of Friendly Local Organizations,* and the *Agreement between the Yunnan Provincial Committee of the Communist Party of China and the Lào Cai Provincial Committee of the Communist Party of Vietnam Concerning Friendly Exchanges among Local Party Committees,* which are conducive to promoting cooperation between Guangxi and Yunnan, China and Vietnam.

In 2015, the South China Sea issue still had not subsided, but the Chinese Government and the countries having claims over the South China Sea, including Vietnam, Malaysia and Indonesia, overcame their difficulties to reach several consensuses on maintaining peace and stability in the South China Sea region, and these consensuses are reflected in four joint documents signed by the Chinese Government and the above-mentioned countries. First, the *China–Vietnam Joint Communiqué* and the *China–Vietnam Joint Statement* issued by China and Vietnam cover two consensuses on the South China Sea issue: (1) Honor commitments and seriously carry out the *Agreement on the Basic Principles Guiding the Settlement of Maritime Issues between China and Vietnam*, address issues through amicable consultations and negotiations; (2) Jointly manage the differences in the maritime affairs, comprehensively and effectively put into practice the *Declaration on the Conduct of the Parties in the South China Sea* (DOC) and establish a *Code of Conduct in the South China Sea* (COC) on the basis of an agreement through consultations as early as possible;[3] second, the *Joint Statement between the*

[3]China–Vietnam Joint Communiqué, Xinhuanet. http://news.xinhuanet.com/world/2015-04/08/c_1114906532.htm; China–Vietnam Joint Statement, Xinhuanet. http://news.xinhuanet.com/world/2015-11/06/c_1117067753.htm.

People's Republic of China and Malaysia issued by China and Malaysia covers three consensuses on the South China Sea issue: (1) The importance of the peace, security, stability and freedom of navigation in the South China Sea shall be safeguarded according to the generally accepted principles of international laws; (2) The directly related sovereign nations shall resolve differences and disputes in a peaceful way through amicable consultations and negotiations according to the generally accepted principles of international laws; (3) The two sides reaffirmed their commitment to comprehensively and effectively carry out the *Declaration on the Conduct of the Parties in the South China Sea*.[4] In addition, the *Joint Statement between the People's Republic of China and the Republic of Indonesia Concerning Strengthening the Comprehensive Strategic Partnership between the Two Countries* issued by China and Indonesia covers two consensuses on the South China Sea issue: (1) Comprehensively and effectively carry out the *Declaration on the Conduct of the Parties in the South China Sea*, and establish a *Code of Conduct in the South China Sea* on the basis of agreements through consultations as early as possible; (2) Resolve the differences and disputes over the South China Sea in a peaceful way through consultations and negotiations.[5] As indicated, although the South China Sea issue became increasingly intense, it is possible for the Chinese Government and relevant countries having claims over the South China Sea to reach consensuses on some aspects. It is difficult for these consensuses to effectively resolve the South China Sea issue in a short period of time, but they can play quite an important role in maintaining regional stability and helping to effectively resolve the issues.

3. The philosophy of a community with a common destiny was enriched to consolidate the foundation for it

In 2015, the philosophy of the China–ASEAN Community of Common Destiny was further enriched and developed. In March, when delivering

[4]Joint Statement between the People's Republic of China and Malaysia, Xinhuanet. http://news.xinhuanet.com/world/2015-11/24/c_128459810.htm.

[5]Joint Statement between the People's Republic of China and the Republic of Indonesia Concerning Strengthening the Comprehensive Strategic Partnership between the Two Countries, http://www.gov.cn/xinwen/2015-03/27/content_2838995.htm.

the keynote speech during the Boao Forum for Asia, Chinese President Xi Jinping stressed, "In order to move towards a community with a common destiny and create a bright future for Asia, Asia must advance amidst the world's progress and develop in the wave of the world's development."[6] In April, when speaking at the Asian-African Leaders' Meeting, Xi Jinping stated, "We should establish a new type of international relations dominated by win–win cooperation, develop an international order and an international system in a fairer and more rational way, build a human community with a common destiny, bring better benefits to the people in Asia, Africa and other regions."[7] In November, in a signed article published in Singapore, Xi Jinping pointed out, "China is committed to maintaining and developing good-neighborly and friendly relations and mutually beneficial cooperation with the surrounding countries, and upholds the philosophy of neighboring diplomacy which features amity, sincerity, mutual benefits and inclusiveness, pushes forward the construction of the Belt and Road, and helps build a closer China–ASEAN community with a common destiny as well as an Asian community with a common destiny."[8] When speaking at the National University of Singapore, Xi Jinping stressed the commitment to building a close China–ASEAN community with a common destiny and an Asian community with a common destiny.[9] Moreover, other Chinese leaders also gave more concrete explanations about the China–ASEAN community with a common destiny. The scope covered by the philosophy of the community with a common destiny was further expanded, and the means of implementation were further enriched.

Meanwhile, a realistic foundation for a China–ASEAN community with a common destiny was further consolidated in 2015. This was first evidenced by the fact that China and ASEAN countries officially signed the outcome

---

[6]Xi Jinping, Move towards a community with a common destiny and create a bright future for Asia, *People's Daily*, March 29, 2015, p. 3.

[7]Xu Jianmei, Huo Xiaoguang, New moment for the cooperative development of Asia and Africa. *People's Daily*, April 25, 2015, p. 3.

[8]Xi Jinping, Serve as a link between the past and the future, keep going to create a bright future for China–Singapore Relations, *Xinhua Daily Telegraph*, November 7, 2015, p. 2.

[9]Xi Jinping, Deepen the cooperative partnership, jointly turn Asia into a beautiful homeland. *Xinhua Daily Telegraph*, November 8, 2015, p. 2.

document for the negotiations on an upgraded free trade area — the *China–ASEAN Protocol to Amend the Framework Agreement on Comprehensive Economic Cooperation between China and ASEAN and Some of Its Agreements* on November 22, which marked the completion of the negotiations on an upgraded free trade area. Furthermore, China and Vietnam maintained high-level contacts and opportunely exchanged views on major issues in the relationships between the two parties and both countries in many flexible ways, including bilateral visits, special envoys, hotlines, annual meetings and multilateral meetings. The Chinese Government and the Government of Singapore positioned bilateral relations as an all-round cooperative partnership keeping up with the times, and initiated China–Singapore negotiations on an upgraded free trade area agreement and the third intergovernmental cooperation project. The Chinese Government and the Government of Indonesia were determined to strengthen the comprehensive strategic partnership between their two countries. China and Malaysia were committed to developing an active and all-round China–Malaysia partnership on the basis of mutual respect and promoting bilateral cooperation in various fields. In addition, China's cooperation with other ASEAN member countries also continued to be intensified and bilateral relations with them were consolidated, thus further bolstering the realistic foundation for a community with a common destiny.

II. Economic Field

In 2015, the international economic situation was severe, but China–ASEAN economic and trade cooperation did not become stagnant, the status of both sides as economic and trading partners was consolidated. China continued to be ASEAN's largest trading partner, while ASEAN was China's third largest trading partner[10]; bilateral investment maintained high growth. With a year-end conclusion of the negotiations concerning the upgrading of the China–ASEAN Free Trade Area, China–ASEAN economic and trade cooperation will usher in a new chapter in 2016.

---

[10]Xu Ningning, *2016: China–ASEAN Economic Cooperation Will Present a New Development Trend*, China–ASEAN Business Council, January 22, 2016.

1. The situation of China–ASEAN Trade in 2015

In 2015, international trade was subject to great downward pressure, exerting a profound impact on China and ASEAN countries. According to the statistical data from China Customs, in 2015, China's total value of imports and exports was USD 3.96 trillion, down 8%. According to relevant data from the World Trade Organization (WTO), six ASEAN countries,[11] Vietnam, Thailand, Malaysia, Singapore, the Philippines and Indonesia, enjoyed a foreign trade surplus in 2015, but the volume of imports and exports decreased by more than 10% in 2014 (Figure 1). In spite of this, China and ASEAN's importations and exportations were still better than the overall situation of the world's economy. China continued to maintain the status of ASEAN's largest trading country, the proportions of the total imports and exports of China and ASEAN (six countries) on the international market increased steadily from 12.4% and 7.1% in 2014 to 13% and 7.2% in 2015.

In 2015, the volume of China and ASEAN's trade reached USD 472.2 billion, down 1.7% over the previous year, lower than the extent to

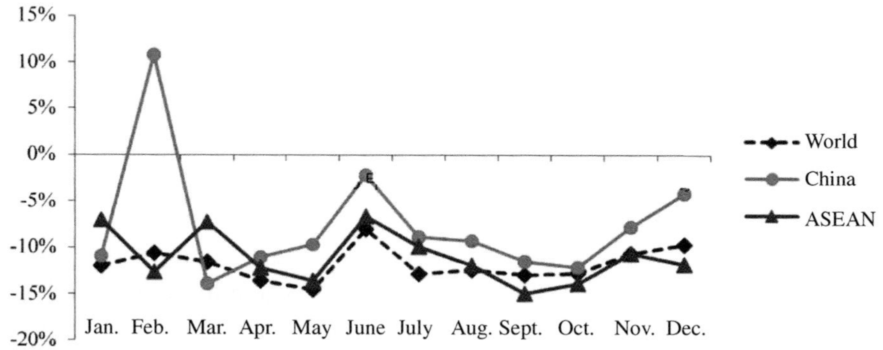

Figure 1. Monthly Statistical Data on the Growth of Foreign Trade between China and the ASEAN Countries in 2015

Note: ASEAN data represent the total value of six ASEAN countries, including Vietnam, Thailand, Malaysia, Singapore, the Philippines and Indonesia.

Source: WTO.

[11] According to relevant data released by the ASEAN Secretariat, in 2014, the foreign trade volume in six ASEAN countries accounted for 97% of ASEAN's total foreign trade volume, it can better represent ASEAN's overall situation.

which the total volume of China's foreign trade declined in the same period of the previous year (8%). China's exports to the ASEAN countries grew by 2.1% over the previous year, while China's imports from those countries decreased by 6.6%,[12] China's surplus reached a new high — USD 82.8 billion; this mainly resulted from the impact of the decreasing prices of bulk commodities, the adjustment of international industrial specialization, the trade substitution effect of the Trans-Pacific Partnership Agreement (TPP) and other factors.[13] The proportion of the volume of China–ASEAN trade in the total volume of China's foreign trade increased slightly and reached 11.9%, with the exports and imports accounting for 12.3% and 11.2%, respectively; the status of the two sides as trading partners was consolidated.

Like the situation in 2014, the ASEAN countries ranked in the decreasing order of the total volume of trade between China and the ASEAN countries in 2015 as follows: Malaysia, Vietnam, Singapore, Thailand, Indonesia, the Philippines, Myanmar, Cambodia, Laos and Brunei. The top six ASEAN countries brought about 94.9% of the total volume of trade volume between China and the ASEAN community, 95.9% of China's imports from the ASEAN community and 94.2% of China's exports to the ASEAN community. Specifically, in 2015, China–Myanmar, China–Laos, China–Brunei, China–Indonesia and China–Malaysia trade grew negatively, while China's trade with five ASEAN countries grew positively — China–Cambodia and China–Vietnam trade grew by 17.9% and 14.7%. Vietnam replaced Singapore to become China's third largest importer in the ASEAN community, and Thailand replaced Indonesia to become China's fourth largest exporter in the ASEAN group. More than 90% of China's trade surplus with ASEAN was concentrated in Vietnam (43.8%), Singapore (29.5%) and Indonesia (17.5%). Only Malaysia and Laos had a trade surplus with China in 2015.

The commodity structure in China–ASEAN trade did not change greatly over 2014. In 2015, the most important goods involved in trade between China and ASEAN remained the goods (electromechanical, audio video equipment and their spare parts, accessories) under the 16th category with the HS Code, accounting for 35.4% of all of the commodities exported

[12]Statistical data from the Ministry of Commerce of China.

[13]Xu Ningning, *2016: The ASEAN Community Planning and Construction Priorities Deserve Attention*, China–ASEAN Business Council, January 22, 2016.

from China to the ASEAN community and 47.6% of all of the commodities imported from ASEAN to China. There was both inter-industry trade and intra-industry trade between China and the ASEAN countries, suggesting that both comparative advantage and the obtaining of a scale economy in the new global division of labor exerted an impact on bilateral trade. According to classified statistics based on the HS code, China–ASEAN's average intra-industry trade index was 0.429 in 2015, a certain decrease over 2014.

Since the financial crisis, the global trade in goods has become sluggish, while the trade in services has maintained its momentum of rapid development and has become a new export growth point under the new normal of China's economy and the important developmental direction for its realization of economic transformation. With the signing and entry into force of the *Agreement on Trade in Services* involving the China–ASEAN Free Trade Area, the market of trade in services between China and the ASEAN countries has been further open to the outside world and trade in services has developed rapidly. According to statistical data from the Ministry of Commerce of China, the service outsourcing contracts concerning services from China to ASEAN countries amounted to USD 8.99 billion and the amount of executed contracts was USD 6.32 billion in 2015, up 30.6% and 17.3% over the previous year, respectively.[14] At present, China has become ASEAN's fourth largest trading partner, while ASEAN has maintained the status of China's fifth largest trading partner.[15]

With slow progress in multilateral trade negotiations, the signing of regional trade agreements has become a trade strategy adopted by many countries. According to the data released by the World Trade Organization, as of December 2015, 10 ASEAN countries and China had signed and implemented nearly 50 regional trade agreements. In October 2015, 12 countries, including Brunei, Vietnam, Singapore and Malaysia, announced in Atlanta, USA, that a consensus had been reached on the Trans-Pacific Partnership (TPP) Agreement. On November 22, 2015, the *China–ASEAN Free Trade Area (CAFTA) Upgrading Agreement* was reached and the *Protocol to Amend the Framework Agreement on Comprehensive Economic*

[14]The official website of the Ministry of Commerce, January 20, 2016.

[15]China–ASEAN Exposition Promoted Great Integration of the Trade in Services between China and the ASEAN countries, *China Industrial Economy News*, September 3, 2015.

Cooperation between the Association of Southeast Asian Nations and the People's Republic of China and Some Agreements under the Framework Agreement ("the Protocol") was signed. The Protocol covers trade in goods, trade in services, investments, economic and technical cooperation; it enriches, improves, supplements and upgrades the original agreements on the China–ASEAN Free Trade Area; it reflects the common aspiration of both sides for deepening and broadening economic and trade cooperation.[16] In addition, the 10th round of ASEAN-led negotiations involving the Regional Comprehensive Economic Partnership (RCEP) ended in the middle of October 2015, and are expected to be concluded in 2016.[17]

With the conclusion of the CAFTA upgrading negotiations and the progress in the RECP negotiations, China–ASEAN trade has been increasingly liberalized, tariff and non-tariff barriers have been reduced substantially, even eliminated, but there are many problems in cross-border logistics, the customs clearance environment, port construction and trade rules; they have imposed certain restrictions on the growth of China–ASEAN trade. According to the *Doing Business 2017* released by the World Bank Group in June 2015, cross-border trade facilitation was greatly different among the 10 ASEAN countries in 2015, seven ASEAN countries, except Singapore, Malaysia and Thailand, and China were at the middle and lower reaches in the world in cross-border trade costs.

2. The current situation of mutual investments between China and ASEAN in 2015

The global foreign direct investment (FDI) flow soared by 36% in 2015; it is estimated to hit USD 1.7 trillion, an all-time high since the global economic and financial crisis in 2008–2009. The foreign direct investment attracted to China reached USD 136 billion in 2015, an increase of 6% over 2014, ranking China the third largest destination for global FDI. The FDI flow to the ASEAN countries generally declined by 7% — FDI flow to Singapore decreased by 4%; it is estimated to reach USD 65 billion.[18]

[16]The official website of the Ministry of Commerce, December 3, 2015.

[17]RCEP Leaders Joint Statement, November 22, 2015.

[18]Global Investment Trends Monitor, January 20, 2016.

According to the statistical data from the Ministry of Commerce of China, in 2015, China–ASEAN two-way investments were about USD 17,092 million, of which China's investments in ASEAN countries totaled USD 9,448 million, up nearly 110% over the previous year,[19] accounting for 55.28% of China's outward investments. China's investments grew in eight ASEAN countries, except the Philippines and Cambodia, in 2015 over 2014; China's investments were fastest-growing in Malaysia, Singapore, Brunei, Laos, Indonesia, and grew by 237%, 120%, 46.4%, 36.2% and 26.2% in these countries, respectively. As of late 2015, the total amount of China–ASEAN two-way investments reached USD 156,469 million — the stock of China's investments in ASEAN was about USD 57,069 million. China's investments in ASEAN were mainly concentrated in Indonesia, Cambodia, Singapore, Laos and Myanmar. As of late 2015, China's investments in the above five countries accounted for 82% of the stock of China's investments in ASEAN.

The investments made in China by ASEAN countries totaled USD 7,644 million in 2015, up 20.6% over the previous year,[20] accounting for 44.72% of China–ASEAN two-way investments and 5.6% of the total actual FDI attracted to China in the same period (USD 136 billion[21]). As of late 2015, ASEAN's total investments in China amounted to USD 99.4 billion, accounting for 8.1% of the foreign capital stock actually attracted to China (about USD 1221.293 billion). ASEAN's direct investments in China mainly came from six old ASEAN countries, which are Singapore, Malaysia, Thailand, Brunei, Indonesia and the Philippines. As of late 2015, the stock of investments made by the above six countries in China amounted to USD 98.93 billion, accounting for 99.5% of the stock of ASEAN's investments in China–Singapore made the most investments in China. In recent years, the Chinese Mainland has always been the largest destination for Singapore's outward investments. In 2015, Singapore's investments in China amounted to USD 6.9 billion, accounting for 90% of the investments made by

[19]According to the data from the China–ASEAN Business Council, the direct investments made by Chinese enterprises in the ASEAN countries amounted to USD 9.13 billion during the period January–November 2015, up 109.9% over the previous year.

[20]Statistical data from the Ministry of Commerce of China.

[21]Global Investment Trends Monitor, January 20, 2016.

10 ASEAN countries in China in that year. As of late 2015, the stock of Singapore's investments in China amounted to USD 79.22 billion, accounting for 79.7% of the stock of the investments made by 10 ASEAN countries in China. Malaysia is in the second place in terms of investments in China; as of late 2015, the stock of Malaysia's investments in China amounted to USD 7.25 billion, accounting for 7% of the stock of the investments made by 10 ASEAN countries in China.

Overall, China–ASEAN two-way investments increased rapidly and steadily during the period 2006–2015, fully demonstrating the developmental prospect of mutually beneficial and win–win bilateral investment cooperation. At the same time, China–ASEAN two-way investments gradually developed from an unbalanced state to a balanced state: Before 2010, the ASEAN countries made substantial investments in China, as evidenced by both the annual investment flow and the cumulative investment stock; after 2010, the investment gap between the two sides narrowed, the proportion of China's investments in the ASEAN community in total two-way investments increased rapidly; in 2014, the flow of China's investments in the ASEAN countries exceeded that of ASEAN's investments in the Chinese Mainland. However, China's direct investments in the ASEAN countries are still at the initial stage, but the potential for development is great.

From an industrial perspective, as of late 2014, China's cumulative investments in the ASEAN community focused on energy and manufacturing and covered three main industries.

The electric power, heat, gas and water production and supply industries received USD 7,226 million in investments from China and were the industries where China's cumulative investments in the ASEAN countries were available in the largest amount, accounting for 15.2% of the investment stock, with these investments mainly distributed in Singapore, Myanmar, Cambodia, Indonesia, Laos, etc.; the manufacturing industry received USD 6,133 million investments, accounting for 12.9% of the investment stock, and it saw China's investments involved in the most extensive ASEAN countries — the countries with USD 100 million in investments include Vietnam (USD 1,403 million), Thailand (USD 1,035 million), Indonesia (USD 985 million), Singapore (USD 741 million), Cambodia (USD 701 million), Malaysia (USD 542 million), Laos (USD 442 million), the Philippines (USD 147 million) and Myanmar (USD 129 million).

Moreover, with respect to the primary industry, the agricultural, forestry, animal husbandry and fishery sectors received USD 2,444 million investments, accounting for 5.1% of the investment stock, mainly distributed in Laos, Indonesia, Cambodia, Singapore, Thailand, Vietnam and Myanmar; the mining sector received USD 6,053 million in investments, accounting for 12.7% of the investment stock, showing China's brisk demand for coal, oil, metal and other natural resources in previous years, mainly distributed in Indonesia, Myanmar, Laos, Singapore, Thailand, Cambodia and the Philippines.

With regard to the construction and real estate sectors, the construction sector received USD 3,362 million in investments, accounting for 7% of the investment stock. The infrastructure construction boom in China greatly increased the level of Chinese enterprises in designing, building and maintaining large-scale infrastructures, with investments mainly distributed in Laos, Cambodia, Singapore, Malaysia, Vietnam, Indonesia and Thailand. The investments in the real estate sector accounted for 2.4% of the investment stock and were mainly available in Singapore. Singapore enjoys many advantages, including complete and strong infrastructures, a livable environment, favorable investment conditions and a business-friendly culture, thus Singapore's real estate sector is highly attractive to international investors.

With regard to the tertiary industry, the leasing and commercial service sectors received USD 6,843 million in investments, accounting for 14.4% of the investment stock, mainly distributed in Singapore, Malaysia, Laos, Vietnam and Thailand. The wholesale and retail sector received USD 5.9 billion in investments, accounting for 12.4% of the investment stock, mainly distributed in Singapore, Indonesia, Thailand, Vietnam, the Philippines and Malaysia. The financial sector received USD 5,879 million in investments, accounting for 12.3% of the investment stock, mainly distributed in Singapore, Thailand, Indonesia, Malaysia and the Philippines. The transportation and warehousing sectors received USD 1,468 million in investments, accounting for 3.1% of the investment stock, mainly distributed in Singapore and Thailand. The investments in the scientific research and technical service sectors accounted for 1.4% of the investment stock. The investments in the information transmission, software and information service sectors accounted for 0.3% of the investment stock. The investments in the resident services and other service sectors accounted for 0.3% of the investment stock, while that in the lodging and catering sectors accounted for 0.2% of the investment stock.[22]

Singapore's investments in China were mainly concentrated in the manufacturing and real estate sectors. The *China–Singapore Free Trade Agreement*, effective as from 2009, focuses on tariff reduction and exemption involving the trade in goods. Singapore's business circle hopes that the upgraded free trade agreement can also extend to the investment and service fields, especially the fields in the modern service sector such as logistics, medical services, education, finance and smart cities. These are Singapore's strong points. Malaysia's investments in China centered on a number of fields, including energy, agriculture, fishery and the green economy. China and Malaysia present respective characteristics and very strong complementarity in resource environment, industrial structure and domestic market demand. Specifically, China enjoys comparative advantages in textiles, clothing, shoes, food, cereal, building materials, and electromechanical and chemical products, while Malaysia is advantageous in such resource products as palm oil, rubber, natural gas and oil. These complementary industries should be the priorities of mutual investments between the two countries. Indonesia's investments in China involved papermaking, real estate and food processing; the Sinar Mas Group (APP) and the Salim Group are well-known Indonesian enterprises.

3. The prospect of China–ASEAN economic and trade cooperation in 2016

As the world economy was generally sluggish, in 2015, great achievements were made in China–ASEAN economic and trade cooperation, but there were also some structural problems, including the following: an imbalance existed in the growth rate and volume of bilateral trade; China's trade surplus reached a new high; it was very hard to resolve the structural contradictions in trade in a short term; the flow of China's investments in the ASEAN community had exceeded that of ASEAN's investments in China, but bilateral investments were still at the initial stage, the focus of investments had just

[22] Statistical Communiqué on China's Outward Direct Investments in 2014.

shifted from the field of resource development to that of infrastructure, there was still a great potential and room for development.

As the economic development in various countries has entered a new stage, the China–ASEAN economic and trade structure will be adjusted to some extent, but the trend of bilateral cooperation will not change greatly. According to the *2016 Evaluation Report on Economic Growth* released by the World Bank, in 2016, the economic growth rate in Cambodia is expected to be 6.9%, in Indonesia, 5.3%, in Laos, 7%, in Malaysia, 4.5%, in the Philippines, 6.4%, in Thailand, 2%, in Vietnam, 6.6%, and in Myanmar, 7.8%. The government work priorities in the economic field in particular countries, e.g., Thailand, will shift in 2016 to increasing domestic demand and reducing the dependence upon the export-oriented economy; however, China and the ASEAN countries will adopt the policy of an open economy; in recent years, various countries have maintained a stable degree of dependence upon foreign trade and have kept their enthusiasm regarding the entry of foreign investors; at the same time, the further construction of the ASEAN Community, the implementation of the Belt and the Road Initiative put forward by China and the official establishment of the Asian Infrastructure Investment Bank will greatly promote the connectivity between China and the ASEAN community, while the initiation of CAFTA upgrading and the development of RECP negotiations will open the post-tariff era for China and the ASEAN community, and the bilateral economic and trade relations will further deepen; it is expected that China–ASEAN bilateral investments will maintain a positive growth and that bilateral trade will grow positively again in 2016.

III. Cooperation in the Fields of Security, the Military and Maritime Activities

1. Cooperation on security

Security is always a major issue in international relations; regional security is the foundation for regional cooperation and development. For a long time, China and the ASEAN community have had a high degree of consensus on the importance of safeguarding regional security, and both sides have made great efforts. With further development of bilateral relations, especially since the establishment of the China–ASEAN Free Trade Area, cooperation has become the main theme between the two sides and has stimulated enormous interest, while the positive expectations regarding cooperation returns and a good developmental prospect further stimulate the two sides to strengthen their cooperation. Thus the two sides have the following common appeals: improving the mechanism for cooperation on security issues; addressing the traditional security issues, including territorial and territorial sea disputes which still exist in China and ASEAN countries, and other non-traditional security issues; creating a good and stable international environment for cooperation between, and development of both sides.

a. *Regional disputes and traditional cooperation on security*

For many years, the greatest goal of traditional cooperation on security between China and the ASEAN community has always been to address the outstanding issue of the South China Sea in a peaceful way. In 2015, the dispute of the South China Sea was still intense. Since China officially claimed the ownership of some islands in the southwestern South China Sea, actively reclaimed and developed land from the sea, Vietnam, the Philippines, Brunei and Malaysia have lodged protests and created friction again and again, the US has actively intervened, sent cruisers and bombers to the South China Sea in the capacity of a supporter of Singapore and the Philippines many times, so the issue of the South China Sea has become more complicated. Furthermore, in 2015, the following disputes broke out: The foreign minister of the Philippines criticized China for threatening the security of the South China Sea in the informal meeting of the foreign ministers of the ASEAN countries; China criticized Vietnam and the Philippines for deploying missiles to the islands and reefs in the South China Sea; the Philippines shot the fishermen from Taiwan, China in the disputed waters; Vietnam groundlessly intervened in China's marine drilling activity; the International Court of Arbitration adjudicated the case in which the Philippines sued China, entered a unanimous judgment about the right of jurisdiction over the South China Sea Arbitration and the admissibility issue and affirmed the right of jurisdiction over the 3rd, 4th, 6th, 7th, 10th, 11th and 13th claims raised by the Philippines, involving whether China enjoys territorial sovereignty over Huangyan Island and part of the islands and reefs in the South China Sea, mainly the islands and reefs controlled by China, and exclusive economic zones, whether China disturbs the Philippines' exercise of rights[23]; the Central Committee of the Vietnam Fatherland Front released a report, alleging that China's action of building islands by reclaiming land from the South China Sea violated Vietnam's sovereignty, illegally invaded and occupied Vietnam's territory, and that Vietnam would resolutely contend against China.[24]

The issue of the South China Sea involves the sovereignty to which no concession can be made, so serious confrontations are self-evident, while international forces take the South China Sea as a game field, making the issue more complicated. The issue of the South China Sea has become the greatest barrier to further deepening the China–ASEAN cooperative relationship. In order to address the issue of the South China Sea to the greatest extent as early as possible, China and ASEAN have made enormous efforts, various parties have striven to settle the dispute of the South China Sea in a peaceful way. Positive progress was made during the senior officials' meeting on the *Declaration on the Conduct of Parties in the South China Sea* and the joint working group meeting on the *Code of Conduct in the South China Sea*; ASEAN countries expressed their willingness to work with China to realistically carry out the *Declaration on the Conduct of Parties in the South China Sea.* Afterwards, the Chinese Foreign Minister Wang Yi put forward the three-point initiative on safeguarding the peace and stability of the South China Sea in the ASEAN–China Foreign Ministers' Meeting and that initiative received positive evaluation from foreign ministers of various countries.[25] Afterwards, China and Vietnam issued the *China–Vietnam Joint Communiqué*, declaring efforts to control the disagreements over the sea and jointly safeguard the peace of the South China Sea. At the same time, in the *Presidential Statement* issued at the 27th ASEAN Summit, the leaders of the ASEAN

[23]An Analysis of the Causes for the Litigation against China Instituted by the Philippines at the International Tribunal for the Law of the Sea and Strategies, *Public Opinion Report*. http://cari.gxu.edu.cn/info/1087/7937.htm.

[24]Foreign Media: Vietnam Released a Report Showing That China and Vietnam Confronted Each Other over the Issue of the South China Sea 22 Times This Year, *Global Times*. http://world.huanqiu.com/exclusive/2015-12/8291988.html.

[25]Wang Yi Put Forward a Three-point Initiative on Safeguarding the Peace and Stability of the South China Sea. http://news.ifeng.com/a/20150805/44357126_0.shtml.

countries once again expressed concern about the issue of the South China Sea and called for guaranteeing the peace, stability and security of the area.[26]

b. *Continued improvement in non-traditional cooperation on security*

Comprehensively pushing forward cooperation in the non-traditional security fields is the inevitable requirement for strengthening the cooperative partnership between the two sides. In particular, since the *Joint Declaration on the Cooperation in the Non-traditional Security Fields* was jointly issued by China and ASEAN in 2002, both sides have engaged in increasingly deep and extensive cooperation in the non-traditional security fields, involving law enforcement and security, security in the navigation channel, anti-terrorism and disaster prevention. In 2015, China and the ASEAN community continued to promote cooperation in the non-traditional security fields, the two sides held talks in this regard in a number of meetings, particularly the "Security for Prosperity" China–ASEAN Ministerial Dialogue on Cooperation on Law Enforcement & Security, and the 1st Foreign Ministers' Meeting on Lancang–Mekong Cooperation; both meetings resulted in the release of achievement documents such as the *Beijing Declaration of "Security for Prosperity" China–ASEAN Ministerial Dialogue on Cooperation on Law Enforcement & Security* and the *Joint Press Communiqué on the 1st Foreign Ministers' Meeting on Lancang–Mekong Cooperation.* The China–ASEAN Ministerial Dialogue on Cooperation on Law Enforcement & Security advocated actions to establish an executive committee on cooperation in fighting terrorism, controlling drugs, cracking down on cyber crimes, organized human smuggling, illegal immigration and other key fields; the participants set up a regular and emergency mechanism of response assistance to jointly enhance the capability for guarding against and resisting regional security risks, and stated that China would provide training to security and anti-riot personnel in ASEAN countries.[27] It is worth mentioning that the Fox

[26]China's New Diplomatic Situation: The Issue of the South China Sea Cannot Be Bypassed, the ASEAN community and China Still Steadily Escalated the Tussle, *The Paper International.* http://www.thepaper.cn/newsDetail_forward_1413996_1.

[27]The China–ASEAN Ministerial Dialogue on Law Enforcement & Security Cooperation Was Held in Beijing. http://news.qq.com/a/20151024/028783.htm.

Hunting 2015 action made great achievements, providing a reliable model for cooperation on law enforcement and security between the two sides. Under the Lancang–Mekong cooperation mechanism, further cooperation agreements were reached in such fields as poverty alleviation, enhanced joint cruising for guaranteeing the safety of navigational security and public health. Furthermore, Chinese Premier Li Keqiang stated during the 18th China–ASEAN Leaders' Meeting that China was willing to work with the ASEAN community to institutionalize the defense ministers' informal meeting, strengthen the cooperation in cracking down on transnational crimes, fighting terrorism and managing disasters; he also declared that China would hold the *China–ASEAN Agricultural Cooperation Forum* in 2016 to enhance agricultural cooperation between the two sides and safeguard regional grain security, and suggested that both sides should adopt the *China–ASEAN Environmental Cooperation Strategy (2016–2020)* as early as possible, build the environmental protection information sharing platform and continuously push forward practical cooperation in such fields as education, science and technology, culture, health, youth, tourism and media,[28] with which various countries highly agreed. At the same time, the two sides also continued to hold consultations on the *Agreement on the Southeast Asian Nuclear-Weapon-Free-Zone Treaty*, and hoped that the regional nuclear issue could be addressed as early as possible.

2. Military cooperation

The military is a matter of paramount importance for a country; it determines the survival of a country, so it has to be valued. The military strength of a country is the sword and shield for that country to safeguard its sovereignty, while military cooperation among countries is the only choice for countries to safeguard regional peace and stability, and cooperation needs to be promoted in order to maintain a peaceful, good international environment. In recent years, China and the ASEAN community have engaged in increasingly close military cooperation, the dispute between the two sides has focused on the South China Sea, so bilateral military cooperation has centered on maritime

[28] Li Keqiang Delivered a Speech during the 18th China–ASEAN Leaders' Meeting, Xinhuanet. http://news.xinhuanet.com/politics/2015-11/22/c_1117218197.htm.

military cooperation. In 2015, the two sides continued their previous plan of cooperation, made great headway and conducted active explorations in addressing the dispute of the South China Sea in a peaceful way.

a. *A link between the past and the future was built to safeguard regional peace*

China–ASEAN military cooperation in 2015 is the continuity of the previous strategy of cooperation and also an exploration of a future path towards cooperation, with the ultimate goal of safeguarding regional peace.

1. **The continuity of the previous strategy:** Both sides continued to strengthen and deepen their cooperation in the non-traditional security issues threatening regional stability, including cracking down on terrorism, transnational crimes and pirates; both sides continued to cooperate in high-level visits, military assistance, military education and training, reciprocal visits to warships, joint training and exercise, national defense industry and other national defense areas; both sides strove to build and develop an ASEAN regional forum, an ASEAN defense ministers' enlarged meeting and other regional multilateral security cooperation mechanisms, and regularize and institutionalize military cooperation.[29] In 2015, the military exercises between China and ASEAN countries included the China–Thailand Air Force "Eagle Strike-2015" joint training activity, multilateral joint exercise and the COBRA GOLD joint military exercise. Moreover, in November, China and Cambodia signed an agreement with a view to strengthening China's military assistance to Cambodia and bilateral cooperation in the military and communication fields; this is a vivid example of further cooperation between the two sides.
2. **An exploration of the future path:** On the one hand, China and the ASEAN community were not content with the present achievements; on the other hand, in order to cope with the new situation, the two sides

[29]Sincerely Pushing Forward China–ASEAN Defense Cooperation, Building the China–ASEAN Community of Common Destiny, *Global Times*. http://world.huanqiu.com/exclusive/2015-10/7769958.html.

worked together in exploring the path for future military cooperation. In September, China and Malaysia conducted the first joint military exercise "Peace and Friendship-2015", the largest bilateral joint military exercise between China and ASEAN countries, achieving huge success. This exercise breaks the previous scale and mode and provides a reliable model for future joint military actions between China and ASEAN countries. In October, China and Malaysia reached an agreement on permitting Chinese naval vessels to only use the Port of Kota Kinabalu in Sabah State as the stopover site, which serves as a paradigm for striking a delicate balance between China and ASEAN countries in responding to the game among great powers. Afterwards, under the theme of "Moving towards the China–ASEAN Community of Common Destiny, Strengthening Security and Defense Cooperation", the China–ASEAN Defense Ministers' Informal Meeting was held successfully, in which Chinese Defense Minister Chang Wanquan put forward five suggestions for jointly identifying the general direction for cooperation, safeguarding regional security and stability, promoting the building of a security mechanism, deepening the practical cooperation in the defense field, properly dealing with disputes and controlling risks,[30] which received an active response from various countries and set the tone for future national defense and military cooperation between China and the ASEAN community.

b. *Regional disputes added difficulties to military cooperation*

Among the ASEAN countries, Vietnam, Brunei, Malaysia and the Philippines had some disputes with China with respect to the sovereignty of islands and reefs; Indonesia had a dispute with China with regard to the demarcation of exclusive marine economic zones; however, with the intervention of the great powers, including the USA and Japan, the dispute of the South China Sea between China and the ASEAN community escalated from a regional issue to a global issue, it became the bargaining chip in the game among great

[30]China–ASEAN Defense Ministers' Informal Meeting was held in Beijing, chinanews.com. http://www.chinanews.com/mil/2015/10-16/7573324.shtml.

powers, thus complicating the issue of the South China Sea and increasing difficulties for bilateral peaceful military cooperation.

1. The dispute over the South China Sea restricted the deepening of bilateral military cooperation. The countries having territorial and territorial sea disputes with China, e.g., Vietnam and the Philippines, were estranged from China for a long time, both sides were caught in repeated bargaining and friction, so both sides had to dedicate great energy to deal with the disputes. In January 2013, the Philippines sued China in the International Court of Arbitration, while in December, 2014, Vietnam submitted a document which favored the Philippines' stand, exacerbating the contradictions between the two sides.
2. The intervention of great powers made the issue complicated. Vietnam, the Philippines and other countries held exercises together with the USA, Japan and other countries in the South China Sea many times to pressurize China. As the main participant in the game over the South China Sea, the USA joined the countries with disputes with China and also tried to forge a Four-country Hidden Alliance with Japan, Australia and India. In 2015, the USA signed the *Enhanced Defense Cooperation Agreement* (EDCA) with the Philippines, advocated the plan for the "freedom of navigation" in the South China Sea, sent the USS Lassen guided missile destroyer to cruise within the scope of 12 sea miles away from China's Bihai Reef and Meiji Reef under the pretext of safeguarding the freedom of navigation, and it even dispatched reconnaissance planes and bombers to invade the territorial air space of the South China Sea many times, thus escalating the issue of the South China Sea.

3. Maritime cooperation

The sea is vast, symbolizing unknown and infinite possibilities. The sea abounds in biological and mineral resources, which became known to all long ago, while marine channels are the main arteries for world trade; developing and utilizing marine resources has become the common goal of various countries around the world; marine cooperation and development has also become a major issue in today's international relations. China is adjacent to the ASEAN community by land and sea, so maritime cooperation naturally becomes their cooperation priority; in fact, China and ASEAN have always been making active efforts and explorations in deepening maritime cooperation.

a. *Strategic connection and pragmatic cooperation*

The year 2015 was the Year of China–ASEAN Maritime Cooperation. With the philosophy of amity, sincerity, mutual benefit and inclusiveness, China and ASEAN engaged in all-round maritime cooperation and deepened their maritime cooperation.

1. **Working on the strategy of integrated development:** China actively advocated the plan of the 21st Century Maritime Silk Road and offered three planning suggestions: (1) giving full scope to the role of the Year of China–ASEAN Maritime Cooperation in immensely driving forward development, focusing on the marine economy, maritime connectivity, marine environment, disaster prevention and reduction, maritime security and maritime humanistic development; (2) enhancing the dialogue and cooperation among various countries along the South China Sea, exploring a mechanism and mode for cooperation which is acceptable to all of the parties involved; (3) holding a dialogue and consultation to push forward joint maritime development,[31] which were recognized by most countries. Furthermore, China connected the strategy of the Belt and the Road connectivity and the overall plan called *ASEAN's Connectivity*, and strove to address the strategy of building the China–ASEAN Community. China made substantive progress in railway transportation together with Indonesia, Laos and Thailand; this becomes the model for successful strategic connection between the two sides.
2. **Carrying out solid work through pragmatic cooperation:** In 2015, China actively prepared to build the ASEAN Maritime Cooperation Center. After its establishment, the Center will organize its efforts to

[31]The Maritime Cooperation Becomes a New Bright Spot in ASEAN, the official website of China–ASEAN Exposition. http://www.caexpo.org/html/2015/bolanhuidongtai_0601/209057.html.

complete the *Research on the Top-level Design and Strategic Planning of the ASEAN Maritime Cooperation Center*, shifting China–ASEAN maritime cooperation from strategic connection to practical operations. In addition, the establishment of the Asian Infrastructure Investment Bank provided strong fund support for building the 21st Century Maritime Silk Road. The application and examination involving the program "China–ASEAN Maritime Cooperation Fund" was underway. The two sides also made substantive headway in route security cooperation, e.g., the military exercise with Vietnam and Malaysia, and the series of consensuses reached during the defense ministers' meeting. China also affirmed that it would participate in joint training, maritime search and rescue, joint exercise in disaster relief involving the *Code for Unplanned Encounters at Sea* in the South China Sea in 2016.

b. *Building a regularized, peaceful and rational mechanism for cooperation*

In 2015, China and the ASEAN community engaged in maritime cooperation by upholding the spirit of the *Declaration on the Conduct of Parties in the South China Sea* and the dual-track thinking, and endeavored to establish a peaceful mechanism for dialogue on the issue of maritime cooperation. In the China–ASEAN Foreign Ministers' Meeting in August, Wang Yi put forward the three-point initiative on safeguarding the peace and stability of the South China Sea: (1) the countries in the South China Sea should undertake to fully and effectively carry out the *Declaration on the Conduct of Parties in the South China Sea*, and more quickly hold consultations concerning the *Code of Conduct in the South China Sea*, actively discuss the preventative measures for controlling maritime risks; (2) the extraterritorial countries should undertake to support the above efforts made by the countries in the region and refrain from taking actions leading to an intense and complicated regional situation; (3) various countries should undertake to exercise and safeguard the freedom of navigation and overflight in the South China Sea according to international laws.[32]

---

[32] Wang Yi Put Forward a Three-point Initiative on Safeguarding the Peace and Stability of the South China Sea, ifeng.com. http://news.ifeng.com/a/20150805/44357126_0.shtml.

The initiative received positive evaluation from various countries and pinpointed the direction for the two sides to build a mechanism for maritime cooperation. Furthermore, on November 17, China announced that it had been approved to join the *Maritime Labor Convention 2006* and would hold the Convention in 2016, suggesting that it endeavored to keep in line with international and ASEAN's practices in maritime systems. This shows that China is an active and responsible large country in regional cooperation and that China has the vision of keeping amity, sincerity and goodwill towards and working with its neighboring countries.

IV. Cultural Field

In 2015, the ASEAN Community was completed and the Belt and Road Initiative by China started to be comprehensively built. In that year, China released the *Vision and Actions on Jointly Building the Silk Road Economic Belt and the 21st Century Maritime Silk Road*, initiated the Year of China–ASEAN Maritime Cooperation and signed the *Protocol* of the agreement on upgrading the China–ASEAN Free Trade Area; China continued to hold the exhibitions, meetings and forums focusing on engagement with ASEAN — mainly the China–ASEAN Exposition and the China–ASEAN Business and Investment Summit — and various cultural exchange activities; the Lancang–Mekong cooperation mechanism was officially established and China–ASEAN people-to-people cooperation was deepened.

1. The maritime cultural exchanges charted a beautiful blueprint for China–ASEAN maritime cooperation

The year 2015 was the Year of China–ASEAN Maritime Cooperation. In 2015, China–ASEAN maritime cultural cooperation was given the humanistic connotation of amity, sincerity, mutual benefit and inclusiveness, actions were taken to boost the full rise and cooperative development of the culture of China–ASEAN marine cultivation and fishery amidst the awareness of a "Common Home" in the South China Sea, the vision and practice of "jointly working on a beautiful blueprint for maritime cooperation".

a. *The maritime cultural activities helped develop the awareness of a China–ASEAN "Common Home" in the South China Sea*

In 2015, the awareness of a "Common Home" in the South China Sea was described as a sea of peace, amity and cooperation. Chinese President Xi Jinping vowed to strengthen maritime connectivity, push forward the building of a mechanism for Asian maritime cooperation, promote cooperation in such areas as marine economy, environmental protection, disaster management and fishery activities so that the sea would become a sea of peace, amity and cooperation connecting Asian countries[33]; the 21st China–ASEAN Senior Officials' Consultation Meeting also expressed the vision of turning the South China Sea into a sea of peace, amity and cooperation; such aspects as the connection between the Maritime Silk Road initiated by China and the Global Maritime Fulcrum envisioned by Indonesia have given expression to a "Common Home" in the South China Sea at the regional and national levels.

With the support of the awareness of a "Common Home" in the South China Sea, China–ASEAN maritime cultural cooperation tended to flourish. In 2015, under the theme of "jointly building the 21st Century Maritime Silk Road and jointly working on a beautiful blueprint for maritime cooperation", the 12th China–ASEAN Exposition put forward the slogans embodying the spirit of maritime cooperation — including "With Maritime Cooperation as a New Bright Spot, the China–ASEAN Exposition Creates Business Opportunities", "Boosting Maritime Cooperation, Sharing ASEAN's Business Opportunities", with cultural activities focusing on maritime cooperation. The participants in the Cities of Charm exhibition within the China–ASEAN Exposition mainly included the important coastal ports, tourist cities or the important port cities connecting sea ports in various countries, such as Riau Province of Indonesia, Zamboanga City of the Philippines, Chon Buri of Thailand, Lao Cai Province of Vietnam, and Hong Kong of China. The China–ASEAN Maritime Cooperation Achievement Exhibition, held during the China–ASEAN Exposition, showcased the all-round maritime cooperation achievements between China and

[33]Xi Jinping: Towards a Community of a Common Destiny and a New Future for Asia — A Keynote Speech at the Boao Forum for Asia Annual Conference 2015, *People's Daily*, March 29, 2015.

ASEAN countries, including the educational cooperation achievements as the focus of this exhibition, e.g., the Maritime Scholarship established by the Chinese Government, 20 students from six ASEAN countries studying for master's and doctoral degrees in China, and preliminary completion of the China–ASEAN Maritime Cooperation College.

China's coastal provinces and cities also actively expanded maritime cultural cooperation with the ASEAN community. For example, with its colorful cultural charm, Xiamen planned to develop into the forerunner area for China–ASEAN maritime cooperation. In September 2015, the China–ASEAN Maritime Cooperation Center was established in Xiamen; during the Xiamen International Maritime Week in November, under the theme of "Jointly Building the 21st Century Maritime Silk Road: Maritime Cooperation between China and the ASEAN community, the Developing Countries", the ASEAN elements were highlighted in three segments including the international maritime forum, maritime exhibition negotiation and maritime cultural activities. Moreover, Qianhai in Shenzhen of Guangdong Province and Indonesia jointly built the international maritime cooperation bank and carried out other projects, designating the tourist cultural exchange as one of the six cooperation priorities and shaping the new mode of regional maritime cooperation.

As shown, as China and the ASEAN countries have continuously enhanced the modern maritime awareness of developing the marine economy to increase its national strength, the South China Sea with its abundant resources and convenient routes has increasingly become the common home in which the countries along the South China Sea share weal and woe as well as their destiny, while the resulting awareness about the maritime community of common destiny with the sea as the bond and life scene can bring maritime interest and well-being to the countries along the South China Sea and also prosperous maritime cultural cooperation and development.

b. *The traditional culture of marine cultivation and fishery development has opened up a new landscape for China–ASEAN maritime cooperation*

The countries and territories along the Maritime Silk Road have emerged along the sea and flourished thanks to the sea, they share the production culture and life memory of marine cultivation and fishery development. In 2015, the cultural activities of carrying forward marine cultivation and fishery development were vigorously carried out; in March, the people in Sanya of Hainan Province celebrated the Dragon-Head-Raising Festival by offering sacrifices to the Dragon King and blessing the South China Sea through traditional Taoist rites, while various recreational activities displayed the folk culture of the fishermen's families. In August, Yangjiang of Guangdong Province, a city hailed as the Capital of Fishery from the South China Sea, witnessed the Fishing Festival under the theme of "Setting Sail along the Silk Road Waterway and Boosting a Green Rise", during which a traditional sailing ceremony, a sea-worshiping activity and other characteristic folk activities in fishing areas were carried out. An art performance "Sea, Listen to Me", which integrates music, dance, poetry and pictures, debuted in Fuzhou, and it was staged in coastal provinces and cities, including Hainan, Qingdao and Dalian.

In 2015, with marine cultivation and fishery development against the background of the Year of China–ASEAN Maritime Cooperation, the connotation of the traditional culture of maritime production was inherited, with a developmental impetus and resources continuously sought from the sea while developing the fishery and shipping industries. Hainan energetically developed the cage culture in the South China Sea, and more effectively developed and utilized blue territorial resources. Fujian Province, which has better governed and used the sea since ancient times, took advantage of the regional characteristics of the marine industry and the marine culture, moved faster to engage in all-round maritime cooperation with the countries along the Maritime Silk Road — in 2015, priority was given to building and transforming comprehensive fishing bases, including those in Indonesia and Rangoon of Myanmar, completing a number of marine product processing trade centers. In October, the China–ASEAN Marine Product Exchange was open for listing and trading, accelerated efforts were made to build characteristic marine industrial parks with high technological content and the Strait Blue Silicon Valley, and to promote the development of agglomeration of the modern marine industry.

The lifestyle of the development of marine cultivation and fishery has also enriched the connotation of modernization amidst inheritance. For example, the Chinese Government has continued to push forward bilateral and multilateral cooperation with ASEAN countries in marine and climate change, marine environmental protection, marine ecosystem and biodiversity, marine disaster prevention and reduction, regional marine research, and marine policy and management. Hainan has learnt from Bali to deeply combine culture with tourism; leverage the rich deposits and realistic resources available to Hainan thanks to the special historical status and historical memory of Hainan strategically located at the "golden waterway" in the South China Sea; carry out literary and artistic creations under the School of Hainan, turn Hainan into an international tourist island with a literary and artistic style. As indicated, marine cultivation and fishery development have undergone innovation amidst inheritance, opening up a new landscape for China–ASEAN marine cultural cooperation under the theme of marine fishery production.

c. *Folk marine culture: the important bond for China–ASEAN marine people-to-people exchanges*

In 2015, the people in the areas along the Maritime Silk Road fully tapped and utilized the rich national and folk traditional cultural treasures to create the distinctive symbols of a marine culture, with cross-border cultural exchanges conducted to turn the folk marine culture into the important bond for China–ASEAN marine people-to-people exchanges.

Guangxi meets Vietnam in waters, and marine folk cultural exchanges have been unabated between the two sides. In 2015, the marine cultural activities were characterized by the crossing of national borders. For example, the annual international marine Dragon Boat Festival was carried out in Fangchenggang City, reputed as the bridgehead for China's access to the ASEAN countries, in June, during which 19 dragon boats from Vietnam, Hong Kong and Guangxi competed with each other, presenting spectacular folk exchanges between China and Vietnam. The Hajie Festival of the Jing nationality is another symbol of marine culture in Guangxi. The Jing nationality is a marine nationality and it is also a cross-border one; it is also called Viet ethnic group in Vietnam. The Hajie Festival is the greatest traditional festival of the Jing nationality; it consists of sea god and ancestor worshiping, local drinking, social contacts and entertainment. In July 2015, many guests from Vietnam were invited to take part in the Hajie Festival, during which more than 120 representative teams from Vietnam presented excellent performances; the university student teams from Vietnam and China took part in the traditional activity of greeting and worshiping gods, with the participation of Viet ethnic group residents from Mong Cai, Vietnam; the people of the Jing nationality from China and Vietnam and tourists sang Chinese and Vietnamese songs at the public places where the Jing nationality worships gods and ancestors, showing a great integration of folk customs and folk culture.

At the same time, Fujian has served as the bond for the folk cultures shared by China and the overseas Chinese in ASEAN countries, including the Mazu culture, the Hakka culture and the Zhuzi culture, so the non-governmental exchanges become an important way to enable China–ASEAN marine cultural cooperation.

2. The belt and road: Synergy with the Silk Road on various fronts

In 2015, under the main theme of peace and harmony for jointly building the Maritime Silk Road, China and the ASEAN community engaged in cultural contacts at multiple levels through various mechanisms, bringing about synergy among exhibitions, meetings, forums, festivals, activities and the Silk Road, between the government and the non-governmental forces.

a. *Synergy among exhibitions, meetings, forums, festivals, activities and the Silk Road*

(i) Synergy between exhibitions and the Silk Road

The year 2015 witnessed an intense synergy between exhibitions and the Silk Road through the China–ASEAN Exposition as a mechanism or platform. The China–ASEAN Maritime Cooperation Achievement Exhibition, based on the 12th China–ASEAN Exposition, fostered a popular cultural atmosphere for China–ASEAN maritime cooperation. The cultural exhibition displayed the characteristic cultural exhibits from ten ASEAN countries, South Korea, Hong Kong, Macao, Taiwan and the rest of China, including a distinctive cultural image, an intangible cultural heritage, publications, films, TV and rosewood carving art, so that culture became the "endogenous variable" for China–ASEAN economic and social development and also a stage for promoting economic, social and cultural integration and coexistence between China and the ASEAN community. Both exhibitions and the 3rd China–ASEAN Publication Exposition & Guangxi Radio, Film and TV Exhibition 2015, the China–ASEAN Exposition Tourism Exhibition, the 9th China–ASEAN Young Artwork Creation Contest Award-winning Works Exhibition, the China–ASEAN Vocational Educational Exhibition, held during the same period, marked a high tide of people-to-people cooperation and exchanges between China and the ASEAN community in 2015. The Long-standing China–ASEAN Friendly Exchange and Feng Shaoxie's Oil Paintings Exhibition held at the ASEAN Secretariat in November, the China–ASEAN (Nanning) International Auto Show held in Nanning, Guangxi in December, etc. became the lingering sound of synergy between China–ASEAN exhibitions and the Silk Road in 2015.

(ii) Synergy among meetings, forums and the Silk Road

In 2015, China's meetings and forums towards the ASEAN community had fantastic synergy with the Silk Road, mainly evidenced in the following respects: The themes of these meetings and forums were associated with the keywords "The Silk Road" and "sea", while the rich connotation of the Silk Road, which incorporates both ancient and modern elements, was explored and spread through meetings and forums, and thus deeply rooted among the people — for example, the theme of the 12th China–ASEAN Exposition highlighted the "sea" and "The Silk Road"; the Information Office of China and China International Studies Foundation, the China–ASEAN Business Council separately held two international seminars on the 21st Century Maritime Silk Road — the former focused on the main theme "Making the Community of Common Destiny, Jointly Building the 21st Century Maritime Silk Road" and the sub-themes "The Maritime Silk Road: Value Idea and Times Connotation", "Joint Building for Common Development and Prosperity", "Seizing the New Developmental Opportunities to Seek New Cooperation Spaces", with an academic seminar in which experts from more than 30 countries participated; the latter mainly discussed "China–ASEAN Relations and the Building of the Silk Road" and

"People-to-People Connectivity and Social People-to-People Exchanges in Building the Silk Road", with attention being paid to the correlation between *ASEAN 2025: Move Forward Together* and the *Vision and Actions on Jointly Building the Silk Road Economic Belt and the 21st Century Maritime Silk Road.* At the same time, the Xiamen International Ocean Forum 2015 & the 5th Ministerial Forum on Marine Sustainable Development for Developing Countries incorporated the session on maritime economic cooperation between China and the ASEAN countries in which experts and scholars conducted in-depth discussions. Furthermore, the China–ASEAN Cultural Cooperation Fair, the 8th China–ASEAN Strategic Think Tank Dialogue Forum, the 2nd China–ASEAN Information Port Forum, the 7th China–ASEAN Summit on Financial Cooperation & Development, the China–ASEAN Business Leaders Forum 2015 under the 12th China–ASEAN Business & Investment Summit Framework, the 8th China Marine Development Forum & the Academic Thinking Seminar on the *Research on China's Marine Developmental Strategy* inherited and developed the spirit of China–ASEAN cooperation featuring peace, friendliness, openness, inclusiveness, mutual learning, mutual building, mutual benefits and win–win results, and also injected the connotation of new times to the ancient Maritime Silk Road.

(iii) Synergy among festivals, activities and the Silk Road

In 2015, China–ASEAN cooperation covered many festivals and activities, such as the 1st China–ASEAN International Children's Cultural Art Festival, the China–ASEAN Opera Concert, the China–ASEAN Micro Film Contest, the activity in which the singers from China and ten ASEAN countries sang friendship songs together in Beijing; the 3rd China–ASEAN Youth Cultural Exchange Festival, the 8th China–ASEAN Educational Exchange Week, the 4th China–ASEAN Music Week, the Thailand Cultural Festival, the China–ASEAN Cultural Exchange Cooperation Fair & Cultural Program Promotion Meeting. In these wonderful celebrations and festival activities, the cultural elements of the Silk Road shone; these activities not only promoted synergy among festivals, activities and the Silk Road, but also provided opportunities for the integration of diverse cultures from China and the ASEAN community.

b. *Synergy between the government and the non-governmental forces*

In 2015, China frequently engaged in exchanges and cooperation with the governments of the ASEAN countries, China had close non-governmental exchanges with those countries, shaping a pattern of synergy between the government and the non-governmental forces in people-to-people connectivity. In 2015, the two sides sent students to study in each other's countries for more than 180,000 person-times, two-way tourism hit 20 million person-times. Under the theme of "Strengthening Non-governmental Exchanges, Jointly Building the Belt and Road", the 2nd China–Southeast Asia Non-governmental High-level Dialogue Meeting, held in Bali, Indonesia, adopted the *Initiative of China–Southeast Asia Non-governmental Exchanges and Cooperation*; under the theme of "Jointly Building Non-governmental Friendship, Sharing Peace and Prosperity", the 10th China–Southeast Asia Non-governmental Friendship Meeting was held in the Arts and Handicrafts Centre, Brunei; the inheritors of China's ventriloquism, a national intangible cultural heritage, together with the Chinese People's Association for Friendship with Foreign Countries and the Beijing People's Association for Friendship with Foreign Countries, attended the 10th ASEAN Non-governmental Friendly Exchange Meeting in Brunei and Indonesia; the China (Sichuan) Malaysia Non-governmental Friendly Exchange Meeting was held in Chengdu. Such synergy between the government and the non-governmental forces made government diplomacy and non-governmental exchanges complement each other to jointly promote people-to-people connectivity between China and the ASEAN community.

3. Review and outlook

A review of the year 2015 shows that China–ASEAN cultural cooperation highlighted the inheritance and innovation of traditional marine culture, the countries and territories along the Maritime Silk Road actively grasped the main theme of China–ASEAN maritime cooperation in the new period, with cultural exchange activities conducted to foster a good atmosphere and build a platform for China–ASEAN maritime cooperation featuring joint consultation, building and sharing. The common marine culture and historical memory have boosted, at the people-to-people level, China–ASEAN maritime cooperation, thus conveying the Silk Road spirit of peace, friendliness, openness and inclusiveness, mutual learning, mutual benefits and win–win results, cultivating the awareness of a "Common Home" in the South China Sea, stimulating people-to-people connectivity, further dispelling the maritime disagreements between China and the ASEAN countries and upgrading maritime cooperation.

Looking into 2016, pushing forward the integration and innovation of the "cultural power" with the sea as a bond and life scene between China and the ASEAN countries will remain a bright spot and a priority in China–ASEAN cultural cooperation; the inheritance and upgrading of the historical culture of the Maritime Silk Road will become a new issue in China–ASEAN cultural cooperation in 2016; the launch of the Year of China–ASEAN Educational Exchanges 2016 and a closer relationship for educational cooperation between China and the ASEAN community will offer new opportunities for China–ASEAN people-to-people cooperation and exchange in 2016.

V. The Outlook for the Development of China–ASEAN Cooperation in 2016

In 2015, China–ASEAN cooperation reached a new high, as evidenced by the facts that China won the bidding for the Jakarta–Bandung High-speed Railway Project in Indonesia, and the construction of the China–Laos and the China–Thailand high-speed railways began; however, the insufficiency of mutual trust is still a key factor affecting China–ASEAN cooperation.

1. The problems in the development of China–ASEAN relations

Generally speaking, the overall China–ASEAN relations are good; however, institutional differences, the dispute over the South China Sea, the USA's intervention in the issue of the South China Sea and trade demarcation caused by the TPP have affected the mutual trust between the two sides.

a. *ASEAN countries have doubts about and guard against the rise of China*

China differs from some ASEAN countries in political system, small countries worry about and guard against the neighboring large countries, ASEAN countries fear that once China becomes powerful, like other superpowers, China will impose its will on other countries and not observe international rules. This mentality is embodied as follows: China's actions in the South China Sea are interpreted excessively and misunderstood. China's reasonable acts in safeguarding its maritime rights and interests are merely a little something done by China in striking contrast to the acts of other countries involved in the dispute of sovereignty over the South China Sea. However, other countries have done many things, but the neighboring countries do not feel there is anything wrong with each other.[34] For the case involving the South China Sea Arbitration initiated by the Philippines, some ASEAN countries criticized the Chinese Government's policy that China will not participate in the case, does not accept and recognize the results of its arbitration, these countries held that this showed China's disrespect for international rules.

b. *The intense situation of the South China Sea has affected the political mutual trust between China and the ASEAN community*

In 2015, after the information that China carried out the construction on the islands and reefs in the South China Sea was exaggerated by Western media, ASEAN countries expressed doubts about the situation of the South China Sea. During the 26th ASEAN Summit in April 2015 and the 27th ASEAN Summit in November, ASEAN countries vowed to ensure the peace, stability and security of the South China Sea region in two *Presidential Statements*. This indicates that the doubts regarding the intense situation

---

[34] Hu Yishan, With a Strong Momentum of Rise, China Becomes Aggressive in the South China Sea, Phoenix Satellite Television. 2015 -04- 20, http://itech.ifeng.com/41061409/news.shtml?&back.

of the South China Sea issue have been prevalent among the leaders of the ASEAN countries.

The military operations of the USA in the South China Sea have further aggravated this situation. In coordination with the strategies of "Pivot to Asia" and "Rebalancing to Asia", the USA has carried out military operations in the South China Sea again and again, and deepened military cooperation with ASEAN countries in 2015.

c. *The TPP has weakened the economic foundation for the mutual trust between China and the ASEAN countries*

In 2015, driven by the USA, TPP negotiations delivered substantive outcomes. After TPP implementation, the US-led economic system will spread to Southeast Asia, the economic alliance consisting of the USA, Japan and the ASEAN will take shape in the Asia-Pacific Region. Such an economic alliance will challenge the cooperation framework established between China and the ASEAN countries, China's leading role in regional cooperation may be weakened, and China may even lose the opportunities for further cooperation with AEAN countries.

d. *The non-governmental cultural exchanges and cooperation between China and the ASEAN countries are relatively weak*

Although China and the ASEAN countries have engaged in extensive cooperation in education, public health, cultural arts and personnel exchange, such cooperation and exchanges have been carried out mainly at the governmental level and have lacked momentum at the non-governmental level. If the close cooperation between China and the ASEAN community at the governmental level is not supported by active participation at the non-governmental level, there will be no solid foundation. The mutual trust between China and the ASEAN countries should start from mutual understanding and trust between the people from China and ASEAN countries. Strengthening non-governmental cultural exchanges and cooperation is the most effective way to facilitate the communication between the people from the two sides.

2. Countermeasures for the development of China–ASEAN relations

Building mutual trust is an important condition and a long-term task for guaranteeing the stable development of China–ASEAN relations. To build mutual trust, it is necessary to proceed in the following respects.

a. *Removing the Theory of a China Threat*

To remove the Theory of a China Threat, first, China should unswervingly implement a foreign policy of bringing harmony, security and prosperity to its neighboring countries. China should firmly believe, regardless of interference and difficulties, that as a neighbor of China and an alliance of medium and small developing countries, the ASEAN community poses no threat to China and can be regarded as a good-neighborly partner for long-term cooperation.

Second, China should actively participate in various regional cooperation forums and mechanisms organized by ASEAN countries, China should voice opinions through various formal and informal meetings to promote mutual trust and avoid misunderstandings. China should observe international mechanisms, actively participate in regional cooperation mechanisms, strengthen cooperation with its neighboring countries and should not challenge international cooperation mechanisms.

Third, China should take concrete actions to enhance trust and clear up doubts, tell the Chinese story in a way that is understandable to other countries, explain China's diplomatic philosophy so that China's stand is fully understood and accepted by the ASEAN community and its member countries. China should proactively improve the transparency of China's national defense and dispel the doubts of the international community and ASEAN member countries.

Fourth, China should increase economic assistance to poor ASEAN countries, narrow their income gap, ensure that the ordinary people in ASEAN countries can enjoy China's developmental achievements, accept and welcome China.

Fifth, China should provide the neighboring countries and the international community with shipping safety and other public goods in the

South China Sea, such as building many visible navigation lights on islands and reefs, and offering meteorological, navigational and logistics support services. Such actions can remove the misunderstanding regarding China, which exists in some countries having disputes with China over the South China Sea.

b. *Enhancing economic cooperation between China and the ASEAN community*

Strengthening China–ASEAN economic cooperation and building an economic community of a common destiny between the two sides is the foundation for guaranteeing mutual trust between the two sides. The priority of China–ASEAN economic cooperation consists in comprehensively implementing the strategy of the Belt and Road and upgrading the China–ASEAN Free Trade Area.

Within the strategy of the Belt and Road, China's high capacity for infrastructure construction is utilized and the areas along the Belt and Road are connected by highways, railways and networks to achieve trade, exchanges and economic development through further connectivity, so that the economic contact between China and ASEAN becomes closer. *The Protocol to Amend the Framework Agreement on Comprehensive Economic Cooperation between the Association of Southeast Asian Nations and the People's Republic of China and Some Agreements under the Framework Agreement*, signed on November 22, 2015, signifies the upgrading of the China–ASEAN Free Trade Area. The upgrading of the China–ASEAN Free Trade Area means that the scale of trade and that of investments between China and the ASEAN community are expected to reach USD 1 trillion and USD 150 billion by 2020, respectively.

c. *Attempting to enable cooperation under the trilateral framework covering China, ASEAN and the USA*

The USA is the greatest external factor in the dispute of the South China Sea and is called "the largest party concerned which is, however, not a real party concerned". There has been a triangle of close interaction among China, the ASEAN community and the USA in the Asia-Pacific region. The ASEAN has played an important role in shaping the new-type great-power relations between China and the USA, while the USA is the most important external force in developing political mutual trust between China and the ASEAN. China, the ASEAN and the USA can attempt to cooperate under the trilateral framework, especially engaging in economic cooperation and low-level military cooperation.

d. *Engaging in non-governmental cooperation and exchanges in various ways*

In the wake of international exchanges with the non-governmental organizations, scholars and think tanks in the ASEAN countries, China and the ASEAN can maintain closer contacts in such key areas as culture, history, politics, security and the economy, and see a more solid foundation for mutual trust. At the same time, various types of forces at different levels in the society are integrated; the industrial associations, intermediaries, private enterprises and voluntary groups in various fields are organized; cooperation is promoted in an informal, unorganized and non-institutionalized way; trans-regional and cross-border industrial alliances are established, so that multilevel cooperation is achieved in more areas in the society.

3. The direction for the development of a China–ASEAN cooperative relationship

The China–ASEAN cooperative relationship in 2016 should be developed by focusing on enhancing mutual trust and consolidating the economic foundation for mutual trust.

a. *Building a community with a common destiny shared by the countries in the Lancang–Mekong region*

In the first meeting on Lancang–Mekong cooperation in March 2016, Chinese Premier Li Keqiang proposed to jointly build a community with a common destiny shared by the countries in the Lancang–Mekong region. The Lancang–Mekong cooperation mechanism is a beneficial supplement to the framework for China–ASEAN cooperation. The community should rely on project implementation with project priorities including connectivity, production capacity, cross-border economy, water resources, agriculture and poverty alleviation.

b. *Establishing the maritime cooperation partnership through connection*

Maritime cooperation is the best way to resolve the conflicts in the South China Sea. China should build a connection with ASEAN's maritime cooperation to further strengthen policy coordination and increase the level of cooperation of cooperative projects. Such a connection covers: (1) Developmental strategy — The 21st Century Maritime Silk Road initiated by China can be connected with the developmental blueprint for the ASEAN Community. (2) Projects — Their connection should center on the marine economy, maritime connectivity, maritime environmental protection and scientific research, maritime search and rescue, fishery cooperation and anti-pirate cooperation. (3) Cooperation on the capacity for maritime production.

c. *Comprehensive implementation of the Belt and Road Initiative*

The Belt and Road Initiative put forward by China should be connected with the developmental strategies of various countries. Future China–ASEAN cooperation on the Belt and Road will focus on such fields as infrastructure, engineering machinery, electrical power, building materials and communication; cooperation on the capacity for production is carried out to increase the level of industrialization of the relatively backward surrounding countries; the Asian Infrastructure Investment Bank, the Silk Road Fund and other platforms are used to support ASEAN countries with respect to cooperative development in infrastructure and other areas.

Part 2

Report on the Cooperation between China and ASEAN Countries 2015

Chapter 2

Report on the Cooperation between China and Thailand in 2015

Yue Guining and Yue Han*

In 2015, Thailand kept calm amidst turbulence. The Prayuth Chan-ocha Military Government, which came into power through a coup d'état in May 2014, continued to maintain the overall stability of the national situation by means of a military iron hand; the military government adopted a series of means, including reshuffling the cabinet and amending the constitution, with attempts to disintegrate relevant camps and absorb political oppositions, to greatly weaken the capacity for action of the two great forces not in power, including the Thaksin Shinawatra Group and the Democratic Party, thus further consolidating the overall control by the military group over various aspects of the country.

Against the overall background of the increasingly stable governance by Thailand's military government, on the one hand, China–Thailand cooperation on various fronts was continued and promoted; on the other hand, the Prayuth Chan-ocha Government's relations with Western countries were continuously at a low level, so the strategic complementation between China

*Yue Guining, Director, Professor at the Thailand Institute of the China–ASEAN Research Institute of Guangxi University. Yue Han, Special Commentator at the Thailand Institute of the China–ASEAN Research Institute of Guangxi University, chief editor of www.taiguo.com.

and Thailand was boosted, the bilateral contacts, including infrastructure construction and military cooperation, were further consolidated. Promoting relevant work in a continued and steady way was the general tone of China–Thailand cooperation in 2015.

I. The Overall Situation of Thailand in 2015

1. Thailand's political situation: The heyday of the military iron hand

When the Prayuth Chan-ocha Government had been in power for one and a half years, in 2015, it comprehensively rebuilt the military government's authority which had collapsed for some time since the 1990s, fully controlled the direction and rhythm of the succession of Thailand's royal family and firmly suppressed the traditional civil official group and the emerging capital-controlled political parties. Although the military power had not played a part in the political circle for more than 20 years, it staged a comeback to seek the royal power, the prime minister's power and the financial power; Thailand essentially returned to the regime adopted during the period 1932–1992, in which the military took power, so the short and tortuous process of democratization was interrupted and the pattern of the distribution of power was reshuffled in Thailand.

In 2015, Thailand's political circle was still dominated by the Prayuth Chan-ocha Military Government, the Thaksin Shinawatra Group (the People's Power Party — the National United Front of Democracy against Dictatorship) and the Democratic Party. With guns at hand, the military government's authority occupied the absolute leading position in the political circle and fully controlled Thailand's administrative, judicial and legislative branches; it enjoyed the overwhelming advantage over two major groups not in power in the political, economic and public opinion fields, it also obtained universal support from the industrial and commercial circles and from the people.

At the beginning of the year, the military government took a sweeping action to cancel Yingluck Shinawatra's right from participating in public affairs in the next 5 years for the reason of insufficient supervision over the Rice Paddy Pledging Scheme, and it instituted criminal charges against

Yingluck Shinawatra. Afterwards, the military government took two major political actions, including reshuffling the cabinet and making a breakthrough in the constitution — completing the reshuffling of the cabinet in late August, appointing a number of non-military personnel represented by Somkid Jatusripitak, the "economic master" during the period of Thaksin Shinawatra, to important posts, weakening the military character of the government, absorbing some forces from two major non-ruling parties, including the People's Power Party and the Democratic Party; meanwhile the military government was aware of the fact that the non-ruling forces, especially the Thaksin Shinawatra-controlled People's Power Party — the National United Front of Democracy against the Dictatorship Group still enjoyed a good reputation, the military government would not venture to hold a general election, therefore it intentionally submitted the "semi-finished" draft constitution with harsh clauses to the interim reform parliament for voting in September. When the draft constitution was voted down, the general election was postponed automatically, thus the period for the military to hold power was legally prolonged for 1 year.

Subject to the pressure from the steady expansion of Prayuth Chan-ocha's political power, two major forces not in power became noticeably divergent, with public division among the appeasing faction of the military and the radical resistance faction within the party. Similar faction strife also occurred within Thailand's police force and the Buddhist circle. With political expansion, faction strife also gradually surfaced within the military, the newly-elected Commander in Chief of the army, Teerachai Nakwanich, attacked the former Commander in Chief Udomdej Sitabutr for the reason of Rajabhakti Park's graft case, but faction strife only existed within the military and did not exert a decisive impact on the overall political situation.

In general, in 2015, continuous expansion of the military governmental group further encroached on the survival space of the two major parties not in power. The Red Shirts (controlled by Thaksin Shinawatra) and the Yellow Shirts (the Democratic Party), which had been extremely antagonistic in the previous decade, declined and disintegrated amidst the pressure from the military. In the future new constitutional framework led by the military, the previous two-party pattern in Thailand's political circle will become fragmented and return to the situation before the promulgation of the constitution in 1997, in which the military is dominant and small parities exist. It is expected that no political force can effectively check the military in a short time; the actual political form under Thailand's representative democracy is that the military supervises the country with state affairs governed behind the scene.

2. Thailand's economy: Slack policy without evident effect

On the economic front, the Prayuth Chan-ocha Military Government appointed Somkid Jatusripitak, the representative figure of Thaksinomics, to take charge of the economic affairs. Somkid Jatusripitak adopted the stimulus-oriented macro-control means to revitalize the sluggish economy, so Thailand's economy, plagued by unrest, recovered to some extent. After the new cabinet took office, it substantially increased budget expenditure and earmarked more than 130 billion Thai baht capital for the market, greatly eased the control over financial credit to support small and medium-sized enterprises, it restored the township enterprise support plan for "one specialty product in one town" during the Thaksin Shinawatra period and extended the repayment period for farmers' loans to 3 years.[1] A series of measures produced a certain effect on expanding investments and boosting consumption, reducing the speed of Thailand's economic contraction.

However, as the international economy was generally stagnant, Thailand was hit hard by drought and the sequela of populist economic policies introduced during the periods of Thaksin Shinawatra and Yingluck Shinawatra loomed large, the military government saw a strained national treasury and the effects of stimulus policies were limited. The Prayuth Chan-ocha Government was less able to cope with the economic difficulties, including a dull sale of bulk commodities, e.g., rubber, rice and palm oil, and a lack of strength in growing investments, consumption and exports.

In 2015, Thailand's exports contracted for 12 consecutive months and declined by 5.5%, while its imports sharply decreased by nearly 10%, and its

---

[1] Tan Liya, Thailand's Cabinet Adopted the 130 Billion Thai Baht Economic Stimulus Measure, www.huanqiu.com. September 2, 2015, http://finance.huanqiu.com/cjrd/2015-09/7406595.html.

economy grew by only 3–4%.[2] Although consumption improved to some extent and economic contraction eased at the year's end, the recovery of the people's consumption ability will entail a long process, and the country's exportations are making efforts to break away from a negative growth. In particular, the collapse of bulk commodities has threatened consumption and worsened the fiscal situation, it even still continues to endanger Thailand's political situation — the rice and rubber producing areas are the traditional bases of the People's Power Party and the Democratic Party, thus the farmers' predicament has become the factor triggering demonstrations incited by the parties in power. Overall, Thailand's economic prospect is worrying; there is a long way to go before recovery.

3. Thailand's society: Fostering "positive energy"

On the social front, the Prayuth Chan-ocha Government sought popular support by revering the royal family and vigorously fighting corruption, it endeavored to create a harmonious social atmosphere, and it also severely suppressed the fabrication and dissemination of "negative information"; overall, a significant effect was produced, the military government authority was gradually recognized and accepted by the ordinary people. In 2015, the Prayuth Chan-ocha Government continued to carry forward 12 values, mainly "being patriotic and loyal to the throne", and carried out the movement of "Bringing Happiness to the People" to improve people's livelihood and enrich their cultural life and entertainment activities. During the birthdays of Thailand's king and queen, the military dedicated massive resources to mobilizing the people and conducting BIKE FOR DAD activity on a large scale; it took the royal family as the bond to develop the people's sense of national identity, downplayed the backlash and opposition, thus nurturing "positive energy" in public opinion.

Furthermore, the sweeping anti-corruption campaign contributed to the popularity of the Prayuth Chan-ocha Government and effectively held down the "centrifugal factors" within the royal family, the government,

---

[2]Thailand's Exports Diminished by 7.42% in November, 2015, the Economic and Commercial Counsellor's Office of the Chinese Embassy in Thailand, December 29, 2015, http://th.mofcom.gov.cn/article/jmxw/201512/20151201222035.shtml.

the military, the police and the religious circles. In 2015, the trusted followers of Thailand's crown prince Maha Vajiralongkorn, considered to favor Thaksin Shinawatra, were almost fully removed, even thoroughly expelled from Thailand's royal family due to the corruption incident within the entire family of the crown prince and princess; in the religious circle, the mighty Wat Dhammakaya got deeply involved in malpractice scandal relating to Thaksin Shinawatra; the Wat Dhammakaya eminent monk's group among the high-level figures in the Buddhist circle, including the acting Supreme Patriarch — which originally occupied the dominant position and was closely related to the Thaksin Shinawatra group — was besieged by the opposing monks and priests apparently from a military background, and even the succession of the new Supreme Patriarch in Thailand was suspended, astonishingly shocking the people.

For the control over public opinion, the military frequently cited the 112th Clause of the Criminal Law (Crime of Insulting the Royal Family) to severely punish the ordinary people who disseminated negative information to the media and online platforms with an anti-government tendency, and the scholars and students with a strong sense of democracy; as a result, the academic and media circles with consistent actions against the military government kept quiet out of fear.

With the above means, the military government's authority generally maintained a stable situation in Thailand's society, Prayuth Chan-ocha's political power was not hit by major public opinion crises and protests, the legitimacy of his governance was increasingly recognized by the people and his public opinion foundation remained be solid in 2015.

4. Thailand's security and diplomacy: Being unswerving in keeping neutral

At the national security level, Thailand faced the most severe terrorist attack in history — the explosion at Erawan Shrine in the Rachaprasong area — in 2015; at the same time, the separatist activities in Southern Thailand remained active. The Prayuth Chan-ocha Government dodged and downplayed the situation, isolated the explosion from China's Xinjiang separatists and Turkey's ultra-right forces, and only considered the explosion as a vindictive act of an overseas group of human smugglers; the Prayuth

Chan-ocha Government internally insisted on holding talks with the mainstream faction of Islamic separatists in Southern Thailand with a view to assuring the people and rebuilding the image of the tourist industry. In coping with the security challenge, the military government showed an Ostrich mentality to a certain degree, but the security situation was not significantly improved.

On the diplomatic front, the new US ambassador to Thailand criticized Thailand as always, while the EU again and again urged the Prayuth Chan-ocha Government to restart a general election, so the relations between Thailand's military government and the Western world deteriorated. As a response, the Prayuth Chan-ocha Government actively engaged in cooperation with China and built a connection with the Belt and Road Initiative, energetically engaged with Russia, Iran and other countries, maintaining its diplomatic need of being independent.

With the establishment of the ASEAN Community on December 31, 2015, Thailand also kept friendly contacts with the countries in the region. Overall, maneuvering among great powers, being independent and neutral, building good neighborly and friendly relations and attempting to act as the leader in ASEAN unification remained the basic direction for Thailand in its diplomatic dealings.

II. Main Achievements in China–Thailand Cooperation in 2015

In 2015, China–Thailand cooperation in various areas developed substantially; in particular, the most significant achievements were made in two main areas that is infrastructure construction and security cooperation. Major cooperation events, such as the initiation of the construction of the China–Thailand railway, a submarine purchase, repatriation and extradition, drew worldwide attention.

Among a number of remarkable cooperation projects, some projects became successful and saw breakthroughs, while some projects were unsuccessful and regrettable; the objective desire of the heads of both countries to engage in cooperation went beyond, to some extent, the boundary of Thailand's bearing capacity, so much cooperation often awaited actions for a long time and underwent shocks. However, overall, China–Thailand cooperation developed rapidly due to the internal developmental needs of both countries and continued pressure from the external environment.

1. The cooperation on the construction of infrastructure was promoted steadily: The construction of the China–Thailand railway was initiated successfully

On December 3, 2015, after repeated bargaining with the Prayuth Chan-ocha Government for a year, China and the Thailand Government ultimately signed the framework document on railway cooperation, the China–Thailand railway cooperation project, which underwent many setbacks, but eventually saw a final decision. Regarding the China–Thailand double-track railway, which costs USD 12.2 billion (about RMB 78 billion), is about 867 km long and its design speed is 250 km/h but its actual operating speed is about 180 km/h, the initial agreement was reached preliminarily during the period of the Yingluck Shinawatra Government; its plan ran aground for a time during the early stage of the Prayuth Chan-ocha Government; its negotiation was restarted during Li Keqiang's visit to Thailand and afterwards, prolonged negotiations were carried out; ultimately, its plan was basically finalized. At the same time, China and Thailand signed an importation contract on 1 million tons of Thailand's rice, thus the plan concerning "rice for high-speed railway", postponed for several years due to political unrest, was finally back on track.[3]

According to this framework document, both sides will carry out the China–Thailand railway cooperation project in design, purchase, construction and other links, and will establish a joint venture for investment and railway operations; China will provide Thailand with a technology license, technology transfer, personnel training, financing and other support. The foundation stone-laying ceremony for the project was held in December, 2015. The Thai Government vowed to fully complete its construction by May 2016.

[3]Yang Fang, The China–Thailand Railway Was Initiated, Li Keqiang's High-speed Railway Diplomacy Yielded Another Encouraging Outcome, *People's Daily Online*, December 29, 2015, http://politics.people.com.cn/n1/2015/1219/c1001-27950565.html.

In fact, strengthening the construction of transportation infrastructures and providing extensive access to the ASEAN community with the support of a network of railway transportation is one of the strategic goals set by successive Thai Governments, so the final initiation of the construction of the China–Thailand railway is just a matter of time. "The dispute over loan interest rates", "the rumor about the ownership of land along the railway" and other matters during negotiations were the means by which the government and non-governmental forces in Thailand made bargains with China and the pretexts used by the forces not in power to attack the military government, rather than the doubts about the project itself. In the subsequent half year, it is expected that the voice similar to "requiring China to increase investments and reduce interest rates" will linger, but it will not fundamentally hinder the project itself.

2. The military cooperation reached a new high: A new pattern took shape in exercise and military purchases

Military cooperation was a bright spot in China–Thailand cooperation in 2015. After the bilateral relations between Thailand and the USA — the original military partner — deteriorated, Thailand actively sought military cooperation with China, Russia and other countries. Thailand's Deputy Prime Minister and Defense Minister Prawit Wongsuwan, in charge of national defense, visited China several times during the year; both countries sent military personnel for reciprocal visits, conducted symbolic joint military exercises and planned to engage in cooperating on massive military purchases.

At the invitation of Thailand's air force, China's Air Force August 1st Aerobatic Team flew to Thailand on November 12, 2015 to participate in the "Eagle Strike — 2015" joint training activity of the China–Thailand air force. In two weeks, the air forces from the two countries received joint training, including aerial confrontation and flying circus, at Thailand's Korat Air Base. China dispatched a J-11A fighter, while Thailand sent a JAS-39 C/D Gripen fighter purchased from Norway to accept the challenge. With this joint exercise, the two sides learnt from each other, enhanced their understanding and deepened their pragmatic cooperation in the military field. It is widely believed in the world that this joint training of air forces from China and Thailand was of more a political significance than a military one. In late 2015, USA, Japan, Vietnam, the Philippines and other countries condemned China over the issue of the South China Sea, while Thailand engaged in close military exchanges with China. Thailand's then foreign minister Tanasak Patimapragorn even humorously made a famous remark that he "loved Chinese foreign minister Wang Yi" on a public occasion, which undoubtedly reaffirmed before the world that Thailand would keep absolutely neutral in the current international security affairs and shake off the political binding with the NATO and the military bloc at the first island chain. As Thailand had always followed the diplomatic principle of keeping neutral and balanced, it was impossible for Thailand to firmly support China, but at that time, Thailand at least had withdrawn from the team of USA's strategy of "Pivot to Asia" and became an independent sideliner in regional affairs from which support might be sought.

For military purchases, Thailand's military reserved 200 billion Thai Baht in a military budget for itself by taking advantage of holding power and made a "surprise military purchase" in 2015, during which it purchased fighters, military helicopters, armored personnel carriers and other heavy equipment from Russia, France, South Korea and other countries. The plan for a submarine purchase from China became the headline news among Thailand's people, and even drew worldwide attention in 2015. In June 2015, Thailand's Deputy Prime Minister and Defense Minister General Prawit Wongsuwan declared that Thailand would allocate 36 billion Thai Baht (about RMB 6.5 billion) to purchase three submarines from China.[4] However, in the middle of July he said that the plan would be postponed for further evaluation.

That purchase plan became controversial and was finally put aside in reality. Regarding the causes, as said by Thailand's Defense Minister, there was excessive opposition and too much attention, so the plan could not be put on the agenda of the parliament unless Thailand's navy better justified the necessity for having submarines. This clearly shows that the purchase crisis was caused by the political factors outside the project rather than the purchase itself. The diplomatic pressure from USA, limited military

[4]Yue Han, Purchase of China's Submarines at a Low Price. July 7, 2015, http://blog.sina.com.cn/s/blog_c11c62120102vlqi.html.

expenditure and the army's action to squeeze out the navy were the most important causes for the failure of the purchase plan. At the same time, immediately after the purchase plan was announced by the navy, the People's Power Party, the Democratic Party, democratic reform organizations and many social activists raised objections against the purchase plan, and they required the government to use the arms purchase funds to lift the country out of economic plight and address social issues, thus the impact of the pressure from public opinion by the opposition parties cannot be neglected.

At present, that purchase plan has been shelved, Thailand's military government and navy still spare no effort to lobby the people for supporting and understanding the purchase plan; however, it can be expected that the plan will be restarted by Thailand's military once the time is ripe. Thailand's military has taken a clear positive attitude towards military cooperation with China.

3. Economic and trade cooperation was continued: Rice purchase under the grand strategy

In 2015, all-round headway was made in economic and trade cooperation between China and Thailand. China included Thailand in the list of RMB overseas investment destinations, while the upper limit of Thailand's investment in China was raised to 50 billion Thai Baht[5]; at the same time, Thailand also seized opportunities to enter the Chinese market and tried every means to increase its exports to China, with the hope of saving the beleaguered industries including rice, rubber, palm oil and tourism by tapping the shrinking — but still huge — market demand in China. Under the principle of reciprocity and mutual benefit, both sides deepened their economic and trade cooperation.

As early as December 19, 2014, China and Thailand signed the *Memorandum of Understanding Concerning China–Thailand Cooperation in Agricultural Products Trade*, under which COFCO would import 1 million tons of rice from Thailand from November 2015 to December 2016.

[5]Yu Yichun, The Pilot Work on RMB Qualified Foreign Institutional Investors Is Extended to Thailand, *People's Daily Online*, December 18, 2015, http://news.sohu.com/20151218/n431710529.shtml.

On December 3, 2015, witnessed by Wang Xiaotao, Vice Minister of the National Development and Reform Commission of China, and Mrs. Apiradi Tantraporn, Thailand's Commerce Minister, Yu Xubo, COFCO's President, and Mrs. Duangporn Rodphaya, Director of the Department of Foreign Trade, Ministry of Commerce of Thailand, officially signed the contract.[6]

For China, the symbolic massive import contract was part of the "High-speed Railway for Rice" program and the strategic arrangement of the Belt and Road Initiative and epitomized the conscious and purposeful deepening and development of China–Thailand economic and trade relations. Compared with the pure economic and trade contacts between Thailand and other countries, the 21st Maritime Silk Road strategy put forward by China represents the unconscious intrinsic goal of bilateral commercial and trade cooperation; it also governs and promotes the deepening of commercial and trade cooperation on various fronts. This was a significant characteristic of bilateral economic cooperation in 2015.

4. Security cooperation advanced under adverse circumstances: Cooperation, amidst turmoil, in cracking down on human smuggling

In 2015, with the discovery of the Rohingya Smuggling Corridor at the Thailand–Malaysia border, Thailand started to get tough with the overseas smuggling act with the third country as a destination. Thailand repatriated about 100 smugglers with a Uygur nationality, which had a bearing on the security strategies of both countries and drew wide attention and criticism around the world.

On July 9, Thailand announced that it had repatriated about 100 smugglers with a Uygur nationality to China.

After the Thai Government weighed the pros and cons, among the nearly 400 smugglers with a Uygur nationality arrested at Songkhla a year earlier, 173 women and children were sent to Turkey, 109 young people were

---

[6]Liu Chenyao, COFCO Signed a Contract for Importing 1 Million Tons of Rice from Thailand, chinanews.com, December 4, 2015, http://www.chinanews.com/cj/2015/12-04/7656652.shtml.

repatriated to China, while there were about 50 people whose identity had not yet been determined.

That decision made by Thailand reflects a smart tradeoff. Within the situation in which China and Turkey "scrambled for" people, Thailand sent women and children to Turkey and young men to China, thus preserving Thailand's humanitarian image, striking a balance between China and Turkey, also thwarting the attempt of the Middle East extremist forces to recruit soldiers overseas and preventing the Uygur nationals from continuing to flow into Thailand.

However, Thailand was still attacked by anti-China forces due to Thailand's repatriation of Chinese smugglers with a Uygur nationality. Thailand's consulate in Istanbul was smashed by extremists holding the banner of East Turkistan Islamism, while Thailand's embassy in Germany was besieged by Turkish nationals residing abroad; Western countries, the United Nations and other non-governmental organizations denounced Thailand. China–Thailand security cooperation in this field was subject to heavy international pressure; such cooperation also reflects Thailand's firm stand about independence and national security, and shows that Thailand deviated from the West and moved towards the east in the diplomatic field to some extent.

5. High-level diplomacy: Thailand's deputy prime minister visited China with the goal of merely focusing on discussing commercial and trade issues

From September 2 to 5, 2015, Thailand's Deputy Prime Minister and Defense Minister General Prawit Wongsuwan, in charge of security affairs, led a delegation to officially visit China, which included the Commander in Chief and Assistant Defense Minister General Udomdej Sitabutr and the Secretary-General of Thailand's Council for National Security. During this visit to China, as the special representative of Thailand's Prime Minister, General Prawit Wongsuwan attended the activity commemorating the 70th anniversary of the victory of the War of Chinese People's Resistance against Japanese Aggression, the military parade held by the Chinese Government and the meetings on national security, the economy, investments and other affairs.

During this visit, General Prawit Wongsuwan deliberately avoided the issue of the explosion in the Rachaprasong area, Bangkok before the public; he said, "I will not discuss this matter with China because it is Thailand's internal affair". In fact, this indicates that Thailand still pays attention to the economic and trade contacts with China and also keeps a certain distance from China in security cooperation and anti-terrorism, maintains the consistent line of thought of "engaging in economic cooperation and being politically neutral" in dealing with external affairs. Thailand will certainly hold consultations with China with respect to this matter, but Thailand has to refrain from discussing political affairs before the public so that Thailand will not be considered to politically favor China, and Thailand's strategic balance with Turkey, the Islamic world and the whole Western world will not be affected.

III. Achievements and Drawbacks in China–Thailand Cooperation in 2015

China–Thailand cooperation during the year was similar to the usual situation of China's cooperation with foreign countries. China's cooperation with Thailand was in a state of strong hardware cooperation but weak software cooperation. On the one hand, China has seized the opportunity from accelerated integration of Southeast Asia, and leverages its capital and technical advantages to enter Thailand, China has swiftly pushed forward cooperation with Thailand in scale, effectiveness, quality, quantity and breadth; however, on the other hand, with regard to publicity and communication, China lacks a deep understanding of the people's conditions and public opinion among the various classes in Thailand, and it does not effectively communicate with and lobby various forces in the political circle, so that the cooperation on many fronts has faced unnecessary negative public opinion and obstacles.

1. Achievements and experience

Based on China's advantages in technical level and comprehensive national strength in recent years, China has seized opportunities in economic, trade, scientific, technological and military cooperation with Thailand, and has achieved the strategic goal of making favorable arrangements. In particular,

China has succeeded in Thailand's railway construction (the construction of the northeastern quasi-high speed railway), equipment application (Thailand's fishing boat satellite navigation system and electric bus system incorporate China's technologies), the standardization in the emerging fields (4G communication contains the technologies from Chinese enterprises); thus China has been universally recognized by various sectors in Thailand; thanks to the achievements made by China in these fields, "Made in China" has been further recognized by Thailand, which has widely acknowledged and accepted the conception of the 21st Century Maritime Silk Road and has clearly expressed the determination and sincerity about China's southward cooperation. The countries in the region generally consider China's economy as a certain policy-oriented market economy, so after the psychological cognition that China–Thailand cooperation is China's national strategy has been created, both the Thai Government and private capital have a redoubled confidence in the Chinese Government, large Chinese state-owned enterprises even common Chinese enterprises, thus effectively expanding the subsequent space for China–Thailand cooperation in the economic and technical areas.

At the same time, besides a good start, correct understanding of and high alignment with Thailand's developmental strategy, is one core factor contributing to smooth economic and trade cooperation between China and Thailand. The elites in Thailand's political and business circles generally have the strategic insight into regionalization. Advocating the establishment of the uniform ASEAN market under the framework of the ASEAN Community by emulating the EU model, obtaining the developmental opportunities and international status in the capacity of main participant (even the leader) in the greater ASEAN community constitutes Thailand's consensus on its future developmental path. With China's strong willingness to cooperate and its powerful comprehensive strength, Thailand has found China as a lever for building an integrated ASEAN community. With cooperation with China, Thailand has fostered advantages in the ASEAN system on the transportation, logistics, trade, scientific and technological fronts, and has thus established a highly connected regional community with Thailand as the core. With mutually beneficial cooperation between China and Thailand, both countries have identified the points at which respective strategies converge. In this regard, Thailand's decision-makers are very willing to cite the Chinese-style expression that Thailand is the best springboard for the

Belt and Road Initiative by China; Thailand's strategic intent of integrating the ASEAN community by virtue of China is evident.

Finally, military security cooperation embodies Thailand's strategic intent of "elevating itself by relying on China" before the Western world, and also enhances Thailand's confidence in practicing this intent. The opening of Thailand's window will be favorable for China to build a secure surrounding environment, and will provide a stable and valuable channel for China to access the Indian Ocean by bypassing Vietnam and India and a neutral buffer zone for the China–US tussle in the Asia-Pacific region. This is also consistent with Thailand's strategic positioning as "corridor and balance". Utilizing and promoting the sharing of respective developmental strategies is the important achievement and guarantee for China–Thailand cooperation, also the most important principle and experience involving cooperation with Thailand.

2. Drawbacks and suggestions

In general, China's cooperation with Thailand was successful in 2015, but the overall success in hardware indicators was accompanied by many regrets in soft power, causing hidden troubles which should not be overlooked in the long-term development of China–Thailand exchanges.

First, as China intensely engaged with the Prayuth Chan-ocha Military Government, China neglected the forces not in power which were suppressed in Thailand and the social mindsets against the military government; this reveals the drawback that China often only valued the authority but missed the grass-roots forces in foreign cooperation, so Thailand's public opinion gradually bound the Chinese Government to Thailand's military.

Since such a binding existed, the forces not in power boycotted China–Thailand cooperation projects to launch a political attack on the military government. The China–Thailand railway project met with public criticism many times during negotiations, there were many objections and malicious rumors which alleged that a high-speed railway was luxurious, China gained extra advantage at Thailand's expense and the ownership of land along the railway was transferred to China. As a result, this project was delayed in the finalization of its plan and commencement of its construction. The submarine purchase, which would naturally become a reality, was unfortunately shelved due to the pressure from public opinion.

Thailand's military government appears to be gaining ground at present, but its foundation is not unshakable. Internal strife between the two major forces not in power was the important cause for keeping the military away from political challenge during the year. Once either of the Thaksin Shinawatra Group and the Democratic Party Group takes a confrontational attitude, even both groups jointly counter the military, Thailand's military government may face the storm of democratic demonstrations like those during the period of the cold war at any time. If China shows excessive preference for the military and cold-shoulders the forces not in power, it is likely that China will become the target of political consumption among various forces and this will be detrimental to China–Thailand relations. Therefore, China should actively keep in touch with the various parties in Thailand through informal channels and offer assistance to the undeveloped areas in Thailand, shift diplomatic efforts from the government as the core and the overseas Chinese groups in the business circle to the extensive social groups and the young generations, so as to mitigate political risks and improve its national image.

Second, on the security cooperation front, China often excessively concentrates on China itself and neglects the sideliners. In a number of incidents, including the case involving smugglers with a Uygur nationality, the explosion in the Rachaprasong area, Bangkok, and anti-China and anti-Thailand actions of Turkish ultra-right organizations, China made stiff and high-profile responses; for example, when China received the repatriated smugglers with a Uygur nationality, the faces of these smugglers were covered by black masks, triggering widespread aversion in Thailand. After the explosion in Bangkok, the people at the non-governmental level believed that Thailand bore the blame on China's behalf, while China gave no explanation in this regard. Thailand was denounced by the United Nations High Commissioner for Refugees because of this situation, the military government lost face totally and China's national image was impaired.

In the future, China–Thailand security cooperation must take into account Thailand's image and stand more. For the less urgent matters, such as repatriation of dissidents, suppression of heresy, Falun Gong and opposition against Tibet separatists, China should refrain from raising excessive requirements for the Thai Government. With respect to the crucial security cooperation, such as shipping in the Mekong River and cracking down on terrorism-related human smuggling, under the condition that Thailand is willing to cooperate, China should act in a low-profile way as far as possible and not give others an excuse, ensuring that China is not victimized due to the political struggle within Thailand and the latter does not become the target of public opinion among the international anti-China forces.

It is necessary to keep a balance, make friends with as many parties as possible, communicate better with and pacify the forces not in power to avoid unexpected problems and self-demonization. This is the most important lesson to be learned from China–Thailand cooperation in 2015.

Chapter 3

Report on the Cooperation between China and Vietnam in 2015

Jin Dan*

In 2015, under the leadership of the Communist Party of Vietnam, Vietnam was politically stable and diplomatically active; its national economy improved in both scale and potential; the country made significant improvement in the people's livelihood and in the educational, scientific, technological and cultural fields; its status in the international arena continued to rise. The year 2015 was the 65th anniversary of the establishment of diplomatic relations between China and Vietnam; although some setbacks occurred in the development of bilateral relations in that year, friendly cooperation was the mainstream in those relations, the two sides supported and helped each other and new progress was made in bilateral cooperation in many fields.

* Jin Dan, Director, Associate Research Fellow at the Vietnam Institute of the China–ASEAN Research Institute of Guangxi University.

I. Review of Vietnam's Situation in 2015

1. Politics

a. *From active preparation for holding the 12th National Congress of the Communist Party of Vietnam to the successful holding of the 12th National Congress*

In 2015, the important event in Vietnam's national political life was its active preparation for holding the 12th National Congress of the Communist Party of Vietnam. During the period January 5–12, 2015, the 10th Plenary Session of the 11th Central Committee of the Communist Party of Vietnam studied the preparatory work on holding the 12th National Congress of the Communist Party of Vietnam. During the days May 4–7, the 11th Plenary Session of the 11th Central Committee of the Communist Party of Vietnam studied the work direction and principles for personnel arrangement in the 12th National Congress of the Communist Party of Vietnam and some concrete issues, such as the quota of delegates to the 12th National Congress of the Communist Party of Vietnam and quota allocation. During the days October 5–11, the 12th Plenary Session of the 11th Central Committee of the Communist Party of Vietnam focused on the personnel work of the 12th Central Committee of the Communist Party of Vietnam and set the goals for Vietnam's economic and social development in 2016. During the period December 14–21, the 13th Plenary Session of the 11th Central Committee of the Communist Party of Vietnam discussed and approved by voting the nominees for the leadership of the 12th Central Committee of the Communist Party of Vietnam. During the days January 11–13, 2016, the 14th Plenary Session of the 11th Central Committee of the Communist Party of Vietnam continued to improve the plan concerning the candidates for the 12th Central Committee of the Communist Party of Vietnam, political bureau and secretariat, and adopted the recommended list of members of the presidium, secretariat and delegate credentials committee involving the 12th Central Committee of the Communist Party of Vietnam. During the period January 20–28, 2016, the 12th National Congress of the Communist Party of Vietnam was held under the theme of intensifying efforts to build a clean and robust Party organization; giving scope to the strength of the whole nation and the democracy of the socialist system; comprehensively pushing forward the cause of reformation in a coordinated way; firmly defending the motherland and safeguarding the peaceful and stable environment; as early as possible making Vietnam basically become an industrialized country which develops in the direction of modernization. The Congress announced the new leadership of the Communist Party of Vietnam and the members of the Central Committee, and adopted a series of important documents, identifying the direction, goal and task for Vietnam's economic and social development in the next 5 years.

b. *Active progress was made in legislation*

In 2015, the work of the National Assembly of Vietnam focused on legislation and law revision under the Constitution (2013). On May 20, 2015, the 9th Session of the 13th National Assembly of Vietnam deliberated and adopted 11 laws, the Order of the President concerning 1 decree and 1 resolution. These acts directly affect human rights, civic rights and the activities of state organs, they overcome various defects and drawbacks to ensure synchronization of the functions and tasks involving state organs under the state framework. The core issues discussed in the 10th Session of the 13th National Assembly of Vietnam on October 20 included legislative work, execution of the Constitution (2013), supervision, evaluation and decision of major state affairs. In the legislation field, worldwide attention was drawn to the first *Referendum Law* in Vietnam, which becomes effective as of July 1, 2016. According to the *Referendum Law*, the Standing Committee of the National Assembly of Vietnam, the President of Vietnam, the Vietnam Government and at least 1/3 of representatives to the National Assembly can submit a proposal to the National Assembly of Vietnam to initiate a referendum. According to the provisions, the issues for which a referendum can be initiated include all of or the main contents of the Constitution, the issues concerning state sovereignty and territory, the national defense security issues having a direct bearing on national interests, and the social and economic issues exerting a great impact on national development. A number of laws adopted by Vietnam, including the *Housing Law*, the *Enterprise Law* and the *Investment Law*, come into force as of July 1, 2015 and January 1, 2016.

c. *The anti-corruption efforts continued to be intensified, the anti-corruption situation remained severe*

In 2015, under the Party and state's leadership in Vietnam, an anti-corruption campaign was carried out and yielded positive results, the modes of anti-corruption publicity were continuously renewed, the functional organs worked more closely, many serious corruption cases were uncovered, investigated and handled in an accelerated way. In the first 9 months of 2015, the supervisory organs conducted 2,842 administrative inspections and 116,334 special inspections, found and imposed disciplinary punishment on 366 people involved in corruption, involving 11.298 trillion Vietnamese Dong (about USD 53.8 billion) in illegal assets and 589 hectares of land.[1] On November 30, the investigatory agencies at various levels prosecuted 460 people in 216 cases, the people's procuratorates at various levels heard 266 cases involving 591 defendants, while the people's courts at various levels conducted first trials of 235 cases involving 531 defendants.[2] The arrest of Nguyen Xuan Son, the former Chairman of PetroVietnam, was approved. Furthermore, the Supreme People's Procuracy of Vietnam approved the recommendation of instituting criminal proceedings against Ms. Chau Thi Thu Nga, a member of Hanoi's delegation to the 13th National Assembly of Vietnam, for the crime of swindling and embezzling property. In December, 2015, the Anti-Corruption Bureau under the Government Inspectorate of Vietnam launched three anti-corruption whistle-blowing hotlines for encouraging citizens to report corruption cases. Although Vietnam had vigorously carried out an anti-corruption campaign, the anti-corruption situation was still severe. According to the *Corruption in Eyes — 2015 Annual Index* released by the Transparency International, Vietnam ranked No.112 in the world,[3] lagging far behind.

---

[1] [Vietnam] Nguyễn Phú Trọng, the General Secretary of the Communist Party of Vietnam: Substantive Progress Was Made in Fighting Corruption, Vietnam News Agency, September 29, 2015.

[2] *Ibid.*

[3] [Vietnam] Transparency International Corruption Perceptions Index 2015: Vietnam Improved by 7 Places, Vietnam News Agency, January 28, 2016.

2. Diplomacy

In 2015, Vietnam made many diplomatic achievements, its overall strength further increased and its international status improved to some extent.

a. *Relations with the USA and Europe: making active progress*

The year 2015 was the 20th anniversary of the establishment of the diplomatic relations between Vietnam and the USA and the 2nd anniversary of the establishment of a comprehensive partnership between the two sides, and the bilateral cooperative relationship was continuously strengthened in various fields. In July 2015, Nguyễn Phú Trọng, the General Secretary of the Communist Party of Vietnam, visited the USA and signed a number of cooperation agreements and memoranda with the US. In addition, the signing of the TPP in February 2016 also substantially promoted the diplomatic relations between the two countries. On December 2, 2015, Vietnam and the EU officially signed the *Vietnam-EU Free Trade Agreement*, opening a new chapter for Vietnam–EU relations. On December 17, the European Parliament officially ratified the resolution concerning the *Vietnam–EU Comprehensive Partnership Agreement*, marking the official shift of the Vietnam–EU relations from trade exchange and assistance to a comprehensive partnership.

b. *Relations with Japan and South Korea: Enhancing cooperation*

Japan is an important source of foreign capital and the largest assistance provider for Vietnam. According to statistics, as of October 2015 Japan ranked No. 3 among 58 countries and territories investing in Vietnam. In September, Nguyễn Phú Trọng met with Japanese Prime Minister Shinzo Abe; the two sides agreed to strengthen security and economic cooperation and improve bilateral relations. In 2015, South Korea continued to become the largest investment source for Vietnam. On May 5, 2015, Vietnam and South Korea officially signed the *Vietnam–South Korea Free Trade Agreement*, which became effective as of December 20, offering an explicit basis and convenience for the import and export trade between the two countries.

c. *Relations with Russia and India: Advancing steadily*

In 2015, the high-level exchanges between Russia and Vietnam maintained a good momentum. In April, the Russian Prime Minister Dmitry Medvedev visited Vietnam. In May, Trương Tấn Sang, the President of Vietnam, attended the activity of commemorating the 70th anniversary of the victory of the Great Patriotic War in Russia. Vietnam and Russia officially signed the *Free Trade Area Agreement between Vietnam and the Member Countries of the Eurasian Economic Union*, thus pushing forward the development of bilateral trade and economic relations. In 2015, Vietnam and India continued to carry out the *Action Plan for a Bilateral Strategic Partnership (2014–2018)* with efforts to strengthen investments and defense cooperation. In October, the Government of India officially approved the *Protocol to Amend the Agreement between India and Vietnam for the Avoidance of Double Taxation and the Prevention of Fiscal Evasion with Respect to Taxes on Income*, promoting the development of trade and investment between the two countries.

d. *Relations with ASEAN: Deepening integration*

The year 2015 witnessed the completion of the ASEAN Community and the 20th anniversary of Vietnam's accession to ASEAN. Active integration into ASEAN brought huge opportunities and challenges to Vietnam. The completion of the ASEAN Community in late 2015 exerted an active impact on Vietnam, including the expansion of the scope of the market, enabling more free and convenient connectivity of personnel and goods; that completion also added more bargaining chips to Vietnam in cooperating with great powers; however, it also made Vietnam subject to fierce competition due to the inflow of a large number of foreign enterprises.

3. Economy

Under the complicated and changing world situation, in 2015, Vietnam released many positive signs in such respects as the GDP, the growth rate of the GDP, foreign trade and the curbing of inflation.

Table 1. Vietnam's GDP, the Growth Rate of the GDP and Per Capita GDP, 2006–2015

Year	GDP constant price (1 billion Vietnamese Dong)	Growth rate of GDP (%)	Per capita GDP (USD)
2006	1699501.00	6.98	796.65
2007	1820667.00	7.13	919.18
2008	1923749.00	5.66	1164.61
2009	2027591.00	5.40	1232.37
2010	2157828.00	6.42	1333.58
2011	2292483.00	6.24	1543.03
2012	2412778.00	5.25	1755.27
2013	2543596.00	5.42	1908.64
2014	2695796.00	5.98	2052.29
2015	2875875.17	6.68	2228.00

Source: Wind Information, the data on the year 2015 come from the General Statistics Office of Vietnam and are the result of the author's calculation.

a. *GDP reached a new high*

In 2015, Vietnam's GDP was about USD 204 billion, up 6.68%; it was the highest growth rate in the past 5 years and exceeded the planned 6.2% for the first time in 8 years; per capita GDP was USD 2,228 (Table 1). A number of industries tended to recover in production, the secondary and tertiary industries accounted for 82.5% of the GDP. The agricultural labor force accounted for only 45% of all of the labor force.[4]

b. *Foreign capital flowing into Vietnam soared*

In 2015, the newly approved and increased foreign direct investments in Vietnam amounted to USD 22.76 billion, up 12.5% over the previous year; the actual foreign capital reached USD 14.5 billion, up 17.4% over the previous year (Table 2). The processing and manufacturing industry attracted

[4]Vietnam's Economic Bright Spots in 2015 and the Outlook for 2016, (Vietnam) *Vietnam Nhân Dân*, December 9, 2015.

Table 2. Foreign Direct Investments in Vietnam

Year	Number of foreign direct investment projects	Total registered capital of foreign direct investment projects (1 million USD)	The appropriated capital in foreign direct investment projects (1 million USD)
2006	987.00	12004.50	4100.40
2007	1544.00	21348.80	8034.10
2008	1171.00	71726.80	11500.20
2009	1208.00	23107.50	10000.50
2010	1237.00	19886.80	11000.30
2011	1191.00	15618.70	11000.10
2012	1287.00	16348.00	10046.60
2013	1530.00	22352.20	11500.00
2014	1588.00	21000.00	12350.00
2015	2013.00	22760.00	14500.00

Source: Wind Information.

the most foreign capital in Vietnam, followed by the electric power industry and the real estate industry. In 2015, South Korea ranked No. 1 among the 58 countries and territories investing in Vietnam; the investments made by South Korea in Vietnam totaled USD 2.68 billion.[5]

c. *Imports and exports surged, trade deficit appeared again*

In 2015, amidst a sluggish aggregate import demand for commodities and ample supply sources on the world market, the export pressure on Vietnam increased, and the prices of export commodities declined. The volume of Vietnam's imports and exports reached USD 165.6 billion and USD 162.4 billion in 2015, up 12% and 8.1% over the previous year, respectively (Table 3); Vietnam saw a relatively high rate of contribution from mobile phones and their parts, computers and their parts, mechanical equipment, shoes, textiles and clothing to export.

[5]The Foreign Capital Flowing to Vietnam Skyrocketed in 2015, (Vietnam) *Vietnam Nhân Dân*, December 29, 2015.

Table 3. Vietnam's Commodity Imports and Exports, 2006–2015 (Unit: 1 million USD)

Year	Total volume of commodity imports and exports	Commodity exports	Commodity imports	Foreign trade gap
2006	84717.30	39826.20	44891.10	−5064.90
2007	111326.10	48561.40	62764.70	−14203.30
2008	143398.90	62685.10	80713.80	−18028.70
2009	127045.10	57096.30	69948.80	−12852.50
2010	157075.30	72236.70	84838.60	−12601.90
2011	203655.50	96905.70	106749.80	−9844.10
2012	228309.60	114529.20	113780.40	748.80
2013	264065.50	132032.90	132032.60	0.30
2014	298066.20	150217.10	147849.10	2368.00
2015	328000.00	162400.00	165600.00	−3200.00

Source: Wind Information.

d. *The inflation rate fell to the lowest level in 14 years*

In 2015, the Government of Vietnam and the State Bank of Vietnam actively and flexibly adopted various financial policy tools, food supply was sufficient in Vietnam and several categories of products experienced declining prices on the world market, so the inflation rate was the lowest in 14 years. In 2015, the basic inflation rate increased by 2.05% over the previous period, while the CPI rose by 0.63% on average over the previous period and was much lower than the upper limit (5%) put forward by the National Assembly of Vietnam.[6]

4. Society

In 2015, the level of social security for the people's livelihood increased to some extent, and great achievements were made in poverty alleviation, medical care, elimination of gender discrimination and the safeguarding of

[6]Vietnam's CPI Declined to a New Low in 2015, (Vietnam) *Vietnam Nhân Dân*, December 24, 2015.

labor rights and interests in Vietnam. According to relevant data from the General Statistics Office of Vietnam, the total size of the poverty-stricken population was 925,300 in Vietnam in the first 11 months of 2015, down 30.4% over the same period of the previous year. In December 2015, the Central Committee of the Vietnam Fatherland Front and Vietnam Social Insurance signed the *Cooperation Plan for Implementing Social Insurance and Medical Insurance Laws, Regulations and Policies (2016–2020)*, stating that by 2020, 50% and 35% of the labor forces would be covered by social insurance and commercial insurance, 80% of the people would be covered by medical insurance in Vietnam. In addition, Vietnam approved the International Labour Organization C100 *Convention Concerning Equal Remuneration for Men and Women Workers for Work of Equal Value* and C111 *Convention Concerning Discrimination with Respect to Employment and Occupation*; Vietnam will strictly observe the principles set in the above conventions and promote the establishment of the *Minimum Wage Law*. In 2015, science and technology flourished in Vietnam, Vietnam ranked 52nd among 141 economies and was listed among the top three in ASEAN countries in the innovation index.[7] The Government of Vietnam continued to intensify the reform of the educational system, and carried out concrete plans for graduation from high middle school and unified the college entrance examination as of 2015. In 2015, Vietnam's cultural construction became distinctive and diversified. Based on advocating and carrying forward the spirit and style of the Vietnamese, the Government of Vietnam energetically pushed forward cultural integration between Vietnam and other countries, enhanced mutual political trust among countries and deepened the mutual understanding among people through cultural diplomacy.

II. Review of China–Vietnam Cooperation in 2015

The year 2015 was the 65th anniversary of the establishment of diplomatic relations between China and Vietnam. In 2015, the bilateral relations continued to improve, high-level reciprocal visits occurred frequently, mutual

[7] [Vietnam] Vietnam Soared by 19 Places in the World in the Innovation Index in 2015, Vietnam News Agency, September 23, 2015.

political trust was enhanced continuously, the level of bilateral economic and social cooperation was on the increase, and bilateral relations presented a pattern of positive and better development.

1. Political cooperation

a. *The high-level reciprocal visits were frequent and the comprehensive strategic partnership was consolidated*

In 2015, China and Vietnam maintained frequent high-level reciprocal visits. During the period of April 7–10, 2015, Nguyễn Phú Trọng, the General Secretary of the Communist Party of Vietnam, paid an official visit to China and held talks with Chinese President Xi Jinping; the two sides jointly issued *the China-Vietnam Joint Communiqué*, signed the *Plan for Cooperation between the Communist Party of China and the Communist Party of Vietnam (2016–2020)*, the cooperation documents in the financial, infrastructural, cultural, judicial, taxation, and peace-keeping areas, with a view to working together to promote sustained, healthy and sound development of the comprehensive strategic partnership. During the two days November 5 and 6, Chinese President Xi Jinping paid a state visit to Vietnam. The leaders of the two countries exchanged profound views on deepening the relations between the two parties and between the two countries and on the international and regional issues of common concern; they reached important consensuses, issued the *China-Vietnam Joint Communiqué*, signed a number of cooperation documents, including the *Agreement between the Government of the People's Republic of China and the Government of the Socialist Republic of Vietnam with Respect to Navigation in the Free Navigation Area at the Estuary of the Beilun River*, further enriching the connotation of the China–Vietnam comprehensive strategic partnership. In 2015, besides General Secretary Nguyễn Phú Trọng's visit to China and President Xi Jinping's visit to Vietnam, other high-level reciprocal visits also frequently occurred between the two countries. During the days of July 16 and 17, Zhang Gaoli, Vice Premier of the State Council and a member of the Standing Committee of the Political Bureau of the CPC Central Committee, visited Vietnam, discussed with the Vietnamese side with regard to concrete measures for strengthening strategic communication, enhancing mutual political trust, promoting pragmatic cooperation and expanding the people-to-people exchanges. During the period of September 15–17, Nguyen Xuan Phuc, a member of the Political Bureau of the Central Committee of the Communist Party of Vietnam and Deputy Prime Minister of the Government of Vietnam, paid an official visit to China and attended the 12th China–ASEAN Exposition and the China–ASEAN Business and Investment Summit in Guangxi. On December 23, Nguyễn Sinh Hùng, Chairman of the National Assembly of Vietnam, visited China and met with Chinese President Xi Jinping, the two sides signed the *Agreement on Cooperation between the National People's Congress of the People's Republic of China and the National Assembly of the Socialist Republic of Vietnam*.

b. *The mutual political trust was enhanced, active progress was made on the issue of the South China Sea*

In 2015, China and Vietnam made active headway regarding the issue of the South China Sea. During the period of April 7–10, Nguyễn Phú Trọng, the General Secretary of the Communist Party of Vietnam, visited China and held talks with Chinese President Xi Jinping. The two sides agreed to jointly control the divergences over the sea, comprehensively and effectively implement the *Declaration on the Conduct of Parties in the South China Sea* (DOC), and establish the *Code of Conduct in the South China Sea* (COC) as early as possible on the basis of consultation, refrain from taking the actions that would complicate and enlarge the relevant dispute, timely and properly address issues to safeguard the general situation of China–Vietnam relations and the peace and stability of the South China Sea. The two sides agreed to promote the work of the working group for consultation on joint maritime development, strengthen cooperation in the less sensitive areas, steadily push forward the negotiations involving demarcation of the open sea area at the estuary of Beibu Gulf; actively propel the joint development of the sea area, and initiate a joint survey on the open sea area at the estuary of Beibu Gulf as early as possible within the year. During the two days of June 3–4, the expert working group for China–Vietnam maritime cooperation in the less sensitive areas held the 7th round of consultation in Hanoi. The two sides reached a consensus on initiating, within the year, the projects "Research on Comprehensive Management and Cooperation in the Marine

Environment and Islands at Beibu Gulf between China and Vietnam" and "A Comparative Study of Holocene Sedimentary Evolution in the Yangtze River Delta in China and the Red River Delta in Vietnam"; the two sides also agreed to continue to put into practice the important consensuses reached by the leaders of both countries and the *Agreement on the Basic Principles for Guiding the Settlement of the Maritime Issue between China and Vietnam*, actively boost their cooperation in the less sensitive areas in the sea. During the period of November 5–6, General Secretary Xi Jinping paid a state visit to Vietnam and frankly exchanged views with the state leaders of Vietnam with regard to the maritime issue; he stressed that both countries should carefully implement the *Agreement on the Basic Principles for Guiding the Settlement of the Maritime Issue between China and Vietnam*, better use the boundary negotiation mechanism between the governments of the two countries, seek the basic and long-term solution acceptable to both sides through friendly consultations and negotiations, actively explore the transitional solution not affecting respective stands, including energetically studying and discussing the issue of joint development.

2. Economic cooperation

In 2015, bilateral trade maintained a sustained and rapid growth, Chinese enterprises quickened the pace of "going global" in Vietnam, both sides made active progress in financial cooperation.

a. *Bilateral trade continued to grow*

In 2015, bilateral trade developed continuously. First, the scale of the bilateral trade expanded rapidly. According to the statistics from China Customs, bilateral trade totaled USD 95,819 million in 2015, up 14.6% over the previous year.[8] China's exports to Vietnam amounted to USD 66,143 million, up 3.8% over the previous year; China's imports from Vietnam amounted to USD 29,676 million, up 49.1% over the previous year. China was the

[8] However, according to the statistical data from the Vietnam Chamber of Commerce and Industry, China–Vietnam import and export trade totaled USD 66.3 billion in 2015, up 12.9% over the previous year.

largest trading partner for Vietnam for 12 consecutive years, while Vietnam was the second largest trading partner for China in the ASEAN community, only second to Malaysia. In 2015, the gap between China–Vietnam trade and China–Malaysia trade was only USD 1.5 billion. Second, the imbalance in China–Vietnam trade changed gradually. In 2015, China's trade with Vietnam grew by 3.8%, while Vietnam's trade with China surged by 49%; Vietnam's trade deficit with China was USD 36.4 billion, down USD 7.4 billion over the previous year. Third, the China–Vietnam trade structure continued to be optimized. The technology and capital-intensive industries gradually replaced agricultural and sideline products, primary industrial finished products and mineral raw materials to become the leading products in bilateral trade; bilateral cooperation was expanded continuously in breadth and depth. Finally, the border trade played an important role in China–Vietnam trade. According to the statistics from the Ministry of Industry and Trade of Vietnam, in 2015, Vietnam's border trade totaled USD 27.56 billion, while China–Vietnam border trade reached USD 23.4 billion, accounting for 85%, up 10.1% over the previous year.[9]

b. *China's investments in Vietnam grew steadily*

In 2015, the direct investments made by Chinese enterprises in Vietnam showed a steady growth and involved multiple fields, various levels and a number of dimensions. As China's domestic labor costs were on the rise and Vietnam joined the Trans-Pacific Partnership Agreement (TPP), more and more Chinese investors entered Vietnam with the hope of sharing the opportunities from the TPP. According to the statistics from Vietnam, in 2014, Chinese enterprises invested in 1,089 projects in Vietnam with the agreement amount totaling about USD 8 billion; however, in 2015, the investors from the Chinese Mainland carried out 1,258 projects in Vietnam with the cumulative amount of about USD 10 billion and the contract amount totaling USD 8.6 billion,[10] ranking China No. 9 among the 105 countries

[9] The Economic and Commercial Counsellor's Office of China's Embassy in Vietnam: China–Vietnam Bilateral Trade Approached USD 90 Billion in 2015, January 20, 2016.

[10] [Vietnam] China–Vietnam Trade Exchange Meeting Was Held in Ho Chi Minh City, *Vietnam News Agency*, January 14, 2016.

(territories) investing in Vietnam. The steady growth of China's investments in Vietnam largely promoted Vietnam's economic development; in particular, these investments played an apparent role in stimulating local employment, improving the structure of Vietnam's industrial chain and pushing forward Vietnam's industrialization. However, the investments made by Chinese enterprises in Vietnam still had the following two problems: First, less attention was paid to investing in Vietnam's agriculture, forestry and fishery, excessive investments were made in resource development; second, most projects were on a small scale, some projects were worth less than USD 1 million, many projects adopted backward technologies, and they might cause pollution of the local environment.

c. *Financial cooperation was deepened*

In April 2015, China and Vietnam announced that the two sides had officially established the working group for cooperation on infrastructures, and the working group for financial and monetary cooperation, and would steadily promote financial cooperation. In July, the Deputy Governor of the People's Bank of China and Vietnam's counterpart co-chaired the first meeting of the working group for China–Vietnam financial and monetary cooperation in Hanoi. The two sides exchanged views on the recent macroeconomic situation and monetary policy of China and Vietnam, the financial stability and the development of the financial market in both countries, bilateral trade, domestic currency settlement in investments and the next work of the working group. On December 11 in Dongxing, a port city on the border of China and Vietnam, the Guangxi Branch of the Postal Savings Bank of China and the Quang Ninh Branch of the Saigon–Hanoi Commercial Bank of Vietnam held the signing ceremony for the agreement for cooperation on the border trade settlement. After signing, the Guangxi Branch of the Postal Savings Bank of China raised the number of Vietnam's commercial banks as its cooperators to three, extended the international service products to international settlement, foreign exchange settlement and sales, cross-border RMB, and made many beneficial attempts to improve the capability of integrated services covering domestic and foreign currencies. In January 2016, the Yunnan Branch of the Bank of China and the Lao Cai Branch of the Bank for the Investment and Development of Vietnam held the signing ceremony for agreement for cooperation on the border trade settlement. With that signing, the customers from both sides would be provided with safer, more convenient and high-quality cross-border integrated financial services.

3. Cultural, scientific, technological and educational cooperation

In 2015, with the 65th anniversary of the establishment of diplomatic relations between China and Vietnam, the two countries held the activities under the theme of signing contest and artistic performance, the China–Vietnam Friendship Concert, the China–Vietnam Cultural Exchange Week and other cultural exchange activities, while the cultural exchange activities in various forms enhanced the relationship between the people and consolidated mutual friendship. On July 16, witnessed by Zhang Gaoli, a member of the Standing Committee of the Political Bureau of the CPC Central Committee and Vice Premier of the State Council, and Nguyen Xuan Phuc, Deputy Prime Minister of Vietnam, Ding Wei, Vice Minister of the Ministry of Culture of China, and Vice Minister of the Ministry of Culture, Sports and Tourism of Vietnam signed the *Execution Plan for China–Vietnam Cultural Exchange 2016–2018* at the Office of the Prime Minister in Hanoi, providing the plan for bilateral cultural exchanges in the next 3 years. On August 19, the China–Vietnam Friendship Concert, jointly planned by the Culture Office of the Embassy of China in Vietnam and the Ministry of Culture, Sports and Tourism of Vietnam, was held in Hanoi. During the period of October 23–30, the Department of Culture of Yunnan Province organized the Yunnan Culture and Art Troupe to visit and stage performances in Ho Chi Minh City and Hanoi City, Vietnam. In 2015, the Government of Vietnam attached great importance to the friendly exchanges with China in the scientific and technological fields. On July 30, the National Office in the Southern Region under the Ministry of Science and Technology of Vietnam and the China–ASEAN Technology Transfer Center held a seminar on technology matchmaking between Chinese and Vietnamese enterprises regarding new energy, renewable energy and hi-tech energy fields in Ho Chi Minh City, in which a number of Chinese and Vietnamese enterprises signed the technology transfer cooperation and connection agreement on production operations. In 2015, China–Vietnam educational cooperation developed continuously. In May, the China–Vietnam Educational Cooperation

Forum was successfully held in Guilin. During the period of August 3–7, the 8th China–ASEAN Educational Exchange Week was held in Guizhou Province, promoting the common development of education in China and Vietnam. In October, Vietnam's Hung Vuong University and the Embassy of China in Vietnam jointly established the Chinese Language and Cultural Research Room with a view to enhancing Vietnam's understanding of Chinese culture.

4. China–Vietnam cross-border economic cooperation zones

In 2015, positive progress was made in the China–Vietnam cross-border economic cooperation zones. As of August 2015, the industrial development plan, the overall plan and regulatory plan of Dongxing Park had been completed, land requisition, road network construction and investment attraction involving Dongxing Park had been pushed forward in an orderly way; Pingxiang Park saw accelerated efforts in project construction concerning the road network project, the channel of connectivity with Vietnam, specialized market construction, supervised goods yards and facilities. At the same time, Dongxing Park and Pingxiang Park also witnessed first-ever implementation of pilot programs in systems and mechanisms, exploring the way for China to expand its development and opening-up along the border and gaining valuable experience. For example, Dongxing City pioneered in reforming the industrial and commercial registration system, officially dealt with non-local tourist visas, pushed forward experiments in chartered services involving RMB-Vietnamese Dong exchanges, tourists' duty-free shopping and overseas service cooperation between the inhabitants of the border areas. Pingxiang City also experimented with customs supervision innovation, cross-border financial services, upgrading of trade between the inhabitants of the border areas and cross-border labor services. Dongxing Port and Pingxiang Port provided customs inspection characterized by "one-off declaration, one-off inspection and one-off release" and permitted the cross-border passage of transportation vehicles and official vehicles between China and Vietnam; the two ports saw actions to initiate the building of the China–Vietnam joint inspection platform.[11] On May 25, the People's Committee of Lao Cai

[11]The Workshop on the Construction and Management of the China–Vietnam Cross-border Economic Cooperation Zones Kicked Off in 2015, *People's Daily Online*, August 7, 2015.

Province, Vietnam and Yunnan Province, China held talks on speeding up the construction of the Lao Cai-Red River Cross-border Economic Cooperation Zone. The two provinces would actively build the Lao Cai-Red River Cross-border Economic Cooperation Zone dominated by Beishan, Hekou, China—Kim Thanh, Lao Cai, Vietnam Trade Complex, with the purpose of building and developing the Kunmng-Lao Cai-Hanoi-Haiphong Economic Corridor as early as possible. On February 3, 2016, the Management Committee of the Dongxing Experiment Zone and the China MCC17 Group jointly invested 1.8 billion yuan to promote the construction of an industrial park and infrastructure in Dongxing, China—Mong Cai, Vietnam Cross-border Economic Cooperation Zone, making four breakthroughs — a new model of government-enterprise cooperation, labor service cooperation, a cross-border self-driving tour and cross-border financing — in the construction of the cross-border economic cooperation zones.

5. Military and national defense security cooperation

In 2015, China and Vietnam continuously strengthened their military and national defense security cooperation. On April 17, Chinese Public Security Minister Guo Shengkun paid an official visit to Vietnam and held talks with Vietnamese Public Security Minister Tran Dai Quang. The two sides signed the *Execution Plan for the Memorandum of the Fourth Meeting on Cooperation in Cracking Down on Crimes between the Ministries of Public Security of China and Vietnam*, both sides agreed that the ministries of public security of both counties should continue to strengthen cooperation, prevent and crack down on various crimes to ensure the order and security of both countries. On October 19, Nguyen Tan Dung, Prime Minister of the Government of Vietnam, met with Chinese State Security Minister Geng Huichang. The two sides agreed to enhance the defense cooperative relationship, continue to actively carry out the military and diplomatic activities, maintain frequent reciprocal visits of delegations at various levels and military officer exchange activities, jointly safeguard the political security of both countries, strengthen information exchange, enhance cooperation in traditional and non-traditional security fields, including cyber security as well as the fight against international terrorism. On October 24, the Vietnamese Public Security

Minister Tran Dai Quang met with the Chinese Public Security Minister Guo Shengkun, and the two sides agreed to continue implementation of the consensuses reached between the leaders of both parties and countries, take vigorous measures to boost the cooperative relationship, in a comprehensive and profound way, in law enforcement, in the fight against organized crime, cross-border crime, terrorist crime, cyber crime and the crime of human trafficking; they also agreed to jointly carry out the activities to crack down on crimes in the border areas, strengthen the measures for safeguarding the safety and security of citizens of both countries, and intensify the cooperation in professional training. On December 31, a direct phone line between the ministries of national defense of China and Vietnam was officially launched. Chinese State Councilor and National Defense Minister Chang Wanquan held the first phone talks with Phung Quang Thanh, Deputy Secretary of the Central Military Commission of the Communist Party of Vietnam and the Vietnamese National Defense Minister. The two sides agreed to seriously carry out the important consensus reached by the secretaries of both parties, turn high-level consensus into concrete achievements and properly manage and control disagreements so as to further develop the bilateral military ties in the new year.

III. Drawbacks in China–Vietnam Cooperation in 2015 and Suggestions for Improvement

1. The political mutual trust between the two countries was low

At present, China and Vietnam have not yet made substantive progress in some cooperation fields, while the biggest obstacle is the insufficiency of mutual political trust between the two sides, which has affected the relationship between Vietnam's Party members, cadres and the people belonging to various classes and China. Therefore, the two sides should take the strategic and long-term perspective to approach and handle China–Vietnam relations, jointly build a community with a common destiny to benefit the people of both countries. The senior leaders of the two parties and the two countries should keep close contacts in various ways, including reciprocal visits, appointment of special envoys and hotlines, timely exchange views on major issues in the relations between the two parties and the two countries, strengthen strategic communication to enhance the mutual political trust, so as to make sure that China–Vietnam relations always advance along the correct track.

2. The economic and trade frictions were intense

First, the deficit of Vietnam's trade with China was excessively large. In 2015, the total deficit of Vietnam's trade with China hit USD 30 billion. Second, the quantities of China's investments in Vietnam were too small, which was not commensurate with China's strength. Finally, the projects contracted by China were inferior in quality and not continuous. Given the above problems, the leaders of the two countries should actively take measures to strike a balance in bilateral trade. Vietnam has encouraged and led enterprises to expand the exportation of the products with competitive advantages to China. China should also energetically introduce measures to stimulate Chinese enterprises to invest in Vietnam, and require Chinese enterprises to observe local laws and regulations and win through high quality when making investments in Vietnam.

3. The issue of the South China Sea

The issue of the South China Sea is always a major issue restricting the development of China–Vietnam relations. In 2015, Vietnam and China carried out representations with respect to the issue of the South China Sea 22 times — Vietnam sent nine written protests to the Chinese Government in seven representations.[12] As the Maritime Silk Road involves the sea, Vietnam has held that it may involve the issue of sovereignty, so China should maintain strong vigilance. The issue of the South China Sea has become the core issue in the 21st Century Maritime Silk Road. In this regard, China should continue to adopt the strategy of "pursuing joint development while shelving

[12]Vietnamese Media, Vietnam and China Carried out Representations with Respect to the Issue of the South China Sea 22 Times, Vietnam Lodged Protests for Many Times, www.huanqiu.com, December 31, 2015.

disputes" put forward by Deng Xiaoping, establish a code of conduct in the South China Sea with the countries along the South China Sea as early as possible, freeze the status quo of the South China Sea, adjust the publicity strategy to rapidly mitigate tensions in the South China Sea, providing a suitable political environment for regular implementation of the Belt and Road Initiative.

Chapter 4

Report on the Cooperation between China and Myanmar in 2015

Huang Ai'lian and Yang Wen*

I. Review of the Situation of Myanmar in 2015

In 2015, Myanmar's general election, which had been drawing attention from the outside world, was finally held. The year 2015 was the crucial year for determining the direction for Myanmar's future democratic transformation. In 2015, significant achievements were made in Myanmar's domestic peace process; although economic slowdown occurred due to floods, the general situation of economic development was unchanged. At the same time, the diplomatic policy still aimed at maintaining a balance among great powers.

1. Politics

a. *Myanmar's general election was concluded, the National League for Democracy gained a complete victory*

In 2015, Myanmar's presidential election was the focus of attention from the people in various sectors, and it would also be the turning point in

---

* Huang Ai'lian, Director, Professor at the Myanmar Institute of the China–ASEAN Research Institute of Guangxi University. Yang Wen, Research Assistant, doctoral student at the Myanmar Institute of the China–ASEAN Research Institute of Guangxi University.

Myanmar's history. On November 8, Myanmar ushered in the second general election after its political transformation. The National League for Democracy, led by Aung San Suu Kyi, obtained 390 seats in the House of Representatives and the House of Nationalities, accounting for 79.4%. This means that the National League for Democracy obtained the power to independently form a new government. However, Myanmar's political situation is complicated, the National League for Democracy faces many challenges in governance. First, the National League for Democracy and Aung San Suu Kyi have no governance experience, the National League for Democracy suffers a severe shortage of talents; second, how to complete democratic reform while properly dealing with the relationship with the military remains an outstanding issue; third, ethnic minority conflicts and religious conflicts are frequent; these problems urgently need to be solved. Therefore, there are still many uncertainties in the stability of Myanmar's political situation.

b. *Northern Myanmar was war-ridden, staged progress was made in peace talks with armed ethnic groups*

Since the Government of Thein Sein came into power, it has always taken national reconciliation as the major goal in its term of office; however, as national peace talks progressed, armed conflicts were unabated. From January 2015, there were fierce wars between Myanmar's governmental army and the Kachin Independence Army, the Myanmar National Democratic Alliance Army, and their conflicts lasted for several months. At the same time, the Government of Myanmar held peace talks with other armed ethnic groups many times. On October 15, witnessed by the representatives of various parties from the international community and Myanmar, the Government of Myanmar and eight armed ethnic groups officially signed the national ceasefire agreement in Naypyidaw, Myanmar. The signing of this agreement marked substantive progress in Myanmar's peace process, the flame of war was ultimately expected to gradually go out.

c. *The government continued to combat corruption and attached importance to people's livelihood*

In 2015, the Government of Myanmar continued to fight corruption and achieved certain results. In 2 years since the establishment of the

Anti-Corruption Commission, 125 corrupt officials were investigated and dealt with, about 20.68 million kyat in money received from corruption was recovered.[1] According to the Corruption Perceptions Index 2015, released by Transparency International, the corruption cases in Myanmar decreased to some extent compared with the previous years, but Myanmar has been included in the worst corruption list and ranks No. 147 among 168 countries.[2] Furthermore, the Government of Myanmar made numerous efforts in improving the people's livelihood, such as establishing health insurance cards for the people of the middle and low classes to provide medical security, appropriating funds to build low-rent houses for addressing the housing issue concerning some ordinary people, and carrying out the plan for making electric power available to every household.

2. The economy

a. *Myanmar introduced economic reform measures, vigorously developed special economic zones*

In 2015, Myanmar carried out a number of economic reform measures to boost domestic investment growth and improve the economic environment. In April, the President of Myanmar Thein Sein signed the *National Plan for the Fiscal Year 2015–2016*, which specifies total consumption and per capita GDP as 51.45 trillion kyat and 1,281,100–1,404,000 kyat on the basis of the prices in the previous years. Regarding concrete measures, Myanmar actively attracted foreign capital to promote its economic development. First, Myanmar energetically developed special economic zones. In September, the Phase I project of Myanmar's Thilawar Special Economic Zone was initiated; the project demonstrates the achievements made by the Government of Myanmar in developing the economy, attracting foreign capital and creating jobs. Second, Myanmar encouraged the development of small and medium-sized enterprises. In March, the Government of Myanmar built the

[1]The Anti-Corruption Commission of Myanmar Investigated and Dealt with 125 Corrupt Officials in the Past Two Years, the website of Myanmar *Golden Phoenix* (Chinese version). http://www.mmgpmedia.com/local-news/11810, December 31, 2015.

[2]There Are Arduous Tasks and a Long Way to Go in Myanmar's Anti-corruption Drive, the website of Myanmar *Golden Phoenix* (Chinese version). www.mmgpmedia.com/general-news/12331, February 19, 2016.

first industrial park for private small and micro enterprises to push forward the development of small and medium-sized enterprises, develop the local economy and stimulate employment. Third, Myanmar relaxed restrictions on foreign investments. In December, the Assembly of the Union of Myanmar announced the amendment to the *Foreign Investment Law*, delegating some foreign investment examination and approval powers to the provincial and state-level agencies.

b. *Myanmar saw an economic slowdown and continuously attracted foreign capital*

Myanmar's economy was highly dependent on traditional agriculture, and natural disasters were prone to exert an appreciable impact on the national economy. During the fiscal year 2014–2015 (April 1, 2014–March 31, 2015), Myanmar's GDP was USD 61,203 million, up 8.5%. Myanmar's outward investments totaled USD 27,771 million in the fiscal year, up USD 3,341 million over the previous year.[3] In addition, Myanmar maintained sustained attraction of foreign capital; during the period April–December, 2015, the investments made by foreign enterprises in Myanmar reached about USD 5 billion; the most massive foreign investments were made in the energy field. However, with the impact of floods in the rainy seasons and an investment slowdown, according to the forecast made by the World Bank, the economic growth rate in Myanmar during the fiscal year 2015–2016 would decrease to 6.5%.

3. Diplomacy

a. *The relations between Myanmar and ASEAN, its member countries*

As Myanmar's political transformation was promoted and realized, the contacts between Myanmar and other member countries of ASEAN became more frequent and deeper, Myanmar delivered an important performance at

[3]Economic and Commercial Section of the Consulate General of the People's Republic of China in Mandalay, http://mandalay.mofcom.gov.cn/article/jmxw/201504/20150400931706.shtml.

the political and economic levels. In November, the President of Myanmar Thein Sein attended the 27th ASEAN Summit held in Malaysia, in which the leaders of 10 ASEAN countries signed the 2015 *Kuala Lumpur Declaration on the Establishment of the ASEAN Community*, and the vision document *ASEAN* 2025: *Forging Ahead Together* was adopted with a commitment to continuously improving the ASEAN Community in the next decade.

On the economic front, according to the data from the Ministry of Commerce of Myanmar, during the period April — late September, 2015, the bilateral trade between Myanmar and ASEAN countries stood at about USD 5,347 million — the trade between Myanmar and Thailand was the largest in volume and reached USD 2.5 billion. Furthermore, continued progress was also made in substantive cooperation between Myanmar and ASEAN countries. For example, Myanmar and Thailand planned to establish economic zones at the border between the two countries to promote bilateral trade cooperation; Myanmar and Singapore signed a memorandum of understanding on technical cooperation, and Singapore increased investments in Myanmar; Singapore ranked No. 1 in Myanmar in hotel investment; the President of Myanmar Thein Sein met with Nguyen Tan Dung, Prime Minister of Vietnam, and vowed to work together to make bilateral trade hit USD 500 million.

b. *The relations between Myanmar and Western countries, including the USA and Japan*

In 2015, USA adopted the strategy of sanctions plus engagement with respect to Myanmar; on the one hand, USA supported Myanmar's democratic reform; on the other hand, it continued to exert pressure on Myanmar with regard to the so-called "problem of human rights". In January, the special envoy for human rights sent by the US. Department of State visited Myanmar and held a conversation regarding human rights with Myanmar. In May, USA extended the sanctions against Myanmar for another year for the reason of the problem of human rights and domestic contradictions in Myanmar. However, in early December, the US Government suspended some sanctions against Myanmar for 6 months. This means that the USA has taken a wait-and-see attitude towards the new Government of Myanmar, and may gradually mitigate the sanctions. In the meantime, Myanmar progressively strengthened the relations with other Western countries. In July, the President of Myanmar Thein Sein met with the delegation of the German Parliament, the two sides exchanged views on intergovernmental cooperation, human resource development, trade and investments as well as other issues. The relations between Myanmar and Japan focused more on pragmatic economic diplomacy. In 2015, Japan offered economic aid to Myanmar many times and increased its investments in Myanmar. In September, the Phase I project of Myanmar's Thilawar Special Economic Zone, aided by Japan, was initiated, this became the milestone event in bilateral relations.

c. *The relations between Myanmar and India, other South Asian countries*

Myanmar and India stand at the intersection between Southeast Asia and South Asia, while Myanmar–India relations also drew attention from the international community. In 2015, both countries were active in developing bilateral relations. In July, the first meeting of the Myanmar–India Joint Consultation Committee was held in New Delhi, India, the two sides discussed bilateral relations and exchanged views on regional and international affairs. At the same time, for the sake of respective strategies, the two sides discussed and exchanged visits regarding cooperation on national defense security. Furthermore, Bangladesh also strengthened its engagement with Myanmar and proposed to sign preferential trade agreements with Myanmar and India with a view to improving bilateral relations.

4. Social culture

a. *Myanmar suffered the worst flood in 40 years*

During the months of July–August, 2015, tropical cyclone Komen caused continuous rainstorms in Myanmar and subjected Myanmar to the severest flood in 40 years. The flood affected 1.60 million people in 12 provinces and caused 117 deaths. The flood incurred huge economic losses, many roads, bridges and houses were destroyed, more than 3,000 school buildings were severely damaged, more than 1 million hectares of crops were hit, crop failure was equivalent to about 2 million tons of rice. A number of the poorest states in Myanmar were most affected by the flood, 140,000 people displaced due to conflicts in local areas faced more difficulties amidst the flood. International organizations and other countries offered aid to Myanmar, while the social groups, the military and some ordinary people in Myanmar also participated in disaster relief.

b. *The promulgation of a new education law triggered controversy*

In March 2015, Myanmar issued the new *National Education Law*. This new law excessively controls the educational system, restricts the school running system and prohibits student organizations and the teaching of minority languages; many objections were voiced. As from March, students conducted demonstrations from Mandalay to Yangon, calling for amending the education law, but they were met with violent suppression from the government. Finally, this incident ended as the demonstrating students agreed to consult with the government and the Assembly of the Union to amend the *National Education Law*.

c. *The Government of Myanmar set the minimum wage*

After negotiations, disagreements and debates lasting for nearly 1 year, Myanmar finally adopted its first minimum wage — 3,600 kyat per person per day — in August. This policy was considered as a measure taken by the government to increase wages and to maintain stability and prosperity, but it dealt a blow to the garment industry; both the labor forces and capital were dissatisfied with the new standard. On September 1, when the minimum wage came into force, about 500 workers in the Hlaingthaya Industrial Zone lost their jobs mainly because the enterprises cut down the number of employees in order to reduce their losses. However, some people supported this measure and held that it was conducive to stimulating the development of the textile industry.

II. China–Myanmar Cooperation

The year 2015 was the 65th anniversary of the establishment of diplomatic relations between China and Myanmar. The bilateral relations were affected by some disharmonious factors due to the wars in Northern Myanmar and political changes in Myanmar. However, overall, in 2015, the bilateral relations withstood many tests and great cooperation achievements were made in various fields.

1. Political and diplomatic cooperation

a. *Disputes were resolved through consultation to maintain the friendly relations between China and Myanmar*

From January 2015, the conflicts in Northern Myanmar escalated, producing many negative effects on the security and stability of the border between China and Myanmar. In the conflict in Kokang, Myanmar, on March 13, three bombs from Myanmar's governmental army fell into the territory of China, causing the death and injury of many Chinese people. This incident drew great attention from the people in various sectors of the Chinese society; the Ministry of Foreign Affairs of China made solemn representations to Myanmar. Finally, Myanmar made a formal apology to China and pledged to give compensation with respect to the deaths and injuries of the Chinese people in border areas caused by bombs from the military aircraft. The handling of this incident reflects China's determination to firmly safeguard the security of the border between China and Myanmar; it also shows one of the core issues of concern to China in coping with these kinds of emergencies. On April 12, when attending the activity commemorating the 60th anniversary of the Asian–African Leaders' Meeting and the Bandung Conference, Chinese President Xi Jinping held talks with Thein Sein. Regarding the situation in Northern Myanmar, Xi Jinping stated that China supported the efforts at seeking a political solution for the issue of Northern Myanmar through peace talks and hoped to see new progress in Myanmar's peace process as early as possible.

Another great incident in China–Myanmar diplomatic relations in 2015 was the timberjack incident in Myanmar. On July 22, 153 Chinese timberjacks were sentenced to 20-year imprisonment, two 17-year-old juveniles were sentenced to 10-year imprisonment by Myanmar. Ultimately, with repeated consultations between China and Myanmar, these timberjacks were released by Myanmar. The handling of the timberjack incident in Myanmar underwent many setbacks, but generally it did not exert much negative impact on bilateral relations; this also indicates that China still had a certain initiative at hand with regard to China–Myanmar diplomatic relations.

b. *High-level reciprocal visits were frequent, the comprehensive strategic partnership was consolidated*

In 2015, the senior leaders of the two governments and relevant political parties frequently exchanged visits; the event which drew the most attention from the outside world was that Aung San Suu Kyi, Chairman of the National League for Democracy, led a delegation to visit China. During the period of June 10–14, at the invitation of the International Liaison Department of the CPC Central Committee, Aung San Suu Kyi led a delegation to visit China for five days. During this visit, she held talks with Chinese leaders including Xi Jinping and Li Keqiang. This visit shows that China became more pragmatic and flexible in dealing with its diplomatic relations with Myanmar. This visit not only helped safeguard China's long-term interests in Myanmar, but it also effectively improved China's image among the Burmese people, thus laying a foundation for achieving benign development of bilateral relations in the future.

In addition, the senior leaders of the two sides also discussed the issues concerning cooperation in economic and other fields. On May 11, the President of Myanmar Thein Sein met with the Secretary-General of the China State Council, Yang Jing, in Naypyidaw; the two sides reached many consensuses on promoting cooperation in the industrial, energy and other fields, developing the Kyaukpyu Special Economic Zone and pushing forward cooperation on China–Myanmar investments and on the Asian Infrastructure Investment Bank. On September 3, at the invitation of China, Thein Sein attended the activity commemorating the 70th anniversary of the victory of the War of Chinese People's Resistance against Japanese Aggression and the victory of the World Anti-fascism War; after the activity, he met with Xi Jinping; this was the second meeting between the top leaders of the two countries in 2015. President Thein Sein also met with Chinese Premier Li Keqiang, and the two sides discussed China–Myanmar and China–ASEAN relations, youth exchanges and other issues. During the two days of

September 17–18, the Vice President of Myanmar, Sai Mauk Kham, attended the opening ceremony of the 12th China–ASEAN Exposition in Nanning, stating that the 21st Century Maritime Silk Road Initiative, put forward by China, would become the supplement to ASEAN's connectivity and be conducive to the infrastructure development and integration of the ASEAN Community. On December 4, Thein Sein met with Chinese Deputy Foreign Minister Liu Zhenmin at the presidential palace in Naypyidaw; the two sides discussed the issues on enhancing bilateral relations, bilateral cooperation and promoting cooperation in more fields.

2. Cooperation on the economy, trade and investments

China and Myanmar are linked by rivers and mountains, so there are natural advantages for bilateral economic and trade cooperation. Overall, China–Myanmar economic and trade cooperation in 2015 presents the following characteristics.

a. *The volume of bilateral trade declined to some extent, but the prospect is bright*

According to the statistical data from China Customs, China–Myanmar trade decreased sharply in 2015 over 2014 (see Table 1). According to Table 1, the total import and export trade between China and Myanmar fell by USD 9.7 billion (38%) in 2015 over 2014. March, August, September and October saw the greatest decrease, the total amount of imports and exports during these months declined by more than 50% over the same period of the previous year.

As shown, bilateral trade encountered some setbacks in 2015; in particular, the severe flood in Myanmar during July and August exerted a sustained impact on bilateral trade in the subsequent months. For the categories of commodities in trade, China mainly exported industrial products and daily necessities to Myanmar, while Myanmar mainly exported crude oil, natural gas and agricultural products to China; more than 93% of the rice exported from Myanmar was sold to China through border trade — border trade played an important role in bilateral trade. At Ruili Port, the largest border trade port in Yunnan Province, the import and export trade reached

Table 1. Statistics on China–Myanmar Trade (Unit: 100 million USD)

Month	China's exports to Myanmar in 2015	China's imports from Myanmar in 2015	Total import and export trade between China and Myanmar in 2015	Total import and export trade between China and Myanmar in 2014	Increase in total imports and exports
1	14.26	1.81	16.06	13.61	18.03%
2	6.35	3.09	9.45	7.18	31.56%
3	5.24	2.62	7.85	17.06	-53.96%
4	6.92	3.26	10.18	15.37	-33.76%
5	7.55	2.52	10.07	13.5	-25.41%
6	6.70	5.69	12.38	17.61	-29.68%
7	7.73	6.50	14.23	16.29	-12.64%
8	5.66	3.24	8.90	19.43	-54.20%
9	6.67	1.22	7.89	57.58	-86.29%
10	7.51	3.28	10.79	40.22	-73.17%
11	8.16	8.03	16.19	18.14	-10.77%
12	13.80	15.00	28.80	13.81	108.52%
Total	96.55	56.25	152.79	249.8	-38.83%

Source: The *Monthly Report on Customs Statistics* covering January–December 2014 and 2015 on the official website of the General Administration of Customs of the People's Republic of China, http://www.customs.gov.cn/publish/portal0/tab68101/.

USD 4.07 billion during the period January–November, 2015,[4] accounting for 33% of the total bilateral trade in the same period.

b. *China remained the largest source of investments for Myanmar*

Although the investment projects of Chinese enterprises in Myanmar have faced many setbacks in recent years, China had always been at the forefront in Myanmar in the amount of investments. As of late December 2015, China had 115 investment projects in Myanmar, with investments amounting to USD 15,418 million, accounting for 26.07% of all foreign

[4]Ruili, Yunnan, Becomes the "Golden Port" on the Border between China and Myanmar, http://city.qq.com/a/20160113/022261.htm, January 13, 2016.

investments in Myanmar; China continued to maintain the status of the largest source of investments for Myanmar, while Singapore and Thailand ranked Nos. 2 and 3, with investments worth USD 11 billion and USD 10 billion, respectively.[5] China's investments in Myanmar were mainly made by state-owned enterprises, China's investment cooperation with Myanmar was concentrated in the government or military-sponsored enterprises, China's investments in Myanmar focused on resource development and were made less in the industries and fields relating to the people's livelihood, including agriculture, tourism and manufacturing; the investments in water conservation, oil, gas and mining constituted almost all of the investments made by China in Myanmar. After Myanmar's general election in November, great progress was made in China–Myanmar cooperation projects. In December, construction began on the Dali–Lincang section of the China–Myanmar international railway; it is an important project for carrying out the Belt and Road Initiative developed by China and for building the Bangladesh–China–India–Myanmar economic corridor. On December 30, the consortium led by China's CITIC Group won the bidding for the deep-water port project in the Kyaukpyu Special Economic Zone; it is the first large project obtained by a Chinese enterprise in Myanmar after Myanmar's general election, which is a good start for the future cooperation between the two countries on the construction of infrastructures.

c. *China–Myanmar financial cooperation accelerated*

In 2015, the two countries actively cooperated in the financial industry and made substantive breakthroughs in that cooperation. In February, the Yunnan Branch of the China Construction Bank and the Myanmar Cooperative Bank signed the agreement on cross-border settlements. It is the second bank as the cooperator of the China Construction Bank in Myanmar after the Myanmar Economic Bank. In late March, the Ruili China–Myanmar Currency Exchange Center was officially established, Ruili City ranked No. 1 in Yunnan Province in the amount of RMB settlements for cross-border trade. On September 8, the Rangoon Branch of the Industrial and

[5]China Remains the Largest Source of Investment for Myanmar, www.huanqiu.com, http://china.huanqiu.com/News/mofcom/2016-02/8569624.html, February 19, 2016.

Commercial Bank of China was established, suggesting that the Industrial and Commercial Bank of China would become the first Chinese-funded bank entering the Burmese market. On September 14, the Rangoon Representative Office of the Bank of China was established. In December, Yunnan's Fudian Bank and Myanmar's Global Treasure Bank reached four intents of cooperation. As a result, China–Myanmar banking cooperation featured an encouraging pattern with participation and common development of Chinese state-owned commercial banks, local legal person financial institutions, Burmese state-owned banks and private banks.

3. The cooperation in other important fields

a. *Scientific, technological and educational cooperation*

In general, China–Myanmar scientific and technological cooperation decreased to a certain degree in 2015 over 2014, but there were a number of bright spots. In July 2015, the China–ASEAN Technology Transfer Center and the Ministry of Science and Technology of Myanmar jointly held the China–Myanmar Technology Matchmaking Meeting on Modern Agriculture and New Energy in Rangoon, in which 27 pairs of Chinese and Burmese enterprises reached the intents of cooperation and signed agreements, mainly involving China's agricultural product seed breeding, processing technology, chemical products, high temperature heat pump drying units, small distributed photovoltaic power generation systems, solar water pumps, solar street lamps and solar aquaculture. In the educational field, the institutions of higher learning in the two countries frequently exchanged visits in 2015. On January 14, the Beijing Foreign Studies University and the University of Yangon and the Yangon University of Foreign Languages signed a memorandum of understanding on cooperation, under which these three universities would conduct exchanges among students and teachers, engage in exchanges and cooperation in academic research and library information. In addition, Yunnan Minzu University, the University of Yangon and the Yangon University of Foreign Languages signed an agreement on interschool exchanges and cooperation. The Government of Myanmar sent more than 120 government-funded students and 100-plus outstanding young people from various government departments to study in and visit China. The exchanges among young people, especially the institutions of higher learning, between China and Myanmar are conducive to the development of education in both countries and to a deeper friendship and more cooperation between the two countries.

b. *Cooperation on culture and tourism*

With the 65th anniversary of the official establishment of diplomatic relations between China and Myanmar in 2015, China and Myanmar carried out a series of celebratory activities and cultural exchange activities. In February, the "Cultures of China, Festival of Spring" Art Troupe, led by the famous Chinese singers Yang Hongji and Guo Rong, attended the "Happy Chinese New Year" performances in Myanmar. In early September, during Thein Sein's visit to China, Chinese Culture Minister Luo Shugang and Burmese Foreign Minister Wunna Maung Lwin signed the *Agreement between the Government of the People's Republic of China and the Government of the Republic of the Union of Myanmar with Respect to the Mutual Establishment of Cultural Centers* on behalf of their respective countries in Beijing. Moreover, certain achievements were also made in China–Myanmar religious cultural exchanges. In November, the Meeting on the Southern Buddhism Cultural Exchange in China–Myanmar Border Areas 2015 was held in Ruili, Yunnan Province, further enhancing contacts and cooperation between the Buddhist circles of the two countries. Regarding cooperation on tourism, as of late November, inbound tourists in Myanmar exceeded 4.20 million person-times in 2015, up more than 1 million person-times over 2014,[6] while China became the second largest tourist source for Myanmar. At present, China has launched direct flights to Rangoon, Naypyidaw, Mandalay and other cities in Myanmar and eight border tourist routes have taken shape; China–Myanmar border tourism has been continuously popular. At the China International Travel Mart Tourism Investment Forum 2015 held in November, the Yunnan Zhonglu International Travel Agency and Myanmar's iHome Group Of Companies, the Myanmar Federal Tourism Association and Myanmar Virgin Travel Agency signed the agreements on a project regarding the tourism

[6]The Prospect of Burmese Tourist Market Is Bright, news.ifeng.com, http://news.ifeng.com/a/20160127/47249073_0.shtml, January 27, 2016.

industry and product cooperation, elevating China–Myanmar cooperation on tourism to a new level.

c. *Cooperation on the military and on security*

China–Myanmar cooperation on the military and security was mainly reflected in high-level military meetings between the two sides. In September, the second strategic military consultation meeting between China and Myanmar was held in Beijing, in which Sun Jianguo, Deputy Chief of the Joint Staff of the Chinese People's Liberation Army, met with Soe Win, Deputy Commander-in-Chief of the Myanmar Armed Forces and Army Commander; the two sides exchanged views on such issues as the situation of regional security and bilateral relations. On December 5, Min Aung Hlaing, Commander-in-Chief of the Myanmar Armed Forces, met with Chinese special envoy and Deputy Foreign Minister Liu Zhenmin. The two sides discussed the issues concerning Myanmar's reform process, the post-election role of the armed forces, further enhancement of military relations between the two countries, the management of border areas and the cooperation between the two countries. For a long time, the military relations between the two countries maintained a healthy developmental momentum and the China–Myanmar comprehensive strategic cooperative partnership also developed smoothly; the two countries worked together at a military level to cope with various challenges and safeguard common interests of the two sides.

Regarding cooperation on security issues, when meeting with the Governor of Yunnan Province Chen Hao in Naypyidaw, Myanmar on May 6, the President of Myanmar Thein Sein exchanged views with the Governor with regard to border stability, drug control and the crackdown on abduction, trade promotion and enhanced judicial cooperation. During the period January–November, 2015, China transferred 86 abducted people rescued by China to Myanmar. On June 3, the police of Ruili, China and their counterparts in Muse, Myanmar, jointly took a sweeping special action on cracking down on drug trafficking and controlling drugs at the border of Ruili, bringing about a new mode under which China and Myanmar sent observers to engage in drug control and law enforcement cooperation at the border. The two sides also reached consensuses on sending observers in the China–Myanmar joint drug control actions in border areas, cracking down on and dealing with drug-related criminals in action, the transfer of criminals and information exchange as well as other issues, laying a solid foundation for future in-depth cooperation in anti-drug police affairs and law enforcement and further deepening China–Myanmar drug control and law enforcement cooperation.

Besides the above cooperation, China also continued to offer various kinds of aid to Myanmar. In the case of the floods in Myanmar, China swiftly expressed sympathy, and solicited and delivered relevant materials to Myanmar, sent a water conservation expert group to Rangoon to conduct surveys and guide the prevention and control of flooding and waterlogging; China also dispatched "China's working group of health and epidemic prevention experts for the projects assisting Myanmar" to Myanmar to conduct post-disaster disease control lectures and give voluntary treatment of ophthalmic diseases. In addition, China also provided relevant technical support to improve the construction of water conservation infrastructures in Myanmar. In general, the above activities of cooperation and assistance deepened the friendship between the two countries and enhanced mutual trust at the non-governmental level, laying a good foundation for the future development of both countries.

III. Drawbacks in China–Myanmar Cooperation in 2015 and Suggestions for Improvement

1. China was relatively passive in getting involved in the issue of Northern Myanmar

The issue of Northern Myanmar has always been one of the sources for domestic turbulence in Myanmar and is closely related to the security of China's surrounding environment, so it is particularly important for China to get properly involved in the issue of Northern Myanmar. For the incident in March in which Myanmar's military aircraft crossed the border and dropped bombs causing the death and injury to Chinese people in the border areas, China had not made full preparations in advance for the deteriorating situation of Northern Myanmar to prevent that incident, while after the incident occurred, some problems existed in diplomatic communication with Myanmar, thus buck-passing took place between Myanmar's governmental army and armed ethnic groups.

2. The fields in which China made investments in Myanmar needed to be further expanded

For a long time, China's investments in Myanmar basically focused on the fields with high energy consumption and low environmental protection, such as energy, mining and electric power. That situation was still not fundamentally improved in 2015. In the future, the intrinsic investment structure will bring a number of hidden troubles to Chinese enterprises in Myanmar, and even to China–Myanmar relations. On the one hand, there have been increasing channels for Myanmar's ordinary people to express their appeals in the democratic process, and NGOs have continuously enhanced their influence in the Burmese society; the current main fields in which Chinese enterprises make investments will face more public opinion risks. On the other hand, the industries relating to the people's livelihood, such as agriculture, tourism and manufacturing, have grown rapidly in Myanmar; a considerable part of new foreign investments in Myanmar entered these fields during the early stage; for example, Singapore ranked No. 1 in Myanmar in hotel investment; if Chinese enterprises do not promptly adjust the structure of their investments, they will become very disadvantaged in competing with their counterparts from other countries in the future.

3. The people-to-people exchange between China and Myanmar was not deep

China and Myanmar have always attached importance to bilateral cultural cooperation. In 2015, certain achievements were made in China–Myanmar cultural cooperation. However, generally, the people-to-people exchange activities between the two countries in 2015 only exerted a limited impact on the Burmese society; they did not publicize Chinese culture in Myanmar in a more widespread way and promote the cultural understanding between the people of the two countries. Specifically, the people-to-people cooperation or exchange activities between China and Myanmar in 2015 were mainly led at the governmental level, while the universality of non-governmental participation needed to be improved; the two countries had not yet developed a regular mechanism for carrying out people-to-people activities with each other. Given the above problems, the two sides should intensify their efforts in the following respects in the development of future cooperation:

First, China should establish an emergency early-warning mechanism for addressing the emergencies in Northern Myanmar. This mechanism requires China's provinces, cities and counties along the border to develop emergency plans in advance; it also requires the departments of foreign affairs, border defense, medical service and health to act in an interactive way, attach importance to identifying and preventing the possible emergencies at the border, and strengthen measures for safeguarding the safety and security of the people and property at the border. At the same time, China should maintain smooth channels for diplomatic communication with various forces and groups in Myanmar; China should work with various parties to establish and carry out the mechanism for the sharing of security information and the mechanism for the coordination of the handling of emergencies.

Second, China should move faster to optimize the investment structure and mode in Myanmar, pay more attention to its input in the industries relating to the people's livelihood, such as manufacturing, and other new and hi-tech industries. Based on Myanmar's accession to the Asian Investment Development Bank and the Silk Road Fund, China should increase its investments and aid in Myanmar's infrastructure, such as transportation, electric power and communications, and properly surrender part of its profits to promote long-term cooperation between the two countries.

Finally, while strengthening cooperation in the economic field, China should, under the strategic frameworks including the Belt and Road Initiative and Bangladesh–China–India–Myanmar Economic Corridor, regularly carry out various people-to-people exchange activities with explicit themes at the non-governmental and social levels in Myanmar to intensify publicity in Myanmar and make it possible for the people of various classes in Myanmar to further understand Chinese culture and society. The Chinese enterprises investing in Myanmar should also fully respect the religious tradition and cultural customs of local communities, actively fulfill their corresponding social responsibilities and extensively develop a positive perception of China's national image among the Burmese people.

Chapter 5

Report on the Cooperation between China and Malaysia in 2015

Mao Wei*

I. Review of the Situation of Malaysia in 2015

The year 2015 saw a highly volatile one in Malaysia. As the financial crisis broke out at the state-owned investment fund 1MDB (the "1MDB incident"), a political wave against Najib Razak surfaced. Against the general background of a global economic slowdown, the 1MDB incident caused Malaysia's political situation and market to get caught in an abyss.

1. Politics: Turbulence

In early 2015, the financial crisis of 1MDB triggered a series of reports on 1MDB's debts and its involvement in corruption cases, causing a political tsunami in Malaysia.

a. *The governing party: The Prime Minister faced a political crisis*

After the 1MDB incident was exposed, Prime Minister Najib Razak was beset by an unprecedented political crisis. The leader of the Democratic Action

* Mao Wei, Director, Assistant Research Fellow at the Malaysia Institute of the China–ASEAN Research Institute of Guangxi University.

Party, Lim Kit Siang, and former Prime Minister Mahathir Mohamad called for removing the state leader; the royal family of Malaysia, which has seldom directly interfered in the politics of the country, also called for completing the investigation of the 1MDB incident as early as possible; international forces, including USA and Hong Kong, also conducted a series of investigations. The opposition party in the Parliament submitted to the House of Representatives the no-confidence motion against Prime Minister Najib Razak, and the approval rating of the Government of Najib Razak dropped to its lowest level (23%). Splits and confrontations occurred within the United Malays National Organization. The people crusading against Najib Razak and demanding he step down included the grassroots forces from the United Malays National Organization, the former senior leaders of the United Malays National Organization and the leaders of its branches. At the same time, some people within the United Malays National Organization — including the Minister of Home Affairs Ahmad Zahid Hamidi, Defense Minister Hishammuddin Hussein and Secretary-General of the United Malays National Organization Tengku Adnan Tengku Mansor — supported Najib Razak, they requested the people to shy away from the impact of provocation and continue to support Najib Razak's leadership. There were unprecedented contradictions within the United Malays National Organization.

Subject to pressure from the opposition party, Prime Minister Najib Razak took a number of measures for consolidating his personal power: restricting, listing as wanted and arresting the dissidents; freezing the party membership of the leaders who "violated the discipline"; suddenly reshuffling the cabinet; postponing the general election of the United Malays National Organization; announcing a political coalition with the former opposition party, the Islamic Party; delegating more powers and allocating more funds to Negeri Sabah and Negeri Sarawak in order to seek support; adopting the national security act to establish the National Security Council led by Prime Minister Najib Razak for supervising and commanding the national security strategy. Amidst the political wave against him, Prime Minister Najib Razak adopted a slew of strong countermeasures to temporarily maintain his status, but the political tsunami was far from over; real maintenance of Najib Razak's status as Prime Minister ultimately depended upon his ability to safeguard the solidarity within the United Malays National Organization and cope with the financial turmoil.

b. *The party out of power: Division occurred within the opposition coalition Pakatan Rakyat*

The opposition coalition suffered much internal strife. The leader of the opposition, Anwar Ibrahim, was put in prison, and so the opposition coalition became leaderless. With the submission of the motion concerning Islamic criminal law, the Democratic Action Party broke off its ties with the Islamic Party and unilaterally announced withdrawal from the Pakatan Rakyat, so the latter existed in name only. In September, three major opposition parties, including the People's Justice Party, the Democratic Action Party and the National Trust Party, formed the Pakatan Harapan. The Islamic Party and the United Malays National Organization forged a political coalition. The intense and complicated internal strife within the opposition parties, especially the division within the Pakatan Rakyat, provided Najib Razak with a breathing space to some extent. The future political situation in Malaysia hinged on the solidarity within the opposition coalition.

c. *Conflicts between the two parties: "Bersih 4.0 Rally" versus "916 Red Shirt Rally"*

In 2015, there were two highly influential rallies in Malaysia: the "Bersih 4.0 Rally" and the "916 Red Shirt Rally". The "Bersih 4.0 Rally" called for ensuring clean elections and clean government, rescuing the economy, guaranteeing the power to raise objections and enhancing the democracy in the parliament. Although it was considered illegal by the government, the solidarity within the United Malays National Organization was greatly compromised as there was the direct participation of former Prime Minister Mahathir Mohamad and Muhyiddin Yassin who had been removed from the post of Deputy Prime Minister but still served as Deputy President of the United Malays National Organization.

In order to counter the "Bersih 4.0 Rally", the Malay organizations, which favored the United Malays National Organization, initiated the "916 Red Shirt Rally" to resist others or other countries' interference in internal affairs, reject those similar to Bersih Rally and safeguard the status of Malays. The "Red Shirt Rally", defended by and saw the appearance of many chiefs and leaders of the United Malays National Organization, tried to create tensions in ethnic relations, which caused social discontent.

2. The economy: Recession

a. *Imports and exports were sagging*

In 2015, with the impact of the decline in global bulk commodities, Malaysia's exports decreased dramatically, with the growth rate of exports plunging from 5.8% in 2014 to 0.4% in 2015 (as shown in Table 1). Malaysia's economy was an outward-looking economy, of which: oil and gas were the pillar industries in Malaysia's national economy, their exports accounted for 22.4% of Malaysia's total exports, and their incomes made up 30% of Malaysia's fiscal revenue.[1] However, exports and foreign exchanges were apparently affected by the international economic environment; the global economic downturn in 2015 affected Malaysia's economy appreciably. Zhao Jianglin, research fellow at the National Institute of International Strategy of the Chinese Academy of Social Sciences, said, "The adjustment of the economic structure becomes stagnant; with the rise of Vietnam, the Philippines and other countries, Malaysia's advantage in exporting the traditional electronic information

Table 1. Malaysia's Foreign Trade in the Past 5 Years

Year	Total export volume (unit: 1 million Malaysian Ringgit)	Total import volume (unit: 1 million Malaysian Ringgit)	Total trade volume (unit: 1 million Malaysian Ringgit)	Import growth rate (%)	Export growth rate (%)	Total growth rate (%)
2011	697861.94	573626.33	1271488.27	9.24	8.47	8.89
2012	702641.25	606676.95	1309318.20	0.68	5.76	2.98
2013	719992.40	648694.87	1368687.27	2.47	6.93	4.53
2014	765416.88	682937.15	1448354.03	6.31	5.28	5.82
2015	779946.58	685652.07	1465598.65	1.90	0.40	1.19

Source: Malaysia's central bank.

[1]Xu Liping, A Political Wave against Najib Razak Was Triggered in Malaysia, *World Affairs*, 2015 (18), pp. 36–37.

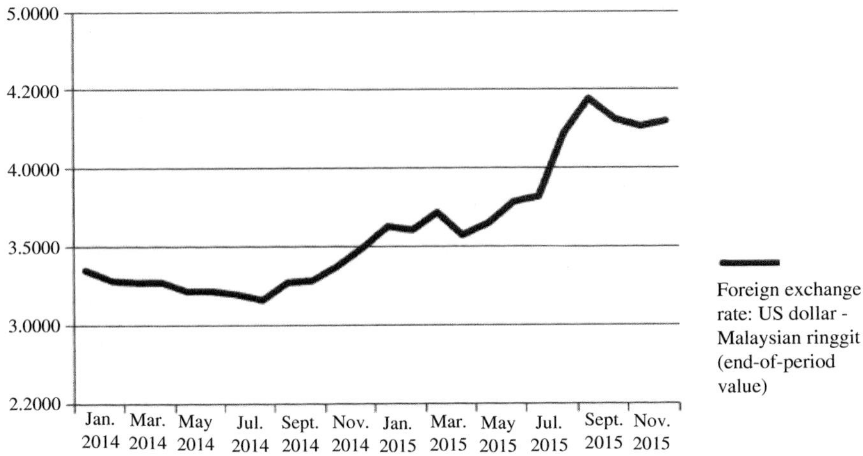

Figure 1. US Dollar–Malaysian Ringgit Trend Chart
Source: Malaysia's central bank.

products is being replaced, external competition is increasingly fierce, but it is difficult for Malaysia to upgrade and transform its industrial sectors in a short time."[2]

b. *Malaysian ringgit depreciated*

In 2015, the Malaysian ringgit depreciated substantially and dropped to an all-time low since the financial storm in 1997. As international oil prices fell and the market showed concerns about 1MDB's debts, the Malaysian ringgit–US dollar exchange rate continuously declined from March. As shown in Figure 1, with the continued depreciation of Malaysian ringgit, import prices rose by at least 20–30%; in the meantime, more and more Malays opened foreign currency deposit accounts to avert risks. However, the Government of Najib Razak did not take capital control measures. This depreciation caused massive capital outflow, further subjecting Malaysia to a foreign exchange reserve crisis. As shown in Figure 2, Malaysia's international reserve decreased greatly in 2015, its greatest decrease was more than 50 billion Malaysian ringgits (about USD 12 billion). Oil prices declined, trade surplus deteriorated

[2]Tao Feng, Will 1MDB Destroy Malaysia?, *Beijing Business Today*, August 5, 2015, p. 8.

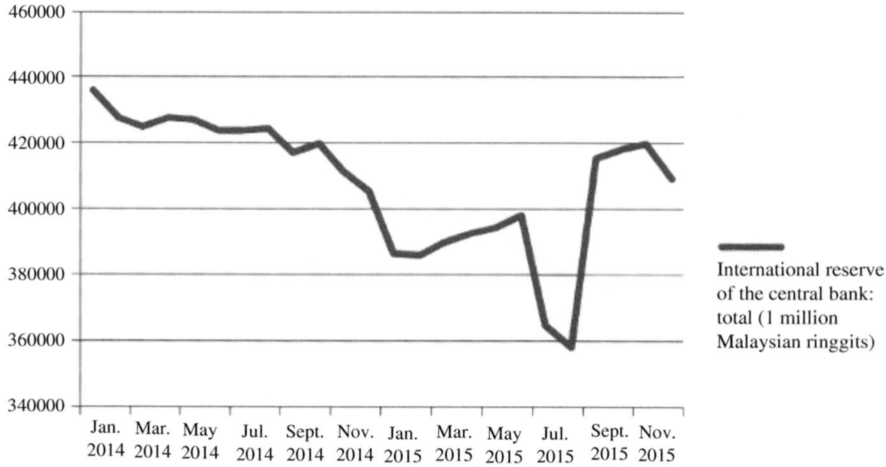

Figure 2. Trend Chart of the Total Amount of Malaysia's International Reserves
Source: Malaysia's central bank.

and 1MDB's debts lingered; Malaysia's fiscal situation became weak, its currency depreciated. At the time of this writing, Malaysia's instability in the financial field is the severest since the global financial crisis in 2008.

c. *Economic slowdown occurred*

With the impact of the global economic recession and the 1MDB incident, the growth of Malaysia's GDP decreased month by month in 2015, the growth rate of its GDP declined from 5.65% in the first quarter to 4.53% in the fourth quarter, down 1% on average over 2014 (as shown in Table 2). The World Bank downgraded the forecast about Malaysia's economic growth in the next 2 years and expected that the country's economic growth rate would remain at 4.7% in 2015 and decrease to 4.5% in 2016 and 2017.

The economic slowdown led to a decrease in the employment rate and an increase in the inflation rate, and the people's dissatisfaction with Najib Razak loomed large. As shown in Table 3, Malaysia's CPI rose to some extent. As both the stock market and the foreign exchange market declined, the national economy lacked strength for recovery, Najib Razak announced the establishment of the Special Economic Council and injected capital to stabilize the stock market. However, the political wrangle strained much energy

Table 2. The Growth Rate of Malaysia's GDP

	2014	2015
The 1st quarter	6.26	5.65
The 2nd quarter	6.49	4.95
The 3rd quarter	5.59	4.74
The 4th quarter	5.68	4.53

Source: Malaysia's central bank.

Table 3. Malaysia's CPI

	CPI: over the same period of the previous year (%)	CPI: over the previous period (%)
January 2015	1.00	–1.10
February 2015	0.10	–0.60
March 2015	0.90	0.90
April 2015	1.80	0.90
May 2015	2.10	0.40
June 2015	2.50	0.60
July 2015	3.30	0.80
August 2015	3.10	0.00
September 2015	2.60	–0.30
October 2015	2.50	0.40
November 2015	2.60	0.60
December 2015	2.70	0.00

Source: Malaysia's central bank.

from the Malaysian Government, so the Malaysian Government failed to deal with many economic problems, and more pressure was put on Malaysia's economy.

3. Society: Chaos

a. *The ethnic problem became salient*

In 2015, with political and economic crises, ethnic sentiment was on the verge of breaking out in the Malaysian society, some people with ulterior motives repeatedly tried to shift the people's attention by creating tension in ethnic relations. First, the Minister of Agriculture and Agro-Based Industry attributed the price problem to an ethnic problem, escalating the issue of people's livelihood to a political issue. Second, an incident of violence occurred at Low Yat Plaza. Originally, it was an incident in which a young Malay stole something at the Low Yat Plaza, but some irresponsible and immature political figures stirred up trouble for a particular political agenda, and as a result, an ethnic riot broke out. Third, in the "Bersih 4.0 Rally", some Malaysian media took the opportunity to play up the ethnic issue and accused overseas Chinese of acting as the main force against the Government of Najib Razak. Ethnic contradictions resurfaced in Malaysian society. Ethnic relations are relatively harmonious in Malaysia compared to in other Southeast Asian countries, but there are difficult tasks to carry out and a long way to go for Malaysia, a multi-ethnic country, to thoroughly achieve peaceful coexistence and common development of ethnic groups.

b. *A hazy situation was severe*

As the mountain fire continued in Indonesia, the haze was grave in Malaysia. Thirty-one areas saw the air pollution index between the unhealthy level and the dangerous level (PSI above 300 points), more than 4,700 schools suspended classes, and the flights at many airports were affected. The Malaysian authorities planned to make a cross-border haze pollution act to crack down on haze-producing enterprises and urgently hoped that the Indonesian Government could convert the "commitment to solving the problem of haze within 3 years" into practical actions, but Malaysia did not exert pressure on Indonesia.

4. The military, security and diplomacy

a. *The anti-terrorism situation was grim*

Malaysia is an Islamic country, its state religion is Islam. With increasingly rampant terrorism in recent years, Malaysia has mostly been accused of acting as the springboard for terrorists, so its anti-terrorism situation was severe. In 2015, the Malaysian police found that some foreign Islamic preachers who had taken charge of Islamic lectures at the local level were actually the leaders of armed groups, and that they had recruited new members in Malaysia. The Malaysian law enforcement department arrested 130 activists who had returned to Malaysia after receiving training at terrorist camps in Syria. The Government of Najib Razak stated that the sprawling terrorist organization Islamic State was the main threat to Malaysia; Malaysia had established a special court under the terrorist prevention measure framework, and had joined the Islamic Military Alliance consisting of 34 countries, including Egypt and Turkey, to actively combat terrorism.

b. *Security and military development*

In 2015, Malaysia made great progress in the military and security fields. Regarding the territorial dispute, the Philippines gave Sabah State, via a territorial dispute between the Philippines and Malaysia, to Kuala Lumpur so as to seek support from Malaysia in the international arbitration case involving the issue of the South China Sea. At the military level, Malaysia and Thailand reached a consensus on establishing five army frontline operational bases on the border between Malaysia and Thailand, with a view to strictly supervising the border areas; Malaysia will participate in the joint live-fire drill "Calfex" conducted by the USA, Thailand and South Korea; Malaysia will also take part in the military exercise "Cobra Gold". This is a positive development of Malaysia's military because, with the participation in the military exercise "Calfex", Malaysia will become one of the active countries in the military exercise "Cobra Gold", thus helping develop its military strength.

c. *New journey in international cooperation*

In 2015, as the rotating ASEAN presidency, Malaysia successfully held the 27th ASEAN Summit; on December 31, Malaysia made a statement that the ASEAN Community was officially established and that establishment was another important milestone in the history of the ASEAN community. Regarding international cooperation, Malaysia firmly supported efforts to further deepen the construction of the ASEAN Community and regional integration. Although the ASEAN Community has been established, many efforts still need to be made before regional integration is really achieved.

II. Bilateral Cooperation between China and Malaysia in 2015

Malaysia and China have been important partners throughout history. In 2015, senior leaders of China and Malaysia frequently exchanged visits; the state visit paid by Chinese Premier Li Keqiang to Malaysia released much good news for economic development and brought hope to Malaysia amidst financial turmoil. With the impact from Malaysia's political and economic turmoil and China's economic structural transformation, China–Malaysia trade declined to some extent; in the meantime, Malaysia joined the TPP and took a tougher stand towards the issue of the South China Sea. Nevertheless, China–Malaysia cooperation was further deepened on the basis of mutual political trust, China and Malaysia held the first joint live-fire military exercise, the two countries also extended cooperation to more fields and the high value-added industries. China–Malaysia cooperation faces new opportunities and challenges.

1. Political and diplomatic cooperation

a. *Li Keqiang paid an official visit to Malaysia, releasing many favorable signs for economic development*

In 2015, as the rotating ASEAN presidency, Malaysia continued to maintain the comprehensive strategic partnership with China. In November, Chinese Premier Li Keqiang paid an official visit to Malaysia, bringing a great deal of good news regarding economic development; that visit was timely help for Malaysia which had been hit hard at the economic level; the visit also mitigated, to some extent, the regional tensions caused by the dispute over the sovereignty of the South China Sea and cemented the comprehensive strategic partnership between China and Malaysia.

The visit focused on economic and trade cooperation. Li Keqiang declared that China would provide Malaysia with RMB 50 billion in Qualified Foreign Institutional Investor (RQFII) quota, help Malaysia build low-cost infrastructures and purchase more Malaysian bonds. These actions were conducive to stabilizing Malaysia's financial system and currency, improving the activity and status of the Malaysian RMB offshore market and increasing the Malaysian market's demand for RMB. The visit consolidated the foundation for the comprehensive strategic partnership between China and Malaysia.

b. *There was a crisis in which Chinese ambassador to Malaysia Huang Huikang was alleged to have interfered in politics*

Amidst continued development of the comprehensive strategic partnership between China and Malaysia, incidents affecting the friendly relations between the two countries occurred occasionally, but they did not substantively harm bilateral relations. The crisis in which Chinese ambassador to Malaysia Huang Huikang was alleged to have interfered in politics was a very good example.

In 2015, as the 1MDB incident caused chain reactions, Malaysia's political situation became turbulent, splits and confrontations occurred within the United Malays National Organization, some groups played up the ethnic issue and tried to shift public attention at the expense of ethnic relations and social harmony; they used external imaginary enemies to arouse new solidarity within the party. At the "Bersih 4.0 Rally", Chairman of the Coalition of Malaysian NGOs Seri Jamal Yunos strongly required actions to ban the "corrupt business activities" at Petaling Street, and cause "half of the stands to be turned over to Malays"; he accused overseas Chinese of acting as the main force against the Government of Najib Razak. The Chinese ambassador to Malaysia Huang Huikang visited Petaling Street and stressed that China opposed any form of terrorism and extremism targeted at particular ethnic groups, severe violent incidents destroying the social order and stability; he affirmed that the Chinese Government neither interfered in nor got involved in the internal affairs of other countries, but China absolutely would not sit idly by in case of violation of China's national interests and the legitimate rights and interests of Chinese citizens and enterprises, and the harming of the friendly relations between China and the countries in which overseas Chinese were settled. His remarks immediately drew attention from the Malaysian Government, which summoned the Chinese ambassador to Malaysia Huang Huikang and required him to make an explanation. The Chinese Foreign Ministry spokesman, Hong Lei, stressed that ambassador Huang Huikang's visit to the Chinese community was a normal goodwill act, and said that China and Malaysia were good neighbors, that China hoped that Malaysia would be able to maintain national solidarity, social stability and ethnic harmony. Although the Chinese ambassador to Malaysia Huang Huikang was alleged to have interfered in politics, the friendly relations between China and Malaysia would not be affected by this crisis and would not continue to be intensified.

2. Economic cooperation

a. *Trade declined*

In 2015, as China entered the new normal of the economy and Malaysia faced a political crisis, China–Malaysia trade decreased to some extent. According to the statistics from China Customs, bilateral trade reached USD 97.42 billion in 2015, down 4.55% over the previous year. China's economic slowdown exerted a particularly apparent impact on Malaysia's exports. As shown in Table 4, China's exports to Malaysia rose by 0.9% in 2014, while China's exports to Malaysia totaled USD 44.19 billion in 2015, down 4.53% over the previous year. On the contrary, China's imports from Malaysia totaled USD 53.23 billion, down 4.56% over the previous year, showing a certain slowdown of the decreasing trend.

The monthly trade volume between China and Malaysia and the growth rates on a month-on-month basis are indicated in Table 5. According to Table 5, China–Malaysia trade declined noticeably in January, February, July and October, 2015 on a month-on-month basis, while bilateral trade grew to varying degrees in other months on a month-on-month basis. As of late 2015, the total China–Malaysia trade in each month was slightly higher than USD 8.7 billion in early 2015.

In the meantime, China–Malaysia trade was to be subject to more uncertainties after Malaysia officially joined the *Trans-Pacific Partnership Agreement* (TPP). From the perspective of Malaysia, the TPP helps Malaysian enterprises get access to more markets and enjoy more financing opportunities, and it increases Malaysia's proportion in the global supply chain and

Table 4. The Volume of China–Malaysia Trade and the Growth Rates (on a Year-on-Year Basis)

	Total (10,000 USD)			Growth rate (%)		
	Total imports and exports	China's exports to Malaysia	China's imports from Malaysia	Imports and exports	Exports	Imports
2014	10206362.86	4629212.99	5577149.88	−3.8	0.9	−7.5
2015	9742109.08	4419393.81	5322715.25	−4.55	−4.53	−4.56

Source: General Administration of Customs of China.

Table 5. The Volume of China–Malaysia Trade and the Growth Rates (on a Month-on-Month Basis)

	Monthly volume (10,000 USD)			Growth rate (%)		
	Total imports and exports	China's exports to Malaysia	China's imports from Malaysia	Imports and exports	Exports	Imports
Jan. 2015	869933.97	454937.88	414996.09	−16.76	−4.00	−27.34
Feb. 2015	702116.78	380222.59	321894.18	−19.29	−16.42	−22.43
Mar. 2015	755299.81	292194.82	463104.99	7.57	−23.15	43.87
Apr. 2015	768718.85	325276.56	443442.29	1.78	11.32	−4.25
May 2015	852930.28	421286.22	431644.06	10.95	29.52	−2.66
June 2015	936339.54	413015.97	523323.57	9.78	−1.96	21.24
July 2015	824536.86	380082.34	444454.52	−11.94	−7.97	−15.07
Aug. 2015	807238.81	354504.59	452734.22	−2.10	−6.73	1.86
Sept. 2015	813947.42	355386.16	458561.26	0.83	0.25	1.29
Oct. 2015	716984.88	314269.47	402715.40	−11.91	−11.57	−12.18
Nov. 2015	777289.45	349756.68	427532.77	8.41	11.29	6.16
Dec. 2015	916772.43	378460.53	538311.90	17.94	8.21	25.91

Source: General Administration of Customs of China.

improves trading performance, but TPP-related rules and regulations will exert a great impact on Malaysian state-owned enterprises and many preferential treatment systems (involving ethnic and non-ethnic groups). According to the experts from the United Nations, Malaysia did not obtain optimal conditions in TPP negotiations, making it unfavorable for the economy. For China, after Malaysia, which has been stating full support for and participation in the construction of the Belt and Road Initiative by China, joined the TPP, Malaysia's accession to the TPP will certainly affect China's imports and exports as China is not a party to the TPP. Therefore, new uncertainties will emerge in China–Malaysia trade.

b. *Cooperation upgrading*

In 2015, the projects in cooperation between China and Malaysia involved such fields as food processing, car making and infrastructure construction, covering governments, state-owned enterprises and private enterprises, bringing about fruitful achievements. In infrastructure, China's Guangxi Beibu Gulf International Group acquired 40% of the equity at the Port of Kuantan, the reconstruction project at the Port of Kuantan was initiated, and it will become an important node of the Maritime Silk Road; China Railway obtained the qualification for carrying out the project of the double-track railway from Gemas, Negeri Sembilan to Johor Bahru, Negeri Sembilan which is estimated to cost 7.1 billion Malaysian Ringgits; the China General Nuclear Power Group allocated USD 2.3 billion to acquire the electric power assets from debt-ridden 1Malaysia Development Bhd; it became the reported largest merger and acquisition transaction in Malaysia and one of the largest transactions in Asia's electric power field in 2015; it is beneficial to improving China's influence in Malaysia and paves the way for cooperation in other projects of the construction of infrastructures.

Regarding cooperation on production, the Haoyue Group in Jilin Province, China, planned to establish the halal product logistics production base in Malacca, Malaysia; a subsidiary of China's listed private company Jereh Oilfield Services Group and TOS signed a cooperation agreement for jointly providing better solutions and services to the Malaysian oil and gas market; China's Geely Auto Group and Malaysia's Proton discussed the issues concerning the establishment of an ASEAN Automobile Hub in Malaysia; China set up the overseas railway equipment manufacturing center in Batu Gajah, Perak State, Malaysia, which makes Malaysia the first country to make products for rail transportation equipment in the ASEAN community and helps China put those kind of products onto the regional market.

As for scientific and technological cooperation, Shanghai Changda Investment Management Co., Ltd., the Malaysia National Information Technology Research and Development Center and Malaysia Softegic Systems Management Sdn Bhd signed a tripartite memorandum, *China–Malaysia Open Innovation Platform*, and China–Malaysia relations officially entered the field of cooperation on information technology. These cooperation projects indicate that China–Malaysia economic cooperation has developed from simple barter trade to the high value-added industries including technical cooperation and production capacity cooperation; at the same time, the demonstration effect of cooperation projects will contribute to the upgrading of China–Malaysia economic cooperation.

3. Cooperation on the military and security fronts

a. *China and Malaysia conducted joint live-fire military exercise for the first time*

In September, 2015, the militaries of China and Malaysia carried out joint live-fire military exercises for the first time; such military exercises were of milestone significance for enhancing the mutual political trust and military and security cooperation between China and Malaysia. China and Malaysia conducted "Peace and Friendship 2015" a joint exercise in the Strait of Malacca and its surrounding waters; so far, it is the largest bilateral joint military exercise between China and ASEAN member countries. During this exercise, USA consulted with Malaysia and sent P-8 and P-3C patrol aircraft of the US military to Malaysia for detecting the activities of China's military in the South China Sea. In response to this action, a Chinese navy spokesperson stressed that this joint exercise aimed at deepening the comprehensive strategic partnership between China and Malaysia, enhancing the defense exchange and cooperation between the two militaries, improving the ability to jointly cope with the realistic security threats and work together to safeguard regional maritime security, and that it was not targeted at the third party and had nothing to do with the regional situation.

Malaysia has kept close economic ties with China, but Malaysia also has closer relations with Western countries at the military level. The first joint live-fire military exercise between China and Malaysia in 2015 was an iconic event in China–Malaysia military cooperation; it demonstrated to the world the profound friendship and mutual political trust between China and Malaysia; it also opened a new chapter for future military cooperation between China and Malaysia.

b. *The issue of the South China Sea*

The issue of the South China Sea has always been one of the main issues affecting China–Malaysia cooperation. In 2015, Malaysia took a tougher attitude toward the issue of the South China Sea; however, in general, Malaysia still showed cold treatment, and China–Malaysia cooperation was not fundamentally affected. In June, the naval vessels of China and Malaysia confronted each other near Qiongtai Jiao in the South China Sea, so the two countries had disputes over the ownership of sovereignty of the place where these coast guard vessels were located; many media reported that the Malaysian Government would lodge a protest against invasion made by the China Coast Guard's vessel, and pointed out that Prime Minister Najib Razak would directly make representations to Chinese President Xi Jinping. In the opening ceremony of the ASEAN Summit, Malaysia expressed, in an anonymous way, the common severe concern to ASEAN countries — the concern of some leaders about the reclamation works in the South China Sea. Although Malaysia had reservations about China's activities in the South China Sea, Malaysia agreed to permit the People's Liberation Army Navy of China to use its Port of Kota Kinabalu near the Nansha Islands. As shown, with respect to the dispute over the South China Sea, as the host country of the 26th ASEAN Summit, Malaysia sought support from USA and strengthened its military presence to counter China's might in the South China Sea on the one hand, but on the other hand, Malaysia did not become estranged from China and strove to keep a balance between China and USA.

4. Cooperation on other fronts

a. *Tourism: Putting in place the electronic visa*

China and Malaysia have maintained frequent tourism contacts and close cultural exchanges at the non-governmental level. In 2015, in order to strengthen contacts between the people of the two countries and stimulate the development of Malaysia's tourism industry, Malaysia gradually deregulated visas for Chinese tourists. In early 2015, in the Boao Forum for Asia, Najib Razak held the fourth bilateral talk with Xi Jinping since he served as prime minister; he also stated that Malaysia would establish visa processing centers in Nanning and Xi'an, China, to attract more Chinese tourists to Malaysia. Afterwards, Najib Razak announced that Malay would introduce the visa-free policy for Chinese group tourists from October 1, 2015 to March 31, 2016. However, the policy was not implemented because there was no coordination among Malaysia's governmental departments. In December 2015, the Malaysian Cabinet decided to carry out the electronic visa measure from January 2, 2016 to attract more Chinese tourists to Malaysia. Malaysia's visa-free policy for Chinese tourists shows that Malaysia hopes to enhance the contacts and understanding between the people of the two countries. Although it has not yet been implemented due to governmental inefficiency, the relationship between the people of both countries has been further improved.

b. *Education: developing diploma certification*

In 2015, the educational cooperation between China and Malaysia developed well, new progress was made in the educational engagement between the two countries. On the one hand, Malaysia and China signed a memorandum of understanding on recognizing the performance in Chinese subjects involving Malaysian Certificate of Education, so that Malaysian students with this certificate can be exempted from taking the entrance examination of Chinese proficiency and those with outstanding performance can apply for scholarship when studying in China. On the other hand, the Malaysian Government and the Chinese Government made good progress in junior college diploma certification; China announced that it would increase the number of the Malaysian Government-sponsored and private junior colleges recognized by China from the original 64 to 76. These measures will help increase the number of Malaysian students in China, and enhance the educational cooperation between the two countries, laying a solid foundation for political and economic cooperation between the two countries.

Besides the above cooperation, Malaysia and China also cooperated in many fields including culture and traditional Chinese medicine research and development, a new model of China–Malaysia cooperation within a wide scope and in various forms took shape, enhancing friendship, mutual political trust and people-to-people connectivity, thus laying a solid foundation for the future cooperation between the two countries.

5. Drawbacks in China–Malaysia cooperation

In 2015, China–Malaysia cooperation continued to be deepened; although many achievements were made, some problems existed. First, economic cooperation faced challenges. China was Malaysia's largest trading partner, while Malaysia was China's largest trading partner in the ASEAN community. However, since China–Malaysia trade declined in 2014, subject to the dual pressure from the entry of China's economy into the new normal and Malaysia's economic turmoil, bilateral trade further decreased in 2015. Malaysia's accession to the TPP posed a challenge to the trade between Malaysia and China which is not a party to the TPP. Second, the issue of the South China Sea hindered the mutual political trust. It may last for a long time, become complicated and international. The issue presented a huge challenge to China's diplomacy. For China–Malaysia cooperation, the issue of the South China Sea was certainly an obstacle. China and Malaysia had a certain tacit understanding on the issue over the previous years; however, recently, as Malaysia changed its strategy for the South China Sea, the mutual political trust between China and Malaysia will certainly be affected and bilateral cooperation may be threatened. Third, the problems of government efficiency and corruption affected the implementation of cooperation. In a country under a democratic system, the government-to-government strategic model is likely to change from opportunity to challenge. In particular, when the implementation of relevant policies only delivers benefits at the governmental level and does not benefit the people and the local market, there will be a negative impact on investment returns. In the meantime, the government's corruption problem and inefficiency of enforcement will hinder bilateral cooperation. Malaysia's delay in implementing the visa-free policy for China–Malaysia contacts is an excellent example.

Therefore, China and Malaysia should intensify their efforts in the following respects in their future cooperation and development: First, a flexible strategy should be adopted for the issue of the South China Sea. For China–Malaysia relations, the proper way to address the issue of the South China Sea at the present stage should be as follows: continuing to shelve disputes, refraining from deliberately stressing the issue. From a relatively realistic perspective, it is difficult to effectively deal with the issue of the South China Sea between China and Malaysia in a short term; China should address the issue of the South China Sea in a low-key way as far as possible and prevent the issue from affecting the construction of the Belt and Road and China–Malaysia cooperation.

Second, actions should be taken to improve the manner of economic cooperation and promote the transformation and upgrading of the economic structure. As the largest economic partner of Malaysia, China has entered the new normal of the economy, exerting a marked impact on Malaysia's exportations; furthermore, with the impact from a sharp decrease in the prices of international bulk commodities and domestic political unrest, Malaysia's economy is worrying. Given the current economic developmental situation of both countries, it is imperative for China and Malaysia to change the traditional manner of their economic cooperation, strengthen their capacity for production and technical cooperation, push forward the upgrading and transformation of the economic structures in both countries, so as to further boost China–Malaysia economic cooperation.

Third, steps should be taken to build multi-level cooperation and exchange mechanisms, enhance the capability of communication between relevant departments of the two countries. At present, the work on the mechanisms of China–Malaysia communication focuses on high-level exchanges, while there is a lack of communication between relevant departments of the two countries with respect to visas and foreign workers, making it difficult to carry out some concrete policies. Therefore, multi-level communication and exchange mechanisms will be conducive to improving the efficiency of cooperation and promoting bilateral cooperation.

III. The Trends of Recent China–Malaysia Cooperation

In 2015, the friendly cooperative relations between China and Malaysia will be steadily promoted. Looking into the future, China–Malaysia cooperation has a bright prospect and shows the following trends.

1. The comprehensive strategic partnership will continue to be maintained

In 2015, the naval vessels of Malaysia and China confronted each other near Qiongtai Jiao in the South China Sea, the Chinese ambassador to Malaysia, Huang Huikang, was alleged to have interfered in politics and summoned by Malaysia; however, the foundation for mutual political trust between China and Malaysia remains firm. This is because Malaysia always upholds the diplomacy of maintaining a balance among great powers. The joint exercise between the Malaysian navy and the Chinese navy in September 2015 and recently concluded TPP negotiations with USA highlight Malaysia's great care for maintaining a balance between China and USA. Based on this factor, the overall tone of the comprehensive strategic partnership between China and Malaysia will not be changed due to the issue of the South China Sea and Malaysia's political dilemma.

2. Cooperation will develop from the economic front to production capacity and technical fronts

China–Malaysia trade declined to a certain degree in 2015, but both the countries signed a memorandum, *China–Malaysia Open Innovation Platform*, initiating bilateral cooperation in the field of information technology. The traditional economic and trade relations between China and Malaysia are very close, but the relations seldom involve technology transfer. Currently, Malaysian enterprises are eager to improve their production efficiency through technical cooperation. Therefore, in parallel to deepening commodity trade, China–Malaysia cooperation should be promoted by gradually shaping the cooperative operational mode which features interdependence, enhancing technology transfer and further reinforcing bilateral cooperation.

3. The cases of cooperation among private enterprises will increase

In the past, China–Malaysia cooperation was pushed forward mainly by governments and central enterprises, more emphasis was placed on short-term political performance and less attention was paid to long-term benefits during cooperation, making it difficult to ensure that local people got the tangible benefits. Such a government-led cooperative operational mode is not suitable for Malaysia as a relatively democratic country. In 2015, some Chinese private enterprises, including the Geely Auto Group and a subsidiary of China's listed private company Jereh Oilfield Services Group, started cooperation with Malaysian enterprises. In the future, the cases of private enterprise cooperation with a focus on long-term benefits will increase in coordination with government policies, and they will undoubtedly elevate China–Malaysia economic and trade cooperation to a new level.

4. Financial cooperation will be deepened

Currently, Malaysia is one of the top 10 RMB offshore centers in the world, while the second largest RMB settlement bank in Southeast Asia is based in Malaysia. Fourteen percent of the merchants in Malaysia have used RMB in cross-border transactions, but the proportion of interbank settlements is very small and less than 2%. In 2015, during his visit to Malaysia, Chinese Premier Li Keqiang declared that China would provide Malaysia with RMB 50 billion in a Qualified Foreign Institutional Investor (RQFII) quota. This measure will be beneficial for improving the activity and status of the Malaysian RMB offshore market and for increasing the Malaysian market's demand for RMB, thus helping Malaysia build a regional financial center, avert financial risks and improve the stability of its financial system.

5. Cooperation will occur in various fields, including infrastructure, tourism, education, science, technology and security

In the future, as China actively pushes forward the construction of the Belt and Road Initiative and Malaysia has an urgent need for overcoming a domestic economic and financial downturn, China–Malaysia cooperation will involve a number of fields, including infrastructure, tourism, education, science and technology and security. For example, a host of projects — including the branch of Xiamen University in Malaysia, the visa-free policy for contacts between the two countries and the Singapore–Kuala Lumpur high-speed railway to be built for which China bids — will bring China–Malaysia cooperation to a new height.

Chapter 6

Report on the Cooperation between China and Singapore in 2015

Wang Juan*

I. Review of the Situation of Singapore in 2015

The year 2015 was the 50th anniversary of the founding of Singapore. In 2015, the Government of Singapore continued to deepen its economic transformation and adjust its social policies; and it was committed to building a fairer and more open society. The People's Action Party actively responded to the trend of political diversity, transformed the governance philosophy, emphasized political inclusiveness, and strengthened communication with the parties out of power. In the meantime, Singapore continued to uphold the strategy of maintaining a balance among great powers to safeguard regional stability and prosperity.

1. Politics

a. *Mr. Lee Kuan Yew passed away, the authoritarian politics ended*

In 2015, the founding father of Singapore, Mr. Lee Kuan Yew, passed away, plunging the Singaporean society into profound grief. Along with expressing

*Wang Juan, Director, Professor at the Singapore Institute of the China–ASEAN Research Institute of Guangxi University.

condolences for the passing away of Mr. Lee Kuan Yew, the international community conducted extensive debates on whether the Singapore Model could continue to be maintained. Under the Singapore Model, the economic system was highly open; the government made extensive interventions in the social and economic fields and the people's lives; the People's Action Party became dominant and governed the country over a long period of time. While praising Singapore for a high degree of economic freedom and openness, the Western society has always raised doubts about the governing position of Lee Kuan Yew and the People's Action Party. With the passing away of Lee Kuan Yew, those doubts became increasingly intense. In fact, the doubts in the Western society represent a misunderstanding of Lee Kuan Yew's governance philosophy and prejudice against a political model that was different from the Western one. The core of the Singapore Model is meritocracy plus a society under the rule of law; its essence is pragmatism; it is not unchanged forever, instead, it advances with the times; after the People's Action Party lost ground in the 2011 election, it actively adjusted its original governance philosophy. The passing away of Lee Kuan Yew only means that Singapore has had no strict father since then and the authoritarian politics have ended in Asia, while the quintessence of the Singapore Model has been retained and Singapore's political situation will remain stable in the long term.

b. *The government transformed the philosophy of development and attached more importance to the issue of social security*

In order to narrow the wealth gap and enhance social cohesion, the Government of Singapore changed the previous non-welfarism philosophy, increased fiscal input in social security, energetically improved the efficiency and quality of public services, and strove to build a harmonious Singapore. The total expenditure of the Government of Singapore was SGD 68.22 billion in the fiscal year 2015, up SGD 11.02 billion over the fiscal year 2014, accounting for approximately 17% of the GDP, up 19.3% over the fiscal year 2014. The expenditure on social development accounted for nearly 50% and reached SGD 33 billion. According to the plan developed by the Government of Singapore, in the next 5 years, the expenditure on public transportation in Singapore will increase from an annual SGD 14 billion to an annual SGD 26 billion, the expenditure on medicine and health care will increase from the current SGD 9 to 13 billion. Furthermore, the government has actively utilized the returns from reserves; at least half of the returns from government reserves have been used in social security each fiscal year since the fiscal year 2001, creating a stable social environment for economic transformation.

c. *The governing party faced the challenge of diversity squarely and put forward the concept of constructive politics*

Given the increasingly powerful opposition parties, the People's Action Party presented, in its administrative policy in 2014, the principle of constructive politics so that priority is given to the country and the people, with a view to preventing the act of opposing for the sake of opposing in the Parliament of Singapore as such an act reduces administrative efficiency and harms Singapore's global competitiveness. The People's Action Party believes that the challenges from the opposition parties are legitimate and policy debates are necessary, but the policies and projects of the governing party cannot be opposed just because parties are different; it is essential to proceed from the long-term interests of most citizens and the country to express constructive opinions. The principle of constructive politics is widely recognized by the people. In the general election in September, 2015, the People's Action Party obtained about 70% of the votes, up 10 percentage points over 2011.

d. *The government put forward the direction of political reform, with the tightening of some criteria of a particular respect and the loosening of those of another respect*

The political reform pushed forward by the Government of Singapore in 2015 can be summarized as the tightening of relevant criteria combined with the loosening of other criteria. The tightening of criteria means that stricter criteria for the eligibility of the democratically-elected president were made. Singapore established the democratically-elected presidential system in 1991 according to which candidates must be the leaders of large companies which pay capital worth more than SGD 100 million. As the time passed by and the situation changed, Singapore's economic aggregate grew by nearly eight times, the number of enterprises paying capital worth more than

SGD 100 million soared to more than 2,100 as compared with 158 in 1993, the original criteria for candidates were no longer able to effectively screen out the outstanding leader, so the government raised the criteria for running in an election to ensure that candidates were competent in leading the national development. The loosening of criteria means that measures were taken to ensure that the Non-Constituency Members of Parliament (NCMP) could enjoy the same voting power as that of the Members of Parliament, so their status was consequently improved. At least 30% of the votes were dissenting ones in each general election in Singapore. When a candidate is not a member of the governing party and fails to be elected by a small margin, he/she enters the Parliament as a Non-Constituency Member of Parliament, and he or she will enjoy the same voting power as other members of the Parliament. This shows that the new-generation of voters have the appeal to listen to more dissenting voices in the Parliament. According to the political reform plan developed by the new government, within the structure of the government, the Parliament is the supreme legislative body, two power centers which shift responsibilities with each other are avoided. In the meantime, as a multi-ethnic and multi-religious country, Singapore always ensures that the rights and interests of minority ethnic groups are protected. This is an indispensable element in Singapore, regardless of the political model.

2. The economy

a. *Intensified efforts were made to improve enterprise productivity*

In 2015, the Government of Singapore continued to focus on enhancing the productivity of small and medium-sized enterprises to push forward economic transformation. Concrete measures covered the following two aspects: First, the government provides assistance, encouraging small and medium-sized enterprises to improve their productivity. The period under the Productivity and Innovation Credit Scheme was extended from 5 to 8 years (2018). Under the Scheme, enterprises can enjoy 400% tax deduction with respect to expenditures of a maximum of SGD 600,000 each year. The activities for which tax reduction can be made include automation, employee training, the obtaining of intellectual property rights, registration of intellectual property rights, research and development or developmental design. On the other hand, the government encouraged enterprises to introduce technologies. With great impetus from the government, enterprises actively adopted measures to enhance their productivity. According to the survey on 756 small and medium-sized enterprises conducted by the Singapore Chinese Chamber of Commerce & Industry, 90% of the enterprises had taken measures to improve their productivity, the proportion of micro enterprises in this respect hit 92%; moreover, 74% of the companies applied once for government assistance. In the meantime, the proportion of companies which purchased automation equipment increased from 42% in 2014 to 51% in 2015.

b. *The economy grew at a low rate*

In 2015, with the impact of the weak recovery of the world's economy and domestic economic transformation, the economic growth rate in Singapore decreased to 2%. According to the statistics from International Enterprise Singapore, the importation and exportation of goods in Singapore amounted to USD 593.27 billion during the period January – November, 2015, down 17.2% over the same period of the previous year (the same below). Exports were USD 319.97 billion, down 15.4%; imports were USD 273.3 billion, down 19.1%; the trade surplus was USD 46.67 billion, up 16.3%. The weak foreign trade data compromised the overall performance of Singapore's economy. Meanwhile, Singapore tightened the overseas labor service policy, exerting an impact on the labor-intensive industries such as construction and catering; both the construction industry and the service industry saw a great decrease in their growth rate. However, overall, Singapore still maintained a low unemployment rate and the growth of the real wage was median, guaranteeing a stable environment for economic transformation. In addition, Singapore attracted foreign investments worth USD 81 billion in 2014; this provided vigorous support for technical and equipment renewal in Singapore. It is expected that Singapore will keep a low growth rate for a period of time yet to come.

c. *The aviation industry grew rapidly*

The aviation industry is a high value-added and hi-tech industry; it is the main representative of Singapore's advanced manufacturing industry. Singapore has continuously increased the technical strength of the aviation industry, offering aircraft design, engineering, production and after-sale services to the world, so as to consolidate its leading position in the aerospace industry of the Asia-Pacific Region. At present, Singapore is the most comprehensive aircraft maintenance, repair and overhaul service center in Asia; ST Aerospace is one of the five top airframe maintenance, repair and overhaul companies in the world; British Rolls-Royce and US Pratt & Whitney have established aircraft maintenance plants in Singapore. In 2015, there were about 20,000 people employed by Singapore's aviation industry, more than 90% of them were technical workers; it enjoyed more than a 10% share in the global market. In order to further expand the influence of Singapore's aviation industry, Singapore has held an air show five times; this show is one of the most important aviation trading platforms in Asia, even in the world. In 2015, the 5th Singapore Air Show attracted more than 1,000 companies from about 50 countries and territories, including 65 of the top aviation companies in the world.

3. Diplomacy

Singapore has always upheld a diplomatic strategy of maintaining a balance among great powers. In 2015, Singapore made full use of its good relations with various countries to stimulate various countries to enhance communication; it served as the regional "buffer" and safeguarded the stability and prosperity of the Asia-Pacific Region.

a. *Singapore kept alliance relations with USA and Japan*

Singapore has always maintained close ties with USA. It is one of USA's most important allies in the Asia-Pacific Region; it welcomes the "Pivot to Asia" strategy of the USA. However, Singapore does not indiscriminately chime in with the USA's policies. In June 2014, during a visit to the USA, Prime Minister of Singapore Lee Hsien Loong expressed the understanding of China's stand towards the South China Sea and concerns about Japan's development in the Asia-Pacific Region. For Japan, which is also an ally of the USA, Singapore did not oppose Japan's bigger role in the Asia-Pacific Region, but it had doubts about Japan's future developmental direction. Prime Minister Lee Hsien Loong believed that Japan should change its historical attitude to develop friendly relations with China and South Korea. On the dispute over Diaoyu Island, Singapore held a neutral position, safeguarded the authority of international laws and stressed a peaceful settlement. Therefore, Singapore's policy towards the Asia-Pacific Region aims at maintaining a balance among the great powers and safeguarding regional stability.

b. *Singapore boosted ASEAN integration*

As a founding member of the ASEAN community, Singapore has attached importance to uniting ASEAN countries and actively pushed forward ASEAN integration, regional prosperity and stability. In May 2015, the ASEAN Forum was held in Singapore, at which various countries discussed the opportunities presented by the construction of the ASEAN Community; they developed the unified regional developmental strategy through consultation, thus vigorously promoting ASEAN integration. Singapore also increased investments in the undeveloped ASEAN countries including Myanmar. In 2015, Singapore was Myanmar's largest source of foreign capital.

II. China–Singapore Cooperation

The year 2015 was the 25th anniversary of the establishment of diplomatic relations between China and Singapore. In 2015, the two sides identified the new positioning of the comprehensive cooperative partnership which advances with the times. Given the continuity and stability of its policies, the passing away of the founding father, Mr. Lee Kuan Yew, will not greatly affect Singapore's foreign policy and China–Singapore relations. China and Singapore will still maintain a good momentum of exchanges; bilateral cooperation has been extensive, substantive, complementary, win–win and it has kept pace with the times and has delivered fruitful results.

1. Political and diplomatic cooperation

Political and diplomatic cooperation is an important part of China–Singapore cooperation. Since the establishment of diplomatic relations, the governments of the two countries have always maintained close relations and learnt governance experience from each other; both sides have built multi-level cooperation communication platforms. In 2015, bilateral political relations continued to develop.

a. *The two sides engaged in frequent high-level exchanges and gained a mutual understanding of major issues*

The friendly diplomatic ties between China and Singapore started with China's reform and opening-up. The year 2015 witnessed frequent high-level contacts between the two countries. In February, Meng Jianzhu, the special envoy of Chinese President Xi Jinping, a member of the Political Bureau of the CPC Central Committee and Secretary of the Central Political and Legal Affairs Commission, visited Singapore. In March, the former Prime Minister of Singapore, Lee Kuan Yew, passed away; Chinese President Xi Jinping, Chinese Premier Li Keqiang, the Chairman of the Standing Committee of the National People's Congress, Zhang Dejiang, Vice Premier Zhang Gaoli separately sent a message of condolence to the leaders of Singapore, while at the invitation of Singapore, as the special envoy of Chinese President Xi Jinping, Chinese Vice President Li Yuanchao attended the state funeral of Mr. Lee Kuan Yew in Singapore. In April, Teo Chee Hean, Deputy Prime Minister, Coordinating Minister for National Security and Minister-in-charge of the Civil Services of Singapore, attended the 5th China–Singapore Leadership Forum in China. In July, the President of Singapore Tan Keng Yam paid a state visit to China. President Tan Keng Yam held talks with Chinese President Xi Jinping, and the two sides agreed to jointly promote China–Singapore relations at a new level. In November, Chinese President Xi Jinping and the leader of Taiwan Ma Ying-jeou held a historic meeting at the Shangri-La Hotel in Singapore; Singapore once again demonstrated its important role in safeguarding regional peace and stability.

High-level meetings between China and Singapore focused on two themes: First, economic cooperation. Singapore actively responded to such programs initiated by China as the Asian Infrastructure Investment Bank and the Silk Road Fund; Singapore welcomed the construction of the Belt and Road and was willing to participate in China's western development, vigorously promoting bilateral economic relations. Second, regional security. Singapore stated that it understood China's stand towards the South China

Sea and Diaoyu Island, but it emphasized a peaceful settlement; this conforms to the diplomatic philosophy consistently upheld by Singapore. Meetings enhanced mutual understanding and mutual political trust between China and Singapore.

b. *The construction of the cooperation mechanism was reinforced to boost the exchanges among young cadres*

China and Singapore have always attached importance to exchanging their experiences in governance experience; in particular, the Chinese Government has advocated learning from Singapore. At present, the two sides have built three cooperation exchange platforms, including the China–Singapore Leadership Forum, the China–Singapore Social Governance Forum, and the China–Singapore Leadership Building in the New Media Environment Forum. The China–Singapore Leadership Forum is mainly designed to discuss national policies and leaders' lines of thought regarding governance; the China–Singapore Social Governance Forum focuses on putting forward the measures for resolving and guarding against various contradictions during social development; the China–Singapore Leadership Building in the New Media Environment Forum aims at discussing how to manage new media, prevent risks and enhance the capability for social governance. These three forums separately meet the exchange needs at different levels and effectively enhance the leadership ability of the government.

The two countries also carried out a number of fruitful programs for young cadre training and exchanges, mainly including: A study carried out by China at the Singapore Advanced Seminar on Economics and Management, a study carried out by the Young Cadre Training Class of the Party School of the CPC Central Committee in Singapore and reciprocal training between the ministries of foreign affairs of the two countries. In July 2015, when meeting with the President of Singapore, Tan Keng Yam, Chinese President Xi Jinping stressed the full implementation of the *Framework Agreement on Middle-level and Senior Officials Exchange Programs*. The cooperation in these respects has broadened the horizon of Chinese officials, improved their ability to handle government affairs as well as making Singaporean officials deepen their understanding of China, laying a foundation for China–Singapore cooperation on other aspects.

2. Cooperation on the economics, trade and investments

The cooperation on economics and trade has always been the main part of China-Singapore contacts. In recent years, great progress has been made in China–Singapore cooperation on economics and trade, the cooperation fields have been increasingly wide, the cooperation mechanisms have been gradually improved, and the cooperation level has been increased constantly. In 2015, China–Singapore cooperation on economics and trade entered a new stage at which cooperation became more mature.

a. *China–Singapore trade declined, but bilateral trade relations were stable*

Amidst the global economic slowdown, China–Singapore trade decreased, but China remained Singapore's largest trading partner, its largest exporting market and its largest source of imports. According to the statistics from China Customs, China–Singapore trade amounted to USD 79.67 billion in 2015, down 0.1% over 2014 — China's exports to Singapore amounted to a value of USD 52.11 billion, up 6.5%, while China's imports from Singapore amounted to a value of USD 27.56 billion, down 10.6%. China's economic slowdown and the decline in the prices of staple products were the main causes for the decrease in China's imports from Singapore.

The mechanical and electrical products were the main products exported from Singapore to China; in 2015, their exports totaled USD 12,797 million, accounting for 46.4% of the total amount of exports from Singapore to China. Special traded goods, unclassified products, plastics, rubber and mineral products were the second–fourth largest categories of commodities exported from Singapore to China; the exports of these products amounted to USD 4,929 million, USD 3,627 million and USD 2,896 million, respectively. The main products exported from China to Singapore were also mechanical and electrical products. In 2015, the exports of these products amounted to USD 28,459 million, accounting for 53.5% of the total amount of exports from China to Singapore. The mineral products, base metals and their products ranked Nos. 2 and 3 in terms of proportion in the products exported from China to Singapore. As shown, there was both inter-industry trade and intra-industry trade between China and Singapore, indicating the technical gap in manufacturing between the two sides.

b. *China and Singapore reached a number of agreements and built multi-level cooperation platforms*

In order to promote economic and trade development, China and Singapore reached a slew of economic cooperation agreements. As of late 2015, the two sides signed the *Memorandum of Understanding on Economic Cooperation, Trade and Investment Promotion*, the *Memorandum of Understanding between China and Singapore on Bilateral Labor Service Cooperation*, the *Investment Promotion and Protection Agreement*, the *Agreement on Avoidance of Double Taxation and Tax Evasion*, the *Agreement on Maritime Transportation*, the *Postal and Telecommunications Cooperation Agreement* and the *China–Singapore Free Trade Agreement*. The *China–Singapore Free Trade Agreement* is of far-reaching significance; it is a milestone in the development of bilateral relations; it comprehensively promotes bilateral economic and trade cooperation and exerts a positive impact on East Asian economic integration.

China and Singapore have also built multi-level cooperation platforms for improving the cooperation efficiency, including the Singapore–China Joint Council for Bilateral Cooperation, the China–Singapore Bilateral Investment Promotion Council, the Joint Steering Committee of the China–Singapore Suzhou Industrial Park, the Joint Steering Committee of the Sino-Singapore Tianjin Eco-city, economic and trade councils established by Singapore and seven provinces including Shandong, Sichuan, Zhejiang, Liaoning, Tianjin, Jiangsu and Guangdong. The Singapore–China Joint Council for Bilateral Cooperation, the Joint Steering Committee of the China–Singapore Suzhou Industrial Park, the Joint Steering Committee of the Sino-Singapore Tianjin Eco-city are the cooperation mechanisms at the vice premier level, while the remaining ones are the cooperation mechanisms at the provincial and ministerial levels. These multi-level and wide-ranging cooperation mechanisms have created a good environment for bilateral economic and trade development. In addition, the non-governmental organizations, represented by the China Council for the Promotion of International Trade and the Singapore Chinese Chamber of Commerce & Industry, have also offered communication platforms for bilateral economic and trade cooperation.

c. *China–Singapore cooperation parks operated well, a new park was officially initiated*

In 2015, Suzhou Industrial Park and Tianjin Eco-city jointly managed by China and Singapore functioned well, their demonstration effect on China's new-type of industrialization and urbanization gradually emerged. Suzhou Industrial Park is positioned as a world-class hi-tech park, it is gradually intensifying investments in nanotechnology, biological medicine and cloud computing; Tianjin Eco-city is designed to build an ecological, livable city, it is actively exploring the development and application of environmental protection technologies and strives to achieve coordination between economic development and ecological protection. In order to consolidate the bilateral cooperative relationship and fully utilize the increasingly mature cooperation model, the governments of the two countries signed the third intergovernmental cooperation project — The China–Singapore (Chongqing) Demonstration Initiative on Strategic Connectivity — in 2015. This project will strengthen bilateral cooperation in finance, transportation logistics and information communication, and will serve the Belt and Road Initiative put forward by China, shaping a new pattern of major project cooperation between the two countries.

d. *China–Singapore financial cooperation deepened constantly, the RMB became gradually international*

China–Singapore financial cooperation can be divided into three stages: Chinese enterprises were listed in Singapore; an RMB offshore market was established in Singapore; the Chinese financial market was open to Singaporean institutions. A loose examination mechanism and high price earnings ratio were the main reasons for the listing of Chinese enterprises in Singapore. However, after 2007, with the impact of the financial crisis, the Singaporean stock market plunged, Chinese enterprises listed in Singapore tended to decrease. During the years 2010–2013, China–Singapore financial cooperation was widened in scope, the two sides cooperated on financial market supervision, access to the banking sector and the construction of the RMB offshore market. During the years 2013–2015, China–Singapore financial cooperation deepened, the two sides worked on opening cross-border RMB settlement and securities markets. In April 2015, the Singapore Exchange and BOC International signed a cooperation framework in Singapore, under which the two sides would cooperate in developing more RMB-denominated products, including bulk commodity futures and foreign exchange derivatives, and strengthen their cooperation on RMB settlement and payment.

As of late 2015, there were more than 8,000 Chinese-funded enterprises in Singapore, with a cumulative investment amount above USD 25 billion. As China–Singapore financial cooperation involves more fields and proceeds in a more profound way, Singapore will certainly become an important platform for RMB regionalization and internationalization.

3. Cooperation in other fields

a. *Scientific, technological and educational cooperation*

China–Singapore scientific and technological cooperation has been extensive and deep. As of 2015, the joint research plan between the two sides had been carried out in 10 phases, covering material development, environmental protection and life health, delivering many innovative achievements and giving a big push to economic growth. In 2014, based on the National University of Singapore (Suzhou) Research Institute, the two sides established the China–Singapore Innovation Center, to which seven programs supported by the Natural Science Foundation of China were immediately granted. This center will become an important platform for bilateral scientific and technological cooperation, and will further promote cooperation between scientific and technological entities or enterprises from Singapore and China. In addition, bilateral educational cooperation also brought about new achievements. The National University of Singapore and Suzhou Industrial Park signed cooperation agreements on jointly building the China Business Research Center, the Suzhou Center of the Lee Kuan Yew School of Public Policy and the GLP (Urbanization Development) Research Center; this marked the entry of China–Singapore educational cooperation into the stage of investing in running schools.

b. *Cooperation on cultural activities and tourism*

In 2015, the two countries carried out a number of activities designed to promote people-to-people exchanges, enhancing the people's understanding of the cultural difference between China and Singapore. In April, the 5th Painting & Calligraphy Art Exhibition was held in Singapore, where painting and calligraphy enthusiasts from the Chinese Mainland, Malaysia and Taiwan were available to exchange painting and calligraphy skills with a view to enhancing mutual understanding. In May, the cultural exchange activity at the Singapore Station of 2015 Retracing the Maritime Silk Road was held at the National University of Singapore, which introduced Chinese ceramics and the culture of tea art to the Singaporean people. In November, the Singapore Chinese Cultural Centre, co-founded by China and Singapore, was established in Queens Street, Singapore; the Centre will further promote cultural exchanges and cooperation between the two countries and enhance the understanding and friendship between the people of the countries. Furthermore, according to the statistics from the Singapore Tourism Board, the tourists from the Chinese Mainland visited Singapore 2.10 million person-times in 2015, up 20%. Frequent non-governmental exchanges will enhance mutual trust between the two countries and lay a good foundation for deepening cooperation between the governments of the two countries.

c. *Cooperation on the military and security*

In 2015, both countries engaged in closer cooperation in military and security fields and consolidated mutual military trust. The navies of the two countries held the China–Singapore Cooperation — 2015 Bilateral Marine Joint Exercise for the first time, the Marine Joint Exercise targeted anti-terrorist efforts, while the joint training of armies elevated, for the first time, the China–Singapore cooperative relationship to the actual combat level. The two sides decided to further increase the level of their military cooperation and exchanges, and increase the scope and frequency of cooperation in the future. Although significant progress has been made in military cooperation between the Chinese Mainland and Singapore, the military cooperation between Singapore and Taiwan has not yet been stopped completely. The Taiwan issue is China's core interest, so properly addressing that issue is the precondition for further deepening the military cooperation between China and Singapore.

Moreover, both countries also engaged in close exchanges and cooperation in such fields as quality inspection and environmental protection;

relevant departments of the two sides separately signed the *Memorandum of Understanding on Cooperation in Entry and Exit Health Quarantine* and the *Memorandum of Understanding on Exchanges and Cooperation in Urban Environmental Governance and Comprehensive Utilization of Water Resources*, further showing that bilateral exchanges are extensive.

III. The Trends of Recent China–Singapore Cooperation

As indicated by the cooperation in 2015, China–Singapore relations were stable and mature, but slight defects still existed. Looking into the next several years, China–Singapore cooperation presents bright prospects.

1. Drawbacks in China–Singapore cooperation in 2015 and suggestions for improvement

a. *The mutual political trust needs to be further enhanced*

Singapore has stated that it understands China's stand towards the South China Sea, but the fact that Singapore welcomes the US. Pivot-to-Asia strategy and strengthens security cooperation with the Philippines and Australia shows that Singapore still has concerns about China's strategic intent. This will cause hidden trouble in deepening China–Singapore cooperation and may affect China–ASEAN relations. China should continue to strengthen communication with the leaders of Singapore, actively publicize China's policies and stands to gain further mutual political trust.

b. *The level of industrial cooperation needs to be increased*

In China–Singapore industrial cooperation, China's role is limited to the manufacturing of goods, and what China utilizes is still the advantage of a cheap labor force. However, with many years of development, China's labor cost has been on the rise, the manner of cooperation using capital plus a cheap labor force has become unsustainable. In the meantime, China has gathered ample human capital through its own development. China–Singapore cooperation should be promoted by using China's intellectual resources to push forward the upgrading of China's industrial functions; otherwise, the products made by China and Singapore will become so akin that the two countries will compete in foreign trade and their common interests will be harmed.

c. *The non-governmental relationship needs to be guided*

A good non-governmental relationship is conducive to win–win cooperation between the two countries. For ethnic and historical reasons, China's non-governmental attitude towards Singapore is complicated. On the one hand, the Chinese people are naturally on intimate terms with Singaporeans thanks to the same clan and origin; on the other hand, the Government of Singapore adopts the strategy of maintaining a balance among great powers, so the Chinese people feel deeply betrayed by Singapore. Such a division in non-governmental sentiment is unfavorable for high-level cooperation between the two sides and the development of China's national consciousness. The Chinese government should actively guide a non-governmental attitude towards Singapore, strengthen the national education and foster a good social atmosphere for deep cooperation between the two sides.

2. The developmental trends of the recent cooperation between China and Singapore

As China's economic development features the new normal, the mode of China–Singapore cooperation will change, and bilateral cooperation will enter a stage of intensive cultivation. In the future, bilateral cooperation will focus on the following aspects.

a. *The two sides will move faster to open the service industry up to each other*

China is currently at the crucial period of economic transformation and upgrading, the backwardness of the service industry is one of the main factors hindering China's economic growth. Singapore's service industry enjoys extremely high international competitiveness, especially in financial, educational and medical fields. At present, progress has been made in bilateral financial and educational cooperation; three main banks based in Singapore have developed new business in China, while the Civil Service College Singapore, Nanyang Technological University and other institutions have formed an educational alliance to jointly develop the Chinese market. China can provide Singapore's service industry with broad developmental space, while Singapore will become the regional headquarters, technology research and development center and the international marketing and international financing center for China, so China–Singapore cooperation in the service industry enjoys broad prospects and exerts a far-reaching impact.

b. *The two sides will further upgrade the functions of China–Singapore cooperation parks*

Suzhou Industrial Park and Tianjin Eco-city, resulting from China–Singapore cooperation, will enter a new stage of development. Suzhou Industrial Park will upgrade its industrial function from manufacturing to research and development, it will transform from an industrial park to an urban complex, it will make beneficial explorations in institutional innovation and social services as well as in other fields. With the goal of building a national demonstration zone for green development, Tianjin Eco-city will promote the development and utilization of environmental protection technologies, they will enable coordination between economic development and ecological protection, which will gather experience and technologies for China's future urban development and management and urban ecological protection. Both cooperation parks will serve as the experimental fields for China's future development and present a new mode of China's mutually beneficial economic cooperation with foreign countries.

c. *Singapore will be attracted to participate in China's western development*

China's economic development is not balanced, there is a huge gap in the level of economic development between the eastern and western regions in China. China's western region is advantageous in low land and labor costs, while local governments energetically attract foreign capital, and the central government also encourages foreign investors to invest in the western region. As Singapore has successful experience in park development in China, the Chinese Government has the desire to stimulate Singapore to participate in China's western development and foster an economic growth pole in the western region. According to the cooperation agreement between the governments of China and Singapore in November 2015, the two sides will carry out the connectivity demonstration project in Chongqing, China to enhance bilateral cooperation in financial, logistics, aviation and communication fields. This cooperation project will contribute to coordinated regional economic development in China and will also offer a new investment space for Singaporean capital.

d. *The two sides will jointly develop projects under the framework of the Belt and Road Initiative*

Singapore is Asia's financial center and also the founding member of the Asian Infrastructure Investment Bank. Under the framework of the Belt and Road Initiative, there are bright prospects for bilateral cooperation in joint financing, financial services, international production capacity and other fields. Since 2015, a number of Chinese and Singaporean banks have signed cooperation agreements with relevant departments in Singapore, they are committed to providing Chinese and Singaporean enterprises with financial support for pragmatic cooperation under the framework of the Belt and Road Initiative. In addition, Singaporean enterprises have advanced philosophies and mature practice in bulk commodity trading, shipping, financial insurance, park development and operations, city and port planning, while Chinese enterprises enjoy advantages in production organization, equipment and capital, so Chinese and Singaporean enterprises work together to complement each other's advantages, contributing to more rapidly pushing forward the Belt and Road projects.

Overall, China–Singapore cooperation aims at delivering mutual benefit and win–win result, it centers on economic and trade cooperation. As Asia's financial center and shipping center, Singapore will be bound to play an important role in China's future development.

Chapter 7

Report on the Cooperation between China and Philippines in 2015

Miao Huixing and Cai Qi*

I. Review of the Domestic Situation of the Philippines in 2015

In 2015, the domestic situation of the Philippines was basically stable. On the one hand, with the arrival of the general election, the political circle was more active than it was in the previous years. On the other hand, some local contradictions and problems left over by history — such as armed conflicts in the southern region and domestic corruption — still awaited effective solutions. On the economic front, the Philippines was affected by the global economic downturn to some extent, but the growth at a medium-high rate was basically maintained in 2015. On the social front, the Philippines still faced complicated social problems, with some contradictions tending to become acute.

* Miao Huixing, Director, Lecturer at the Philippines Institute of the China–ASEAN Research Institute of Guangxi University. Cai Qi, Research Assistant at the Philippines Institute of the China–ASEAN Research Institute of Guangxi University.

1. Review of the political situation of the Philippines in 2015

a. *Domestic environment: The overall situation was stable, but local contradictions still lingered*

In 2015, the domestic political situation of the Philippines was generally calm, and the people's trust in the Government of Benigno Aquino III was kept at a relatively high level, thus laying a good foundation for economic and social development. However, amidst a stable political situation, some long-standing ethnic problems — especially the conflicts between the Government of the Philippines and the non-governmental armed forces on the Mindanao Island in the south — still failed to be solved. In January 2015, the Mamasapano incident occurred in Maguindanao in the southern region of the Philippines, in which 44 Special Action Force members of the Philippines governmental troops died in combating the Moro Islamic Liberation Front. After this incident, the people from various sectors of the society condemned the wrong decision made by the Government of Benigno Aquino III. Although the government repeatedly denied the connection between President Benigno Aquino III and the bloody clash, the investigative group under the Senate of the Philippines still gave a ruling that President Benigno Aquino III was responsible for this incident.

In 2014, with the efforts of the current government, the Government of the Philippines separately signed peaceful cease-fire agreements with the Moro Islamic Liberation Front and the Moro National Liberation Front. The main contents of the peaceful cease-fire agreements reflected the appeal of the Philippine Islamic World; they hoped to found Bangsamoro with more autonomy. In this regard, in 2015, the Government of Benigno Aquino III actively sought the adoption, by the Congress of the Philippines, of the Bangsamoro Basic Law representing the Bangsamoro "entity". However, the Catholic-dominated Congress of the Philippines had some reservations about the Bangsamoro Basic Law; some members of the Congress were absent at the meeting on discussing the Bangsamoro Basic Law for various reasons and under various pretexts, so there was a man-made delay in discussing and adopting it. The allies of the Philippines, such as the USA and Australia, actually had concerns about the high requirement of the Philippine Islamic World for autonomy. As the Bangsamoro Basic Law was not adopted in the specified time, the Chairman of the Moro Islamic Liberation Front and the leader of the Moro National Liberation Front held a meeting in December 2015, with the purpose of exerting pressure on the government again. If the Congress still took a negative attitude, the situation in the southern region of the Philippines would become highly uncertain.

Furthermore, the local situation of the Philippines was unstable in 2015, partly because the Government of the Philippines still constantly exchanged fire with the New People's Army led by the Communist Party of the Philippines and the terrorist group of Abu Sayyaf in the southern region of the Philippines. As it was very difficult to resolve the contradictions in a short time, the unstable state of the local political situation of the Philippines would last for a long time.

b. *Game playing in the 2016 general election: ups and downs*

The year 2015 was the last year during which President Benigno Aquino III was in power; the year 2016 ushered in the general election of the President of the Philippines. Game playing was full of twists and turns before the general election. The current Vice President of the Philippines, Jejomar Binay, was the candidate who announced at the earliest that he would run for presidency; he led the way in approval rating as shown by polls in the first half of 2015. However, in the second half of 2015, Jejomar Binay was reported to have been involved in a series of corruption scandals; his son Junjun Binay, Mayor of Makati, was even sued by the court, thus Jejomar Binay suffered a declining approval rating.

With the impact of Jejomar Binay's corruption scandals, another candidate for presidency, Grace Poe, gained popularity, the people pinned their hopes on the clean background of Grace Poe to make the Philippines completely rid itself of corruption. Originally, it was believed that game playing occurred basically between the candidate of the Liberal Party and Grace Poe in the 2016 general election; however, in October 2015, it was suddenly reported that Grace Poe was ineligible for running for presidency on the grounds that: First, she was an abandoned baby and could not prove that she was born in the Philippines[1]; second, she had resided in the Philippines for fewer than 10 years, so the Commission on Elections of the Philippines made

[1] It means that when a baby was born, his/her parents had the Philippines nationality.

an adjudication that she was not eligible for running for presidency. In order to seek the qualification for running for presidency, Grace Poe filed a lawsuit concerning this election with the Supreme Court of the Philippines; however, her approval rating declined before the Supreme Court made a decision involving her eligibility.[2]

Afterwards, Rodrigo Duterte, Mayor of Davao City, a place of strategic importance in the southern region of the Philippines, announced in November that he would run for presidency. Rodrigo Duterte, 70 years old, originally hoped to retire or continue to serve as Mayor of Davao City; however, with constant encouragement from his family members and supporters, Rodrigo Duterte officially applied for running for presidency. Although Rodrigo Duterte was the last to announce that he would run for presidency, thanks to meeting the aspirations of the people, a poll conducted in December 2015 showed that he ranked No.1 as his approval rating reached 30.25%. As Rodrigo Duterte decided to run for presidency, the pattern of the presidential election changed and competition became increasingly fierce.

c. *Domestic politics: political corruption remained severe*

Corruption is a long-standing problem in the Philippines. According to the statistics from the World Bank, 40% of the state revenue of the Philippines was lost due to official corruption.[3] Shortly after President Benigno Aquino III came into power, he took cracking down on corruption as an important administrative program, but the corruption problem in the Philippines failed to be solved and became more and more serious immediately before he left the post of president. In 2015, Vice President of the Philippines, Jejomar Binay, and his family were reported to have gotten involved in the corruption incident in the construction of a government building in Makati City; his son was suspended from work and sued; moreover, Mar Roxas, the candidate

[2] In March 2016, the Supreme Court of the Philippines ruled that Grace Poe was eligible for running for presidency and she could participate in the presidential election of the Philippines in May 2016.

[3] In an Effort to Prevent Officials from Seeking Tips, Sending Greetings by Saying "Merry Christmas" Was Banned at the Airports in the Philippines, http://news.sina.com.cn/w/2005-12-19/13047745895s.shtml.

of the Liberal Party in power, was also reported to have been involved in the corruption case concerning the No. 3 urban railway line in Manila when he served as the Secretary of Transportation in 2012. In addition, the notorious Napoles List incident[4] exposed in May 2014, remained unsolved.

2. Review of the economic situation of the Philippines in 2015

a. *The GDP grew at a medium-high rate, there was a balance of payments surplus*

According to the data from the Philippine Statistics Authority, the Philippines' GDP was 7,579.94 billion pesos in 2015, up 5.81% over 2014, which was lower than the growth rate in 2014 (6.13%). The service industry greatly contributed to the economic growth; it grew by 6.7% in 2015, up 0.8% over 2014. The industrial and agricultural growth rates declined by varying degrees; the industrial growth rate was 6% in 2015, down 1.9% over 2014; the agricultural growth rate was only 0.2%, down 1.4% over 2014.

The final household consumption expenditure in the Philippines grew by 6.2%, while the government's final consumption expenditure grew by 9.4%. The investments in the Philippines reached 661.83 billion pesos in 2015, higher than the 634.24 billion pesos in 2014, up 4.4%. The investments in the Philippines in 2015 resulted in the execution of 358 projects, which were expected to create 58,252 jobs.[5] In 2015, the Philippines enjoyed USD 2.62 billion in a balance of payments surplus, reversing the situation of a USD 2.9 billion balance of payments deficit in 2014. The Philippines' exports grew by 5.5% in 2015, showing a great decrease over the growth rate in the previous year (it was 11.3% in 2014), which was mainly due to the excessively slow growth of the exportation of goods which grew by only

---

[4]The Napoles List incident is also called the PDAF scam or the pork barrel scam; it refers to the political scandal exposed in May 2014, in which the Philippine businesswoman Janet Lim-Napoles colluded with government officials to misuse fiscal appropriation from the government's Priority Development Assistance Fund by fictitiously establishing projects, non-governmental organizations and foundations.

[5]The Investments in the Philippines Increased in 2015, the Ministry of Commerce of the People's Republic of China, http://www.mofcom.gov.cn/article/i/jyjl/j/201601/20160101229960.shtml.

2.4%. Although the exportation of services grew by 18.7%, its proportion was relatively small, thus the exportation of services cannot stimulate the overall increase in export trade. The growth rate of imports increased to some extent in 2014, trade in goods grew almost in sync with trade in services. The Philippines' importations totaled USD 66.69 billion in 2015, up 2% over 2014.[6] For the product category, electronic products remained the main products imported by the Philippines, their importation amounted to USD 20.2 billion in 2015, accounting for 30.2%, up 32% over 2014, followed by mineral fuels and lubricating oil, whose importations amounted to a value of USD 7.9 billion, accounting for 11.8%, down 40% over 2014; the third largest category was transportation equipment, whose import value was USD 5.9 billion, accounting for 8.8%, down 5.2% over 2014.[7]

b. *The fiscal deficit was on the increase, risks were controllable*

According to the statistics from the Department of Finance of the Philippines, the government deficit of the Philippines reached 121.7 billion pesos in 2015, revenue and expenditures rose by 11% and 13% over 2014. The deficit ratio in the Philippines reached 0.9% of the GDP, up 0.3% over 2014. At present, the deficit level in the Philippines is controllable, and the expansion of fiscal expenditure will not increase the fiscal risks in the Philippines. Purisima, the Secretary of Finance of the Philippines said: "In the past 5 years, the Philippines has always upheld the theory of prudent fiscal management, so currently, we have more fiscal resources to invest in our people, build a more powerful social safety net and better connect the islands."[8]

c. *The infrastructure investment and construction were insufficient*

Infrastructure weakness is a long-standing problem in the economic and social development of the Philippines. This problem was not better solved

---

[6] The data from the Philippine Statistics Authority.

[7] China Remained the Largest Source of Imports for the Philippines in 2015, the Ministry of Commerce of the People's Republic of China, http://www.mofcom.gov.cn/article/i/jyjl/j/201602/20160201262774.shtml.

[8] National Government Posts Deficit at 0.9% of GDP for 2015, http://www.dof.gov.ph/.

any better in 2015. For example, water and power supply facilities were extremely underdeveloped in the Philippines, so the Government of the Philippines needed to control water and power supply for the people many times in 2015. In addition, the transportation facilities were very bad; the Philippines was low-ranking in the global transportation environment scoring in 2015. As the transportation facilities were underdeveloped, on the one hand, the Philippine people suffered a lot due to traffic jams; on the other hand, roads, airports and ports were so irregular for transportation that a large quantity of goods in the Philippines could not move quickly, economic operations became inefficient. Although the Philippines' economy grew at a medium-high rate and its government intensified the input in the people's livelihood in 2015, an excellent infrastructure environment cannot be fostered overnight, so there is still a very large investment space for infrastructures in the Philippines.

3. Review of the social situation of the Philippines in 2015

a. *The religious problem was complicated*

The Philippines is a Catholicism-dominated country. The Constitution of the Philippines makes it clear that the Philippines is a country where religion is separated from government, but it is very hard to separate history from reality. Besides the fact that the Bangsamoro Basic Law failed to be adopted by the Congress due to pressure from Catholicism as mentioned above, a Christian demonstration incident occurred at Edsa Boulevard, in 2015; both incidents highlighted the difficulties in separating religion from government in the Philippines. This demonstration arose because some ministers of the Christian Church of the Philippines claimed that they had been kidnapped by church leaders, and required the Department of Justice of the Philippines to intervene; the Department of Justice of the Philippines immediately conducted investigations. Such a move aroused the dissatisfaction of the Christian Church of the Philippines which believed that the Department of Justice had interfered in the internal affairs of the religion and called on believers around the country to carry out a demonstration at Edsa Boulevard, causing a traffic tie-up. Afterwards, the Department of Justice softened its tone, and the demonstration then came to an end.

b. *Natural disasters frequently occurred*

As an island country, the Philippines is affected by typhoons throughout the year. In 2015, it suffered typhoons Linfa, Melor and Koppu. The reconstruction work, initiated due to the previous super typhoon Haiyan, had not yet been completed. The typhoon Melor in December 2015 caused the evacuation of more than 700,000 people in order to take refuge elsewhere; as shown, typhoons are the major natural disaster affecting the safety of the Philippine residents. In addition, another major natural disaster in the Philippines was the Nino phenomenon. In 2015, the Nino phenomenon led to the failure of many crops in the Philippines, so the Philippines had to import more rice to meet the domestic grain demand.

II. Review of China–Philippines Cooperation in 2015

In 2015, China–Philippines political relations met with great obstacles due to the issue of the South China Sea; after many setbacks, the tension eased slightly at the end of 2015. In the economic, social and cultural exchange fields, China–Philippines cooperation was promoted steadily and progressed in a gratifying way.

1. The bilateral political relations developed tortuously

Although the year 2015 was the 40th anniversary of the establishment of diplomatic relations between China and the Philippines, in the first half of 2015, China–Philippines relations plunged to the ice point, bilateral high-level political exchange was nearly interrupted due to the issue of the South China Sea. In January 2015, Albert del Rosario, Secretary of Foreign Affairs of the Philippines, publicly required, for the first time, the ASEAN countries to express their stand on China's land reclamation in the South China Sea; he warned that China's acts would eventually pose a threat to ASEAN countries. Afterwards, bilateral relations worsened drastically, the Philippines even allied itself with Vietnam many times to require the ASEAN community to voice opinions on the issue of the South China Sea at ASEAN meetings, further casting a shadow over the bad relations between China and the Philippines. In October, the International Court of

Arbitration adjudicated the right of jurisdiction over the issue of the South China Sea and the admissibility of the case involving the South China Sea arbitration,[9] but China's Ministry of Foreign Affairs held that such adjudication was invalid and was not binding upon China. Therefore, the stalemate in bilateral relations continued until the second half of 2015. However, as the bad political relations did not conform to the interest appeal of the two countries, the countries had the desire to improve their bilateral relations. The APEC meeting held in Manila in 2015 provided an opportunity for easing the tension between these two countries. On November 17, 2015, Chinese President Xi Jinping arrived at Manila, the capital of the Philippines, and attended the 23rd APEC Leaders' Meeting. Chinese President Xi Jinping's participation in the meeting demonstrated China's active role in APEC and also mitigated the tension between the two countries, so his participation was of great significance.

2. China–Philippines economic and trade cooperation developed steadily

a. *Bilateral trade grew amidst adverse situations*

With the global economic downturn, various countries faced great downward pressure on foreign trade, but China–Philippines trade grew in 2015. According to the data from China Customs, China–Philippines trade totaled 283.5 billion yuan in 2015, up 2.7%, China's exports to the Philippines were 165.7 billion yuan, up 13.7%, while China's imports from the Philippines were 117.8 billion yuan, down 9.6%. In bilateral trade, China enjoyed a surplus, while Philippines suffered a deficit. In the meantime, China remained the Philippines' second largest trading partner and its largest importer. China–Philippines trade maintained a positive growth rate as compared with a 1.7% decrease in the overall trade between China and the ASEAN countries, further demonstrating the great vitality of bilateral trade (see Table 1).

[9]The Philippines Unilaterally Submitted the Issue of the South China Sea to International Arbitration in 2013.

Table 1. The Import and Export Trade between China and the Philippines During the Period January–December 2015 (Unit: 10,000 yuan)

Time	Total imports and exports	Exports	Imports	Import–export gap
Jan. 2015	2237913	1357317	880596	476721
Feb. 2015	1920473	1175588	744885	430703
Mar. 2015	1955719	917465	1038254	-120789
Apr. 2015	2191548	1210235	981313	228922
May 2015	2292433	1352112	940321	411791
June 2015	2333719	1385264	948445	436819
July 2015	2489406	1349964	1139442	210522
Aug. 2015	2366895	1364251	1002644	361607
Sept. 2015	2691288	1585483	1105804	479679
Oct. 2015	2417690	1504341	913349	590992
Nov. 2015	2809786	1789207	1020579	768628
Dec. 2015	2688578	1595336	1093242	502094
Total	28355090	16574083	11781007	4793076

Source: China's General Administration of Customs.

b. *Cooperation on investments was strengthened constantly*

In 2015, bilateral investments were boosted steadily, both sides showed great confidence in investment cooperation.

First, the cooperation fields were on the increase; for example, in 2015, China's NARI Solar Technology Co., Ltd. built a 30 MW photovoltaic power station on an island in the Philippines; it is the ground photovoltaic power station with the largest installed unit capacity in the Philippines; the China Energy Engineering Group and PCPC signed an operations maintenance contract for the Concepcion Power Plant located in the Municipality of Concepcion in lloilo Province on Panay Island, the Philippines; the SM Group, the largest shopping mall operator in the Philippines, announced that it would expand business in China, develop a residential project in Chengdu — its first residential project in China — and build four residential apartments near the SM shopping mall in Chengdu; the Jollibee Group with a number of brands, including Jollibee, Chowking and Greenwich, the largest fast-food company in the Philippines, increased investments in China's food industry; its Yonghe King owns 321 restaurants in China, the business turnover of Yonghe King on the Chinese market accounted for 10% of that on global market in 2015. Tony Tan Caktiong, Chairman of Jollibee, said that the Chinese market would be one of Jollibee's business priorities.

Second, the willingness to invest was strengthened continuously. For a long time, the investments between China and the Philippines had lagged behind those between China and other ASEAN countries for various reasons, but both sides always endeavored to reverse that situation. In April 2015, the Bureau of Commerce of Xiamen City, Fujian Province, China, acknowledged that the Philippines was one of the nine key countries under the action plan of Xiamen City for carrying out the Belt and Road Initiative; nine projects out of 39 projects currently pushed forward by Xiamen City were related to the Philippines. In September 2015, the Deputy Secretary of Trade and Industry of the Philippines led a Philippine delegation of more than 120 people to attend the 12th China–ASEAN Exposition in Nanning, Guangxi. The delegation carried out the Philippines national investment promotion event at the Nanning International Convention and Exhibition Center to actively discuss the issues concerning cooperation between China and the Philippines. On December 30, 2015, President Benigno Aquino III authorized the Philippine ambassador to China to sign the agreement on the Asian Infrastructure Investment Bank, which meant that the Philippines could catch up with the last train of the founding members of the Asian Infrastructure Investment Bank.

Third, the supporting facilities for investment had been improved continuously. On the financial front, in March 2015, the Philippine Business Bank announced its cooperation with the Bank of China, under which the RMB would be used as the foreign currency only second to the USD for real-time domestic settlement. The Philippine Business Bank also became the 11th bank for providing RMB-denominated products and services in the Philippines. In the meantime, as the IMF included the RMB into its special drawing rights (SDR) currency basket, the central bank of the Philippines announced that it would hold more RMB assets and actively study the suggestion on making peso-RMB direct exchange arrangements. If the suggestion was adopted, China–Philippine trade and investment would be promoted greatly. Furthermore, China also made efforts to build a bridge for boosting bilateral trade; for example, in September 2015, the Makati Branch of the Bank of China held the Bridge-PPP Project and Financial Service Forum, serving as the bridge for Chinese-funded enterprises to participate in PPP projects launched by the Philippines. As continuous improvement has been made in the supporting work on mutual investments between China and the Philippines, the investment potential of both sides will increase greatly, and the space for investment cooperation will be expanded.

3. The social and cultural exchanges continued to be carried forward

a. *Cooperation on tourism reached a new height*

In 2015, China–Philippines cooperation on tourism was elevated to a new level. According to the data from the Department of Tourism of the Philippines, in 2015, Chinese tourists visited the Philippines 490,000 person-times, accounting for 9.16% of all tourists who visited the Philippines, ranking China No. 4 as a tourist source for the Philippines. Chinese tourists who visited the Philippines increased by 88.34% in 2015 over 2014; China ranked No. 1 among all countries as a tourist source for the Philippines in this respect. Chinese tourists visiting the Philippines increased thanks to the following factors: On the one hand, the income of the Chinese people was on the rise; on the other hand, the Philippines changed its tourism policy. In early 2015, the Philippines announced that the tourists with a Chinese passport could apply for visa-free treatment if they stayed in the Philippines for fewer than 7 days; such a move greatly stimulated Chinese tourists to visit the Philippines. The Philippine tourism department also paid particular attention to the Chinese market. According to the Philippine ambassador to China, Erlinda F. Basilio, the Philippines had become the hot destination for Chinese people to enjoy family tours and honeymoon tours; China and the Philippines should strengthen their cooperation on tourism, the Philippines should introduce more policies for promoting China–Philippines cooperation on tourism in the future.[10]

---

[10] Last Year, Chinese Tourists Received by the Philippines Increased by More Than 20%, Xinhuanet, http://news.xinhuanet.com/overseas/2016-02/13/c_128714578.htm.

b. *The cultural exchanges became increasingly rich*

In 2015, bilateral cultural exchanges became closer than ever before, as evidenced by:

First, the actors engaged in the exchanges became diverse. In 2015, various actors participated in the cultural exchanges between China and the Philippines, various forms of cultural exchange activities were carried out between governments and non-governmental organizations. At the governmental level, the Government of the Philippines actively promoted Filipino martial arts in China, and established the Rizal Center under the theme of Filipino art, culture and language within the Philippine Embassy in China which is located in Beijing. The Rizal Center will serve as a venue for Chinese people to learn about Philippine history, culture and traditions. In addition, Zhao Jianhua, the Chinese ambassador to the Philippines, and Felipe M. de Leon Jr., Chairman of the National Commission for Culture and the Arts of the Philippines, met at the Department of Foreign Affairs of the Philippines and signed the *Execution Plan for China-Philippines Cultural Exchanges 2015–2018*, continuing to write a better chapter for bilateral cultural exchanges. Regarding the non-governmental exchanges, the actors in China–Philippines non-governmental exchange activities in 2015 included schools, hospitals, non-governmental organizations and enterprises; for example, nearly 1,000 overseas Chinese students from the Philippines took part in the Fujian Jimei Chinese summer camp; the Philippine Chinese Table Tennis Federation and the affiliated Competitive Sports School of the Capital University of Physical Education and Sports signed a letter of intent on cooperation in Beijing, under which reciprocal visits and exchanges involving table tennis programs would be conducted regularly each year; the Confucius Institute of Ateneo De Manila University participated in the annual charity activity of the Philippine General Hospital, the largest public hospital in the Philippines, and donated books and Chinese traditional game devices to the hospital. Compared with the governmental cultural exchanges, China–Philippines non-governmental cultural exchanges are more diverse in form and type, and can better promote understanding and communication between the peoples of the two countries.

Second, the exchange achievements were fruitful. For example, in July 2015, Huaqiao University held the graduation ceremony of the 10th Chinese

Class for Foreign Government Officials, while students from the Philippines, Thailand and Indonesia attended the class to learn Chinese, gain an understanding of Chinese history and culture, and deepen their understanding of the Chinese society and local customs and practices. Furthermore, during the China–ASEAN Exposition in September, 2015, Isabelle Climaco-Salazar, Mayor of Zamboanga City, the Philippines, and Li Xinyuan, Mayor of Guigang City, Guangxi Zhuang Autonomous Region, China, signed a letter of intent on the establishment of sister-city relations; the two sides agreed to strengthen exchanges and cooperation on various aspects on the basis of mutual benefit. Regarding the achievements in cultural exchanges between China and the Philippines, even the ASEAN countries, the Philippine ambassador to China said: "I feel China's great sincerity in promoting cultural exchanges and mutual understanding between China and the ASEAN community, and I hope that China and ASEAN countries can constantly push forward cultural exchanges, deepen mutual understanding, exchanges and integration in various fields so that China and the ASEAN countries can form an integral whole".[11]

[11] Philippines Ambassador to China: I Feel China's Great Sincerity in Promoting Cultural Exchange with the ASEAN, *Chinese Commercial News*, September 20, 2015.

Chapter 8

Report on the Cooperation between China and Laos in 2015

He Zheng*

I. Review of the Situation of Laos in 2015

In 2015, Laos' situation was stable, the government's efforts in poverty reduction produced a marked effect, the diversified diplomacy helped improve Laos' international status; economic growth slowed down, but its potential was high; the government's finances were relatively strained, the inflation rate fell to a new low; the official development aid decreased to some extent compared with the previous year; population growth was relatively slow; the educational situation improved to a certain degree; skilled labor force had been lacking for a long time, and the welfare security system developed slowly.

1. Politics

a. *The political situation maintained a stable state, the anti-corruption situation remained severe*

Since the 9th National Congress of the Lao People's Revolutionary Party elected the new central collective leadership in 2011, Laos' political and

* He Zheng, Director, Senior Economist at the Laos Institute of the China–ASEAN Research Institute of Guangxi University.

the central leadership has been basically stable. With respect to personnel affairs, Laos' leadership basically maintained the status quo and did not change greatly. According to the newly amended Constitution, the tenure of the President of Laos shall not exceed two consecutive terms. The upper age limit for the President of Laos is 65. Where work is outstanding, retirement can be postponed until the end of the tenure; where work is fair, retirement occurs in the year of reaching the upper age limit. Therefore, a number of leaders, including the current General Secretary Choummaly Sayasone, will retire in 2016, and the Lao People's Revolutionary Party is planning to form a new leadership collective. As regards institutional reform, Laos adopted the newly-amended Constitution to permit, for the first time, the establishment of Provincial Assemblies (PAs). Like local assemblies, provincial assemblies have similar functions to those of the National Assembly; their basic task lies in deliberating and adopting the laws proposed by local governments, deliberating and approving the social and economic development and the national budget plans and supervising the administrative performance of local governments, including the economic development plan.

Furthermore, corruption was relatively serious among Laos' officials, the anti-corruption situation was grim. According to the 2015 Report released by the Procuratorial Committee of the Government of Laos, corruption caused a loss of 2.42 trillion kip, 95 officials were punished, the transparency of the Government of Laos was not enough, the working efficiency of the government was not high, and bureaucracy remained severe.

b. *The government achieved some success in poverty reduction, but Laos remained an underdeveloped country*

In 2015, Laos made significant progress in reducing poverty, and the proportion of poor families decreased to 6.59%, much better than the original target (10%). However, in order to remove poverty in this underdeveloped country, Laos should continue to intensify its economic transformation and structural adjustment; the tasks are heavy and the journey ahead is long for the Government of Laos.

c. *The diversified diplomatic strategy of maintaining a balance contributed to improving Laos' international status*

The diversified diplomatic strategy carried out by Laos for many years has undoubtedly been successful. In 2015, Laos made fruitful diplomatic achievements, its international status improved significantly. Laos not only chaired a number of important ASEAN meetings, but was also elected to the rotating ASEAN presidency for the year 2016. Within the ASEAN community, Laos serves as the strategic center in ASEAN energy cooperation thanks to its abundant hydropower resources; Laos has vowed to act as the "storage battery" for the ASEAN community and deliver its electric power to ASEAN countries. In this regard, Laos has, through a diversified kind of diplomacy, signed electric power supply agreements with Vietnam, Thailand, Myanmar, Malaysia and Singapore. Externally, Laos has drawn attention from the developed countries, including USA, the European countries, Japan, Australia and South Korea, thanks to its strategic location.

2. The economy

a. *Economic growth declined, but the potential remained huge*

In the fiscal year 2015, Laos' GDP grew by 7.5% and stood at USD 12.8 billion, the per capita GDP was USD 1,970. The economic growth rate was equivalent to the GDP growth rate in 2014, but the economic growth rate decreased to some extent as compared with the average economic growth rate (7.9%) in Laos in the past 10 years. The main causes were the government's fiscal constraints, income decrease in the mining industry and China's economic slowdown.

(i) With the impact of natural disasters such as droughts and floods, the harvest of the main agricultural products declined

In 2015, a drought inhibited the yield of rice, vegetables and fish in some parts of Laos, agriculture and forestry grew by 3%, the annual rice yield was 3,872,000 t. Subject to a dual impact from natural disasters and industrialization, the proportion of agriculture and forestry continued to plunge, and it declined sharply from 28.9% during the fiscal year 2009–2010 to 23.7% during the fiscal year 2014–2015. The exportation of forestry products decreased by more than 20%; in particular, with the impact of the decline in coffee prices around the world, the exportation of coffee, deemed as one of the main export products of Laos, fell from 30,000 t in 2013 to 23,000 t in 2015, its total export value was only USD 50 million.

(ii) The share of the industrial sector gradually increased, the industrial sector progressively developed in the direction of industrialization

In 2015, Laos' industrial growth rate was 8.9%; the proportion of industry in its national economy rose from 25.6% during the fiscal year 2009–2010 to 29.1% during the fiscal year 2014–2015. Such sectors as clothing, building material and electric power developed rapidly. In the meantime, Laos planned to build 10 hydropower stations, delivering an additional 2,000 MW power each year; it is expected that the annual power generation will reach 5,000 MW in the future; the domestic electric power demand can be satisfied greatly and electric power exportation can be promoted. However, overall, Laos' industry remained weak, its export growth mainly relied on the increase in electric power sold to Thailand, while most industrial products in Laos were mainly imported.

(iii) The service industry saw a decreasing proportion in GDP, the tourism sector developed vigorously

The proportion of Laos' service industry in the GDP declined from 44.2% during the fiscal year 2012–2013 to 39.8% during the fiscal year 2014–2015. In 2015, although the developmental rate declined to some extent, the service industry still grew by about 9.1%; the service industry made the greatest contribution to the growth of the national economy among the primary, secondary and tertiary industries. Such service sectors as tourism, finance and telecommunications underwent the most vigorous expansion. As the flagship of Laos' service industry, the tourism sector developed rapidly in 2015; according to statistics, tourists visited Laos 4.33 million person-times in 2015, up 4% over the previous year; they generated USD 670 million in tourist income. China was Laos' largest source of tourists, followed by Thailand and Vietnam.

b. *Fiscal dilemma and foreign debts put a burden on the progress in large projects*

In 2015, Laos still faced fiscal difficulties, the budget for government projects was insufficient, there was a delay in putting funds in place, the fiscal expenditures of the government still outstripped its fiscal income. During the fiscal year 2015–2016, as the government adjusted the national budget, the deficit accounted for 5.7% of the GDP,[1] suggesting that budget deficit remained a huge challenge for the Government of Laos. On the one hand, the government approved too many projects; according to statistics, in the first 11 months of the fiscal year 2014–2015, the government departments at various levels had 1,589 projects not approved by the National Assembly, with the cumulative amount above USD 2,899 million, the investment projects involving concession amounted to USD 1,206 million; this was the greatest cause of Laos' fiscal expenditure exceeding the standard; on the other hand, the government's tax oversight was so insufficient that tax arrears caused by enterprises were severe, and the period of tax exemption granted to investors during the early stage of investment attraction had not yet expired. Subject to a dual dilemma, the government decided to postpone the construction of some large projects and only retain the projects which could deliver quick economic benefits. The current decrease in tax revenue and continued growth of the importation of machinery, oil and other commodities have harmed Laos' international trade balance. Laos' foreign debts have accounted for 62.51% of the GDP[2]; Laos can be considered a country with a relatively high proportion of foreign debts in the world. Therefore, the Government of Laos must properly address the issue of fiscal balance, increase the exportation of electric power to reduce its trade deficit, and anchor its hope on private investments to boost Laos' economic growth and create more jobs.

c. *The inflation rate was on the decrease*

In 2015, Laos' monthly inflation rate was 1.28% on average, the lowest one in 6 years, much lower than the 4.62% in the same period of 2014. This is

[1] Economists Warned That Laos' National Budget Deficit Exceeded the Standard, http://news.news-com.cn/a/20151111/8237346.shtml.

[2] *Source*: WIND economic database (EBD), IMF's statistics on July 10, 2015.

because the decline in global fuel prices helped Laos mitigate its trade imbalance and inflation.

d. *The official development aid (ODA) decreased to some extent over 2014*

With the impact of the international macroeconomic situation, there was a certain decrease in the international aid received by Laos compared with 2014, though Laos received a lot of international aid in 2015. According to the statistical data from the World Bank, as of late 2015, the total official development aid received by Laos exceeded USD 421 million, less than USD 600 million in 2014.

3. Society

a. *The population growth slowed down, urbanization accelerated*

According to the data from China's latest population census 2015, as of March 2015, Laos' total population size was 6.50 million, the population growth rate declined from 2.08% during the decade 1995–2005 to 1.45% during the decade 2005–2015, showing a decrease in population growth. Laos' male population was larger than its female population, and the ratio of male population to female population was 100.5:100. In 2015, Laos' population density was 27 people/km^2; there were 148 cities in Laos, the average population size in cities across the country was about 44,000, and the urbanization rate increased from 27% in 2005 to 33% in 2015.

b. *The enrollment rate in vocational education rose to some extent, the educational level of the domestic population still needed to be further increased*

In order to ensure high-quality educational development and promote further development of human resources, the National Assembly of Laos ratified the amendment to the *Education Law* in July 2015. In 2015, the Ministry of Education of Laos provided financial assistance and support for vocational education and training, the enrollment rate in vocational education rose by

11.3%; in the meantime, Laos started to incorporate vocational education into the national public education system. The literacy rate of Laos' domestic population reached 70–80%, an intermediate level; nationals were generally at or below the level of secondary education; most of the population had received primary education; the dropout rate in primary education reached 30%; only Sainyabuli Province saw popularization of junior middle school education; and only 17% of the people could receive higher education nationwide.

c. *The shortage of specialized labor forces was still acute*

Laos' special economic zones created more than 22,000 jobs for Laotian people, greatly reducing the loss of domestic workers and illegal immigration to the neighboring countries; however, as a large number of skilled Lao workers migrated to the neighboring Thailand, Laos suffered a shortage of workers, and the problem was the severest in the clothing industry; in 2015, the clothing industry showed a gap of more than 30,000 workers. A shortage of ordinary domestic workers and a lack of professional technical workers have been the long-standing social problems in Laos, which has severely hindered its economic development. The fundamental way to mitigate labor shortage consists in increasing the educational level, improving labor quality and developing a strategy for human resource development that is suited to the national conditions.

d. *The social security system scheme developed slowly*

In late 2015, the coverage rate of Laos' social security system (SSS) was only 30.22%, much lower than the target set for the fiscal year 2014–2015 (50%). The failure of the SSS coverage rate to meet the target was mainly due to the following two factors. First, after the social security law was promulgated in 2013, the ordinary citizens in society joined the social security system, while previously only civil servants and enterprise employees joined this system. Second, the medical security scheme operated by the Ministry of Health of Laos (part of the SSS) faced fiscal difficulties; as the scheme relied heavily on external assistance, it developed slowly. The Government of Laos planned to increase the coverage rate of the social security system to about 80% by 2020.

II. China–Laos Cooperation

In 2015, there were frequent high-level contacts between China and Laos, bilateral cooperation was impressive. China has attached great importance to consolidating and developing friendly cooperative relationship with Laos. Under the policy of maintaining long-term stability, good neighborly and friendly relations, a high degree of mutual trust and engaging in comprehensive cooperation, and the principle of being good neighbors, friends, comrades and partners, the two sides strengthened their amicable cooperation in various fields and pushed forward long-term healthy and stable development of a comprehensive strategic cooperative partnership.

1. Political cooperation — Mutual trust was enhanced

Laos actively sought integration into China's neighboring diplomatic strategy characterized by the Belt and Road Initiative, while the iconic event was the initiation of the Lancang–Mekong Cooperation Mechanism. On November 12, 2015, the first foreign ministers' meeting under the Lancang–Mekong Cooperation Mechanism was held in Jinghong City, Yunnan Province; this indicates that China, Myanmar, Laos, Thailand, Cambodia and Vietnam would initiate a new attempt in sub-regional cooperation. The initiatives put forward by China in coordination with a neighboring diplomatic strategy generally received vigorous support and active response from the state leaders of Laos. For example, when the President of Laos, Choummaly Sayasone, visited China in September, the two sides discussed the issues concerning cooperation on the high-speed railway project; he attended the activity commemorating the 70th anniversary of the victory of the War of Chinese People's Resistance against Japanese Aggression and the victory of the World Anti-Fascist War. The senior leaders of Laos stated that with joint efforts from the leaders of the two parties and the two countries, great progress was made in the comprehensive strategic cooperative partnership between Laos and China; Laos was willing to more rapidly cooperate with China on major projects, including railway projects, constantly tapping the potential for cooperation. On October 20, 2015, Pany Yathotou, a member of the Politburo of the Central Committee of Laos and the President of the National Assembly of Laos, made a statement that Laos fully supported the Silk Road Initiative put forward by China. In addition, Yu Zhengsheng, Chairman of the Chinese People's Political Consultative Conference, met with Executive Vice President of the Central Committee of the Lao Front for National Construction in July. All contacts among and political views of senior leaders of the two countries show that the relations between China and Laos have entered a better historical period of rapid development.

2. Economic cooperation — It developed in a profound way

In 2015, Laos obtained generous support from China in domestic economic construction; the two sides made great achievements in economic cooperation. With the rapid development of bilateral economic and trade cooperation in recent years, bilateral economic cooperation has gradually advanced from pure trade in goods in the early period to high-end areas. The two sides have built connections in their developmental strategies, energetically pushed forward the construction of infrastructures for connectivity, including railways and highways; the two sides have actively cooperated on their capacity for production in energy, mining, agriculture and other areas to promote the prosperity and stability of the border areas of both countries, making new achievements in bilateral relations and pragmatic cooperation.

a. *The economic and trade relations developed in an unbalanced way, the growth of bilateral trade declined slightly*

In 2015, China's project contracting in Laos grew substantially, with the contract amount above USD 5 billion, the contracts newly-signed by Chinese enterprises in Laos amounted to USD 5.16 billion, up 39.8% over 2014; the business turnover stood at USD 3.22 billion, up 38.2%; it ranked No. 3 among ASEAN countries, only second to Indonesia and Malaysia, and it ranked No. 4 among Asian countries. The projects involved roads, bridges, water conservation facilities, agriculture, real estate, building material, hotels, communication and park development. According to statistics from China, as of late 2015, the cumulative actual investments made by Laos in China were USD 45.49 million,[3] while China's direct investment stock in Laos

[3]The Department of Asian Affairs, the Ministry of Commerce of the People's Republic of China, http://yzs.mofcom.gov.cn.

was USD 5.85 billion. China's non-financial direct investment flow in Laos surpassed USD 1 billion to reach USD 1.36 billion, up 36.2%, overtaking that of Indonesia for the first time, following Singapore.

Currently, China has become Laos' largest foreign capital source, its largest aid-giving country and its second largest trading partner; bilateral economic and trade cooperation has really featured reciprocity and mutual benefit as well as common development. However, bilateral trade declined to a certain degree in 2015. According to statistics from China Customs, in 2015, bilateral trade amounted to USD 2.78 billion, down 23.1% — China's exports were USD 1.23 billion, down 33.3%; imports were USD 1.55 billion, down 12.6%. The main causes are as follows: First, with the impact of price fluctuation on the international market, the export prices of gold, copper and other raw materials from Laos fell to a certain extent; second, since 2015, the investment and engineering contracting projects initiated by Chinese-funded enterprises in Laos have decreased, the exportation of infrastructure construction materials declined. The positive aspect of bilateral trade was that Laos obtained more opportunities for getting access to the Chinese market. On October 27, 2015, the Administration of Quality Supervision, Inspection and Quarantine of China issued Announcement No. 129, permitting Laos to deliver rice to China. If other agricultural products of Laos are given access to the Chinese market in the future, they will help bilateral trade become balanced.

b. *New breakthroughs were made in cross-border economic cooperation*

On August 31, 2015, the governments of the two countries officially signed the *Overall Plan for the Joint Construction of the China–Laos Mohan-Boten Economic Cooperation Zone*. The signing of the plan was an important milestone in the bilateral economic and trade cooperation and development. The China–Laos Mohan–Boten Economic Cooperation Zone is the second cross-border economic cooperation zone between China and the adjacent country; it is an important move for both countries to innovate their cooperation mode and accelerate the opening-up. The plan will further promote the complementation of the economic advantages of both countries, facilitate trade investment and personnel contacts and push forward bilateral industrial cooperation; it will also speed up the development of the border areas of the two countries, benefit the border areas and the people of both countries. At present, construction has been basically completed in the commercial, trade and financial zone, the tourist and cultural zone, and the logistics processing park on the Boten, Laos side; some of them have been put into use, laying a solid foundation for the development of the cross-border economic zone and providing more conveniences for the flow of port factors. In addition, the Vientiane Saysettha Development Zone, 21 km away from the downtown area of Vientiane, Laos, and jointly built by the two countries, has signed contracts with 19 enterprises, among which Dongyan Petrochemical's Laos Oil Refining Project, the Thailand DSG Logistics Park and Laos Tobacco Co., Ltd., and they have seen the initiation of construction. The developmental zone has become an important project in the construction of the Belt and Road; it is a new carrier for Chinese-funded enterprises to achieve sustainable development and whole industrial chain operations in Laos and to engage in economic cooperation with Laos.

c. *Cooperation on hydropower reached a new level*

In 2015, bilateral hydropower cooperation deepened and bore fruit: three transformer substations at the first stage of the EPC power grid project in North Laos — in which Yunnan International Co., Ltd. of China Southern Power Grid serves as general contractor — were successfully put into grid-connected operations; Laos' Houay Lamphan Gnai Hydropower Station, built by China Gezhouba Corporation, was officially completed and delivered on October 14; the river was successfully dammed for Laos' Namtha River No. 1 Hydropower Station Project, that is controlled, developed and built by China Southern Power Grid; its construction was officially started at the Nam Ngum III Hydropower Station, the largest hydropower station in Laos, built by Sinohydro Group Ltd.; the 230 kV interconnection project in North Laos, the first power grid project under the Belt and Road Initiative between China and Laos, was officially put into operation. These projects have proved the close hydropower cooperation between China and Laos. Regarding Laos, as Laos has cooperated with Chinese enterprises to carry out water conservation projects, the country can enjoy convenience in financing and obtaining technical support. Therefore, many hydropower projects in Laos have been mainly outsourced to Chinese enterprises or developed in cooperation with Chinese enterprises, such as the EPC contract on Vientiane's loop-network power transmission and transformation project signed between China Electric Power Equipment and Technology Co., Ltd. and Electricite du Laos in 2015; the Laos NN hydropower station project in which Fengfan Power Equipment Co., Ltd. and Laos Hydropower Investment Consulting Co., Ltd. engage in cooperation; the H.La-Nge 50,000-kW Hydropower Station Project in Xekong Province, Laos signed by HeBei Construction & Investment Group Co., Ltd.; the EPC contract on the power transmission and transformation project from Laos' Xekong No. 1 Transformer Substation to a hydropower station in Laos signed between Pinggao Group of the State Grid Corporation of China and Electricite du Laos in Vientiane. These cooperation projects, beneficial to both sides, have greatly boosted Laos' economic and social development.

d. *"Shaking heaven" and " moving earth" are the two greatest bright spots in China–Laos economic and trade cooperation*

In late 2015, Laos' first satellite Laos No.1 was launched successfully at Xichang Satellite Launch Center, China, which marked the beginning of the comprehensive strategic partnership between China and Laos. With the official signing of the China–Laos railway project, the cooperation agreement between the governments of the two countries entered the stage of execution. December 2 witnessed the opening ceremony of the China–Laos railway project connecting Vientiane, the capital of Laos, with Kunming, Yunnan Province. The railway, which is 427.2 km long and will cost RMB 38.7 billion (USD 6.04 billion), is expected to be completed by 2020; it will help Laos realize its great dream of transforming from a landlocked country into a land-connected country; it will also make Laos actively integrated into China's neighboring diplomatic strategy characterized by the Belt and Road Initiative.

Overall, China–Laos cooperation has been in full swing from trade in goods, logistics, farming and mineral development to hydropower stations, transportation and electric power infrastructures, development zones, satellites and railways. With a high degree of mutual political trust and win–win economic cooperation, the two countries have worked together from simple trade to the export of complete equipment and hi-tech cooperation; this shows that bilateral cooperation is a process of progressive development from the shallow level to the deep level and from the primary level to the high level; in particular, the realization of two landmark projects which "shake the heaven" (satellite) and "move the earth" (railway) embodies the community with a common destiny shared by the two countries and further consolidation of the comprehensive strategic cooperative partnership between the two countries. As mentioned by Zhao Wenyu, the economic and commercial counselor of the Chinese Embassy in Laos, with Laos' rapid economic development, bilateral economic cooperation will become increasingly rich in content and wider in area, especially developing towards the hi-tech field; it is believed that bilateral economic and trade cooperation will get better and better since Laos' satellite was launched and the construction of the China–Laos railway began.[4]

3. Cooperation in social and other areas

In 2015, bilateral cultural exchanges brought forth something new again and again, scientific and technological exchanges and cooperation were fruitful.

a. *The Center for Chinese Studies at the National University of Laos was established*

On November 19, 2015, the opening ceremony of the Center for Chinese Studies at the National University of Laos was held at the National University of Laos. As the important think tank of the National University of Laos and the bridge for connecting the academic institutions of the two countries, the center will enhance cooperation and exchanges between research institutions of the two countries, and make the people from various sectors of Laotian society better understand China.

b. *Media and cultural communication was intense, cultural blending and symbiosis was achieved between the two countries*

In 2015, the bilateral cultural exchanges went beyond the traditional cultural blending mode and entered the era of media information and cultural

[4] From Satellite to Railway, China–Laos Economic Cooperation in the New Period Moves towards the High End, Xinhuanet, December 3, 2015.

communication; movies and TV dramas, book translations and productions, audio programs, bilingual magazines, and tourist products became the media for China to disseminate its culture. The special news issue of *China–Yunnan* (English), jointly launched by the media organizations of the two countries, was first published in Vientiane; Laos' Chinese Radio started to broadcast; both events indicated that learning Chinese had become a fashion and tide in Laos. According to the Confucius Institute, in Laos, many people believe that learning Chinese well can secure employment at Chinese companies in Laos, suggesting an increasing influence of Chinese culture in Laos. Furthermore, the Chinese Embassy in Laos separately established one Ambassador Study at one middle school and one primary school in Vientiane; China's original children's books and a periodical exhibition tour were held in Vientiane, Laos; China Radio International and Lao News Agency signed a cooperation agreement. Various forms of media cultural exchanges will lay a good mass base for expanding bilateral cooperation and further promoting cultural blending and symbiosis between the two countries.

c. *Both countries enhanced cooperation on human resources, science and technology*

In 2015, under project contracting projects, the number of people sent by China to Laos increased substantially, their number exceeded 11,000, ranking it No. 1 among the ASEAN countries, even the Asian countries. In the meantime, China also strengthened the training of human resources for Laos through bilateral cooperation projects. For example, on December 20, in order to enhance scientific and technological talent exchanges and cooperation between the two countries, the Yunnan Association for Science and Technology and the Lao Chinese Chamber of Commerce signed the *Memorandum between the Lao Chinese Chamber of Commerce and the Yunnan Association for Science and Technology with Respect to Cooperation on Overseas Intellectual Resources*, under which the Yunnan Association for Science and Technology establishes the scientific and technological talent exchange platform at Vientiane Sky City, Laos with a view to boosting bilateral cooperation in human resources and scientific and technological projects.

4. Problems in China–Laos cooperation

a. *The fiscal difficulties in the Government of Laos and the destabilizing factors hindered bilateral cooperation*

Regarding the political security, Laos' political situation was generally stable; however, the wealth gap between urban and rural areas widened increasingly, the government paid insufficient attention to the development of the areas inhabited by ethnic groups and corruption worsened, and the people's discontent with the Lao People's Revolutionary Party increased to some extent. In particular, Laos' fiscal difficulties, insufficiency of budget for government projects and delay in putting funds in place impeded the development of many cooperation projects between the two sides. According to the *Debt Sustainability Analysis 2014* released by the IMF and the World Bank, the increase in the amount of foreign debts may trigger a foreign debt crisis. Therefore, when going global, Chinese-funded enterprises must carefully deal with foreign debts.

b. *The operating costs for enterprises were high, there were difficulties in financing, and the market system was underdeveloped*

When investing in Laos, foreign enterprises first faced a number of dilemmas, including poor infrastructures, low transportation capacity, a limited level of logistics and insufficient electric power. These dilemmas posed a very severe test on enterprises and might cause capital flight. However, the Government of Laos required enterprises to independently address the issues concerning water supply, roads and electric power necessary for investment projects, and help local areas get rid of poverty and become better off. This exerted a great pressure in costs on enterprises. Second, enterprises encountered difficulties in project financing. Take Chinese-funded enterprises as an example; the financial resources at Lao banks were limited, the ability of these banks to offer loans was insufficient; Chinese banks set a number of examination and approval procedures for overseas projects. However, it was difficult for these enterprises to obtain credit support from Lao banks and Chinese banks. Furthermore, Laos' market system and financial system were still at the initial stage and were underdeveloped, they lagged far behind the socialist market economic system built by China, so it was relatively hard to build connections between the former and the latter.

c. *There were contradictions between the pursuit of economic interest by Chinese capital and Laos' sustainable development*

As stated by the Minister of Planning and Investment of Laos, Somdy Douangdy, the Government of Laos would focus on sustainable development in the new period and maintain a balance between social and economic development and the environment, and he hoped that Chinese-funded enterprises would attach greater importance to improving the quality of investments. As some Chinese-funded enterprises brought some "bad habits" developed in China to foreign countries, in that they disregarded the rights and interests of local workers, causing labor disputes, or they ignored the differences in culture and customs, incurring hatred from local people, or they blindly pursued economic benefits, leading to environmental pollution and ecological damage; some enterprises paid no attention to contract procedures, resulting in disputes arising out of breaking contracts; as a result, they were severely punished by local governments, or projects got nowhere, even worker strikes occurred, causing bloody conflicts and incurring unnecessary safety risks to the people of the Chinese side. In the meantime, the bad behavior of one Chinese-funded enterprise would engender a negative image among local people, so other Chinese-funded enterprises might pay higher reputation costs, and even safety costs. Therefore, in the future, as Chinese-funded enterprises and overseas branches more rapidly increase service outlets, they should improve the quality of their investments, better adjust the investment structure, and pay more attention to the local environment and people's livelihood.

d. *Bilateral relations and cooperation were constantly subject to interference and challenges from external factors*

Throughout their history, Laos and Vietnam have had special relations, so Vietnam is still able to exert a certain influence on Laos. For example, Laos and Vietnam signed a bilateral border trade agreement on June 29, 2015, under which the import tariff rates for the products of both countries and those made by Vietnamese investors in Laos would be reduced to zero. For Laos, the special relations between Laos and Vietnam intersect China–Laos relations featuring the community with a common destiny, thus Laos plays a very delicate role; it has also learnt to maintain a balance among various countries in the diplomatic field. Meanwhile, the development of Laos' relations with Japan, USA and other countries has also affected China–Laos relations. For example, the President of Laos, Choummaly Sayasone, met with US President Barack Obama in New York on September 7; Assistant Secretary of State Daniel Russel visited Laos during the days of December 17–18, making way for US President Barack Obama's visit to Laos in 2016, and Laos–US relations improved continuously.

Therefore, China–Laos relations were affected by Vietnam and were also subject to restrictions and interference from ASEAN countries and other countries, adding more uncertainties to the development of China–Laos relations.

Chapter 9

Report on the Cooperation between China and Brunei in 2015

Huang Ying, Huang Qin and Wang Yong*

I. Review of the Situation of Brunei in 2015

In 2015, a sharp decline in international oil prices and the persistent issue of Islam exerted an adverse impact on Brunei's economic and social development. In the complicated international environment, the Government of Brunei continued to transform its functions, strengthen the centralization of the Sultan's power, carry forward the traditional culture, enhanced cooperation with private enterprises and pushed forward diversification of the industrial structure, so Brunei developed steadily in the political, economic and diplomatic fields.

* Huang Ying, Director, Associate Professor, master supervisor at the Brunei Institute of the China–ASEAN Research Institute of Guangxi University; Huang Qin, part-time Research Fellow at the China–ASEAN Research Institute of Guangxi University, Lecturer at the Faculty of Education of Guangxi Normal University; Wang Yong, Research Assistant, doctoral student at the Brunei Institute of the China-ASEAN Research Institute of Guangxi University.

1. Politics — Reinforcing the centralization of the Sultan's power, improving the government's efficiency

a. *Reshuffling the government's cabinet to strengthen the Sultan's power*

In 2015, the Sultan announced the new list of the cabinet members for reshuffling. After reshuffling, the Crown Prince Al-Muhtadee Billah continued to serve as the senior minister of the Prime Minister's Office of Brunei, Mohamed Bolkiah, the brother of the Sultan and the Minister of Foreign Affairs and Trade of Brunei, was dismissed from office, while the Sultan concurrently served as the Minister of Foreign Affairs and Trade of Brunei. This cabinet reshuffling meant that the Sultan would serve as the Minister of Foreign Affairs and Trade of Brunei in addition to serving as Prime Minister, Defense Minister and Finance Minister; the Sultan had the intent of further centralizing power.

b. *Transforming government functions, stressing the improvement of efficiency*

Given huge government institutions, red tape and high administration costs, the Government of Brunei intensified its reforms, carried out the 2015–2020 Digital Government Strategy, speeded up the construction of e-government, promoted interdepartmental collaboration and cooperation and built the platform for two-way communication between the people and the government. In the meantime, the Prime Minister's Office established four new departments at the Ministry of Energy and Industry — including the Department of Technical Innovation and Industrial Creative Affairs, the Department of the Development of the Global Halal Industry, the Department of the Handicraft Industry, Cooperatives and Business Environment — to develop the new forms of service business. Moreover, the government introduced the items for scoring the performance in the public sector to stimulate civil servants to improve the quality of their services and the efficiency of their work.

c. *Advocating the leading role of religion, improving the legal system*

In 2015, Brunei continued to serve the governance purpose: peace and security. In response to the impact from extremism and modernization on religion, while emphasizing the importance of the Islamic belief, Brunei united and understood the people who were not believers of Islam, so as to prevent the radical reform forces from damaging the process of democracy in Brunei.

Furthermore, the Sultan promulgated and revised a series of laws and regulations, including an anti-corruption law, and continued to carry out the *Islamic Criminal Law* to strengthen the leading position of Islam in the Bruneian society and consolidate the Islamic monarchy in Brunei. The government also started to regularize financial order and the financial market; for example, the Monetary Authority of Brunei issued a number of regulations for market rectification, paving the way for attracting foreign capital and promoting diversified economic development. These measures helped improve the domestic system of Islamic law and modernize the capital market laws and regulations.

2. Diplomacy — Focusing on the neighboring countries, actively expanding the diplomatic space

In 2015, with a focus on the diplomatic affairs concerning the Southeast Asia Region, Brunei continued to adopt a moderate and prudent all-round diplomatic policy, energetically broadening its diplomatic space and carrying out diplomatic work through consultation and dialogue. First, the unity of ASEAN member countries is the cornerstone for Brunei's diplomatic policy; Brunei has always stressed close diplomatic relations with other ASEAN member countries, especially Singapore, Malaysia and Thailand. Brunei has sent a permanent mission to East Timor and has supported East Timor's accession to the ASEAN community. Furthermore, Brunei continued to maintain friendly relations with Japan and South Korea. As the China–ASEAN Free Trade Area was upgraded and the Belt and Road Initiative was put forward, Brunei attached greater importance to friendly relations with China, actively participating in building the Asian Infrastructure Investment Bank and supporting the "dual-track channel" approach to the issue of the South China Sea. Brunei also further enhanced regional economic cooperation, became a member of the Trans-Pacific Partnership Agreement (TPP), kept close ties with Germany, France, India, Russia, Latin America, Saudi Arabia and other Arab countries.

3. The economy — Developing slowly amidst change

In 2015, Brunei's stable political situation, preferential tax policy and relatively transparent market made Brunei attractive for foreign-funded enterprises. Government departments achieved a lot in actively promoting economic diversification, improving the business environment, sharpening the competitive edge of the private sector and developing small and medium-sized enterprises. However, Brunei was still characterized by the industrial pattern in which the oil and gas industries are dominant and other industries are small.[1] With the impact of various factors including a drastic decrease in international oil prices, as a resource-based outward-looking economy, Brunei saw an economic slowdown evidenced by a decrease in the GDP growth rate, CPI fall and slow adjustment of the industrial structure.

a. *GDP growth slowed down and became negative for a time*

Brunei's nominal GDP totaled 17,777 million Brunei Dollars in 2015, down 18.1%. As the proportion of oil and gas resources in Brunei's GDP was high, subject to the complicated international oil price situation, in 2015, Brunei's quarterly GDP declined continuously, the growth rate fell markedly, the quarterly nominal GDP was negative in several quarters (see Table 1).

b. *CPI declined noticeably*

With the impact of the economic situation, Bruneian residents' consumption of daily necessities and their willingness to invest in education contracted in 2015, CPI decreased by 0.4 percentage points in 2015 over 2014, especially in such expenditure items as clothing, footwear, transportation and education (see Table 2).

c. *Trade surplus was maintained, imports and exports tended to decrease*

In 2015, Brunei generally maintained a trade surplus, but the overall imports and exports declined (see Figure 1). The value of imports was 4,180.7 million

[1]The oil and gas industries are the absolute pillars in the national economy, while other industries are small and weak.

Table 1. Brunei's Quarterly GDP, 2014–2015 (Unit: 1 million Brunei Dollars)

	2014				2015			
Time Item	First quarter	Second quarter	Third quarter	Fourth quarter	First quarter	Second quarter	Third quarter	Fourth quarter
Nominal GDP	5738	5490.6	5738	5490.6	5738	5490.6	5738	5490.6
Real GDP	4776.5	4664.4	4776.5	4664.4	4776.5	4664.4	4776.5	4664.4
Nominal growth rate (%)	−5.4	−2.4	−5.4	−2.4	−5.4	−2.4	−5.4	−2.4
Real growth rate (%)	−5.9	−3	−5.9	−3	−5.9	−3	−5.9	−3

Source: http://www.depd.gov.bn/.

Table 2. Brunei's CPI, 2014–2015

Type	Weight	2014	2015	Change (%)
General price index	10000	100.4	100	−0.40
Food and non-alcoholic beverages	1911	99.7	100.6	0.90
Clothing and footwear	424	99.2	95.7	−3.53
Housing, water, electricity, gas and other fuel	1114	99.2	101.3	2.12
Furniture and household articles	1101	97.1	96.4	−0.72
Health care	132	100.2	101.2	1.00
Transportation	1883	102.6	99	−3.51
Communication	601	99.9	100.6	0.70
Culture and leisure	913	99.1	99.2	0.10
Education	390	105.2	102.5	−2.57
Restaurant and hotel	885	102.4	103.6	1.17
Bulk commodity and service	646	101.7	102.2	0.49

Source: http://www.depd.gov.bn/.

Brunei Dollars, down 8.24%, while that of exports was 8,716.9 million Brunei Dollars, down 35.1%, the total amount of imports and exports decreased by 28.3%.

In 2015, Brunei mainly imported mechanical and transportation equipment, finished products, fuel and lubricants, chemical products, beverages

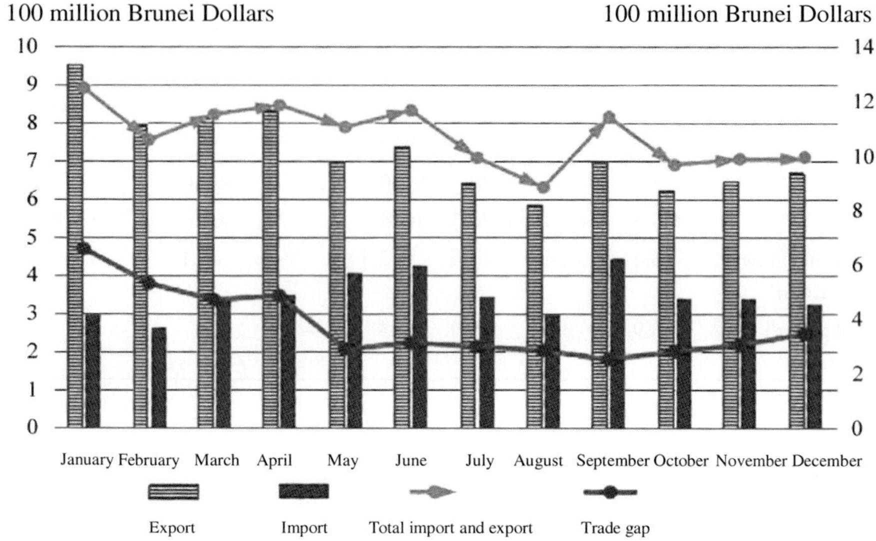

Figure 1. Brunei's Import and Export Trade in 2015
Source: http://www.depd.gov.bn/.

and tobacco, and it chiefly exported oil and gas; their exports amounted to 8.11 billion Brunei Dollars, accounting for 93.04% of total exports.

d. *A number of measures were taken to promote the transformation of the industrial structure, the business environment improved to some extent*

In 2015, the Government of Brunei mainly adopted the following measures to transform the industrial structure and support the development of private enterprises:

First, continuing to steadily develop the energy industry. In 2015, Brunei's national economy still heavily relied upon the oil and gas industries. Given this situation, the Government of Brunei renewed oil and gas exploitation equipment to increase the level of exploration and drilling; it also actively introduced foreign capital from the downstream industries of oil and gas, developed deep processing of oil and gas to extend its footprint along the value chain of the oil and gas industries.

Second, placing emphasis on developing the high value-added industries. In 2015, Brunei focused its developmental goal on the high value-added industries — such as halal food production, information and communication technology, new and high technology, software services, other manufacturing and service sectors — to foster new economic growth points. To attract foreign capital, Brunei gave priority to the high value-added industries and encouraged technical localization and technical innovation.

Third, creating a good business environment for economic development. In 2015, main government departments of Brunei zealously promoted reform to develop an excellent business environment: the Ministry of Home Affairs and the Ministry of Industry and Primary Resources announced the enforcement of new business regulations for permitting enterprises to register companies before determining the nature and place of business, and the enforcement of the 2015 sundry goods license act (amendment) for building a fair business environment; the Ministry of Finance launched a special website for handling the matters concerning enterprise name and company registration, shortening the period for registering an enterprise to one day; the system for scoring the performance of the public sector was carried out to increase the level of services of the public sector; the Monetary Authority of Brunei issued new regulations, requiring all Bruneian banks, financial companies and Islamic trust funds to adopt the overall debt repayment rate for all of their loan clients, so as to reduce the excessively high household debt ratio, regularize the lending behaviors of financial institutions and promote healthy development of the credit market.

The above measures greatly improved Brunei's business environment. According to *Doing Business* released by the World Bank, Brunei ranked 84th in the world in the Ease of Doing Business Index in 2015, up 21 places over the previous year. The proportion of the costs for starting a business in the per capita national income declined from 10.5% in 2014 to 1.2% in 2015; the time for starting a business was shortened from 104 to 14 days; the number of procedures initiated for enterprise registration decreased from 18 to 7; the total tax rate declined from 15.8% to 8.7%.[2]

---

[2] *Data source*: http://www.worldbank.org.cn/.

4. Society — Continuing to improve the people's livelihood

Ranking Brunei among the top ten in the world with regards to the quality of the people's lives is one of the three main goals set in Brunei Vision 2035. In 2015, Brunei's national housing scheme was implemented well, which had provided houses to nearly 30,000 residents without land. There was a certain decrease in the number of criminal cases nationwide. However, with the impact of the decline in the per capita national income, Brunei's United Nations Human Development Index fell by one place in 2015 over the previous year. Furthermore, the *Islamic Criminal Law* was enforced well, while the non-Muslim people started to be accustomed to and accept the law. Brunei imposed restrictions on non-Islamic cultures and religious activities — for example, the Sultan announced that citizens were prohibited from celebrating Christmas, but overseas Chinese in Brunei were not prohibited from celebrating Chinese festivals. Overseas Chinese enjoyed an increasing status in Brunei. After cabinet reshuffling, Vice Minister of Finance Liu Guangming became another overseas Chinese person entering the cabinet following Lin Yucheng, but overseas Chinese still have a long way to go and heavy tasks to fulfill in seeking civic rights.

Moreover, Brunei constantly improved the quality of education, strengthened supervision over education, and supported the non-governmental forces dedicated to developing higher education; it also stressed equal access to education — such as letting more women receive education – and increased the coverage of domestic scholarships, cooperated with foreign countries, provided such countries as Laos with scholarships to attract foreign talents.

Overall, the measures taken by the Government of Brunei for improving the people's livelihood were conducive to promoting administration and people-to-people harmony within Brunei. Brunei's people generally live and work in peace and contentment, so it is hard to breed radical Islamic behavior in Brunei.

5. Culture — Safeguarding and carrying forward the traditional culture

In 2015, with a number of great activities, Brunei continued to carry forward its fine cultural traditions, maintain ethnic characteristics and Islamic lifestyle, use its traditional values to lead the basic code of conduct in the whole society; Brunei attached importance to protecting historical sites and ruins as well as its ethnic heritage, pushed forward sustainable development and utilization of tourist resources. Brunei made a lot of international achievements in cultural and sports events. Besides its excellent performance in The World Championship of Performing Arts and Special Olympics World Summer Games, Brunei also successfully held the 7th ASEAN School Sports Meeting. As the second largest ethnic group in Brunei, overseas Chinese highly value the education of native language Chinese. In 2015, some Chinese schools increased grants, adjusted fees to improve the quality of the teaching while attracting more non-overseas Chinese people to learn Chinese.

6. Military security — Attaching importance to regional cooperation

In 2015, the Royal Brunei Armed Forces actively conducted external exchanges, engaging in military security cooperation with China, Malaysia, Bangladesh, Pakistan and USA; it also carried out military exercises with Malaysia, USA and other countries, and it donated four second-hand Black Hawk helicopters to Malaysia. In 2015, Brunei controlled the national defense budget, which decreased by 25.6% over 2014. In general, Brunei focused military development on regional cooperation, and it strictly controlled and utilized its military budget. On the security front, in 2015, Brunei placed emphasis on international cooperation to combat terrorism, corruption, smuggling, drug trafficking and other transnational crimes.

II. China–Brunei Cooperation in 2015

In 2015, China–Brunei relations developed smoothly, cooperation fields increased continuously and strategic mutual trust between the two countries was further consolidated. Brunei upheld the view that the issue of the South China Sea should be addressed through the "dual-track channel" in a peaceful way. The upgrading of the China–ASEAN Free Trade Area and the Belt and Road Initiative put forward by China highly tallies with Brunei's economic diversification strategy and the goals set in Vision 2035, and it offers a broad developmental platform and space for bilateral economic and trade cooperation.

1. Political cooperation

China and Brunei are different in ideology and political system, but the two countries always respect each other's sovereignty and territorial integrity, and they refrain from interfering in each other's internal affairs; the momentum of mutual political trust and cooperation between the two countries has been good. Based on this situation, in 2015, the heads of the two countries continued to maintain close exchanges and deepen their political friendship through various channels. On the one hand, the heads of the two countries paid high attention to and engaged in timely communication with each other's great events; for example, the Sultan and the royal family members participated in the New Year Gala 2015 held by overseas Chinese in Brunei to celebrate the New Year together with the overseas Chinese in Brunei; Brunei sent a message of condolence to China after the ferry sinking in the Yangtze River and the extraordinarily serious fire accident at the Port of Tianjin, China; Chinese President Xi Jinping separately expressed congratulations on the 31st anniversary of Brunei's independence and the 69th birthday of the Sultan. On the other hand, senior leaders of both countries made unremitting efforts to further deepen the exchanges and cooperation in various fields, and to promote regional peace and prosperity. The two sides held the same stand towards major issues, including cracking down on violent international terrorism, improving global climate governance and opposing hegemony.

2. Economic cooperation

a. *Bilateral trade*

(i) Bilateral trade declined markedly

According to the data from the General Administration of Customs of China, bilateral importations and exportations varied greatly each month. In the first 10 months of 2015, China's exports to Brunei generally decreased; in various months of 2015, China's imports from Brunei were small in number, with the largest volume of imports (USD 29.2 million) and the smallest volume of imports (USD 200,000) occurring in December and September, respectively. China always maintained a trade surplus with Brunei (Table 3).

Table 3. China's Exports to Brunei in 2015 (Unit: USD 100 million)

Month	1	2	3	4	5	6	7	8	9	10	11	12
Exports	1.591	1.318	0.506	2.358	0.903	0.840	0.955	1.566	0.900	0.753	1.163	1.236
Imports	0.003	0.038	0.041	0.016	0.003	0.035	0.065	0.354	0.002	0.064	0.059	0.292
Gap	1.588	1.280	0.466	2.341	0.900	0.806	0.890	1.212	0.897	0.689	1.104	0.944

Source: http://www.customs.gov.cn/.

Table 4. Statistics on China's Trade with Brunei During the Period January–December 2015 (Unit: USD 100 million)

	Import and export		Export		Import		Trade gap	
	Amount	Increase or decrease (%)	Amount	Increase or decrease (%)	Amount	Increase or decrease (%)	The current year	The same period in the previous year
Brunei	15.1	−22.2	14.09	−19.34	0.97	−48.78	13.12	15.57

Source: http://www.mofcom.gov.cn.

The volume of China–Brunei trade was the smallest among that between China and the ASEAN countries; it was only 1.55% of the volume of China–Malaysia trade — Malaysia is the largest trading partner of China in the ASEAN community; in 2015, the volume of China–Brunei trade declined greatly. According to the data in Table 4, the volume of China–Brunei trade was USD 1.51 billion in 2015, down 22.2%; China's exports were USD 1,409 million, declining sharply by 19.34%; imports were USD 97 million, down 48.78%. China's trade surplus was USD 1,312 million, down 18.67% over the previous year.

According to statistics from China Customs, the top five products imported by China from Brunei in 2015 included organic chemicals, instruments and equipment, products of stones and similar materials, wood pulp and other fibrous cellulose pulp, and machinery. The top five products exported from China to Brunei were furniture, iron and steel products, ceramic products, toys and sports products and machinery, accounting for 54.98% of China's exports to Brunei; furniture was the product whose exports from China to Brunei were the largest in number.

The continued decline in crude oil prices on the international market and the product structure in China–Brunei imports and exports determined a sharp decrease in bilateral trade in 2015. Regarding the structure of Brunei's imports and exports, Brunei mainly exported oil and gas, but the importers were Japan, South Korea and other countries, while the proportion of exports to China was relatively small; Brunei mainly imported mechanical and transportation equipment and food, accounting for 50.13% of total imports, the main sources of imports were Malaysia and Singapore, while the imports from China made up a relatively small proportion. Therefore, as international oil prices plummeted, organic chemicals which ranked No.1 in Brunei's exports to China, mainly crude oil, showed an increasing quantity but a decreasing price, so the total volume of exports decreased; on the other hand, Brunei's domestic market is small, with a decrease in the exportation of oil and gas as the economic pillars, national income shrank, Brunei's imports from China declined. Furthermore, the reduction of excessive production capacity and the industrial structural transformation and upgrading in China's economy under the new normal were also the important factors leading to a decrease in bilateral trade.

(ii) Accelerated efforts were made in building the framework for bilateral trade cooperation

Given the small domestic market, Brunei needs to rely on regional economic and trade cooperation agreements to connect the international market, draw upon foreign capital, technology and management experience to develop its domestic economy and achieve economic diversification. With smooth negotiations involving the upgrading of the China–ASEAN Free Trade Area (CAFTA) and the Regional Comprehensive Economic Partnership (RCEP), China and Brunei continued to speed up the building of the trade cooperation framework. Brunei actively responded to the Asian Infrastructure Investment Bank Initiative put forward by China. On June 29, 2015, the Second Finance Minister of the Prime Minister's Office of Brunei officially signed the *Asian Infrastructure Investment Bank Agreement* on Brunei's behalf in Beijing, showing Brunei's determination to promote infrastructure construction and connectivity in Asia.

b. *Bilateral investments*

Brunei's investment environment is extremely attractive for Chinese-funded enterprises: First, Brunei abounds in resources, it enjoys a stable political situation and obvious location advantages; second, its policies are transparent, tax policies are preferential, the costs of such factors as land are low; third, China and Brunei are highly complementary in the economic field. The diversified economic developmental strategy adopted by the Government of Brunei offers new opportunities for Chinese-funded enterprises to develop in Brunei, while the huge market demand and a wealth of technical, management and capital resources in China also become the potential forces for driving Brunei's economic growth and industrial structural transformation and upgrading.

(i) Chinese-funded enterprises paid increasing attention to investment in Brunei

In 2015, more and more Chinese-funded enterprises registered companies and normally carried out business in Brunei, with business covering telecommunication services, real estate development, geological exploration, traditional Chinese medicine, fishery, agriculture, hydropower and road construction. Marked effects were produced in bilateral cooperation in investment and contractual services and other respects; for example, Beijing Sesame World established the Overseas Intelligent Hardware R&D Center in Brunei, which highly accords with Brunei's intent to actively introduce high and new technology industries, and has received vigorous support from the Government of Brunei and has officially become the major project in the Belt and Road Initiative by China; Hengyi Petrochemical, the first Chinese-funded enterprise investing in Brunei, raised 3.8 billion yuan through non-public offerings and invested all of the funds so raised in Brunei's PMB Petrochemical Project so as to ensure that the integrated oil refining and chemical project — with crude oil and gas condensate as raw materials – carried out in cooperation with the Government of Brunei could be smoothly put into production; the China Harbour Engineering Company won the bidding for the EPC project of the Pulau Muara Besar Bridge — the project includes the design and construction of one 2.7 km four-lane sea-crossing bridge, one 3 km island four-lane highway, one supporting electrical network, one communication network and one water supply pipe network; its construction period is 36 months and its amount is about USD 200 million; Beijing New Oriental Star Petrochemical Engineering Co., Ltd. conducted a preliminary investment feasibility assessment and planned to establish a wholly-owned subsidiary in Brunei — which engages in project contracting involving oil and gas resource exploration and design as well as other areas — to further develop the Southeast Asian market. Moreover, China's provinces and autonomous regions, including Guangxi, Yunnan, Fujian, Hainan and Hubei, sent business delegations to Brunei for surveying the investment environment in energy, agriculture, fishery, tourism, halal food and logistics, they actively sought the opportunities for enhancing economic and trade cooperation with Brunei.

(ii) The pragmatic cooperation in the Brunei–Guangxi Economic Corridor took shape

The *Memorandum of Understanding on Economic and Trade Cooperation in the Brunei–Guangxi Economic Corridor* was officially signed in 2014. In late March 2015, Peng Qinghua, Secretary of the Party Committee of the Guangxi Zhuang Autonomous Region, led a delegation to visit Brunei, proposing to engage in early cooperation in the following areas: making the Beibu Gulf International Port Group participate in operating the Port of Muara; building the Nanning–Brunei Agricultural Industrial Park and the Yulin–Brunei Traditional Chinese Medicine Health Industrial Park; carrying out aquaculture, oyster cultivation and rice planting in Brunei. The two sides ultimately reached the letters of intent in 12 projects involving agriculture, fishery, food processing, tourism and transportation logistics; the two sides agreed to strengthen the joint committee mechanism between them. In May, Guangxi's delegation arrived in Brunei to attend the International Food and Biotechnology Investment Meeting, and conducted discussions with relevant departments of Brunei, the two sides signed the letters of intent in four projects including the China (Nanning)–Brunei Agricultural Industrial Park, the China (Yulin)–Brunei Traditional Chinese Medicine Health Industrial Park, and mariculture and rice planting in Brunei. In September, the Government of Brunei and the Guangxi Beibu Gulf International Port Group signed the letter of intent on jointly building Brunei into the shipping center for the ASEAN community and the East ASEAN Growth Area, thus laying a solid foundation for Brunei–Guangxi cooperation and development in more fields and at a deeper level. The Brunei–Guangxi Economic Corridor becomes a new bright spot in China–Brunei cooperation and a new platform for industrial cooperation in the Belt and Road Initiative.

Overall, China–Brunei economic and trade cooperation in 2015 showed the following four characteristics. First, with a weak recovery of the world's economy and a fall in international oil prices, Brunei saw a downward economic development; as there was dislocation in the structure of China–Brunei import and export trade under the new normal of China's economy, bilateral trade shrank greatly. Second, territorial disputes did not hinder bilateral cooperation. On the issue of the South China Sea, unlike Vietnam and the Philippines, Brunei actively advocated a peaceful solution to the dispute over the South China Sea, and resolutely elected to continue deepening economic and trade cooperation with China. Third, the upgrading of CAFTA and the Belt and Road Initiative put forward by China offered new platforms and opportunities for deepening China–Brunei economic, trade and investment cooperation, the Brunei–Guangxi Economic Corridor became the China–ASEAN cooperation innovation demonstration project and set a good example for economic and trade cooperation between China and other ASEAN countries. Fourth, Brunei's strong desire to "bring in" played a significant role. In 2015, Chinese enterprises were awarded many investment cooperation projects in Brunei, which was closely related to the preferential policies adopted by the Government of Brunei for introducing foreign capital.

3. Exchanges and cooperation in other fields

a. *The work priority in military and defense security shifted to international judicial cooperation*

Bilateral military exchanges and cooperation became increasingly close and diverse. Brunei's domestic situation was stable, Brunei took a consistent attitude toward the issue of the South China Sea; moreover, in 2014, the militaries, especially the navies, of the two countries engaged in frequent exchanges, the Royal Brunei Armed Forces participated in the maritime exercises jointly conducted by many countries on the day of the establishment of the People's Liberation Army Navy of China, so the work priority of the two countries in military and defense security shifted to enhanced international judicial cooperation in light of both sides' domestic needs and international environmental governance in 2015. The Energy Minister of Brunei praised China for its contributions to the regional bloc in China–ASEAN defense cooperation, and also expressed the necessity for expanding the areas of cooperation with China; deepening bilateral pragmatic cooperation in law enforcement and security; jointly combating various transnational criminal activities including terrorism, cyber crimes, telecommunication fraud, drug-related crimes, illegal human smuggling; working together to cope with various risks and challenges; when attending the 9th China–ASEAN Procurators-General Conference held in Nanning, China in November 2015, the Attorney General of Brunei stressed that the necessary legal framework should be made and that it was essential to strengthen relevant cooperation, including international judicial cooperation.

b. *Educational cooperation was deepened continuously*

China–Brunei educational cooperation is an important bridge for reinforcing talent cultivation, enhancing mutual understanding and deepening bilateral friendship. In 2015, the Chinese Government provided two Bruneian students with full scholarships to help them complete their studies in China. The second group of Chinese young volunteers dedicated to assisting Brunei carried out teaching at the Business School, Faculty of Health Sciences, and Language Center of the University Brunei Darussalam for one year, promoting cultural and educational exchanges between the two countries. Moreover, Chinese-funded enterprises in Brunei energetically engaged in cooperation on industrial talent training in order to achieve localized operations and cultivate local talents; for example, the Hengyi Group set up the Hengyi Petrochemical Talent Class at the University Brunei Darussalam, with a view to working with Brunei to cultivate petrochemical talents; Huawei (Brunei) initiated the Future Seed Program to discover and develop the talents in Brunei's information, communication and technical fields. At present, Brunei lacks industrial technical management talents; given the developmental needs of the private sector and small and medium-sized enterprises, vocational skill educational training will become the new content in the area of educational cooperation between China and Brunei.

c. *Cultural cooperation was rich and colorful*

In 2015, the two countries jointly carried out a number of cultural exchange activities and international events, covering many fields. For the international events, the Minister of Industry and Primary Resources of Brunei attended the 12th China–ASEAN Expo held in Nanning, Guangxi, China; the 10th Brunei–China People-to-People Friendship Conference, organized by the Brunei China Friendship Association and co-organized by China and Brunei, was held with the participation of the representatives from China, 10 ASEAN countries, organizations of friendship, business associations, entrepreneurs, experts and scholars for discussing how to jointly build the platform for people-to-people friendship and friendly contacts, share peace and prosperity. It was the second event after the China–ASEAN people-to-people 10+1 cooperation mechanism was upgraded. Furthermore, the 3rd China–ASEAN Martial Arts Festival, which enjoys great popularity among the people of ASEAN countries, was held in Liuzhou, Guangxi, China; it enhanced the exchange between China and ASEAN countries in martial arts. There was also cooperation in other fields as follows: The officials of the Brunei History Center visited Nanning and Guangzhou to gain insights into the commercial and trade relations between Brunei and China in ancient times and the historical process, especially the history of the Maritime Silk Road. The two countries have learnt from each other through cultural exchanges and cooperation, resulting in enhancing cohesion between the people of the two countries, strengthening bilateral relations, promoting the common development of the two countries, thus better boosting the implementation of the Belt and Road Initiative.

4. Drawbacks in bilateral cooperation

In 2015, bilateral cooperation in various fields developed well and brought about significant achievements, but some drawbacks still existed:

Politically, bilateral relations remained at the level of strategic cooperation, the concrete framework for carrying out cooperation had not yet been fully built, mutual political trust still needed to be further enhanced.

Economically, bilateral trade declined greatly, mismatch occurred in the trade demand structure. The increment of China's investments in Brunei was insufficient, Chinese-funded enterprises in Brunei faced difficulties in localized operations. The early cooperation projects in the Brunei–Guangxi Economic Corridor were initiated and executed slowly, the bilateral economic and trade consultation and cooperation mechanisms urgently needed to be improved.

On military security, the two countries are maritime neighbors, the space for bilateral maritime security cooperation is huge; however, current bilateral cooperation is limited to China–ASEAN regional cooperation without substantive cooperation on military security.

Regarding educational and cultural exchanges, bilateral educational cooperation still focused on sending students to study in the counterpart country, dispatching volunteers for teaching assistance and as enterprise employees; the cooperation in talent cultivation, vocational and technical education was still at the initial stage; the institutions of higher education in the two countries have not yet jointly run schools. The areas of cultural exchange and cooperation between the two countries needed to be broadened, and the level of bilateral cooperation should be deepened. In the meantime, Bruneian traditional culture was less disseminated and exchanged in China, intensified efforts should be made in this regard.

III. Suggestions for Enhancing Bilateral Cooperation

1. Countermeasures and suggestions for bilateral political and diplomatic relations

In 2016, bilateral political cooperation can be deepened in the following three respects.

a. *Continuing to leverage the advantages of people-to-people diplomacy*

Actions should be taken to further support the people-to-people exchange activities of the friendship association of the two countries, the China–ASEAN

Friendship Association, the Ningxia Islamic Council for the Promotion of International Economic and Cultural Friendship, other overseas Chinese cultural organizations and groups, the institutions of higher learning and research institutions in the two countries; importance should be attached to the role of the overseas Chinese of one blood in Brunei as the bridge and bond for bilateral exchange.

b. *Pushing forward cultural diplomacy, enhancing the influence of China's cultural soft power*

The Chinese Government should carry out diplomatic work among the general public in Brunei and strengthen cooperation with the institutions which are influential among the general public in Brunei. The media agencies of the two countries should send personnel to work in the counterpart countries; international cooperation in education should be reinforced; students and volunteers should be exchanged, the two countries should jointly run schools, schools in both countries should forge alliances and exchange visits, so as to further experience local conditions. Based on promoting outstanding traditional culture, the Chinese Government should dedicate more energy to introducing the cultural developmental philosophies, policies and achievements of contemporary China. China should also draw upon the beneficial experience from Brunei and other ASEAN countries in the cultural field to improve its cultural soft power.

c. *Carrying out country-specific training among Chinese-funded enterprises, respecting Brunei's religions and customs*

Currently, Chinese-funded enterprises generally have no research on Brunei's local religions, Islamic culture and customs, they pay less attention to assuming social responsibilities, their external contacts mainly take place within the circle of overseas Chinese, and it is hard for them to integrate into the mainstream society. Given this situation, it is essential to cooperate with relevant research organizations and training institutions to help enterprises foster the awareness of transnational public service. Steps should be taken to strengthen the awareness and behavior of Chinese-funded enterprises about the assumption of social responsibilities in Brunei.

2. Countermeasures and suggestions for deepening bilateral economic and trade relations and cooperation

a. *Bilateral relations should be developed under the trade law system within the framework of upgraded CAFTA*

First, both countries should further improve their respective foreign investment law systems to ensure that they conform to international treaties including WTO rules. Second, both sides should more rapidly build the trade law systems within the framework of upgraded CAFTA, and optimize their legal environments for bilateral investment.

b. *Focusing on promoting pragmatic cooperation in the Guangxi–Brunei Economic Corridor*

Relevant supporting service systems should be developed and improved; standards should be unified; funds should be raised through multiple channels; Brunei–Guangxi industrial cooperation should be deepened in food processing, pharmaceuticals, traditional Chinese medicinal products, cosmetics, biotechnology research, and medical and health care products; first-ever implementation of pilot programs should be enabled in some key fields to make breakthroughs through the Guangxi–Brunei Economic Corridor in deepening China–Brunei economic and trade cooperation.

c. *Bringing about closer cooperation in upgrading the energy industry*

Brunei encourages foreign capital to participate in oil and gas exploration and exploitation. China has well-proven deep-water oil exploitation and exploration technologies and petrochemical technologies, abundant capital and a vast market, so there are bright prospects for China's cooperation with Brunei in upgrading the energy industry, including oil and gas exploration and exploitation, in the renewal of related equipment, and in the deep processing of oil and gas resources.

Chapter 10

Report on the Cooperation between China and Cambodia in 2015

Liu Yaping*

Cambodia still enjoyed stable economic development in 2015, which can also be seen in 2014. In 2015, the GDP growth rate was kept at 7% for the 5th consecutive year, the industries of ready-made garments, tourism, construction and agriculture leading the way. Cambodia remained relatively stable in politics, various parties were active as they prepared for the 2018 general election, and there was the risk of political unrest. Corruption was still rampant in Cambodia, so the Government of Cambodia faced more difficulties in combating corruption, and the current government lacked credibility of governance; Cambodia was still low-ranking among 168 countries in the Corruption Perceptions Index 2015 and ranked last among the 10 ASEAN countries in this regard. Although maintaining active bilateral relations, characterized by a high degree of mutual trust, with China, Cambodia expanded the modes and ways of cooperation with other countries.

* Liu Yaping, Director, Professor, doctoral supervisor at the Cambodia Institute of the China–ASEAN Research Institute of Guangxi University.

I. Review of the Situation of Cambodia in 2015

1. Politics

a. *The general situation was relatively stable, various parties were active in preparation for the 2018 general election*

In 2015, the Government of Hun Sen basically maintained a stable political situation; however, as the 2018 general election drew near, various parties frequently carried out a number of activities. The governing party the People's Party canceled the "dialogue culture" with the National Rescue Party due to discontent with the behavior of Sam Rainsy, the President of the National Rescue Party — the "dialogue culture" had been maintained between the two parties for a certain period of time,[1] while the National Rescue Party boycotted the Parliament for a period of time. As the government issued a warrant for the arrest of Sam Rainsy, he fled to a foreign country, a split occurred within the National Rescue Party — some leaders changed their jobs, members withdrew from the National Rescue Party, greatly weakening the ability of the party to win in the 2018 general election. In the meantime, various parties were established in Cambodia, with eight new political parties registered with the Ministry of the Interior in 2015.[2] Although Norodom Ranariddh returned to the Funcinpec Party early in 2015, he established the Monarchist People's Socialist Party in June,[3] Nhek Bun Chhay, former Vice President of the Funcinpec Party, also broke away from the party and applied for setting up a new party. As indicated, the political parties were complicated in Cambodia, adding uncertainties to the governing party in 2018.

b. *The anti-corruption efforts were intensified to some extent, concrete anti-corruption measures were developed*

According to the Corruption Perceptions Index 2015 released by Transparency International, Cambodia ranked No. 150 among 168 countries under survey; although it's ranking improved by six places over 2014, it still ranked last

[1]The People's Party: the Dialogue Mechanism Was Suspended, *Sin Chew Daily*, December 8, 2015.

[2]In 2015, Politics Were Changeable, Online Public Opinion Rose, *Khmer Daily*, January 2, 2016.

[3]http://cn.thekhmerdaily.com/home/detail/9203.

among the ASEAN countries. In the Corruption Perceptions Index, Cambodia obtained 21 points, equivalent to what it had in the previous years, but its position in the Corruption Perceptions Index was still lower than that of Thailand, Vietnam, Laos and Myanmar, and it was considered a country with a high degree of corruption.[4] However, in 2015, Cambodia developed some anti-corruption measures, pushed forward the national property declaration system for officials, distributed anti-corruption materials to the teachers and students at middle schools,[5] and made laws to limit the amount of gifts received by officials.

c. *Cambodia upheld an active diplomatic policy to improve its international status*

In 2015, Cambodia continued to practice an active diplomatic policy, energetically seeking new partners while maintaining and consolidating the original relations. On the one hand, Cambodian leaders met with the leaders of various countries and organizations, including China, Japan, USA, Russia, Malaysia, Indonesia, Egypt and the EU; on the other hand, Cambodia attended the 6th Ayeyawady–Chao Phraya–Mekong Economic Cooperation Strategy (ACMECS) Summit, the 7th Cambodia–Laos–Myanmar–Vietnam Summit, the ASEAN Summit 2015 to enhance its status in the ASEAN community, Cambodia also signed a cooperation strategy agreement with Asian and European countries to obtain financial aid and expand its influence. In 2015, with a series of diplomatic activities, Cambodia received more attention from the international community and sought favorable conditions for its development.

2. The economy

a. *The macroeconomic growth rate was stable, the economic situation was good*

According to Figure 1, in 2015, Cambodia continued to achieve steady economic growth, the GDP grew by more than 7% for the 5th consecutive year; its per capita GDP reached USD 1,225, up 8.4% over 2014; its inflation rate was kept

---

[4] In the Corruption Perceptions Index Released by Transparency International, Cambodia Ranked 150th, *Sin Chew Daily*, January 28, 2016.

[5] Soghidda. The Ministry of Education Distributed Anti-corruption Materials to the Teachers and Students at Middle Schools, *Khmer Daily*, January 17, 2015.

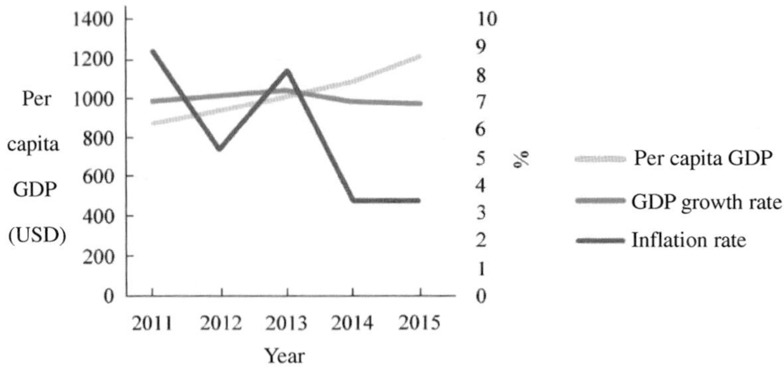

Figure 1. Trend Chart of Cambodia's GDP Growth Rate, Per Capita GDP and Inflation Rate, 2006–2015

Source: The data covering the period from 2011 to 2014 come from the World Bank database, while the data on the year 2015 come from Global Economic Data Online.

at 3.5%.[6] The industries of ready-made garments, tourism, construction and agriculture remained the four main industries in Cambodia's economic development. Agriculture grew by 3.8%, up 1.2% over the previous year; the industry grew by 9%, down 0.6%; the service industry grew by 7.1%, down 0.4%, it was kept at relatively low levels for five consecutive years; the Cambodian Riel–USD exchange rate was 4,040:1; although Cambodian Riel depreciated by 0.7% over 2014, it remained generally stable.[7] According to the data from The Council for the Development of Cambodia, Cambodia attracted investments worth USD 4.64 billion in 2015, up 18% over the previous year.[8]

b. *The yield of agricultural products decreased, the export volume increased steadily*

As Cambodia suffered a drought in 2015, Cambodia's rice yield was affected, the total yield was about 9,227,000 metric tons,[9] down nearly 100,000 metric

---

[6]Last Year, Cambodia's Inflation Rate Was 1.2%, *Phnom Penh Evening*, January 28, 2016.

[7]Cambodia's Economic Situation in the First Half of 2015 and the Trend in the Second Half of the Year, http://cb.mofcom.gov.cn/article/zwrenkou/201510/20151001148002.shtml.

[8]Cambodia attracts investment worth 4.64 bln USD in 2015, up 18 pct, https://www.glofang.com/news/show/31947/.

[9]The Rice Yield Declined Slightly in Cambodia in 2015, http://www.chinagrain.cn/dami/2015/12/29/201512298285336012.shtml

tons over 2014. The production of agricultural and sideline products covered an area of 67,000 hectares, the plantation of economic plants covered an area of 11,000 hectares, down 458 hectares over 2014.[10]

Cambodia's rice exportation was 538,000 t in 2015, up 39.1% compared with 336,000 t in the same period of 2014. China was the largest importing market for Cambodia, with Cambodia's exports to China accounting for 20% of Cambodia's total exports, followed by France (14%), Poland (11%) and Malaysia (11%).[11] As of November 2015; Cambodia exported 8,500 t fishery products from fresh water and sea water, down 23% compared with 11,000 t in the same period of 2014[12]; rubber output was about 111,000 t, exports exceeded 100,000 t, but the export price was USD 1,030/t, down USD 700–800/t over 2014.[13]

c. *The ready-made garment and footwear industries remained the leading industries in Cambodia*

The ready-made garment industry is Cambodia's traditional advantageous industry; Cambodia's exportation of garments and footwear totaled USD 7.1 billion in 2015, up 14.5% compared with USD 6.2 billion in 2014,[14] and so the garment and footwear industries still enjoyed an important position in Cambodia's economic development; Cambodia's garments and footwear were mainly exported to Europe, USA and Canada. However, with worker strikes, rising labor costs and low competitiveness, 130 garment and footwear factories were closed in 2015. After the signing of the Trans-Pacific Partnership Agreement (TPP), Vietnam's investment environment for the garment industry will be optimized, it is expected to exert a great impact on

---

[10] Rice Harvest Exceeded 7 Million Tons in Cambodia during the Rainy Seasons, *The Commercial News*, January 22, 2016.

[11] In 2015, Cambodia's Rice Export Was Nearly 540,000 t, up 40%, China Was the Largest Importing Market for Cambodia, Cambodia's Exports to China Accounted for 20% of Cambodia's Export, *Phnom Penh Evening*, January 8, 2016.

[12] Cambodia's Fishery Exports Declined by 23% in the First 11 Months, *The Commercial News*, December 31, 2015.

[13] The Export Prices of Cambodia's Rubber Decreased to USD 1,030/t, *Phnom Penh Evening*, January 15, 2016.

[14] Cambodia earns 7.1 billion USD from garment, footwear exports in 2015, http://www.xinhuanet.com/english/2016-02/01/c_135063970.htm.

garment enterprises in Cambodia. In order to maintain a stable development of the garment industry, Cambodia had increased the base pay in the garment and footwear industries from USD 128 to USD 140.

d. *The tourist industry showed sustained prosperity, the room for improvement was still large*

The tourist industry is another pillar industry in Cambodia; it can provide jobs to 620,000 Cambodian citizens.

In 2015, Cambodia maintained a strong momentum of continued growth of inbound tourism thanks to further improvement of infrastructures in the country and its increased influence on the international market. According to statistics, tourists visited Cambodia 4.80 million person-times in 2015, up 6.1% over the 4.50 million person-times in 2014; 75% of them came from the Asian-Pacific Region, 18.2% from Europe, 72% from USA, and the remaining ones from Africa and other countries.[15] Cambodia's tourist income reached USD 3.5 billion in 2015, up 16.7% over the USD 3 billion in the previous year[16]; Sihanoukville Province and Siem Reap Province are the main tourist destinations.

e. *International loans and aid continued to grow, helping Cambodia gradually improve its infrastructure*

In 2015, the Government of Cambodia continued to make significant achievements in improving the social environment, benefiting the people, vigorously carrying out the construction of electric power and transportation infrastructure. On the one hand, Cambodia increased its electricity output and reduced the electricity prices; on the other hand, it obtained loans and aid worth nearly USD 100 million to build the tap water system and help residents in many provinces and cities get access to clean water. The *Telecommunication Law* was adopted in 2015, which will play an active role in

---

[15]Tourism Minister: Four Main Economic Pillars: 620,000 People Lived on the Tourism Industry, *Sin Chew Daily*, February 17, 2016.

[16]Last Year, Tourists Visited Cambodia for 4.80 Million Person-times, Vietnam Became the Largest Source of Tourists, *The Commercial News*, January 25, 2016.

promoting the construction of communication infrastructure in Cambodia. Moreover, with financial support from the financial institutions in China, Japan, South Korea, the EU and other countries and territories as well as the Asian Infrastructure Investment Bank and the Asian Development Bank, Cambodia continuously improved such infrastructure as roads, medical institutions and educational institutions in urban and rural areas.

f. *The total number of imports and exports grew, special zones played an important role in exports*

Cambodia's total imports and exports hit USD 20 billion in 2015, up 13%; however, its trade surplus remained at a relatively high level and was about USD 3.4 billion. Cambodia's exports totaled USD 8,519 million in 2015, up USD 1,111 million over the USD 7,408 million in 2014. Garment exports reached USD 6 billion, accounting for about 70% of its total exports. The total value of Cambodia's imports was USD 11,996 million in 2015, up 13%.[17] Many exported products came from the special economic zones, and they amounted to USD 1,212 million, up 78% over the USD 672 million in 2014.[18]

3. Society

a. *Worker welfare increased, the ratio of labor strikes declined*

With the introduction and continued revision of the draft *Trade Union Law*, the level of workers' wages was gradually raised and guaranteed by policies; the new worker health security act and pension system also provided effective guarantee for the physical health of workers, and the Ministry of Labor carried out the zero work-related injury strategy for workers,[19] so the working

[17]Last Year, Cambodia's Imports and Exports Totaled USD 20 Billion, Up 13%. With Rising Labor Costs and Decreasing Competitiveness, the Garment Industry Will Face a Dilemma This Year, *Phnom Penh Evening*, January 28, 2016.

[18]The Special Economic Zones across the Country Generated Increasing Profits, *Khmer Daily*, December 29, 2015.

[19]1,161 Workers Felt Dizzy When Working in the First 10 Months, the Ministry of Labor Will Implement the Zero Work-related Injury Strategy for Workers, *Khmer Daily*, November 17, 2015.

environment for workers improved greatly, the ratio of strikes gradually decreased.

b. *Illegal clinics were shut down, attention was paid to children's health*

In 2015, Cambodia closed nearly 1,000 illegal clinics. On December 1, 2015, Cambodia launched a campaign of injecting a new poliomyelitis vaccine nationwide,[20] while Type B poliomyelitis vaccine is scheduled to be disused as from April 19, 2016,[21] and Cambodia planned to vaccinate 4 million children nationwide for meningitis in 2016. All of these actions show that the Government of Cambodia made continued efforts to guarantee children's health.

c. *The AIDS injection rate was high, the spread of AIDS was grim*

In Cambodia, the AIDS injection rate remained high, an average of two people were infected with AIDS every day. So far, there are about 70,000 people infected with AIDS nationwide, among whom about 53,000 have received anti-AIDS drug treatment. The AIDS patients who have received treatment are fewer than the people infected with AIDS, so it is hard for the National Center for AIDS Prevention and Control to track the AIDS infection; more people are subject to injection. According to statistics, nearly 1,000 people die of AIDS each year on average in Cambodia. Against such a background, the National Anti-AIDS Center of Cambodia has planned to keep the number of the people infected with AIDS within 300/year by 2020,[22] but the task is very arduous.

---

[20] A Campaign of Injecting a New Poliomyelitis Vaccine Was Carried Out Nationwide, https://www.58cam.com/thread-15564-1-1.html.

[21] Cambodia Will Disuse Type B Poliomyelitis Vaccine in April Next Year, *Phnom Penh Evening*, December 29, 2015.

[22] In Cambodia, Two People Are Infected with AIDS Each Day on Average, Nearly 1,000 People Die of AIDS Each Year, *Khmer Daily*, November 4, 2015.

II. China–Cambodia Cooperation

1. The mutual political trust remained stable

a. *Visits were exchanged frequently between senior leaders and at a people-to-people level, China–Cambodia relations entered the best period in history*

Cambodia is a good reliable partner for China, the senior leaders of the two sides frequently exchanged visits, there was a high degree of mutual political trust, and mutually beneficial cooperation yielded great achievements. At present, China–Cambodia relations have been in their best period in history. In 2015, the senior leaders of the two countries engaged in reciprocal visits and exchanges on the cooperation on the Belt and Road Initiative, the issue of the South China Sea and on national and regional security; both sides attended the 26th ASEAN Summit, the Asia Cooperation Dialogue, the China Southeast Asia High-level People-to-People Dialogue, the First Lancang–Mekong Cooperation Foreign Ministers' Meeting, the China ASEAN Ministerial-level Security Meeting, the 6th Xiangshan Forum and the Asian Parliamentary Assembly 8th Plenary Session. Besides close coordination in and cooperation on international and regional affairs, Norodom Ranariddh visited China on behalf of the Funcinpec Party for the first time after he was elected President of the Funcinpec Party; in October 2015, Hun Sen, the Prime Minister of Cambodia, visited China and held talks with Chinese President Xi Jinping, and the Prime Minister of Cambodia visited Macao, China, for the first time in nearly 60 years since the establishment of diplomatic relations between China and Cambodia.

b. *China and Cambodia still resolutely supported each other on core interests*

In 2015, the two sides jointly planned the new development of bilateral relations; China supported Cambodia's political and economic reform and its social development, while Cambodia strengthened the comprehensive strategic cooperative partnership with China. In September 2015, His Majesty King Norodom Sihamoni was invited to attend the activity commemorating the 70th anniversary of the victory of the War of Chinese People's Resistance against Japanese Aggression and the victory of the World Anti-fascist War; when meeting with the King, Xi Jinping pointed out, "China and Cambodia are good neighbors and intimate brothers". Cambodia upheld, "China is a close and great friend of Cambodia", Cambodia firmly supported China on the Taiwan issue and adhered to the one-China policy. Furthermore, bilateral people-to-people exchanges developed rapidly and became the people-to-people foundation for mutual support between the two countries. At present, with impetus from the Belt and Road Initiative, China and Cambodia work together on making the Cambodian Sihanoukville Special Economy Zone into a "Shenzhen" in Cambodia in the future; the Port of Qingdao and the Sihanoukville Autonomous Port have become sister ports, while Phnom Penh City and Hefei City are sister cities, as are Siem Reap City and Huangshan City.

2. Economic cooperation continued to expand

a. *Bilateral trade showed continued growth, the growth of China's exports to Cambodia increased*

As shown in Figure 2, China–Cambodia trade was only USD 480 million in 2004, while it soared to USD 4.43 billion in 2015, an increase of 823% in 11 years. According to the data from China Customs, in 2015, bilateral trade grew by 18%, Cambodia's exports to China were USD 670 million, accounting for 8.5% of Cambodia's exports in 2015; as China enjoyed advantages in economic development and technology, bilateral trade deficit grew, and it was hard to improve this situation in a short time. Specific causes are as follows: In 2015, Cambodia's economic growth rate generally declined, the people believed that the prices of products exported to the rest of world, including China, especially agricultural products, were generally low, and they were on the verge of suffering a loss. Therefore, in order to protect the interests of Cambodians, the Government of Cambodia adjusted relevant policies and plans, such as allocating USD 20 million to increase the output of its agricultural products and thus reduce the imports from China.

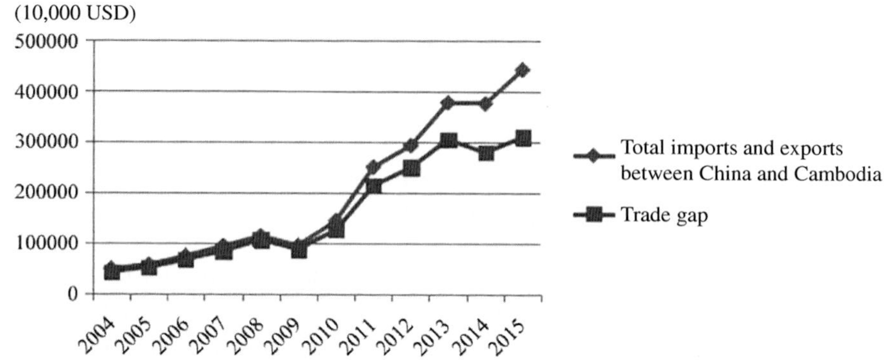

Figure 2. Total Imports and Exports between China and Cambodia and the Trade Gap, 2004–2015
Source: The data from the Ministry of Commerce of the People's Republic of China

b. *China became a large exporting market for Cambodia's rice, the cooperation on agricultural projects was promoted steadily*

In 2015, the quantities of rice and cassava exported from Cambodia to China increased. China gave 100,000 t rice in import quota to China in 2015, up 100% over 2014, accounting for about 20% of the rice exported by Cambodia in 2015; China replaced the EU to become Cambodia's largest buyer, and China agreed to keep 100,000 t of its rice import quota for Cambodia each year from 2016. In the meantime, Chinese-funded enterprises planned to invest USD 400 million to build rice warehouses in Cambodia, and make rice-drying equipment available to boost the exportation of Cambodia's rice to more international markets. Furthermore, the National Development and Reform Commission of China issued the *Medium and Long-term Development Plan for Renewable Energy*, making China's import demand for cassava increase by 60–70%. Obviously, this will help China become the new market for the export of Cambodia's cassava. Moreover, Cambodia utilized the preferential loans offered by China to carry out its water conservation project — the Weigu irrigation project, its Phase I was completed in 2015; it is so far the largest agricultural water conservation project in Cambodia; it can ensure the irrigation of farmland covering an area of more than 30 hectares. The China–Cambodia Agricultural Promotion Project, based on assistance provided to Cambodia by China, was launched on September 17; this will greatly speed up China–Cambodia exchanges and cooperation on multiple areas of agriculture.

c. *Cooperation on tourism was unabated, driving rapid development of the aviation industry*

Chinese tourists visited Cambodia 694,700 person-times in 2015, up 24%, accounting for 14.5% of the international tourists to Cambodia; China became Cambodia's second largest source of tourists, only second to Vietnam. As tourists increased year by year, cooperation on tourism has become the hotspot in China–Cambodia cooperation in recent years. In October 2015, Hun Sen led a delegation to China and attended the Global Tourism Economy Forum under the theme of "The Belt and Road — Unleashing a New Driving Force for Cultural Tourism", and the two sides discussed the issues concerning the development of the tourism industry. In November, Cambodia launched the customized (CHINAREADY) service standard system to Chinese tourists with the hope that Cambodia could reach a certain level of quality when receiving Chinese tourists. Cambodia also planned to carry out the visa-free entry system for China, and establish more consulates in China with a view to attracting more tourists from the second largest economy in the world and pushing forward the development of the tourism industry. Chinese-funded enterprises planned to invest in building eco-tourism areas in Cambodia and developing resorts. The growth of Chinese tourists stimulated the development of Cambodia's aviation industry. At present, direct flights can be achieved between 10 and 20 Chinese cities and Cambodia; Cambodia Bayon Airlines, in which China invested, developed rapidly; the tourist flow at airports soared.

d. *Cooperation on the construction of infrastructures brought about fruitful achievements by virtue of the Belt and Road*

In 2015, Cambodia fully supported the Belt and Road Initiative and the China-led Asian Infrastructure Investment Bank (AIIB). In February, the Ministry of Public Works and Transportation of Cambodia was invited to attend the 5th International Infrastructure Investment and Construction

Summit held in Macao, China, where they discussed the topic of international cooperation on regional infrastructures for connectivity and they actively responded to the Belt and Road Initiative. Furthermore, China–Cambodia cooperation also delivered substantive results; for example, the Mekong China–Cambodia Friendship Bridge in Stung Treng Province and Highway No. 9 connecting Stung Treng Province with Preah Vihear Province were completed; Highway No. 41, Takhmao Bridge crossing the Tonle Bassac River, the China–Cambodia Friendship Bridge and the Chroy Changvar Bridge, built based on preferential loans from China, were officially open to traffic; the round-trip international route between Sihanoukville Autonomous Port and Kunming was launched; the Tatay Hydropower Station BOT Project, in which the China National Heavy Machinery Corporation invested, underwent an acceptance check and was put into operation. These infrastructure projects have greatly improved the living standard of the local people and brought enormous impetus to the overall economic improvement in Cambodia. Besides the completed projects, construction of Highway No. 55 and Highway No. 1577, built based on assistance from China, started in 2015; Highway No. 58, the Phnom Penh–Sihanoukville Highway, and a 230 kV high-voltage power transmission and transformation network are under construction.

e. *The industrial cooperation proceeded in an all-round way, special economic zones created new opportunities*

China–Cambodia industrial cooperation in 2015 was mainly reflected in the following two aspects; First, the number of Chinese enterprises investing in Cambodia increased. Shangtex, Shanxi Dayun Automobile, Ledx (North Sea) and the State Development Investment Corp entered the Cambodian market to expand bilateral cooperation on automobiles, electronic components and textiles. In particular, Chinese and Cambodian enterprises signed a contract on production lines with a daily capacity of 5,000 t of cement; the successful signing of the contract means that the largest cement plant in Cambodia will be built and it will further expand the brand influence of Chinese complete cement equipment suppliers and service providers in the Southeast Asian market and their global competitive advantages. Second, the construction of special economic zones was carried out. Chinese-funded enterprises planned to build special economic zones in Cambodia, with the main purpose of introducing new science and technology, thus creating new opportunities for Cambodia's industrial development.

f. *Cooperation on information boosted connectivity and injected new vitality into the construction of the Belt and Road*

In 2015, the Ministry of Post and Telecommunications of Cambodia and the Ministry of Industry and Information Technology of China signed a cooperation agreement within the field of information communication technology, with a view to strengthening the exchange, cooperation and human resource training in the field of information communication. The Export–Import Bank of China offered USD 50 million export buyer's credit to Cambodia, which was used to build Cambodia's optical fiber communication network for a national information superhighway and boost China–Cambodia connectivity. In September 2015, the China–ASEAN Information Harbor Forum, under the theme of "Internet + Maritime Silk Road – Cooperation · Mutual Benefit · Win–win Outcome", was held in Guangxi, in which China put forward eight-point cooperation initiative, and Cambodia stated that deepened understanding can bring about more cooperation. In the meantime, during the China–ASEAN E-commerce Summit, the Ministry of Commerce of Cambodia stressed that against the background of the Belt and Road Initiative, China and the ASEAN community should strengthen e-commerce cooperation and upgrade the China–ASEAN Free Trade Area (CAFTA). As shown, China–Cambodia cooperation on information was elevated to a new height, injecting new vigor into the construction of the Belt and Road.

g. *Financial cooperation was pushed forward steadily, regional financial and economic integration was promoted*

In August 2015, the Bank of China and the Cambodia–China Friendship Association signed a memorandum on an international financial exchange and cooperation project in the Belt and Road to boost the governmental and non-governmental exchanges between the two countries. In September 2015, the Guangxi Beibu Gulf Bank and the Canadia Bank of Cambodia signed the *Strategic Cooperation Agreement*, under which the two sides provide convenience for each other's businesses. In November 2015, the Phnom Penh Branch of the Bank of China and Cambodia's small loan lender PRASAC MFl LTD signed an agreement under which the Bank of China extends USD 10 million in loans to support PRASAC's funding of small and medium-sized enterprises and rural households. The financial cooperation on these respects has further consolidated bilateral relations and played an active role in the rapid development of regional financial and economic integration.

3. Cooperation continued to be expanded in a number of fields, including culture, education and environmental protection

a. *Mass media communication was widely promoted, cultural cooperation was gradually strengthened*

With the Belt and Road Initiative as an opportunity, China and Cambodia further enhanced their mass media and cultural exchanges and cooperation. In 2015, more than 60 Chinese media based in Cambodia attended the Belt and Road World Chinese Media Economic Forum, and in March 2015, they participated in the Media Leaders Roundtable Conference at the Boao Forum for Asia 2015. The Department of Publicity of Yunnan Province, China and the Ministry of News of Cambodia signed a memorandum of understanding for cooperation on news. In the meantime, China planned to establish a digital TV station in Cambodia. Furthermore, the first overseas Home of Chinese Culture was inaugurated in Phnom Penh; it has become the bridge and platform for enhancing mutual understanding and friendship between the people of the two countries; the ministries of culture of both countries signed the *Agreement on Preventing Theft, Surreptitious Excavation, Illegal Entry and Exit of Cultural Properties* to further strengthen cooperation on the protection of cultural properties.

b. *Educational cooperation developed constantly, bilateral amicable relations continued to be maintained*

China–Cambodia educational exchanges are an important part of bilateral amicable relations. First, Cambodian students studying in or visiting China grew in number. So far, there are more than 800 Cambodian students in various parts of China, about 700 Cambodian students obtained Chinese scholarships in the past 5 years. Second, Chinese language education was highly valued, the Ningbo Chamber of Commerce in Cambodia donated USD 5,000 for supporting the Khmer–Chinese Association in the Kingdom of Cambodia to develop Chinese language education and cover the funds for the Association's development. Third, China–ASEAN Educational Exchange Week became an important platform for China–Cambodia educational exchanges. During the activity of the China–ASEAN Educational Exchange Week under the theme of "Learning From Each Other for the Well-being in the Future", Deputy Prime Minister of Cambodia Sok An expressed the willingness to send more students to study in China and further reinforce bilateral exchanges and cooperation in the field of education.

c. *Cooperation on law enforcement entered a new stage, the two sides reach a consensus on solving crime problem*

In 2015, cooperation on bilateral law enforcement ushered in a new stage of development. The senior leaders of the two countries met many times to reach consensuses on enhancing their cooperation on bilateral law enforcement and security, jointly cracking down on transnational trafficking crime, strengthening regional drug control cooperation and working together to combat cybercrimes. Significant effects were produced in cooperation on law enforcement: China and Cambodia signed a memorandum of understanding on cooperation in the field of discipline inspection and supervision; a branch of the China–ASEAN Legal Cooperation Center will be established in Cambodia. Based on the continued increase in the level of cooperation on law enforcement, the two countries enhanced their mutual political trust, laying a foundation for long-term stable development of bilateral amicable relations.

d. *Cooperation on environmental protection was carried out in new areas, both countries jointly pushed forward environmental protection*

The Belt and Road Initiative put forward by the Chinese Government received an active response from the countries along the Belt and Road, especially Cambodia. For the construction of the Belt and Road, intensified efforts were made in their cooperation involving ecological environment, and they proposed building the Belt and Road jointly in a green way. This will certainly offer new opportunities for expanding and deepening China–Cambodia environmental cooperation. On June 12, 2015, the senior leaders of the two sides exchanged views on the issues concerning bilateral environmental cooperation in the future, they signed the *Memorandum of Understanding on Cooperation in China–Cambodia Environmental Protection*; with the signing and execution of the memorandum, China and Cambodia can establish a mechanism of constructive cooperation and jointly push forward environmental protection.

e. *The aid provided to Cambodia by China remained stable and the friendship between the two countries continued to deepen*

The Chinese Government has always attached importance to bilateral amicable relations and has offered aid to Cambodia in the fields of infrastructure, medicine, the military and education. As of late 2015, China provided aid to build six hydropower stations, seven bridges (currently 12 bridges in Cambodia) and 2,000 km of roads (currently 5,760 km roads across Cambodia) in Cambodia.[23] In the meantime, 12 water conservation hub facilities have been improved, consultation is also underway with respect to the support for garbage disposal, sewage treatment and the construction of highways and a national multi-purpose sports stadium. The aid on these aspects demonstrates China's international image characterized by peace and friendship, and it also deepens China–Cambodia friendship and reflects the international humanistic care which China shows.

3. Suggestions for China–Cambodia Cooperation

a. *Continuing to increase the scope of all-round cooperation so as to achieve common stability and prosperity*

In 2016, both countries should continue to maintain high-level exchanges, further strengthen their strategic communication, and support each other in

---

[23]China's Aid Has Delivered Tangible Benefits to Cambodia, *Khmer Daily*, http://cn.thekhmerdaily.com/homepage/detail/14422.

the most important and major interests of common concern; both countries should enhance their coordination and cooperation on international and regional issues; they should strengthen economic and trade cooperation to promote common development, carry out cooperation projects in the fields of economic and trade investment, infrastructure, agriculture and water conservation; and they should expand people-to-people exchanges, engage in closer cooperation in education, culture, health and tourism, broaden media and think tank exchanges, as well as deepen their cooperation on security to achieve common stability, make greater progress in their capacity for the development of defense and law enforcement.

b. *Keeping up various forms of high-level engagement, consolidating mutual political trust*

In 2016, China should maintain various forms of high-level engagement with Cambodia to lay a solid foundation for mutual trust. On the issues concerning major interests in national territorial sovereignty, both sides should uphold a policy of mutual non-interference under the principle of mutual respect. China hopes that Cambodia can support China in properly addressing the issue of the South China Sea with the ASEAN countries having disputes with China according to the "dual-track thinking", and that Cambodia can agree that disputes are settled by the countries involved through negotiation and consultation, that Cambodia can cooperate in stimulating China and the ASEAN countries to jointly safeguard the peace and stability of the South China Sea, in order to guarantee a good international environment for the Southeast Asia Region. Meanwhile, both sides should reach a consensus on continuing to strengthen their cooperation in regional and international arenas. China should continue to resolutely support the construction of the ASEAN community, ASEAN integration and the important role of the ASEAN community in Asia's regional cooperation. Both countries should also continue to reinforce their pragmatic cooperation in the United Nations, in the China–ASEAN community and the recently established Lancang–Mekong Cooperation Mechanism Framework, thus consolidating and enhancing their mutual political trust.

c. *Further relying on the Belt and Road Initiative to strengthen economic and trade cooperation*

The Belt and Road Initiative opens up a broader stage for the common prosperity of China and its neighboring countries, including Cambodia. The Asian Infrastructure Investment Bank, initiated by China and jointly built by China and other countries, including Cambodia, and the Silk Road Fund, established with USD 40 billion from China, can fund China–Cambodia connectivity and the construction of Cambodia's national infrastructure to narrow the trade gap between China and Cambodia, improve Cambodia's economy and the people's livelihood. Regarding economic and trade cooperation, China should continue to develop more special preferential policies for Cambodia, take advantage of the Belt and Road, strengthen industrial cooperation in light of both sides' comparative advantages, stimulate the exportation of more Cambodian products to the Chinese market, gradually change the trend of the continued expansion of Cambodia's trade deficit, and promote bilateral trade to hit USD 5 billion in 2017.

d. *Continuing to beef up cooperation projects in agriculture, infrastructure and tourism*

Regarding agriculture, the agricultural products directly exported from Cambodia to China are relatively small in quantities; at present, only rice and cassava can be directly exported to China; this inhibits China–Cambodia agricultural cooperation. It is hoped that the two sides can adjust their policies on export trade for agricultural products in 2016 and for several years in the future; for example, promoting the direct exportation of Cambodia's fruit to China. It is necessary to enable, as early as possible, the signing of the fruit import and export agreement between China and Cambodia; Cambodia should fully leverage the complementary advantages and strictly execute its trade testing system for agricultural products to ensure that its products reach relevant standards before exportation. Meanwhile, Cambodia's relevant departments should also actively communicate with the Administration of Quality Supervision, the Inspection and Quarantine of China to obtain the approval for access involving relevant products as early as possible, and increase the varieties and export quota of agricultural products exported from Cambodia to China.

Regarding infrastructure, besides free aid, interest-free credit and preferential loans offered to Cambodia, Chinese enterprises should also be encouraged to invest in Cambodia, such as adopting the BOT mode to build railways and highways to improve Cambodia's transportation capacity. It is suggested that in the next several years, China and Cambodia should continue to deepen tourism exchanges and cooperation and utilize the Belt and Road strategic platform to attract Chinese enterprises to invest in Cambodia's tourist industry, especially hotels, restaurants and green scenic spots in Cambodia's major tourist cities, and help it improve the infrastructure in the tourist industry and make the people engaged in Cambodia's tourist industry understand the demand of Chinese tourists. In the meanwhile, the opportunities from the Belt and Road Initiative should be fully utilized to help Cambodia realize the goal of attracting 2 million Chinese tourists by 2020.

Chapter 11

Report on the Cooperation between China and Indonesia in 2015

Wei Qianqing and Tan Chunzhi*

I. Review of the Situation of Indonesia in 2015

The year 2015 was the first full year after the new President of Indonesia, Joko, came into power. In 2015, Indonesia developed steadily in the political, diplomatic, economic, cultural and social fields; bright spots and drawbacks existed at the same time.

1. Politics

a. *The opposition coalition restricted Joko's governance to some extent*

Although Joko won the 2014 Indonesian presidential election, in the new Parliament, the Prabowo Subianto-led opposition coalition KMP obtained 353 seats, while the Joko-led KIH held only 207 seats. Prabowo Subianto advocated the coexistence of cooperation and competition, so Joko's governance was restricted to a certain degree. This phenomenon improved

* Wei Qianqing, Deputy Director, Doctor, Professor at the Indonesia Institute of the China–ASEAN Research Institute of Guangxi University; Tan Chunzhi, Director, Doctor, Professor at the Indonesia Institute of the China–ASEAN Research Institute of Guangxi University.

to a certain extent on September 2, 2015: The Zulkifli Hasan-led National Mandate Party announced separation from the KMP and accession to the KIH. The number of political parties in both coalitions became six, showing that they were neck and neck; however, the opposition coalition was a majority coalition. How to unite the opposition parties and the members of parliament of the opposition parties is an issue for Joko in his future governance.

b. *Joko's approval rating declined*

According to a poll conducted on the 100th day after Joko took office (January 2015), his approval rating reached 70%; however, as economic development was unsatisfactory and there was a political struggle from Budi Gunawan, the candidate for a position at the Corruption Eradication Commission and the Chief of Police, Joko's approval rating decreased rapidly in May; his approval rating was lower than 50% on the 1st anniversary after Joko took office (October 2015).[1] In order to reverse the situation, Joko made efforts accordingly: canceling the nomination of Budi Gunawan for the Chief of Police, and in August, reshuffling the cabinet, replacing the Minister of Economy and Trade in an attempt to reverse economic sluggishness.

c. *Corruption was severe, there were heavy tasks and a long way to go in combating corruption*

In Indonesia, corruption was rampant. According to a survey carried out by the Abu Dhabi Gallup Center, 91% of Indonesians thought that corruption was very widespread in the government.[2] At present, Indonesia's anti-corruption situation is complicated, and the anti-corruption drive entails heavy tasks and a long journey.

---

[1]The Approval Rating of the President of Indonesia, Joko, Plummeted on the 1st Anniversary after He Took Office, www.huanqiu.com, October 19, 2015, http://world.huanqiu.com/exclusive/2015-10/7791281.html?agt=15438.

[2]What Is Wrong with Indonesia as the Candidate for the Chief of Police Got Involved in Corruption, www.hexun.com, January 14, 2015, http://opinion.hexun.com/2015-01-14/172375872.html.

(1) **Anti-corruption cases frequently occurred:** In January 2015, Indonesia's police arrested Vice Chairman of the Corruption Eradication Commission, Bambang Widjojanto, for instigating a witness to provide false evidence in a case 5 years ago. In February, under pressure, Joko canceled the nomination of Budi Gunawan as the only candidate for the Chief of Police because the latter was identified as a corruption suspect by the Corruption Eradication Commission after his nomination. In December, the Parliamentary Ethics Committee overwhelmingly affirmed that the Speaker of the People's Representative Council, Setya Novanto, had violated the Parliament's code of ethics, and investigated him for usurping the name of president and vice president to extort the shares of free ports; Setya Novanto resigned due to this incident.

(2) **There was fierce strife between the Corruption Eradication Commission and other organs of power:** According to statistics, since 2003, the Corruption Eradication Commission has put dozens of members of parliament into prison. Joko attached great importance to the role of the Corruption Eradication Commission in the process of combating corruption. In early 2015, the contradictions between the Corruption Eradication Commission and the police surfaced due to the Budi Gunawan and Bambang Widjojanto incidents. In 2015, the fight between the Corruption Eradication Commission and the Parliament was more intense; the Parliament twice presented acts for amending the act of the Corruption Eradication Commission in less than 1 year; this was understood to aim at weakening and dissolving the Corruption Eradication Commission.[3] As Indonesia adopts the system of thorough separation between the President and the Parliament in functions and powers, Joko faced a dilemma in dealing with this matter.

2. Diplomacy

Indonesia upheld the diplomatic policy of "having one thousand friends rather than one enemy" during Susilo's governance. After Joko came into power, he

[3]Indonesia: Heavy Tasks and a Long Way in the Anti-corruption Drive, *People's Daily Online*, December 18, 2015, http://world.people.com.cn/n1/2015/1218/c1002-27943354.html.

carried out a more pragmatic kind of diplomacy: delivering tangible benefits to the Indonesian people through diplomacy while defending sovereignty. Economic diplomacy was a great bright spot — seeking further economic cooperation with other countries, especially the great powers in the world, through diplomacy. "Indonesia makes friends with whosoever can invest in Indonesia and promote Indonesia's economic growth" is the diplomacy characterized by extraordinary pragmatism.[4]

a. *Indonesia resolutely safeguarded sovereignty*

Defending state sovereignty is a priority in the diplomacy of every country. In 2015, Indonesia had some friction with other countries while defending state sovereignty. This epitomized the increasingly complicated international diplomatic situation and frequent disputes among countries.

(i) Indonesia defended judicial sovereignty

Indonesia upheld judicial sovereignty and firmly imposed the death penalty on foreign drug dealers in an effort to crack down on drug-related crimes. In January and April, 2005, Indonesia sentenced a number of foreign drug dealers to death. During this period, Brazil, Australia and other countries raised strong opposition and recalled ambassadors.

(ii) Indonesia safeguarded the fishery right

In order to preserve the fishery rights and show determination regarding defending territorial and sovereign rights and interests, Indonesia took strict measures towards the foreign fishing vessels engaged in fishing in its sea areas; for example, the Indonesian navy sank, through bombs, 41 foreign fishing vessels involved in illegal fishing in Indonesia's sea areas on May 20.

---

[4]The President of Indonesia, Joko, Carried Out Pragmatic Diplomacy, 8 Cooperation Agreements on Infrastructure Were Signed during His Visit to China, https://www.thepaper.cn/newsDetail_forward_1315395.

b. *Indonesia pushed forward the strategy of building a maritime power*

Indonesia is the largest island country in the world; it borders on the Pacific Ocean and the Indian Ocean; as it is situated in the Strait of Malacca, its strategic position is very important, it enjoys the prerequisite for serving as the global maritime fulcrum. Joko's strategy of building a maritime power focuses on strengthening Indonesia's role in the Indian Ocean and the Pacific Ocean, such as actively promoting the settlement of regional territorial and maritime disputes, enhancing the diplomacy of the developing countries, making Indonesia an important country in safeguarding regional peace and stability, and boosting regional prosperity and development.[5]

c. *Indonesia attached importance to developing the relations with the great powers in the world*

In 2015, Indonesia actively engaged with major powers in the world through economic diplomacy; for example, Indonesia and Russia signed a memorandum of understanding on nuclear energy cooperation; Indonesia and Japan initiated negotiations involving an equipment and technology agreement, Japan promised to invest in building automobile production bases in Indonesia; Indonesia and USA signed a memorandum of understanding on maritime cooperation; Indonesia and UK signed a cooperation agreement on ocean and aerospace engineering, the eradication of terrorism and transnational crimes, and UK promised to offer at most one billion pound sterling in loans to Indonesia for funding Indonesia's infrastructure projects.

d. *Indonesia was generous in spearheading the ASEAN community*

Indonesia is the most populous country with the greatest economic aggregate in the ASEAN community; the ASEAN community has always been the cornerstone in Indonesia's previous diplomatic policies. After Joko came into power, Indonesia seemed to no longer give priority to the ASEAN, thus

---

[5]Indonesia Faces Many Challenges as It Is on the Way to Realizing its Dream of Becoming a Maritime Power, www.sina.com, January 29, 2015, http://world.huanqiu.com/hot/2015-01/5447621.html.

causing some concerns among its neighboring countries.[6] However, these concerns were essentially unnecessary, as Indonesia remains pleased to head the ASEAN community. In the future, Indonesia will share a common fate with the other ASEAN countries and endeavor to gradually build a democratic and prosperous ASEAN community.

e. *Indonesia's relations with China entered its best period in history*

Indonesia–China relations did not develop well and Chinese exclusion incidents often occurred in Indonesia due to ethnic and religious factors; however, this situation cannot hinder better long-term cooperation between the two countries. With the establishment of the Asian Infrastructure Investment Bank in 2015 — Indonesia is one of the prospective founding members — and the widespread implementation of the Belt and Road Initiative developed by China, the bilateral comprehensive strategic partnership ushered in its best period in history.[7]

(i) Senior leaders engaged in frequent contacts

In March 2015, Xi Jinping met with Joko in the Great Hall of the People, the two sides decided to establish the China–Indonesia Vice Premier-level People-to-People Exchange Mechanism. In May, Joko met with Chinese Vice Premier Liu Yandong in Jakarta, the two sides held the first meeting under the China–Indonesia Vice Premier-level People-to-People Exchange Mechanism. In July, Yu Zhengsheng visited Indonesia. In September, Zulkifli Hasan visited China. In November, Xi Jinping met with Joko in Antalya, Turkey.

(ii) Project cooperation progressed rapidly

In 2015, a number of large cooperation projects were carried out, such as the Jakarta–Bandung high-speed railway project, the Phase I and Phase II

---

[6]"Has Jokowi put ASEAN on the sidelines?", *The Jakarta Post*, June 01, 2015, http://www.thejakartapost.com/news/2015/06/01/has-jokowi-put-asean-sidelines.html.

[7]Yu Zhengsheng: China-Indonesia Relations Are Currently in their Best Period in History, *China Today*, July 29, 2015, http://www.chinatoday.com.cn/chinese/news/201507/t20150729_800035897.html.

projects of the Indonesia Morowali Industrial Park (IMIP) controlled by the Tsingshan Group and the coal gasified dimethyl ether (DME) project with an annual production capacity of 400,000 t carried out by SEDIN Engineering Co., Ltd.

3. The economy

a. *Overall development*

In 2015, Indonesia's economy was generally sluggish, but some economic data showed a turnaround in the fourth quarter.

(i) The economic growth rate was lower than expected

Indonesia's GDP grew by 4.79% in 2015, lower than the expectation of the World Bank at the beginning of 2015 and the 3-year target set by President Joko (7%); it was the lowest since 2009. However, the GDP grew by 5.04% in the fourth quarter, higher than the market expectation.

(ii) The overall pressure of inflation tended to decrease

In the second half of 2015, Indonesia's inflation rate declined from 7.26% in June to 3.35% in December, the lowest since April 2010; the overall level of inflation fell to within the 3–5% low-end target range established by the central bank, providing some space for the central bank to stimulate economic growth.[8]

(iii) Currency depreciated continuously

The Indonesian rupiah kept depreciating against the USD in 2015, breaking the lowest level of the financial crisis in 1998. The exchange rate increased slightly only in the fourth quarter. The currency depreciation incurred a huge loss to the manufacturing industry, such as the printing and dyeing sector, with imported raw materials. In the meantime, as the prices of bulk

---

[8]Indonesia's Inflation Declined Greatly. Reaching its Lowest Level in Six Years, January 6, 2016, http://mt.sohu.com/20160106/n433618633.shtml?qq-pf-to=pcqq.c2c.

commodities were low on the international market, the exporting industries were also subject to pressure, making it difficult to improve the deficit in Indonesia's current account.

(iv) Overall foreign trade decreased

With the domestic and global economic downturn, Indonesia's foreign trade totaled USD 292,991 million in 2015, down 17.34%. Its exports totaled USD 150,252 million, down 14.62%; its imports totaled USD 142,739 million, down 19.89%. According to the statistics on non-oil and gas products, China's trade totaled USD 42,476 million, down 9.47%.[9]

b. *Industrial development*

In agricultural development, the backwardness of production technology and dependence on grain importation remained the principal problems. Indonesia should speed up its agricultural modernization and enhance exchanges and cooperation with various countries around the world in the agricultural field.

Regarding its industrial development, infrastructure, especially in the transportation industry, was underdeveloped. In November 2015, Indonesia stated that it planned to apply for USD 38 billion from the Asian Infrastructure Investment Bank (AIIB) to carry out the construction of infrastructures. In the meantime, subject to a global economic recession and declining prices of bulk commodities, Indonesia saw decreases in the output and exportation of minerals. In late 2015, Indonesia returned to OPEC in the capacity of net oil importer. As Indonesia once again became an OPEC member country, Indonesia's cooperation with oil-producing countries will be strengthened, and it will help Indonesia build connections with crude-oil suppliers and become the bridge for connecting energy companies with consumers.[10]

---

[9]Indonesia's Foreign Trade in 2015. January 17, 2016, http://china.huanqiu.com/News/mofcom/2016-01/8396656.html.

[10]The Net Oil Importer Indonesia Returned to OPEC, China Research Institute of Global Energy Public Opinion, October 16, 2015, http://www.energypo.org/net-oil-importer-indonesias-return-to-opec/.

Concerning financial development, the non-performing loan ratio increased to some extent in Indonesia's banking sector. In 2013 and 2014, the non-performing loan ratio in Indonesia's banking sector was 1.77% and 2.16%. In late April 2015, that figure rose to 2.48%.[11]

The rapid development of the tourist industry became a bright spot. Indonesia abounds in tourist resources; however, Indonesia's tourist industry was less developed as compared with more than 10 million tourists visiting Malaysia and Thailand each year. In 2015, Indonesia introduced a number of measures to attract foreign tourists. In February, Indonesia launched the tourist route "the Route along Which the Famous Chinese Voyager Zhenghe Traveled to the West", with a view to attracting more Chinese tourists. In June, the Government of Indonesia announced the visa-free policy for tourists from 30 countries, including China. These measures produced a certain effect. In 2015, foreign tourists visited Indonesia 5.10 million person-times, up 4.8% over the previous year — 3.26 million tourists entered Indonesia on a visa-free basis, up 100% over the previous year. Chinese tourists soared by 20%, ranking China No. 1 among various countries in growth rate.[12]

4. Culture

a. *Indonesia engaged in cultural exchanges with China*

Indonesia is the country with the largest number of overseas Chinese, thus Indonesia–China cultural exchanges were frequent. In 2015, the two countries worked together to hold a series of cultural exchange activities, including the Chinese Traditional Calligraphy and Painting Exhibition; the Picture Show "Solidarity, Friendship and Cooperation — the Zhou Enlai and Bandung Conference"; the ASEAN Countries Series Exhibition II — the 2015 Indonesia Exhibition; the Indonesia Confucius Institute China Summer Camp and the Large Picture Show Commemorating the 70th Anniversary of

---

[11] Scholars Warned the Government of the Upward Trend of the Non-performing Loan Ratio in Indonesia's Banking Sector, www.huanqiu.com, July 24, 2015, http://china.huanqiu.com/News/mofcom/2015-07/7092862.html.

[12] The Roads for Chinese People to Go Global Have Been Increasingly Wide, Chinese People Have Become the Important Force for Driving the Growth of the Global Tourist Industry, https://finance.sina.com.cn/roll/2016-02-04/doc-ifxpfhzk8864066.shtml.

the Victory of the War of the Chinese People's Resistance against Japanese Aggression.

b. *Indonesia held the 2015 World Bang Shu Expo*

The 2015 World Bang Shu Expo, held by the Indonesia Branch of the World Federation of Bang Shu Calligraphy for the first time, was inaugurated in Jakarta on October 3, 2015. This expo exhibited 280 Bang Shu works created by famous calligraphers from 24 countries and territories throughout the world; it was the largest Bang Shu calligraphy art event in Indonesia, even in the world. Bang Shu is a form of expression in Chinese traditional calligraphy. This expo made important contributions to carrying forward Chinese traditional culture around the world, especially in the circle of overseas Chinese.

5. Society

a. *Large transportation accidents occurred frequently*

In 2015, Indonesia saw a number of serious traffic accidents: three air crashes occurred in June and August, causing the death of more than 300 people; in December, one passenger ferry sank 12 sea miles away from Siwa Wharf, Sulawesi, in which more than 60 people died. These accidents took place for objective reasons, including the natural environment and weather, but subjective human factors cannot be neglected. In recent years, the Indonesian budget airline market has developed rapidly, and budget airlines have excessively reduced their operating costs, thus increasing the risks of air accidents. Moreover, negligence and corruption have existed in the management in Indonesia's aviation industry; after the AirAsia Flight accident, many people in Indonesia held that this accident was closely related to corruption in the aviation industry; seven officials approved the operation of the flight without a permit for the sake of their own interests, leading to tragedy.[13] Owning to the physical geography, Indonesia relies heavily upon maritime transpor-

[13]Why Do Air Crashes Frequently Occur in Indonesia?, http://www.thepaper.cn/baidu.jsp?contid=1365183.

tation and inland water transportation, but relevant management costs are high, so it is easy to cause omission in management.

b. *The poverty-stricken population increased*

The Government of Joko had always taken the narrowing of the wealth gap and the reduction of the poverty-stricken population as important goals. However, poverty reduction did not deliver good results. In September 2015, 28.60 million people had monthly incomes of less than 23 USD on average in Indonesia, accounting for 11.3% of Indonesia's total population, up 300,000 people over the same period of 2014.[14] Considering this situation, Indonesia unveiled the Nine Comprehensive Plans for Poverty Alleviation, but it was hard to fulfill the task of reducing the poverty-stricken population amid unsatisfactory economic development.

c. *A large number of residents joined the Islamic State (IS)*

In recent years, IS has been increasingly active in the world. Indonesia is the country with the largest Muslim population in the world and is a fertile soil for IS to spread thoughts, so IS has taken Indonesia as its best stronghold in the ASEAN community. In March 2015, Indonesia's national police spokesman Colonel Rikwanto said, "Most residents in Indonesia are Muslims, many people can become extremists and the supporters of Caliph".[15] In November, the Indonesian media pointed out that IS was recruiting weapon experts and bombs in Malaysia and Indonesia. During the same period, the Indonesian National Counterterrorism Agency conducted an evaluation showing that more than 350 Indonesians had joined IS.[16]

---

[14] Indonesia Vowed to Make All-round Efforts to Fight Poverty, October 15, 2015, http://finance.china.com.cn/roll/20151015/3382428.shtml.

[15] Indonesia Has Become a Fertile Soil for IS to Spread Extreme Thoughts, *Indonesia International Daily News*, March 24, 2015, http://www.guojiribao.com/shtml/gjrb/20150324/212306.shtml.

[16] Extremist Groups Extended to Southeast Asian Countries, While Indonesia and Malaysia Intensified Counter-terrorism Efforts, www.sina.com, November 16, 2015, http://news.sina.com.cn/o/2015-11-16/doc-ifxksqku3090689.shtml.

In order to curb the dissemination of IS, Indonesian police carried out a series of activities for cracking down on IS organizations within Indonesia in 2015. In the future, Indonesia will also need to enhance cooperation with various countries in the world in the counterterrorism field. It is still necessary to speed up economic development since many Indonesians joined IS in order to seek a better life.[17]

II. China–Indonesia Cooperation in 2015

The year 2015 was special for bilateral cooperation. It was the 65th anniversary of the establishment of diplomatic relations between China and Indonesia. In 2015, the two sides engaged in more frequent exchanges in the political, diplomatic, economic and cultural fields, vigorously promoting the development of a bilateral strategic comprehensive cooperative partnership.

1. Bilateral political and diplomatic cooperation

a. *The 65th anniversary of the establishment of diplomatic relations between China and Indonesia*

On April 13, 1950, China and Indonesia announced the establishment of diplomatic relations. The year 2015 was the 65th anniversary of its establishment. In these 65 years, bilateral relations once fell to its lowest point and reached the peak, historic progress was made in bilateral relations, bringing enormous benefits to the people of both countries and exerting an active impact on regional peace, stability and prosperity.

With the 65th anniversary of the establishment of bilateral diplomatic relations in 2015, the leaders of the two countries frequently exchanged visits, while these reciprocal visits vigorously deepened the understanding between the two sides and promoted bilateral cooperation; for example, the President of Indonesia, Joko, paid a state visit to China during the period of March 25–28, 2015, obtaining a number of important achievements.

---

[17]Indonesian Police: More than 500 Citizens Want to Join IS Allegedly Due to Economic Problems, www.huanqiu.com, March 14, 2015, http://world.huanqiu.com/hot/2015-03/5910826.html.

These achievements mainly include: (1) The two countries signed a joint statement on strengthening the comprehensive strategic partnership between them; (2) the two countries signed several cooperation agreements on the Jakarta–Bandung High-speed Railway, the avoidance of double taxation, maritime search and rescue, the China–Indonesia aerospace cooperation program 2015–2020, and on infrastructure and production capacity.[18]

In 2015, frequent reciprocal visits and benign interactions between the heads of the two countries broadened the strategic consensus on deepening their cooperation and pursuing common development; these visits and interactions vigorously promoted excellent connections between China's strategy of the 21st Century Maritime Silk Road and Indonesia's strategy of building a maritime power, and consolidated the political foundation for deepening bilateral cooperation, thus they were of great significance for friendly cooperation between and development of the two countries.

b. *The two sides engaged in cooperation under the Belt and Road Initiative*

The Belt and Road Initiative was initiated by China; it caters to the common needs of the countries along it; it opens a new window of opportunity for those countries to complement each other's advantages and pursue open development; it offers a new platform for international cooperation. As the initiator of the Belt and Road, China needs to stimulate the development of the Belt and Road Initiative to boost the enthusiasm and initiative of other countries along the Belt and Road. Therefore, with respect to the Belt and Road, a model country for cooperation is urgently needed for dispelling international concerns, while as the largest economy in the ASEAN community, Indonesia is certainly the best choice for serving as the model country for cooperation. Furthermore, after Joko became the new President of Indonesia, he took the strategy of a global maritime fulcrum as the priority of future work to be carried out by the Government of Indonesia, which tallies exactly with the strategy of the 21st Century Maritime Silk Road put forward by China.

[18] Zhang Tianyu, Joint Statement between the People's Republic of China and the Republic of Indonesia on Strengthening their Bilateral Comprehensive Strategic Partnership, March 26, 2015, http://www.xinhuanet.com/world/2015-03/26/c_127625705.htm.

In the meantime, Indonesia has the need to carry out massive construction of infrastructures, while China has a surplus of advantageous production capacity, so the two sides are highly complementary in cooperation. The perfect connection between both strategies developed by China and Indonesia is of far-reaching significance for promoting the modernization of both countries and improving their international political statuses.

In 2015, China and Indonesia made great efforts in cooperation under the Belt and Road Initiative. Regarding diplomacy, the two countries exchanged views on the future strategic plans, enhancing the understanding and exchange between them. Concerning the economy, Indonesia wanted to remove the economic developmental obstacles to Indonesia through strategic cooperation with China, and hoped that Chinese enterprises would be able to invest in Indonesia. The Chinese Government stated that China would support the projects for the construction of industrial zones in various parts of Indonesia, participate in building 35 million kW power generation and supply facilities and assist in the construction of new ports.[19]

2. Bilateral economic and trade cooperation

Bilateral economic and trade cooperation in 2015 is characterized by complementation, wide areas, inclusiveness and coordination. There are close bilateral investment relations between China and Indonesia. Indonesia has become the main investment destination for Chinese enterprises in the Southeast Asia region. According to the statistics from the Indonesia Investment Coordinating Board, from October 22, 2014 to October 16, 2015, overseas investment commitments received by Indonesia amounted to about USD 156 billion — the amount of planned investments from China was the largest investment and reached USD 61 billion, accounting for 39.1% of the total amount.[20] China further deepened and expanded its investments in Indonesia, with investments gradually extending from small

[19]Indonesia and China Are Committed to the Maritime Silk Road, *Indonesia International Daily News* (Indonesian Edition), March 28, 2015, p. A3.

[20]Various Investors Undertook to Invest USD 156 Billion, China Invested USD 61 Billion, the Largest Amount, Accounting for 39.1%, *Indonesia International Daily News* (Indonesian Edition), October 21, 2015, p. A3.

processing, assembly and production projects to communication equipment, finance, infrastructure, construction, tourism, energy development and trade. In 2015, China's investment projects involved 35 million kW of power generation, 1 million in a housing construction plan, a 6 million-ton steelworks, a 900 MW power station, communication equipment, an airport, a port, the Jakarta–Bandung high-speed train, a mobile phone factory and an automobile factory. Indonesia's Jakarta–Bandung High-speed Railway Project was the bright spot in bilateral economic and trade cooperation in 2015.

a. *The Jakarta–Bandung High-speed Railway Project*

The project was the hotspot in bilateral economic and trade cooperation in 2015. It is a high-speed railway between Jakarta and Bandung. Its full length is 144.6 km. According to the relevant plan, with its operation, the time for traveling between Jakarta and Bandung will be shortened from 2–3 h to about 36 min. The investment in the project amounts to about 67 trillion Indonesian rupiahs.[21] As China and Indonesia are working together to carry out the Jakarta–Bandung High-speed Railway Project, China can leverage the economic advantage as a great power of the high-speed railway to obtain a vast market and interests, the project deepens the railway cooperation between China and relevant Southeast Asian countries, and it enables transportation infrastructure connectivity between China and the countries along the Belt and Road. For Indonesia, the construction of the Jakarta–Bandung High-speed Railway provides more space and opportunities for Indonesia's economic development and meets Indonesia's economic and development needs.

b. *China's investments in Indonesia*

In 2015, bilateral consensus on cooperation under the Belt and Road Initiative further stimulated Chinese enterprises to enter Indonesia. On April 23, 2015, China's Sedin Engineering Co., Ltd. and Indonesia's Manggala Motor

---

[21] China Promised to Build the Jakarta–Bandung High-speed Railway, Fully Accepted Indonesia's Requirements and Would Build Carriages and an Aluminum Factory, *Indonesia International Daily News* (Indonesian Edition), September 19, 2015, p. A3.

Listrik Pertama signed an agreement on the investment and construction of a coal gasified dimethyl ether (DME) factory with an annual production capacity of 400,000 t.[22] In order to promote Chinese enterprises' investments in Indonesia, the Chinese Government and banks offered many loans. On April 25, 2015, the Chinese Government planned to extend USD 50 billion loans for Indonesia's infrastructure projects.[23] On September 25, 2015, the PT Bank ICBC Indonesia and the Indonesia Exim Bank signed a 5-year USD 500 million working capital loan agreement for supporting Indonesia's infrastructure and economic development. On October 1, 2015, Indonesian state-owned enterprises obtained USD 3 billion in loans from the China Development Bank (CDB), which did not require any guarantee from the Government of Indonesia.[24]

c. *Indonesia's economic and trade exchange in China*

Indonesia has also attached great importance to economic and trade exchanges with China. In order to promote cooperation with China under the Belt and Road Initiative, on January 31, 2015, the Indonesia–China Silk Road Committee was established. The committee is designed to utilize the people-to-people exchanges between the two countries and mainly proceed from economic and trade development to learn from each other, so as to bring about reciprocity, mutual benefit and a win–win outcome between the two sides and promote China–Indonesia cooperation in the 21st Century Maritime Silk Road. The China–ASEAN Expo also serves as an excellent venue for Indonesian enterprises to recommend themselves to Chinese consumers. At the China–ASEAN Expo held in Nanning, China in September 2015, 101 Indonesian enterprises were available to exhibit various kinds of advantageous products, such as food and drinks, furniture, interior design,

---

[22] Zhou Shunyi, China–Indonesia Economic and Trade Investment and Cooperation Forum, *Indonesia Shang Bao*, April 24, 2015.

[23] China Will Offer 647 Trillion Indonesian Rupiahs in Loans to Support Indonesia's Infrastructure Construction, Including Electric Power and a High-speed Railway, *Indonesia International Daily News* (Indonesian Edition), April 25, 2015, p. A3.

[24] China Offers USD 3 Billion in Loans without Sovereign Guarantee, *Indonesia International Daily News* (Indonesian Edition), October 1, 2015, p. A3.

fashionable garments, ornaments and consumer products. Besides these advantageous products, Indonesia also promoted its potential investment projects and introduced the Indonesia Chamber of Commerce in China.[25] Indonesian enterprises' support for the China–ASEAN Expo reflects Indonesia's sincerity in helping market construction in the Belt and Road and is also conducive to further connection and integration between Chinese and Indonesian markets and smooth trade activities.

3. Bilateral tourism and cultural cooperation

Besides political, diplomatic, economic and trade cooperation, China and Indonesia also strengthened their cooperation and exchanges in tourism and culture. As from January 1, 2015, Indonesia has carried out the visa-free policy for tourists from five countries, including China.[26] The visa-free policy means that every Chinese tourist to Indonesia can save the visa fee; more importantly, it can arouse the enthusiasm of Chinese tourists for traveling to Indonesia, boost the development of Indonesia's tourism industry and promote bilateral cultural exchanges.

On May 28, 2015, the launching ceremony of the Chinese program channel, jointly established by the China International Television Corporation and PT Elnet Media Bersama, was held.[27] The two countries enhanced radio, film and television cooperation so that the Indonesian people can watch Chinese films and television programs at home; the bridge for people-to-people cultural exchanges between the two countries can be built and the bond for connecting the people of the two countries can be forged to deepen the friendship between the people of the two countries, promote the development of bilateral relations and achieve a mutually-beneficial and win–win outcome.

[25] 101 Indonesian Enterprises Will Attend the 2015 China–ASEAN Expo, *Indonesia Shang Bao*, September 3, 2015.

[26] Li Xiaoming, Indonesia Implements the Visa-free Policy for Chinese Tourists from Now On, Providing Free Access to Bali, *Morning Post*, January 1, 2015.

[27] Shen Weizhen, The Launching Ceremony of the China–Indonesia Radio and Television Cooperation Was Held in Jakarta, *Harian Nusantara*, May 28, 2015.

4. Cooperation on bilateral security

In order to safeguard regional security, the two countries cooperated on security, involving countering terrorism and cracking down on human trafficking. On February 12, 2015, the two countries agreed to cooperate on combating cyber terrorist activities, while these activities are joint efforts to implement the anti-terrorist cooperation agreement signed by the two countries in 2014.[28] With the anti-terrorist cooperation mechanisms among the governments, organizations and enterprises of the two countries, these countries effectively strengthened bilateral exchanges and communication, exchanged information, jointly built a firm defense line for cracking down on cyber terrorism, thus improving the people's well-being and safeguarding world peace. On October 26, 2015, Indonesian and Chinese police once again discussed the extension draft of the memorandum of understanding in cooperation, which expired in 2009, so as to consolidate bilateral security and legal cooperation relations. Indonesia's cooperation projects included in the extension draft involve transnational crimes, corruption, illegal mining, cybercrimes and human trafficking.[29]

III. Problems and Challenges in Bilateral Cooperation

Although bilateral cooperation developed in an extensive way in the special year 2015, bilateral cooperation still faces many problems and challenges, which are mainly reflected in economic, trade and political cooperation.

1. Problems and challenges in economic and trade cooperation

a. *Bilateral trade was imbalanced*

Given the size of the population, the resource endowment and the advantages of the location, there is a huge potential for future bilateral cooperation and investment. However, at present, the scale of bilateral trade is extremely inconsistent with bilateral political relations. China–Indonesia trade makes up a very low proportion of China's foreign trade, while it makes up a very

[28] *Data source*: http://qiandaoribao.com/news/60265.

[29] *Data source*: http://indonesia.sinchew.com.my/node/57146?tid=5.

high proportion of Indonesia's foreign trade. According to the data from Badan Pusat Statistik, in 2015, Indonesia–China trade totaled a value of USD 42,476 million — Indonesia's exports to China were a value of USD 13,259 million, accounting for 10.07% of Indonesia's total exports of non-oil and gas products, while Indonesia's imports from China were of a value of USD 29,217 million, accounting for 24.73% of Indonesia's total imports of non-oil and gas products. In terms of total imports and exports, in 2015, China remained Indonesia's largest trading partner in non-oil and gas products, followed by Japan and USA. As from 2008, Indonesia suffered a deficit in China–Indonesia trade, and the deficit amount has increased year by year; in 2015, Indonesia's trade deficit rose by 13.97%. The continued imbalance in China–Indonesia trade is the hidden trouble for future bilateral cooperation.

b. *Mutual trust is insufficient*

The two main causes for insufficient mutual trust are as follows. First, the proportion of investments realized by China was low. According to statistics, the proportion of foreign investments realized in Indonesia was 40% on average, the proportion of investments realized by Japan and South Korea was 60%, while that of investments realized by China in Indonesia was only 7%. After China and Indonesia established the comprehensive strategic cooperative partnership, with enhanced bilateral trade cooperation, the proportion of investments realized by China in Indonesia increased continuously, but the low historical proportion often dented Indonesia's confidence in Chinese enterprises and hindered bilateral economic cooperation. Second, Indonesia's infrastructure is obsolete and outdated, the overall domestic economic level is low, the infrastructure input is severely insufficient, causing high transportation costs and a low degree of efficiency. According to statistics, logistics costs accounted for 25–30% of Indonesia's GDP; furthermore, Indonesia's ports and wharfs are extremely saturated; these factors restrict the development of Indonesia's foreign trade and affect Chinese enterprises' investment confidence in Indonesia.

c. *Indonesia's overall investment environment is not good*

First, at present, Indonesia's political situation is less stable; policies are changeable; Indonesia lacks a regularized and transparent legal system; many laws are extremely irrational; the existing laws are not observed and not strictly enforced. Indonesian government departments are inefficient; corruption has been a major problem for restricting its economic development. Second, the efficiency of production and the technical levels of workers in Indonesia are relatively low; although the government revised the labor law in order to attract foreign capital, that revision met with strong opposition from trade unions and workers and failed to be realized. Moreover, Indonesia also has some investment barriers; for example, the controlling stake held by foreign capital cannot exceed 95% in infrastructure, including ports, power stations and railways, as well as medical service and health; the controlling stake held by foreign capital cannot exceed 49% in air transportation and telecommunications; engaging in fishing, fish farming, printing of negotiable securities is subject to licensing from the Government of Indonesia; foreign investments are prohibited in the nursing of seedlings of rare species, forest exploitation, the processing of red wood, the right to operate natural forests and forest harvesting; many restrictive measures still exist on the labor market. Furthermore, the wealth gap is wide in the Indonesian society; terrorist and religious extremist activities often occur. Therefore, Indonesia's overall investment environment is not good, thus affecting bilateral trade contacts and economic cooperation.

2. Problems and challenges in political cooperation

a. *Indonesia's attitude towards cooperation with China is unclear*

Although China and Indonesia have established a comprehensive strategic cooperative partnership, Indonesia's attitude towards China is still unclear. On the one hand, Indonesia clearly states that developing amicable relations with China can bring huge benefits to Indonesia; on the other hand, considering the asymmetry in the strength between the two countries, Indonesia's attitude towards bilateral cooperation is uncertain. Moreover, Indonesia attempts to adopt the strategy of keeping a balance among the great powers and striking a balance among China, USA and Japan, so as to maintain its diplomatic independence, but this easily affects friendly cooperation between the two countries at times.

b. *Indonesia's domestic political relations are complicated*

Complicated political relations within Indonesia constitute one of the obstacles to bilateral political cooperation. Joint governance by multiple parties is currently the main political form in Indonesia; various parties wane and wax in strength; it is likely that the strategy of the global maritime fulcrum put forward by the current President Joko will be thwarted by the opposition parties.

c. *The third countries exert an adverse impact on China–Indonesia political cooperation*

The geopolitical relations along the Belt and Road are complicated and the Belt and Road is situated in the sensitive areas where the strategies of great powers contend with each other. The strategies and policy stands of major powers and the international community may greatly affect China–Indonesia cooperation. If USA, Japan and other countries deliberately incite various international forces to set up barriers to strategic connection between China and Indonesia, bring shame on China's strategic intent or impose pressure in the maritime field and deepen Indonesia's concerns about China's strategies, China–Indonesia economic cooperation, mutual political trust and security coordination will be subject to great obstacles.

Part 3

Special Reports on China–ASEAN Cooperation in 2015

Chapter 12

Report on China–ASEAN Investments in 2015

Sun Shuo*

I. Overview of the Development of China–ASEAN Two-way Investments

The flow of global foreign direct investments (FDIs) soared by 36% in 2015, it is estimated to reach USD 1.7 trillion, the highest level since the global economic and financial crisis in the period 2008–2009; the FDIs flowing to the developed economies surged by 90%; this was the main factor contributing to a global investment rebound. According to statistics, the FDIs flowing to the EU and the USA in 2015 quadrupled the historical low level of 2014; the flow of FDIs to the developed countries accounted for 55% of the global investment flow. Furthermore, FDI inflow to the developing economies increased by 5% and reached USD 741 billion, a record high. The FDIs attracted by China grew by 6% over 2014 and reached USD 136 billion, making China the third largest destination for global FDIs; FDI inflow to

*Sun Shuo, Doctor of Economics at the China–ASEAN Research Institute of Guangxi University. This chapter is jointly funded by a special research project of the China–ASEAN Collaborative Innovation Center for Regional Development and the Cheung Kong Scholars and Innovation Team Development Program initiated by the Ministry of Education (contract number: CW201603).

the ASEAN community generally fell by 7% — FDI inflow to Singapore deceased by 4% and is estimated to be USD 65 billion.[1]

Investment is one of the 11 principal areas of cooperation between China and the ASEAN community and also the priority in the upgrading of the China–ASEAN Free Trade Area (CAFTA). In 2014, the cumulative investments made by the ASEAN community in China exceeded that from such countries as Australia, the USA and Russia, the ASEAN community became China's third largest source of foreign capital. China's investments in the ASEAN countries have developed rapidly in recent years. In 2013, China became the ASEAN community's third largest source of foreign capital.[2] According to statistics from the Ministry of Commerce of China, in 2015, China's investments in the ASEAN community amounted to USD 9,448 million, while the ASEAN's investments in China stood at USD 7,644 million. As of late 2015, the cumulative two-way investments between China and the ASEAN community had reached USD 156,469 million. The stock of investments made by ASEAN countries in China exceeded USD 99.4 billion, while that of investments made by China in the ASEAN community was about USD 57,069 million. Compared with 2014, China's investments grew in eight ASEAN countries, all except the Philippines and Cambodia. Overall, the ASEAN community is one of the regions where China's investments are the fastest-growing and that region is also one of China's important sources of foreign capital.

1. China's investments in the ASEAN community

The ASEAN community has a population of 620 million; the combined GDP of all ASEAN countries reached USD 2.3 trillion, higher than that of Brazil and Russia, following that of the UK.[3] In the past 15 years, the average GDP growth rate in the ASEAN community reached 6%. Few regions in the rest of the world can achieve such a growth rate. Australia & New Zealand Banking (ANZ) took the ASEAN as the third pole of Asia's economic growth, next only to China and India. According to the Ministry of Trade

[1] Relevant data come from *Global Investment Trends Monitor*, January 20, 2016.

[2] Relevant data come from *ASEAN Investment Report 2015*.

[3] Relevant data come from the World Development Index.

and Industry of Singapore, in 2013, the five largest economies in Southeast Asia obtained USD 1.3 trillion in foreign investments, exceeding the foreign investments in China for the first time. However, direct investments between China and the ASEAN community were unilateral — investments mainly came from the ASEAN countries to China — for a long time. With globalization and the rapid growth of China's economy, China started to actively seek overseas investment opportunities for domestic capital and carried out the economic strategy of "going global". In recent years, China's investments in the ASEAN community have grown continuously. In 2009, the Chinese Government established USD 10 billion in the China–ASEAN Investment Cooperation Fund for investing in major cooperation projects between the two sides in infrastructure, energy resources and information communication. The Chinese Government also offered USD 15 billion in credit to ASEAN countries with a view to providing financial support for investment cooperation among the enterprises of the two sides. Under the initiative of the Chinese Government, the China–ASEAN Investment Cooperation Fund and the China–ASEAN Inter-bank Association were established, which became important platforms for bilateral investment and financing cooperation. During the APEC meeting held in Beijing in November 2014, the Chinese Government vowed to allocate USD 40 billion to establish the Silk Road Fund for providing investment and financial support for the connectivity projects in the countries along the 21st Century Maritime Silk Road in infrastructure, resource development, industrial and financial cooperation. The Asian Infrastructure Investment Bank, pushed forward by China, was established in January 2016; it is designed to realize the Belt and Road Initiative focusing on connectivity. In 2014, the investment flow from China to ten ASEAN countries was USD 7,809 million, accounting for 6.3% of the total outward investment flow from China and 9.2% of the outward investment flow from China to Asia; the stock was USD 47,633 million (Figure 1), accounting for 5.4% of the total stock of outward investments from China and 7.9% of the stock of outward investments from China to Asia. In late 2014, there were more than 3,300 enterprises in the ASEAN community in which China made direct investments; they employed 159,500 foreigners.[4]

[4]2014 Statistical Communiqué on China's Outward FDIs.

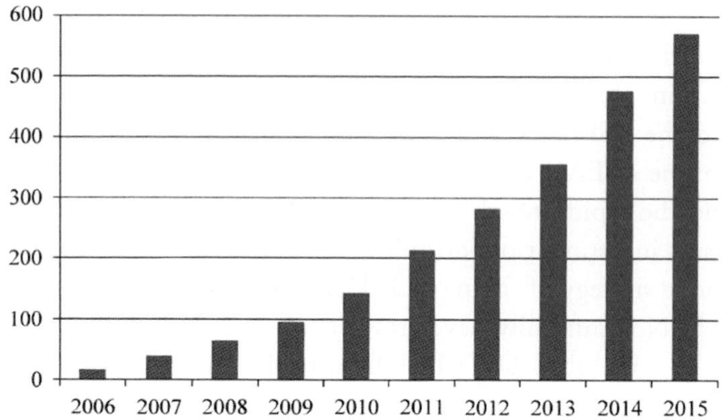

Figure 1. The Stock of China's Investments in the ASEAN Community, 2006–2015 (USD 100 million)
Source: Statistical Communiqué on China's Outward FDIs.

In the meantime, China's direct investments in the ASEAN community were distributed within the ASEAN community in an extremely unbalanced way; they were concentrated in Indonesia, Cambodia, Singapore, Laos and Myanmar. As of late 2015, the investments received by the above countries from China accounted for 82% of the stock of China's investments in the ASEAN community (Figure 2). Of course, this was closely related to the economic and investment environment in these countries and their long-term economic and trade contacts with China. Singapore is, to a larger extent, becoming one regional center for the enterprises with the desire to enter the fast-growing economies in the ASEAN community. It should also be noted that China's investments in several other ASEAN countries have also grown gradually.

2. The ASEAN's investments in China

China has been highly attractive thanks to its huge economic scale. The ASEAN countries have invested in China since the 1980s.

In 2015, the investment flow from the ASEAN countries to China reached USD 7,644 million, accounting for 5.6% of total FDIs actually received by China in the same period (USD 136 billion). As of late 2015, the cumulative investments made by the ASEAN community in China

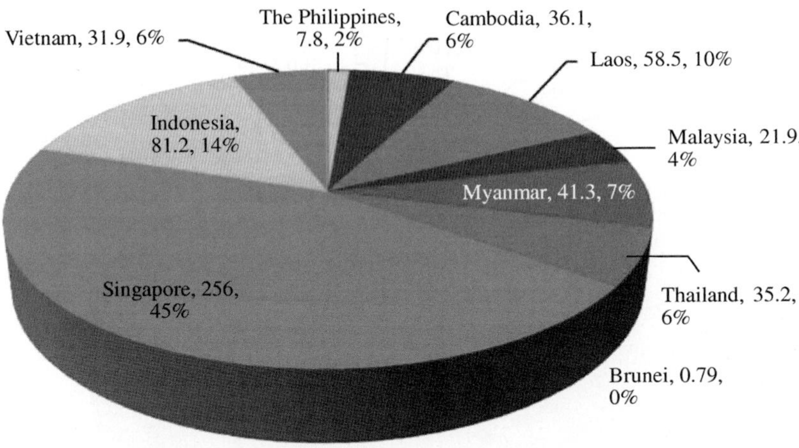

Figure 2. The Make-up of the Stock of China's Investments in the ASEAN Community by Country in 2015 (USD 100 million)
Source: The Ministry of Commerce of China.

amounted to USD 99.4 billion, accounting for 8.1% of the stock of foreign investments actually received by China (about USD 1,221,293 million). The ASEAN's investments in China mainly came from six old member countries including Singapore, Malaysia, Thailand, Brunei, Indonesia and the Philippines, while the investments from other ASEAN countries were small in quantity (see Figure 3).

As of late 2015, the stock of the investments made by the above six countries in China was USD 98.93 billion, accounting for 99.5% of the stock of the ASEAN's investments in China. Among these six countries, Singapore made the most investments in China; it was the largest investor in China in 2013 and 2014[5]; the Chinese Mainland had always been the largest destination for Singapore's outward investments.[6] In 2015, the investment flow from Singapore to China was USD 6.9 billion, accounting for 90% of the investment flow from 10 ASEAN countries to China. As of late 2015, the stock of Singapore's investments in China was USD 79.22 billion, accounting for 79.7% of the stock of the investments made by 10 ASEAN countries

[5] November 8, 2015, http://www.zaobao.com.sg/special/sg-cn/business/story20151108-546470.
[6] Singapore's Direct Investments Abroad, 2014.

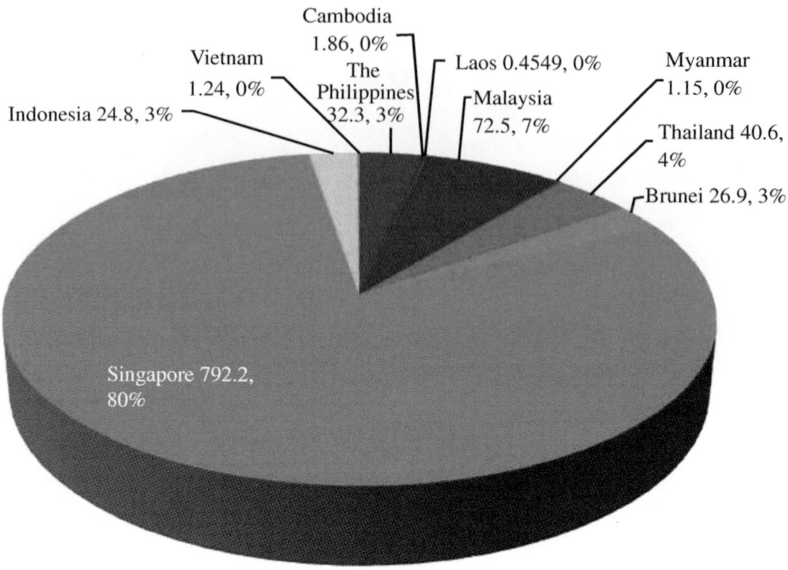

Figure 3. The Make-up of the Stock of China's Investments in the ASEAN Community by Country in 2015 (USD 100 million)
Source: The Ministry of Commerce of China.

in China. Singapore was followed by Malaysia; as of late 2015, the stock of Malaysia's investments in China was USD 7.25 billion, accounting for 7%.

Overall, China–ASEAN two-way investments expanded and developed rapidly and steadily during the period 2006–2015, fully demonstrating the developmental prospect of mutual benefit and a win–win outcome from bilateral investment cooperation. In the meantime, China–ASEAN two-way investments gradually developed from an unbalanced state to a balanced state. Before 2010, the amount of the ASEAN's investments in China was large in terms of the investment flow in the current year and the cumulative investment stock. After 2010, the investment gap between the two sides narrowed gradually, the proportion of China's investments in the ASEAN community in total two-way investments increased rapidly. In 2014, the investment flow from China to the ASEAN countries exceeded that from the ASEAN countries to the Chinese Mainland. However, the direct investments between China and the ASEAN community are still at the initial stage, the potential for development remains huge.

II. Analysis of China–ASEAN Investments in 2014–2015

1. Scale of investments

According to the Ministry of Commerce of China, China–ASEAN two-way investments totaled about USD 17,092 million in 2015 — the investments made by ASEAN countries in China totaled USD 7,644 million, accounting for 44.72%; China's investments in ASEAN countries totaled USD 9,448 million, accounting for 55.28% of the total investments.[7] Compared with 2014, China's investments grew in 8 ASEAN countries except the Philippines and Cambodia.

The growth of China–ASEAN investments in 2015 was mainly attributable to: first, in August 2014, the upgrading of the CAFTA was initiated, and the policies and efforts for deepening regional integration enabled closer connections between China and the Southeast Asia Region. China and the ASEAN community intensified their industrial cooperation, the governments of member countries introduced a number of policies and measures for trade and investment facilitation, the investment environment tended to improve, bringing new vitality to the development of bilateral cooperation. Second, the policy measures for deepening connectivity — such as the Belt and Road Initiative developed by China — and the policy of ASEAN members for opening the transportation industry to foreign investors stimulated the construction of ports, transportation of goods and the rapid development of economic trade in the (CAFTA), especially creating new investment opportunities in the infrastructure field. Third, the economic situation in the China–ASEAN Area was generally stable. China's economic growth decreased, the expectations about the economic growth rates in most ASEAN countries were lowered, but Cambodia, Myanmar, Malaysia and Vietnam showed sound economic growth; there was benign economic development and enterprises' investment confidence improved in China and ASEAN countries.

[7] Statistical data from the Ministry of Commerce of China and their calculations.

2. Investments by country

According to statistical data from the Ministry of Commerce of China, 10 ASEAN countries ranked in the order of decreasing flow of direct investments from China in 2015 (Figures 4 and 5): Singapore (USD 4.96 billion, up 120%), Laos (USD 1.36 billion, up 36.2%), Indonesia (USD 1.33 billion, up 26.2%), Thailand (USD 440 million, up 21.1%), Malaysia (USD 408 million, up 237%), Cambodia (USD 390 million, down 26.3%), Vietnam (USD 320 million, up 1.9%), Myanmar (USD 206 million, up 16.3%), the Philippines (USD 24 million, down 58.9%), and Brunei (USD 10 million, up 46.4%). China's investments in Singapore, Indonesia, Laos, Thailand and Malaysia accounted for 89.94% of China's total investments in the ASEAN community. As the financial center in 10 ASEAN countries, Singapore remains attractive for Chinese companies thanks to its low corporate tax rate (about 17%), complete legal and commercial services, and basically an absence of corruption.

Compared with 2014, the countries where China's investments showed the fastest growth in 2015 ranked as follows: Malaysia, Singapore, Brunei, Laos, and Indonesia. In recent years, China's direct investments in ASEAN

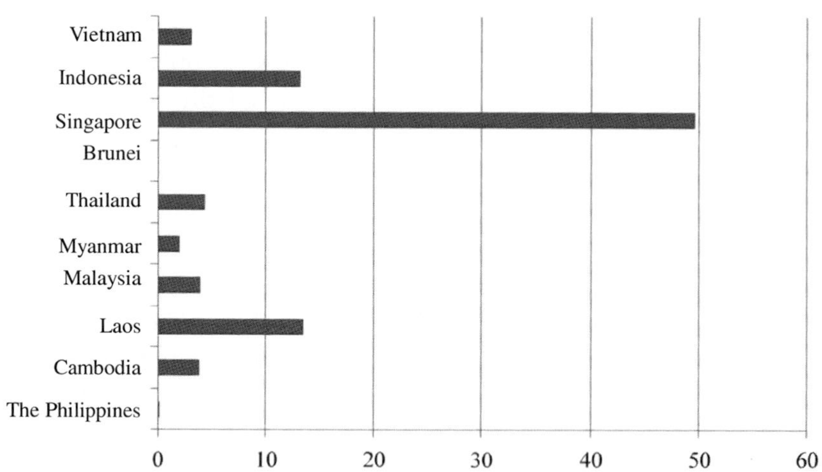

Figure 4. The Investment Flow from China to ASEAN Countries in 2015 (USD 100 million)

Source: The Ministry of Commerce of China.

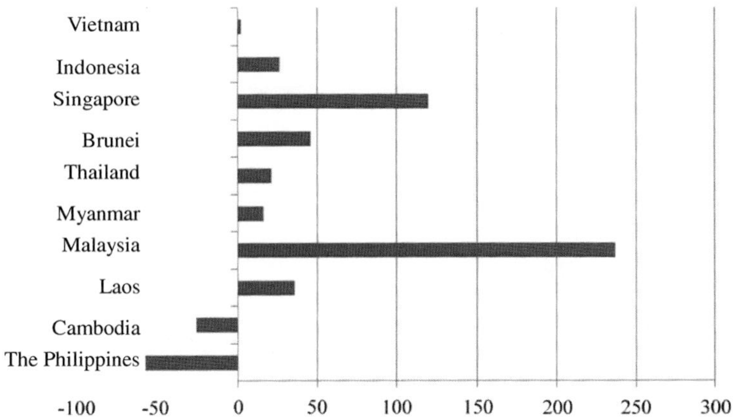

Figure 5. The Growth of Investment Flow from China to ASEAN Countries in 2015 (%)
Source: The Ministry of Commerce of China.

countries have grown rapidly due to the facts that, on the one hand, China's economy has grown steadily and it has adopted open economic policies; and on the other hand, as more and more countries have introduced or announced the measures beneficial for FDI, the investment environment in the ASEAN community has further improved. The strong economic fundamentals in the ASEAN community — such as cost advantage and market factors, including ASEAN integration — have also attracted investments from China and exerted an impact on the strategy formulation by Chinese enterprises.

The ASEAN countries in which China made direct investments mainly included Singapore, Thailand, Malaysia, the Philippines, Brunei and Indonesia. The above six countries ranked in terms of the investment flow to China in 2015 (Figure 6) as follows: Singapore (USD 6.9 billion, up 18.5%), Thailand (USD 44 million, down 26.7%), Malaysia (USD 480 million, up 205%), Indonesia (USD 108 million, up 37.8%), the Philippines (USD 39 million, down 60.2%), and Brunei (USD 73 million, up 2.3%), while the investments made by other ASEAN countries in China were negligible. For many years, these six countries maintained a steady growth of investments in China, the direct investments made by Singapore in China accounted for 90% of the total investment flow from ASEAN countries to China in 2015, Singapore continued to rank No. 1 among ASEAN countries

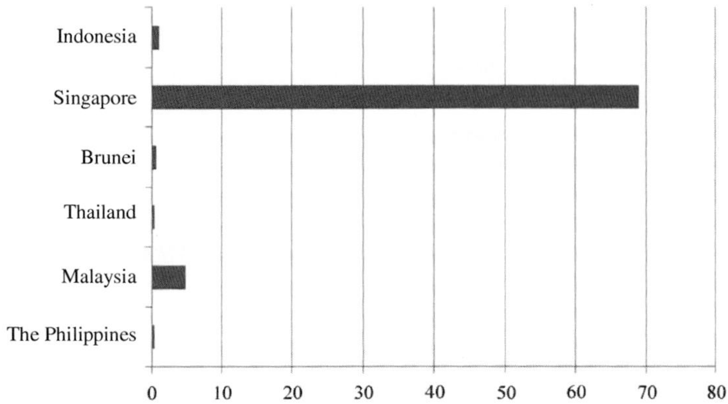

Figure 6. The Investment Flow from Six ASEAN Countries to China in 2015 (USD 100 million)
Source: The Ministry of Commerce of China.

in investments in China. In terms of absolute value, China's present 5% growth of its GDP is equivalent to double-digit growth, even higher growth 10 years ago; the challenges for a company in China do not greatly differ from that in other developing markets; however, China has provided many opportunities for continued growth, the government's policy of supporting a growth goal is a favorable factor. Therefore, although problems exist in China's economy at present, ASEAN investors and multinational corporations do not exclude China.

3. Investment fields

China's investments in the ASEAN countries in 2014 mainly flowed to: manufacturing in the amount of USD 1,522 million, up 28%, accounting for 19.5%, mainly distributed in Indonesia, Singapore, Thailand, Vietnam, and Cambodia; leasing and commercial services in the amount of USD 1,239 million, accounting for 15.9%, mainly distributed in Singapore and Laos; wholesale and retail in the amount of USD 1,118 million, accounting for 14.3%, mainly distributed in Singapore, the Philippines, Indonesia, and Thailand; construction in the amount of USD 797 million, accounting for 10.2%, mainly distributed in Laos, Singapore, Cambodia, Malaysia, and Indonesia; agriculture, forestry, animal husbandry and fishery in the amount

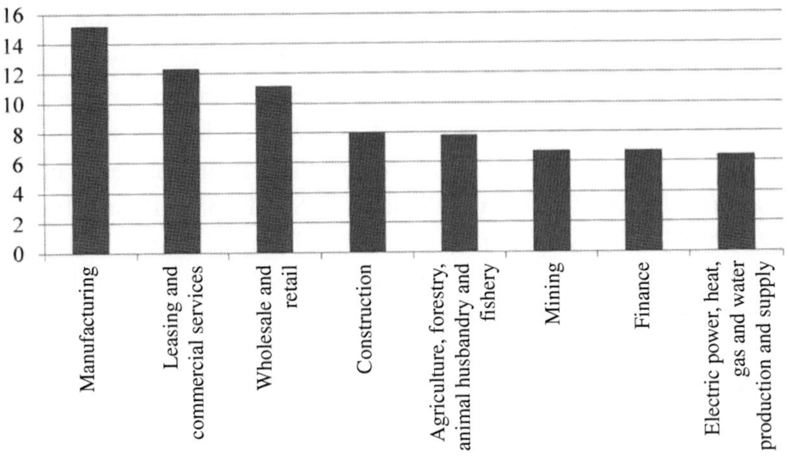

Figure 7. Distribution of China's Investments in the ASEAN Community by Industry in 2014 (USD 100 million)
Source: Statistical Communiqué on China's Outward FDIs, 2014.

of USD 783 million accounting for 10%, mainly distributed in Indonesia, Laos, and Cambodia; mining in the amount of USD 674 million, accounting for 8.6%, mainly distributed in Myanmar and Indonesia; finance in the amount of USD 673 million, accounting for 8.6%, mainly distributed in Thailand, Malaysia, the Philippines, and Cambodia; electric power, heat, gas and water production and supply in the amount of USD 646 million, accounting for 8.3% (Figure 7).[8]

As of late 2014, the cumulative investments made by China in the ASEAN countries were as follows by industry: USD 7,226 million in electric power, heat, gas and water production and supply — the industry saw the most cumulative investments made by China in the ASEAN community — accounting for 15.2% of the investment stock, mainly distributed in Singapore, Myanmar, Cambodia, Indonesia, and Laos; USD 6,843 million in leasing and commercial services, accounting for 14.4%, mainly distributed in Singapore, Malaysia, Laos, Vietnam, and Thailand; USD 6,133 million in

[8] *Source*: *Statistical Communiqué on China's Outward FDIs* (the data concerning the areas in which China's investments in the ASEAN community were made in 2015 have not yet been published).

manufacturing, accounting for 12.9% — in this industry, China's investments in the ASEAN community involved the most extensive number of countries; the East Asian Region gradually became a uniform market (except North Korea), the degree of interdependence was very high in industrial connections, the countries with USD 100 million in investments included Vietnam (USD 1,403 million), Thailand (USD 1,035 million), Indonesia (USD 985 million), Singapore (USD 741 million), Cambodia (USD 701 million), Malaysia (USD 542 million), Laos (USD 442 million), the Philippines (USD 147 million), and Myanmar (USD 129 million); USD 6,053 million in mining, accounting for 12.7% of its investment stock, reflecting China's brisk demand for natural resources, including coal, oil and metals, in previous years, mainly distributed in Indonesia, Myanmar, Laos, Singapore, Thailand, Cambodia, and the Philippines; USD 5.9 billion in wholesale and retail, accounting for 12.4% of its investment stock, mainly distributed in Singapore, Indonesia, Thailand, Vietnam, the Philippines, and Malaysia; USD 5,879 million in finance, accounting for 12.3%, mainly distributed in Singapore, Thailand, Indonesia, Malaysia, and the Philippines; USD 3,362 million in construction, accounting for 7% — the infrastructure construction boom in China greatly increased the level of Chinese enterprises in the design, construction and maintenance of large infrastructure projects — mainly distributed in Laos, Cambodia, Singapore, Malaysia, Vietnam, Indonesia, and Thailand; USD 2,444 million in agriculture, forestry, animal husbandry and fishery, accounting for 5.1%, mainly distributed in Laos, Indonesia, Cambodia, Singapore, Thailand, Vietnam, and Myanmar; USD 1,468 million in transportation and warehousing, accounting for 3.1%, mainly distributed in Singapore and Thailand; the investments in real estate accounted for 2.4% of the investment stock, mainly distributed in Singapore — Singapore enjoyed many advantages, including complete and powerful infrastructure, a livable environment, favorable investment conditions, a business-friendly environment, which attracted international buyers to Singapore's real estate industry; the investments in scientific research and technical services accounted for 1.4% of the investment stock; that in information transmission, software and information services accounted for 0.3% of the investment stock; that in resident services and other services accounted for 0.3% of the investment stock; that in lodging and catering accounted for 0.2% of the investment stock.

Singapore's investments in China were concentrated in manufacturing and real estate. The China–Singapore Free Trade Agreement, effective as from 2009, focuses on tariff reduction and exemption for trade in goods; Singapore's business circles hope that the upgraded free trade agreement can be extended to the investment and service fields, especially modern services, such as logistics, medical service, education, finance and smart cities, all of which are Singapore's strong points. Malaysia's investments in China centered on such fields as energy, agriculture, fishery and green economy. China and Malaysia had respective distinctive features in resource environment, industrial structure and domestic market demand, the two countries were highly complementary; specifically, China enjoyed comparative advantages in textiles, garments, shoes, food, cereal, building material, mechanical and electrical products and chemical products, while Malaysia was advantageous in resource products, including palm oil, rubber, gas and oil; these complementary industries became the priorities of mutual investments between the two countries. Indonesia's investments in China involved papermaking, real estate, and food processing; Indonesia's APP and Salim Group are famous enterprises in this regard.

4. Investment gap

In 2015, China's investments in the ASEAN community and the ASEAN community's investments in China were USD 9,448 million and USD 7,644 million, respectively. As of late 2015, the cumulative two-way investments between China and the ASEAN community were USD 156,469 million — the investments made by ASEAN countries in China exceeded USD 99.4 billion, the cumulative investments made by China in the ASEAN community were about USD 57,069 million, the investment gap between the two sides was USD 42,331 million, the ratio of inflow to outflow was 1.35:1,[9] but the proportion of China's investments in the ASEAN community in total two-way investments grew rapidly. As from 2014, the inflow of China's direct investments in the ASEAN community was smaller than its outflow, the gap in the amount of investment stock between the two sides decreased gradually. However, China's investments in the ASEAN

[9]The Ministry of Commerce of China.

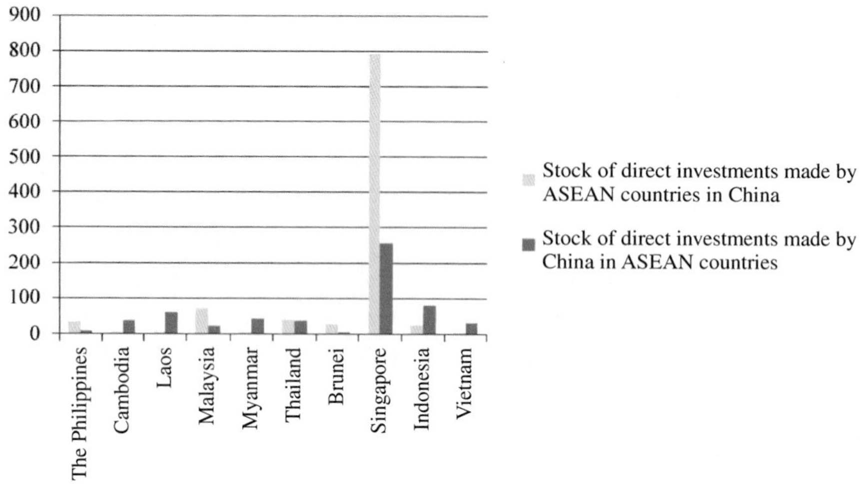

Figure 8. The Stock of Mutual Investments between China and the ASEAN Community in Late 2015 (USD 100 million)
Source: The Ministry of Commerce of China.

countries are still at the initial stage, a huge potential for development still exists. The distribution of the investment gap between China and the ASEAN community by country is shown in Figure 8.

Singapore: as of late 2015, the cumulative investments made by Singapore in China were USD 79.22 billion, and the stock of China's direct investments in Singapore was USD 25.6 billion. The cumulative mutual investments between China and Singapore were USD 104.82 billion; Singapore's investment outflow exceeded its inflow.

Malaysia: as of late 2015, the cumulative actual investments made by Malaysia in China were USD 7.25 billion, and the stock of China's direct investments in Malaysia was USD 2.19 billion. The cumulative mutual investments between China and Malaysia were USD 9.44 billion; Malaysia's investment outflow exceeded its inflow.

Thailand: as of late 2015, the cumulative actual investments made by Thailand in China were USD 4.06 billion, and the stock of China's direct investments in Thailand was USD 3.52 billion. The cumulative mutual investments between China and Thailand were USD 7.58 billion; Thailand's investment outflow exceeded its inflow.

Indonesia: as of late 2015, the cumulative actual investments made by Indonesia in China were USD 2.48 billion, and the stock of China's direct investments in Indonesia was USD 8.12 billion. The cumulative mutual investments between China and Indonesia were USD 10.6 billion; China's investment outflow exceeded its inflow.

The Philippines: as of late 2015, the cumulative direct investments made by the Philippines in China were USD 3.23 billion, and the stock of China's direct investments in the Philippines was USD 780 million. The cumulative mutual investments between China and the Philippines were USD 4.01 billion; the Philippines' investment outflow exceeded its inflow.

Brunei: as of late 2015, the cumulative actual investments made by Brunei in China were USD 2.69 billion, and the stock of China's direct investments in Brunei was USD 79 million. The cumulative mutual investments between China and Brunei were USD 2,769 million; Brunei's investment outflow exceeded its inflow.

Myanmar: as of late 2015, the cumulative actual investments made by Myanmar in China were USD 115 million, and the stock of China's direct investments in Myanmar was USD 4.13 billion. The cumulative mutual investments between China and Myanmar were USD 4,245 million; China's investment outflow exceeded its inflow.

Cambodia: as of late 2015, the cumulative actual investments made by Cambodia in China were USD 186 million, and the stock of China's direct investments in Cambodia was USD 3.61 billion. The cumulative mutual investments between China and Cambodia were USD 3,796 million; China's investment outflow exceeded its inflow.

Vietnam: as of late 2015, the cumulative actual investments made by Vietnam in China were USD 124 million, and the stock of China's direct investments in Vietnam was USD 3.19 billion. The cumulative mutual investments between China and Vietnam were USD 3,314 million; China's investment outflow exceeded its inflow.

Laos: as of late 2015, the cumulative actual investments made by Laos in China were USD 45 million, and the stock of China's direct investments in Laos was USD 5.85 billion. The cumulative mutual investments between China and Laos were USD 5,895 million; China's investment outflow exceeded its inflow.

5. Investment mode

In 2015, China–ASEAN two-way investments were made in the following ways: joint venture cooperative development, engineering contracting, greenfield investment, cross-border merger and acquisition, TOT, BOT and direct investments; they covered sole proprietorship, direct investment and cooperation, etc, and joint venture cooperation was dominant; for example, a high-speed railway project signed between China and Indonesia in 2015; nearly 98% of the investments made by Chinese enterprises in Laos' mining industry were under the joint venture mode. Furthermore, some investments were under the franchising mode led by investment and financing.

III. Opportunities and Challenges in China–ASEAN Two-way Investments in 2016

In the opening ceremony of the China–ASEAN Expo in September, 2013, Chinese Premier Li Keqiang said that China hoped to increase China–ASEAN bilateral trade to USD 1 trillion and expand China–ASEAN bilateral investments by 7 times to USD 150 billion by 2020.

The year 2016 was crucial for China to comprehensively carry out the Belt and Road Initiative. China–ASEAN two-way investments face the following favorable opportunities.

First, the ASEAN community has a huge demand for infrastructure investment, as infrastructure plays an important role in regional economic, social and environmental development, promotes regional connectivity and reduces regional transaction costs. The improvement of infrastructure in ASEAN member countries is conducive to enhancing the ASEAN's investment environment. The connectivity of the transportation infrastructure improves the efficiency of logistics and supports the growth of investments, trade and other commercial activities. The investments in electric power infrastructure guarantee energy security and meet the people's demand for electric power in their daily life and production. Like other infrastructures, information and communication technology-related infrastructure supports enterprises' e-commerce and cross-border commercial connections.

The ASEAN community has a huge demand for investments in infrastructure, including electric power, transportation, information and communication technology, water supply and public health facilities, from the present to 2025. The annual demand for infrastructure investments in these fields hits USD 110 billion.[10] Given the current payment capacity of ASEAN member countries for infrastructure, the investment gap in their infrastructure is huge. In order to fill the current investment gap and meet the future demand, it is necessary to find new resources. China's investments can play a bigger role in filling that gap.

Although the global interest rates are relatively low, the funds for infrastructure investments are scarce. The financial crisis in 2007–2008 has reversed the trend of the steady growth of overseas direct investments (ODIs). The new Basel rules increase the infrastructure financing costs and risk management difficulties, so the multinational banks which funded infrastructure in the past are no longer willing to do so. Pension funds and sovereign wealth funds still express interest in infrastructure investments, and their investments focus on the long term, thus they are the most suitable sources of funds. However, these funds often lack the necessary professional competence. Other developmental agencies do not have sufficient funds to meet the ASEAN's demand for the construction of infrastructure.

In many other countries, including Indonesia, the insufficiency of infrastructure remains a problem. Generally, infrastructure can create extensive welfare for the society, while that creation is unprofitable for the private sector. The responsibility for infrastructure investment rests with the government; however, amidst a global economic slowdown, policymakers have given priority to fiscal prudence. Although the private sector is encouraged to make contributions, especially through public–private partnerships, these contributions are often highly inadequate to solve real problems. The Asian economic crisis during the period 1997–1998 has made Asian countries generally averse to foreign loans. The Chinese Government has offered loans according to commercial terms without imposing the following prerequisite: the borrowers shall carry out structural reform. This approach has been more acceptable to many developing countries from a political perspective.

Second, the ASEAN Economic Community (AEC) officially came into force on December 31, 2015. As envisioned, the ASEAN Economic Community will become a zero-tariff single market and production base, so that the

[10] Data come from *ASEAN Investment Report* 2015: *Infrastructure Investments and Connectivity.*

cross-border migration of service enterprises within the region will be basically free from any restrictions. Theoretically, a uniform product and service market is established, making way for free movement of people, legal and regulatory coordination. Economic growth and the expectations regarding AEC stimulate the multinational enterprises within and outside the ASEAN region to expand their investments in the region; the ASEAN community may benefit from relatively low wage costs and an ample labor supply in the next 20 years. With the rapid economic growth of the ASEAN region and the expansion of the middle class, Chinese manufacturers who transfer production to foreign countries have also made arrangements in the ASEAN community with a view to seeking a share from the ever-increasing consumer market.

Third, Chinese enterprises transferred production capacity. As China carries out its strict family planning policy, the United Nations expect that China's labor force may decrease by 70 million during the period 2010–2030; the current labor shortage has driven up wages, and enterprises have to pay more generous social welfare. According to a manufacturer survey conducted by Standard Chartered in the Pearl River Delta in February and March 2015, in China's export base in the Pearl River Delta Region, about 1/3 of the manufacturers planned to transfer production capacity to the domestic regions with lower labor costs or Southeast Asia, Bangladesh, India and Sri Lanka. According to Standard Chartered, 36% of the enterprises under survey which planned to transfer production capacity to foreign countries had the desire to transfer to Vietnam, 25% to Cambodia, 10% to Bangladesh, 10% to Indonesia, 5% to India, 5% to Sri Lanka, 5% to Thailand, and 3% to the Philippines. As indicated by the survey, the 10 ASEAN countries would enjoy the greatest benefit from the decrease in the competitiveness of the Pearl River Delta Region. The Pearl River Delta Region contributed 27% of China's exports and received nearly 20% of FDIs in China. Given that FDI flow in the Pearl River Delta Region made up a large proportion of global FDI flow, even a small-scale transfer of production capacity might also exert a huge impact on investment recipients. For example, in 2013, FDI flow to the Pearl River Delta Region totaled USD 106.1 billion, almost four times the FDI flow to India and nearly five times that to Indonesia and 12 times that to Vietnam. The annual amount of exports from the Pearl River Delta Region (USD 607 billion in 2013) much exceeded that from ASEAN countries. However, opportunities are often accompanied by challenges. With different regulatory systems, corporate cultural conflicts and commercial misjudgment, Chinese enterprises are still not fully understood overseas, cultural fusion may also be a challenge. In 2015, the USD 5.5 billion high-speed railway project undertaken by China in Indonesia was suspended a week after the cornerstone laying ceremony. This sends a warning that Chinese enterprises may encounter a variety of problems in the emerging markets.

A new wave of China's outward FDIs (OFDIs) is supported by the efforts of the Chinese Government in actively carrying out reform and relaxing supervision over overseas investments. We can anticipate that more progress in this respect will be made in the near and medium-term future. For example, as Chinese enterprises speed up their overseas expansion, the RMB-denominated transactions may be promoted in overseas mergers, acquisitions and expansions. Chinese state-owned and private enterprises flocked to any promising project during the flourishing period of oil and bulk commodities, so new projects for which transactions have been concluded must either make profits at relatively low prices or be provided with great subsidies from the Chinese Government. The potential host countries have reduced investments to safely survive the expected economic downturn, so they cannot be relied on to provide funds.

Although tariff rates become zero at 95% of tariff lines, there are non-tariff barriers ranging from differences in supervision criteria to failure of ports to perform normal operations, making the trade among ASEAN countries difficult and frustrating. The ASEAN community is unable to sanction the countries which defy its rules. The ASEAN Model stresses consensus; this is either an advantage or a disadvantage. A huge divide still exists between gorgeous publicity and the reality.

Since 2015, China's real economy has deteriorated in profitability and has been subject to heavy debts, so China's financial system has been unstable. On March 2, 2016, the rating agency Moody's downgraded China's sovereign bond rating from outlook to negative; on March 3, Moody's downgraded the rating of many Chinese financial institutions and state-owned enterprises from outlook to negative. The confidence of domestic and foreign markets in China's economy was therefore inevitably further compromised. Whether the economic operation policies expected to be introduced will consequently change after two sessions will be the focus of attention within the market.

The United Nations Conference on Trade and Development expects that the global FDI flow will decrease in 2016, showing the fragility in the global economy, fluctuations on the global financial market, a sluggish global aggregate demand and a noticeable decrease in the growth of some large emerging market economies. High geopolitical risks and regional tensions may further enlarge some economic challenges. With the reduction of an excess inventory in real estate, the decreasing RMB exchange rate and the removal of an excess production capacity from state-owned enterprises, China's economic growth rate will decline to about 6.9%. In the meantime, global trade and investment protectionism is getting strong, USA is carrying out the strategy of Pivot to Asia, Chinese enterprises are facing the underdevelopment of the industrial chain when investing in the ASEAN community, the political situation is unstable in some countries, so China–ASEAN two-way investments are subject to heavy pressure and many challenges.

Chapter 13

Report on China–ASEAN Trade in 2015

Sheng Yuxue*

Against the background of globalization and regionalization, carrying out an open economic policy is an inevitable choice for China and ASEAN countries. In 2015, the international economic situation was severe, but China–ASEAN trade did not become stagnant. With progress in the Belt and Road Initiative, the establishment of the ASEAN Community in late 2015 and the conclusion of negotiations involving the upgrading of the China–ASEAN Free Trade Area (CAFTA), China–ASEAN trade will usher in a new chapter in 2016.

* Sheng Yuxue, Doctor of Economics at the China–ASEAN Research Institute of Guangxi University. This chapter is jointly funded by the special research project of the China–ASEAN Collaborative Innovation Center for Regional Development and the Cheung Kong Scholars and Innovation Team Development Program initiated by the Ministry of Education (contract number: CW201520).

I. The Total Volume and Structure of China–ASEAN Trade in 2015

1. Overview of bilateral trade

a. *The foreign trade of various countries faced a great downward pressure but was better than the overall situation of the world economy*

In 2015, the international situation regarding trade was grim and complicated, exerting a profound impact on China and ASEAN countries. According to statistics from China Customs, in 2015, China's imports and exports totaled USD 3.96 trillion, down 8%. The exports amounted to USD 2.28 trillion, down 2.8%; the imports were USD 1.68 trillion, down 14.1%.[1] The ASEAN community was also subject to heavy downward pressure. According to the data released by the WTO, the ASEAN community of six countries[2]: Vietnam, Thailand, Malaysia, Singapore, the Philippines and Indonesia — maintained a trade surplus in 2015, but both imports and exports declined by more than 10% over 2014. Nevertheless, China–ASEAN imports and exports remained better than the overall performance of the world's economy. China continued to keep its status as the largest trading country, the proportions of total imports and exports between China and the ASEAN countries (six countries) on the international market increased steadily from 12.4% and 7.1% in 2014 to 13% and 7.2% in 2015.

b. *China–ASEAN trade showed a negative growth but the status of the two sides as trading partners was consolidated*

Since the CAFTA was launched in 2010, China has become its largest trading partner, while the ASEAN community has served as China's third largest trading partner, its fourth largest exporting market and its second largest source of imports. With the impact from the world's economic slowdown

[1] The official website of the Ministry of Commerce of China, January 20, 2016.

[2] According to the data released by the ASEAN Secretariat, in 2014, the foreign trade of six ASEAN countries accounted for 97% of the ASEAN community's overall foreign trade, these six countries can better represent the ASEAN community's overall situation.

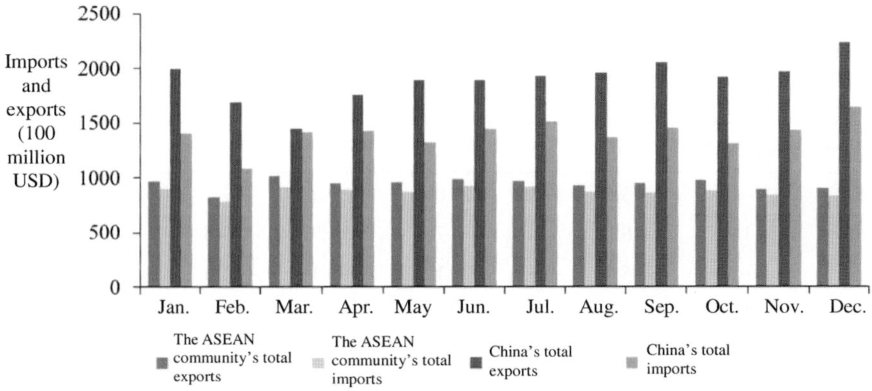

Figure 1. Monthly Statistics on the Total Imports and Exports of the China–ASEAN Group in 2015

Note: The data on the ASEAN community are the total value of Vietnam, Thailand, Malaysia, Singapore, the Philippines and Indonesia.

Source: The data from the WTO.

and decreases in the prices of bulk commodities on the international market, China–ASEAN trade reached USD 472.2 billion in 2015, down 1.7% over 2014, lower than the rate of decrease in China's foreign trade in the same period (8%). The proportion of China–ASEAN trade in China's foreign trade increased slightly from 11.2% in 2014 to 11.9% in 2015 — the exports and imports rose from 11.6% and 10.6% to 12.3% and 11.2%, so the status of the two sides as trading partners was sealed (see Figure 1 and Table 1).

2. The country-specific structure of bilateral trade

a. *The pattern in which six countries played the leading role was unchanged, Vietnam and Cambodia performed well*

Like 2014, the ASEAN countries ranked in the order of decreasing trade with China in 2015 as follows: Malaysia, Vietnam, Singapore, Thailand, Indonesia, the Philippines, Myanmar, Cambodia, Laos and Brunei. The trade of the first six countries accounted for 94.9% of China–ASEAN trade, their imports and exports accounted for 95.9% of China's imports from the

Table 1. Monthly Statistics on the Growth Rates of China–ASEAN Imports and Exports in 2015 (Unit: %)

	Export growth rate				Import growth rate			
Month	ASEAN	China	Asia	World	ASEAN	China	Asia	World
1	−4.5	−3.5	−3.1	−10.4	−9.7	−19.7	−14.3	−13.7
2	−14.6	48.2	5.5	−7.8	−10.7	−20.5	−16.2	−13.5
3	−5.6	−15.1	−10.7	−11.9	−9.1	−12.5	−14.1	−11.2
4	−10.7	−6.6	−8.9	−12.9	−13.7	−16.0	−14.3	−14.2
5	−11.1	−3.4	−8.5	−13.3	−16.2	−17.3	−16.2	−15.6
6	−7.8	1.5	−5.1	−7.2	−5.7	−6.7	−9.8	−8.7
7	−8.8	−9.2	−8.7	−12.4	−10.8	−8.4	−11.3	−13.0
8	−12.5	−5.8	−10.5	−12.1	−11.1	−13.7	−13.3	−12.5
9	−13.0	−3.9	−9.0	−11.5	−17.2	−20.2	−19.0	−14.7
10	−10.8	−7.0	−10.2	−12.1	−17.3	−18.6	−17.7	−13.5
11	−11.7	−7.0	−9.6	−10.9	−9.6	−8.8	−12.8	−10.5
12	−10.8	−1.6	−6.9	−8.5	−12.9	−7.4	−11.1	−10.8
Total	−10.1	−2.8	−7.4	−10.9	−11.9	−14.1	−14.1	−12.6

Note: The data on the ASEAN community are the total value of Vietnam, Thailand, Malaysia, Singapore, the Philippines and Indonesia.
Source: The data from the WTO.

ASEAN community and 94.2% of China's exports to the ASEAN community; these three figures increased to some extent over 2014, suggesting that China–ASEAN trade was dominated, to a certain degree, by the trade of these six countries. Specifically, in 2015, China–Myanmar trade, China–Laos trade, China–Brunei trade, China–Indonesia trade and China–Malaysia trade showed a negative growth, while China's trade with the remaining five ASEAN countries grew positively; China–Cambodia trade and China–Vietnam trade grew by double-digit rates (17.9% and 14.7%). Vietnam and Cambodia were two countries with a positive growth of China's imports from the ASEAN community in 2015; Vietnam replaced Singapore to become China's third largest importing country in the ASEAN community. China's exports to Malaysia, Indonesia, Laos and Brunei grew negatively, while China's exports to the remaining six ASEAN countries showed a positive

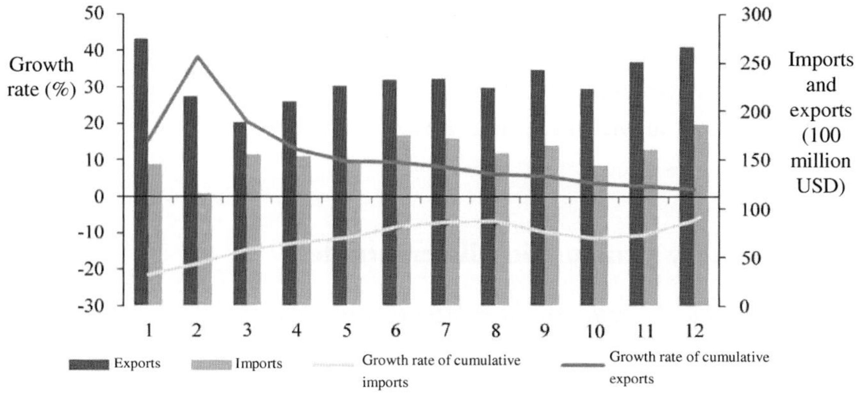

Figure 2. Monthly Statistics on China–ASEAN Bilateral Import and Export Trade in 2015
Source: China Customs.

growth to varying degrees — China's exports to Cambodia, the Philippines and Thailand indicated a double-digit growth; Thailand replaced Indonesia as China's fourth largest exporting country in the ASEAN community (see Figure 2).

b. *China's trade surplus reached a new height, the trade surplus with Vietnam, Singapore and Indonesia accounted for 90%*

According to statistics from China Customs, in 2015, China's exports to the ASEAN community grew by 2%, while China's imports from the ASEAN countries decreased by 6.5%, China's trade surplus reached an all-time high and hit USD 82.8 billion. The surplus expansion was mainly due to the fall in the prices of bulk commodities, adjustment of international industrial division and the trade substitution effect of the Trans-Pacific Partnership Agreement (TPP).[3] China's trade surplus with the ASEAN community was concentrated in Vietnam (USD 36.3 billion, 43.8%), Singapore (USD 24.5 billion, 29.5%) and Indonesia (USD 14.5 billion, 17.5%). In 2015, China changed from a deficit-ridden country into a country with a surplus in China–Thailand trade and China–Myanmar

[3]The official website of the Ministry of Commerce of China, January 22, 2016.

trade; China changed from a country with a surplus into a deficit-ridden country in China–Laos trade. Malaysia continued to maintain a USD 9.3 billion surplus with China; Malaysia and Laos were the only two major countries with a surplus in China–ASEAN trade in 2015 (see Figures 3, 4 and Table 2).

3. Commodity structure in bilateral trade

a. *The commodity structure in bilateral trade was stable, the mechanical and electrical products ranked No. 1 in bilateral trade*

The commodity structure in China–ASEAN trade did not change greatly over 2014. In 2015, the uppermost commodities in China–ASEAN trade remained the commodities (mechanical and electrical products, audio and video equipment and their parts, accessories) under the 16th category with customs code (HS code), accounting for 35.4% of all commodities exported from China to the ASEAN community and 47.6% of all commodities imported by China from the ASEAN countries. Furthermore, the commodities which ranked Nos. 2 and 3 among those exported from China to the

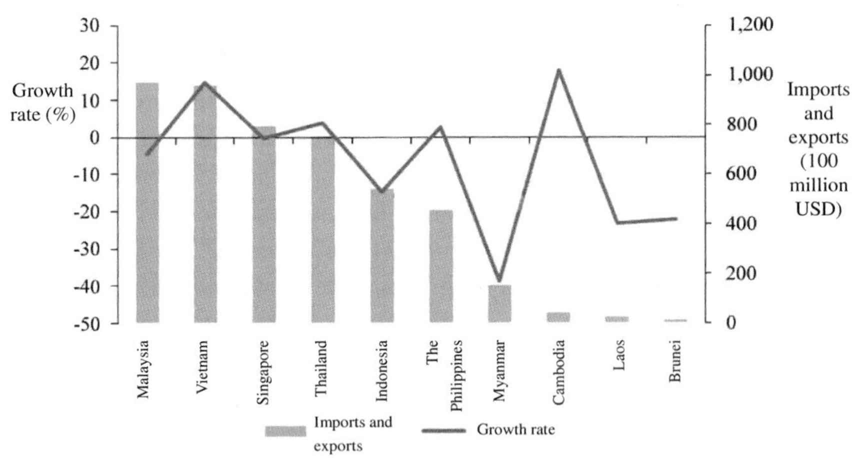

Figure 3. Distribution of China–ASEAN Total Trade in 2015
Source: China Customs.

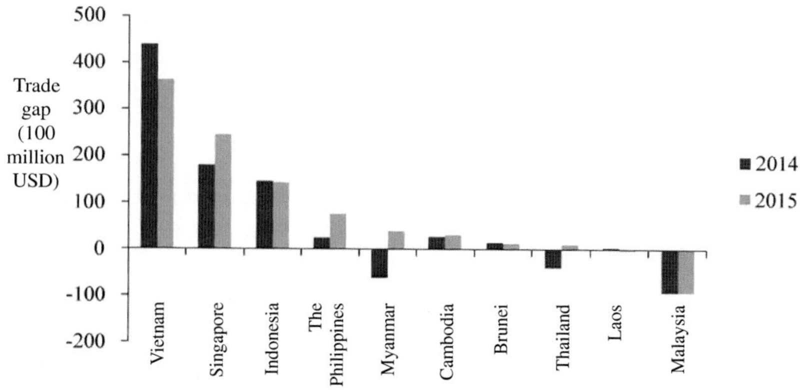

Figure 4. Distribution of China's Surplus in China–ASEAN Trade in 2015
Source: China Customs.

Table 2. Distribution of China–ASEAN Imports and Exports by Country in 2015

	China's exports		China's imports	
Country	Exports (USD 100 million)	Growth rate (%)	Imports (USD 100 million)	Growth rate (%)
Malaysia	439.90	−5.1	533.00	−4.2
Vietnam	661.24	3.8	298.42	49.9
Singapore	520.08	6.3	275.56	−10.6
Thailand	382.93	11.7	371.70	−3.0
Indonesia	343.42	−12.1	198.88	−18.8
The Philippines	266.73	13.6	189.76	−9.6
Myanmar	96.55	3.1	56.25	−63.9
Cambodia	37.65	15.0	6.67	38.0
Laos	12.27	−33.3	15.54	−12.6
Brunei	14.09	−19.4	0.97	−48.8
ASEAN	2774.87	2.0	1946.75	−6.5

Source: China Customs.

ASEAN community remained the commodities (textile raw materials and products) under the 11th category and the commodities (plastics, rubber and their products) under the 7th category, accounting for 12.8% and 8.53%. Similarly, the commodities which ranked Nos. 2 and 3 among those imported by China from the ASEAN community remained the commodities (mineral products) under the 5th category and the commodities (base metals and their products) under the 15th category, accounting for 12.7% and 9.28%.

b. *Bilateral trade encompassed inter-industry trade and intra-industry trade, the average intra-industry trade index declined slightly*

There was both inter-industry trade and intra-industry trade between China and the ASEAN community, showing that comparative advantages and the acquisition of a scale economy in the new global labor division exerted an impact on bilateral trade. According to the classification based on HS code, the China–ASEAN average intra-industry trade index was 0.429 in 2015, a certain decrease over 2014. The intra-industry trade index of the commodities under each of the 16th, 2nd, 10th, 18th, 7th, 6th and 4th categories exceeded 0.7, while that of the commodities under the 21st category declined greatly (see Table 3).

4. Bilateral trade in services and technology

a. *The bilateral trade in services grew rapidly, the potential for development is great*

Since the financial crisis, global trade in goods has become sluggish, while trade in services has maintained a momentum of rapid development; it has become a new export growth point under the new normal in China and an important developmental direction for China's economic transformation. In 2007, the CAFTA *Service Trade Agreement* was signed and came into force; afterwards, the two sides opened a service market with each other, and trade in services developed rapidly; in 2014, bilateral trade totaled USD 62.66 billion, up 44.7%.[4] Service outsourcing has been an emerging field in trade in services; China's service outsourcing industry generally developed in a positive way amidst the slow recovery of the global economy and an increasing downward pressure on the domestic economy.

[4]The official website of the Ministry of Commerce of China, November 22, 2015.

Table 3. The Proportions of Commodities Under the Various Categories in China–ASEAN Trade and the Intra-industry Trade Indexes (2014–2015)

Commodity category (HS)		Proportion of commodities exported from China (%)		Proportion of commodities imported by China (%)		Intra-industry trade index	
		2014	2015	2014	2015	2014	2015
Second category	Plant products	2.46	2.85	3.55	3.92	0.926	0.993
Third category	Animals, plant oil, fat, wax; refined edible fat and oil	0.03	0.02	2.78	2.55	0.024	0.023
Fourth category	Food; beverages, spirits and vinegar; tobacco and products	1.59	1.53	0.96	1.16	0.655	0.719
Fifth category	Mineral products	4.54	3.23	15.26	12.74	0.541	0.512
Sixth category	Chemical industry and its related industrial products	6.18	5.91	6.07	4.69	0.882	0.738
Seventh category	Plastics and its products; rubber and its products	3.85	3.82	9.57	8.53	0.667	0.755
Eighth category	Leather, fur and products; bags and suitcases; catgut products	1.01	1.17	0.31	0.43	0.399	0.424
Ninth category	Wood and products; charcoal; softwood; knotwork	0.53	0.54	2.19	1.91	0.463	0.552
Tenth category	Wood pulp etc.; waste paper; paper, paperboard and its products	1.05	1.15	1.03	1.08	0.882	0.818
Eleventh category	Textile raw materials and textile products	13.15	12.80	1.88	2.24	0.205	0.229

(*Continued*)

Table 3. (*Continued*)

Commodity category (HS)		Proportion of commodities exported from China (%)		Proportion of commodities imported by China (%)		Intra-industry trade index	
		2014	2015	2014	2015	2014	2015
Twelfth category	Shoes, hats and umbrellas, etc.; processed feathers and their products; artificial flowers; human hair products	1.99	2.11	0.48	0.74	0.326	0.411
Thirteenth category	Mineral material products; ceramics; glass and products	3.01	3.60	0.25	0.25	0.124	0.098
Fourteenth category	Jewelry, precious metal and products; imitation jewelry; coins	0.58	0.28	6.45	2.65	0.2	0.248
Fifteenth category	Base metals and their products	10.10	9.29	2.24	1.95	0.303	0.268
Sixteenth category	Mechanical and electrical products, audio and video equipment and their parts, accessories	34.45	35.35	43.20	47.61	0.996	0.996
Seventeenth category	Vehicles, aircraft, ships, transport equipment	5.68	6.59	0.55	0.58	0.144	0.122
Eighteenth category	Optical, medical equipment, etc.; clocks; musical instruments	3.18	3.00	2.35	2.81	0.745	0.817

Notes: (1) China Customs only released the table showing the amounts of import and export commodities under various subcategories and categories between China and seven ASEAN countries, including the Philippines, Vietnam, Myanmar, Singapore, Malaysia, Indonesia and Thailand. The trade between China and the above seven countries accounted for more than 98% of the trade between China and the ASEAN community (exports 97.7%, imports 98.8%) in 2015, these countries are highly representative. (2) The intra-industry trade index = 1 – |imports – exports|/(imports + exports).

Sources: China Customs. The data on the commodity categories whose proportion was less than 1% are not listed; the readers with interest can contact the author to obtain the data.

According to the Ministry of Commerce of China, the service outsourcing contracts awarded to China in the Southeast Asian countries amounted to USD 8.99 billion and the amount of the executed contracts was USD 6.32 billion in 2015, up 30.6% and 17.3%.[5] At present, China has become the fourth largest trade in services partner of the ASEAN community, while the ASEAN community has maintained its status as China's fifth largest trading partner.[6]

b. *Platforms were built to push forward the trade in technology, China improved its capability for making its technologies go global*

Against the background of implementing the strategy of innovation-driven development, China has surpassed USA to become the largest patent applicant in the world. In 2015, the contractual transactions amounted to 1 trillion yuan on the domestic technology market.[7] In parallel with enhancing its capability for technical innovation, China greatly improved its ability to make technologies go global and get access to the ASEAN community; trade in technology became an important means for both sides to climb the global value chain. The technology matchmaking platforms substantially pushed forward bilateral trade in technology. At present, China and the ASEAN community have jointly built the China–ASEAN Technology Transfer Center (CATTC) dedicated to promoting scientific and technological cooperation between China and the ASEAN countries in modern agriculture, new energy and renewable energy, electronic information, energy conservation and environmental protection. As of March 2015, the number of CATTC collaborative network members had reached 1,188, with 393 members from ASEAN countries, the amount of cooperation reached by enterprises of the two sides through the CATTC was nearly 310 million yuan. In 2015, CATTC successfully held technology matchmaking meetings between China and Singapore, Cambodia, Myanmar and Vietnam. In the 3rd China–ASEAN Technology

[5] The official website of the Ministry of Commerce of China, January 20, 2016.

[6] The China–ASEAN Expo Promotes Great Trade Integration between China and the ASEAN community, *China Industrial Economy News*, September 3, 2015.

[7] Vice President of the Hong Kong Trade Development Council: the Belt and Road Boosts the Trade of Intellectual Property, *Xinhuanet*, November 23, 2015.

Transfer and Innovation Cooperation Conference held in November, Thailand and China decided to expand the cooperation agreement signed by the two countries in 2013, with a view to strengthening their cooperation in such scientific and technological fields as space technology, remote sensing satellite, solar energy and electric vehicles.

II. The Network Under the China–ASEAN Regional Trade Agreement was Expanded in 2015

With slow progress in multilateral trade negotiations, the international trade order has become more complicated due to the networking under the regional trade agreement (RTA). The year 2015 was important for some countries to expand their RTA network; for example, Vietnam separately signed free trade agreements with South Korea, the Eurasian Union and the EU; Vietnam also signed the TPP, so that Vietnam concluded negotiations involving 12 free trade areas; after China successfully signed and executed the free trade agreements between China and South Korea, between China and Australia, the number of China's free trade agreements reached 14. In the meantime, the negotiation involving the upgrading of the CAFTA was concluded on schedule, substantive progress was made in the negotiations concerning the agreement on the Regional Comprehensive Economic Partnership (RCEP).[8] According to the data from the WTO, as of December, 2015, 10 ASEAN countries and China had signed and executed nearly 50 RTAs.

1. The CAFTA upgrading agreement was reached

On November 22, 2015, China and the ASEAN community agreed upon the upgrading of the free trade area and signed the *Protocol to Amend the Framework Agreement on Comprehensive Economic Cooperation between the Association of Southeast Asian Nations and the People's Republic of China and Some Agreements under the Framework Agreement* ("the Protocol"). The Protocol covers the trade in goods, trade in services, investments, and

[8]The official website of the Ministry of Commerce of China, January 6, 2016.

economic and technical cooperation; it enriches, improves, supplements and enhances the original CAFTA agreements; it embodies the common desire of both sides to deepen and broaden economic and trade cooperation.[9] In the field of trade in goods, the Protocol comprehensively upgrades the rules of origin concerning CAFTA so that they become more similar to those in other free trade agreements in the area. The Protocol also adds the content of customs procedures and trade facilitation and proposes to build the electronic customs operating system; it ensures that relevant laws and regulations of the two sides are open and transparent; it introduces the risk management system, the pre-ruling system and the authorized operator system; it improves the customs clearance environment and reduces the export costs.[10] In the field of trade in services, China promised to make improvements in such sectors as constructional engineering, securities, travel agencies and tourist operators, while the ASEAN countries made the following commitment to China: increasing the level of openness in about 70 subsectors of eight sectors including commerce, communication, construction, education, the environment, finance, tourism and transportation.[11]

2. RCEP negotiations were promoted steadily

The 10th round of RCEP negotiations was concluded in mid-October, 2015; RCEP negotiations are expected to be completed in 2016.[12] The population of RCEP member countries accounts for about 50% of the global population. GDP, trade volume and the absorbed foreign capital make up nearly 1/3 of those in the world; it is currently the largest free trade agreement negotiation in Asia; it is also the largest, most influential free trade area negotiation with the largest number of members in which China participates; its objective is to reach a modern, comprehensive, high-quality and mutually beneficial free trade agreement. The agreement will help various countries obtain low-cost

[9]The official website of the Ministry of Commerce of China, December 3, 2015.

[10]The Upgraded Free Trade Area Will Help Deeply Tap the Potential for China–ASEAN Trade, www.chinanews.com, January 18, 2016.

[11]The official website of the Ministry of Commerce of China, November 22, 2015

[12]Joint Statement of RCEP Leaders, November 22, 2015.

raw materials in a wider scope, enjoy tariff reductions and exemptions and enhance the competitiveness of export products.

3. Substantive breakthroughs were made in TPP

Since the official negotiation kicked off in March 2010, as the first group of negotiating member countries, some ASEAN countries actively moved to make substantive breakthroughs in TPP. On October 5, 2015, 12 participating member countries — including New Zealand, Brunei, Canada, Chile, Japan, Malaysia, Mexico, Singapore, the USA and Vietnam — announced in Atlanta, in USA, that they agreed upon the TPP. The TPP is characterized by wide coverage, strict agreement terms and high standards. The GDP of the participating countries accounts for 40% in the global economy; the economic scale surpasses that of the current EU, and the TPP exerts an important impact on reshaping the global trade and investment rules and order (see Figure 5).

4. The construction of the ASEAN Community

The ASEAN Community was officially established on December 31, 2015; that establishment indicated that ASEAN integration had reached a new level and that new opportunities were provided for expanding intra-trade in the ASEAN community. In recent years, intra-trade in the ASEAN community has grown by more than 10%; it accounted for 24.1% of total regional trade in 2014[13]; however, the room for improvement is still very large compared with the EU (60%). Therefore, the ASEAN group announced the initiation of the ASEAN Pathfinder Project in October, 2015, and the ASEAN members signed and adopted a number of documents in the 27th ASEAN Summit held in November, including the *2015 Kuala Lumpur Declaration on the Establishment of the ASEAN Community*, and the *ASEAN 2025: Forging Ahead Together*, identifying expansion of the intra-trade as one of the priorities in the construction of the ASEAN Community.

---

[13] Xu Ningning, *2016: the Priorities in the Planning and Construction of the ASEAN Community Deserve Attention*, China–ASEAN Business Council, January 22, 2016.

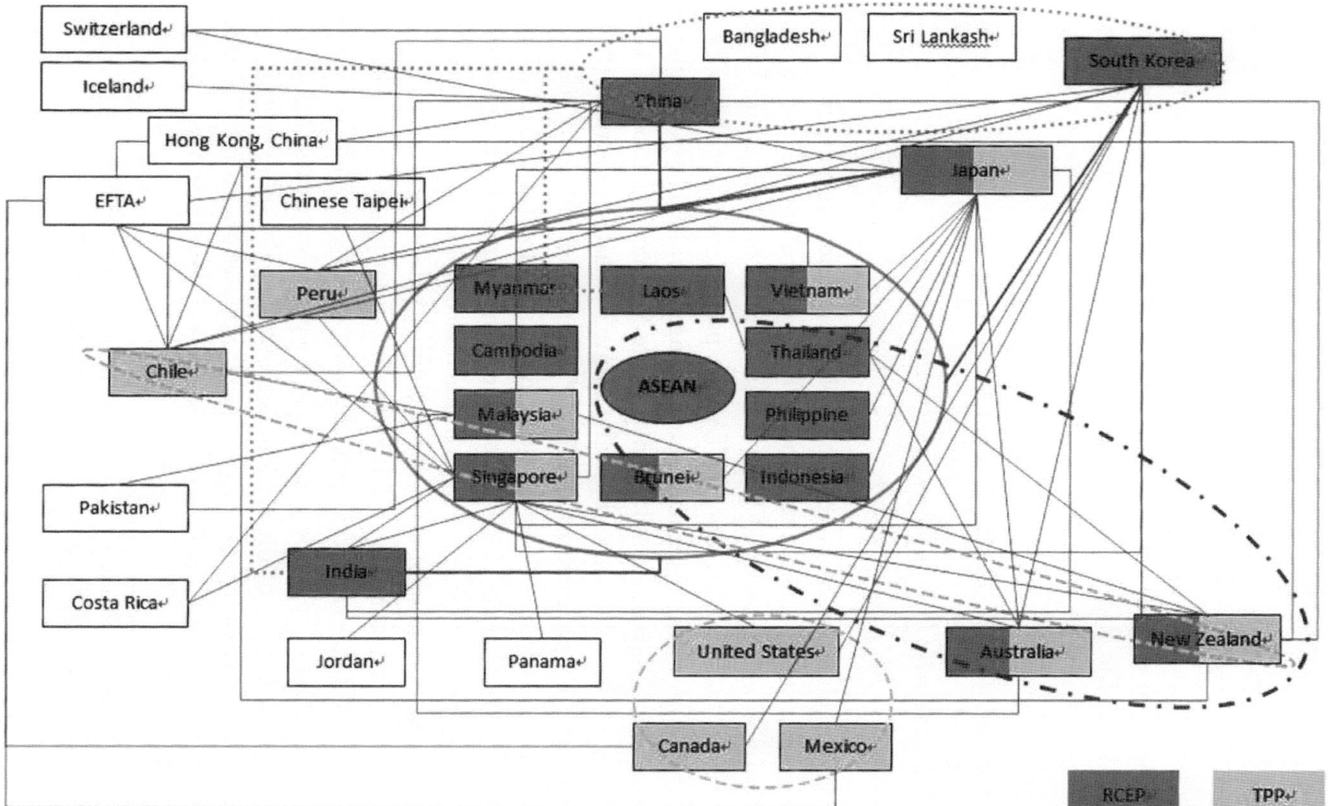

Figure 5. The Network Under the China–ASEAN Regional Trade Agreement
Source: The data from the WTO.

III. Costs in China–ASEAN Trade in 2015

With the conclusion of the negotiations involving CAFTA upgrading, the liberalization of trade between China and the ASEAN community has been expanded continuously, the tariff and non-tariff barriers have been reduced greatly, and even eliminated; however, many problems still exist in cross-border logistics, the customs clearance environment, port construction and trade rules, imposing certain restrictions on the growth of bilateral trade.

1. Overview of costs in bilateral trade

a. *Various countries have adjusted tariffs and quotas to promote trade liberalization*

The greatest achievement in the ASEAN Economic Community is the liberalization of trade in products; the ASEAN community has achieved a success in eliminating internal tariff barriers under the framework of the ASEAN Free Trade Agreement (AFTA). At present, zero tariff has been realized for 99% of the categories among Singapore, Malaysia, Thailand, Indonesia, the Philippines and Brunei, while Vietnam, Cambodia, Laos and Myanmar have planned to basically eliminate tariffs prior to 2018. In 2015, the ASEAN countries, including Vietnam and Myanmar, adopted a number of measures, such as adjusting tariffs and quotas, thus affecting import and export trade; besides approving the importation of second-hand machines at suitable prices,[14] Myanmar also reduced the import and export trade taxes concerning jewelry, including jade.[15] Vietnam increased the import quotas of cane sugar, salt and eggs.[16] In order to protect domestic producers, Malaysia carried out the zero export tax rate policy for crude palm oil as of September, 2014[17]; as the prices were expected to rise, Malaysia restored 4.5% of the export tax on crude palm oil in April 2015. In July 2015, the Government of Indonesia increased the import taxes for 24 categories of commodities. With more than a decade of development,

---

[14] The official website of the Ministry of Commerce of China, March 23, 2015.
[15] The official website of the Ministry of Commerce of China, April 8, 2015.
[16] The official website of the Ministry of Commerce of China, January 14, 2015.
[17] The official website of the Ministry of Commerce of China, March 18, 2015.

zero tariff has been realized for nearly 95% of the products between China and the ASEAN[18] community, and the trade in goods between China and the ASEAN community has reached a very high level of liberalization. According to the CAFTA upgrading agreement, both sides will further promote trade facilitation and reduce trade costs.

b. *It is still necessary to increase the degree of cross-border trade facilitation*

The negative relation between cross-border time, costs and trade volume has been empirically verified in many countries around the world.[19] As most ASEAN member countries are highly homogeneous in production and export structure, trade protectionism remains prevalent; in particular, the adoption of non-tariff barriers — for example, the extended customs clearance time for imports and exports, the technical barriers to trade (TBT), Sanitary and Phytosanitary (SPS) measures — has severely weakened the growth potential of total intra-regional trade.[20] According to the *Doing Business 2016: Measuring Regulatory Quality and Efficiency* released by the World Bank Group in June 2015, 10 ASEAN countries differ greatly in the degree of cross-border trade facilitation; the remaining seven countries, except Singapore, Malaysia and Thailand, rank in the medium and lower positions in the world. Given the special features of agricultural products, the ASEAN countries which mainly export agricultural products face higher trade costs; the resulting trade substitution effect cannot be neglected. In the meantime, ASEAN countries differ widely in the level of their transportation infrastructure, so reducing the logistics costs while simplifying, regularizing and coordinating customs procedures remains an urgent task for these countries in their task of opening up (see Table 4).

[18]The official website of the Ministry of Commerce of China, December 3, 2015.

[19]The Secretariat of the China–ASEAN Business & Investment Summit: Research Report on China–ASEAN (Cambodia, Laos, Myanmar, Vietnam) Trade Facilitation (Draft), September 2015. According to an estimation, once the customs clearance environment of an importing country improves by 1%, trade flow will increase by 0.745%; once the quality of infrastructure improves by 1%, trade flow will increase by 0.326%.

[20]Xu Ningning, *2016: the Priorities in the Planning and Construction of the ASEAN Community Deserve Attention*, China–ASEAN Business Council, January 22, 2016.

Table 4. Estimation of Costs in Cross-border Trade between China and ASEAN Countries (2015)

Country (territory)	Cross-border costs									Infrastructure	
		Exports				Imports					
		Boundary and rules		Documents and rules		Boundary and rules		Documents and rules			
	World ranking	Time	Expenses	Time	Expense	Time	Expense	Time	Expense	World ranking	Score
Brunei	121	72	340	168	90	48	395	144	50	—	—
Indonesia	105	39	254	72	170	99	383	144	160	62	4.19
Cambodia	98	45	375	132	100	4	240	132	120	101	3.19
Laos	108	3	73	216	235	5	153	216	115	98	3.23
Myanmar	140	144	432	144	140	120	367	48	115	134	2.09
Malaysia	49	20	321	10	45	24	321	10	60	24	5.51
The Philippines	95	42	456	72	53	72	580	96	50	90	3.44
Singapore	41	12	335	4	37	35	220	1	37	2	6.49
Thailand	56	51	223	11	97	50	233	4	43	44	4.62
Vietnam	99	57	309	83	139	64	268	106	183	76	3.84
China	96	26	522	21	85	92	777	66	171	39	4.73
Taiwan, China	65	17	335	31	84	47	389	41	90	12	5.87
Hong Kong, China	47	19	282	1	52	19	266	1	130	1	6.69
The Netherlands	1	0	0	1	0	0	0	1	0	3	6.30

Notes: (1) Time is determined by hour; expenses are denominated in USD; the infrastructure score is 1–7 points. (2) According to the new methodology introduced in 2015, the *Doing Business 2016* measures the cumulative time and costs relating to three procedures in the whole process of the import and export of goods (excluding tariffs). The report covers 189 economies around the world and shows that 16 Eastern European countries, including the Netherlands, enjoyed the lowest cross-border trade costs in 2015. (3) The *Global Competitiveness Report 2015–2016* covers 140 economies throughout the world and shows that Hong Kong, China ranked No. 1 in infrastructure.

Source: The World Bank Group: *Doing Business 2016: Measuring Regulatory Quality and Efficiency*; World Economic Forum: *Global Competitiveness Report 2015–2016*.

2. Construction of trade channels

a. *Significant progress was made in the construction of a network of sea–land–air transportation*

Regarding the shipping channel, the main ports in the ASEAN community, including the Cai Mep International Port in Vietnam, improved substantially in container throughput, and China–ASEAN port cooperation was carried out smoothly in 2015. Based on leveraging its geographical advantages, Guangxi actively built hub port cities along the Belt and Road and worked with 46 cities and ports in the ASEAN community to establish a city and port cooperation network.[21] The following supporting projects have been launched: a liner ship line and shipping service between the Port of Qinzhou and the main ports in the ASEAN countries; the Phase I China–ASEAN Port Logistics Information Center and maritime search and rescue center; a marine meteorological monitoring and early warning base.[22] Moreover, after the memoranda of understanding on cooperation was signed with seven major ports including Ningbo, Shanghai and Tianjin, China, Port Swettenham, the largest port in Malaysia, established sister port ties with the Port of Haikou in November, 2015. Both ports will engage in exchange and cooperation in information, technical assistance and transportation.[23]

Regarding the land transportation route, great progress was made in the construction of the Trans-Asian Railway in 2015: in August, construction began on the Yuxi–Mohan railway, on the China section of the China–Laos Railway; in December, the cornerstone laying ceremony of the Boten–Vientiane railway project was held, construction officially began on the Baoshan–Ruili and the Dali–Lincang sections of the China–Myanmar International Railway; on December 4, China and Thailand signed the intergovernmental railway cooperation framework. Furthermore, breakthroughs were made in the construction of the highway network in China's border provinces in 2015; in Guangxi, two highways connecting ASEAN

[21] Guangxi Beibu, Gulf Economic Zone Sees Accelerated Efforts in China–ASEAN Port Information Construction, www.chinanews.com, November 23, 2015.

[22] Qinzhou Pushes Forward the Construction of a China–ASEAN Port City Cooperation Network, *Guangxi Daily*, April 24, 2015.

[23] www.10s1.com, November 13, 2015.

countries and 10 highways connecting neighboring provinces were completed, the main backbone of the provincial highway network was basically completed, the goal of building the highway network connecting the surrounding provinces, the sea and border was basically achieved,[24] and the role of a large international route has been increasingly prominent.

Regarding the air transportation route, various provinces and autonomous regions in China actively developed ASEAN aviation routes to promote bilateral exchange and cooperation. In 2015, Guangxi's Nanning Airport earnestly developed air routes and flights connecting ASEAN countries, with 27 ASEAN air routes (including overtime charter flights) in service, there were 20 flight connecting points in the ASEAN community, including Bangkok and Chiengmai, passenger throughput reached 581,000 person-times, up 50.5%.[25]

b. *Cyberspace cooperation progressed smoothly*

The construction of regional information network infrastructures is an important part of efforts in strengthening international trade and building a regional common market of the Internet economy in the new period. China's online cross-border shopping consumption grew by 10 times in 2014 over 2010,[26] the volume of cross-border e-commerce transactions accounted for 14.5% of the total volume of imports and exports[27]; IT application and networking have brought opportunities for China–ASEAN trade. As various countries are at different stages of information development, there is a huge potential for China–ASEAN cyberspace cooperation. As early as 2010, China Unicom set up four international communications gateway exchanges of China in Nanning, and subsequently launched Nanning

[24] Guangxi's Highway Network Was Basically Completed, Connecting 87 Counties and ASEAN Countries, *Guangxi Daily*, December 28, 2015.

[25] Naning Airport: ASEAN Air Routes Grew by More Than 50% in 2015, People's Daily Online, January 6, 2016.

[26] The China–ASEAN Information Harbor Forum Was Inaugurated, Cross-border E-commerce Is a Hot Topic, *China Daily*, September 14, 2015.

[27] Good News and Anticipations: National Cross-border Trade E-commerce Service Is Piloted in Guangxi, Xinhuanet, September 16, 2015.

international direct access data, direct connection between Guangxi and ASEAN countries was built through land cables and a submarine cable.[28] In the 1st China–ASEAN Cyberspace Forum in September 2014, China and 10 ASEAN countries reached consensus on the initiative for joint construction of the China–ASEAN Information Harbor. In June 2015, Nanning Integrated Service Platform for Cross-border E-commerce Trade was officially launched, and the China–ASEAN (Nanning) Cross-border E-commerce Industrial Park was established.[29] With the introduction of e-commerce enterprises, such as Jingdong, Tencent, Alibaba, propelled by the construction of Guangxi's national border pilot area for comprehensive financial reform, Guangxi's ASEAN e-commerce project vigorously promoted bilateral trade. During the China–ASEAN Information Harbor Forum under the theme of "Internet + Maritime Silk Road — Cooperation · Mutual Benefit · Win–win Outcome" in September, the China National Internet Information Office and the Ministry of Posts and Telecommunications of Laos signed the *Memorandum of Understanding on Cyberspace Cooperation and Development*, and China and Indonesia reached the letter of intent on extensive cooperation (see Table 5).[30]

3. The development of trade facilitation

a. *Various countries carried out customs reforms to optimize the customs clearance environment*

In recent years, China Customs has taken a number of measures to improve the facilitation of customs clearance, including comprehensively pressing ahead with reforms in classified customs clearance, paperless customs clearance, the customs inspection mode of one-off declaration, one-off inspection and one-off release, and building the four-in-one logistics monitoring system. On December 30, 2015, the Guangxi International Trade "Single

[28] Guangxi Becomes the Core Fulcrum for the China–ASEAN Information Harbor, *China Daily*, September 13, 2015.

[29] The official website of the Ministry of Commerce of China, June 27, 2015.

[30] China–ASEAN Information Harbor Forum Was Concluded, China Put Forward the Eight-point Cooperation Initiative, www.cac.gov.cn, September 14, 2015.

Table 5. The Internet Users in China and ASEAN Countries (Per 100 People) (2000–2014)

Country (territory)	2000	2014
Brunei	9.0	68.8
Indonesia	0.9	17.1
Cambodia	0.0	9.0
Laos	0.1	14.3
Myanmar	—	2.1
Malaysia	21.4	67.5
The Philippines	2.0	39.7
Singapore	36.0	82.0
Thailand	3.7	34.9
Vietnam	0.3	48.3
China	1.8	49.3
East Asia and the Pacific	1.9	42.1
Hong Kong, China	27.8	74.6
Macao, China	13.6	69.8

Window" Customs Clearance Platform — China's first regional customs clearance public service platform towards the ASEAN community — was officially put into operation. The platform was jointly built by the departments of customs, inspection and quarantine, border defense and maritime affairs; it enables entry of all data within 1 h, and vessel declaration and release within 2 h; it is a milestone in boosting the steady growth of China–ASEAN trade.[31] ASEAN countries also enhanced the customs clearance efficiency by carrying out the single-window program and electronic customs clearance and strengthening consultation among customs offices. As early as 2008, six ASEAN countries put into use the single window. After Vietnam established the single window in 2011 and realized electronic customs declaration nationwide in 2013, Myanmar signed the ASEAN

[31] China's First Customs Clearance Public Service Platform towards the ASEAN Was Launched, www.chinanews.com, December 30, 2016.

single-window agreement during the 19th ASEAN Finance Ministers' Meeting in March 2015,[32] and initiated the national single-window mode nationwide in 2016. Laos and Cambodia piloted the one-stop customs clearance at their main ports, and the latter planned to build a national single window in 2018.

b. *The bilateral mutual recognition mechanism was carried out extensively*

The unified standard is an important tool for trade facilitation. China has actively built the bilateral mutual recognition mechanism for certification and accreditation to effectively reduce technical barriers and transaction costs while guaranteeing quality. As of late October 2015, China had acceded to 20 international certification and accreditation organizations, 13 multilateral mutual recognition agreements, and had signed 93 bilateral cooperation agreement documents with 28 countries and territories; China had cumulatively issued more than 1.40 million valid authentication certificates and accredited 7,474 conformity assessment bodies; it became a large certification and accreditation country with the largest number of certificates and the most extensive mutual recognition,[33] thus greatly promoting trade facilitation. ASEAN countries further revised domestic technical regulations under the framework of ASEAN trade facilitation so that they could be consistent with the ASEAN community's unified standards. The mutual recognition agreements (MRAs) for conformity assessment currently executed in the ASEAN community cover a number of fields, including electrical and electronic products, communications, drugs and cooked food. China and the ASEAN countries have signed multiple cooperation agreements in SPS standards, technical regulations and conformity assessment (TBT), and the regular consultation mechanism called the "China–ASEAN Ministerial Meeting on Quality Supervision, Inspection and Quarantine" has been established.[34] Meanwhile,

---

[32] The official website of the Ministry of Commerce of China, April 1, 2015.

[33] The Certification and Accreditation Administration of China: a Chinese Representative Was Elected Chairman of the International Accreditation Forum (IAF) for the First Time, November 9, 2015.

[34] The Secretariat of the China–ASEAN Business & Investment Summit: Research Report on China–ASEAN (Cambodia, Laos, Myanmar, Vietnam) Trade Facilitation (Draft), September 2015.

China Customs and Singapore Customs comprehensively carried out mutual recognition of Authorized Economic Operators (AEO) as from 2013. After Chinese enterprises became AEOs, only 0.1% of the goods exported by Chinese enterprises to Singapore were inspected by local customs, and so the customs clearance time was saved by 60%.[35]

IV. Challenges and Opportunities for China–ASEAN Trade in 2016

The year 2016 is the 25th anniversary of the establishment of dialogue relations between China and the ASEAN community. In 2016, the trend that the two sides will enhance trade cooperation will not change, and the upgrading of CAFTA and the construction of the Belt and Road will create new opportunities for bilateral trade and offer a new solution to the ailments within the trade structure and trade costs which have beset both sides for many years.

Challenges in China–ASEAN trade and countermeasures

a. *Trade costs: Increasing the level of trade facilitation through multiple channels*

Although the liberalization of China–ASEAN trade has been extended continuously as the negotiation involving the upgrading of CAFTA has been concluded, trade costs caused by such factors as cross-border logistics and the customs clearance environment remain so high that the growth of bilateral trade is restricted. Amidst the slow recovery of the world's economy, bilateral trade is highly vulnerable to negative impacts; moreover, both sides heavily rely on the markets outside the ASEAN community, including USA, Japan and Europe, and the accession of some ASEAN countries to the TPP may produce a certain substitution effect on China–ASEAN trade. In order to achieve the goal of making bilateral trade reach USD 1 trillion by 2020, China and ASEAN countries should actively respond to the Belt and Road Initiative, and while strengthening infrastructure connectivity, study measures

---

[35] The Customs Clearance Time for the Goods Exported to Singapore Was Saved by 60%, *Nanjing Daily*, December 31, 2015.

to facilitate trade, remove the barriers to trade, including engaging in multilateral cooperation on intensifying customs, inspection and quarantine, certification and accreditation, supervision efforts and conducting AEO mutual recognition; they should also push forward the entry into force and implementation of the WTO's *Trade Facilitation Agreement*, improve the customs clearance facilities and conditions at border ports, speed up the construction of the single window at border ports, enhance the customs clearance capability, lower the non-tariff barriers, jointly improve the transparency of technical trade measures, leverage multiple channels to promote China–ASEAN trade facilitation and guarantee the steady growth of trade.

b. *Trade structure: tapping new trade growth points to promote a trade balance*

In China–ASEAN trade, the traded goods are less diverse, their structure seems to be unchanged, and trade imbalance is severe: China has surplus in its trade with ASEAN countries in most cases, the surplus still tends to increase. In the new year, China and ASEAN countries should further discover new points for the growth of trade, expand trading areas, optimize the structure of trade, including innovating the trading mode, developing new forms of business, such as cross-border e-commerce, activating the regional common market of the Internet economy, establishing and improving the system for the promotion of trade in services, consolidating and broadening traditional trade, vigorously developing the modern trade in services and trade in services. In the meantime, in an effort to promote the construction of the Belt and Road, bilateral investments should be perfectly combined with trade and the development of trade should be stimulated through trade to boost a trade balance.

Chapter 14

Review of the Progress in China–ASEAN Financial Cooperation in 2015

Fan Zuojun and Wen Jianchun*

On November 23, 2015, the document of negotiation achievements concerning the upgrading of the China–ASEAN Free Trade Area (CAFTA) was officially signed. In late 2015, the ASEAN Community was officially established, continued progress was made in ASEAN financial integration, and China–ASEAN financial cooperation ushered in a new period of golden opportunities. In 2015, China–ASEAN financial cooperation maintained a good momentum of active development, the two sides gradually built an institutional framework for financial cooperation, and financial cooperation entered the "deepwater zone".[1] In particular, with constant progress in the strategic vision of the Belt and Road, finance became an important entry point for China to push forward the construction of the Belt and Road; as the Asian Infrastructure Investment Bank was officially established on

* Fan Zuojun, Executive Deputy Director, Professor, doctoral supervisor at the China–ASEAN Research Institute of Guangxi University; Wen Jianchun, Research Assistant, doctoral student at the Indonesia Institute of the China–ASEAN Research Institute of Guangxi University.

[1] China–ASEAN Financial Cooperation Enters the "Deepwater Zone", http://news.xinhuanet.com/2015-09/19/c_1116614548.htm.

December 25, and the Philippines officially signed the *Asian Infrastructure Investment Bank Agreement* in Beijing on December 31, all of the 10 ASEAN member countries became the founding members of the Asian Infrastructure Investment Bank, and China–ASEAN financial cooperation could be bolstered by an inter-country platform at a higher level. In the meantime, China's banking sector "went global" and got access to the ASEAN community, the financial institutions of ASEAN countries entered China, the financial support system for cross-border trade was built, the bulk commodity trading center was established, the two sides advanced from cross-border insurance cooperation to cross-border small and micro financial services, thus bilateral financial cooperation was expanded and deepened ceaselessly. This chapter first provides a brief review of the course of China–ASEAN financial cooperation in 2015 and then presents the corresponding comments and outlook for bilateral financial cooperation.

I. Review of the Course of China–ASEAN Financial Cooperation in 2015

With the continued growth of bilateral trade and unceasing development of cross-border real economy, financial cooperation has been deepened continuously as it is needed to support and serve the real economy. In 2015, China–ASEAN financial cooperation was earnestly promoted, the two sides gradually deepened their financial cooperation from governmental support to innovative cooperation between financial institutions and then non-governmental multilevel and diversified exchanges, with the coexistence of problems and achievements: the financial branches mutually established by both sides were on the increase, but the subsequent full services and technical support still need to be provided; platforms for bilateral currency swap agreements continued to be developed, but measures should be studied and improved to more flexibly utilize them to serve bilateral trade settlements. Therefore, with respect to China–ASEAN financial cooperation, it is necessary to explore and find the modes suited to bilateral cooperation while gradually identifying and making the relevant framework, and make innovations and integration for technical support while building the cooperation platform, so as to enhance financial cooperation between and financial development of the two sides.

1. Financial branches were mutually established

Cross-border mutual establishment of financial branches is an effective way to engage in bilateral financial cooperation. In 2015, Chinese financial institutions continued to actively set up branches on the ASEAN market, and China's banking forces led by the Bank of China continuously exploited the ASEAN financial market. As of late 2015, the top five Chinese banks set up branches in the ASEAN community as follows: the Bank of China established branches in nine countries (except Brunei) among the 10 ASEAN countries; afterwards, the Industrial and Commercial Bank of China set up operating units in eight ASEAN countries (except the Philippines and Brunei); the China Construction Bank, the Agricultural Bank of China and the Bank of Communications of China separately established branches in Singapore and Vietnam. The development of Chinese financial institutions on the ASEAN financial market since 2015 is shown in Table 1.

As shown in Table 1, it should be noted that the central bank-type institutions of ASEAN countries — including the Government of Singapore Investment Corp., the Monetary Authority of Singapore, the Bank Indonesia, the Bank of Thailand — were filed with the China Foreign Exchange Trade System and officially entered China's interbank foreign exchange market.

As China adopted the two-way opening-up financial policy, financial institutions obtained the opportunity for setting up branches in the ASEAN community. For ASEAN countries, this measure could meet the increasing needs of future economic and social development for the financial industry. The People's Bank of China announced in September 2015 that the overseas central bank-type institutions can enter China's interbank foreign exchange market in the following three ways: the People's Bank of China and the members of China's interbank foreign exchange market serve as agencies, and these overseas institutions directly become the members of China's interbank foreign exchange market.[2] This shows that the financial institutions of ASEAN countries can "interact" with Chinese financial institutions through new channels, that China has steadily opened the financial industry to the outside world and has taken effective measures to "bring in" and enhance

[2]The official website of the People's Bank of China.

Table 1. The Development of Chinese Financial Institutions on the ASEAN Financial Market Since 2015

October 2014	The Phnom Penh Branch of the Bank of China held a ceremony in Phnom Penh, the capital of Cambodia, on the 8th day, celebrating the new establishment of the Olympics Sub-branch of the Bank of China in Cambodia.
January 2015	The Bank of China was approved to serve as the RMB clearing bank for Kuala Lumpur, Malaysia.
	The Industrial and Commercial Bank of China was approved to serve as the RMB clearing bank for Bangkok, Thailand.
March 2015	The Vientiane Branch of the Bank of China was open for business.
September 2015	The Bank of China established the Rangoon Representative Office in Myanmar.
	The Rangoon Branch of the Industrial and Commercial Bank of China was officially open for business.
November 2015	The first batch of overseas central bank-type institutions, including the Government of Singapore Investment Corp., were filed with the China Foreign Exchange Trade System and officially entered China's interbank foreign exchange market.
December 2015	The Bank of China set up three branches in Thailand, including the Bangna Branch, the TaladThai Branch and the Khon Kaen Branch.
January 2016	The second batch of overseas central bank-type institutions, including the Monetary Authority of Singapore, the Bank Indonesia, the Bank of Thailand, were filed with the China Foreign Exchange Trade System and officially entered China's interbank foreign exchange market.

Source: The official websites of the People's Bank of China, the Bank of China, the CAFTA, Xinhuanet.

bilateral financial cooperation for a time, that China opened the interbank bond market to overseas central bank-type institutions for investing and that at present, overseas central bank-type institutions can directly enter China's interbank foreign exchange market. This will greatly beef up the driving forces for holding RMB and is conducive to further promoting the RMB to the ASEAN community and to the world, enabling the RMB to be further recognized by the international community and thus pushing forward the internationalization of the RMB.

2. Cooperation agreements, initiatives or memoranda were signed

The financial agreements signed between China and the ASEAN community in 2015, as shown in Table 2, mainly cover economic dialogue and cooperation, currency clearing and payment, financial exchange and cooperation and the establishment of new platforms for transaction cooperation. With the signing of cooperation agreements, initiatives or memoranda, China and the ASEAN community have engaged in all-round cooperation from the real economy to finance and from finance to the real economy. The actual needs of the real economy are identified to promote financial innovation, exploit and develop diverse financial products, financial services and financial instruments, which can also meet the financial service needs in economic development. For bilateral financial cooperation, the respective advantages of both sides can also be fully leveraged to complement each other and achieve mutually beneficial and win–win outcomes in the increasingly fierce market environment.

3. Bilateral currency swap agreements were signed

As of 2015, the People's Bank of China had signed bilateral currency swap agreements with four countries (Indonesia, Malaysia, Singapore and Thailand) among the 10 ASEAN countries. As of September 2013, the total amount under the bilateral currency swap agreements signed between the People's Bank of China and ASEAN countries had exceeded RMB 1,400 billion yuan.[3]

In April 2015, China and Malaysia renewed a currency swap agreement which maintains the RMB 180 billion yuan swap quota determined in 2012. With economic development in China and Malaysia, financial support needed to be furthered in order to promote bilateral trade and investment activities. In November 2015, the Monetary Authority of Singapore and Indonesia's central bank agreed to renew currency swap agreements, as shown in Table 3.

The signing of bilateral currency swap agreements between China and ASEAN countries can stimulate merchants of the two sides to use domestic

---

[3] *Source*: The Total Amount under the Bilateral Currency Swap Agreements Signed between the People's Bank of China and ASEAN Countries Exceeded RMB Yuan 1,400 Billion, http://news.hexun.com/2013-09-04/157729775.html.

Table 2. Relevant Financial Agreements Signed between China and the ASEAN Community

January 2015	China and Indonesia signed the *Minutes of the First Meeting on the High-level Economic Dialogue between the People's Republic of China and the Republic of Indonesia*.
April 2015	The Bank of China and the Singapore Exchange signed the Cooperative Innovation Development Agreement; the two sides vowed to jointly research and develop more RMB-denominated products, including RMB-denominated bulk commodity futures and foreign exchange derivatives, and strengthen cooperation in RMB clearing and payment.
August 2015	The Bank of China and the Cambodia–China Friendship Association signed a memorandum on international financial exchanges and cooperation projects for the Belt and Road.
November 2015	The Industrial and Commercial Bank of China and International Enterprise Singapore (IE Singapore) signed a memorandum on strategic cooperation in Singapore, with a view to jointly building the cross-border e-commerce platform for B2C and B2B transactions.
	The Bank of China and the Singapore Business Federation signed a global strategic cooperation agreement for the Belt and Road.
	The Bank of China held the opening ceremony of a global energy and bulk commodity operations center and a global bulk commodity repurchase center, and separately signed memoranda of understanding and cooperation agreements with International Enterprise Singapore and the Singapore Exchange.
	Chinese Commerce Minister Gao Hucheng and the ministers of 10 ASEAN countries signed the document of negotiation achievements concerning the upgrading of the CAFTA — the *Protocol to Amend the Framework Agreement on Comprehensive Economic Cooperation between the Association of Southeast Asian Nations and the People's Republic of China and Some Agreements under the Framework Agreement* ("the Protocol") — on behalf of the Chinese Government and the governments of 10 ASEAN countries in Kuala Lumpur, Malaysia. ASEAN countries made the following commitment to China: opening-up wider in about 70 subsectors of eight sectors including finance. The two sides made the following concrete improvement measures: expanding the areas of service opening-up, permitting the two sides to establish sole proprietorship or joint ventures, relaxing restrictions on the shareholding ratio in establishing companies, increasing the scope of business, reducing geographical restrictions.
January 2016	The Yunnan Branch of the Bank of China and the Lao Cai Branch of the Bank for Investment and Development of Vietnam successfully held the signing ceremony of cooperation on border trade settlements.

Source: The official website of the CAFTA, www.ce.cn, People's Daily Online, NetEase News.

Table 3. Bilateral Currency Swap Agreements between China and the ASEAN Community

April 2015	China and Malaysia renewed a currency swap agreement which maintains the RMB 180 billion yuan or 90 billion Malaysian Ringgit swap quota and is valid for 3 years.
November 2015	The Monetary Authority of Singapore (MAS) and the People's Bank of China agreed to renew and strengthen a bilateral currency swap agreement. Indonesia's central bank and China renewed a currency swap agreement; Indonesia's central bank expanded its currency swap agreement with China to USD 20 billion.

Source: Sina Finance, People's Daily Online, Reuters' international financial and economics articles, finance.ifeng.com, the official website of (CAFTA).

currency in trade settlements. This can ensure that both sides largely defuse the exchange rate risk caused by USD exchange and reduce transaction costs; this can make it easier to use domestic currency for financing and further promote the use of the RMB in ASEAN countries, thus pushing forward the internationalization of the RMB.

4. Financial services

As of September 2014, the RMB can be directly swapped for the currencies of seven ASEAN countries without using the USD as an intermediary. As of December 31, 2015, RMB Qualified Foreign Institutional Investor (RQFII) was piloted in three ASEAN countries, including Singapore (100 billion yuan), Malaysia (50 billion yuan) and Thailand (50 billion yuan), with a total investment quota reaching RMB 200 billion yuan. The areas for piloting RQFII were extended to the ASEAN community; that extension is an important embodiment of deepened financial cooperation between China and ASEAN countries; it greatly broadens the channels for the overseas investors in the ASEAN to allocate RMB assets; it is conducive to opening the domestic capital market to the outside world and further facilitating China–ASEAN trade and investment.[4]

In 2015, the performance of China–ASEAN financial services was better than that in previous years. As Chinese financial institutions actively exploited the ASEAN financial market, the financial institutions of ASEAN

[4]The official website of the People's Republic of China

Table 4. China–ASEAN Financial Services

January 2015	On January 16, the Bank of China successfully handled the first cross-border RMB loan transaction in the experimental border area for financial reform in Yunnan Province by offering a loan of RMB 200 million yuan to a client in Yunnan Province.
March 2015	The Philippine Business Bank and the Bank of China established a cooperative partnership with respect to RMB remittance and transfer services, the Philippine Business Bank will become one of the 11 banks providing RMB-denominated products and services, such as RMB deposits, remittance and trade settlements.
April 2015	The Industrial and Commercial Bank of China (Thai) Public Company Limited announced in Bangkok, Thailand that it had officially launched RMB clearing bank services, the commercial banks of Thailand and other relevant countries can directly handle RMB transactions through the accounts opened with the Industrial and Commercial Bank of China (Thai) Public Company Limited.
	The Tianjin Branch of the Bank of China and the Singapore Branch officially signed overseas direct loan agreements with three leading industrial enterprises within the Tianjin Port Free Trade Zone, including the China Railway Major Bridge Engineering Group Co., Ltd., the Sinohydro Harbour Co., Ltd. and the Tianjin Motor Dies Co., Ltd. According to these agreements, the Singapore Branch of the Bank of China will offer working capital loans to these three enterprises for daily production operations.
October 2015	The Bank of China (Malaysia) Berhad helped Oriental Pacific Futures successfully complete the settlement of the first RMB margin deposit. This margin deposit also became the first RMB trading margin deposit received by the Malaysia Derivatives Exchange.
November 2015	With the approval of the State Council, the areas for piloting RMB Qualified Foreign Institutional Investor (RQFII) were extended to Malaysia, with the investment quota being RMB 50 billion yuan.
	China Unionpay, the China Development Bank and the Bank of Lao PDR announced that the three sides would help Laos complete the construction of the national bank card payment system.
December 2015	With the approval of the State Council, the areas for piloting RMB Qualified Foreign Institutional Investor (RQFII) were extended to Thailand, with the investment quota being RMB 50 billion yuan.
	The Index Institute of the China National Financial Information Center and the Nanning Municipal Government released the RMB Exchange Rate Index for the ASEAN community for the first time — China ASEAN (Nanning) Monetary Index (Nanning CAMI).
January 2016	Myanmar issued the first bank credit card with the signs of Myanmar Payment Union (MPU) and China UnionPay.

Source: The official websites of the Bank of China, the Ministry of Commerce, the People's Bank of China, the CAFTA, www.yuncaijing.com, www.chinanews.com.

countries also initiated cooperation with Chinese financial institutions; for example, in March, the Philippine Business Bank and the Bank of China established a cooperative partnership with respect to RMB remittance and transfer services; in January 2016, Myanmar issued the first bank debit card with the signs of the Myanmar Payment Union (MPU) and China UnionPay. Although ASEAN countries are less active in engaging in financial cooperation with China, it is believed that bilateral cooperation will be further deepened given the developmental trend (Table 4).

5. Talks were held and initiatives were put forward

The talks and initiatives between China and ASEAN countries in 2015 are shown in Table 5. In 2015, with the strategic vision of the Belt and Road as a new starting point, besides annual regular meetings, the two sides also made new attempts and had new expectations; for example, the China–ASEAN Expo was held in ASEAN countries (Thailand, Indonesia) for the first time; the upgrading of the CAFTA was completed on schedule in November, the agreements including those on promoting financial development were signed; in January 2016, the Asian Infrastructure Investment Bank was officially launched, while the Bank can serve as the bond in the financial field and also help realize the vision of the ASEAN Community; these activities suggested that bilateral cooperation and development went beyond quantitative accumulation and underwent qualitative transformation.

II. Review of China–ASEAN Financial Cooperation

Finance has become an important economic and diplomatic means for China to seek a diplomatic status in the world, participate in global governance and assume the responsibilities of a great power. Like connection with the Chinese Dream and the World Dream, China should ensure that other countries, especially the surrounding countries, enjoy the dividends and benefits from China's development, achieve self-development in the process of China's development, while finance is an important node. In 2015, in general, China–ASEAN financial cooperation went smoothly and showed a good momentum of development. The following part discusses the role of and constraints on China–ASEAN financial cooperation.

Table 5. Talks and Initiatives between China and the ASEAN

April 2015	The China–ASEAN Expo was inaugurated in Bangkok, Thailand; it was held in an ASEAN country for the first time in its 11 times.
	China and Indonesia issued a joint press communiqué. The heads of the two countries agreed to encourage more effective execution of the 3-year bilateral currency swap agreement signed between the two sides in March 2009 and renewed in October 2013. The heads of both countries agreed to more rapidly use domestic currency to promote bilateral trade and investment. The heads of both countries affirmed the significance of the bilateral currency swap agreement in safeguarding the stability of the financial market by guaranteeing short-term liquidity.
	A new round of consultation involving the *Agreement between China and Vietnam on Cooperative Protection and Development of the Detian* (*Ban Gioc*) *Waterfall Tourism Resources* and the *Agreement between China and Vietnam on Navigation in the Free Navigation Area at the Estuary of the Beilun River* ("two agreements") was held in Hanoi, Vietnam.
May 2015	The 2015 China–ASEAN Expo Indonesia Exhibition was held in Jakarta, Indonesia.
	The China–ASEAN (Maritime Silk Road) Business Forum was held in Beijing.
June 2015	China and Southeast Asia issued the non-governmental cooperation initiative: supporting the joint construction of the Belt and Road.
	The 21st China–ASEAN Senior Officials' Consultation was held in Beijing.
September 2015	The 8th China–ASEAN Think Tank Strategic Dialogue Forum, the 12th China–ASEAN Expo, the China–ASEAN Business & Investment Summit were held in Nanning, Guangxi.
	The China–ASEAN Summit on Financial Cooperation & Development was held in Nanning.
November 2015	The upgrading of the CAFTA was carried out on schedule.
January 2016	The opening ceremony of the Asian Infrastructure Investment Bank (AIIB) was held in Beijing; ASEAN member countries (all of them are the founding members of the Asian Infrastructure Investment Bank) will become the largest beneficiaries because they have many projects which await investments, especially the projects proposed in the *Master Plan on ASEAN Connectivity*.

Source: The official websites of the CAFTA, *China Daily*.

1. Mutual promotion and common development in China–ASEAN financial cooperation

China–ASEAN financial cooperation has produced multidimensional promotional effects. It promotes China's two-way financial opening-up; it boosts ASEAN financial integration; it is conducive to safeguarding regional financial stability in the East Asian region.

a. *Promoting China's two-way financial opening-up*

The Recommendations to the 13th Five-Year Plan identify the expansion of two-way financial opening-up as the direction for development. From China's perspective, China–ASEAN financial cooperation contributes to realizing China's two-way financial opening-up. The financial cooperation with ASEAN countries is helpful for facilitating an orderly flow of China's domestic factors and international factors so that financial resources are allocated efficiently and the financial market is integrated deeply. As China has engaged in tangible interactions with the institutions, enterprises and markets of ASEAN countries, there are increasing needs for China's financial services in terms of motive force or need; given the upgrading of the CAFTA and the strategic background of the Belt and Road, besides continued deepening of trade contacts, financial cooperation also promotes China's two-way financial opening-up. While sharing advanced financial technologies, instruments and services with ASEAN countries, Chinese financial institutions can also get access to more extensive financial market platforms for achieving self-development. ASEAN countries meet the needs of economic and trade development for financial services through cooperation, they also share more financial cooperative opportunities to deliver mutually beneficial and win–win outcomes in the financial field.

b. *Boosting ASEAN financial integration*

Financial integration is greatly beneficial to the development of the ASEAN economy. In ASEAN countries, especially the countries at the primary stage of development, the financial system is mostly dominated by the banking sector. However, in the relatively developed countries, such as Singapore and

Malaysia, the insurance and fund sectors, in addition to the banking sector, exert an increasing amount of influence on the financial system. With deepening financial cooperation between China and the ASEAN community, measures are being taken to stimulate the development and product innovation in the financial sector of ASEAN countries, enhance the competitiveness and efficiency of the financial institutions in ASEAN countries, so as to boost economic growth, increase employment and promote financial inclusion. The deepening financial cooperation between China and the ASEAN community is also conducive to making the market bigger, deeper and more fluid, thus greatly reducing capital cost, optimizing resource allocation and effectively spreading risks; with regard to financing, it can also extend the financing term, lower transaction costs and improve the efficiency of settlement. Furthermore, it can also impose more constraints on the government, banking institutions and non-banking institutions, enhance the capability of the ASEAN economy for withstanding the impact from the economic crisis and the financial crisis.

c. *Safeguarding financial stability in East Asia*

China–ASEAN financial cooperation plays a very important role in the financial stability and economic integration in East Asia. As the two sides engage in financial cooperation, both of them can, under the principle of voluntariness, equality and mutual benefit, intensify communication and exchange among financial institutions, reinforce the coordination in macroeconomic policies, which is conducive to orderly and coordinated development of the financial system in East Asia and, to a certain extent, safeguards the financial stability in East Asia.

2. Constraints on China–ASEAN financial cooperation

China–ASEAN financial cooperation is developing positively, but there is still a large room for improvement. The following section presents brief discussions about the constraints on bilateral financial cooperation.

1. The development of the financial market is unbalanced and financial infrastructure is underdeveloped in ASEAN countries. Chinese financial

institutions have energetically marched toward the ASEAN financial market, but many areas have failed to effectively utilize the advanced financial instruments and technologies due to the underdevelopment of financial infrastructures, so the efficiency of financial operations is still low.

2. The operational systems for financial cooperation have not yet been better improved. China–ASEAN financial cooperation has entered the "deepwater zone", but its relevant operational systems still need to be further developed and enhanced, so that systems are available for governing China–ASEAN financial cooperation, and the cooperation in various respects can become more regularized and in-depth.
3. There are restrictions from political factors. Bilateral financial cooperation can bring about considerable economic benefits; however, the financial cooperation between ASEAN countries and China will be inevitably affected by geopolitical and other factors.

III. Suggestions for Enhancing China–ASEAN Financial Cooperation

Against the general background of the plan for the regional development strategy for the Belt and Road, as the core of the modern economy, finance is the key to connecting China with the countries along the Belt and Road to share opportunities and achieve common development. However, as the advocate of the Belt and Road, China must have a financial support system commensurate with its international status and the implementation of the Belt and Road Initiative in the process of realizing the Belt and Road Initiative; only in this way can the measures in the Belt and Road Initiative be effectively carried out. China–ASEAN financial cooperation is the crucial and important strategic step for establishing a China–ASEAN Community of Common Destiny, upgrading the free trade area and building the 21st Century Maritime Silk Road; this cooperation can further help deepen and broaden the financial cooperation between China and ASEAN countries, so benign development of China–ASEAN relations can be ultimately realized. With a review of China–ASEAN financial cooperation in 2015, looking into the increasing opportunities for cooperation in the future, the author offers the following suggestions for deepening that cooperation.

1. The existing platforms should be fully utilized to expand the scope of financial cooperation. In 2015, the upgraded CAFTA, the 21st Century Maritime Silk Road and the Asian Infrastructure Investment Bank were launched in an all-round way. They are new developmental platforms which urgently need to be effectively used. The conveniences and opportunities provided by these platforms can be exploited to obtain more new forms of cooperation and opportunities, and play should be given to the positive effect from a structured combination of policy-oriented finance, development-oriented finance, commercial finance and informal finance, with a view to increasing the scope and level of bilateral financial cooperation.
2. Importance should be attached to cooperation and technical support in infrastructures. In some ASEAN countries, financial infrastructure is at the primary stage, thus strengthening bilateral financial cooperation in infrastructure, intensifying financial technical assistance and support are very crucial to fostering the financial development of ASEAN countries and improving their capability to offer financial services. Laying a good foundation for financial infrastructure can generate more business opportunities. At present, financial institutions mutually establish branches; subsequently, actions can be taken to assist ASEAN countries in building a securities exchange and performing such financial services as insurance, so there is still a very large space for financial infrastructure cooperation; this will play an active role in spurring ASEAN's development and China–ASEAN financial integration.
3. The People's Bank of China should set up representative offices in ASEAN countries to further strengthen the mechanism of high-level dialogue and exchange with the central banks of ASEAN countries and enhance the coordination of international financial supervision, and the top-level design should be carried out to make top-down institutional innovations and build a market-oriented, regional and international financial cooperation system suited to bilateral cooperation development and operations. The mechanism for the management of bilateral currency cooperation should be established, consensuses should be reached on the management of cross-border currency swaps, allocation and transportation and storage. Moreover, a support system for top-down financial innovation should be provided, and the advantages and high

flexibility of micro players should be leveraged to enable two-way interaction between lower and upper levels and promote two-way financial cooperation.

4. China and the ASEAN countries should also enhance regional cooperation in stock and bond markets, share experiences, further communicate with each other to boost their capacity for the building of stock and bond markets. Besides stock and bond markets, fund and futures markets can also be included in cooperation and exchange in due time, with participation of relevant regulators, and the market standards should be regularized and unified to push forward cross-border transactions. Furthermore, measures should also be adopted to stimulate financial institutions to set up branches in other countries and carry forward cross-border RMB loans, so as to ensure that various countries open their financial markets to each other within the region.
5. A China–ASEAN RMB-denominated currency settlement system should be established. Such a system can greatly reduce transaction costs in bilateral trade and help build a China–ASEAN common financial market. China can support Singapore to establish an RMB offshore market, enable more bulk commodities to be denominated in RMB in the ASEAN community, improve the mechanism for issuing RMB to and withdrawing RMB from the ASEAN community, and make RMB gradually become the leading currency in the ASEAN group.
6. China can give priority to opening the financial field to the ASEAN community in due time. Specifically, China can first engage in exchange rate cooperation with ASEAN countries, permit the financial institutions with a certain qualification in ASEAN countries to enter China's interbank lending market and interbank market, expand the pilot areas and quotas of RMB Qualified Foreign Institutional Investor (RQFII) in ASEAN countries, and lower the threshold for permitting financial institutions to enter China.

Looking into the future, China–ASEAN financial cooperation will certainly involve China–ASEAN exchange rate cooperation and the opening-up of the open financial support system. As mentioned by Chinese Premier Li Keqiang, China and ASEAN countries should actively explore and draw up the roadmap for the future development of regional financial cooperation to the Asian currency stabilization system, the Asian credit system and the Asian investment and financing cooperative system. These measures are part of the strategic plan for the future financial cooperation between China and the ASEAN community. In the meantime, the strategy of China–ASEAN financial cooperation should cover not only the upgrading of the CAFTA, the construction of pilot areas of the 21st Century Maritime Silk Road, but also the construction of the China–ASEAN Community with a Common Destiny and financial support under the China–ASEAN "2+7" cooperation framework. In order to achieve the above goals and build a closer China–ASEAN Community with a Common Destiny, the strategy of future China–ASEAN financial cooperation must be re-planned, rearranged and readjusted to practically guide the process of China–ASEAN financial cooperation and provide the route and steps for financial cooperation. In general, on the one hand, it can be promoted gradually in terms of time; on the other hand, it can proceed from internal development to external development. Specifically, this can be realized by carrying out institution building, reshaping the organizational system, resource allocation and the market system, the product innovation and financial service system and the financial security and financial supervision system.

As the ASEAN community is an important region in China's diplomacy with its neighboring countries and the pilot region for the construction of the 21st Century Maritime Silk Road, if China's external financial strategy is changed, ASEAN's strategy of financial cooperation with China should also be adjusted accordingly. The adjustment of that strategy should be made by utilizing China's great financial strength and a mix of policy-oriented finance, development-oriented finance, commercial finance and private capital for ASEAN financial cooperation to deepen China–ASEAN cooperation. Commercial finance is the support for China–ASEAN financial cooperation and a key part of the strategy of China–ASEAN financial cooperation; policy-oriented finance provides a guarantee for China–ASEAN financial cooperation and supplements commercial finance, while development-oriented finance can enable a seamless connection in China–ASEAN financial cooperation; essentially, development-oriented finance can be deemed to upgrade a combination of commercial finance and policy-oriented finance; private capital can further enrich China–ASEAN financial cooperation.

Overall, from the perspectives of China–ASEAN financial cooperation and financial cooperation platforms built thanks to deepened exchanges as well as prevention of financial crisis, financial cooperation provides a vigorous guarantee for the development of bilateral economic and trade relations. As the two sides gradually move towards higher-level cooperation, obstacles and fetters are inevitable; however, with joint efforts from China and the ASEAN countries, a path towards development which can address the interests of both sides can be ultimately found.

Chapter 15

Overview of China–ASEAN Environmental Cooperation under the Belt and Road Initiative (2015)

Xiong Jianhua and Wang Yinghui*

I. The Background of China–ASEAN Environmental Cooperation

During visits to the Central Asian and Southeast Asian countries in September and October 2013, Chinese President Xi Jinping put forward the major initiatives of jointly building the Silk Road Economic Belt and the 21st Century Maritime Silk Road (collectively, the "Belt and Road Initiative"). During the 2013 China–ASEAN Expo, Chinese Premier Li Keqiang vowed to build the Maritime Silk Road for the ASEAN community and foster the strategic fulcrum for stimulating the development of the hinterland. The Belt and Road Initiative emphasizes the construction of a community of shared interests for mutually beneficial and win–win development and a community with

* Xiong Jianhua, Deputy Director, Associate Professor, Master Supervisor at the Institute of Ecology, the China–ASEAN Research Institute of Guangxi University. Wang Yinghui, Director, Professor, doctoral supervisor at the Institute of Ecology, the China–ASEAN Research Institute of Guangxi University.

a common destiny for common prosperity and development; it has drawn wide attention from the international community. In March 2015, China released the document *Vision and Actions on Jointly Building the Silk Road Economic Belt and the 21st Century Maritime Silk Road*,[1] further stressing that it is necessary to highlight the philosophy of ecological civilization in investment and trade, strengthen the cooperation on an ecological environment, biodiversity and climate change, jointly build a green Silk Road. This provides new opportunities for broadening and deepening China–ASEAN environmental cooperation.

II. Content and Effects of China–ASEAN Environmental Cooperation in 2015

The year 2015 was crucial for global sustainable development. In the Third International Conference on Financing for Development held in Addis Ababa in July 193 countries reached an action agenda. During the UN Development Summit held in September, the *2030 Agenda for Sustainable Development* was adopted. At the Climate Conference in Paris in December, various countries expected to reach a new global climate agreement and made efforts at controlling global temperature rise within 2°C by 2050. These three high-level international conferences presented new routes to achieving human sustainable development in the future.

In 2015, the Chinese Government actively pushed forward the construction of the Belt and Road. The year 2015 was the Year of China–ASEAN Maritime Cooperation; both sides energetically carried out the *Strategy of China–ASEAN Environmental Cooperation* (*2009–2015*) and the *Action Plan for China–ASEAN Environmental Cooperation* (*2014–2015*),[2] as well as a series of fruitful cooperation activities; the two sides built platforms for high-level

---

[1] *Vision and Actions on Jointly Building the Silk Road Economic Belt and the 21st Century Maritime Silk Road.*

[2] The *Strategy of China–ASEAN Environmental Cooperation* (*2009–2015*) identifies six cooperation priorities: public awareness and environmental education; environmentally sound technology, environmental labeling and clean production; biodiversity conservation cooperation; environmental management capacity building; environmental product and service cooperation; global environmental issues.

exchanges and reciprocal visits, signed a number of cooperation memoranda, and they conducted joint research; the two sides pragmatically pushed forward the construction of the demonstration base for China–ASEAN environmental protection technology and industrial cooperation exchanges, China and ASEAN countries engaged in multi-level and multi-faceted environmental protection cooperation, exchange and training. China–ASEAN environmental cooperation has delivered fruitful outcomes and it has effectively boosted regional sustainable development. At present, both sides are developing the *Strategy of China–ASEAN Environmental Protection Cooperation (2016–2020)*. China–ASEAN environmental cooperation has developed well and has become the model for regional environmental cooperation and South–South environmental cooperation. The main achievements in China–ASEAN environmental cooperation are summarized as follows.

1. Platforms were built, high-level exchanges and meetings were held

a. *The 14th ASEAN–China, Japan and South Korea Environment Ministers' Meeting was held*

On October 29, 2015, the 14th ASEAN–China, Japan and South Korea Environment Ministers' Meeting was held in Hanoi, the capital of Vietnam. Wan Bentai, the special representative of the Chinese Environmental Protection Minister Chen Jining, the chief engineer of the Ministry of Environmental Protection, led a delegation to the meeting and introduced the new progress in China's environmental protection to the representatives of various countries. The meeting is an important part of the ASEAN–China, Japan and South Korea leaders' meeting mechanism and a high-level platform for regional environmental cooperation. The Ministry of Environmental Protection had formed groups to attend the meeting in the past.

b. *The 4th Greater Mekong Sub-region Environment Ministers' Meeting was held*

On January 29, 2015, the 4th Greater Mekong Sub-region Environment Ministers' Meeting was held in Naypyidaw, Myanmar. Under the theme of

"Increasing Natural Capital Investments in the Sub-region", the meeting discussed and adopted the *Joint Statement of the 4th Greater Mekong Sub-region Environment Ministers' Meeting*. The joint statement stressed the importance of natural resources for the inclusive and sustainable development of the Greater Mekong Sub-region; it showed the consensus on jointly promoting and increasing the natural resource investments in the Greater Mekong Sub-region; it requires the Working Group for the Environment of the Greater Mekong Sub-region to, with the support of the Asian Development Bank, better execute the core environmental projects and provide effective support for the plan for the implementation of the regional investment framework. The meeting is the highest decision-making mechanism for sub-regional environmental cooperation; it is held every 3 years. China held the 1st Greater Mekong Sub-region Environment Ministers' Meeting in Shanghai in 2005.

c. *The Lancang–Mekong cooperation mechanism was officially established in the 1st Lancang–Mekong Cooperation Foreign Ministers' Meeting*

On November 12, 2015, the 1st Lancang–Mekong Cooperation Foreign Ministers' Meeting was held in Jinghong, Yunnan Province. Foreign ministers of China, Thailand, Cambodia, Laos, Myanmar and Vietnam attended the meeting. Under the theme of "Sharing the Same River and a Common Destiny", participants conducted in-depth discussions on further strengthening the cooperation among the countries relating to Lancang and Mekong and reached an extensive consensus, they agreed to officially initiate the process of Lancang–Mekong cooperation and announced the official establishment of the Lancang–Mekong cooperation mechanism. China held that the Lancang–Mekong cooperation mechanism should be used to engage in cooperation in three key areas, including political security, economic and sustainable development, social humanity, and to build a complete connection with the three pillars in the construction of the ASEAN Community. Relevant work should be gradually pushed forward in the order of increasing difficulties; in light of the reality and developmental needs of the sub-region at the present stage, priority should be given to connectivity, production capacity cooperation, cross-border economic cooperation, water resource cooperation, agricultural and poverty reduction cooperation; important support should be provided at the policy, financial and intellectual levels, the project-led actions should be taken and emphasis should be placed on implementation. The three important cooperation fields put forward by China tally with the three pillars in the construction of the ASEAN Community; they constitute the core of Lancang–Mekong cooperation development; various parties reached cooperation consensuses. The meeting deliberated and adopted the conceptual documents concerning Lancang–Mekong cooperation; participants agreed to study and as early as possible execute a number of "early harvest" projects, the Lancang–Mekong cooperation mechanism was officially established, and a joint press communiqué was issued.

d. *The 10th semiannual meeting of the Working Group for the Environment (WGE) of the Greater Mekong Sub-region (GMS) and relevant meetings were held*

During the two days of November 11–12, 2015, the 10th semiannual meeting of the Working Group for the Environment of the Greater Mekong Sub-region and relevant meetings were held in Chiengmai, Thailand. The meeting was divided into the 10th semiannual meeting of the Working Group for the Environment of the Greater Mekong Sub-region and the meetings of the Technical Working Group. The 10th semiannual meeting focused on discussing the execution of core environmental projects (CEPs), the rectification after mid-term project evaluation, the work plan for 2016, CEP and EOC mechanism design and transformation, fund demand and financing options, main achievements in the 20th GMS ministerial meeting, the next arrangements for CEP participation in the GMS regional investment framework (RIF); a meeting resolution was completed in the closing meeting. The meetings of the Technical Working Group focused on in-depth discussions about the development of CEP and EOC mechanisms.

e. *The 2015 China–ASEAN Environmental Cooperation Forum was held*

During the three days of September 18–21, 2015, under the theme of "Jointly Building the 21st Century Maritime Silk Road—Drawing a Beautiful Blueprint for Maritime Cooperation", the 12th China–ASEAN Expo and the Business & Investment Summit were held in Nanning, Guangxi. In order to carry out the initiative of strengthening China–ASEAN environmental cooperation as put forward by state leaders, the Ministry of Environmental Protection, the People's Government of the Guangxi Zhuang Autonomous Region and the ASEAN Secretariat co-hosted the 2015 China–ASEAN Environmental Cooperation Forum during the China–ASEAN Expo; the forum covered a series of activities, including the Environmental Sustainable Development Dialogue and Seminar, the Environmental Protection Industry Cooperation and Development Exchange Roundtable Conference, the Environmental Protection Industry and Technology Exhibition. The Environmental Sustainable Development Dialogue and Seminar was designed to carry out policy dialogues and learning and exchange activities with ASEAN countries to publicize China's philosophies of the construction of an ecological civilization and environmental protection, make participants understand China and the ASEAN countries' environmental policies, enhance the ecological environmental protection cooperation and exchange under the framework of the Belt and Road Initiative and the capability for regional environmental sustainable development; under the theme of "Boosting China–ASEAN Environmental Protection Cooperation — Government and Social Capital Cooperation Mode (PPP)", the China–ASEAN Environmental Protection Industry Cooperation and Development Exchange Roundtable Conference was aimed at publicizing the achievements in China–ASEAN environmental protection cooperation, enhancing the influence of China's environmental protection products and technologies in ASEAN countries, showcasing the development of China's environmental protection industry, building the technical exchange and cooperation platform for the environmental protection industry and promoting China–ASEAN pragmatic cooperation in the field of environmental protection.

China's Environmental Protection Industry and Technology Exhibition was held under the theme of "Promoting Industrial Cooperation, Jointly Seeking Green Business Opportunities for the Belt and Road". The platform of the China–ASEAN Expo was relied upon to display the latest environmental protection technologies and products from China, introduce China's environmental protection industry parks and stimulate Chinese enterprises to "go global". The China–ASEAN Environmental Cooperation Forum is an important platform for China and ASEAN countries to engage in dialogue, promote exchanges and pragmatic cooperation in the environmental field. It had been held four times since its launch in 2011.

f. *The Theme Forum on the Green Belt and Road was held*

On November 11, 2015, the 2015 Annual Conference of the China Council for International Cooperation on the Environment and Development — Theme Forum on the Green Belt and Road was held in Beijing. The forum discussed how to realize the great vision of the Belt and Road and build a green Belt and Road; the participating domestic and foreign members and experts of the China Council for International Cooperation on the Environment and Development witnessed wonderful keynote speeches and conducted heated discussions. The objective of building the Belt and Road, as put forward in the forum, is to pursue common, mutually beneficial and win–win development together with the countries along the Belt and Road, share China's developmental experience and achievements, and turn China's achievements into the world's opportunities. The construction of a green Belt and Road is an important part of efforts in promoting green development of the countries along the Belt and Road and sustainable regional development. The forum focused on policy coordination, facilities connectivity, unimpeded trade, financial integration and people-to-people bonds; the forum gave prominence to the construction of an ecological civilization and the joint construction of a green Belt and Road.

2. Memoranda of cooperation were signed

a. *The Memorandum of Understanding between China and Cambodia on Cooperation Regarding Environmental Protection was signed*

On June 11, 2015, Chinese Deputy Minister of Environmental Protection Li Ganjie met with the State Secretary of the Ministry of Environment of Cambodia in Beijing. The two sides exchanged views on the future environmental cooperation between China and Cambodia, and signed the *Memorandum of Understanding between China and Cambodia on Cooperation*

Regarding Environmental Protection. The Belt and Road Initiative put forward by the Chinese Government received active response from the countries along the Belt and Road, especially Cambodia. Li Ganjie presented the following three-point initiative on the future environmental cooperation between China and Cambodia: first, actively implementing the memorandum, endeavoring to turn China–Cambodia environmental cooperation into the model of South–South environmental cooperation; second, energetically exploring and building China–Cambodia exchange platforms and demonstration bases for environmental protection technologies and industries to promote China–Cambodia cooperation in the environmental protection industry; third, exploring and promoting the China–Cambodia Green Angel Program, developing it into the China–Cambodia flagship program in the fields of building up the capacity for environmental protection and carrying out environmental education.

b. *The Memorandum of Cooperation between the United Nations Environment Program and the China–ASEAN Environmental Cooperation Center was signed*

On June 3, 2015, Chinese Deputy Minister of Environmental Protection Li Ganjie met with Ibrahim Thiaw, Deputy Executive Director of the United Nations Environment Program. After the meeting, Deputy Executive Director Ibrahim Thiaw and the Director of the China–ASEAN Environmental Cooperation Center Guo Jing signed the *Memorandum of Cooperation between the United Nations Environment Program and the China–ASEAN Environmental Cooperation Center*. According to the memorandum, the two sides will cooperate on biodiversity protection and ecological system management, environmental law, sustainable development and green economic policy and financing, resource efficiency and sustainable production and consumption, knowledge sharing and other fields.

c. *Guangxi and the environmental protection department of Cao Bằng Province, Vietnam signed a memorandum of cooperation*

On May 12, 2015, the Department of Environmental Protection of the Guangxi Zhuang Autonomous Region and the Department of Natural

Resources and Environment of Cao Bằng Province, Vietnam, signed the *Memorandum of Cooperation between the Department of Environmental Protection of the Guangxi Zhuang Autonomous Region, China and the Department of Natural Resources and Environment of Cao Bằng Province, Vietnam, on Biodiversity Protection* in Cao Bằng City, Cao Bằng Province, Vietnam. As one of the important subsequent actions for carrying out the achievements of the 4th Greater Mekong Sub-region Environment Ministers' Meeting, it is the first memorandum of understanding on cross-border cooperation in seven cross-border biological landscape hot spots in the Greater Mekong Sub-region. Meanwhile, as a beneficial attempt for working with the surrounding countries to explore joint construction of the green Belt and Road, it is also the first memorandum of bilateral cooperation on environmental protection successfully signed between China and the provincial-level environmental protection department of a Southeast Asian country. The memorandum of understanding confirms that the two sides will strengthen their cooperation in six fields including mechanism cooperation, monitoring and evaluation, planning management and capacity building. The two sides will also put into practice their cooperation in the above fields through policy dialogues, personnel exchanges and joint research. In order to promote further cooperation between the environmental protection departments of the two sides, the Department of Environmental Protection of Guangxi offered the following proposals: First, further giving play to Guangxi's locational advantage, engaging in inter-provincial cooperation to boost the cooperation between countries; second, further enabling multi-level, wide-ranging cooperation by means of implementing the memorandum of understanding; third, jointly building a green Belt and Road, fostering a community of regional environmental cooperation; fourth, taking the China–ASEAN Environmental Cooperation Forum as a platform for initiating a new mode of regional environmental cooperation.

d. *Yunnan Province and a province of Laos signed a memorandum of cooperation*

In November 2015, the Department of Environmental Protection of Yunnan Province and the Department of Natural Resources and Environment of Luang Prabang Province, Lao People's Democratic Republic, signed the *Memorandum of Cooperation in Environmental Protection* in Kunming. Both sides agreed to give priority to cooperating on urban environmental management, environmental planning and environmental scientific research, environmental publicity and education, environmental management training and capacity building as well as other fields upon which both sides agreed, with a view to jointly promoting sustainable green regional development. Under the memorandum of cooperation, the two sides will cooperate by exchanging relevant environmental information and data, enabling personnel exchanges and reciprocal visits, holding seminars and professional training, jointly carrying out environmental science research and pilot demonstration programs.

3. China carried out multi-level and multi-faceted environmental protection cooperation, exchanges and training with ASEAN countries

a. *The first China–Singapore Environmental Cooperation Policy Dialogue was held in Beijing*

On December 2, 2015, the first China–Singapore Environmental Cooperation Policy Dialogue was held in Beijing. It is the first department-chief-level environmental policy dialogue aimed at implementing the memorandum of understanding on inter-departmental environmental cooperation renewed by China and Singapore in 2014. The dialogue focused on the priorities and difficulties in China's current environmental protection in light of Singapore's advantageous fields; the dialogue covered such topics as balance between environmental protection and economic development, enforcement and observance of environmental laws, green finance, urban environmental management; during the dialogue, the two sides exchanged views on their cooperation in the fields in which the two sides were interested, including the management of hazardous wastes, green supply chain cooperation, environmental protection technologies and industry. After the dialogue, the working groups of the two sides held consultations on future cooperation projects, and a Singaporean delegation visited the Satellite Application Center of the Ministry of Environmental Protection.

b. *The Chinese delegation attended the 17th Intergovernmental Conference on the Acid Deposition Monitoring Network in East Asia (EANET)*

During two days of November 24–25, 2015, the 17th Intergovernmental Conference (IG17) on the Acid Deposition Monitoring Network in East Asia was held in Bangkok, Thailand. The Chinese delegation, made up of the Monitoring Department, the Department of International Affairs of the Ministry of Environmental Protection of China, the China National Environmental Monitoring Centre, the Chinese Research Academy of Environmental Sciences and the China–ASEAN (Shanghai Cooperation Organization) Environmental Cooperation Center, attended the conference. The conference focused on deliberating the 2015 Financial Report and Work Report of the Network Center and the Secretariat, the framework document for the Secretariat's institutional transformation arrangements, the measures for saving network expenditures, the next medium-term plan (2016–2020) and the revision of the guide rules for administrative and financial management of the Secretariat and the Network Center.

c. *The Seminar on China–Thailand Cooperation in Environmental Protection Technology was held*

On November 26, 2015, the Seminar on China–Thailand Cooperation in Environmental Protection Technology, jointly organized by the China–ASEAN Environmental Cooperation Center and the Department of Pollution Prevention of the Ministry of Resources and Environment of Thailand, was held in Bangkok, Thailand. The representatives of the management committees of and enterprises from the China–ASEAN Environmental Protection Technology and Industry Cooperation Demonstration Base (Yixing) and the China Yixing Environmental Protection Science & Technology Industrial Park, the Department of International Affairs of the Ministry of Environment of Thailand, and industrial associations attended the seminar. The seminar was designed to serve the exchanges in environmental protection industry and technology for the Belt and Road, carry out the framework of China–ASEAN cooperation in environmental protection technology and industry, push forward the matchmaking and exchanges of environmental protection technology and industry between China and Thailand, support the overseas development of the China–ASEAN Environmental Protection Technology and Industry Cooperation Demonstration Base. The representatives present at the seminar introduced the current situation of the environmental protection industry of the two sides, conducted heated discussions on the topics of common concern such as environmental protection technology and environmental standards. The Thai representatives inquired about the particulars of the Belt and Road Initiative put forward by China and showed strong interest in it. After the seminar, the Chinese representatives were invited to visit the Monitoring Center under the Department of Pollution Prevention of Thailand to learn about the technologies and equipment mainly adopted by Thailand at present for the monitoring of air, water and soil pollution, and Chinese representatives exchanged views with working personnel with respect to environmental monitoring data indicators.

d. *The Seminar on China–Indonesia Cooperation in Environmental Protection Technology was successfully held*

On November 23, 2015, the Seminar on China–Indonesia Cooperation in Environmental Protection Technology, jointly organized by the China–ASEAN Environmental Cooperation Center and the Ministry of Environment and Forestry of Indonesia, was held in Jakarta, Indonesia. The seminar was aimed at serving the exchanges in environmental protection industry and technology for the Belt and Road, carrying out the framework of China–ASEAN cooperation in environmental protection technology and industry, promoting technology matchmaking and transfer between China and Indonesia, supporting the development of the China–ASEAN Environmental Protection Technology and Industry Cooperation Demonstration Base. The seminar was co-chaired by China and Indonesia. The officials from Indonesia's departments of industry, environment and forestry and the representatives of the China–ASEAN Environmental Protection Technology and Industry Cooperation Demonstration Base (Yixing) and the China Yixing Environmental Protection Science & Technology Industrial Park attended the seminar and exchanged views on the current situation of the environmental protection industry in Indonesia and its relevant international cooperation.

e. *The Seminar on Cooperation under the China–ASEAN Partnership for Eco-friendly Urban Development was held*

During the two days of November 17–18, 2015, the Seminar on Cooperation under the China–ASEAN Partnership for Eco-friendly Urban Development, jointly organized by the China–ASEAN Environmental Cooperation Center and the ASEAN Biodiversity Center, was held in Beijing. The representatives present at the seminar conducted exchanges and discussions on the current situation and trends of regional urbanization and sustainable development, the opportunities and challenges in urban biodiversity and ecological protection, foreign policies, experiences, measures and technologies in urban ecological development; they discussed how to give scope to the constructive role of enterprises and social organizations in the development of ecological cities. The seminar adopted the *Recommendations on the Establishment of the China–ASEAN Eco-friendly City Partnership*, offering concrete cooperation recommendations on building the China–ASEAN Ecological City Alliance, strengthening the capacity building of the urban environmental departments of China and ASEAN countries, sharing the experience in the development and management of ecological cities, encouraging exchange, cooperation and joint research on laws and regulations, the system of standards, the incentive and financial mechanism and the best practice involving ecological cities, enhancing the enterprises' participation in developing the eco-friendly cities, advocating sustainable production and consumption modes, spreading the urban ecological environmental protection technologies and reinforcing the cooperation between enterprises and social organizations.

f. *The China–ASEAN Environmental Cooperation Personnel Exchange Activity was successfully held*

During the period June 25–27, 2015, 11 representatives from the ASEAN Biodiversity Center and Cambodia, Laos, Malaysia, Myanmar, Thailand, Singapore and other ASEAN countries visited China to carry out exchanges, learning activities and surveys involving China–ASEAN cooperation on biodiversity and ecological protection. During the activities, ASEAN's representatives and the experts from the Biodiversity Committee of the Chinese Academy of Sciences conducted special discussions on China–ASEAN cooperation on biodiversity data and information; they attended the Exchange Meeting on China–ASEAN Biodiversity Protection Cooperation, and the Theme Forum "Biodiversity and Green Development" held in Guiyang during the 2015 Guiyang Eco Forum Global Annual Conference. The activity was part of the "China–ASEAN Biodiversity and Ecological Protection Cooperation Program (Phase II)" jointly developed by the ASEAN Center and the ASEAN Biodiversity Center; the activity was designed to exchange experiences and capacity building to help ASEAN countries improve their awareness of and capability for biodiversity and ecological protection, and build a regional cooperation network for biodiversity and ecological protection.

g. *The Seminar on Building up the Capacity of China–Cambodia Industrial Pollution Prevention and Control was held*

On the morning of June 11, 2015, the Seminar on Building up the Capacity of China–Cambodia Industrial Pollution Prevention and Control, organized by the China–ASEAN Environmental Cooperation Center, was officially held in Beijing. A delegation of 18 people, led by SAO Sopheap, Director (vice-ministerial level) of the General Office of the Ministry of Environment of Cambodia, attended the opening ceremony of the seminar. In the opening ceremony, Guo Jing, Director of the China–ASEAN Environmental Cooperation Center, shared the progress made by China in environmental protection, introduced the background of the establishment of the ASEAN Center, and reviewed China's cooperation with ASEAN countries in environmental protection since the establishment of the ASEAN Center; he also offered three suggestions on future environmental protection between China and Cambodia: first, deepening the existing cooperation, innovating the cooperation mode; second, executing the China–Cambodia Green Angel Environmental Cooperation Program, jointly carrying out the flagship projects for building up of the capacity of China–Cambodia environmental protection and the environmental awareness of the public; third, pushing forward the construction of the China–Cambodia Environmental Protection Technology Cooperation Center, and building the platform for China–Cambodia exchange and cooperation in the environmental protection industry.

4. Joint research projects were carried out

a. *The program for preparing the China–ASEAN Environmental Outlook was jointly carried out*

The program was a joint research program conducted by China and the ASEAN community and completed by Chinese and foreign experts; it was designed to analyze and evaluate the current environmental and developmental cooperation between China and the ASEAN and the future developmental trends from the regional perspective. As the program executor and coordinator, the ASEAN Center was responsible for relevant research and management work including building up the teams, the coordination of the research and report preparation, peer review organization, project monitoring and evaluation as well as quality control. On July 17, 2015, the China–ASEAN (Shanghai Cooperation Organization) Environmental Cooperation Center organized and held a discussion meeting of Chinese experts on the *China–ASEAN Environmental Outlook* in Beijing. The experts who led the chapters of the *China–ASEAN Environmental Outlook* gave a detailed introduction to the work carried out by them on various chapters; the expert group fully affirmed the exiting research achievements, they discussed how to improve the existing reports and determined the research priorities and key time nodes in the second half of the year.

b. *The Strategy of China–ASEAN Environmental Cooperation 2016–2020 was developed*

During the period June 3–4, 2015, the seminar on developing the Strategy of China–ASEAN Environmental Cooperation 2016–2020 was held in Beijing, China. The seminar was organized by the China–ASEAN Environmental Cooperation Center, with the participation of nearly 30 representatives from the Department of International Cooperation of the Ministry of Environmental Protection of China, the ASEAN Secretariat, and the environmental protection departments of relevant ASEAN countries (Cambodia, Indonesia, Laos, Malaysia, Myanmar, the Philippines, Singapore, Thailand, and Vietnam). The seminar reviewed the progress in various fields concerning China–ASEAN environmental cooperation, and conducted exchanges on China's and ASEAN countries' latest policies in the environmental field. Finally, the seminar discussed a strategy document and reached a consensus on it.

c. *The Meeting on the Inspection and Acceptance of Environmental Cooperation Projects of the Developing Countries under the Leadership Mechanism was held*

On February 3, 2015, the 2014 Meeting on Inspection and Acceptance of Environmental Cooperation Projects of the Developing Countries under the Leadership Mechanism was held in Beijing, China. The meeting focused on listening to the report on research achievements in regional environmental cooperation issues and mechanism research, the environmental impact assessment of ASEAN countries, the assessment of the China–ASEAN environmental impact, the international environmental protection cooperation information platform under the leadership mechanism and the environmental cooperation among the developing countries under the leadership mechanism; those participating in the meeting discussed the project-related work plan and arrangements for 2015. The meeting called for further refining of and improving project achievements to provide technical support for preparing the 13th Five-Year Plan for international environmental protection cooperation and engaging in regional environmental protection cooperation, well executing and managing the project fund budget in 2015, carrying out innovative research in close coordination with the leadership mechanism and better serving the national political and diplomatic situation and the work of the environmental protection center.

5. China–ASEAN cooperation and exchanges in the environmental protection industry were promoted

The environmental protection technology and industry is one of the cooperation priorities specified in the *China–ASEAN Environmental Protection Cooperation Strategy* (*1999–2015*). In order to carry out the guiding principles of the speech "China–ASEAN Environmental Protection Industry Cooperation Initiative" delivered by Chinese Premier Li Keqiang during the 16th China–ASEAN Leaders' Meeting, it was suggested that ASEAN countries should take as the key areas for China's environmental protection industry the idea of "going global", and efforts should be made to support the pilot work of the China–ASEAN Environmental Protection Technology and Industry Cooperation Demonstration Base in Guangxi and the China Yixing

Environmental Protection Science & Technology Industrial Park.[3] The construction of the China–ASEAN Environmental Protection Technology and Industry Cooperation Demonstration Base (Yixing) was officially initiated in 2014; the Demonstration Base engaged in various forms of exchange and cooperation with ASEAN countries in 2015. Work is being carried out to actively push forward the China–ASEAN Environmental Protection Technology and Industry Cooperation Demonstration Base to be built in the Guangdong–Guangxi Interprovincial Pilot Cooperation Special Zone in Wuzhou, Guangxi.

a. *The ASEAN Center and the Yixing Environmental Protection Science & Technology Industrial Park jointly held the international seminar on the developmental plan for Yixing's environmental protection industry*

On the afternoon of January 6, 2015, the China–ASEAN Environmental Cooperation Center and the China Yixing Environmental Protection Science & Technology Industrial Park organized and held the international seminar on the developmental plan for Yixing City's environmental protection industry. The participating experts fully exchanged views on their main tasks, developmental direction and key projects in the *Developmental Plan of Yixing City for Increasing the International Level of the Environmental Protection Industry*, and expressed many constructive opinions on the internationalization of Yixing City's environmental protection industry. They held that the plan was logically clear, and that it was comprehensive and detailed; in particular, the developmental opportunities and challenges were duly analyzed, the main tasks and concrete projects were highly operable, thus the plan can play an active role in guiding the international development of Yixing's environmental protection industry and Yixing's economic and social development. In the meantime, consensuses were reached on the 2015 work plan for the China–ASEAN Environmental Cooperation Center and the China Yixing Environmental

[3] Zhou Guomei, Discussions on the Opportunities and Paths for the Environmental Protection Industry to "Go Global" against the Background of the Belt and Road Strategy, *Environmental Protection*, 2015(8).

Protection Science & Technology Industrial Park, their working mechanisms, main tasks and enhanced personnel exchange.

b. *The Symposium on International Cooperation in the Belt and Road Environmental Protection Industry and Technology was held*

On July 13, 2015, the China–ASEAN Environmental Cooperation Center held the Symposium on International Cooperation in the Belt and Road Environmental Protection Industry and Technology in Beijing. The symposium discussed issues concerning the construction of the Belt and Road Environmental Protection Technology and Industry Cooperation Demonstration Base. The representatives present at the symposium proceeded from their work to exchange views and ideas on Belt and Road environmental protection industry cooperation, and put forward excellent opinions and suggestions on the construction of the Demonstration Base. Song Xiaozhi, Deputy Director of the Department of International Cooperation under the Ministry of Environmental Protection of China, offered the following three suggestions on the construction of the Demonstration Base: First, the top-level design should be strengthened and the construction of the Demonstration Base should be planned well during the period of the 13th Five-Year Plan; second, provincial-ministerial cooperation should be enhanced, the construction of the Demonstration Base should be carried out to stimulate the development of the environmental protection industry in relevant provinces and cities; third, reform and innovation should be persevered and the horizon should be broadened in the construction of the Demonstration Base.

c. *Yixing Demonstration Base took the opportunity of the China Environmental Protection Technology & Industry Development Promotion Meeting to boost cooperation with ASEAN countries*

On October 29, 2015, during the 3rd China Environmental Protection Technology & Industry Development Promotion Meeting, the China–ASEAN Environmental Cooperation Center and the Yixing Environmental Protection Science & Technology Industrial Park jointly held a small seminar on China–ASEAN environmental protection industry cooperation, in which four government officials from the environmental protection departments of Thailand and Cambodia and eight enterprises from the China–ASEAN Environmental Protection Technology and Industry Cooperation Demonstration Base (Yixing) engaged in exchanges and matchmaking involving environmental protection industry technology. The seminar was designed to explore different forms of communication and exchange, help Chinese enterprises learn about the industrial development and investment environment in ASEAN countries, promote pragmatic cooperation in the environmental protection industry between China and ASEAN countries, speed up the construction of the China–ASEAN Environmental Protection Technology and Industry Cooperation Demonstration Base, and help with the construction of the green Belt and Road. With communication, the environmental protection enterprises present at the seminar further understood the environmental protection policies, developmental trends and industrial needs of Cambodia and Thailand, and reached a letter of intent with the environmental protection departments of Cambodia and Thailand with regard to investment in the environmental protection industry. This seminar was a new attempt made by the Yixing Demonstration Base to serve the environmental protection enterprises as they "went global"; it produced a good effect.

d. *There were visits to and symposiums at Indonesia's Cikarang Industrial Park and the Thai–Chinese Rayong Industrial Zone*

On November 24, 2015, the Department of Technical Exchange of the China–ASEAN Environmental Cooperation Center visited Cikarang Industrial Park in Jakarta, Indonesia, and held a symposium with the Indonesian Industrial Park Association. During the symposium, the Indonesian Industrial Park Association and the China–ASEAN Environmental Protection Technology and Industry Cooperation Demonstration Base (Yixing) signed a letter of intent on cooperation; the two sides agreed to strengthen their cooperation and jointly carry out research on and development of relevant technologies and products, put them into practice and gradually establish a cooperation exchange mechanism in the future, so as to further reinforce China–Indonesia exchanges and cooperation on environmental protection technologies and the environmental protection industry. The survey group also surveyed the sewage treatment facilities at EJIP Industrial Park in the Cikarang Area. On November 28, 2015, the Department of Technical Exchanges of the China–ASEAN Environmental Cooperation Center visited the Thai–Chinese Rayong Industrial Zone, and held talks with the Industrial Zone's management personnel. The Thai–Chinese Rayong Industrial Zone is mainly available to Chinese enterprises with the intention of carrying on business in Thailand; it was jointly developed by China's Holley Group and Thailand's Amata Group in Thailand; it is among the first batch of overseas economic and trade cooperation zones approved by the Ministry of Commerce of China. The China Rayong Industrial Zone and the China–ASEAN Environmental Protection Technology and Industry Cooperation Demonstration Base (Yixing) signed a letter of intent on cooperation; the two sides agreed to establish a long-term strategic partnership to jointly promote the development of Thailand's environmental protection industry, the China–Thailand exchanges and cooperation on environmental protection technology and on the environmental protection industry.

e. *The China–ASEAN Environmental Protection Technology and Industry Cooperation and Exchange Demonstration Base (Wuzhou) was built*

On January 17, 2015, a delegation from the Leading Group Office of the Guangdong–Guangxi Interprovincial Pilot Cooperation Special Zone, Wuzhou, Guangxi, visited the China–ASEAN (Shanghai Cooperation Organization) Environmental Cooperation Center. The two sides agreed upon building the China–ASEAN Environmental Protection Technology and Industry Cooperation and Exchange Demonstration Base ("the Base") in the Guangdong–Guangxi Interprovincial Pilot Cooperation Special Zone; the two sides held discussions and reached a consensus with respect to the Base's construction plan, implementation scheme and working mechanism, and regarding other matters. On November 12, 2015, the Department of Technical Exchanges of the China–ASEAN Environmental Cooperation Center visited the Guangdong–Guangxi Interprovincial Pilot Cooperation Special Zone, and held a symposium with relevant departments of the Guangdong–Guangxi Interprovincial Pilot Cooperation Special Zone.

The symposium focused on discussing the developmental plan for the Base and exchanging views on the Base's functional orientation, line of thought regarding its development and the next steps to be taken. The symposium held that the Base's construction should be carried out by fully leveraging the policy superposition advantage and location advantage of the Guangdong–Guangxi Interprovincial Pilot Cooperation Special Zone, focusing on serving international cooperation in China's environmental protection technology and industry, turning it into the China–ASEAN Environmental Protection Technology and Industry Cooperation Service Platform, by designing a relevant policy and building a platform for the construction of the Base; the symposium also affirmed that full play should be given to respective advantages, enhancing cooperation to build and improve the Base's functions in serving national strategy and international cooperation on environmental protection. The survey group also made a field visit to the construction area of the Base.

III. The Outlook for China–ASEAN Environmental Cooperation against the Background of the Belt and Road Initiative

Chinese President Xi Jinping advocated that China and the ASEAN countries should jointly build the 21st Century Maritime Silk Road and create a closer China–ASEAN Community with a Common Destiny. Chinese Premier Li Keqiang stated that the "2+7" cooperation framework was a great cause for promoting regional economic cooperation, peaceful development of the world and benefiting the people around the world. The construction of the Belt and Road is a major strategic decision made by the Party Central Committee and the State Council in light of the changes in the global situation, the new situation and new tasks for China's development. The Belt and Road Initiative takes into account both domestic and international situations; it is of great significance for safeguarding national political and military security, reshaping the global governance system, breaking domestic environmental and resource constraints and for expanding developmental space to maintain the forces for driving sustained economic growth. Ecological environmental protection is the key to the successful construction of the Belt and Road; on the one hand, ecological environmental protection is one of the eight major areas under the Belt and Road Initiative, and state leaders attach great importance to the construction of a green Belt and Road; on the other hand, with the intensification of the construction of the Belt and Road, many environmental risks have loomed large, and so environmental topics have been elevated to the political and diplomatic levels. Ecological environmental protection should provide effective support for policy coordination, facilities connectivity, unimpeded trade, financial integration and people-to-people bonds; ecological environmental protection should help guard against ecological environmental risks and serve Chinese enterprises as they "go global".

The ASEAN countries are the important areas for the construction of the Belt and Road. Engaging in ecological environmental cooperation with the ASEAN countries, enhancing the dialogue and communication, increasing the depth and breadth of the existing cooperation mechanism are the inevitable requirements for the construction of the Belt and Road; these actions will promote policy coordination, facilities connectivity and people-to-people bonds between China and the ASEAN countries. In order to further deepen China–ASEAN environmental cooperation, we offer the following five suggestions for cooperation:

1. Building the China–ASEAN regional environmental cooperation platform, establishing and improving a service security system. The China–ASEAN Environmental Cooperation Center advocated by Chinese leaders, the China–ASEAN Environment Ministers' Meeting Mechanism, and the Lancang–Mekong Cooperation Mechanism initiated this year will complement and develop in coordination with the existing ASEAN environmental cooperation mechanisms; they will play an active role in enhancing the overall development of the sub-region and regional cooperation in East Asia. Actions should be taken to support the China–ASEAN Environmental Cooperation Center in playing a bigger role under the Shanghai Cooperation Organization and the Lancang–Mekong cooperation framework, to build communication and exchange platforms and dialogue mechanisms to share the experience of various countries in an in-depth way and to push forward regional environmental cooperation between China and ASEAN member countries.

2. Carrying forward the *Strategy of China–ASEAN Environmental Protection Cooperation (2016–2020)* and deepening that cooperation. The *Strategy of the China–ASEAN Environmental Cooperation 2016–2020* should be adopted as early as possible; priority should be given to policy communication, capacity building, technical exchanges and industrial cooperation; China–ASEAN environmental protection cooperation should be actively carried out in a high-level policy dialogue, through research on cross-border environmental issues, biodiversity and ecological protection, environmental sustainability and urban construction. The *Strategy of China–ASEAN Environmental Protection Cooperation (2016–2020)* should be pushed forward in a pragmatic way; steps should be taken to build a China–ASEAN high-level platform for a dialogue on environmental protection policies, a platform for sharing environmental protection information, a platform for the environmental protection think tank exchanges, a platform for the building up of environmental protection capacity and knowledge exchanges, as well as the China–ASEAN Partnership for Eco-friendly Urban Development; steps should also be taken to energetically engage in cooperation on environmental technology and on the environmental protection industry and to establish the China–ASEAN Environmental Protection Industry and Technology Cooperation Demonstration Base in order to achieve regional environmentally sustainable development.
3. Broadening financing channels, exploring China–ASEAN cooperation on international production capacity. Most ASEAN countries are pushing forward industrialization and urbanization, and they have a brisk demand for the construction of infrastructures and for the development of their manufacturing industries. As China takes the ASEAN community as an important direction for engaging in cooperation on international production capacity, it should actively give play to the roles of financing platforms including the Asian Infrastructure Investment Bank, the Silk Road Fund, and it should leverage the technical and cost advantages of Chinese enterprises in building green infrastructures, in cooperation on production capacity to promote the construction of green infrastructure, make Chinese enterprises "go global", provide financing support for green, ecological and environmental protection projects and boost the construction of the China–ASEAN environmental protection industry.

4. Building an ASEAN environmental alliance of international scientists and think tanks to propel international ecological environmental cooperation. At present, China lacks systematic and comprehensive research on the basic situation, the impact and developmental trends of environmental problems in the ASEAN community, thus directly imposing restrictions on China's ability to make internal and external strategies and measures for coping with regional environmental problems in the ASEAN community. Therefore, efforts should be made to intensify the building of institutions and capacity and to set up a dedicated research team for researching environmental problems in the ASEAN community; emphasis should be placed on building an environmental protection information support system, strengthening communication with the countries involved with respect to environmental laws, regulations, policies and standards, and reinforcing research on cross-border environmental protection and regional environmental protection issues. In the meantime, relevant domestic research institutions should be organized to carry out long-term and systematic basic observation and research on the ASEAN community; actions should be taken to enhance communication with international think tanks and to build a number of internationally influential think tanks for ASEAN environmental and developmental research.
5. Further engaging in maritime cooperation, establishing maritime partnerships. In 2016, China and the ASEAN community should enhance pragmatic cooperation in marine economy, maritime connectivity, scientific research, environmental protection, maritime security and maritime humanity as well as in other fields; moreover, they should press ahead with joint maritime development, turn maritime cooperation into a new bright spot and a new driving force for the development of China–ASEAN relations. The year 2016 is identified as the Year of China–ASEAN Educational Exchanges. It has been suggested that the China–Southeast Asian Countries Marine Science and Technology & Environmental Protection Cooperation Forum should be held regularly, that the construction of the China–ASEAN Academy of Marine Sciences should be supported and the construction of the China–ASEAN Maritime Cooperation Center should be promoted.

Chapter 16
Report on the China–ASEAN Expo in 2015

Qin Weibing*

The year 2015 was the Year of China–ASEAN Cooperation and the first year for comprehensively implementing the construction of the Belt and Road. With the Year of China–ASEAN Cooperation as an opportunity, under the theme of "Jointly Building the 21st-Century Maritime Silk Road — Drawing a Beautiful Blueprint for Maritime Cooperation", the 12th China–ASEAN Expo was held with a series of friendly exchanges, economic, trade and people-to-people activities, making new achievements in deepening China–ASEAN cooperation.

I. Basic Information

The 12th China–ASEAN Expo was successfully held during the period of September 18–21, 2015. Zhang Gaoli, a member of the Standing Committee of the Political Bureau of the CPC Central Committee and Vice Premier of the State Council, the Deputy Prime Minister of Thailand Tanasak Patimapragorn, the Vice President of Myanmar Sai Mauk Kham, the Deputy Prime Minister of Laos Somsavat Lengsavad, the Deputy Prime Minister Nguyen Xuan Phuc, and the State and Commerce Minister of

* Qin Weibing, Director of the Department of Development of the China–ASEAN Expo Secretariat.

Cambodia Sun Chanthol attended the exposition. The leaders of China and ASEAN countries delivered speeches at the opening ceremony. A total of 269 ministerial-level guests of honor were present at the exposition, three more than those present at the previous exposition, including 129 guests of honor from the ASEAN community and the countries and territories outside the region. The diplomatic envoys of various countries, presidents of business associations, famous entrepreneurs, experts, scholars and celebrities from various sectors of the society attended the exposition. The Country of Honor, Thailand, carried out diverse theme activities, including the Country of Honor's pavilion opening ceremony with the participation of Chinese and Thai leaders, a round table dialogue between Thai leaders and the CEOs of some Chinese enterprises, Thailand's national promotional event and people-to-people exchange activities. The China–ASEAN Economy and Trade Ministers' Luncheon Party, ministerial-level consultations and exchange activities in various fields were held during the exposition.

The exposition continued to feature the Nanning International Convention and Exhibition Center, the Guangxi Exhibition Hall and China South City, Nanning. There were 4,600 booths, including 1,296 booths for the enterprises from the ASEAN community and outside the region, and 2,207 enterprises participated in the exhibition. At the Nanning International Convention and Exhibition Center, foreign booths accounted for 38.1%. 65,000 attended the exposition and exhibition. There were 85 purchasing groups, up 5% over the previous exposition; the number of organized professional purchasers was 2,500, larger than that in the previous exposition.

A total of 1,226 journalists from 205 media in 22 countries and territories covered the exposition, with news dispatches on the rise. Besides the media from China and the ASEAN countries, the media and journalists from other countries along the Belt and Road present at the exposition increased substantially. During the exposition, Chinese and foreign media distributed more than 15,700 news dispatches, 26 online special reports were made, thus expanding the brand influence of the exposition. Focus on CAEXPO: Asia Media Forum was held during the exposition, in which the mainstream media from Asian countries reached an extensive consensus on utilizing the exposition and Business & Investment Summit to enhance exchanges and cooperation and to promote the construction of the Belt and Road.

With emphasis placed on the upgrading of the China–ASEAN Free Trade Area (CAFTA) and cooperation on international production capacity, the exposition featured a number of fruitful high-level friendly contacts, economic and trade promotions and multi-field exchange activities, further promoting the recognition of strategies, connecting developmental plans, enabling the execution of preferred projects and pushing forward the construction of major projects, including the China–ASEAN Information Harbor. Based on China–ASEAN "10+1" cooperation, actions were taken to engage in cooperation involving the Regional Comprehensive Economic Partnership (RCEP) and the countries along the Belt and Road, to address the WTO's trade facilitation to help achieve mutual benefit and win–win outcomes in a wider scope, at a higher level and in a deeper way, to further put into practice policy coordination, facilities connectivity, unimpeded trade, financial integration and people-to-people bonds, so as to make new achievements in deepening China–ASEAN cooperation in multiple fields and stimulating Guangxi's open cooperation, and its economic and social development.

II. Main Characteristics

1. Senior leaders of various countries attended the exposition, the consensus on jointly building the 21st Century Maritime Silk Road was deepened, enhancing China–ASEAN friendly cooperation

The leaders of various countries spoke highly of the achievements from China–ASEAN friendly cooperation and the important role which the exposition played in the process, and they deepened their consensus on jointly building the 21st Century Maritime Silk Road. The participants vowed to connect the Belt and Road Initiative with the developmental strategies of their countries and territories, take the exposition as a platform to deepen cooperation, jointly participate in and promote the construction of the 21st Century Maritime Silk Road, achieve mutual benefit and win–win outcomes at a higher level and work together to build the China–ASEAN Community with a Common Destiny.

2. With a focus on the upgrading of the China–ASEAN Free Trade Area and international production capacity cooperation, efforts were made to put into practice some major projects including the China–ASEAN Information Harbor, so economic and trade results improved significantly

The exposition further served the upgrading of the CAFTA; it included a series of economic and trade activities, which witnessed a brisk trade in commodities, including rice, coffee, solid wood furniture, handicrafts from ASEAN countries, food processing and packaging machinery, and electrical and electronic products from China. Investment cooperation delivered significant outcomes. The investment amount in the signed international cooperation projects increased by 8.8% over the previous exposition, while that in the signed domestic cooperation projects grew by 9.2% over the previous exposition. In the meantime, the exposition saw the 2015 Series of Activities Regarding the China–ASEAN Cooperation on the International Production Capacity. These activities were jointly organized by the National Development and Reform Commission, the Ministry of Foreign Affairs, the Ministry of Commerce of China and the People's Government of the Guangxi Zhuang Autonomous Region; this was the first time that national ministries and commissions utilized an international exhibition platform to serve the cooperation on the international production capacity in the region. These series of activities included the 21st Century Maritime Silk Road & Promoting International Production Capacity and Equipment Manufacturing Cooperation Forum, the International Economic and Production Capacity Cooperation Exhibition, the Project Matchmaking Fair and bilateral talks; the exhibition, the meeting, the fair and the talks were integrated to build a new platform for production capacity cooperation among China, the ASEAN community and the countries and territories along the Maritime Silk Road. In the forum, the participants reached a consensus on building the 21st Century Maritime Silk Road and promoting cooperation on international production capacity. China held bilateral talks with relevant departments of ASEAN countries, including Malaysia, Indonesia, Myanmar, Vietnam and Cambodia. The International Economic and Production Capacity Cooperation Exhibition mainly displayed electric power equipment, engineering machinery, transportation vehicles, building materials and electronic communications, with the participation of more than

20 large enterprises and relevant organizations, including the China Railway Corporation, CRRC and the China North Industries Corporation. In the Production Capacity Cooperation Project Matchmaking Fair, more than 60 Chinese enterprises met with the industrial parks in ASEAN countries, they reached letters of intent on cooperation in 11 projects. According to incomplete statistics, the exposition witnessed the successful signing of 34 international production capacity cooperation projects through various project fairs, involving mechanical manufacturing, auto parts, energy construction, building material production, non-ferrous metals and mineral development.

3. New breakthroughs were made in cooperation with the economies outside the region, more opportunities were created

The exposition made new breakthroughs in the level and mode of exhibition participation from the specially invited countries. As the Special Guest Country, South Korea separately set up a commodity exhibition area; Moon Jae-do, Vice Minister of the Ministry of Trade, Industry and Energy of the Republic of Korea led a government delegation and important figures from the business circles to attend the exposition, and South Korea's National Promotion Event was carried out during the exposition. The cooperation area in the exposition extended services from the "10+1" to the RCEP and the countries along the Belt and Road.

New breakthroughs were also made in substantive cooperation between the exposition and international organizations. The exposition witnessed, for the first time, the substantive business activity of international organizations — High-level Seminar on Trade Facilitation and the 20th Anniversary of the Establishment of the WTO; the WTO officially became the supporter of the exposition, injecting new vitality into it to make the exposition better serve the upgrading of the CAFTA and for global trade facilitation.

4. The series high-level forums and exchange activities yielded new results and expanded all-round cooperation

Twenty-seven high-level forums were held during the exposition; the number reached an all-time high. The multi-level and multi-field exchange activities facilitated ministerial-level consultations, dialogues and communication among government officials, entrepreneurs, experts, scholars and celebrities from various sectors of the society; more cooperation mechanisms were established; a number of major projects were launched or executed; Nanning Channel was enriched, thus propelling progress on the 21st Century Maritime Silk Road.

Regarding network information, the China–ASEAN Information Harbor Forum brought about communication in network information cooperation; the opening ceremony of the China–ASEAN Information Harbor Base was held; the China National Internet Information Office and the Ministry of Posts and Telecommunications of Laos signed the *Memorandum of Understanding on Cyberspace Cooperation and Development*, China and Indonesia reached the signing of a letter of intent on extensive cooperation; the Xinhua News Agency initiated the preparation, research and development of the China–ASEAN (Nanning) Currency Index and the Pan-Beibu Gulf Economic Index, playing an active role in turning the information harbor into the information hub on the 21st Century Maritime Silk Road.

Concerning connectivity and the construction of an economic corridor, the China–ASEAN Customs Connectivity High-level Workshop adopted the *Meeting Consensus*, with the signing of customs cooperation documents between China and Vietnam, as well as China and Cambodia. The China–Indochina Peninsula International Economic Corridor (Nanning–Singapore) Cooperation & Development Round Table Conference focused on discussions and communication about connectivity, customs facilitation, investments and trade facilitation, the construction of multinational (cross-border) economic and trade parks, and released the *Nanning Consensus*.

On financial cooperation, the China–ASEAN Summit Forum on Financial Cooperation & Development witnessed the signing of the *Framework Agreement on Guangxi Beibu Gulf RMB International Investment and Loan Fund*, so the China–ASEAN Currency Center of the Postal Savings Bank of China launched services in Dongxing, Pingxiang and Jingxi.

Regarding maritime cooperation, the major activity in the Year of the China–ASEAN Maritime Cooperation — the China–ASEAN Countries Maritime Cooperation Achievements Exhibition — was held. The State Oceanic Administration and Guangxi signed a cooperation agreement.

Regarding scientific and technological cooperation, the China–ASEAN Technology Transfer & Innovation Cooperation Conference launched the webpage of the China–Thailand Technology Transfer Center, initiated such projects as the China–ASEAN Innovation Center and the China–ASEAN Scientific and Technological Innovation Policy Research Center.

Other forums also delivered fruitful results. A series of non-governmental friendly and people-to-people exchange activities were carried out during the exposition. Guangxi and Ho Chi Minh City, Vietnam; Chongzuo City, Guangxi and Thakhek City, Khammouane Province, Laos; Guigang City, Guangxi and Zamboanga City, the Philippines, established sister region and sister city relations. The Nanning Folk Song Arts Festival, the China–ASEAN (Nanning) Drama Week Gala, the International Sister City Exhibition & Art Show Activity unfolded amazingly, enhancing mutual understanding and friendship between the people of China and the ASEAN community.

III. Drawbacks

1. The professional level needs to be further increased

The international experience in exhibition development shows that taking a professional developmental path is the inexorable trend. At present, the exposition has produced certain effects in exhibition contents and the degree of professionalization of exhibition services, but it cannot meet the needs of professional traders for deepening cooperation. The drawbacks are mainly reflected in the following respects: The commodities of ASEAN countries were displayed mainly through national pavilions rather than the industries in the places where products were made; the number of professional purchasers, especially the purchasers from countries outside the region, such as European countries and USA, was not big enough; the exposition should improve in these aspects.

2. The measures for elevating economic and trade cooperation to a higher level still need to be further reinforced

Initially, the exposition focused on the trade in goods; now it places equal emphasis on the trade in goods and investments; the exposition has made outstanding contributions to promoting China–ASEAN economic and trade cooperation. However, with the full implementation of the Belt and Road

Strategy and deepening upgrading of the CAFTA, there are higher requirements for the service capability and platform functions of the exposition; in particular, as Chinese enterprises "go global" to engage in international production capacity cooperation with ASEAN countries, it is necessary to upgrade the exposition. The China–ASEAN "2+7" cooperation framework also presents more requirements for the exposition in serving both sides in park, production capacity, finance, science and technology and environmental protection. Given the new situation and new requirements, it is also necessary for the exposition to further extend and improve the exhibition value chain, comprehensively deepen bilateral economic and trade cooperation to achieve mutual benefit and win–win outcome at a higher level.

3. Exhibition infrastructure and supporting service facilities need to be further improved

With increasing popularity and the influence of the exposition, domestic and foreign enterprises have become increasingly interested in attending the exposition; however, subject to restrictions from the venue of the Nanning International Convention and Exhibition Center, the unmet needs for booths exceed 20% each year. The Nanning International Convention and Exhibition Center is characterized by an insufficient area, incomplete supporting facilities and unsmooth transportation, severely hindering the development of the exposition and Guangxi's convention and exhibition industry. We are working with Nanning City to upgrade and renovate the existing exhibition halls, build new supporting service facilities and expand the existing ones so as to satisfy the needs of a professional and long-term exhibition development.

IV. Development Suggestions

1. Actively professionalizing exhibitions, improving their comprehensive service capability

Professional exhibitions and overseas exhibitions should be better held within the exposition. Based on the original exhibitions relating to culture, forest trees, tourism, Thailand and Indonesia, the exposition should add overseas exhibitions and professional exhibitions covering more ASEAN countries and industries, so that the series of exhibitions within the exposition are available throughout the year. More promotional activities should be carried out to attract more exhibitors, so that improvement is made in the number of booths for ASEAN countries and other countries and territories along the Belt and Road, as well as the number and quality of purchasers. Better work should be done to conduct trade matchmaking, bring more tangible benefits in the economic and trade fields, build a good economic and trade service brand of the exposition. There should be active participation in the construction of the China–ASEAN Information Harbor; the service platform resources at the website of the ASEAN–China Center should be fully utilized; the official website of the exposition and the China–ASEAN Business Database should be further improved to improve daily commercial and trade services, including trade and project matchmaking, investment policy and environmental consulting.

2. Energetically enhancing the investment promotion function, pushing forward investment cooperation

The requirements of the Belt and Road Initiative should be carefully carried out; with close attention paid to the needs of boosting cooperation in international production capacity and equipment manufacturing, exhibitions and investment promotion activities should become more well-targeted and result-oriented in the major fields, including railways, the aerospace field, electric power and new energy equipment, infrastructure construction, finance, culture, science and technology as well as environmental protection; actions should be taken to pragmatically serve Chinese enterprises and ASEAN countries so that they engage in multi-field and in-depth exchanges and cooperation. The existing senior officials' meeting and round table conference mechanisms of the exposition for investment promotion should be improved; efforts should be made to intensify information cooperation with ASEAN investment promotion agencies and the competent departments for industrial parks, and improve cooperation effectiveness.

3. Holding a series of high-level meetings, forums and activities

Measures should be taken to promote China–ASEAN cooperation in multiple areas. Under the China–ASEAN "2+7" cooperation framework, a series of high-level meetings, forums and activities should be continuously held during the exposition; the multi-field cooperation mechanism should be built, providing more institutional guarantees for China–ASEAN all-round cooperation.

4. Pushing forward institutional and mechanism reforms, cultivating the leading players in Guangxi's convention and exhibition industry

The leading players in Guangxi's convention and exhibition industry should be nurtured in a professional, international, brand-focused and market-oriented way to effectively integrate venue resources, human resources and market resources for the development of the convention and exhibition industry, and a professional force for leading the development of Guangxi's convention and exhibition industry should be built; scope should be given to the role of the convention and exhibition industry in promoting opening-up and economic development; they become the main engine for stimulating the growth and development of Guangxi's convention and exhibition industry.

5. Supporting and cooperating in the improvement of infrastructure and ancillary service facilities in the Nanning International Convention and Exhibition Center and the surrounding areas

There should be active involvement in speeding up the reconstruction and expansion of the Nanning International Convention and Exhibition Center, enhancing the convention and exhibition hardware and ancillary service facilities in Nanning City and improving the environment for the development of the convention and exhibition industry and related service sectors in Nanning City.

Chapter 17

Review of the ASEAN's Perceptions and Responses Involving the Belt and Road Initiative

Li Hao*

In September and October 2013, Chinese President Xi Jinping put forward the initiative of the Silk Road Economic Belt and the 21st Century Maritime Silk Road (collectively, the "Belt and Road Initiative") in Kazakhstan and Indonesia. The initiative has received great attention and has had an active response from the international community; it has gradually become China's major national strategy for opening-up and diplomacy with neighboring countries. According to the document *Vision and Actions on Jointly Building the Silk Road Economic Belt and the 21st Century Maritime Silk Road* jointly released by the National Development and Reform Commission, the Ministry of Foreign Affairs and the Ministry of Commerce on March 28, 2015, the Silk Road Economic Belt focuses on the unimpeded exchange and cooperation routes from China to Europe (the Baltic Sea) via Central Asia

---

*Li Hao, Executive Deputy Director, Associate Professor, Master Supervisor at the 21st Century Maritime Silk Road Research Center of Guangxi University. The paper is jointly funded by the China–ASEAN Collaborative Innovation Center for Regional Development and the Cheung Kong Scholars and Innovation Team Development Program initiated by the Ministry of Education (contract number: BY201501).

and Russia, from China to the Persian Gulf and the Mediterranean Sea via Central Asia and West Asia, from China to Southeast Asia, South Asia and the Indian Ocean; the 21st Century Maritime Silk Road mainly addresses the routes from China's coastal ports to the Indian Ocean and Europe via the South China Sea, from China's coastal ports to the South Pacific Ocean via the South China Sea. In the process of pushing forward the strategy, whether the surrounding countries support the Belt and Road becomes an important indicator for observing their attitudes towards the rise of China.[1] The ASEAN countries are in the unparalleled strategic position in both the overland Silk Road Economic Belt and the Maritime Silk Road; furthermore, in the recent decade or so, as China–ASEAN economic and trade cooperation has soared, a solid foundation has been laid, so the ASEAN countries have become the cooperation priorities for China as China moves forward in the Belt and Road Initiative. If the landmark projects jointly carried out by China and the ASEAN community in the Belt and Road can be duly executed and yield fruitful results, these projects can produce a very significant demonstration effect for other countries along the Belt and Road. Therefore, China must fully understand the ASEAN community's perceptions, responses and interest appeals involving the Belt and Road Initiative; this is an important guarantee and precondition for the smooth implementation of the Belt and Road Initiative in Southeast Asia. Given these considerations, the China–ASEAN Research Institute of Guangxi University and the China–ASEAN Collaborative Innovation Center for Regional Development initiated the emergency program "The Belt and Road Plan and an Analysis of Interest Appeals of ASEAN Countries" in 2015; the Research Institute and the Innovation Center took 1 year to go deep into the ASEAN countries, conduct in-depth surveys, from the perspective of social cognition, among various classes in the ASEAN community — including the political, academic and business circles and the ordinary people — with respect to their basic perceptions and attitudes towards the Belt and Road. In the following part, the Research Group provides an overview of the perceptions and attitudes of various classes in ASEAN countries towards the Belt and Road Initiative.

[1] Lin Minwang, India's Perception of the Belt and Road and China's Policy Options, *World Economics and Politics*, 2015(5), p. 43.

I. The Perceptions and Responses of the Political Circle in ASEAN Countries regarding the Belt and Road Initiative

1. Cambodia and Laos expressed resolute support and gave active responses

The focus of the Belt and Road Initiative lies in connectivity and cooperation on production capacity; this highly accords with the interest appeals of Cambodia and Laos for economic development. Moreover, there are traditional, good and stable political relations between China and Cambodia and between China and Laos, thus the senior leaders of both Cambodia and Laos have firmly supported and actively responded to the Belt and Road Initiative. When delivering the opening speech during the 2nd China–Southeast Asia High-level People-to-People Dialogue in May 2015, Deputy Prime Minister of Cambodia Sok An compared the Belt and Road Initiative to "two wings" indispensable for Asia to "Fly to the Clouds"[2]; Cambodian Ambassador to China Khek Cai Mealy Sysoda believed that the cooperation in two major fields can turn China–Cambodia mutual political trust, geographical proximity, economic complementation and other advantages into pragmatic cooperation in transportation infrastructure, trade and investment, energy, mining and regional integration. During the 2014 APEC CEO Summit, the President of Laos Choummaly Sayasone made it clear that the 21st Century Maritime Silk Road would promote cooperation among ASEAN countries, between China and the ASEAN community so as to achieve common development.[3] Lattanamany Khounnyvong, Vice Minister of Public Works and Transportation of Laos and the Leader of Laotian Side at the Joint Working Group for the China–Laos Railway Project, said that the Belt and Road Initiative would help Laos transform itself from a landlocked country into a land-lined country.[4]

[2] Common Destiny: Spearhead the Drive at the People-to-People Level, *Phnom Penh Evening*, June 1, 2015.

[3] Jiang Tao, Laos Stressed that the 21st Century Maritime Silk Road Would Promote the ASEAN's Regional Development, *China Daily*, November 9, 2014.

[4] Rong Zhongxia, The Belt and Road Helps Laos Become a Land-linked Country, *Xinhua Daily*, June 4, 2015.

2. Indonesia, Malaysia, Singapore and Brunei took a welcoming and cooperative attitude, but cooperate prudently

The senior leaders of Indonesia, Malaysia, Singapore and Brunei believed that the Belt and Road highly tallied with the developmental strategies of their countries, so they took a welcoming and cooperative attitude. Indonesian Ambassador to China Soegeng Rahardjo stated that the 21st Century Maritime Silk Road Initiative put forward by China was highly consistent with Indonesia's strategy of building a maritime power, so Indonesia supported the 21st Century Maritime Silk Road Initiative and was willing to work with China in developing it. The focus of Malaysia's *11th Five-Year Plan* (*2016–2020*) consists in strengthening the construction of public transportation and infrastructures; this coincides with China's future 5-year developmental goal, thus Malaysia welcomed the initiative of "jointly building the Silk Road Economic Belt and the 21st Century Maritime Silk Road" put forward by China; the two sides agreed to enhance the connection of developmental strategies under the framework with a view to advancing pragmatic cooperation.[5] In the opinion of the Prime Minister of Singapore, Lee Hsien Loong, as Asia's financial, trade and logistics center, Singapore is the highpoint in the strategic blueprint for the Belt and Road, and Singapore can provide the full amount of services necessary for rebuilding the Maritime Silk Road to boost trade contacts among the economies in the region. According to Bruneian Ambassador to China, Ms. Magdalene Teo, the strategic initiative of building the 21st-Century Maritime Silk Road put forward by China fits in with Brunei's leading role in the East ASEAN Growth Area and its diversified economic strategy (i.e., the Brunei Vision 2035); Brunei hopes to further cooperate with China under the framework of the Belt and Road in infrastructure development, tourism, education and cultural exchanges.[6]

However, the senior leaders of the above four countries were also generally confused about the Belt and Road Initiative. First, they hoped that the

---

[5] Wang Xinyi, Helping China and Malaysia Cross the Middle-income Trap, *National Business Daily*, November 25, 2015.

[6] Dong Yan, Wei Jialin, Bruneian Ambassador to China, Ms. Magdalene Teo: Brunei Actively Participates in the Construction of the Belt and Road, *China Report*, 2015(10).

Chinese Government can, as early as possible, present a clear and feasible roadmap and plan for putting the initiative into practice. Only in this way can various countries understand what they can do in the Belt and Road Initiative and rationally evaluate the actual benefits which the initiative can bring to them. Second, some countries worry that the Belt and Road may become a tool used by China to forcibly export production capacity and industries to other countries. For example, Indonesia's former Minister of Trade, Mari Pangestu, expressed her concern, at the Boao Forum for Asia, that China would use the strategy of the Maritime Silk Road to push its products, services and companies to the countries along the Belt and Road through a hard-sell approach. Finally, such countries as Singapore and Brunei were also anxious about the fact that China's influence might expand too fast in the region, thus they actively persuaded great powers in other regions to get involved in cooperation projects though they also cooperate with China.

3. Thailand and Myanmar showed enthusiasm, but they were highly uncertain

The mainstream participants in Thailand's political circle, especially the governing party, had always been enthusiastic about the Belt and Road Initiative. In 2015, the current President of Thailand, General Prayuth Chan-ocha, expressed his positive intention regarding the Belt and Road on different occasions many times — on February 6, 2015, when meeting with Chinese State Councilor and Defense Minister Chang Wanquan, he stated that Thailand welcomed the major cooperation initiatives put forward by China, including the Belt and Road Initiative, and was willing to participate in them; Thailand hoped to take the 40th anniversary of the establishment of diplomatic relations between China and Thailand as an opportunity to actively push forward bilateral cooperation in railway, agriculture, tourism and other fields, enhance personnel contacts and traditional friendship. However, the forces out of power and the factions on the fringe of the political circle generally emphasized that the Belt and Road will bring many disadvantages to Thailand: If Thailand was excessively involved in China's external expansion, Thailand would lose its status of independence and neutrality in diplomacy. However, according to surveys on the parties out of power, these factions raised objections and doubts mostly due to a habitual "vicious consumption" by the parties out of power for the purpose of attacking the governing party, and they did not challenge the Belt and Road Initiative. The parties out of power were generally less active than the governing party in Thailand when it comes to the Belt and Road; however, as the cooperation with China had nothing to do with domestic political strife, and various factions hoped to amicably deal with China, the politicians of various parties more or less had a stake in bilateral cooperation; at present, two major parties out of power including the People's Power Party (Thaksin Shinawatra family) and the Democratic Party, the political forces out of power including small and medium-sized parties in Thailand mainly take a positive attitude toward the Belt and Road.[7] Therefore, once the forces out of power come into power, their attitudes toward the Belt and Road will be reversed, thus Thailand's political circle shows this characteristic: Whosoever comes into power supports the Belt and Road Initiative, whosoever is out of power challenges it.[8]

The attitudes of Myanmar's political circle towards the Belt and Road Initiative were more complicated and changeable than those of Thailand. The former governing party of Myanmar, the Union Solidarity and Development Party, once declared that it highly supported the Belt and Road Initiative. When attending the Dialogue on Strengthening the Connectivity Partnership in China in November 2014, the former President of Myanmar, Thein Sein, praised the Belt and Road Initiative and believed that this would bring peace, stability and prosperity to the region, and even to the world.

---

[7] Phinij Jarusombat, the representative figure of the People's Power Party and former Deputy Prime Minister of Thailand, stated that the Asian Infrastructure Investment Bank would provide financial support for many major projects in Thailand, Thailand was willing to fully support the joint construction of the Belt and Road and work together to develop Asia's infrastructure; the leader of the Democrat Party Abhisit Vejjajiva also stressed that Thailand should actively request China to participate in Thailand's rail transportation and other economic stimulus projects.

[8] When the Belt and Road Initiative was put forward, the government of Yingluck Shinawatra massively introduced China's infrastructure construction projects, and that introduction met with strong objection from the opposition parties out of power. After Prayuth Chan-ocha came into power in 2014, the popular plan of "rice for a high-speed railway" was immediately stopped. However, in less than a year, the government of Prayuth Chan-ocha, gradually gained a firm foothold, re-launched the plan of China–Thailand railway cooperation; it also became one of the driving forces for the Belt and Road in Thailand.

The National League for Democracy of Myanmar came into power in April 2016, which occurred for the first time in Myanmar, and it became the majority party at the Assembly of the Union; its leader Aung San Suu Kyi would become the key figure in Myanmar's political circle in the future, so her attitude towards the Belt and Road was extremely important. On November 17, 2015, after Aung San Suu Kyi won the election, she gave an exclusive interview to the journalist from the Xinhua News Agency, and she said that she had heard of the Silk Road as a child, that the Silk Road was very artistic and splendid, that she appreciated the Belt and Road Initiative put forward by China, and hoped that the Belt and Road Initiative would be able to yield results beneficial for various sides. This is the only opinion on the Belt and Road Initiative so far publicly expressed by Aung San Suu Kyi. Although she did not express very explicit support, she at least suggested that Myanmar, governed by the National League for Democracy, did not oppose the initiative. Furthermore, recently, Aung San Suu Kyi has mentioned "Paukphaw" (fraternal) friendship between Myanmar and China on different occasions and many times. The investigation report on the Letpadaung Copper Mine Project released by the Investigation Committee led by Aung San Suu Kyi concludes that the project should continue to be executed. All this indicates that she took a realistic attitude toward China–Myanmar economic and trade cooperation.

It should be noted that when Aung San Suu Kyi talked about China's investments in Myanmar before the journalist from the Xinhua News Agency, she stressed, "The most important factor for making China's investments in Myanmar more successful is the acceptance by our people rather than the policy adopted by the National League for Democracy. Our people hope that investments are beneficial to our country and helpful to our economy. If investments can noticeably show this result, we will welcome the investments."[9] Since 2011, with the operations of the National League for Democracy, the Myitsone Power Station and the Kunlong Power Station projects were put aside; the Letpadaung Copper Mine Project suffered setbacks; the China–Myanmar oil and gas pipeline was battered by criticism;

[9] Myanmar Becomes More Prudent and Smarter in Dealing with China, It Will Be Friendly to China, www.huanqiu.com, November 19, 2015, http://news.china.com/zh_cn/international/1000/20151119/20779991.html.

the China–Myanmar railway agreement was terminated under pressure; these incidents were related to the people's livelihood; therefore, if the strategies for executing the Belt and Road Initiative in Myanmar are not promptly adjusted, uncertainties still exist. Moreover, the parties out of power in Myanmar, mainly the National League for Democracy, had a certain positive attitude towards China; however, most parties out of power knew little about China and their understanding of China was not comprehensive, they often had some misunderstandings, even some extreme anti-China consciousness.[10] In order to go along with these extreme public opinions, expand influence and seek more supporters, some parties out of power repeatedly called for re-examining the bills concerning large cooperation projects signed by China and the former Government of Myanmar at the Assembly of the Union. These factors may add uncertainties and political risks to the Belt and Road in Myanmar.

4. The Philippines and Vietnam were hesitant, cautious and took a wait-and-see attitude

With the impact from the issue of the South China Sea, the relations between China and the Philippines obviously became worse during the period of Benigno Aquino III. The current Government of the Philippines appears to show a certain interest in the Belt and Road, but in fact, it nurses a grievance and is on the alert. On the one hand, some government officials of the Philippines believe that the Philippines has been excluded from the Belt and Road and express discontent; for example, when attending the APEC Ministerial Meeting in Beijing, Deputy Foreign Minister of the Philippines Laura del Rosario said before the *Wall Street Journal* that the 21st Century Maritime Silk Road planned by China apparently bypassed

[10] On the one hand, with regard to the members of the parties out of power in Myanmar, their perceptions of China were often affected by the negative public opinion from Myanmar and the Western world, it was difficult for them to obtain comprehensive and objective information; on the other hand, the people ruled by the military for a long time did not know much about the democratic philosophies and rules in the Western world, there was a certain amount of extremism in Myanmar, such as "being opposed to the military and China means being democratic".

the Philippines, so the Philippines felt very alone. On the other hand, the Government of the Philippines also has the concern that rash participation in the Belt and Road would destroy the strategic partnership between the Philippines and the USA and the strategic ally relations between the Philippines and Japan.

In Vietnam, the senior leaders of Vietnam have not yet reached a consensus on the issue of the Belt and Road. Although Vietnam seems to support the Belt and Road Initiative put forward by China, essentially Vietnam is very cautious. When meeting with Chinese President Xi Jinping during his visit to China this year, the General Secretary of the Communist Party of Vietnam Nguyen Phu Trong only expressed a vague opinion on the Maritime Silk Road Initiative, and he said, "Vietnam attaches great importance to developing sustained and stable amicable relations with China"; his doubt and caution were evident. Furthermore, in 2015, Vietnam strengthened its cooperation with the countries outside the region and signed the TPP, the Vietnam–EU FTA and the Vietnam–South Korea FTA to balance China's influence in Vietnam. The talks with the government officials of Vietnam also revealed that they knew little about the specific content and details of the Belt and Road; Vietnam would not really consider the next step unless the Chinese Government made authoritative and sufficient explanations. Vietnam has signed the TPP and conducted an evaluation, and the TPP will become the focus of Vietnam's foreign trade and economic cooperation in the future.

II. The Perceptions of the Academic Circle in ASEAN Countries about the Belt and Road Initiative

The academic circle in ASEAN countries has shown a great amount of attention to the Belt and Road Initiative; in particular, the academic circle has conducted heated discussions regarding China's strategic intent (or motive). The important think tanks, experts, scholars and analysts of ASEAN countries are obviously different in research and perception regarding the intent of the Belt and Road due to the impact from respective research preferences and ideological philosophies. In sum, ASEAN's think tanks, experts, scholars and media mainly hold the following views.

1. The Belt and Road is the necessity for transforming China's economy and reshaping China's new pattern of opening up; it is the strategic innovation involving China's integration into the global economy

According to Zheng Yongnian, Director of the East Asian Institute, National University of Singapore, the Silk Road is part of Chinese ancient civilization and an effective way to build the self-confidence of and achieve the revival of contemporary Chinese civilization in the international political arena; it is also the spirit of the times for supporting the rise of a great power. In his opinion, the Belt and Road Initiative is China's internal demand for economic development and also the environmental requirement from external economic imbalance in the world.[11] In the view of Win Tin, Chief Editor of Myanmar's *Union Daily*, Chinese leaders put forward the Belt and Road Initiative with great foresight in order to address the issues concerning peaceful development and common development.[12] Li Mingjiang, an expert from The S. Rajaratnam School of International Studies, Singapore, also criticized the influential view in the international community that the Belt and Road was a modern Marshall Plan, believing that the Belt and Road Initiative was, to a certain extent, a response to the US strategy of the Asia-Pacific Rebalancing, but that China had no intention of countering the US, thus there was a difference from the background of the Marshall Plan.

2. The Belt and Road is beneficial to promoting the economic development of the countries concerned and pushing forward regional economic connectivity and cooperation

According to David Arase from the Institute of Southeast Asian Studies, Singapore, the initiative is aimed at establishing an integrated economic

[11] Zheng Yongnian, Major Speeches Provide an In-depth Analysis of the Belt and Road Strategy, http://www.china.com.cn/opinion/think/2015-03/27/content_35169987.htm.

[12] Jiang Xiheng, Cheng Guoqiang, Overview of Viewpoints in the Research on the Belt and Road, *Beijing Daily*, October 20, 2014.

connection network across Asia and Europe, which will bring China and Southeast Asia closer once it is implemented.[13] In the opinion of Chanthaphilith Chiemsisouraj, the President of the Laos Academy of Historical Sciences and Society, the China–Indochina Peninsula Economic Corridor built under the Belt and Road Initiative will transform Laos from a closed landlocked country into an open country with access to both land and sea, and it will help Laos eliminate poverty in a few years. Surakiart Sathirathai, President of the Saranrom Institute of Foreign Affairs, Thailand, said that the Belt and Road, the Asian Infrastructure Investment Bank and other initiatives would greatly promote Asia's economic cooperation.

3. The Belt and Road is conducive to promoting and safeguarding regional peace and stability, cracking down on the Three Evil Forces — terrorism, splittism and extremism

According to Zheng Yongnian, Director of the East Asian Institute, the National University of Singapore, with participation in the construction of the Belt and Road, the relatively backward countries will obtain the opportunity to rejoin the world's economic mainstream and gradually wipe out poverty and it will help get rid of the Three Evil Forces.[14] In a paper, Li Mingjiang, an expert from The S. Rajaratnam School of International Studies, Singapore, pointed out that the Belt and Road could ease the recent tensions between China and its neighboring countries, and was conducive to regional peace and stability.[15] Meanwhile, some scholars do not know much about the Belt and Road Initiative, so they have many misgivings and misunderstandings. The relatively typical views are as follows:

---

[13] David Arase, China's Two Silk Roads Initiative: What It Means for Southeast Asia, Southeast Asian Affairs, Vol. 2015, pp. 25–45.

[14] Feng Wei, Cheng Guoqiang, The International Community's Evaluation of the Belt and Road Initiative, *China Economic Times*, July 15, 2014.

[15] Li Mingjiang, China's "One Belt, One Road" Initiative: New Round of Opening Up? http://www.rsis.edu.sg/rsis-publication/rsis/co15050-chinas-one-belt-one-road-initiative-new-round-of-opening-up/#.VpeO-vnbpG8.

4. There is a concern that the Belt and Road will challenge the existing regional cooperation mechanisms

Some Vietnamese scholars believe that the Belt and Road is a strategy adopted by China to offset the US's and Japan's influence and to seek hegemony in Asia, that it will lead to the Asian order, similar to the US Hub-Spoke scenario, in which China plays the dominant role and ASEAN countries are heavily swayed by China. As a response, some Cambodian scholars think that the Belt and Road will weaken the ASEAN community's leading role and result in the ASEAN-advocated RCEP being compromised.[16] Some Singaporean scholars hold the same view, and believe that the Belt and Road may cause RCEP to become marginalized.[17] Some Indonesian scholars warn that the Maritime Silk Road may squeeze Indonesia's strategic space.

5. The philosophy and connotation of the Belt and Road are misunderstood

According to some Vietnamese scholars, China hopes to use the Belt and Road to build China into a regional hegemonic power. In their opinion, China's strategy lies in inducing the neighboring countries with economic benefits to downplay their disagreements with China. China leverages the Belt and Road to change the balance of power in Southeast Asia, thus taking advantage of its favorable position to impose pressure on related parties on the issues concerning sovereignty and the jurisdiction of the ocean. In the perspective of some Philippine scholars, the Belt and Road is designed to serve the Chinese Dream put forward by Xi Jinping, create conditions for helping China enhance the capability of China's navy and marine forces, thus laying the foundation for establishing overseas military bases and facilities. According to some Cambodian scholars, Cambodia has the

---

[16] Wang Yiwei, Cambodia's Ten Concerns about the Belt and Road, http://www.guancha.cn/WangYiWei/2015_12_24_345761.shtml.

[17] Zhang Ming, Singapore and the Maritime Silk Road, *Bloomberg Businessweek*, November 26, 2015.

memory of China's exportation of revolution, and the current efforts in building connectivity may help China export its model and interfere in Cambodia's internal affairs.[18]

6. The concept of the Belt and Road is too generalized, its details are not available and it is less transparent

Many ASEAN scholars generally believe that the concept of the Belt and Road Initiative is excessively generalized, its details are lacking and communication with the countries along the Belt and Road is insufficient, thus there is much bewilderment, and even doubts. For example, some Indonesian scholars hold that the details about the 21st Century Maritime Silk Road Strategy have not yet been provided, so we only know a very grand strategy but do not know how to execute it, and Indonesia does not know how to effectively participate in this process. According to former Deputy Director of the Institute of Chinese Studies of the Vietnam Academy of Social Sciences, the implementation plan, measures and guidance documents of the Chinese Government for the Belt and Road are less concrete and complete, and Vietnam cannot gain more understanding of the initiative. The President of the Thailand Institute of Future Developmental Studies, Kriengsak Chareohwongsak, suggests that the Belt and Road should be institutionalized as early as possible; for example, the current ten ASEAN countries should change the concept into the form of a certain organization. In his opinion, at present, the most pressing issue is institutionalization of the Belt and Road. According to the scholars from academic groups, including the East Asian Institute, the National University of Singapore and the GIC, the Chinese Government should further set forth the nature and scope of the Belt and Road, and present the action plan covering the specific areas and major projects. Only in this way can it help the countries along the Belt and Road understand the intent of the Chinese Government and dispel their other doubts. Moreover, they do not know which agency is responsible for coordinating, as a whole,

[18] Wang Yiwei, Cambodia's Ten Concerns about the Belt and Road, http://www.guancha.cn/WangYiWei/2015_12_24_345761.shtml.

the efforts to implement the Belt and Road Initiative and develop a relevant plan, so it is urgently necessary for the Chinese Government to give clear and concrete explanations on these aspects.[19]

III. The Perceptions of the Business Circle in ASEAN Countries about the Belt and Road Initiative

According to the survey conducted by the Research Group, most ASEAN enterprises, especially Chinese businessmen, thought a great deal of the vast international market with unlimited business opportunities behind the Belt and Road Initiative, and they expressed strong interest and firm support. The Chinese businessmen in Malaysia said that their investment operation activities were subject to severe restrictions due to the impact of such factors as domestic ethnic contradictions, and they hoped to find new markets and solutions by virtue of the Belt and Road.[20] As the largest trading partner of China in the ASEAN community, Malaysia pays more attention to the following aspect: With the construction of the Belt and Road, bilateral trade can be expanded, and more enterprises can enter China and further develop the Chinese market for trade in services. Pattarapong Kanhasuwan, the First Senior Vice President of KASIKORNBANK, said that the implementation of the Belt and Road Initiative would stimulate the construction of local infrastructures, the movement of international trade and personnel, while these economic activities would generate a brisk demand for financial services, and so this would present a great developmental opportunity for financial enterprises. Singaporean entrepreneurs hoped that Singapore can become the springboard for cooperation on the advantageous production capacity between China and ASEAN countries, and believed that there was a broad space for cooperation with China in third-party development, such as the

---

[19] Zhang Ming, Singapore and the Maritime Silk Road, *Bloomberg Businessweek*, November 26, 2015.

[20] The above viewpoints come from the persons in charge of main Chinese businessmen organizations, including Malaysia–China Friendship Association, the Federation of Chinese Associations Malaysia and The National Council of the Associated Chinese Chambers of Commerce and Industry of Malaysia, who gave an interview to the Research Group.

joint establishment of industrial parks in other ASEAN countries.[21] Sumadi Kusuma, a well-known Indonesian marine logistics entrepreneur, Chairman of Global Putra International Group, specially stated that the Chinese Government utilized the 21st Century Maritime Silk Road to encourage investment in overseas marine infrastructures, that this was consistent with Indonesia's plan for building a marine power in the world, thus Chinese and Indonesian enterprises can cooperate in developing the marine cause, including the construction of such infrastructures as ports, logistics warehousing, marine transportation and fisheries.[22] Furthermore, the overseas Chinese businessmen in the Philippines had special considerations; besides the hope that the Belt and Road can benefit the enterprises in all countries along the Belt and Road, they further expect the Belt and Road, as an economic channel, to improve the currently unharmonious political and diplomatic relations between the two countries, curb the simmering anti-Chinese sentiment possibly caused by the worsening bilateral relations.[23] The enterprises of overseas Chinese in Southeast Asian countries generally have strong economic strength, they lean politically towards the Chinese Mainland, and the Belt and Road is highly attractive at the economic level, thus there is an upbeat prospect for carrying out the Belt and Road Initiative in the ASEAN's business circle and they will become the main participants and direct beneficiaries in ASEAN countries with respect to the Belt and Road.

In the meantime, some entrepreneurs expressed reservations about the Belt and Road Initiative. Some had a sober understanding of possible risks arising out of implementing it; for example, some Singaporean businessmen held that the construction of the Belt and Road was dominated by cross-border infrastructure investment, it was characterized by a large scale of

---

[21] Zhang Ming, Singapore and the Maritime Silk Road, *Bloomberg Businessweek*, November 26, 2015.

[22] Kuang Yaozhang, Logistics Entrepreneur Sumadi Kusuma Talked about the Maritime Silk Road, Expressed Full Support for Indonesia and China's Marine Construction, *Indonesia Shang Bao*, February 13, 2015.

[23] The viewpoints of the Philippines' business circle and overseas Chinese businessmen about the Belt and Road come from Carlos Chan (Honorary Chairman of Qishi (International) Co., Ltd.), Teresita Ang See (Executive Trustee of the the Kaisa Heritage Foundation Inc.), Chito Sta Romana (professor at the Asian Center, University of the Philippines, once serving as chief correspondent of ABC in China) who gave an interview.

investments, a long investment recovery period and a low investment return; if there were not good project options and project design, it would be very difficult to attract private capital; finally, the Chinese Government may become one of the main investors, subsequently great economic risks may occur. Some Bruneian entrepreneurs equated the Belt and Road with bridge and road construction and they had doubts about the continuity of the policies adopted by the Chinese Government. Some people warned that the Belt and Road might let more Chinese enterprises occupy the ASEAN market and disturb the normal market order; for example, some Bruneian entrepreneurs cautioned that with progress in the Belt and Road, the Government of Brunei must strengthen its examination of market access for Chinese-funded enterprises, to curb unscrupulous Chinese merchants from engaging in dishonest and illegal operations. In Thailand, the business circle expressed the concern that after the powerful Chinese capital entered Thailand, it would "eat up" resources in Thailand, it would not moderately surrender some of the profits to Thailand's business circle, and that it would not create social benefits and employment in Thailand. In Vietnam, some entrepreneurs had more straightforward views, in that they worried that the Belt and Road would lead to the situation in which more Chinese products — including many inexpensive shoddy products — would, like fierce floods and savage beasts, flock to the markets in the countries along the Belt and Road, and they would exert a severe impact on local enterprises.

IV. The Perceptions and Responses of the People in ASEAN Countries about the Belt and Road Initiative

According to the survey conducted by the Research Group, the ordinary people in ASEAN countries know little about the Belt and Road and relevant issues — in the Philippines, with the impact of the issue of the South China Sea, backward communication infrastructure and official guidance of public opinion, the people basically know nothing about the Belt and Road; in Cambodia, the people had no historical experience and concept about the Silk Road, so it was difficult for them to understand the Belt and Road; in Brunei, most local young people — even local young overseas Chinese — know little about China, some only know Chinese Kung fu but do not know about the Belt and Road; the elder overseas Chinese know that the Belt and Road Initiative was put forward by Chinese President Xi Jinping, but they know nothing of its details; in Malaysia's Chinese community, the people have never heard of the Belt and Road or only know of its concept but they do not know its details; in the Philippines' Chinese community too, the people know almost nothing about the Belt and Road.

For the people surveyed by the Research Group who had gained some understanding of the Belt and Road, many of them expressed support for the initiative,[24] while many others expressed concerns and doubts. According to statistical data from the survey, 45.4% of the ordinary people in Myanmar supported China–Myanmar cooperation under the Belt and Road Initiative, while 28.1% did not support it and 26.5% did not express an opinion.[25] According to the survey results obtained by Horizon Group, among the ASEAN countries, Singapore, Malaysia and Thailand were the countries where the ordinary people generally tended to show a good attitude towards China; Indonesia was the country where the ordinary people lacked trust in China; Vietnam was the country where the ordinary people had a completely negative attitude towards China.[26] In the opinion of the Research Group,

[24]Most respondents who expressed support believed that the Belt and Road Initiative can promote economic development, increase local employment in their countries; for example, according to the survey, 72.6% of the respondents in Myanmar held that the implementation of the Belt and Road Strategy would generate more foreign exchange earnings to Myanmar, while 77.4% of them believed that the Belt and Road Strategy would create more jobs for the people in Myanmar.

[25]Statistical data come from the questionnaires distributed by the Research Group in Myanmar. According to the actual survey, the Research Group distributed 339 questionnaires in such Burmese cities as Naypyidaw, Rangoon, Mandalay, Pegu, Moulmein, 339 questionnaires were recovered, the recovery rate was 100%; there were 336 valid questionnaires, accounting for 99.1% of those distributed.

[26]Horizon Group surveyed the ordinary people in 18 countries along the Belt and Road with respect to their attitudes towards China via the Internet during the period April–May, 2015, with the total sample size being 14,522. The survey covered 10 indicators, including the overall favorability of the ordinary people towards China, the degree of appreciation of Chinese culture, the degree of recognition of China's path, the degree of confidence in China's developmental prospects, the favorability towards Made in China and Chinese brands, the degree of attention to Chinese leaders, the degree of confidence in Chinese leaders in terms of correctly

in the past, when "going global", Chinese enterprises paid more attention to contacts with governments but ignored the wishes of the people, thus causing huge losses, similar to the dilemma for which Myanmar's Myitsone Power Station was put aside indefinitely. In view of this situation, the Research Group specially collected, reorganized and summarized the data on the negative evaluation from the ordinary people in various countries about the Belt and Road Initiative so that relevant departments and investment organizations can gain a comprehensive understanding.

1. The Belt and Road Initiative did not directly benefit the ordinary people

Some Lao people believed that the China–Laos railway under construction would lead to an increasing budget deficit for Laos, that this would greatly affect the grass-roots civil servants and other ordinary people living on the fiscal revenue of the government, and that their life would become very difficult. Some people pointed out that their purchasing power was so limited that they cannot afford a trip on the China–Laos railway even if the railway was built, so they thought that this was favorable for the government but meant more burdens on the ordinary people. In Thailand, the people's attitudes were deeply affected by domestic media and online media. Since 2015, the rumors that China's loan conditions for railway construction are strict and the land along the railway is managed by China have gone viral online, and the objections from the ordinary people have been on the rise.

2. The Belt and Road is a tool used by China to achieve "economic control"

In Malaysia, most non-ethnic-Chinese Malaysian people under our survey said that they were fearful of China as a superpower and were worried about the sovereignty issue; they feared that Malaysia would be reduced to China's

---

handling domestic and international affairs, the degree of recognition of bilateral relations between their countries and China and the degree of trust in the economic relations between their countries and China; on this basis, the surveyed countries were classified. For details, see the Horizon Research Consulting Report.

economic colony. In Cambodia, some ordinary people thought that as China promoted the Belt and Road in Cambodia, China hoped to turn Cambodia into one of China's protectorate states through a continuous flow of investment and aid.

3. The Belt and Road would destroy the local environment and result in looting resources

In particular, in the underdeveloped ASEAN countries, such as Cambodia, Laos and Myanmar, the following view became prevalent: The construction of the Belt and Road was aimed at guaranteeing resources and an energy supply for China by looting resources from other countries. In Vietnam, some people believed that the 21st Century Maritime Silk Road made it plausibly justifiable for China to develop marine resources in Vietnam, especially the oil and gas resources that are much needed by China. The Lao people believed that the China–Laos railway would deteriorate Laos' ecological environment as the railway crossed the vast stretches of forests and mines in Laos and extensive tracts of the people's land. In Koh Kong Province in West Cambodia, the plan for a hydropower station project based on assistance from China had to be changed as the local people launched a campaign against the project due to migration and the possible destruction of the precious ecosystem. In Phnom Penh, the concrete bridge undertaken by China on the National Highway No. 6 had been completed, but the surrounding residents complained that dust was severe after the bridge was completed, and some people had to move to other places.[27] These circumstances were very common in Cambodia, making the people more concerned about the environmental problems caused by the Belt and Road.

Overall, although the Belt and Road Initiative was put forward by China, the Belt and Road cannot be built unless the countries along the route to be used for the Belt and Road, including ASEAN countries, join hands in this endeavor. According to the survey on the perceptions and responses of various classes in the ASEAN community conducted by the Research Group, priority should be given to the following work: First, planning and

[27] [Japan] Murakami Daki: China's Foreign Aid Needs to Transform from Quantitative Change to Qualitative Change, *Nikon Keizai Shimbun*, January 5, 2015.

implementation must take into account domestic and international factors to avoid self-talk and one-sidedly presenting China's intent and to better understand and consider the interest appeals of the countries along the Belt and Road, thus removing estrangement and doubts and obtaining active support and cooperation from the other side.[28] Second, the construction of the Belt and Road must serve the purpose of promoting the economic modernization of ASEAN countries, and the construction must be performed by innovating the cooperation mode on the basis of the common interests of the various parties. Only when the construction of the Belt and Road responds to the appeal of the developing countries for achieving modernization can it be really accepted by these countries. For such consideration, the author suggests that as China pushes forward the Belt and Road in Southeast Asia, it must base that effort on the common interests of the two sides and the appeal of the countries along the Belt and Road for pursuing development, with a focus on project cooperation in the construction of infrastructures (such as Laos, Cambodia, Thailand), industrial production capacity (such as Indonesia, Malaysia, Singapore, Vietnam) and the people's livelihood and well-being (such as Myanmar).[29] Third, China must further refine and deepen the preliminary policy communication, as well as further broadening the areas of policy communication; for example, it is necessary to clearly explain the goals and connotation of the strategy to ASEAN countries, develop an explicit roadmap, carry out publicity work in the international community in a more attractive, acceptable and understandable way; finally, China should actively draw upon experience from Europe, USA and Japan, rationally define and address the roles of the Chinese Government, enterprises, think tanks and other NGOs, and create synergy in the construction of the Belt and Road.

---

[28] Some researchers attributed the misunderstandings and speculations — such as China's Marshall Plan — arising during overseas communication of the Belt and Road Initiative to the following factors: on the one hand, some western media deliberately brought shame on China; on the other hand, China adopted the mode of one-way inculcation, commonly used in China, to disseminate the Belt and Road Initiative overseas, irrespective of different circumstances at home and abroad. For details, see Wang Linggui, Anticipation, Welcome and Anxiety: Foreign Think Tanks View the Belt and Road, *Beijing Daily*, November 30, 2015.

[29] Jiang Xiheng, Cheng Guoqiang, Overview of Viewpoints in the Researches on the Belt and Road, *Beijing Daily*, October 20, 2014.

Chapter 18

The Implementation of the Belt and Road Initiative in the ASEAN Community: Achievements and Problems

Lu Jianren and Cai Qi*

The Belt and Road Initiative, put forward by Chinese President Xi Jinping in October 2013, has aroused great repercussions around the world. As the important region for pushing forward the Belt and Road Initiative, the ASEAN community is of great significance. The implementation of the Belt and Road Initiative in the ASEAN community covers two parts: one part is the sea route, mainly the 21st Century Maritime Silk Road,[1] involving five ASEAN marine countries (Malaysia, Indonesia, the Philippines, Singapore, Brunei); another part is the land route, mainly the China–Indochina

* Lu Jianren, Chief Researcher at the China–ASEAN Research Institute of Guangxi University, research fellow at the National Institute of International Strategy, Chinese Academy of Social Sciences; Cai Qi, Research Assistant at the China–ASEAN Research Institute of Guangxi University.

[1]According to the document *Vision and Actions on Jointly Building the Silk Road Economic Belt and the 21st Century Maritime Silk Road* officially issued by several departments including the National Development and Reform Commission, the 21st Century Maritime Silk Road also includes the route from China to the South Pacific countries.

Peninsula Economic Corridor, involving five ASEAN continental countries (Vietnam, Myanmar, Cambodia, Laos, Thailand). So far, outstanding achievements have been made in implementing the Belt and Road Initiative in the ASEAN community, but many problems exist and deserve a great amount of attention.

I. The Responses of ASEAN Countries to the Belt and Road Initiative

The Belt and Road Initiative has received enthusiastic responses from ASEAN countries; their views are roughly classified as follows.

1. Positive

This view holds that China upholds the philosophy of respecting different developmental paths and values of various countries in the Belt and Road Initiative; compared with the US-led Trans-Pacific Partnership Agreement (TPP), the Belt and Road Initiative is more inclusive and diversified in access conditions, so that it is easier for it to be accepted by the ASEAN countries. The Belt and Road Initiative can promote the development of the ASEAN community, ease the financial strain in the ASEAN community and it is conducive to the economic development of the ASEAN countries; the Belt and Road Initiative and the construction of the ASEAN Community echo each other.[2]

a. *At the governmental level*

In 2015, Win Tin, Chief Editor of the *Union Daily*, the newspaper of the Union Solidarity and Development Party, the then governing party in Myanmar, said that as the Belt and Road can promote regional economic development and regional peace and stability, Myanmar fully supported China's stand and also fully believed that China was able to unite the

[2] Jeremy Koh, ASEAN diplomats welcome China's One Belt, One Road initiative, https://www.channelnewsasia.com/news/asiapacific/asean-diplomats-welcome/2265422.html.

surrounding countries to jointly build the Silk Road and achieve win–win outcomes.[3]

According to former Foreign Minister of Singapore, George Yong-Boon Yeo, the Belt and Road Initiative will bring more opportunities to Singapore for obtaining benefits; in particular, with respect to logistics, Singapore and Hong Kong can work together. Thanks to Singapore's influence in Southeast Asia, China and Singapore can also play an important role in shipping and in the shipping route.[4]

b. *At the non-governmental level*

There are the following main views: With participation in the construction of the Belt and Road, the relatively backward countries will gain opportunities for rejoining the world's economic mainstream.[5] According to Cambodian economist Sotha, the establishment of the Asian Infrastructure Investment Bank is a new opportunity for Cambodia's development, the Asian Infrastructure Investment Bank offers loans with lower interests in a more convenient way than the World Bank and the Asian Development Bank and it is easy for Cambodia to apply for obtaining loans from the Asian Infrastructure Investment Bank.[6] Huang Bin, Director of the Department of Chinese Studies at Thailand's Kasikorn Research Center, said that the Belt and Road Initiative was highly compatible with ASEAN's goal of building a community of political security, an economic community and a sociocultural community to achieve all-round connectivity.[7] In a paper, Lucio Blanco Pitloiii, a member of the Philippine Society of Chinese Studies, said that

[3] How Foreign Media and Scholars View the Belt and Road, www.globalview.cn, http://www.globalview.cn/html/zhongguo/info_7590.html.

[4] George Yong-Boon Yeo: The Belt and Road Brings Opportunities to Singapore, *Reference News,* http://column.cankaoxiaoxi.com/2015/0720/857716.shtml.

[5] How Foreign Media and Scholars View the Belt and Road, www.globalview.cn, http://www.globalview.cn/html/zhongguo/info_7590.html.

[6] Foreign View on the Opening of the Asian Infrastructure Investment Bank: the Establishment of the Asian Infrastructure Investment Bank Is a New Opportunity for Cambodia, http://news.ifeng.com/a/20160119/47136949_0.shtml.

[7] Huang Bin, The Belt and Road Initiative Is Highly Compatible with the ASEAN's Goal of Achieving Connectivity, Xinhuanet, http://sg.xinhuanet.com/2016-03/08/c_128782820.htm.

as the Belt and Road Initiative was combined with the *Master Plan for the ASEAN's Connectivity*, the Chinese Mainland was connected with the land and sea of Southeast Asia.[8] Chanthaphilith Chiemsisouraj, the President of the Laos Academy of Historical Sciences and Society, stated that if the China–Indochina Peninsula Economic Corridor under the Belt and Road Initiative was completed, Laos would change from a closed landlocked country into a country with access to both land and sea, and it would be conducive to boosting Laos' economy and eliminate its poverty.[9] In the view of Burmese media, the Belt and Road is also the Belt and Road for the people of Myanmar; Myanmar is the central intersection of the Belt and Road, and the Belt and Road Initiative put forward by China would play to Myanmar's geographical advantage and bring opportunities to the weak infrastructure in Myanmar.[10] According to Philippine media, even if the relations between China and the Philippines sour due to the issue of the South China Sea, joining the Belt and Road Initiative and the Asian Infrastructure Investment Bank will do more good to the Philippines than harm, and developing good economic relations with China will be beneficial to the long-term development of the Philippines.[11] Teo Tiou Seng, Managing Director of Pacific International Lines, believes that the Belt and Road Initiative will bring huge opportunities for development to Singapore, a financial center in Southeast Asia, Singapore can also become the transfer, supply and repair center on the 21st Century Maritime Silk Road.[12]

---

[8]Lucio Blanco Pitlo III, ASEAN Connectivity and China's "One Belt, One Road" — could there be a convergence of interests between these two grand projects? http://thediplomat.com/2015/03/asean-connectivity-and-chinas-one-belt-one-road/.

[9]David Arase, China's Two Silk Roads Initiative: What It Means for Southeast Asia, *Southeast Asian Affairs*, Vol. 2015, pp. 25–45.

[10]Nan Lwin, The Belt and Road for the People of Myanmar: Myanmar Is the Central Intersection of the Belt and Road, www.webaobo.com, *The Modern Weekly*, January 15, 2016 (No. 493).

[11]Boo Chanco, Joining the Belt and Road Initiative and the Asian Infrastructure Investment Bank Will Do More Good to the Philippines than Harm, http://mp.weixin.qq.com/s?__biz=MjM5MjE3NDkyMw==&mid=400308793&idx=7&sn=175b51ea43d888c26a68bd860ca18d03&scene=23&srcid=1107Ml0Owvtmno1HiDDg9GIs#rd.

[12]Teo Tiou Seng: Singapore and China under the Belt and Road Initiative, news.ifeng.com, http://inews.ifeng.com/yidian/46055620/news.shtml.

2. Sceptical

This view doubts China's intention under the Belt and Road Initiative, and holds that ASEAN countries will become the areas where China will dump its products, or that China will interfere in the ASEAN's and regional affairs by means of the Belt and Road Initiative.

a. *There is a concern that ASEAN countries will become the areas where China will dump its products*

Some people in the ASEAN community have doubted that China would use the Belt and Road Initiative to export its influence to ASEAN countries. The Former Minister of Trade of Indonesia, Mari Pangestu, said, at the Boao Forum for Asia in 2015, that the people were concerned about the Maritime Silk Road Initiative put forward by China: Will China use its might to push its products and services to other countries through a hard-sell approach or export its companies to other countries?[13] The above view was proved by some Thai media, who believe that the Belt and Road Initiative put forward by China conflicts with Thailand's interests, once China's manufacturing industry is transferred to Thailand thanks to convenient transportation, it would exert an impact on the manufacturing industry owned by non-Chinese foreign capital in Thailand. Furthermore, China would take Thailand as the dumping market for its products by virtue of its powerful manufacturing industry, "Created in Thailand" would no longer be able to rise again. As a result, Thailand's trade deficit would accelerate, massive funds would flow out of Thailand, and Thailand would fall into a vicious circle in the fiscal respect.[14] Some people think that as a large number of Chinese enterprises will enter Thailand through the Belt and Road, they would endanger Thailand's economic security, and an excessive inflow of Chinese people would affect job opportunities for Thai people.[15]

---

[13] Former Minister of Trade of Indonesia: The Belt and Road Has Three Pillars, http://business.sohu.com/20150327/n410429466.shtml.

[14] See: Chinese Greengrocers Massively Enter the Thai Market, They Enjoy the Overwhelming Advantages in Price, Exerting an Impact on Local Vendors in Thailand, *Sing Sian Yer Pao Daily News*, May 4, 2016.

[15] Zhang Xizhen, In the Eyes of Thai People, the Belt and Road Sheds Light on the Strife between China and the USA over Southeast Asia, http://finance.huanqiu.com/cjrd/2015-12/8287523.html.

b. *There is a concern that the Belt and Road Initiative will interfere in the ASEAN-led affairs*

The ASEAN community worries that the Belt and Road Initiative put forward by China will weaken or replace the ASEAN-led regional affairs. The Minister of Defense of Malaysia, Hishammuddin Hussein, stated outright, "It is necessary for China to announce the intention of the initiative; China should not regard the Maritime Silk Road Initiative put forward by it as China's plan, while the plan should not bypass the existing regions or processes, such as the ASEAN community."[16] Moreover, ASEAN countries hope to have a greater say on this aspect. Singaporean Ambassador to China, Stanley Loh Ka Leung, pointed out that as China pushes forward the Belt and Road Initiative, it should engage in more bilateral communication with other countries.[17]

c. *There is a concern that the strife between China and USA over Southeast Asia will endanger the ASEAN community*

According to Zhang Xizhen, professor at Pridi Banomyong International College, Thammasat University, some people in Thailand believe that as China promotes the Belt and Road in Southeast Asia, essentially, China and USA will vie for Southeast Asia, the game between China and USA will increase regional tension and may exert an adverse impact on Thailand's economic development and social stability.[18] Some Thai media hold that before the win–win mode of the Belt and Road takes shape, it will be necessary to be cautious about China's goal, while the issue of the South China Sea is the important indicator for sounding out China's sincerity — whether China aims at achieving common development of the disputed areas through

[16] Translated by Zhang Yuan'an, The Economist: The Foresight of Chinese Leaders in the Belt and Road, *China Daily*, http://translate.chinadaily.com.cn/article-304760-1.html.

[17] See: Loh Ka Leung, Incorporating ASEAN's Connectivity into the Belt and Road, *Lianhe Zaobao*, http://www.zaobao.com/special/report/supplement/futurechina2015/forum/story20150722-505592.

[18] Zhang Xizhen, In the Eyes of Thai People, the Belt and Road Sheds Light on the Strife between China and the USA over Southeast Asia, http://finance.huanqiu.com/cjrd/2015-12/8287523.html.

cooperation or confrontation.[19] For many years, the ASEAN community has adopted the dual structure of diplomatic policy — economically relying on China but depending upon USA in the security field, so the ASEAN community worries that closer cooperation with China in the Belt and Road would displease USA and harm its interests.

d. *There is a concern that the ASEAN community's opportunities and interests may not be guaranteed*

The ASEAN countries have paid attention to whether China attaches importance to transferring technology to ASEAN countries and training local workers as it pushes forward the Belt and Road Initiative; for example, Vietnam holds that Chinese companies have always been used to sending their construction teams to Vietnam, they seldom provided jobs to local people in Vietnam. With the implementation of the Belt and Road Initiative, Vietnam would further rely on China's economy.[20] They are also anxious about whether China will respect the cultural and social customs in ASEAN countries, and whether the projects will cause environmental pollution. Cambodia worries that as the recipient of the route and rules involving the Belt and Road Initiative, Cambodia will suffer loss in sharing returns and risks; Cambodia believes that it is so poor that it cannot afford the basic expenditures relating to cooperation, and hopes that China can provide convenience to help Cambodia develop; for example, helping Cambodia first achieve domestic connectivity and then connect with the Belt and Road projects.[21] Furthermore, Japan, Europe and USA have made massive investments in the ASEAN countries; in particular, Japan is currently the country with the most direct investments in the ASEAN community, many ASEAN countries are worried that cooperation with China will produce a crowding-out effect on Western investments. The ASEAN

---

[19] Maritime Silk Road runs into South China Sea tension, https://www.nationthailand.com/noname/30269414.

[20] Wei Qiang, Mou Shan, Evaluation and Analysis of the Vietnamese People's Mentality towards China, http://www.21ccom.net/articles/world/zlwj/20150620125973_all.html.

[21] Wang Yiwei, Cambodia's Ten Concerns about the Belt and Road, http://pit.ifeng.com/a/20151224/46818018_0.shtml.

community hesitates and is taking a wait-and-see attitude with respect to its participation in the construction of the Belt and Road.

ASEAN countries also have their own calculations and are weighing the benefits from participation in the construction of the Belt and Road. For example, the Philippines doubts that it would be "bypassed" by the roadmap of the 21st Century Maritime Silk Road; moreover, the relations between China and the Philippines have plunged to an icy point due to the dispute over the South China Sea, so the Philippines remains passive in joining the Belt and Road Initiative and the Asian Infrastructure Investment Bank. However, after the Philippines has weighed the advantages and disadvantages in various aspects, in particular, the remaining ASEAN countries would join the Asian Infrastructure Investment Bank in the capacity of founding members, the Philippines is fearful that it would suffer a loss, and has finally decided to join the Asian Infrastructure Investment Bank.

The Asian Infrastructure Investment Bank serves as the touchstone for measuring the ASEAN community's willingness to participate in the construction of the Belt and Road. Ling Teck Soon, senior lecturer at the Institute of China Studies, the University of Malaysia, said that the charter of the Asian Infrastructure Investment Bank and its operational mechanism would be the indicators for observing whether China is sincere.[22] The ASEAN community was very concerned about its say in the Asian Infrastructure Investment Bank; if China imposes pressure by money in its words and deeds when China leads the Asian Infrastructure Investment Bank, the ASEAN community will certainly doubt the Asian Infrastructure Investment Bank.

3. Neutral

A Neutral view holds that the Belt and Road Initiative is an open option where the ASEAN community enjoys a high degree of autonomy, and it can strike a balance between the US-led TPP and the China-led Belt and Road Initiative. While being aware of the huge repercussion provoked by the Belt and Road Initiative, some ASEAN people are worried that it would be

[22] How the Ten ASEAN Countries Respond to the Belt and Road Draws Much Attention, http://www.chinairn.com/news/20150413/164506166.shtml.

uneasy to carry out the initiative. Singaporean scholar Rajiv R. Chaturvedi pointed out that the construction of the Belt and Road would exert a positive impact on regional stability and global peace, but it also faces challenges, including the Three Evil Forces, ethnic conflicts and the sovereignty dispute.[23] Tang Zhimin, Director of the China ASEAN Studies Center at Panyapiwat Institute of Management, hopes that the Belt and Road Initiative can be refined and carried out in coordination with the construction of the ASEAN Community.[24] In short, the neutral ASEAN people hope more that the developmental strategies of their countries can connect with the Belt and Road Initiative so that their countries can have the initiative in their hands.

It should be noted that unlike the governments of the ASEAN countries which have actively discussed the feasibility of participating in the Belt and Road Initiative, the ordinary people in the ASEAN countries know little about the initiative, as does the community of overseas Chinese. This is due to the following factors: on the one hand, the initiative was put forward not long ago, many projects are at the initial stage of implementation and thus are less known to the ordinary people in ASEAN countries; on the other hand, China's publicity efforts are not sufficient, China is pushing forward the initiative mainly at the high level, and it does not effectively arouse the enthusiasm of the ordinary people in ASEAN countries for participation.

Geographically, the five ASEAN continental countries (Myanmar, Laos, Cambodia, Thailand, Vietnam) are more enthusiastic than the five marine countries (Indonesia, the Philippines, Malaysia, Singapore, Brunei). The five continental countries are traditionally friendly countries to China, and they generally recognize the Belt and Road Initiative. The five ASEAN marine countries have many concerns for the following reasons: as an ally of USA, the Philippines adopts the policy towards China in alignment with that of USA, it becomes extreme in the issue of the South China Sea and has strained relations with China; Singapore usually seeks a balance among great powers, it considers the response of USA on a wide range of issues; Malaysia's political situation has fluctuated recently, the policy towards China adopted by senior

[23]The Evaluation of the Belt and Road Initiative by the International Community, http://www.cet.com.cn/plpd/zfff/1249914.shtml.

[24]The Belt and Road Initiative Leads the Efforts to Break New Ground in the ASEAN community's Connectivity, http://world.huanqiu.com/hot/2015-11/8012243.html.

leaders is subject to restrictions; Indonesia is highly vigilant against China, its relations with China have always been sensitive. Furthermore, the five ASEAN marine countries are less close to China than the five ASEAN continental countries in terms of geography and economic ties, so it is not surprising for the five ASEAN marine countries to take vague attitudes toward the Belt and Road Initiative.

II. Achievements and Problems in the Implementation of the Belt and Road Initiative in the ASEAN Community

1. Achievements in the implementation of the Belt and Road Initiative in the ASEAN community and causes for making these achievements

a. *Achievements in the implementation of the Belt and Road Initiative in the ASEAN community*

In 2015, great progress and significant achievements were made in carrying out the Belt and Road Initiative in the ASEAN community. They are mainly reflected in the following aspects:

First, the construction of the Asian Infrastructure Investment Bank was supported by the ASEAN community. As of late 2015, all of the 10 ASEAN countries joined the Asian Infrastructure Investment Bank as the prospective founding members. The ASEAN community took a positive attitude towards the construction of the Asian Infrastructure Investment Bank from the beginning. In March 2015, soon after the *Asian Infrastructure Investment Bank Agreement* came into force, the rotating ASEAN presidency, Malaysia, stated that the ASEAN group was fully assisting the establishment of the Asian Infrastructure Investment Bank, and hoped that the Asian Infrastructure Investment Bank can work with the ASEAN Infrastructure Fund to provide more financial support for regional development. On June 29, 2015, the signing ceremony of the *Asian Infrastructure Investment Bank Agreement* was held in Beijing, all of the ASEAN member countries, except Malaysia, Thailand and the Philippines, signed the agreement. These three countries separately signed the agreement on August 21, September 29 and December 31, respectively. Amidst doubts in the international community, the Philippines finally caught up with the last train of the founding members of the Asian Infrastructure Investment Bank. The Secretary of Finance of the Philippines, Cesar V. Purisima, said that after the Philippines joined the Asian Infrastructure Investment Bank, the financing capability of the Philippines would be improved and the Philippines would obtain benefits in infrastructure construction.[25] Thus all of the 10 ASEAN countries had officially joined the Asian Infrastructure Investment Bank. The construction of the Asian Infrastructure Investment Bank will provide a fund accommodation guarantee for the Belt and Road Initiative. This platform demonstrates the diversity and inclusiveness of the Belt and Road Initiative; it also arouses the enthusiasm of ASEAN countries and is conducive to steadily pushing forward the Belt and Road Initiative.

Second, China's high-speed train "went global" more rapidly. On October 16, 2015, the consortium of Chinese enterprises led by the China Railway Corporation and the consortium of Indonesian state-owned enterprises led by PT Wijaya Karya Tbk officially signed a China–Indonesia joint venture agreement. The joint venture will be responsible for building and operating the Jakarta–Bandung High-speed Railway Project in Indonesia; this marks a historic breakthrough in the "going global" drive of China's railway, especially the high-speed railway. Furthermore, the China–Laos railway cooperation developed smoothly, both sides signed a cooperation agreement on November 13; the cornerstone laying ceremony of the Laos section (Boten–Vientiane) was held on December 2; it became the overseas railway project directly connected by China's railway network. On March 25, 2016, the Government of Thailand announced that Chinese enterprises would appoint Chinese experts and use China's technology to build the 250-km/h 250-km long Bangkok–Nakhon Ratchasima Railway, with the adoption of trains made by China. Before long, the railways in Indonesia, Laos and Thailand will be connected to shape the Trans-Asian Railway as a whole and thus form a railway-linked Silk Road, laying the foundation for shaping a

[25] See: The Philippines Announces That It Will Sign the *Asian Infrastructure Investment Bank Agreement*, *Philippine World News*, December 31, 2015.

China–ASEAN industrial chain and building the China–ASEAN greater economic region. More importantly, the construction of connectivity marked by the railway will produce a demonstration effect on the implementation of the Belt and Road Initiative, so that China and the ASEAN form a closer community of shared interests.

Third, industrial cooperation was promoted intensely. With the impact of the global economic recession, China–ASEAN trade declined by 1.7% in 2015, but bilateral economic relations improved; this was closely associated with China–ASEAN industrial cooperation under the Belt and Road Initiative. At present, China–ASEAN industrial cooperation is dominated by the establishment of industrial parks, while the existing industrial parks include the China–Malaysia Qinzhou Industrial Park, the Malaysia–China Kuantan Industrial Park, the China–Thailand Chongzuo Industrial Park, the China–Vietnam (Shenzhen–Haiphong) Economic and Trade Cooperation Zone, the China (Guangxi)–Indonesia Economic and Trade Cooperation Zone, the Thai–Chinese Rayong Industrial Zone, and the China–Brunei Industrial Park and the Guangxi (China–ASEAN) Grain Logistics Industrial Park. In 2015, the China–Malaysia Qinzhou Industrial Park basically satisfied the conditions for entering the industrial park; the construction of supporting infrastructure, including water, electricity, roads and communications, began in the Malaysia–China Kuantan Industrial Park; the project of the Guangxi (China–ASEAN) Grain Logistics Industrial Park broke the ground; the intent of cooperation was determined with respect to the China (Nanning)–Brunei Agricultural Industrial Park and the China (Yulin)–Brunei Traditional Chinese Medicine Health Industrial Park as the pioneering projects of the Brunei–Guangxi Economic Corridor. With joint operation by multiple parties, industrial parks have gradually become the bridges for China–ASEAN industrial cooperation on the Belt and Road. Industrial parks serve as the "strongholds" for the ASEAN community to attract capital from China; industrial parks are the "safety valves" for China's mitigating the risks arising out of going global.

Moreover, in 2015, construction was initiated on the China–ASEAN Cereals and Oil Processing Park Project; the signing and groundbreaking ceremony of the Muara Bridge Project in Brunei, undertaken by the China Harbour Engineering Company under the China Communications

Construction Co., Ltd., was held at Muara Port; with positive impact from the China–ASEAN Free Trade Area (CAFTA), the China–ASEAN Mining Cooperation Forum has enabled more than 810 projects to be promoted and discussed since 2010 — more than 80 projects have been signed, involving more than 48 billion yuan.[26] With impetus from the Belt and Road Initiative, China–ASEAN industrial cooperation has reached a new height.

Fourth, the implementation of the Belt and Road Initiative promoted China–ASEAN connectivity. The Belt and Road Initiative tallies with the needs of the ASEAN countries. With the driving force from the initiative, progress accelerated the connectivity between China and the ASEAN countries. Regarding pipeline construction, in January 2015, the China–Myanmar oil pipeline was fully open to traffic; it is a new route for China's importation of oil via a land route; it is conducive to mitigating China's dependence upon the Strait of Malacca; it expands the common interests of China and Myanmar while guaranteeing China's energy security.[27] Concerning road transportation, in March 2015, direct connection for freight transportation was launched at the China–Vietnam border port, which marked the official launch of a multinational cross-border transportation route connecting Vietnam with the Suzhou–Manzhouli–Moscow–Warsaw Railway via Guangxi.[28] Regarding railway construction, gratifying achievements have been made on the China–Thailand Railway, the China–Laos Railway and the China–Indonesia Railway Projects. Moreover, as an important part of the Belt and Road, the Trans-Asian Railway will see the initiation of construction soon; the China–Singapore Economic Corridor has progressed from consensus to practice; the China–ASEAN Maritime Channel is also actively being studied. The financing platforms, including the Asian Infrastructure Investment Bank, the Silk Road Fund and the China–ASEAN Cooperation

[26] 2015 China–ASEAN Mining Cooperation Forum: A New Journey in Cooperation Involving the Belt and Road, *People's Daily* (Overseas Edition), October 1, 2015, p. 8. http://news.cnpc.com.cn/system/2015/02/05/001527782.shtml.

[27] See: How Important Is the Completion of the China–Myanmar Oil Pipeline for China?, http://world.huanqiu.com/hot/2015-03/5939565.html.

[28] See: Direct Connection for Freight Transportation Is Launched at the China–Vietnam Border Port, Connecting the Suzhou–Manzhouli–Moscow–Warsaw Cross-border Transport Route, www.huanqiu.com.

Fund, provide financial guarantees for China–ASEAN connectivity. At present, China is continuing to work on building and improving the sea–land–air transportation channels with ASEAN countries, strengthening the connectivity planning and construction in such fields as communications, electric power and networking, improving the soft environment for connectivity, including customs clearance facilitation, market supervision and standards specification.

b. *Causes for obtaining achievements in the implementation of the Belt and Road Initiative in the ASEAN community*

Overall, significant achievements have been made in the implementation of the Belt and Road Initiative in the ASEAN community, which are attributable to the following factors:

First, the senior leaders of China and the ASEAN community reached important consensuses and supported each other. In the 17th China–ASEAN (10+1) Leaders' Summit in late 2014, the leaders of ASEAN countries praised China's initiative of building the China–ASEAN Community with a Common Destiny and jointly building the 21st Century Maritime Silk Road, they reaffirmed their firm commitment to further strengthening the China–ASEAN strategic partnership and put forward China–ASEAN Belt and Road plan and the list of project implementation.[29] During Chinese President Xi Jinping's visits to Vietnam and Singapore in November 2015, the Belt and Road was the important topic for discussion between China and Vietnam and Singapore. During his visit to Vietnam, Xi Jinping stated that China was willing to expand investment and financing in Vietnam, and promote balanced and sustainable development of bilateral trade. The *Joint Statement between China and Vietnam* issued by the two sides shows that China and Vietnam should strengthen cooperation on production capacity in building material, supporting industries, equipment manufacturing, electric power, renewable energy and other fields. When meeting with the Prime Minister of Singapore Lee Hsien Loong, Xi Jinping stated that the two sides

[29]See: China and the ASEAN Community Sealed Great Deals Involving the Belt and Road, the official website of the CAFTA, http://www.cafta.org.cn/show.php?contentid=73630.

should push forward the third intergovernmental cooperation project with Chongqing as the project operation center and actively explore the cooperation mode under which the enterprises of the two countries can develop the third-party market under the framework of the Belt and Road Initiative. China and Singapore will also upgrade the existing *China–Singapore Free Trade Agreement*.

In late 2015, the ASEAN Community was officially completed, bringing enormous opportunities for cooperation to the countries in the region, including China. The ASEAN community is the key and priority region for the construction of the Belt and Road in terms of geography and economic and trade ties. The construction of the ASEAN Community has been resolutely supported by China; likewise, the Belt and Road Initiative has also received vigorous support from the ASEAN community. Mutual support between the two sides is the guarantee for obtaining great success.

Second, the mechanisms for carrying out the Belt and Road Initiative were improved continuously. The original China–ASEAN cooperation mechanisms included reciprocal visits between heads, a China–ASEAN Leaders' Summit (10+1), the Greater Mekong Sub-region (GMS) Leaders' Meeting and decision-making mechanisms, more than 20 ministerial and senior officials' meeting execution mechanisms as well as some semi-official or non-governmental cooperation mechanisms, involving political, economic, cultural, educational, security, maritime and other fields. With many years of operations, these mechanisms have provided a vigorous guarantee for China–ASEAN cooperation. In 2015, new progress was made on China–ASEAN cooperation mechanisms — on November 12, the Lancang–Mekong Cooperation Mechanism was officially established. This Mechanism covers multi-level cooperation mechanisms, such as leaders' meetings, foreign ministers' meetings and the working groups in other fields; China will cooperate with the countries in the Mekong River Basin on political security, economic and sustainable development, social humanity, with complete connection to the three pillars involved in the construction of the ASEAN Community; they complement the original sub-regional cooperation mechanisms — including the Greater Mekong Sub-region economic cooperation, the ASEAN–Mekong River Basin development cooperation and the Mekong River Committee — to earnestly promote regional integration.

Moreover, with regard to the next institutional construction under the Belt and Road Initiative, China proposed to have a discussion with the ASEAN members to formulate the *Master Plan for China–ASEAN Connectivity*.[30] The ASEAN community has carried out the *Master Plan on ASEAN Connectivity* as of 2010, and has developed a Five-Year Plan for the construction of infrastructures, institutional buildings and people-to-people exchanges. In 2016, the ASEAN started implementing the second Five-Year Plan. The plan can be connected with the Belt and Road Initiative put forward by China to form the master plan for China–ASEAN connectivity. This new mechanism will certainly deepen bilateral connectivity.

Third, China–ASEAN cooperation started early and has featured a good foundation. Compared with other countries along the Belt and Road, the ASEAN community has many advantages for carrying out the Belt and Road Initiative: First, China and the ASEAN countries have established the legal framework for economic cooperation and the code of conduct, including *the Framework Agreement on Comprehensive Economic Cooperation between the Association of Southeast Asian Nations and the People's Republic of China*, laying the foundation for implementing the Belt and Road Initiative. Second, detailed economic cooperation plans have been developed. As of 2004, the two sides developed and implemented the Five-Year *Action Plan for Implementing the Joint Declaration between China and the ASEAN Community on the Strategic Partnership for Peace and Prosperity*. At present, the *Phase III Action Plan (2016–2020)* is being carried out. Many details in these plans accord with the Belt and Road Initiative. Third, besides the official mechanism, the diversified and multi-level cooperation platforms have also been established — such as the China–ASEAN Expo, the China–ASEAN Business & Investment Summit and bilateral matchmaking meetings in various industries, creating the conditions for the implementation of the Belt and Road Initiative. Fourth, there is support from various types of fund platforms; the China–ASEAN Investment Cooperation Fund, the China–ASEAN Maritime Cooperation Fund, China–ASEAN Special Loans for Infrastructure, and the Economic Cooperation Fund under the framework of the CAFTA

[30] Wang Yi, China Is Willing to Discuss with the ASEAN Community to Formulate the Master Plan for China–ASEAN Connectivity, August 6, 2015, the official website of the CAFTA, http://www.cafta.org.cn/show.php?contentid=75674.

can be utilized to implement the Belt and Road Initiative in addition to the loans from the Silk Road Fund and the Asian Infrastructure Investment Bank.

2. Problems in the construction of the Belt and Road Initiative in the ASEAN community

Although the Belt and Road Initiative has delivered good performance in the ASEAN community, some problems exist: First of all, plans and details are too limited to meet the ASEAN community's needs. The Belt and Road Initiative has been recognized by most ASEAN countries, but the released action plans and details are limited during implementation so that the ASEAN community does not know how to participate in it; in particular, some key elements — including executors, the mode of pushing forward the initiative, fund application — have not yet been clearly explained by China, so even if ASEAN countries want to engage in cooperation, they cannot find channels for communication. As ASEAN countries have different national conditions, they have different needs for infrastructure and production capacity; however, so far no well-targeted schemes or action plans are available. These schemes and plans cannot be carried out and will be reduced to blindfold actions unless there are connections and consultations with relevant ASEAN countries. China has not yet identified the department(s) responsible for doing these things. If all of these things are done by the National Development and Reform Commission, it will be very difficult to draw up the plans covering more than 60 countries along the Belt and Road.

Second, the localities in China rushed headlong into mass action and lacked coordination. After the Belt and Road Initiative was released, various provinces and autonomous regions in China scrambled for projects for fear of suffering a loss. Many provinces and autonomous regions sent visiting missions to recommend projects; some ASEAN countries were overwhelmed by too many visitors and did not know how to distinguish confusing information. Some private enterprises sought preferential policies from local governments in the name of the Belt and Road, some launched land-related enclosure efforts in ASEAN countries, some seized the opportunity to promote shoddy products; this certainly aroused disgust among ASEAN countries.

Third, emphasis was placed on "exportation", while "bringing in" was ignored and there was no thinking of any win–win cooperation. The implementation of the Belt and Road Initiative is based on win–win cooperation with the countries along the Belt and Road. Take the ASEAN community as an example; if China unilaterally exports excess production capacity and does not open its market to ASEAN countries, the enthusiasm of ASEAN countries will be affected. For example, Malaysia and Singapore — which enjoy excellent infrastructures — hoped to, by virtue of the Belt and Road Initiative, push their competitive industries (such as finance, telecommunications, foreign trade and other service sectors) to the Chinese market or the third-party markets cooperating with China. The state-owned enterprises in Thailand, Vietnam and Brunei worried that as Chinese enterprises entered their countries, their interests would be eroded, thus there was resistance from them. Therefore, it is not easy to really achieve win–win cooperation between China and ASEAN countries through the implementation of the Belt and Road Initiative.

Fourth, the preparations for projects were not sufficient enough, the decision-making departments of the two sides lacked coordination. For example, as China carried out the high-speed railway project in Thailand, surveys were not sufficiently conducted, the loans offered by China were those with a relatively high interest rate, so the Government of Thailand thus sought low-interest loans from Japan; finally, the Government of Thailand awarded part of the project to Japan.[31] Delay thus occurred on initiating the construction of the China–Thailand High-speed Railway Project to be built by China. Afterwards, the Government of Thailand announced independent financing rather than the planned construction of the railway under the mode of a China–Thailand joint venture, and only the Bangkok–Nakhon Ratchasima section was awarded to China. This change was due to decentralization of power in the decision-making departments of the two sides, the diversity of stakeholders, decision-making from multiple departments and difficulty in coordination.[32]

[31] See: The Ministry of Transport of Thailand: As China's Loans Involve High Interest, the High-speed Railway Project Will Be Awarded to Japan, www.xilu.com, http://www.xilu.com/20150303/1000010000749224.html.

[32] See: Zhong Jiabin, Railway Politics Uncovers the True Features of China–Thailand Relations, http://www.zaobao.com/forum/views/opinion/story20160330-598867.

Fifth, China fell into a passive position in project negotiation without the ability to consider all matters at the same time. Cooperation on the China–Indonesia high-speed railway also suffered setbacks. China and Japan fiercely competed with each other in bidding, both China and Japan made all-round efforts to win the bidding and the Government of Joko even canceled the high-speed railway project in order to keep a balance between China and Japan. Before long, the Government of Joko awarded the high-speed railway project to China since China offered more favorable terms. However, this triggered discontent from Thailand. Thailand imposed a deep price cut in high-speed railway negotiations with China by mentioning the project in Indonesia. The rate of preferential loans offered by China to Thailand's high-speed railway project was 2.5%, lower than 3%, the lowest interest rate offered by the Export–Import Bank of China to an overseas project, but Thailand required China to reduce the loan interest rate from 2.5% to 2% according to the terms given to Indonesia. The setbacks in Thailand's high-speed railway show that China upheld the tradition of addressing issues case by case in negotiations and failed to develop a whole set of criteria, communication among relevant departments was unsmooth and an effective balance could not be achieved, so a special case was misunderstood by the other side as the model which can be duplicated, and thus China fell into a passive position in negotiation.

Sixth, risk awareness was not strong. The implementation of the Belt and Road Initiative is accompanied by risks, including political and economic risks. At present, the political situation in the ASEAN community is generally stable, but the situation is volatile in particular countries, such as Malaysia; the legal system is not well-developed in some ASEAN countries, such as Myanmar, Laos and Cambodia; some countries, e.g., the Philippines, change foreign investment laws and regulations quickly; some NGOs raised strong objections in such countries as Myanmar and Laos; these are the risks that are involved. As China invests in these countries, China must consider political and economic risks and cannot ignore costs because relevant tasks are ultimately carried out by enterprises and enterprises must consider profit or loss in the projects. China should learn a lesson from the three projects with setbacks and a huge loss in Myanmar, and enhance the risk awareness.

Seventh, as China's trade surplus expanded, the ASEAN community was subject to heavy pressure. With the global economic slowdown and sharp decline in international trade, China–ASEAN trade decreased to some extent in 2015 over 2014; this is not difficult to understand. It should be noted that China's trade surplus with the ASEAN community continued to increase amidst a decline in total trade, and the trade imbalance between the two sides worsened. From 2002 to 2015, China's trade with the ASEAN community featured a deficit in the first 8 years, but it became a surplus as of 2012; the surplus expanded continuously and reached a record high USD 83.2 billion in 2015. Some people in the ASEAN community believed that Chinese commodities were highly competitive, making it difficult for the ASEAN countries to compete with China; many small enterprises in the ASEAN community were thus closed down, so the ASEAN community was locked in a debate on whether or not cooperation with China can benefit the ASEAN community. The ASEAN countries worried that like the (CAFTA), the Belt and Road Initiative would ultimately increase the ASEAN community's economic dependence upon China, so the ASEAN community was very cautious about the Belt and Road Initiative and stressed the freedom and flexibility of cooperation more, adding more difficulties to the implementation of the initiative.

Eighth, the issue of the South China Sea dented the ASEAN community's political trust in China and increased its concerns about China. On the issue of the South China Sea, as of 2013, the ASEAN community has changed its past attitude to break the silence; the ASEAN countries collectively voiced their opinions and raised requirements to China. In July 2015, Vietnam, Malaysia, Indonesia and Thailand, in addition to the Philippines, sent representatives to attend the hearing held at the International Court of Arbitration. The Minister of Maritime Affairs and Fisheries of Indonesia publicly required China to change the nine-dotted line. ASEAN countries were generally vigilant against China's military presence in the South China Sea. The disputes over the South China Sea severely affected the political relations between China and the claimant countries in the ASEAN community and compromised the ASEAN community's political trust in China, exerting an adverse impact on the implementation of the Belt and Road Initiative in the ASEAN countries.

III. Policy Suggestions for Carrying out the Belt and Road Initiative in ASEAN Countries

1. Intensifying intergovernmental cooperation between China and the ASEAN community, putting into practice relevant agreements

The year 2016 marks the beginning of the period of China's 13th Five-Year Plan and is the first year after the completion of the ASEAN Economic Community. China should strengthen its strategic connection with the ASEAN community, seize the opportunities from the completion of the ASEAN Economic Community to deepen China–ASEAN economic and trade relations and increase mutual investments so that common development is boosted through economic and trade cooperation. Pushing forward the Belt and Road Initiative calls for carrying out relevant agreements. In the 18th "10+1" Leaders' Meeting held on November 21, 2015, Chinese Premier Li Keqiang stated that China was willing to make the Belt and Road Initiative connect with the developmental strategies of the countries in the region, to actively participate in the *Master Plan on ASEAN Connectivity* and to continue to energetically promote the construction of the Trans-Asian Railway; China would sign the China–Laos–Thailand tripartite transportation facilitation agreement as early as possible, China would also study and develop the *China–ASEAN Transportation Facilitation Agreement*; China would work on establishing the China–ASEAN Countries Mechanism for Cooperation on Computer Emergency Response Organization and jointly building the China–ASEAN Information Harbor.[33] These initiatives relating to the construction of the Belt and Road are very concrete but need to be actively promoted and gradually carried out by the governmental departments of the two sides. Furthermore, it is also necessary to reinforce relevant safeguard measures, give full scope to the roles of the Asian Infrastructure Investment Bank, the Silk Road Fund, the China–ASEAN Investment Cooperation Fund and other platforms. At present, the Asian Infrastructure Investment Bank has been put into substantive operations; experience

[33] See: The ASEAN Summit Focuses on Upgrading Regional Trade Cooperation, http://www.baminxw.com/guojijujiao/103452.html.

should be summarized timely so that the Asian Infrastructure Investment Bank can play a more important role in the joint construction of the Belt and Road by China and the ASEAN community.

2. Giving prominence to the principle of achieving shared development through consultation and collaboration, fully arousing the ASEAN community's enthusiasm

Achieving shared development through consultation and collaboration is an important principle which governs the construction of the Belt and Road. It is imperative to highlight this principle for active publicity to fully arouse the enthusiasm of ASEAN countries. Cooperation should be based on equality and really yield win–win outcomes. In reality, publicity efforts can be made by combining this principle with win–win cooperation.

Moreover, China should, as early as possible, unveil more details of the plan or scheme for the construction of the Belt and Road, so that ASEAN countries can fully understand it/them; China should seek advice from ASEAN countries by carrying out the principle of consultation. Rules should be jointly made to ensure fairness and impartiality. It is necessary to fully identify the common interests of the two sides by putting into practice the principle of achieving shared development.

3. Ensuring that the government is in the right position, giving full play to the role of enterprises as the main players

The construction of the Belt and Road is carried out by enterprises rather than by the government. As China put forward the Belt and Road Initiative, one of its objectives is to make Chinese enterprises "go global" to exploit foreign markets. Thus the Belt and Road Initiative should be implemented by enterprises with platforms built by the government. The government should give full scope to the role of enterprises as the main players in the construction of the Belt and Road; the government should not go beyond its responsibilities and should make a macro plan and provide overall guidance, create cooperation platforms for Chinese enterprises to "go global", as well as provide policy support and facilitation services. As Chinese enterprises may encounter some difficulties when entering ASEAN countries — for example, they may be unfamiliar with local political, economic and investment environments, laws and regulations, overseas projects may suffer a shortage of professional talents, so government departments should improve the supporting policies for "going global", assist with the introduction of talents and organize the training and it should communicate with the governments of the ASEAN countries. Furthermore, actions should also be taken to encourage non-governmental chambers of commerce, associations and other social organizations to provide enterprises with supporting services. It is necessary to ensure the role of enterprises as the main players, observe the internationally recognized business rules, and leverage comparative advantages to carry out the development of the project and market-oriented operations. The government should refrain from seeking unrealistic quick results and creating excessive administrative intervention.

4. Properly addressing the issue of the South China Sea

With the announcement of the final verdict by the International Court of Arbitration on the case of an appeal instituted by the Philippines, some claimant countries in the ASEAN community may take the opportunity to impose pressure on China. Under such a circumstance, the mutual political trust between China and the ASEAN community will be subject to impact, which will be unfavorable for carrying out the Belt and Road Initiative.

On the issue of the South China Sea, in 2014, China put forward the "dual-track line of thought" by which relevant disputes are directly settled by the parties involved in a peaceful way through amicable consultation and negotiation, while the peace and stability of the South China Sea are jointly safeguarded by China and the ASEAN countries. In November 2015, in the 10th East Asia Summit, Chinese Premier Li Keqiang put forward a five-point initiative on jointly safeguarding the peace and stability of the South China Sea by various countries. On this basis, further scope should be given to the role of the ASEAN community in addressing the issue of the South China Sea, the consultation on the *South China Sea Code of Conduct* (COC) should be accelerated, and intensified efforts should be made to prevent the issue of the South China Sea from continuing to worsen in 2016.

5. Promoting China–ASEAN sociocultural exchanges

Once a cultural atmosphere in which the people of China and the ASEAN community depend on and help each other is created, it will greatly boost the implementation of the Belt and Road Initiative. In late 2015, the ASEAN Community was established. The construction of the ASEAN Sociocultural Community — one of the three pillars of the ASEAN Community — is beneficial for ASEAN countries to strengthen solidarity and external exchanges. China and the ASEAN community should take this historic opportunity to enhance bilateral social and cultural exchanges. The governments and non-governmental forces of the two sides should cooperate with each other to jointly promote the implementation of the Belt and Road Initiative in ASEAN countries.

Moreover, it is also necessary to speed up the cultivation of talents involving minority languages of the ASEAN community. Most ASEAN countries are minority language-speaking countries; however, currently, China is weak in the discipline of minority languages of the ASEAN community, so more cultivation efforts should be made. It is necessary to integrate the knowledge in various respects — including the political, historical, cultural and ethnic characteristics of ASEAN countries — in conjunction with mastering languages, so as to cultivate all-round interdisciplinary talents and improve the system of a knowledge reserve. The year 2016 is the Year of China–ASEAN Educational Exchanges. Both sides can take this opportunity to expand their bilateral cultural and educational contacts, enhance bilateral exchanges and consolidate and develop bilateral cooperation, thus contributing to the construction of the Belt and Road.

Chapter 19

Report on Guangxi–ASEAN Cooperation in 2015

Qin Jianwen*

In 2015, China–ASEAN relations witnessed progress in several fields, such as politics, security, economic cooperation, as well as social and cultural and other fields; the two sides basically achieved the goals for the development of bilateral relations specified in the *Action Plan for Implementing the Joint Declaration between China and the ASEAN on the Strategic Partnership for Peace and Prosperity* (2011–2015). As the important bridge for China–ASEAN contacts and cooperation, Guangxi developed good relations with the ASEAN community and made encouraging achievements to promote China–ASEAN cooperation in 2015.

* Qin Jianwen, Professor, doctoral supervisor at the Business School, Guangxi University, research fellow at the China–ASEAN Fiscal and Financial Policy Research Center of the China–ASEAN Research Institute of Guangxi University.

I. The Political and Diplomatic Cooperation Was Further Deepened

1. Guangxi–Vietnam exchanges developed in an increasingly extensive way

In 2015, Guangxi–Vietnam exchanges were on the rise and significant achievements were made in bilateral diplomatic ties.

Regarding the contacts between senior government officials, Peng Qinghua, the Secretary of the Party Committee and Chairman of the Standing Committee of the People's Congress of the Guangxi Zhuang Autonomous Region, met with the delegation led by Võ Trọng Việt, Commander of the Vietnam Border Defense Force, the two sides reached a consensus on building a secure and stable border environment; Peng Qinghua met with Nguyen Xuan Phuc, a member of the Political Bureau of the Central Committee of the Communist Party of Vietnam and Deputy Prime Minister of Vietnam, the two sides expressed the willingness to strengthen economic and trade contacts, connectivity and cross-border cooperation.[1] Peng Qinghua met with Vietnamese Ambassador to China Dang Minh Khoi, the two sides reached a consensus on the development of future cooperation in connectivity, cross-border economic and other fields. As the senior government officials of Guangxi and Vietnam engaged in exchanges and discussed matters regarding cooperation; these exchanges and discussions will be beneficial for scientifically and rationally guiding bilateral construction investments, promoting the common development of the two sides.

Regarding the cooperation between cities of the two sides, the Party and government delegation led by Mo Xiaolin, the Secretary of the Party Committee of Fangcheng District, Fangchenggang City, was invited to Hải Hà District, Vietnam, for engaging in friendly exchanges and signing the agreement on the establishment of amicable relations between Fangcheng District and Hải Hà District. The delegation met with the Vietnamese counterpart with respect to relevant matters including the work on promoting the construction of the Tongzhong–Dang Mo Port and expansion of trade, and the two

[1] Wei Heng, Peng Qinghua Met with the Deputy Prime Minister of Vietnam, Nguyen Xuan Phuc, *Guangxi Daily*, September 18, 2015(1).

sides reached an extensive consensus on the exchange and cooperation in various fields. The Party and government delegation of Dongxing City of Fangchenggang led by Zhou Shijun, the Secretary of the Party Committee of Dongxing City, met with the Party and government delegation of Mong Cai City, Vietnam, led by the Secretary of the Party Committee of Mong Cai City, and the two sides established the sister-city ties between Dongxing City and Mong Cai City. Ban Zhongbai, a member of the Standing Committee of Nanjing City and Director of the Organization Department of Nanjing City, met with the delegation of Hạ Long City, Vietnam, and the two sides agreed to expand bilateral exchanges and cooperation in a number of fields for achieving common prosperity and development. The amicable cooperation and contacts between the cities of Guangxi and relevant provinces and cities of Vietnam are conducive to enhancing the mutual political trust and on this basis, pushing forward bilateral exchanges and cooperation in the economic, trade, cultural and other fields.

2. Close cooperation between Guangxi and Brunei, Thailand

In 2015, Guangxi and Brunei engaged in close cooperation, obtaining great achievements, while the construction of the Brunei–Guangxi Economic Corridor became a new bright spot in China–Brunei cooperation.

Peng Qinghua, the Secretary of the Party Committee and Chairman of the Standing Committee of the People's Congress of the Guangxi Zhuang Autonomous Region, led Guangxi's delegation to visit Brunei, and the two sides reached a consensus on more rapidly promoting the construction of the Brunei–Guangxi Economic Corridor, encouraging and supporting bilateral cooperation in various fields; the Mayor of Yulin City, Su Haitang, met with the advisor to the Government of Brunei, and the two sides engaged in extensive exchanges in cooperation matters including the introduction of Bruneian businessmen; Chen Wu, Chairman of the Guangxi Zhuang Autonomous Region, met with Pehin Yahya, the Minister of Industry and Primary Resources of Brunei, and the two sides reached a shared vision on engaging in multi-field and in-depth cooperation and exchanges between Brunei and Guangxi.

In 2015, Guangxi and Thailand kept close contacts and further deepened their cooperation in various fields.

Peng Qinghua met with the Prime Minister of Thailand, Prayuth Chan-ocha, and the two sides reached an extensive consensus on bilateral cooperation in the political, economic and other fields[2]; the Deputy Mayor of Baise City, Zhao Guilan, and Mayor Zhou Yijue met with Thailand's delegation, and the two sides reached a consensus on further cooperation and exchanges. Furthermore, Guangxi also held a Round Table Dialogue among State Leaders of Thailand and CEOs from China aimed at promoting bilateral economic and trade relations and achieving common development; the Deputy Director of the Division of East Asian Affairs at the Ministry of Foreign Affairs of Thailand led a delegation to visit the Qinzhou Free Trade Port Area, Guangxi, expressing the intent on and vision of deepening wharf and port cooperation.

Both Brunei and Thailand are the economically developed countries among the 10 ASEAN countries. Deepening the cooperation between Guangxi and the two countries in the fields of economics, trade, port, cultural exchanges, investment and other fields can boost the development of Guangxi, Brunei and Thailand, and help build a good image of Guangxi–ASEAN cooperation, thus quickening the pace of friendly exchanges between Guangxi and other ASEAN countries.

3. Guangxi continued to maintain amicable cooperative relations with other ASEAN countries

In 2015, Guangxi continued to keep friendly contacts with other ASEAN countries, including Malaysia, Singapore, Laos, Myanmar, Cambodia and the Philippines.

Regarding the contacts between senior government officials, the senior leaders of Guangxi met with the important figures of ASEAN countries many times. Peng Qinghua, the Secretary of the Party Committee of the Guangxi Zhuang Autonomous Region, met with Deputy Prime Minister of Cambodia Hor Nam hong, the Second Minister for International Trade and Industry of Malaysia, Dato' Seri Ong Ka Chuan, the Senior Minister of State at the Ministry of Trade and Industry and the Ministry of National Development of

[2] Li Pan, Peng Qinghua Met with the Prime Minister of Thailand, Prayuth Chan-ocha, in Bangkok, *Guangxi Daily*, April 4, 2015(1).

Singapore, Lee Yi Shyan, the Minister of Trade of Indonesia, Thomas Lembong; Chen Wu, Chairman of the Guangxi Zhuang Autonomous Region, met with Malaysian ambassador to China, Zainuddin Yahya, the Vice President of Myanmar, Sai Mauk Kham, the Deputy Prime Minister of Laos, Somsavat Lengsavad, the State and Commerce Minister of Cambodia, Sun Chanthol, the Deputy Prime Minister of Cambodia, Keat Chhon and other important government officials; they attended the 12th China–ASEAN Expo and Business & Investment Summit. The Mayor of Nanning City, Zhou Hongbo, met with consul generals of Cambodia, Myanmar, Laos and Malaysia, he met with Laos' delegation and commission, and attended the 1st China–ASEAN Mayor's Forum.

Regarding city and enterprise cooperation, Guigang City, Guangxi and Zamboanga City, the Philippines became sister cities; Chongzuo City, Guangxi and Thakhek City, Khammouane Province, Laos established international sister city ties; Guangxi's Beibu Gulf International Port Group and PSA Singapore successfully signed an agreement for cooperation.

In 2015, Guangxi and the senior leaders of the above countries maintained close contacts and established friendly cooperative relations with a number of ASEAN countries. This is conducive to enhancing the mutual political trust between China and ASEAN countries and establishing stable and good political relations between the two sides; this also deepens the cooperation between Guangxi, and even between China, and ASEAN countries in the economic, trade, cultural exchange, investment development, border security and other fields; this also helps China successfully carry out the Belt and Road Initiative, promotes cross-border cooperation, the sharing of cooperation achievements and the delivery of win–win outcomes for various parties.

4. Guangxi became the key node of the China–ASEAN multi-level cooperation mechanism

In 2015, Nanning witnessed the convening of a number of important meetings, including the China–ASEAN Statistics Forum, the 1st China–ASEAN Mayors' Forum, the China–Indochina Peninsula International Economic Corridor (Nanning–Singapore) Cooperation and Development Round Table Conference, the 12th China–ASEAN Expo and Business & Investment

Summit. Furthermore, other cities and areas, including Fangchenggang, also became the hot spots for ASEAN countries to visit and engage in exchanges with China. As the most important node in China–ASEAN cooperation, thanks to its special location advantage, Guangxi will play a more important role in China–ASEAN cooperation, and will boost China–ASEAN cooperation in connectivity projects and promote the construction of the Belt and Road.

II. The Military and Security Cooperation Became More Pragmatic

1. Guangxi and Vietnam deepened exchange and cooperation in border security

a. *The cooperation and exchanges among the border defense forces became closer*

In 2015, the Guangxi Public Security and Border Defense Corps and the border defense forces of four provinces of Vietnam, including Quang Ninh Province and Lang Son Province, jointly held the meeting on summarization of the work in jointly building friendly stations (teams) and villages as well as a safe border; the meeting recognized the border defense forces of China and Vietnam for active mutual assistance and excellent work.[3] The win–win cooperation between the border defense forces is beneficial to guaranteeing the security of the border between the two sides and the social and economic development of the border areas of both sides.

Furthermore, the representatives from the Border Defense Corps of Fangchenggang City and the border defense station of Mong Cai International Port, Vietnam, jointly inaugurated the China–Vietnam Border Defense Force Friendship Forest in the China–Vietnam People's Friendship Park, Dongxing, and carried out the tree planting activity. The activity of jointly building the friendship forest embodies the enhancement of exchange and cooperation by China and Vietnam's border defense forces and is conducive to further bilateral cooperation in the field of border security.

[3] Shi Baihua, Huang Chunyun, Inheriting the Traditional Friendship, Expanding the Areas of Cooperation, *China Border Police*, June 15, 2015 (1).

b. *The cooperation in cracking down on crimes was deepened*

Regarding preventing and guarding against smuggling, in 2015, under the cross-border cooperation mechanism, Dongxing Customs and Dang Mo Customs Suboffice, Vietnam jointly cracked the case of endangered animal product smuggling at the Tongzhong–Dang Mo Port. Concerning the issue of cracking down on drugs, China and Vietnam carried out the second joint campaign against drug trafficking at the China–Vietnam border during the months September–November, 2015, which was aimed at investigating and seizing those engaged in cross-border drug trafficking and intensively cracking down on drug-related criminal gangs detrimental to both countries. This joint campaign helps both countries increase the degree of cooperation in safeguarding security and makes the public security at the border areas of both countries orderly and regularized.

Regarding border inspection, the Dongxing Border Inspection Station and the border defense station of Mong Cai International Port, Vietnam, held the Activity of the Chinese Border Defense Service Brand Publicity and China–Vietnam Joint Enhancement of Border Inspection Services. The activity is conducive to improving the mechanism of bilateral cooperation in law enforcement services and enhancing the border inspection services of the two sides.

2. Guangxi and ASEAN countries deepened the cooperation on health safety

1. The 9th China–ASEAN Procurators-General Conference, under the theme of "Cooperation in the International Pursuit of Stolen Goods", was held in Nanning. The conference reflects the great importance attached by the Chinese Government to the international pursuit of stolen goods in the fight against corruption and the Chinese Government's determination in working with ASEAN countries to crack down on transnational corruption crimes.[4]

---

[4] Chen Wenfeng, Pushing Forward Judicial Cooperation in the International Pursuit of Stolen Goods, Joining Hands at the International Level to Fight and Punish Corruption Crimes, *Guangxi Fa Zhi Ri Bao*, November 27, 2015, A01.

2. The China–ASEAN Cross-border Infectious Disease Surveillance and Response Seminar, under the theme of "Strengthening Exchanges, Establishing a Mechanism, Working Together, Actively Responding", was held in Nanning, in which the representatives of ASEAN countries introduced the experience of their respective countries in infectious disease surveillance and response. The seminar indicates China and ASEAN countries' determination to enhance their cooperation on health safety.

Deepening the cooperation between Guangxi and ASEAN countries in the military, border security, anti-crime, health safety and other fields is conducive to promoting the friendly relations between China and ASEAN countries and guaranteeing the economic development and social stability of various countries, thus boosting exchanges and cooperation in other fields and achieving win–win outcomes.

III. Economic and Trade Cooperation Became Closer

1. The ASEAN community remained the largest trading partner of Guangxi

During the period of January–December, 2015, Guangxi's import and export trade totaled 286,804 million yuan, up 15.13% over the same period of the previous year. The importation and exportation of goods between Guangxi and the 10 ASEAN countries totaled 146.8 billion yuan, accounting for 56.66% of Guangxi's total imports and exports, up 20.15% over the same period of the previous year — the export trade totaled 120,658 million yuan, up 15.02%; the import trade totaled 26,142 million yuan, up 51.32%; the trade surplus was 94,516 million yuan, up 10.79%. The importations and exportations between Guangxi and Vietnam, Thailand, Singapore and Malaysia among the 10 ASEAN countries were noticeable. The total amount of trade between Vietnam and Guangxi still ranked No. 1 and accounted for 85% of the importations and exportations between Guangxi and the 10 ASEAN countries, as shown in Table 1.

Overall, in 2015, the pattern of Guangxi's main trading partners was stable, the ASEAN community remained Guangxi's largest trading partner,

Table 1. Import and Export Trade between Guangxi and ASEAN Countries in 2015 (Unit: RMB 1,000 yuan)

	January	February	March	April	May	June	July	August	September	October	November	December	Total
Myanmar	24513	18285	19587	18115	18898	329356	284450	12832	17139	14173	22128	29785	809261
Cambodia	24568	17548	17029	13931	11660	16174	14055	18719	24547	38250	30874	49033	276388
Brunei	2295	1513	194	0	235	378	0	252	168	0	192	292	5519
Indonesia	268532	70562	302233	227872	177919	361144	311118	189024	474390	368579	206937	234227	3192537
Laos	5281	7059	6170	11206	9896	5343	4243	3596	5114	6246	7640	12694	84488
Malaysia	407374	325737	294826	323597	340662	498949	365993	306672	361237	203751	465868	270998	4165664
Singapore	102239	37016	883746	86798	259688	1077134	505824	560870	681630	427674	59228	397504	5079531
Thailand	761790	448966	812815	636747	1007901	757517	819220	777392	891251	708476	1008920	1266644	9897639
Vietnam	13730148	6453938	10899306	8065471	6055636	7888806	7450664	7183027	9407436	11792965	13207757	17569928	119705082
The Philippines	184974	178707	234119	174508	283419	698481	413308	365678	333941	251844	258516	206682	3584177
Guangxi's total imports and exports	26300799	14947355	23548598	19272114	19123752	24155114	21813938	22723864	27344887	24288937	27512476	35772578	286804412

(Continued)

Table 1. (*Continued*)

	January	February	March	April	May	June	July	August	September	October	November	December	Total
Guangxi's imports and exports with Asia	19846119	10137951	19233544	13779827	12132076	17222433	15155463	16102256	19032901	19156895	21060097	27837744	210697306
Guangxi's imports and exports with the ASEAN community	15326740	7380624	13235906	9383737	7882495	10934801	9755567	9052384	11862912	13560114	15009544	20037786	146800106
The proportion of imports and exports with Vietnam in those with the ASEAN community	89.58%	87.44%	82.35%	85.95%	76.82%	72.14%	76.37%	79.35%	79.30%	86.97%	88.00%	87.68%	85.00%
The proportion of imports and exports with the ASEAN community in total imports and exports	58.27%	49.38%	56.21%	48.69%	41.22%	45.27%	44.72%	39.84%	43.38%	55.83%	54.56%	56.01%	56.66%

Source: The Monthly Total Import and Export of Goods in 2015 by Country (Territory) at Nanning Customs Online.

trade contacts were on the rise, the role in stimulating the development on other fronts was enhanced continuously, and win–win outcomes for multiple parties gradually emerged.

2. A number of exhibitions and summits were successfully held in Nanning

a. *The China–ASEAN Expo and the China–ASEAN Business & Investment Summit were successfully concluded*

In September, 2015, the four-day 12th China–ASEAN Expo and the China–ASEAN Business & Investment Summit were successfully held in Nanning, Guangxi.[5] The expo featured the theme of "Jointly Building the 21st Century Maritime Silk Road — Drawing a Beautiful Blueprint for Maritime Cooperation". A total of 65,000 people participated in the exhibition and meeting; there were 85 purchasing groups. The expo witnessed 84 investment promotion activities, the investment promotion meetings of several ASEAN countries, a series of high-level forums and exchange activities, including the 3rd China–ASEAN Technology Transfer and Innovation Cooperation Conference, the China–ASEAN E-commerce Summit, the 7th China–ASEAN Summit on Financial Cooperation & Development, the China–ASEAN Mining Cooperation Forum and the 1st China–ASEAN Statistics Forum. During the expo, the China–ASEAN cross-border e-commerce platform and China–ASEAN trade facilitation research were launched, and the first research report on China–ASEAN (Cambodia, Laos, Myanmar, Vietnam) trade facilitation was released.

The China–ASEAN Expo and the China–ASEAN Business & Investment Summit have further improved the "Nanning Channel" for deepening the exchanges between China and the ASEAN community in various fields and have built a fruitful exchange platform characterized by win–win cooperation for promoting China–ASEAN cooperation and development.

[5] Wei Jing, The 12th China–ASEAN Expo Was Inaugurated Today, *Nanning Daily*, September 18, 2015, p. 1.

b. *A number of exhibitions and forums were successfully held*

The overseas exhibitions of the China–ASEAN Expo were carried out in several ASEAN countries for the first time in 2015. In 2015, the Thailand Exhibition, the Indonesia Exhibition and the Guilin Tourism Exhibition were organized, thus a main exhibition and several special exhibitions were held concurrently; under the theme of "Jointly Building the 21st Century Maritime Silk Road — Strengthening Investment Cooperation to Promote Common Development", the East Asian Investment Seminar was held in Nanning, which further reinforced the investment cooperation between Guangxi and East Asian countries; the 5th China–ASEAN (Liuzhou) Automobile, Construction Equipment and Components Expo was held in Liuzhou; the China–ASEAN Information Harbor Forum, under the theme of "The Internet + the Maritime Silk Road — Cooperation · Mutual Benefit · Win–win Outcome", was held in Nanning, during which the China National Internet Information Office and the Ministry of Posts and Telecommunications of Laos signed the *Memorandum of Understanding on Cyberspace Cooperation and Development*, and China and Indonesia also reached an intent of cooperation in cyberspace; during the 8th China–ASEAN Think Tank Strategic Dialogue Forum, the Guangxi Academy of Social Sciences and the Royal Academy of Cambodia signed a memorandum of cooperation; the launching ceremony of the sharing of scientific and technological innovation achievements and cooperation between 100 enterprises of Nanning and ASEAN countries was held.

These exhibitions, seminars and forums have provided excellent opportunities and platforms for extensive exchange and cooperation between China and various countries in various fields; they have played an important role in building the China–ASEAN Community with a Common Destiny and are of great realistic significance for Guangxi to carry out the Belt and Road Initiative.

3. New progress was made in Guangxi–ASEAN land and sea connectivity

The direct container liner route between the Port of Qinzhou and the Port of Ho Chi Minh was officially launched; at present, Nanning Airport has connected 13 cities in ASEAN countries and ranks No. 5 nationwide; the bridge approach of the Beilun River No. 2 Bridge connecting Mong Cai City, Vietnam with Dongxing City, China, officially broke ground; construction began on the middle section of the Hanoi–Friendship Pass Highway; Longzhou Port of the China–ASEAN Border Commodity Circulation General Station was officially opened; the master plan for the construction of Qinzhou, serving as the base of the China–ASEAN port city cooperation network has been completed, the first batch of three projects have been approved by the Ministry of Foreign Affairs for initiation, and relevant supporting projects have been launched; the multinational cross-border transportation route connecting Vietnam with the Suzhou–Manzhouli–Moscow–Warsaw Railway via Guangxi was officially open to traffic; Pingxiang City continued to press ahead with three major actions to make available three major channels, ceaselessly reinforced the construction of its port and further consolidated the foundation of the land route toward the ASEAN countries; the representatives from the customs offices of the two sides held the second border meeting, in which the two sides engaged in in-depth exchanges on cooperation matters, including innovation in customs clearance operation cooperation and pilot operations, so as to further push forward the reform of trade facilitation; the consensus reached in the 9th China Border Port City Mayor Forum was released.

In 2015, Guangxi intensified transportation construction towards the ASEAN countries and made fruitful achievements in the construction of a land route and an air route as well as port customs clearance, making outstanding contributions to Guangxi–ASEAN sea, land and air connectivity.

4. The construction of the Guangxi–ASEAN industrial parks reached a new level

In 2015, the construction of the China–ASEAN Cereals and Oil Processing Park Project was initiated; the number of companies among the global 500 companies which settled in the Guangxi–ASEAN Economic Development Zone was increased from eight to 10, while six projects — including the warehousing logistics project of the Guangxi Materials Group — had been carried out within the Guangxi–ASEAN Economic Development Zone; the industrial avenue was open to traffic in the China–Thailand (Chongzuo) Industrial Park, one of the two sister parks in the two countries, while large enterprises — including COFCO, Mitrphol — had settled in the industrial park; the Guangxi China–ASEAN Youth Industrial Park saw vigorous efforts in pushing forward park planning, investment attraction, the construction of projects settled in the industrial park and infrastructures, and the industrial park showed a good momentum of rapid growth in major economic indicators; the China–Malaysia Qinzhou Industrial Park basically satisfied the condition for developing vast stretches of area and providing industrial projects with access upon arrival, while a large number of traditional advantageous industrial projects from the ASEAN community had settled in the industrial park; the Malaysia–China Kuantan Industrial Park Project went well in general; at present, the construction of the supporting infrastructure — including water, electricity, roads and communications — has been carried out in the industrial park; Chongzuo City and Mitrphol intensified cooperation to jointly build the China–Thailand (Chongzuo) Industrial Park; the Guangxi (China–ASEAN) Grain Logistics Industrial Park Project broke ground, and it will become the hub for delivering grain from China to the south and importing grain from the ASEAN countries to China.

The fruitful construction of the Guangxi–ASEAN Industrial Park will continuously promote cooperation and development in such areas as the Pan-Beibu Gulf, the Greater Mekong Sub-region, two corridors and one circle, the Nanning–Singapore Economic Corridor, thus gathering experience for upgrading the China–ASEAN Free Trade Area (CAFTA).

5. The platforms for multi-channel cooperation and exchanges between Guangxi and the ASEAN community were upgraded continually

a. *The construction of cross-border cooperation platforms was in full swing*

The ASEAN Cross-border E-commerce Headquarters Base — jointly built by the Guangxi–ASEAN Economic & Trade Promotion Association and the International Development Co., Ltd. of the Zhongwang E-commerce Group — was officially launched in Nanning[6]; the 2015 China–ASEAN

[6] Li Shize, Guangxi's Development Gave a Vital Push to the Belt and Road, *The Guangxi Today Magazine*, 2015(7), pp. 45–46.

(Jingxi) Cross-border E-commerce Forum was held in Jingxi City. The construction of the above cross-border e-commerce cooperation platform will offer a new business model and trading platform for China–ASEAN import and export trade.

b. *Cooperation in commercial and trade logistics was promoted steadily*

The ASEAN (Vietnam)–Guangxi (Nanning)–Pearl River Delta highway-railway combined transportation route — which is based in Nanning as the freight logistics hub and is the new route for the Silk Road — was open to traffic; six projects — including the warehousing logistics project of the Guangxi Materials Group — broke ground within the Guangxi–ASEAN Economic Development Zone; the liner routes and shipping services between the Port of Qinzhou and the main ports in ASEAN countries, the Phase I project of the China–ASEAN Port Logistics Information Center and other supporting projects were launched; the Pingxiang China–Vietnam International Logistics Association was inaugurated in the Pingxiang Logistics Park, bringing together more than 100 logistics enterprises involving a cold chain, warehousing, less-than-carload freight and full carload freight; construction began at the special channel project for (China–Vietnam cross-border) goods at the Pingxiang Border Goods Logistics Center. Such projects as the logistics hub, logistics warehousing and a liner route were completed, which will fully boost China–ASEAN economic and trade cooperation and development as well as the smooth implementation of the Belt and Road Initiative.

c. *Cross-border financial reform was deepened continuously*

The Guangxi Branch of the Postal Savings Bank of China and the Lang Son Branch of the Vietnam Bank for Agriculture and Rural Development signed a border trade settlement cooperation agreement in Nanning, the capital of Guangxi; the Guangxi Beibu Gulf Bank and the Canadian Bank of Cambodia signed a *Strategic Cooperation Agreement*, under which the two sides will leverage their respective resource advantages to provide convenience for both sides to carry on business; the border banks of China and Vietnam signed a memorandum of cooperation in combating counterfeit currency. The intensification of the cross-border financial reform will inject new vigor into the healthy development of China–ASEAN cooperation.

d. *Cooperation on energy and communications advanced smoothly*

The China–Myanmar oil pipeline project (Myanmar section) was basically completed and the ceremony of its trial operation was held in Rangoon; construction began on the Phnom Penh-Bavet 115 kV power transmission line project, whose construction was undertaken by the Power Transmission & Distribution Co., Ltd. of the Guangxi Power Grid; the China–Myanmar international overland optical cable project — whose investment came solely from China Unicom — was fully put into operation, and the completion of the project will greatly enhance the quality of communication between Guangxi and the ASEAN community in voice, data communication and the Internet. The deepening cooperation on energy and communications will provide a vigorous basic guarantee for China–ASEAN cooperation. The multi-channel cooperation and exchange platforms have been upgraded continuously, bringing about closer economic and trade cooperation between China and the ASEAN community, thus promoting the economic and social development of China and ASEAN countries.

IV. The Exchange and Cooperation in the Social and Cultural Fields Reached a New Height

1. The cultural exchanges and cooperation continued to be deepened

a. *Cooperation in the cultural industry embarked on a new track*

In 2015, the China–ASEAN (Nanning) Public Cultural Construction Seminar and the 8th China–ASEAN Think Tank Strategic Dialogue Forum were held in Nanning; Guangxi's media established workstations in ASEAN countries, including Laos, for the first time, which marked closer news media cooperation and exchanges between Guangxi and the ASEAN community; The Chinese magazine *China–ASEAN Panorama* and the Thai magazine *ASEAN Business* signed a cooperation agreement on distribution, landing, manuscript and advertising exchanges as well as on other aspects; the Museum of Guangxi and the National Museum of Vietnamese History signed the *Cooperation Agreement on the Protection and Utilization of Cultural Heritage* in

Nanning; the Information Office of the Government of the Guangxi Zhuang Autonomous Region held the activity of the 2015 Beautiful South– ASEAN Overseas Chinese Language and Culture Media's Tour in Guangxi, organized and invited the mainstream overseas Chinese language and culture media from the 10 ASEAN countries to visit Guangxi.

b. *The cultural exchange was colorful*

In 2015, the 1st China–ASEAN International Fashion Week, the China–ASEAN Music Week, the China–ASEAN Drama Week, the 11th China–ASEAN Etiquette Contest, the 10th China–ASEAN Culture Forum, the 17th Nanning International Folk Song Art Festival, the 12th Focus on CAEXPO: the Asia Media Forum and other activities were held in Nanning City.

In May 2015, the cultural exchange activities "the Red Tour Following the Footstep of Uncle Ho Chi Minh" and the "China–Vietnam Borderers Gala" were carried out at the Dongxing People's Hall. These activities were attended by the Vice Chairman of the Vietnam–China Friendship Association, the Deputy Director of the Office of Foreign Affairs of the Guangxi Zhuang Autonomous Region, relevant leaders of Nanning City, a Vietnamese delegation led by the Vice Chairman of the Central Committee of the Vietnam Fatherland Front and the Vice Chairman of the Vietnam–China Friendship Association, as well as more than 200 Chinese and Vietnamese borderers.

c. *The cultural and sports contests continued to be held*

In 2015, Guangxi and ASEAN countries held a variety of cultural and sports contests, such as the lion king championship and the Dragon Boat Race with folk characteristics, chess competitions, a half marathon, a cycling cross-country race, a youth football match and a youth piano competition; the 3rd China–ASEAN Martial Arts Festival was held in Liuzhou City, the Guangxi Zhuang Autonomous Region. The rich and colorful cultural and sports exchange activities have enhanced social contacts between Guangxi and ASEAN countries, bilateral cultural fusion and the people's friendship.

2. The educational and academic exchanges and cooperation yielded notable results

a. *The cooperation among the institutions of higher learning became closer*

Regarding higher education, China–ASEAN cooperation continued to increase. In 2015, the number of overseas students studying at the institutions of higher learning in Guangxi still grew by more than 20%, and Guangxi became the province with the largest number of students from ASEAN countries in China.

In 2015, the China–ASEAN Vocational Education Exhibition and Forum was held in Nanning; more than 60 institutions of higher learning — including Guangxi University, Guangxi Normal University, Guangxi Medical University, Guangxi University for Nationalities, Guilin University of Technology and Guilin University of Electronic Technology — held talks with regard to vocational education and teaching as well as cooperation, with the KLC School of Education, the Hanoi Open University, the University of Cambodia, East Timor's Instituto Superior Cristal, Thailand's Rangsit University, the University of the West of England and other universities. The Department of Culture and Education of the China Overseas Exchange Association, the Guangxi Arts University, the Guangxi Overseas Chinese School, the Baise University separately signed the memoranda of cooperation on education and relevant agreements with the Government of Khon Kaen City, Thailand, the Panyapiwat Institute of Management, the Sawang Boriboon Wittaya School in Pattaya, Thailand, the consulate generals of Krabi, Thailand, and the Kingdom of Cambodia in Nanning.

b. *The academic exchanges were increasingly extensive*

In 2015, the Confucius Institute, jointly established by Guangxi Normal University and the Prince of Songkla University, carried out the Phase One Chinese culture camp activity of the year 2015; a 2015 workshop on economic and trade journalists of ASEAN countries, the 40th senior workshop on international young cadres (Cambodia, Myanmar) and the China–ASEAN (Vietnam) women's learning exchange class were opened in Nanning; the Seminar on Chinese Literature in Southeast Asia, the 2nd International Seminar on Overseas Chinese and Overseas Chinese Hometown Culture in

China were held in Qinzhou University; the chairman of a well-known public school of Chinese language and culture in Phetchaburi Province, Thailand, led a delegation, and the chairman of a time-honored public school of the Chinese language and culture in Laos led a Chinese language and cultural education delegation consisting of members from two public schools of the Chinese language and culture in Laos to the Guangxi Overseas Chinese School to hold talks on cooperation and exchanges in Chinese language and cultural education; the Center of Thai Culture Studies was established in Guangxi University for Nationalities.

The China–ASEAN Commercial Legal Cooperation Seminar was held in Nanning, in which the *Joint Declaration on China–ASEAN Legal Cooperation* and the *China–ASEAN Joint Commercial Mediation Agreement* were signed; two special classes on legal training were held. Furthermore, the Singaporean Law Workshop was smoothly opened in Nanning.

c. *The workshops on industrial cooperation were successively opened*

The Workshop on China–ASEAN Economic and Trade Relations, the Economic and Trade Journalist Workshop, the Workshop on Convention and Exhibition Affairs were opened in Nanning; the Workshop on the Construction and Management of the China–Vietnam Cross-border Economic Cooperation Zone was opened in Nanning; the Workshop on China–ASEAN Cooperation in the Tourism Industry was opened at the Guangxi International Business Vocational College; the international workshop on agricultural technology for ASEAN countries was opened at the Guangxi Academy of Agricultural Sciences.

The increasing educational cooperation and academic exchange activities between Guangxi and the ASEAN community will provide strong talent support and intellectual guarantees for expanding Guangxi–ASEAN political, economic and social cooperation.

3. Scientific and technological cooperation was deepened in an all-round way

Regarding technical cooperation, the 3rd China–ASEAN Technology Transfer and Innovation Cooperation Conference was held in Nanning, during which seven major activities were carried out, including the Joint Committee on China–ASEAN Scientific and Technological Cooperation, the High-level Cooperation Forum on China–ASEAN Technology Transfer and the Innovation Cooperation Conference, the East Asia Summit New Energy Forum, the China–ASEAN Expo Advanced Technology Exhibition, the China–ASEAN Technology Matchmaking Fair, the Thailand Industrial Cooperation Promotion Fair, the China–ASEAN Scientific and Technological Innovation Policy Seminar.[7] These activities covered various levels and a number of major industrial fields, mainly including new energy and renewable energy, biological medicine, marine science and technology and modern agriculture; they were rich in content and pragmatic.

Regarding information cooperation, China and the ASEAN community speeded up the construction of an information harbor, and made all-round efforts to build the "Information Maritime Silk Road" for "10+1" cooperation. The China–ASEAN Information Harbor generally relies on Guangxi in cooperation with the ASEAN countries to jointly build an infrastructure platform, an information-sharing platform, a technical cooperation platform, an economic and trade service platform and a people-to-people exchange platform, with efforts made to push forward the construction of information communication infrastructure, the Beidou Navigation Satellite System, the industrial base, the smart power grid and cybercultural exchange and other aspects, so as to promote regional economic and social development.

Regarding environmental cooperation, the China–ASEAN Environmental Cooperation Forum was inaugurated in Nanning, in which activities were carried out under the theme of "Environmental Sustainable Development Dialogue and Workshop"; the *Memorandum of Cooperation between the Department of Environmental Protection of the Guangxi Zhuang Autonomous Region, China, and the Department of Natural Resources and Environment of Cao Bằng Province, Vietnam, on Biodiversity Protection* was officially signed in Cao Bang City, kicking off a new project of cooperation between the environmental protection departments of the two countries in the new period and providing an important platform for dialogue and cooperation between

[7] Jiang Dongzhou, Liu Hao, The 3rd China–ASEAN Technology Transfer and Innovation Cooperation Conference Was Held in Nanning, *Science and Technology Daily*, September 19, 2015, p. 3.

Guangxi, China and Vietnam in the field of cross-border biodiversity protection.

With regard to medical service and health, the 2015 Asian Society of Cardiology China–ASEAN Coronary Intervention Summit & the 12th Guangxi Coronary Intervention Forum were held in Nanning, with a focus on engaging in international exchange and cooperation, concurrently advancing the cultivation of cardiovascular specialists in Guangxi and jointly promoting the healthy development of Guangxi's cause of coronary heart disease prevention and treatment.

Regarding agriculture, forestry and animal husbandry, Vietnam and the Guangxi Forestry Research Institute signed a memorandum on scientific and technological cooperation with respect to afforestation and tree planting; the Vietnam and Laos International Workshop on Agricultural Technology was opened at the Guangxi Forestry Research Institute, boosting agricultural development in Vietnam and Laos, enhancing the exchanges between China and Vietnam and Laos, for greater solidarity and mutual assistance. In recent years, the forestry cooperation between Guangxi, the place for holding the China–ASEAN Expo, and the ASEAN community has developed rapidly. At present, Guangxi's forestry industry has seen the preliminary formation of eight major advantageous forestry industries, including forestry, pulp paper, wood processing, sasanqua, flowers, forest tourism, bamboo and rattan processing and wild animal and plant breading and utilization.

The scientific and technological exchanges and cooperation are conducive to propelling economic and trade cooperation between Guangxi and ASEAN countries, laying a good foundation for bilateral trade cooperation.

4. The people-to-people exchanges flourished

In 2015, Guangxi–ASEAN people-to-people exchanges became more frequent, a variety of exchange activities were carried out, mainly including: the Brunei–China Friendship Association established the first club in Nanning; Dongxing City, Guangxi and Mong Cai City, Vietnam, became international sister cities; the "Embrace China" performance aimed at expressing gratitude was staged; the Spring Lantern Festival football match between Dongxing, China and Mong Cai, Vietnam, was conducted in Dongxing City; the Ho Chi Minh and the People of Zhuang Nationality Exhibition

Hall was officially completed and inaugurated in Jingxi County, Baise City; the Confucius Institute of Mahasarakham University organized the Kalasin Chinese summer camp group to visit and study at Guangxi University for Nationalities; during China's National Day in 2015, the borderers at Tansan Village invited the borderers at a village in Vietnam to take part in the activity of celebrating the 66th anniversary of the founding of the People's Republic of China; the exotic culture experience camp of Guangxi Normal University was inaugurated at the Confucius Square on the Yanshan Campus of the university; Chinese and Vietnamese young people gathered and sang in antiphonal style along the banks of the Beilun River, a boundary river between China and Vietnam.

The people-to-people activities have enhanced the cultural exchange and understanding between Guangxi and ASEAN countries as well as the exchange and friendship between the people of the two sides; they have also pushed forward the cooperation between and development of Guangxi and ASEAN countries.

5. Cooperation on tourism reached a new level

In 2015, the 2015 China–ASEAN Expo Tourism Exhibition, jointly organized by the China National Tourism Administration and the People's Government of the Guangxi Zhuang Autonomous Region, was inaugurated at the Guilin International Convention and Exhibition Center[8]; a charter flight between Nanning City and Cebu, the Philippines, was launched, so nine countries among the 10 ASEAN countries had launched air routes in Nanning; the *Agreement on Scenic Area Cooperation between the Jiangshan Peninsula Bailangtan Scenic Area in Fangchenggang City, the Guangxi Zhuang Autonomous Region, China, and the Tra Co Beach Scenic Area in Mong Cai City, Quang Ninh Province, Vietnam,* was successfully signed, indicating that both scenic areas had officially initiated cross-border tourism cooperation; Longzhou County separately signed the memoranda of China–Vietnam cross-border red tourism with the Culture, Sports and Tourism Bureau of Cao Bang Province, Vietnam, and the Party Committee of Phục Hoa District,

[8] Liu Qian, Guilin Strives to Build a New Brand through China–ASEAN Expo and Tourism Development, *Guilin Daily*, July 29, 2015, p. 1.

which helps more rapidly build the International Area of China–Vietnam Cross-border Red Tourism.

The cooperation between Guangxi and ASEAN countries in the tourism industry is conducive to promoting multilateral trade and cultural exchanges, deepening the development of multilateral relations and elevating economic and cultural cooperation to a new level.

V. Main Problems in Guangxi–ASEAN Cooperation

1. There were disputes involving the sovereignty over territorial waters, political disputes frequently occurred and the economic and trade contacts were hindered

In 2015, disputes and military intervention frequently took place among China and Vietnam, the Philippines and Malaysia with respect to the issue of the South China Sea, which was further internationalized. As Guangxi is situated at the land and sea junction between China and the ASEAN community, the disputes over the South China Sea will, to a certain extent, affect the mutual political trust between Guangxi and ASEAN countries; they will also exert an impact on the shipping in the South China Sea and will be unfavorable for China–ASEAN maritime trade contacts.

2. The structure of import and export trade was unbalanced, the main players engaged in trade were subject to risks

The import and export trade between Guangxi and the 10 ASEAN countries grew substantially in 2015 over 2014, but the structure of import and export trade was very unbalanced. First, the structure was unbalanced among countries, as evidenced by the fact that Guangxi's import and export trade with Vietnam, Thailand, Singapore and Malaysia made up a relatively large proportion — Guangxi's trade with Vietnam still ranked No. 1, accounting for 85% of the total import and export trade between Guangxi and the 10 ASEAN countries. Second, the structure of import and export commodities was unbalanced since the import and export commodities were not diverse in structure, most of them were primary products and semi-finished products, and they were dominated by resource and labor-intensive products. Third, the structure of the main players involved in trade was unbalanced since the import and export enterprises were mostly small private enterprises, and they were subject to high credit, financial and market risks.

3. There were frequent cultural frictions between the two sides, contradictions between social groups occurred occasionally

In the process of cultural fusion, cultural differences led to frictions, triggering processions, protests and demonstrations, thus affecting the normal cultural exchange between the two sides and producing an unfavorable effect on the normal contacts between non-governmental organizations and societies of the two sides. The economic, trade and political ties between the two sides were often adversely affected within a certain scope for a certain period of time.

4. The regional economic competition became fiercer, countries frequently contended with each other in trade

All of the ASEAN countries engaged in trade with China under the overall framework of the CAFTA, and regional economic competition was increasingly fierce; in order to vie for the most favorable trade conditions and resources and seize the best strategic highland, countries frequently adopted various means of trade protection, including increasing technical barriers and restrictions on import and export quotas.

VI. Relevant Policy Suggestions

1. Seeking common grounds while reserving differences, building the China–ASEAN Regional Economic Community

China and most ASEAN countries are developing countries, so development is their shared vision and is of overriding importance for them. Moreover, there are a solid foundation and rare and unique conditions for development-oriented cooperation between Guangxi and ASEAN countries; only when there is cooperation can common development be achieved and can both sides jointly address the threats and challenges from the developed countries; this is sufficiently proved by the fact that the ASEAN community was Guangxi's largest trading partner for 14 consecutive years. In the future economic and trade contacts, Guangxi and the ASEAN community should, under the framework of China–ASEAN cooperation, proceed from common interests and seek common grounds while shelving differences and disputes, deepen regional economic integration, continue to maintain economic and trade cooperation and steady growth of the import and export trade, respect history and culture to correctly handle the issue of sovereignty and cultural differences, follow the Five Principles of Peaceful Coexistence as the core to make continued efforts to promote bilateral social, economic and cultural exchanges and political mutual trust, improve geographical relations and push forward trade facilitation.

2. Accelerating the construction of the Belt and Road, fostering an ecological environment for win–win cooperation

The year 2016 marks the beginning of implementing the 13th Five-Year Plan and is crucial for the construction of the Belt and Road. Guangxi and ASEAN countries should fully tap their respective comparative advantages, jointly build the bilateral or multilateral cooperation mechanism, work together to study the industrial layout and cooperation in the industrial chain, land and sea transportation construction and the information network; both sides should press ahead with industrial optimization and industrial upgrading, create an industrial chain which features complementation of each other's advantages to increase the overall regional economic strength, and both sides should speed up financial cooperation, promote investment and financing cooperation and development, thus injecting new vitality into economic and trade cooperation; both sides should accelerate regional integration, establish and improve a bilateral or multilateral risk prevention mechanism and foster a stable and harmonious regional economic ecological environment. The two sides should work together to cultivate a number of multinational corporations with high core competitiveness and high ability to withstand risks, so as to spur the healthy development of small and medium-sized enterprises at the upper and lower sections of the industrial chain.

3. Pushing forward scientific, technological and cultural cooperation, enhancing the people-to-people communication

Scientific, technological and cultural cooperation is an important support for deepening Guangxi–ASEAN development. It is necessary to further establish and improve a cultural exchange and cooperation mechanism, respect each other's cultural traditions and social customs and actively push forward cultural cooperation. It is essential to energetically promote the construction of the China–ASEAN Union University and expand the scale of the students mutually sent by the two sides. It is necessary to further strengthen scientific and technological research, technology development and cooperation on cultural innovation, with a view to improving the region's overall capability for innovation. Joint actions should be taken to delve into the foundation for bilateral and multilateral economic and trade cooperation, future development prospects and developmental path, uncover the basic, key, focal and growth points of win–win cooperation and gradually make recommendations from points to lines and then areas, so as to seek a balance. It is necessary to promote cross-border personnel and vehicle movement by continuing to develop the groups of sister cities, offering the landing visa for tourism or making tourism visa-free and shopping duty-free. It is essential to continue to enrich the multi-level and diversified cultural, entertainment, sports and cultural exchange activities, expand long-term active and healthy social and people-to-people exchanges, improve the people's well-being through culture and promote development and harmony through culture. Efforts should be made to strengthen enterprise management and corporate cultural exchanges and enhance the soft power of enterprises in market competition.

4. Continuing to better carry out the Expo, Summit and Festival, improving the cooperation and exchange platforms

The China–ASEAN Expo, the China–ASEAN Business & Investment Summit and the Nanning International Folk Song Festival are the important platforms for deepening China–ASEAN cooperation. It is necessary to make careful preparations for the annual Expo, Summit and Festival, enrich their themes, contents and forms. It is necessary to, through the Expo, Summit and Festival, jointly study the issues concerning China–ASEAN collaborative innovation and industrial chain cooperation and extension, study the issues involving deepened cooperation in the Greater Mekong and Pan-Beibu Gulf regions, as well as the cooperation and development of the Belt and Road; it is essential to, by means of the Expo, Summit and Festival, stimulate various countries to focus on the general situation and long-term development, jointly creating a community of regional interests; it is necessary to, by virtue of the Expo, Summit and Festival, further improve the China–ASEAN dialogue consultation mechanism, properly address the issues concerning exchange and cooperation in the political, economic, trade, cultural and other fields and appropriately resolve contradictions and disputes to steadily promote the healthy development of bilateral and multilateral relations.

Part 4

Evaluation and Analysis of Hot Issues Concerning the Southeast Asian Region in 2015

Chapter 20

The Disputes over the South China Sea Amid Strife between China and the United States: 2015

Nong Fang and Li Hong*

The South China Sea is situated between the south of the Taiwan Straits and Billiton Island, between the east of the Strait of Malacca and Bashi Channel; covering an area of approximately 3.50 million km^2, it includes Beibu Gulf and the Gulf of Thailand and features a semi-closed rhombus. The sea area owned by China in the South China Sea covers an area of approximately 2.05 million km^2, accounting for about 58.6% of the whole South China Sea; it has long been marked on the maps published by China and most versions of the world map; it is shown to feature a dotted national boundary line, called the U-shaped line or nine-dotted line.[1] The so-called disputes over the South China Sea refer to the disagreements among the countries

* Nong Fang, Research Assistant at the Institute of International Relations, the China–ASEAN Research Institute of Guangxi University; Li Hong, Director, Professor at the Institute of International Relations, the China–ASEAN Research Institute of Guangxi University. This paper is the staged achievement made under the Program of the National Natural Science Foundation of China (41561026).

[1] Zhao Huanting *et al.*, The Road to Achieving Harmony in the South China Sea, *Tropical Geography*, 2015(5), pp. 687–700.

surrounding the South China Sea over the ownership of the islands and reefs in it and the division of sea areas in it. The disputes involve the Chinese Mainland and Taiwan, Vietnam, the Philippines, Malaysia, Brunei — "five countries and six parties"; the disputes present a complicated situation in which relevant countries separately control or claim the ownership of the sovereignty over various islands and reefs.[2] USA is not part of these "five countries and six parties"; however, as the South China Sea is strategically located, USA got increasingly involved in the issue of the South China Sea after the Second World War.

Since the United Nations deliberated the demarcation case according to the *United Nations Convention on the Law of the Sea* in 2009, the US factor has become increasingly strong in the issue. The issue of the South China Sea has gradually become an important topic in China–US relations, and China and USA have wrangled over the issue of the South China Sea again and again.

I. The Evolution of the US Policy Toward the South China Sea after the Second World War

USA has been active in the South China Sea for more than 200 years. As early as the 18th century, the Empress of China, the first US merchant ship which came to China, entered the Port of Guangzhou via the South China Sea; this was the first recorded time that USA contacted the South China Sea; this is also recognized by the academic circle as the beginning of China–US relations. In the subsequent two and a half centuries, the US policy toward the South China Sea changed from "insouciance" to "active control" before the Second World War and from "active containment" to "neutrality and nonintervention" for a certain period of time after the Second World War, thus avoiding the situation of complicating the issue of the South China Sea for a long time.

However, with the changes in the world pattern and regional environment after the collapse of the Soviet Union, driven by the US Asia-Pacific strategy, the US policy toward the South China Sea has gradually turned to

---

[2] Lu Fanghua, An Analysis of the US Factor in the Issue of the South China Sea, *Southeast Asia & South Asian Studies*, 2009(4), pp. 6–10.

"active intervention", so USA has become the primary factor outside the region in the international development of the issue of the South China Sea.

1. The first change: From "deliberation" to "active neutrality"

As of the 1980s, as the Government of the Soviet Union gradually gave up military deployment in Vietnam, the US withdrew part of its military strength from the Southeast Asian Region, but such partial withdrawal of military strength did not mean that the US Government had fully abandoned its involvement in the South China Sea; instead, it deliberated a new policy.[3]

In 1995, a number of diplomatic and military confrontations occurred between China and the Philippines, while the most famous one is the so-called Incident of Mischief Reef. Given the ally relations between the US and the Philippines, the Clinton Administration politically leant towards the Philippines while calling for settling disputes in a peaceful way; in April 1995, the Clinton Administration explicitly stated that the US would protect the Philippines from military attack from any country. The then Assistant Secretary of Defense Joseph Nye stressed, "the essence of the US policy toward the South China Sea is 'active neutralism'"[4]; this marked a fundamental change in the US policy toward the South China Sea and entry into the developmental stage of "active neutrality". Against the background of the situation at that time, the US Government showed great concerns over China's military threat to the South China Sea amidst continued rapid economic growth in China, and was actively committed to playing its role in maintaining a balance of power. In this sense, the US Government initiated intensified military deployment after it officially unveiled the policy of "active neutrality".

2. The second change: From "strengthened presence" to "deep involvement"

In the late 1990s, at the turn of the century, with the improvement of China's overall strength and international status, China gradually became

---

[3] Yang Dejun, A Brief Analysis of the US Policy towards the Dispute of the South China Sea, master's thesis at Fudan University, 2012, pp. 14–21.

[4] Liu Qing, New Changes in the US Strategic Deployment in the Asia Pacific, *Contemporary International Relations*, 2011(5), pp. 13–20.

the potential competitive force for the US in the Asia-Pacific Region. In 1998, the US Government released the *Security Report on East Asia and the Pacific*, identifying the security of the South China Sea and the surrounding Asia-Pacific Region as the priority of US global strategy and stating efforts in further deepening military visits and joint exercises in the region, thus comprehensively heightening its military deterrence in the region. In 2002, USA and the Philippines signed the *Cooperative Logistic Support Agreement*, under which the US military can freely traverse the Philippines' territorial airspace and sea. The US Government also provided USD 700 million in financial aid to the Philippines. In return, the Government of the Philippines granted the US the right to use two major military bases, including Subic and Clark, in case of an emergency. During this period, some Southeast Asian countries, such as Singapore, Malaysia and Brunei, signed the military access agreements with the US Government. Since the 21st century, the US has conducted a number of military exercises in the South China Sea — only in 2000, the US carried out 16 military exercises — and has maintained a continued growth in the number of exercises.

After 2009, the US increasingly criticized China for sovereignty over the South China Sea, and clearly expressed its stand. In March 2009, soon after President Barack Obama took office, the US naval surveillance ship USNS Impeccable conducted illegal surveying in the exclusive economic zone of the South China Sea, causing a confrontation between the US and Chinese ships in the South China Sea, so the US criticized China profusely; the US publicly denied China's ownership of sovereignty over the South China Sea, and also openly supported the territorial claims of relevant ASEAN countries over the Nansha Islands. Afterwards, the US and the countries surrounding the South China Sea carried out a growing number of military exercises in various names and forms. In July 2010, when attending the 17th ASEAN Regional Forum (ARF) in Hanoi, Vietnam, Secretary of State Hillary Clinton emphasized that the US had national and international interests in the South China Sea, and she believed, "All parties to the disputes must claim marine rights and interests through the channel of international maritime law".[5] During the

[5] Stephen Kauf-man, Clinton Urges Legal Resolution of South China Sea Dispute, July 23, 2010, http://www.america.gov/st/peacesec-english/2010/July/20100723154256esnamfuak4.879177e-03.html.

period October–November, Hillary Clinton visited such countries as Vietnam, Cambodia, Malaysia, New Zealand and Australia, and frequently mentioned the disputes over the South China Sea during her visit.[6]

Various signs show that since the beginning of the 21st century, the US Government has gradually deviated from its policy toward the South China Sea — "active neutrality" — that it had adopted for a long time, and further increased its involvement in the disputes over the South China Sea. The US policy toward the South China Sea is undergoing a new round of adjustment, the time that the US has "deep involvement" in the issue of the South China Sea has arrived.[7] The trends in the issue of the South China Sea will be closely associated with the development of China–US relations.

II. Specific Practice of US Involvement in the Issue of the South China Sea: 2015

The South China Sea was destined to be turbulent during the past year 2015. During the year, "seeking huge benefits at a low cost" was another factor contributing to the escalation of tension in the South China Sea[8]; the case of arbitration involving the South China Sea, orchestrated by the Philippines over two years, eventually came to a conclusion, and the Ad Hoc Arbitration Tribunal made a ruling unfavorable for China to safeguard its sovereignty; China came under unprecedented international pressure in the issue of the South China Sea. During the year, the strife among the great powers over the issue of the South China Sea loomed large and became the determining factor for leading the trends in the South China Sea. USA unprecedentedly increased its involvement in the issue, it switched from indirect involvement to direct intervention, the tension in the South China Sea continued to escalate, the US took frequent actions, sent military aircraft and warships

[6] Ge Hongliang, The US Policy towards the South China Sea after the Cold War and Its Impact on China–US Relations, *Southeast Asia & South Asian Studies*, 2012(2), pp. 16–21.

[7] Satu Limaye, Boom Times in U.S.–Southeast Asia Relations, October 27, 2010, http://asiafoundation.org/in-asia/2010/10/27/boom-times-in-u-s-southeast-asia-relations/.

[8] 2015, the South China Sea Was Rough, www.haiwainet.cn, December 11, 2015, http://news.k618.cn/kx/201512/t20151211_6357487.html.

to intrude into the sea areas and sky near China's Fiery Cross Reef, Mischief Reef and Subi Reef in Nansha for close-in reconnaissance; the US and China fell into frictions and conflicts at sea on many occasions. A series of incidents show that the US is never a country which keeps its nose clean; it is adopting the economic, military, diplomatic and other means to get involved in the bilateral disputes over the South China Sea which essentially only involves China and part of the ASEAN countries.

1. With the thought of hegemony, the US interfered in China's land reclamation from the sea

"The American people seldom show concern over moral issues when pursuing their national self-interests, they are too arrogant and have a strong desire to lead others."[9] Since the Second World War, the US has gradually established a complete global order which reflects its values and power advantages, including the United Nations focusing on promoting human rights, the IMF and the WTO centering on boosting trade and financial liberalization and other important international organizations. These international organizations and mechanisms have brought enormous benefits to the US so that the US has spared no effort to carry out hegemony worldwide.[10] On May 20, 2015, the US P-8A reconnaissance plane flew over the islands and reefs being built by China in the South China Sea; Chinese Navy sent warnings eight times. With regard to this, on May 21, the US Assistant Secretary of State Daniel Russel said that the US reconnaissance action was absolutely proper and the US would continue to exercise the right to freedom of navigation in the South China Sea. In the 14th Shangri-La Dialogue on May 30, the US Secretary of Defense Ashton Carter delivered a speech "Challenges to the US and Asia-Pacific Security", and made a criticism that China's reclamation of land from the sea was unprecedented in scale and speed, it exceeded the combined land reclamation by other claimants, he stated that the US was very worried about the prospect of militarization of the islands and reefs in the South China Sea and possible misjudgments and

---

[9] Wang Jisi, The Logic of the US Hegemony, *American Studies Quarterly*, 2003(3), p. 28.

[10] Yang Dejun, A Brief Analysis of the US Policy towards the Dispute of the South China Sea, master's thesis at Fudan University, 2012, pp. 14–21.

conflict risks and he called upon various parties to immediately stop the reclamation of land from the sea.[11]

As we know, there are severe confrontations and disagreements between USA and China on the issues concerning military activities in the exclusive economic zone, including military surveying, espionage reconnaissance and joint exercises. This is because the *United Nations Convention on the Law of the Sea* ("the Convention") does not explicitly regulate "military activities". The focus is whether military activities cannot be freely conducted within the exclusive economic zone unless the coastal countries grant approval.[12] The two countries have different understandings, so both countries act in different ways in national practice. Although USA is not a member country of the Convention, the exclusive economic zone system has become a customary international law, and this has been confirmed by international judicial precedents and national practice, thus USA should also observe the exclusive economic zone system specified in the Convention. Undeniably, as China has expanded and reinforced the islands and reefs of China's Nansha Qundao since 2014, its objective is to improve the infrastructure environment and conditions, create conditions for providing public goods, also strengthen control over the territory and sea areas of the Nansha Islands as well as substantively utilize the right to autonomous development in order to promote cooperative and joint development. As stated by the Ministry of Foreign Affairs of China, as we take actions at home, we do not violate anyone's rights,[13] so China will not stop relevant acts and activities due to strong opposition from other countries.

2. The US frequently posed military threats and provocations

On October 27, 2015, the US naval missile destroyer USS Lassen cruised within 12 sea miles off China's artificial islands and reefs in the South China

[11] Expert: It Is Reasonable and Legitimate for China to Reinforce the Islands and Reefs of China's Nansha Qundao, China Will Not Stop Due to Objections from Other Countries, www.chinadaily.com.cn, May 27, 2015, http://chinadaily.com.cn/2015-05/27/content_20835822.htm.
[12] Shi Xiaoqin, On Sea Power and China–US Relations, Military Science Publishing House, 2012, pp. 255–258.
[13] The Ministry of Foreign Affairs Responds to the Expansion of the Islands and Reefs of China's Nansha Qundao: China Does Not Target Any Country, www.chinanews.com, April 9, 2015, http://news.china.com/domesticgd/10000159/20150409/19503857_1.html.

Sea. According to the US Department of Defense, the USS Lassen cruised for several hours within its scope, including Subi Reef and Mischief Reef, which are controlled by China. The Ministry of Foreign Affairs of China described this action as a political provocation; Deputy Foreign Minister Zhang Yesui summoned the US ambassador to China, Max Baucus, lodged a strong protest and criticized the US act as extremely irresponsible.[14] It can be confirmed that the USS Lassen was only the beginning, the US military took actions again and again. Early on the morning of December 10, 2015, two US B-52 strategic bombers trespassed into the air space near relevant islands and reefs of China's Nanhai Qundao. The Chinese military kept close watch over the activities of the US military aircraft. The troops garrisoning the reefs were on high alert, and they warned and expelled the US military aircraft. In the meantime, the US Department of Defense claimed that the military aircraft wrongly flew into relevant air space and was investigating the incident. The B-52 strategic bomber, nicknamed Stratofortress, is the main bomber of the US Air Force; its maximum range is 16,000 km, its maximum flight altitude is 16,700 m (55,000 feet). The B-52 is the core type capable of carrying nuclear weapons among the strategic bombers of the US military.[15]

Meanwhile, conducting military exercises with other countries was also an important means adopted by the US to pose military threats. The annual Exercise Balikatan, jointly conducted by USA and the Philippines, was held on April 20, 2015. The exercise took place in the western part of Palawan Island, Pangasinan Province and Zambales Province. The naval base in Zambales is only 220 km from China's Huangyan Island. The exercise was a large-scale regular annual joint exercise between the US and the Philippines. It was held in 1991 for the first time and suspended in 1995, but resumed in 1999. It was held for the 31st time in 2015. According to the information from the Armed Forces of the Philippines, in the Exercise Balikatan in the

---

[14]The US Sent a Warship to the South China Sea for Surveillance and Warning, China Lodged a Strong Protest against the Entry of the US Warship into 12 Sea Miles from Artificial Islands, www.zaobao.com, October 28, 2015, http://www.zaobao.com/special/report/politic/southchinasea/story20151028-542305.

[15]Two US B-52 Strategic Bombers Intruded into China's Islands and Reefs in the South China Sea, Chinese Troops Garrisoning the Reefs Warned and Expelled Them, www.ifeng.com, December 20, 2015, http://news.ifeng.com/a/20151220/46751395_0.shtml.

year 2015, the US sent 6,656 soldiers, 76 airplanes and three warships, while the Philippines sent 5,023 soldiers and Australia sent 61 soldiers; the total strength in the exercise was 11,740 people, and it witnessed the largest number of participating soldiers in the past 5 years.[16]

3. The US built multilateral mechanisms to internationalize the issue

From the point of view of USA, the way to addressing the issue of the South China Sea should not be restricted to bilateral diplomatic consultations; instead, more multilateral settlement mechanisms should be established. This strategy for complicating the issue of the South China Sea and internationalizing the issue in a multilateral way exactly resulted from elaborate planning and long-term deliberation by the US.

On October 5, 2015, substantive breakthroughs were made in the Trans-Pacific Partnership Agreement (TPP) in the negotiations in Atlanta, USA; the 12 countries participating in the negotiations — including USA, Japan, Canada, Australia, Mexico, Vietnam, Peru, Malaysia, Brunei, Chile, New Zealand and Singapore — jointly held a press conference after negotiations, in which they stated that they had reached an agreement on the TPP. With protracted negotiations for five and a half years, the largest free trade area in the world, covering a population of about 800 million and whose GDP accounts for about 40% of the world's GDP, emerged. The TPP was led by USA; negotiations over it consisted of two parts: First, the fields were jointly determined by all 12 negotiating countries, including the intellectual property protection rules; second, other fields were determined through bilateral consultations, such as tariff reduction and exemption for certain goods.[17]

The US Government has regarded the TPP as the key to implementing the US Pivot-to-Asia strategy. In recent years, economic integration has obviously accelerated in the Asia Pacific, a number of economic and trade cooperation

[16]The US, the Philippines and Australia Sent about 10,000 Soldiers to Participate in the Exercise Balikatan 2015, www.huanqiu.com, April 7, 2015, http://world.huanqiu.com/hot/2015-04/6110463.html.

[17]The TPP Has Been Reached, a Huge Economic Circle Led by the US Will Emerge, www.ifeng.com, October 6, 2015, http://finance.ifeng.com/a/20151006/14005612_0.shtml.

mechanisms, including the "10+1", "10+3" and "10+6", have taken shape. The US has been worried that once regional integration organizations are established, as a potential competitor with the US, China will play a crucial role in them thanks to its geographical advantages, while USA will be excluded since it does not have the status of an East Asian country. From this perspective, USA needs to serve its interest appeals by developing multilateralism, while the TPP can curb the integration of the East Asian Region through trans-regional integration, thus further weaken China's influence, expand the presence of the US, making the issue of the South China Sea increasingly complicated.

III. China's Countermeasures

1. China took a firm stand to safeguard its sovereignty

On August 20, 2015, the State Council issued the *National Plan for Main Marine Functional Areas* ("the Plan") after it was signed by Chinese Premier Li Keqiang. According to the Plan, it is necessary to rationally identify the main functions of different sea areas in light of different characteristics of internal waters, territorial sea, exclusive economic zone, continental shelf and other sea areas under jurisdiction, as well as the resource and environmental carrying capacity, the existing intensity of and potential for development of the different sea areas, with a focus on promoting transformation towards a recycling-oriented development of the sea and building a pattern of marine development which features land–sea coordination and man–sea harmony. The introduction and implementation of the Plan suggests that the national strategy for the main functional areas enables full coverage of territorial land and sea spaces; it is of great strategic significance for carrying out the strategy of building a maritime power, enhancing the capability of marine development, transforming the mode of marine development, protecting the marine ecological environment and safeguarding the national maritime rights and interests.[18] On February 25, 2016, when delivering the speech entitled "China under Development and China's Diplomacy" at the US Center for Strategic and International Studies, Chinese Foreign Minister Wang Yi stated

[18]The State Council Issued the National Plan for Marine Main Functional Areas, Xinhuanet, August 20, 2015, http://news.xinhuanet.com/politics/2015-08/20/c_1116317876.htm.

that, at present, the situation in the South China Sea was generally stable, the security and freedom of navigation had never been affected, China upheld its efforts in resolving differences through dialogue and negotiation, and firmly safeguarded national security and legitimate interests.[19]

In response to the troubles made by such countries as the Philippines and Vietnam on the issue of the South China Sea, China started to adjust countermeasures; in 2015, China speeded up the development of and construction in the South China Sea. On June 16, the Ministry of Foreign Affairs of China announced that China would complete the land reclamation project at some garrisoned islands and reefs of China's Nansha Qundao in the near future, and after that completion, China would, at the next stage, build the functional facilities necessary for serving military defense and meeting civil needs. On June 25, the Maritime Safety Administration of China announced that the Hai Yang Shi You 981 drilling platform of the China National Offshore Oil Corporation would carry out drilling operations about 139 km southeast of Sanya, Hainan Province. On August 24, China successfully completed the drilling of the Ling Shui 25-IS-1 well, the first deep-water high-temperature and high-pressure prospecting well in China drilled by the Hai Yang Shi You 981 drilling platform; it is another important prospecting well in the South China Sea; it will help China further verify the reserves of natural gas in the South China Sea. Two months later, the Ministry of Communications of China held the completion ceremony of the Huayang Lighthouse and the Chigua Lighthouse at the Huayang Reef in the South China Sea, and announced that the two large multifunctional lighthouses were officially put into use. These two lighthouses fill the gap in terms of navigation and navigation aid facilities in the Nansha water area, they greatly improve the navigational environment in the water area of the South China Sea, they provide navigation service, safety information, emergency rescue and other public benefit services to the vessels of various countries passing through the waters of the sea, thus reducing marine accidents.[20]

---

[19] Wang Yi Delivered a Speech at the US Center for Strategic and International Studies, Consulate General of the People's Republic of China in San Francisco, February 26, 2016, http://www.fmprc.gov.cn/ce/cgsf/chn/zgxw/t1343592.htm.

[20] The Chronicle of Events in the South China Sea in 2015, National Institute for South China Sea Studies, January 8, 2016, http://zizhan.mot.gov.cn/zhuanti/2016jiaotonggongzuo_HY/beijingziliao/201512/t20151228_1966501.html.

China's continued development of and construction in the South China Sea Region were excellent in both scale and speed, so this naturally stirred anxiety among some countries that had claims to the South China Sea and great powers outside the region. However, China's development and construction behaviors in the South China Sea — including island reef expansion, military defense, comprehensive service guarantee and fishery service — constitute a testament to an indisputable fact: China's construction is carried out fully in its sovereign territory and is completely above criticism, beyond reproach, reasonable and legitimate.

2. China sought to build international consensus to weaken the US factor

During the two days of March 13–14, 2015, the China–Vietnam Working Group for Consultation on Common Development held the fourth round of consultation in Da Nang, Vietnam. The two sides agreed to observe the important consensuses reached by the leaders of the two countries and the *Agreement on the Basic Principles for Guiding China and Vietnam in Addressing the Maritime Issues*, and continue to make active progress in maritime common development between China and Vietnam. On April 8, China and Vietnam signed the *Joint Communiqué between China and Vietnam*. According to the communiqué, the two sides should jointly manage maritime differences, fully and effectively carry out the *Declaration on the Conduct of Parties in the South China Sea*; establish the *Code of Conduct in the South China Sea* as early as possible through consultation; refrain from taking actions that would complicate and enlarge the disputes; promptly and properly deal with problems to safeguard the general situation of China–Vietnam relations and the peace and stability of the South China Sea.[21] On August 3, when holding a press conference in Singapore, Chinese Foreign Minister Wang Yi stressed that China would uphold the following principles in dealing with the issue of the South China Sea: safeguarding the peace and stability of the South China Sea, settling the disputes in a peaceful way through consultation, managing differences through a mechanism of rules,

[21] Joint Communiqué between China and Vietnam, People's Daily Online, November 7, 2015, http://paper.people.com.cn/rmrbhwb/html/2015-11/07/content_1630402.htm.

preserving the freedom of navigation and overflight in the South China Sea, and achieving win–win outcomes through cooperation.[22] Two days later, in the China–ASEAN Foreign Ministers' Meeting in Kuala Lumpur, he put forward a three-point initiative: the countries in the South China Sea Region should pledge to fully and effectively carry out the *Declaration on the Conduct of Parties in the South China Sea*, move faster to hold consultations on the *Code of Conduct in the South China Sea* and actively explore the preventive measures for managing maritime risks; the countries outside the region should pledge to support the above efforts made by the countries in the region, refrain from taking actions causing tension in the region and complicating the situation of the region; various countries should pledge to exercise and safeguard the freedom of navigation and overflight that they enjoy in the South China Sea.[23]

With respect to the disputes concerning the sovereignty over the South China Sea between part of Southeast Asian countries and China, although USA is the largest external force of the former, the issue of the South China Sea should absolutely not become the issue between China and USA; it is most unadvisable to put the issue between China and USA. As specified in the five-point initiative for various countries jointly safeguarding the peace and stability of the South China Sea as put forward by Chinese Premier Li Keqiang in the East Asia Summit on November 22,[24] the countries outside the region should pledge to respect and support the efforts made by the countries in the region in safeguarding the peace and stability of the South China Sea, play an active and constructive role, and refrain from taking actions causing tension in the region. This suggests that particular great powers outside the region should not, without restraint, find fault with China on the issue of the South China Sea, and the countries having disputes

---

[22] Wang Yi: China Always Upholds Five Principles in Addressing the Issue of the South China Sea, Xinhuanet, August 3, 2015, http://news.xinhuanet.com/2015-08/03/c_128088772.htm.

[23] Wang Yi Put Forward a Three-Point Initiative for Safeguarding the Peace and Stability of the South China Sea, Xinhuanet, August 5, 2015, http://news.xinhuanet.com/world/2015-08/05/c_1116158507.htm.

[24] Li Keqiang Put Forward a Five-Point Initiative for Addressing the Issue of the South China Sea in the 10th East Asia Summit, the official website of the Chinese Government, November 22, 2015, http://www.gov.cn/guowuyuan/2015-11/22/content_2970188.htm.

over the South China Sea should work together to jointly turn the South China Sea into a sea of harmony in the true sense.[25]

3. China developed maritime forces to strengthen its military presence

Although China stresses peaceful development, this does not mean that it will renounce military construction and the readiness of a military force. Peaceful development is based on a powerful military force; the objective of peaceful development is to safeguard the dignity of a great power rather than succumb and concede. Since 2010, China has conducted large-scale naval exercises in the South China Sea, which were much more comprehensive, complex and larger than ever before.

In August 2015, the Chinese navy successfully held a live-fire combat exercise in the airspace of a certain sea area in the South China Sea. The exercise was large and involved 100 naval ships, tens of airplanes and the launch of dozens of missiles and torpedoes. According to naval military expert Yin Zhuo, the exercise targeted military operations in the entire South China Sea, with a view to safeguarding the security of all of China's islands and reefs within the nine-dotted line, and the exercise was not directed at any particular country.[26] Furthermore, in the exercise, shipborne antiaircraft missiles, YJ-8 anti-ship missiles and various types of torpedoes attacked targets and missiles were launched in salvo attacks many times. In the one-day exercise, dozens of missiles and torpedoes were launched, which was not common in the world. On October 30, the missile destroyer Yuncheng, owned by a destroyer division of the South China Sea Fleet under the Chinese Navy, and French navy's missile destroyer Vendemiaire conducted a joint maritime exercise — which focused on the occupation of a replenishment position and a formation movement — in a sea area of the South

[25] Gao Jianzhi, The Prospect for the Dispute of the South China Sea — A Path Analysis Based on the Thinking of Seeking Common Grounds While Shelving Differences, *Journal of Guangxi University*, February 2016, pp. 105–111.

[26] Expert: The Naval Exercise in the South China Sea Was a Battle-level One, the Missiles of the Second Artillery Corps Can Counterattack the Bases of Other Countries, People's Daily Online, July 30, 2015, http://military.people.com.cn/n/2015/0730/c1011-27384352.html.

China Sea according to the *Code for Unplanned Encounters at Sea*, thus enhancing bilateral exchanges and mutual trust.[27] Moreover, the US missile destroyer USS Lassen cruised within 12 sea miles off Subi Reef in the Nansha Islands on October 27; as a response, Chinese Foreign Ministry spokesman Lu Kang pointed out on October 28, "China will firmly respond to deliberate provocations from any country; we will continue to put relevant airspace of the sea under close surveillance, and take all necessary measures in light of needs." Chinese Foreign Minister Wang Yi stressed that USA should think carefully before taking actions, refrain from acting rashly to make trouble out of nothing.[28] The spokesperson for the Chinese Embassy in the US, Zhu Haiquan, said in Washington that no country should take the freedom of navigation as an excuse for harming the sovereignty and security of other countries.

According to the report of the Philippine media, Daniel J. Kritenbrink, Senior Director for Asian Affairs in the National Security Council of the White House, said at the US Center for Strategic and International Studies on February 26, 2016, that USA hoped that China could extend its commitment about demilitarization to the entire South China Sea Region. He added that the ruling made at the case of arbitration involving the South China Sea would be equally binding upon China and the Philippines since both countries were the members of the *United Nations Convention on the Law of the Sea*. With regard to this, during a regular press conference of the Ministry of Foreign Affairs held on February 29, 2016, the Chinese Foreign Ministry spokesman, Hong Lei, stated that as China deployed the necessary and moderate national defense facilities on its territory, it exercised the right of self-preservation and the right of self-defense granted to a sovereign state by international laws, that this matched the environment and threats for relevant islands and reefs of China and had nothing to do with militarization. There was a sufficient basis of international laws for China not to accept and

[27] Chinese and French Navies Conducted a Maritime Joint Exercise in a Sea Area of the South China Sea, www.huanqiu.com, November 1, 2015, http://mil.huanqiu.com/china/2015-11/7883587.html.

[28] The Latest News on the Situation of the South China Sea: China Protested against the Entry of the US Warship within 12 Sea Miles off the Artificial Islands and Reefs, www.zaobao.com, October 28, 2015, http://www.80sd.org/junshi/jun/2015/10/28/88434.html.

participate in the case of arbitration involving the South China Sea initiated by the Philippines; this stand was clear-cut and consistent; China urged USA to refrain from acting as an "international judge" to find fault with China's behaviors.[29]

A series of military exercises, tough stands and measures demonstrated China's capability and confidence in safeguarding state sovereignty, maritime rights and interests. Only when the maritime forces are developed constantly can a military presence be strengthened and can China always stand ready to defend its sovereignty over the South China Sea; only when one dares to fight can peace be made, only when the preparation for fighting is made can war be avoided.[30] In the meantime, when dealing with the US military, the Chinese military should adopt the tactic of conquering the unyielding with the yielding and should not take tough measures, the Chinese military should actively engage in the regional military cooperation led by USA and properly address the sensitive military issues so that China's military strength can improve steadily in the absence of head-on confrontation with USA.

IV. Analysis of the Driving Factor behind the China–US Game

USA is the traditional maritime power and enjoys the dominant position in the maritime order of the Asian Pacific, while China is an emerging large maritime country. At present, there is no strategic mutual trust between China and the US; China and the US interpret international maritime law in different ways; the US interferes in the affairs of Taiwan and the South China Sea; these factors make it more likely that China and the US will clash at sea, so the power game will occur between the US, the traditional maritime power, and China, a developing emerging maritime power.

---

[29] China Urged the US to Refrain from Acting as an "International Judge", www.ifeng.com, February 29, 2016, http://news.ifeng.com/a/20160229/47632961_0.shtml.

[30] Xi Jinping's Strategies for the South China Sea, www.gmw.cn, October 12, 2015, http://politics.gmw.cn/2015-10/12/content_17319912_2.htm.

1. The important geographical location and resource advantages of the South China Sea

The South China Sea offers one of the important shipping routes in the world, the total amount of transportation in the South China Sea accounts for more than 50% of the world's total maritime transportation. It is situated at the intersection of sea, land and air transportation, it connects Asia and Europe and provides access to the Pacific Ocean and the Indian Ocean; it always serves as the shortest important international shipping route that is indispensable for East Asia in terms of connecting South Asia, the Middle East, Africa and Europe, so it is of an important geostrategic value. Meanwhile, the South China Sea is also the inevitable route for Japan to follow in transporting oil and other strategic resources, it is the main channel for the US navy to follow to enter the Indian Ocean via the Pacific Ocean, so it is hailed as the Mediterranean Sea of Asia.[31]

Besides its important geographical advantages, the South China Sea also abounds in oil, gas, combustible ice, fishery resources, solar energy, wind energy, wave energy resources as well as unique tourist resources and it enjoys a huge potential for development, so it is of important economic and strategic value.

2. The US geographical goals

a. *Safeguarding the enormous economic interests of the US in the South China Sea*

US enterprises have important business interests in the South China Sea, while the exploration and development of oil and gas in the South China Sea are the most important part of those business interests. The US oil and gas companies have cooperated on or are cooperating with the countries having disputes over the South China Sea, including Vietnam and the Philippines, in the exploration and development of oil and gas. These companies include CRESTONE Energy Corporation and Mobil Oil Corporation. Besides oil

[31] She Fei, China–US Game behind the Issue of the South China Sea, *Business*, 2013(9), pp. 166–167.

and gas interests, the security of the shipping routes in the South China Sea, which is directly associated with US overseas trade and investments, is the consistent interest appeal of the US policy toward the South China Sea which has changed from neutrality to involvement and from involvement to deep involvement.[32] Take the US trade with China and the ASEAN community as an example; according to the *2005–2014 Exports by US States to China* released by the US China Business Council, over the past decade, the US exports to China soared by 198%, China was the fastest-growing export destination for the US and the US's third largest export market. Meanwhile, the US also had enormous economic interests in Southeast Asia with a population of more than 600 million. During the years 2010–2014, the cumulative investments made by the US in the ASEAN community totaled USD 54 billion, the bilateral trade exceeded USD 212 billion; USA became the third largest investment source and the fourth largest trading partner of the ASEAN community. However, these business interests are not all of the pursuits of the US policy towards the South China Sea; they are fundamentally subject to the US regional strategy and are greatly affected by the US policy towards China.

b. *Strengthening USA's position as a leader in the strategically located Southeast Asia*

In recent years, such countries as China, Japan, South Korea and India have substantially expanded their political and economic influence in the Southeast Asia Region, and the US has regarded that expansion as a potential challenge to its regional political and economic clout. From the perspective of military strategy, the South China Sea is an important part of the US's first island chain, it is also the hub for the US to connect its military bases in the Western Pacific Region, the Indian Ocean and the Persian Gulf Region. Therefore, the Obama administration actively participated in regional affairs, strongly emphasized USA's "national interests" and "international interests"

[32] Ge Hongliang, The US Policy toward the South China Sea after the Cold War and Its Impact on China–US Relations, *Southeast Asia & South Asian Studies*, 2012(2), pp. 16–21.

in the South China Sea, and tried to take the issue of the South China Sea as the pivot for restoring and reinforcing USA's position as leader in the region.[33]

Overall, USA has declared that it takes no position on the sovereignty dispute, but it has put more stress on the freedom of navigation in the South China Sea, on a peaceful way to settling disputes, on opposition against the use of military force for changing the status quo and on the maintenance of regional peace and stability. In particular, the freedom of navigation has always been the "public reason" and "moral banner" for the strong involvement of USA in the issue of the South China Sea; USA has specially emphasized its right to conduct military activities within the exclusive economic zone — close-in reconnaissance by warships and airplanes for various kinds of intelligence gathering — to preserve its role as "offshore balancer" and its right to dominate the Western Pacific Region.[34]

c. *Obstructing and containing the rise of China in the region*

The issue of the South China Sea has always been an important issue used by the US for containing the rise of China. Since 2009, as the rise of China has been increasingly evident, the US intention to contain the rise of China by means of the issue of the South China Sea has become more apparent. For the sake of saving face and safeguarding its international reputation, as well as pacifying its allies and stabilizing the alliance system, the US has — under the strategies of "Pivot to East Asia", "The Asia Pacific First" and "the Asia-Pacific Rebalancing"[35] — made troubles on the issue of the South China Sea to force the ASEAN community to take a consistent stand towards China on the issue of the South China Sea, spread the China Threat Theory and stepped up efforts to reinforce the security relations with the countries surrounding the South China Sea, with extensive military deployment in the Asia-Pacific Region; the US has also wielded the TPP to compete with the

[33] *Ibid.*

[34] Zhou Wei. Islands and Reefs Construction in the South China Sea: Secret Warfare between China and the US, *WEISHI*, 2015(8), pp. 91–94.

[35] Chen Xiangyang, Operations of China's Asia-Pacific Strategy, *Journal of Jiangnan Social University*, 2012(4), pp. 1–5.

East Asian cooperation in which China participates, with a view to fundamentally undercutting China's influence in the issue of the South China Sea.

3. China's core interests

The discovery and naming of the South China Sea Islands by China date back to 2,000 years ago. Since ancient times, China has owned the indisputable sovereignty over the Nansha Islands and the adjacent waters, the South China Sea Islands have been China's territory. In the past 60 years, China has also always publicly declared that the sovereignty over the South China Sea Islands is owned by China, and China has legitimately and appropriately expanded relevant sovereignty interests in light of the development of international maritime law. The white paper *China's Peaceful Development*, issued by the State Council Information Office in September 2011, explicitly and correctly points out, "China's core interests include state sovereignty, national security, territorial integrity and national reunification, China's political system established by the Constitution and overall social stability, and the basic safeguards for ensuring sustainable economic and social development"[36]. With regard to the significance of the South China Sea for China at present and in the future, the South China Sea is naturally China's core interest. Therefore, China fears no challenge on the issue of the South China Sea, which has a vital bearing on China's core interests.

V. The Impact from the Development of China–US Relations on the Disputes over the South China Sea

China–US relations have been at the stage of building the new-type relations between great powers. The new-type relations between great powers feature a mode of relations of benign interaction which goes beyond the conventional mode under which great powers strive for hegemony.[37] Under

---

[36] Zeng Yong, A Study of the Issue of the South China Sea from the Perspective of China–US Relations, doctoral dissertation at the Party School of the CPC Central Committee, 2013, pp. 205–209.

[37] An Analysis of the Path for Building the New-type Relations between Great Powers, www.faobserver.com, July 8, 2014, http://www.faobserver.com/NewsInfo.aspx?id=10234.

this mode, China and the US either compete or cooperate with each other, the two countries either compete amidst cooperation or cooperate amidst competition, the bilateral relations present the characteristic of sustainable benign interaction. Correctly judging the state of bilateral relations plays an active role in the benign development of bilateral relations, while the basis for judgment often comes from some developments in the issues which exert a great impact on the balance of power between the two sides. The issue of the South China Sea has developed into one of the barometers for judging bilateral relations since that issue has been increasingly elevated to a strategic level.

If the model of the prisoner's dilemma in the game theory is used to analyze China–US cooperation in maritime security, two factors — benefit and cost — are considered to arrive at the outcome: both sides take a cooperative attitude, the Pareto Optimality is achieved, both sides obtain benefits; if both sides, driven by self-interest, elect to betray the other side or refrain from cooperating with the other side, neither side will obtain benefits. Therefore, if China and the US cooperate on maritime security, that cooperation will play a positive role in safeguarding the security of shipping routes and coping with the non-traditional security threats, and a win–win outcome will be achieved; however, if one side takes the cooperative attitude but another side does not do so, the experience and funds paid by the cooperating side will become futile; if neither side takes a cooperative attitude, the benefits for both sides will not change.[38]

At present, the really overarching strategic dilemma for the East Asian Region is that there is dual separation between the China-centered economic system and the US-centered security system, the policy choice and behavioral orientation of either side toward the affairs of the region will be inevitably subject to structural restrictions from this unique "dual leadership system".[39] For the US, the most fundamental focus lies in maintaining a strategic balance and regional stability, the US does not hope that the region once again falls into a cold-war confrontation, nor will the US be willing to be

[38]Wang Jia, An Analysis of the Driving Factors behind the U.S. Policy toward the South China Sea and China's Countermeasures, master's thesis at Yunnan University, 2014, pp. 43–44.

[39]Wang Junsheng, China–U.S. Dual Leadership System and the Security of the East Asia: Structural Imbalance and Order Reconstruction, *International Politics Quarterly*, 2013(4), pp. 99–113.

"kidnapped" by the Philippines and Vietnam and thus engage in a military conflict with China.[40] For China, the "maintenance of stability", as part of China's policy towards the South China Sea, has two implications: First, safeguarding the stability of the relations between China and the countries surrounding the South China Sea; second, maintaining the stability of the scenario in which the overall situation of the South China Sea is within China's control; both respects supplement rather than contradict each other.

Therefore, currently, the core issue in China–US relations is how both sides identify the strategic orientation of each other. Subject to structural contradiction between the rise of China and US hegemony, China should manage to fully play the role of a responsible large regional country, while the US should embrace the rise of China in an open-minded and confident way and better play the role of stabilizer in the strategic balance among great powers; this is the key to promoting a long-term healthy development of bilateral relations.[41] Although the issue of the South China Sea essentially involves the territorial disputes between China and such countries as Vietnam and the Philippines, in fact, it has become an issue which China and the US must face together in the development of China–US relations, and the way to address the issue will also largely depend upon the future form of bilateral relations and the state of confrontation between the respective policies. In this process, neither China nor the United States should only pay attention to the gain and loss in a certain field, the two sides must actively engage in high-level strategic dialogue, and continuously strengthen the global strategic cooperation, thus persistently enhancing strategic mutual trust, helping to find the way to fundamentally settling the disputes over the South China Sea. Possibly, the issue of the South China Sea will not become an issue which cannot be addressed amidst concerns from the international community, and the establishment of the new-type great-power relations between China and the US will become a reality.

Overall, with continuous development in the issue of the South China Sea, China should, on a new basis, think the whole picture through and make

---

[40] Bonnie Glaser. China–US Relations: The run-up to President Xi Jinping's State Visit. Comparative Connections, No. 2, 2015, pp. 27–41.

[41] Wang Chuanjian, The Issue of the South China Sea and China–U.S. Relations, *Journal of Contemporary Asia-Pacific Studies*, 2014(2), pp. 4–26.

overall arrangements, including how to achieve diversified development and open cooperation in expansion of island and reef functions, how to carry out a new policy design to manage the disputes over the South China Sea and guide that situation towards negotiation and cooperation, how to uphold the "dual-track line of thought" and properly deal with the bilateral relations with the ASEAN community, how to safeguard the rights and interests of the South China Sea and promote the construction of the 21st Century Maritime Silk Road in a coordinated way, how to push forward the construction of the more vibrant China–ASEAN Community with a Common Destiny, how to establish the new-type great-power relations between China and the US characterized by a non-conflict and non-confrontation posture, mutual respect and win–win cooperation[42]; all this should be carefully considered and scientifically planned by China in top-level design, so that it can more smoothly achieve the strategic layout of its peaceful development and finish the historical task of bringing about national rejuvenation while taking practical actions to respond to the questions from the neighboring countries and the international community.

[42] Xi Jinping Summarizes the New-type Great-power Relations between China and the US: Non-conflict, Non-confrontation Posture, Mutual Respect and Win–win Cooperation, The Beijing News, 2013-06-10, http://cn.chinausfocus.com/news/20130610/18997.html.

Chapter 21

The Case of the South China Sea Arbitration Initiated by the Philippines

Cai Qi*

Since the Government of Benigno Aquino III, the President of the Philippines, initiated the so-called case of the South China Sea arbitration in 2013, the situation of the South China Sea has drawn global attention, and unprecedented challenges were posed to China's diplomatic activities.

I. Overview of the Case of the South China Sea Arbitration

1. Timeline

a. *Cause: The Philippines lost control over Huangyan Island*

On April 10, 2012, the Philippine navy attempted to detain Chinese fishermen near Huangyan Island in the South China Sea; the attempt was stopped by a Chinese marine surveillance ship; subsequently, a stand-off occurred between the two sides. After the incident of Huangyan Island

* Cai Qi, Research Assistant at the Institute of Philippine Studies, the China–ASEAN Research Institute of Guangxi University.

unfolded, Chinese maritime safety department started regular cruising near Huangyan Island, and the Philippines lost control over Huangyan Island.

b. *Preparation*

The Philippines' efforts to internationalize the issue of the South China Sea started from December 2012 when the Philippines invited Vietnam, Malaysia and Brunei to discuss how to deal with China, but only Vietnam accepted the invitation to attend the meeting.

On January 22, 2013, the Government of the Philippines unilaterally initiated the so-called arbitration involving the disputes between China and the Philippines over the right of maritime jurisdiction over the South China Sea. The Chinese Government solemnly stated on many occasions that China did not accept or participate in the arbitration initiated by the Philippines.

The Secretary of Foreign Affairs of the Philippines, Albert del Rosario, was the most active pusher behind the case of the so-called South China Sea arbitration. To a certain extent, the Government of Benigno Aquino III went further and further on the wrong path involving the issue of the South China Sea because it was "kidnapped" by Albert del Rosario. Afterwards, Albert del Rosario misused the *United Nations Convention on the Law of the Sea* on different international occasions to preach the settlement of the issue of the South China Sea through international arbitration, without regard to China's position of addressing the issue in a bilateral way.

Later, on January 4, 2014, the US Assistant Secretary of State required China to explain the nature of the nine-dotted line and claimed that no international law served as the basis for China to claim sovereignty over the South China Sea.

c. *Official submission*

On March 30, 2014, the Philippines instituted the litigation concerning the issue of the South China Sea at the Ad Hoc Arbitration Tribunal for the case of the South China Sea arbitration. The Ad Hoc Arbitration Tribunal in The Hague announced official acceptance of the litigation instituted by the Philippines, and it required China to respond to the litigation before December 15, 2014; otherwise, it would make judgment by default with respect to China. China's position was clear-cut: China did not accept or participate in the arbitration, even if the ruling was made in the future, China would not recognize and execute it. The Chinese Government expressed this position on many occasions.

2. The main points of the litigation instituted by the Philippines

The litigation concerning the issue of the South China Sea instituted by the Philippines mainly involved three appeals: First, clearing up the international law force of China's nine-dotted line in the South China Sea; second, ascertaining the statuses of particular islands and reefs and the maritime rights involving them; third, the legitimacy of some actions taken by China in the South China Sea.[1] As shown in Table 1, the Philippines raised 15 appeals and requested the tribunal to make a ruling. The Ad Hoc Arbitration Tribunal for the case of the South China Sea arbitration held that the requests over which it had jurisdiction were mainly the 3rd, 4th, 6th, 7th, 10th, 11th and 13th appeals put forward by the Philippines, mainly involving whether Huangyan Island and several other islands and reefs can generate an exclusive economic zone or a continental shelf and territorial sea and whether China illegally disturbed the Philippines' rights; the requests whose jurisdiction had not yet been made clear were the 1st, 2nd, 5th, 8th, 9th, 12th and 14th appeals put forward by the Philippines, mainly involving whether the nine-dotted line was rational, whether China's historical rights were valid, how to ascertain China's maritime rights in the South China Sea and whether China's activities at such islands and reefs as Mischief Reef contravened the *United Nations Convention on the Law of the Sea*.[2]

---

[1]The Arbitral Tribunal in The Hague Held a Hearing for the Case of the South China Sea Arbitration, *Philippine World News*, November 25, 2015.

[2]China's Strategies in the Arbitration Case Involving the Disputes over the South China Sea and the Ruling on the Right of Jurisdiction, www.sina.com, http://finance.sina.com.cn/sf/news/2015-11-04/17449441.html.

Table 1. The Appeals Put Forward by the Philippines in the Case of the South China Sea Arbitration

Serial No.	Content	Whether there is a right of jurisdiction
1	China's maritime rights in the South China Sea, like the Philippines, cannot exceed the scope permitted by the *United Nations Convention on the Law of the Sea* ("the Convention")	To be determined
2	The sovereign rights, the right of jurisdiction and the "historical rights", over the South China Sea, claimed by China within the scope of the nine-dotted line violate the Convention; these claims do not have legal force to the extent of exceeding the geographical and physical constraints on China's maritime rights as permitted by the Convention	To be determined
3	Exclusive economic zone or continental shelf cannot emerge at Huangyan Island	Support
4	Mischief Reef, Ren'ai Reef and Subi Reef are low-tide elevations, they cannot generate a territorial sea, an exclusive economic zone or a continental shelf, and they are landforms which cannot be obtained by pre-occupation or by other means	Support
5	Mischief Reef and Ren'ai Reef are part of the Philippines' exclusive economic zone and continental shelf	To be determined
6	Nanxun Reef and Ximen Reef, including Dongmen Reef, are low-tide elevations, they cannot generate a territorial sea, an exclusive economic zone or a continental shelf, but their low-tide lines can be taken as the baselines for separately measuring the breadth of the territorial sea at Hongxiu Island and Jinghong Island	Support
7	Chigua Reef, Huayang Reef and Yongshu Reef cannot generate a territorial sea, an exclusive economic zone or a continental shelf	Support
8	China illegally disturbed the Philippines from enjoying and exercising the sovereign rights over the biological and non-biological resources in its exclusive economic zone and continental shelf	To be determined

9	China illegally refrained from preventing its nationals and ships from developing the biological resources within the Philippines' exclusive economic zone	To be determined
10	China disturbed the traditional fishery activities conducted by the Philippines' fishermen at Huangyan Island and thus illegally prevented them from seeking a livelihood	Support
11	China violated, at Huangyan Island and Ren'ai Reef, the obligation for protecting and preserving the marine environment under the Convention	Support
12	China's occupation and construction activities at Mischief Reef: (a) violated the stipulations concerning artificial islands, facilities and structures under the Convention; (b) violated China's obligation for protecting and preserving the marine environment under the Convention; (c) constituted the illegal act of attempting to possess something under the Convention	To be determined
13	China conducted dangerous operation of its law enforcement ships, posing a risk of a severe collision with the Philippine ships sailing near Huangyan Island and violating the obligation under the Convention	Support
14	Since arbitration began in January 2013, China has illegally aggravated and enlarged the disputes, including: (a) Disturbing the Philippines' right of navigation in the sea area of Ren'ai Reef and the adjacent sea areas (b) Preventing the rotation and supplement of the Philippine personnel stationed at Ren'ai Reef (c) Jeopardizing the health and well-being of the Philippine personnel stationed at Ren'ai Reef	To be determined
15	China should stop further illegal claims of rights and activities, and stop requesting the Philippines to clarify appeals	To be determined

Source: The *Decision on the Right of Jurisdiction over the South China Sea Arbitration* (Chinese and English versions).[3]

[3] *Decision on the Right of Jurisdiction over the South China Sea Arbitration* (Chinese and English versions), www.china-arbitration.com, http://www.cnarb.com/Item/7814.aspx.

3. The responses from various parties to the case of the South China Sea arbitration

a. *China*

For the case of the South China Sea arbitration initiated by the Philippines, China has always maintained the position that it does not accept or participate in it, China holds that the issue of the South China Sea needs to be addressed through consultation and negotiation in a bilateral and peaceful way; it opposes the actions which complicate and multilateralize the issue of the South China Sea and China has expressed opinions on the issue of the South China Sea on many occasions. When acceding to the *United Nations Convention on the Law of the Sea*, China stated that the Convention was not applicable to addressing the territorial issues related to China, and it absolutely does not accept the way of resorting to the third party for settling the disputes over territorial sovereignty, maritime rights and interests. China did not participate in the arbitration; the *Position Paper of the Government of the People's Republic of China on the Matter of Jurisdiction in the South China Sea Arbitration Initiated by the Republic of the Philippines*, issued by China on December 7, 2014, stressed, "Transmission of the above position paper cannot be construed as China's acceptance of or participation in this arbitration".

On addressing the issue of the South China Sea, Chinese Foreign Minister Wang Yi put forward the "dual-track" line of thought by which disputes are settled between China and the countries to disputes and within the China–ASEAN framework, China does not hope that the Philippines comes to a dead end on the path of the South China Sea arbitration, claiming that the correct way to address the issue of the South China Sea is through bilateral negotiation in a peaceful way. In the 10th East Asia Summit in 2015, Chinese Premier Li Keqiang put forward a five-point initiative for addressing the issue of the South China Sea, with the hope of addressing it by means of an amicable consultation.[4]

[4] Li Keqiang Put Forward a Five-Point Initiative for Addressing the Issue of the South China Sea in the 10th East Asia Summit, www.chinanews.com, http://www.chinanews.com/gn/2015/11-22/7635502.shtml.

b. *Taiwan, China*

When the case of the South China Sea arbitration initiated by the Philippines had not yet involved the legal status of Taiping Island, Taiwan was calm; as Taiwan was not the direct party to the arbitration case, Taiwan showed restraint. However, after the Philippines denied the status of Taiping Island, Taiwan quickly made a response, Ma Ying-jeou inspected Taiping Island and invited foreign journalists to visit and learn about Taiping Island, demonstrating the status of Taiping Island to the outside world.

c. *The United States*

The US once stated that it took no position on the issue of the South China Sea,[5] but essentially the US again and again instigated the Philippines to provoke China on the issue. In the second half of 2015, the US increasingly got involved in the issue, and was even unsatisfied with operating behind the scene, and gradually began to act openly. The commander of the US Pacific Fleet took a P-BA reconnaissance plane to cruise in the South China Sea in a high-profile manner; afterwards, the US warship USS Lassen cruised within 12 sea miles off China's islands and reefs in the South China Sea. In December, a B-52 bomber flew into the airspace two sea miles off the islands in the South China Sea; these actions showed that the US was overtly interfering in the issue of the South China Sea. In the public opinion, the US actively voiced support for the Philippines. According to Singapore's *Lianhe Zaobao*, the Commander of the US Pacific Fleet, ADM Scott H. Swift, believed that the South China Sea may trigger an arms race, while the cause for instability in the region was that some countries hoped to settle territorial disputes by resorting to force rather than through the international law; this remark was directed at China. US President Barack Obama reaffirmed the US–Philippines alliance relations on many occasions; he boarded a warship of the Philippines to expound this position during the APEC meeting, while

---

[5]The US Secretary of Defense: The South China Sea Was Not an Issue between China and the US, the US Took No Position on the Issue, www.sina.com, http://news.sina.com.cn/c/2015-06-12/104531943678.shtml.

the US never stopped its military aid to the Philippines; recently, the military aid from the US has shown an apparently rapid growth.

d. *Japan*

Japan is the largest investor in the Philippines and also a strategic partner of the Philippines. As Japan and the Philippines are the allies of the US in Asia, they have a "profound" friendship. It is common for the Philippines, Japan and the US to conduct exercises in the South China Sea. Japan also supported the South China Sea arbitration initiated by the Philippines in various respects, including supporting the Philippines' building up of its army, and giving advice to the Philippines in the South China Sea arbitration. Chu Hao, associate research fellow at the China Institute of Contemporary International Relations, believed that Japan constantly gave secret support to the Philippines in the South China Sea arbitration. Japanese judge Ryui Junji, the then Presiding Arbitrator of the Ad Hoc Arbitration Tribunal, played an "important role" in appointing arbitrators in the South China Sea arbitration — all four of the other arbitrators, except one arbitrator appointed by the Philippines, were appointed by him. Japan also actively applied for becoming an observer at the hearing involving the South China Sea arbitration, giving encouragement to the Philippines.[6]

e. *Vietnam*

Like the Philippines, Vietnam also has territorial disputes with China over the South China Sea. Within the ASEAN community, Vietnam and the Philippines often jointly requested the ASEAN community to express opinions on the issue of the South China Sea, and condemned China's "misconducts" there. On the arbitration case, Vietnam hoped to, by virtue of the Philippines, exert pressure on China in the international community, so that Vietnam could obtain a favorable position in negotiations with China over the South China Sea. Vietnam showed much more restraint than the Philippines on the issue of the South China Sea; however, in December 2014,

---

[6]Chu Hao, The Strategic Game over the South China Sea Arbitration Fully Escalates, http://paper.dzwww.com/dzrb/content/20150720/Articel06002MT.htm.

Vietnam submitted its position paper on the case of the South China Sea arbitration initiated by the Philippines in support of the arbitration. Vietnam also sent representatives to attend the hearing involving the arbitration. Vietnam and the Philippines interacted with each other more frequently over the issue of the South China Sea. On May 27, 2015, Vietnamese and Philippine soldiers held a gala on the Northeast Cay Island in the South China Sea. On October 21, 2015, the Secretary of Foreign Affairs of the Philippines Albert del Rosario visited Hanoi, Vietnam; he and Pham Binh Minh, Deputy Prime Minister and Minister of Foreign Affairs of Vietnam, co-chaired the 8th meeting of the Philippine–Vietnam Joint Committee on Bilateral Cooperation, and the Prime Minister of Vietnam Nguyen Tan Dung met with Albert del Rosario.

f. *Others*

The countries involved in the issue of the South China Sea include Malaysia and Brunei in addition to China, the Philippines and Vietnam. Malaysia and Brunei were more moderate than the Philippines and Vietnam. In particular, Malaysia confronted China less over the issue; it hoped that disputes could be settled through consultation in a peaceful way, and China–Malaysia relations also developed steadily. However, with the escalation of the case of the South China Sea arbitration initiated by the Philippines and an increasing presence of China in the South China Sea, Malaysia guarded against China more and more. The most typical example was that Malaysia also sent an observer to attend the hearing involving the South China Sea arbitration.

Moreover, recently Australia has frequently gotten involved in the issue of the South China Sea. Australia is an outsider on the issue, but as an ally of the US, Australia never stopped its support of the Philippines. On January 29, 2015, Australia announced that it would donate two decommissioned heavy-duty landing boats to the Philippines. Afterwards, the Australian Minister for Defense, Kevin Andrews, showed concerns over China's construction of islands and reefs in the South China Sea. Australia always worried that China's efforts in safeguarding the maritime rights and interests in the South China Sea might endanger Australia's economic and trade interests there. This was more evident in the second half of 2015. In December, 2015, Australia sent additional military aircraft to patrol China's islands and reefs in the South China Sea.

In early 2016, the Minister for Foreign Affairs of Australia, Julie Bishop, required China to "explain" the issue of the South China Sea, and anticipated the result of the case of the South China Sea arbitration initiated by the Philippines; she believed that the Philippines had the right to address the issue through arbitration. As proven by the above facts, Australia orally stated that it took no position on the issue of the South China Sea, but it actually supported the Philippines in the case of the South China Sea arbitration.[7]

II. Analysis of the Causes of the Philippines' Initiation of the South China Sea Arbitration

1. China–Philippines economic relations were unbalanced

For a long time, imbalance occurred in China–Philippines economic relations, and the Philippines never gained great benefits from China's development. In terms of trade volume, China was the Philippines' second largest trading partner and its largest importing country, China maintained a large trade surplus. Even former President of the Philippines, Gloria Macapagal Arroyo, friendly to China, thought that importing inexpensive products from China raised the competition which many small and medium-sized enterprises in the Philippines failed to survive, and so the development of the Philippines' manufacturing industry was affected adversely.[8] China's investments in the Philippines were very limited; China only ranked No. 9 among the Philippines' sources of FDI in 2014. The proportion of China's investments in the Philippines in China's investments in the ASEAN community was much smaller than that of China's investments in other ASEAN countries. The poor investment environment of the Philippines was an important factor affecting China's investments in the Philippines, but undeniably, China ignored China–Philippines economic and trade relations for a long time, sowing the seeds of misfortune in China–Philippines relations. As the Philippines

[7]The Minister for Foreign Affairs of Australia: Australia Welcomes China's Peaceful Rise and Takes No Position on the Issue of the South China Sea, www.huanqiu.com, http://mil.huanqiu.com/observation/2016-02/8558913.html.

[8]Zhang Yunling, Between Ideal and Reality — My Research, Involvement and Thinking Regarding East Asian Cooperation, China Social Sciences Press, 2015, pp. 117–118.

did not benefit a lot from its economic contacts with China, when initiating the South China Sea arbitration, the Philippines did not consider the arbitration as an important factor affecting China–Philippines economic and trade relations. Even to a certain extent, the Philippines regarded the arbitration as an important means for containing China.

2. The mutual trust between China and the Philippines was limited, mutual misunderstanding increased

As we know, with the transfer of political power in the Philippines, the new government often liquidated the previous government to safeguard its status.[9] President Gloria Macapagal Arroyo, the predecessor of President Benigno Aquino III, was friendly to China, while President Benigno Aquino III was highly pro-American; immediately after President Benigno Aquino III took office, he liquidated the corruption problem which occurred when President Gloria Macapagal Arroyo was in office. Because it was reported that such companies as Chinese ZTE obtained the Philippines' national projects by means of bribery, this stirred a great backlash and the image of China suffered a disastrous decline among the Philippine people. According to the Government of Benigno Aquino III, joint development of oil and gas resources in the South China Sea by the Philippines and China, was considered by other countries during the period of Gloria Macapagal Arroyo as the "sale" of the Philippines' national interests. The national sentiment was strong in the Philippines, thus the misunderstanding between China and the Philippines deepened.

3. It was instigated by foreign factors

In early 2012, US President Barack Obama put forward the Pivot-to-Asia strategy, before long the US unveiled the strategy of the Asia-Pacific rebalancing. In the view of many media, although China was not the only factor resulting in the introduction of the Pivot-to-Asia strategy, China was an important

[9]Liquidation was very common in the Philippines' political circle. After President Benigno Aquino III took office, former President Gloria Macapagal Arroyo was under house arrest in hospital due to corruption; when Gloria Macapagal Arroyo was in office, her predecessor Joseph Ejercito Estrada was under house arrest due to corruption.

factor. The US exploited the concerns of China's neighboring countries about China to achieve its goals, while the Philippines became an important puppet. As President Benigno Aquino III had just come to power, he needed to clean up the influence of former President Gloria Macapagal Arroyo, thus it was very good for him to adopt a diplomatic strategy different from that carried out by Gloria Macapagal Arroyo. The US and the Philippines quickly became partners, and the Government of Benigno Aquino III provoked disputes over Huangyan Island with the support of the US. After the incident, the Secretary of Foreign Affairs of the Philippines, Albert del Rosario, issued a statement, suggesting that the Philippines should submit the issue of the South China Sea to the International Court of Arbitration. The Secretary of National Defense and the Deputy Secretary of Foreign Affairs of the Philippines and the Secretary of State and the Secretary of Defense of the US held a "2+2" meeting on April 30, 2012, in which the US decided to provide the Philippines with patrol ships with the hope that the Philippines could settle the disputes over the South China Sea according to the *United Nations Convention on the Law of the Sea*, and the two sides reaffirmed the mutual defense treaty between the US and the Philippines. Afterwards, the US did not renounce the support for the Philippines in military expenditure, arms and public opinion. The two countries conducted military exercises in the South China Sea many times, and the US even roped in Japan to get involved in the issue. Since 2015, it has been increasingly apparent that the US has disturbed the status quo of the South China Sea, it has not been satisfied with operating behind the scenes, and it flagrantly meddled in the issue of the South China Sea. The public opinion in the Philippines held that the Philippines was low-ranking in Asia regarding military strength, the Department of National Defense, led by the Secretary of National Defense, Voltaire T. Gazmin, was only a shell institution; if there was no help from the US, the Philippines, a militarily weak country, did not dare to provoke China on the issue of the South China Sea.

III. Analysis of the Philippines' Strategies for the Case of the South China Sea Arbitration

1. Full early-stage preparations were made

After the Philippines decided to sue China on the issue of the South China Sea, it made full preparations. First, it actively launched an extensive propaganda campaign, unilaterally initiated and promoted the South China Sea arbitration in the name of the *United Nations Convention on the Law of the Sea*, and politically provoked China under the disguise of laws. Second, it appointed Western lawyers at high cost to defend the Philippines; this is because Western lawyers are familiar with the legal mechanism and evaluation perspective of the International Court of Arbitration, so they are better equipped to help the Philippines gain the upper hand in the South China Sea arbitration. Thus, this evidently showed the Philippines' great care and efforts in the South China Sea arbitration.

2. The government provided vigorous support

The Government of the Philippines played up the "theory of the China threat in the South China Sea" on many occasions, and claimed that the Philippines had been "forced" to refer the case of the South China Sea arbitration to the Ad Hoc Arbitration Tribunal. The delegation for the case of the South China Sea arbitration initiated by the Philippines was led by the Secretary of Foreign Affairs of the Philippines, Albert del Rosario, with representatives from the administrative, legislative and judicial branches of the Philippines, indicating that the Government of the Philippines attached importance to the South China Sea arbitration. In recent years, the Philippines has been financially strained, but the Government of the Philippines still paid a heavy price to appoint Western lawyers in the South China Sea arbitration, and it also continuously provided financial support to relevant working personnel involved in the South China Sea arbitration. Many people in the Philippines criticized the government; they argued that the government spent the taxpayers' money to do a meaningless thing, did not allocate fiscal funds to the areas where money was needed most — for example, work was often stopped or delays frequently occurred in the delivery of projects in the field of infrastructure construction because fiscal funds were not put in place; however, the Government of the Philippines still took its own course to move forward the South China Sea arbitration.

3. The Philippines actively built the image that the Philippines was in the "disadvantaged" position

When reporting the issue of the South China Sea, the Philippine media always used the word "bully" to describe China's "bad behavior", creating the impression that China, a great power, bullied the Philippines, a weak country. Reports often added the pictures of Chinese warships, highlighting China's "hegemony". The Philippine media portrayed, with indignation and frustration, the miserable life of coastal fishermen after they lost their economic source, giving a false impression that China was the root of evil. On the issue of the Ren'ai Reef, the Philippines claimed that China had impeded the Philippines from delivering the basic necessities to the personnel on the aground warships at sea, the freedom of navigation in the South China Sea cannot be guaranteed. As the official language of the Philippines is English, the "misery" of the Philippines was publicized widely throughout the Western world, and its efforts at building the image of "disadvantaged" indeed produced some effects.

4. The Philippines downplayed historical evidence

The national history of the Philippines originated from Spain's colonial rule. After the Spanish discovered the archipelago in Southeast Asia, they named it the "Philippines". Before that, the Philippines was ruled by tribes and small kingdoms, there was no unified concept of a State. Regarding the historical evidence proving the governance of the Islands in the South China Sea, the Philippines has been keenly aware that it cannot contend with China, a country with a long history, so it mainly based its claims on its proximity to the Nansha Islands and generations of Philippines fishermen making a living there. The Philippines also tried to deny, in various ways, China's historical sovereignty over the South China Sea — for example, the Philippines held that some islands were unsuitable for human life, and thus denied, on this ground, that China had discovered and governed these islands very early, saying that ancient Chinese fishermen only lived on these islands while fishing, thus making the outside world believe that China's claims of sovereignty were unreasonable.

5. The Philippines took pains to multilateralize and complicate the issue of the South China Sea

In December 2014, Vietnam submitted its position paper on the South China Sea arbitration initiated by the Philippines to support the arbitration.

In 2015, the US warship USS Lassen entered the area within 12 sea miles off the islands and reefs controlled by China in the South China Sea, and the Government of the Philippines supported this action. In December 2015, the President of the Philippines welcomed Australian military aircraft patrolling the airspace in the South China Sea. President Benigno Aquino III called on, on various occasions, the ASEAN community to intervene against China. The Philippines, in conjunction with USA, Japan, Vietnam and other countries, conducted military exercises in the sea areas surrounding the South China Sea on many occasions. The involvement of great powers further complicated the issue of the South China Sea.

IV. Analysis of China's Countermeasures for the Case of the South China Sea Arbitration Initiated by the Philippines

There has been an unquestionable fact that the case of the South China Sea arbitration has increasingly internationalized and complicated the issue of the South China Sea, so China must make responses as quickly as possible to prevent the enlargement of the unfavorable situation from exerting an adverse impact.

1. China should take certain actions to actively cope with the case of the South China Sea arbitration

China has stated that it does not accept or participate in the case of the South China Sea arbitration initiated by the Philippines, but this does not mean that China remains inactive. In fact, since the Philippines unilaterally initiated the arbitration, China has adopted various means to safeguard its legitimate rights and interests through various channels. On December 7, 2014, the Chinese Government issued the position paper on the matter of jurisdiction in the South China Sea arbitration initiated by the Philippines. In the opinion of some scholars, this document was the iconic action taken by the Chinese Government.

First, China should take a firm stand, introduce its stand to the international community and refute the Philippines' misconducts through various channels and in many ways. "The Philippines stubbornly, unilaterally initiated the South China Sea arbitration; essentially its objective was to possess the islands and reefs, illegally occupied by the Philippines, of China's Nansha Qundao by means of arbitration". China does not under any circumstances accept the way of resorting to the third party for settling the disputes over territorial sovereignty, maritime rights and interests.

Second, China should divert attention. The Western world led by USA has been hyping the issue of the South China Sea. China needs to cool down the issue in due time, mitigate the diplomatic pressure on China, give prominence to China's international role, stress that it is a responsible great power and takes actions in the South China Sea only for the purpose of safeguarding its own sovereignty interests, thus reducing the negative impact of the South China Sea arbitration on itself.

Third, China should engage in dialogue with the Philippines. The ultimate peaceful way to settling territorial disputes is nothing but dialogue. The 2016 general election in the Philippines will be an important opportunity for easing the bilateral relations; it is estimated that the Philippines' policy will change to some extent. At present, the presidential candidates in the Philippines have relaxed their attitudes towards the issue of the South China Sea to a certain degree; after all, the worsening of relations with China is not good for the economic development of the Philippines. On March 7, 2016, the Secretary of Foreign Affairs of the Philippines, Albert del Rosario, well-known for taking a tough stance towards China, left office, so bilateral relations may usher in new hope. Given the reality, China should adopt diplomatic means, in good time, to reverse the Philippines' tough stand towards the issue of the South China Sea, which is not impossible.

Fourth, China should seek support from other countries. There are no firm supporters for China in the surrounding environment, as a result of which China is in a relatively passive position in addressing international issues, including the issue of the South China Sea; therefore, seeking support from other countries, especially other countries which lay claim to the South China Sea, is very critical. Currently, among the countries which lay claim to the South China Sea, only the Philippines has resorted to international arbitration for addressing the issue, while it is still possible that other parties will endeavor to settle disputes through bilateral negotiations. Taiwan's attitude toward the South China Sea arbitration initiated by the Philippines is similar to that of the Chinese Mainland, so the two sides across the Taiwan Straits should cooperate with each other to create synergy. China should also energetically negotiate with such countries as Malaysia, Vietnam and Brunei to reach consensuses and set good examples, convey to the world its sincerity in addressing the issue of the South China Sea and stress that only bilateral negotiation is the true way to settling territorial disputes, thus weakening the impact of the South China Sea arbitration.

Fifth, China should work together with the ASEAN community. China has put forward the "dual-track" line of thought to address the issue of the South China Sea, and the ASEAN community will play a constructive role in that issue, while addressing the issue within this framework can prevent it from becoming more complicated and from falling into a vicious circle. It is crucial to speed up consultations under the *Code of Conduct in the South China Sea* and ensure that various countries act in accordance with the *Declaration on the Conduct of Parties in the South China Sea.*

2. China should actively convey its voice to the world

It is necessary to further make China's voice heard in the Western world. On the issue of the South China Sea, China has not yet enjoyed the leading position in the Western world in terms of say. When the information on the issue of the South China Sea is searched for in English, relevant reports becoming available through search are still controlled by Western media, so China has no sufficient initiative in claiming rights and sovereignty on the issue of the South China Sea, and it only passively responds. At present, the global institutions, including the International Court of Arbitration, remain controlled by Western countries, thus China has no choice but to improve the situation by changing its publicity strategy. The Chinese Government, domestic research institutions, even the ordinary scholars, should communicate China's voice on the issue of the South China Sea to the world through English channels as much as possible. Furthermore, in order to increase China's say in the Western world, it is also essential to increase the "volume of voice" and combine voice with affection. China still claims the sovereignty over the South China Sea only by means of "reiterating" and "lodging a protest", and this way of claiming produces, to a certain extent, less force of impact than the Philippines' fabrication of the information that China "destroyed" the South China Sea and thus local fishermen suffered losses.

3. China should enhance its transparency and ensure the freedom of navigation and overflight in the South China Sea

China's neighboring countries and the Western world have a concern that China will turn the South China Sea into its backyard garden, impeding the freedom of navigation and overflight in that Sea. Such a concern is absolutely ridiculous. China has stated on many occasions in the international community that there is no problem in the freedom of navigation and overflight in the South China Sea, that China's construction of civil facilities on relevant islands and reefs in the South China Sea aims at safeguarding and guaranteeing the freedom of navigation and overflight in the South China Sea. However, amidst the concern of the international community about the freedom of navigation in the South China Sea, China should move further to hold the forum on the freedom of navigation and overflight there and invite the surrounding countries, USA, Japan and other countries to discuss the rules for navigation and overflight in that sea; this is conducive to dispelling the doubts in the international community. China should intensify maritime cooperative construction in the South China Sea and push forward the building of regional mechanisms to remove the concerns of the surrounding countries about the freedom of navigation and overflight there.

Chapter 22

The Progressive Construction of the ASEAN Community

Wang Yuzhu and Wang Wei*

The plan for the ASEAN Community, composed of three pillars including a political and security community, an economic community and a sociocultural community, was officially put forward in October 2003. Twelve years later, on December 31, 2015, the ASEAN Community was officially established. The inception of the concept of the ASEAN Community dates back to December 1997, when the *ASEAN Vision 2020* was issued, but the vision, to a larger extent, stresses the identity of the ASEAN community and depicts the future of the ASEAN Community, it does not present the specific connotation of the community and the path for realizing that community. The construction of the ASEAN Community was put forward for the first time in the *Declaration of ASEAN Concord II* adopted during the 9th ASEAN Summit in 2003, while the issuance of such documents as the action program, the community blueprint and roadmap in the subsequent leaders' meetings marked the official launch of the construction of the ASEAN Community.

* Wang Yuzhu, Research Fellow at the National Institute of International Strategy, the Chinese Academy of Social Sciences, Research Fellow at the China–ASEAN Research Institute of Guangxi University; Wang Wei, doctoral candidate at the University of International Business and Economics.

For the researchers focusing on ASEAN integration, the construction of the community was announced as expected; however, for the researchers paying attention to bilateral interests or regional prospects,[1] it is more important to evaluate the value of the declaration and the next actions taken by the ASEAN in community construction. According to the core goals pursued by ASEAN for promoting the building of a community and the *Post-2015 Vision*, the ASEAN community has identified its construction as a process; in other words, the declaration in late 2015 should be regarded as the new starting point in the process of progressive construction of the ASEAN Community.

I. Economic Cooperation in Community Construction and the Appeal for Maintaining a Central Position

For the construction of the ASEAN Community, it is necessary to enhance regional cohesion and promote internal cooperation on the one hand; reinforce the central position of the ASEAN countries in regional cooperation through community construction on the other hand. The ASEAN Free Trade Area was officially initiated among the six old member countries in 2002. The preparation for building the ASEAN Free Trade Area was officially launched in 1993, with work accelerated many times; the ASEAN Free Trade Area was first established among the old member countries; however, the level of the ASEAN community's economic integration was not increased substantially, as evidenced by the widening income gap among member countries and the lack of a significant increase in trade volume within the area. On the elimination of non-tariff barriers, the ASEAN community's performance also failed to meet the expectations. Therefore, in order to increase the level of regional economic integration, economic cooperation in the ASEAN community during the next stage should focus on stimulating more countries to

[1]The attention paid to the construction of the ASEAN Community involves bilateral factors and regional interests. For example, [Japan] Kazushi Shimizu, The ASEAN's Regional Integration — Centering on the Progress in the ASEAN Community, *Southeast Asian Studies* (A Quarterly Journal of Translation), 2014(2), pp. 12–20.

join the ASEAN Free Trade Area as early as possible and work on building an economic community. It should be noted that the concept of community was put forward by the ASEAN countries amidst the outbreak of the Asian financial crisis in 1997 when the ASEAN countries were caught up in an unprecedented crisis, member countries generally suffered an economic recession, but the ASEAN countries did not retreat to protectionism, instead, they accelerated regional integration. The vision of the community helped boost the confidence of member countries in coping with the crisis and also reflected the resilience of the ASEAN countries in promoting regional cooperation.

The ASEAN has always emphasized its efforts at pushing forward regional cooperation to the degree of comfort acceptable to member countries, while the emergence of the community is a natural process of development. In the early 1990s, great changes took place in the world's economic and political landscape; economic globalization and regional integration accelerated; the external environment changed and economic growth in the region decreased to some extent, so the construction of the ASEAN Free Trade Area was gradually put on the agenda. With the end of the cold war, the ASEAN countries gradually changed their previous dependence on Western countries, mainly USA, and carried out the "strategy of keeping a balance among great powers" characterized by equidistant diplomacy with major powers outside the region. In late 1997, according to the ASEAN's initiative, the ASEAN–China, Japan and South Korea leaders' meeting was held, during which the ASEAN community separately held unofficial meetings with the leaders of these three countries; afterwards, these arrangements gradually developed into "the ASEAN +" mechanism.

The "the ASEAN +" mechanism gradually became an ASEAN-led mode with priority given to the ASEAN community's interest appeals, and deepened the central position of the ASEAN in East Asian cooperation; however, the outside world had doubts about the capability of the ASEAN community as the leader in East Asian cooperation.[2] The biggest challenge for safeguarding the central position of the ASEAN community came from the buildup of solidarity and cohesion among member countries. From the perspective of

[2]Li Xiangyang, *The Developmental Direction for Asia-Pacific Regional Economic Cooperation and China's Choices*, Social Sciences Academic Press, 2015, p. 91.

consolidating the status of the ASEAN in cooperation, the ASEAN's efforts at promoting the construction of the community were aimed at reinforcing the core status of the ASEAN and enhancing its ability to exchange interests and bargain with the outside world.[3] Given the special cooperation mode in the East Asian Region, the construction of the community is crucial for the central position of the ASEAN in East Asian cooperation. Against such a background, in order to maintain its existing position in East Asian cooperation, externally, the ASEAN must build an image of close cooperation in the international community; internally, the ASEAN should increase the level of integration and enhance the cooperative ability of member countries to deal with regional affairs. Therefore, on the one hand, the construction of a community, advocated by the ASEAN, was designed to increase the integrality of the ASEAN as a regional cooperation organization; on the other hand, the construction of a community was aimed at enhancing the international status of the ASEAN by strengthening cooperation among member countries so as to safeguard the central position of the ASEAN in East Asian cooperation.

II. Analysis of the Goals of the ASEAN Community

The ASEAN Community includes a political and security community, an economic community and a sociocultural community. The ASEAN hopes to promote cooperation among member countries in these three fields to bring about lasting regional peace, stability and prosperity.

1. The ASEAN community's cooperation in the political and security fields under collective consensus

The ASEAN political and security community represents the overall framework and direction for the ASEAN's cooperation in the political and security fields during the next stage; it is designed to increase the level of ASEAN's cooperation in those fields, and to ensure that member countries and the

[3]Wang Yuzhu, *The ASEAN in 40 Years: the Mechanism of Driving Forces for Regional Economic Cooperation (1967–2007)*, Social Sciences Academic Press, 2011, p. 209.

countries outside the region coexist in a relatively fair, democratic and harmonious atmosphere. According to the *Blueprint for the ASEAN Political and Security Community*, the political and security community has three key characteristics: First, it is a rule-oriented community in which member countries have shared value standards and codes of conduct; second, it is a cohesive, vibrant, peaceful and stable area, member countries assume shared responsibility for their overall regional security; third, it maintains vitality and externality in a world of deepening integration.[4] In order to realize the above three characteristics, the blueprint also presents 142 action plans with a focus on deepening the political cooperation among member countries, developing the measures for prevention and peaceful settlement of conflicts, dealing with non-traditional security issues and emergencies, and reinforcing the central position of the ASEAN community in regional cooperation.

For the ASEAN community, cooperation aimed at safeguarding security is necessary; essentially, such cooperation has a political nature. The ASEAN political and security community is different from any form of military alliance, and it will not develop into a mutual defense treaty and a military alliance. The ASEAN political and security community exhibits the following characteristics: First, the ASEAN community copes with regional conflicts by reaching collective consensuses characterized by the "ASEAN way", and thus pushes forward the development of regional security cooperation.[5] In other words, the ASEAN does not safeguard regional common security by enhancing a collective defense capability or building a joint regional military force; instead, the ASEAN community works on enabling internal coordination and reaching a certain consensus at a collective level to regulate the behaviors endangering peace so as to reduce the possibility of the occurrence of conflict. Second, the ASEAN community's cooperation on security involves external relations, so it is particularly important to properly handle the relations with the countries outside the region, especially the great powers, during the construction of the political and security community. The ASEAN community extends the principles which govern cooperation among

---

[4]ASEAN Secretariat, ASEAN Political-Security Community Blueprint, Jakarta: ASEAN Secretariat, June 2009, p. 2.

[5]Zheng Xianwu, The Theory of the Security Community and Practice in the ASEAN, *World Economics and Politics*, 2004(5), p. 23.

member countries — respecting sovereignty and territorial integrity, peacefully settling disputes, keeping equality in status, refraining from interfering in the internal affairs of various countries — to the whole East Asian, and even to the Asian-Pacific Region, by engaging in dialogue and cooperation with the countries outside the region. For example, the ASEAN community has worked out the *Treaty of Amity and Cooperation in Southeast Asia* and the *Southeast Asian Nuclear-Weapon-Free Zone Treaty*; ASEAN requires all of the partners engaging in dialogue with them to sign both treaties and pledge to observe the principles specified in the two treaties.[6] With the construction of the political and security community, the ASEAN community attempts to build an image of a regional organization which features solidarity and cooperation; compared with single member countries, the security interests in some key fields can be guaranteed in a more effective way.

2. The ASEAN economic community as the core of community construction

Three pillars — a political and security community, an economic community and a sociocultural community — were identified at the time of planning the ASEAN Community. The *Blueprint for the ASEAN Economic Community* was signed and adopted during the 13th ASEAN Summit in 2007, while the other two blueprints were issued in the 14th ASEAN Summit in 2009. ASEAN did not issue the blueprints for these three communities at the same time possibly for the following reasons: On the one hand, member countries paid more attention to economic development compared with the fields of political, security and sociocultural cooperation, and economic cooperation was also the focus of ASEAN's attention; on the other hand, it was easier to build the economic community among these three pillars by utilizing more than 10 years of construction experience and achievements in the ASEAN Free Trade Area and the construction of the economic community can yield results more quickly at the initial stage of construction. During the early stage of the construction of the ASEAN Community, more resources were allocated to engage in economic cooperation so that the blueprint for the

[6] Zhang Yunling, *Between the Ideal and Reality — My Research, Involvement and Line of Thought Regarding East Asian Cooperation*, China Social Sciences Press, 2015, pp. 75–76.

economic community was executed smoothly during the start-up stage; this was conducive to boosting the confidence of member countries in ultimately completing the ASEAN Community and stimulating member countries to cooperate in the political, security and sociocultural fields.

The construction goals for the ASEAN Economic Community have been specified in a series of plans for the ASEAN community as made in the ASEAN Charter. These goals are as follows: build a stable, prosperous, highly competitive and economically integrated single market and production base to effectively promote trade and investment, enable the free flow of goods, services and investments; propel the movement of commercial personnel, professional personnel, talents and labor forces; make capital flow more freely; eliminate poverty and the developmental gap within the ASEAN community through mutual assistance and cooperation.[7] More specific goals are planned in the *Blueprint for the ASEAN Economic Community*, including four characteristics: turning the ASEAN into a single market and production base, which is the core and main characteristic of the construction of the economic community; a highly competitive economic zone; an area with balanced economic development; an area integrated into the global economy.[8] The blueprint provides a further detailed explanation of each characteristic of the ASEAN Economic Community. With respect to the four construction goals for the ASEAN Economic Community, the ASEAN has identified 17 core factors and 176 developmental priorities. In order to better carry out the plans for the ASEAN Community, the ASEAN has also developed the *Declaration on the Roadmap for the ASEAN Community 2009–2015*; the ASEAN has worked out four 2-year plans as of 2008, specified the construction period for each field and adopted the scorecard system to supervise the implementation of the plans for the ASEAN Economic Community.

According to the developmental plan specified in the blueprint for the economic community, the initial general goals for ASEAN economic integration have been developed into the strategy with very clear steps and measures. The blueprint provides a detailed time frame for ASEAN's integration; on the one hand, it deepens and develops the existing process of the ASEAN's

---

[7]ASEAN Secretariat, the ASEAN Charter, Jakarta: ASEAN Secretariat, January 2008, pp. 3–7.
[8]ASEAN Secretariat, ASEAN Economic Community Blueprint, Jakarta: ASEAN Secretariat, January 2008, pp. 5–6.

economic integration; on the other hand, it sets out specifics and makes supplementary actions about the areas which were missing or ignored in ASEAN's previous economic cooperation, so that the economic community, as a form of realizing the integration of the ASEAN countries, becomes more operable and also lays a solid foundation for ultimate establishment of the future ASEAN Community.

3. The construction of the ASEAN sociocultural community aimed at cultivating the sense of regional identity

The ASEAN community's design of a sociocultural community exceeds the scope of the ASEAN's previous cooperation in the sociocultural field. Its prominent feature is that it not only involves the traditional issues of social equity and cultural identity, but it also incorporates environmental protection and sustainable development of resources, and touches upon the impact of economic integration on the society and environment.[9] The main objective of the ASEAN Sociocultural Community is to build a people-oriented community with a sense of social responsibility, and thus promote the solidarity and unity of the whole ASEAN Region. A common identity is built in the region and the life and well-being of the ASEAN people are improved to build an inclusive and harmonious society with humanistic care and a spirit of sharing.[10] The specific tasks for building the ASEAN Sociocultural Community cover the following six aspects: the development of the ASEAN people, social welfare and security, social equity and civil rights, sustainable development of the environment, the building of an ASEAN identity and the narrowing of the developmental gap among member countries. For the strategic goals under each construction task, the ASEAN community has developed 339 concrete measures.

In the opinion of the former ASEAN Secretary-General Rodolfo C. Severino, the core of the ASEAN Community should be the sociocultural community from the perspective of cultivating a sense of identity about the

---

[9]Wei Hong, The Construction of the ASEAN Sociocultural Community and Its Significance for China, *Journal of Contemporary Asia-Pacific Studies*, 2006(5), p. 54.

[10]ASEAN Secretariat, ASEAN Socio-Security Community Blueprint, Jakarta: ASEAN Secretariat, June 2009, p. 2.

Southeast Asian Region, building a regional consciousness and promoting mutual understanding of the ASEAN people.[11] The formation of an ASEAN identity and an ASEAN consciousness will play a great substantive role in building the ASEAN Community: the construction of a sociocultural community is conducive to stimulating member countries to accept the common norms and share the common values, promoting smooth regional cooperation in the security field, while the development of the consciousness of mutual trust and mutual understanding can boost the confidence of various countries in the mechanism for regional economic cooperation and promote economic integration. Furthermore, the construction of a sociocultural community can also play the role of signal transmission — the ASEAN community does not merely pay attention to cooperation in the traditional fields of politics, security and economics, but it also shows great concern for such issues as the well-being of the ASEAN people and the rights and interests of the disadvantaged groups.

III. Evaluation of the Achievements in the Construction of the ASEAN Community

Since the roadmap for community construction was released, the ASEAN community has basically achieved the preset goals. As of late October, 2015, the ASEAN countries had completed 97% of the work specified in the roadmap — 100%, 100% and 93% of the preset goals for the three pillars including a political and security community, a sociocultural community and an economic community were achieved.[12] In November 2015, the 27th ASEAN Summit adopted the *2015 Kuala Lumpur Declaration on the Establishment of the ASEAN Community* and decided to officially announce the establishment of the ASEAN Community on December 31; it also pledged to strengthen the post-2015 construction of the community under the ASEAN

[11] [The Philippines] Rodolfo C. Severino, *Southeast Asia in Search of an ASEAN Community Insights — From the Former ASEAN Secretary-General*, trans. by Wang Yuzhu, Social Sciences Academic Press, 2012, p. 314.

[12] The ASEAN Secretary-General Le Luong Minh: the Preparatory Work for Completing the ASEAN Community Has Been Basically Finished, see http://zh.vietnamplus.vn/东盟秘书长黎梁明东盟共同体建成各项筹备工作基本就绪/44781.vnp, accessed on July 20, 2016.

Charter. The Declaration stresses that the establishment of the community is a milestone in the process of the ASEAN countries' integration and is conducive to safeguarding the long-term peace and stability of the region, injecting new vitality into economic development and elevating integration to a higher level, thus building an inclusive and people-oriented society.

The establishment of the ASEAN Charter in 2007 was an important turning point for the building of the community. As the first legally-binding instrument in 40 years since the establishment of the ASEAN group, the ASEAN Charter identifies the ASEAN as a regional organization with an independent legal personality and provides a legal guarantee for the ASEAN community to achieve strategic goals. The ASEAN Charter legally establishes the organizational status, goals and principles of the ASEAN community. It stipulates the identity of the ASEAN as a regional organization with a legal status, so the ASEAN community can carry out diplomatic activities as a whole and sign agreements with other countries or organizations. Thus, the ASEAN community has developed from a loose platform of cooperation into a regional organization for cooperation with a legal status and decision-making power. This is a foundation for the ASEAN community, to advance from functional cooperation to the construction of a community.[13]

1. Promotion of political development and cooperation on security in building mutual trust

The most prominent achievement made by the ASEAN community in political development is embodied in the promotion and protection of human rights. The ASEAN Charter establishes human rights as the legal principles for the ASEAN's member countries in the form of regional constitution. In 2009, the 15th ASEAN Summit adopted the *Cha-am Hua Hin Declaration on the Intergovernmental Commission on Human Rights*, and the mechanism of the ASEAN Intergovernmental Commission on Human Rights (AICHR) was officially launched. The ASEAN community took the establishment of

[13]Zhang Yunling, How to Understand the ASEAN — The Principle of Inclusiveness and the Successful Experience of the ASEAN, *Journal of Contemporary Asia-Pacific Studies*, 2015(1), pp. 4–20.

the Commission as a milestone in the process of building the community.[14] Immediately after the Commission was established, the *2010–2015 Five-Year Work Plan for Human Rights* was developed, work was carried out to draft the *ASEAN Human Rights Declaration* (AHRD), and it was finally signed and adopted at the 2012 Phnom Penh Summit. The Declaration offers a normative framework for the ASEAN community's human rights cooperation regarding four aspects: civic and political rights; economic, social and cultural rights; developmental rights; the right to seek peace.[15] After the Declaration was adopted, the focus of the work of the ASEAN Intergovernmental Commission on Human Rights shifted to publicizing and popularizing the Declaration. Specific actions include the following: translating the Declaration into the languages of the various countries and issuing it at the 46th anniversary of the establishment of the ASEAN; carrying out human rights training programs; holding youth workshops and debate competitions on the issue of human rights. The 48th ASEAN Foreign Ministers' Meeting in 2015 announced that the ASEAN community had entered the second stage of human rights cooperation. The *Five-Year Work Plan for the ASEAN Intergovernmental Commission on Human Rights (2016–2020)*, adopted during the Foreign Ministers' Meeting, stresses a continued commitment to promoting and protecting human rights in the ASEAN Region so as to fully achieve the long-term goals specified in the Declaration.

Regarding the field of cooperation on security issues, when the *Declaration of ASEAN Concord II* put forward the vision of the ASEAN Community for the first time in 2003, the instruments available for the ASEAN to observe in the field of cooperation on security were only the *Treaty of Amity and Cooperation in Southeast Asia*, the *Southeast Asian Nuclear-Weapon-Free Zone Treaty* and the *Declaration on the Conduct of Parties in the South China Sea*; the mechanism of dialogue regarding security was only the ASEAN Regional Forum (ARF) established in 1994.[16] The ASEAN revised and supplemented, to varying degrees,

[14]ASEAN Secretariat, Cha-Am Hua Hin Declaration on the Intergovernmental Commission Human Rights, Jakarta: ASEAN Secretariat, October 2009, p. 1.

[15]ASEAN Secretariat, ASEAN Human Rights Declaration and Phnom Penh Statement on the Adoption of the ASEAN Human Rights Declaration, Jakarta: ASEAN Secretariat, February 2013, p. 2.

[16]Luo Youngkun, The Process, Driving Factors and Prospects for the Construction of the ASEAN Community, *Guo Ji Yan Jiu Can Kao*, 2016(2), pp. 1–7.

the above treaties during the construction of the ASEAN Community, with a view to enabling more effective execution of these declarations. As an achievement made under the action plan for the security community, the ASEAN Defense Ministers' Meeting (ADMM) mechanism was established in May 2006, and it became the main platform for discussing the issues concerning regional security. At this point, the ASEAN community's cooperation mechanisms in building up confidence regarding security, the prevention of conflicts and defense mainly include the ARF and the ASEAN Defense Ministers' Meeting; the former is the core of the ASEAN community's security framework, while the latter is the ASEAN's highest defense mechanism.[17] The ASEAN Defense Ministers' Meeting makes it convenient for the defense ministers of various countries to discuss and exchange views about the current defense issues and security threats, and helps enhance the defense transparency of and mutual trust among member countries. In order to guide cooperation, the ASEAN community has developed a work plan every 3 years since 2008, with cooperation and actions focusing on strengthening regional cooperation on defense and security issues; reinforcing the existing cooperation, increasing the possibility of cooperation on defense and security, enhancing contacts with dialogue partners and making and sharing norms. Under the mechanism of the ASEAN Foreign Ministers' Meeting, the ASEAN community established the network of peacekeeping centers, held the meetings on collaboration in the defense industry and engaged in cooperation on providing quick responses.

During the construction of the political and security community, the ASEAN group provided the dialogue platform for traditional security, and also attached importance to the cooperation in non-traditional security fields such as counter-terrorism and response to disasters. Regarding counter-terrorism, the ASEAN countries and all of the countries as dialogue partners issued joint declarations on anti-terrorism cooperation, and developed the corresponding action plans. The *ASEAN Convention on Counter-Terrorism* was signed in 2007, offering a regional framework of cooperation for combating and preventing terrorism, with a view to deepening the anti-terrorism cooperation between law enforcement departments and other organs of power. The ASEAN community also developed a series of declarations on the

[17]Zhou Yuyuan, *From the ASEAN to the ASEAN Community: The ASEAN's Decision-making Mode and Practice*, World Affairs Press, 2015, p. 201.

non-traditional security fields, including the action plan for combating transnational crimes, the *Joint Declaration for a Drug-Free ASEAN* and the convention on combating human trafficking.

The construction of a political and security-focused community cannot be carried out without interaction with the countries and organizations outside the region; the ASEAN community continuously strengthened its position in East Asian cooperation in this process. The ASEAN countries' cooperation with the outside world on security mainly relies on such mechanisms as the ARF, the East Asia Summit (EAS), "The ASEAN +" meeting and the ASEAN Defense Ministers' Meeting-Plus (ADMM-Plus). With 27 members, the ARF has become the largest and most influential multilateral platform for dialogue on political and security issues in the region. At present, the ARF is at the stage of preventive diplomacy marked by the *Preventive Diplomacy Work Plan of the ASEAN Regional Forum* signed and adopted in July 2011.[18] In order to support the construction of a community and improve the functional mechanism of forums, the ARF is advocating that the achievements of the preventive diplomacy should be tested in an action-oriented way, with the gradual expansion and deepening of cooperation fields. Furthermore, in order to continue deepening the cooperation with dialogue partners on security and defense, the ASEAN community established the ADMM-Plus mechanism in Hanoi, Vietnam, in October, 2010, pushing forward the cooperation in a number of fields including maritime safety, counter-terrorism, humanitarian aid, response to disasters, peacekeeping actions, military medical service and subsequently supplemented humanitarian demining actions. An expert group was established for each cooperation field and co-chaired by the ASEAN member countries and dialogue partners, and they separately held meetings to initiate cooperation plans.

2. The progressive construction of the ASEAN Economic Community

For the overall construction of the ASEAN Economic Community, the Presidential Statement of the 27th ASEAN Summit intentionally

[18]Zhao Haili, The Construction of the ASEAN Political and Security Community: Achievements and Problems, *Southeast Asian Affairs*, 2015(4), p. 44.

downplayed specific data, it did not present the completion ratios like the previous presidential statements, and it only adopted "the blueprint plan for near completion" to make vague descriptions. This indicates that the ASEAN community's efforts in some key fields did not go as smoothly as expected in the process of pushing forward the economic community. Detailed data were shown in the *ASEAN Economic Community 2015: Progress and Key Achievements* released during the summit — as of October 31, 2015, the ratio of completion of the ASEAN Economic Community was 92.7%, 469 out of all 506 action arrangements were completed.[19] Specifically, 256 action arrangements (277 in total) were completed in the construction of a single market and production base, 154 action arrangements (170 in total) were completed in building the competitive economic zones, the ratio of completion reached 100% in the remaining two pillars.

Regarding tariff reduction, under the framework of the *ASEAN Trade in Goods Agreement* (ATIGA), six old member countries of the ASEAN planned to eliminate all import tariffs for trade within the ASEAN community by 2010, while the time limit for four new countries — Cambodia, Laos, Myanmar and Vietnam (CLMV) — in terms of that elimination was extended to 2015–2018. In 2014, the average tariff rate under ATIGA had been reduced to 0.54%, while the tariff rate for the countries outside the region, which enjoyed the ASEAN's most-favored-nation treatment, hit 6.9%. So far, six ASEAN countries have canceled 99.2% of the import tariffs for the goods within the region, and that proportion in CLMV reached 90.86%.[20] Merely tariff reduction cannot bring about an open market. Thus the ASEAN community also actively engaged in cooperation in the non-tariff field by taking convenient country of origin certification measures, developing the action plan for trade facilitation, building the ASEAN trade information base, eliminating the non-tariff barriers to trade, developing the ASEAN's single window system and signing the mutual recognition agreement (MRAs). With the ASEAN community's efforts in reducing tariffs and non-tariff barriers, the trade within the ASEAN soared by 58.9% in 2014

[19]ASEAN Secretariat, ASEAN Economic Community 2015: Progress and Key Achievements, Jakarta: ASEAN Secretariat, November 2015, p. 17.

[20]ASEAN Secretariat, ASEAN Integration Report 2015, Jakarta: ASEAN Secretariat, November 2015, p. 22.

over 2007, slightly higher than the growth of external trade, but the proportion of the trade within the ASEAN in the ASEAN community's total trade remained at a relatively low level (24.1%).

In parallel to the reduction of the tariffs for trade in goods, the ASEAN community also continuously accelerated liberalization of trade in services, and gradually canceled restrictive measures for trade in services. The ASEAN's service market integration was based on the *ASEAN Framework Agreement on Services* (AFAS). In 2014, the negotiations involving the ASEAN's liberalization of trade in services generated the 9th package plan. At present, at least 80 service sectors have been opened to foreign capital and seen the relaxation of equity restrictions on foreign capital. Before 2015, at least 70% of the service sectors in ASEAN countries were open to foreign capital.[21] With the ASEAN community's continued efforts in relaxing investment restrictions in service sectors, the exports from the ASEAN's service sectors grew rapidly, their trade deficit decreased from USD 27.3 billion in 2005 to USD 8.2 billion in 2014. In 2013, service sectors in ASEAN countries contributed nearly half to the actual output, the proportion in some relatively developed member countries, such as Singapore and Malaysia, reached 66.6% and 55.2%.

Regarding investment liberalization, in August 2007, the ASEAN Investment Area Council (AIA Council) integrated the *1987 ASEAN Agreement for the Promotion and Protection of Investments* and the *1998 Framework Agreement on the ASEAN Investment Area* into the *ASEAN Comprehensive Investment Agreement* (ACIA). The ACIA officially came into effect in March 2012; its main characteristics include the following: comprehensive clauses on investment liberalization and promotion, the explicit investment liberalization schedule for the ASEAN Economic Community, greater preferential policies for exclusively foreign-owned enterprises investing in and building factories in the ASEAN; reservation of preferential arrangements for the ASEAN Investment Area; the building of a more liberalized, convenient, transparent and competitive investment environment.[22]

[21]Wang Qin, The Process of the Construction of the ASEAN Economic Community and Its Effectiveness, *Southeast Asian Affairs*, 2015(4), p. 6.

[22]AIA Council, Joint Media Statement of The Tenth ASEAN Investment Area Council Meeting, Makati City, August 23, 2007.

In 2014, the ASEAN revised and supplemented the ACIA, and gradually relaxed or canceled investment restrictions, mainly involving such fields as manufacturing, agriculture, fishery, forestry, mining and service. The ASEAN Investment Area has more than 10 years of construction experience and has significantly improved attraction as an investment destination. The flow of foreign investments to the ASEAN countries accounted for 11% of the global flow in 2014, while that figure was 5% in 2007. The FDI flow within the region accounted for 17.9%, only second to the EU's investments in the region.

Regarding integration into the global economy, a series of achievements have also been made in the ASEAN community. In January 2010, five ASEAN-centered free trade areas — the free trade areas between the ASEAN countries and China, Japan, South Korea, India, Australia and New Zealand — were launched at the same time. These five FTAs include 16 founding members of the East Asia Summit. On this basis, in order to further promote regional economic cooperation, the ASEAN put forward the Regional Comprehensive Economic Partnership (RCEP) plan at the 19th Summit in 2011. The guidance document for RCEP positions it as a modern, comprehensive, high-level mutually beneficially economic cooperation, mainly involving trade in goods, trade in services, investments, economic and technological cooperation, intellectual property, a mechanism for competition and a mechanism for the settlement of disputes; its level will be higher than that of the existing FTA but it does not replace the existing FTA; it is open to other countries willing to participate in it, which can join it through consultation.[23]

Moreover, in order to keep in coordination with the construction of the economic community, narrow the economic developmental gap among member countries and strengthen the infrastructure construction in the region, the ASEAN group put forward the *Master Plan on ASEAN Connectivity* during the 17th Summit in 2010, covering more than 700 projects and programs, with the investment scale reaching about USD 38 million, with a view to promoting infrastructure connectivity, mechanism connectivity and people-to-people exchanges within the ASEAN community

[23] Zhang Yunling, *Between Ideal and Reality — My Research, Involvement and Thinking Regarding East Asian Cooperation*, China Social Sciences Press, 2015, pp. 148–150.

to strengthen connection and cooperation among member countries, narrow development gap and further speed up the construction of the community.

3. Emphasis on humanistic care amidst the cultivation of an ASEAN consciousness

The sociocultural community stresses the building and recognition of an ASEAN identity; it is designed to improve the living standard and social welfare of the people in the ASEAN community. Since the declaration of the roadmap was issued, the ASEAN member countries have continuously strengthened their cooperation in the social and cultural fields so as to ensure that the construction of the ASEAN Community can be completed on schedule. An outstanding contribution to the construction of the socio-cultural community lies in promoting the building and recognition of an ASEAN identity, which is achieved mainly by carrying out various kinds of cultural activities so that the people, especially the young people, understand the conditions of the ASEAN community and its member countries. Specifically, mainstream media, network and new media are utilized as the important means of communication and interaction focusing on the ASEAN community to promote the dissemination of an ASEAN consciousness; with the young people as the main educatees, education is taken as the main means for developing the recognition of an ASEAN identity and an ASEAN consciousness, and incorporate ASEAN knowledge as part of the course for learning.

The achievements of the ASEAN community in promoting human development are embodied in enhancing the happiness of the ASEAN people and ensuring equal opportunities for their personal development. In order to increase the educational level of member countries, the ASEAN community has relied on the existing organizations for and networks of educational cooperation to enhance the cooperation on the advantageous resources among member countries: First, the Southeast Asian Ministers of Educational Organization, established in 1965, is relied upon; the ASEAN Secretariat and the Secretariat of the Southeast Asian Ministers of Educational Organization convene meetings, and the resources within and outside the region are utilized to increase the educational level of the ASEAN people. In 2011, the ASEAN community unveiled the *Five-Year Plan for Education in the ASEAN community* (*2011–2015*) for guiding member countries to develop their educational undertaking. Second, the ASEAN University Network (AUN), established in 1995, is relied upon. By promoting exchanges and research in the fields in which priority is given to development, the AUN strengthens the cooperation among the institutions of higher learning in the ASEAN community, especially by promoting cooperation among scientists and scholars of the various countries, pushing forward the human resource development of local professional talents.[24] According to the *Mid-term Evaluation of the Sociocultural Community* released by the ASEAN group, the number of years of education involving adults in the six old ASEAN countries and the CLMV increased from 7.5 and 4.6 in 2005 to 8 and 5, respectively. The youth literacy rate in the six old ASEAN countries approached 100%, while the CLMV also made significant progress in the youth literacy rate — it reached 92% in 2010.[25] The Human Development Index (HDI) also indicated that the human development gap between the six old ASEAN countries and the CLMV further narrowed, with the gap narrowing from 25% in 2005 to 22.9% in 2010.

In 2010, the ASEAN community established the ASEAN Commission on the Promotion and Protection of the Rights of Women and Children, which aims at safeguarding the social welfare of women and children and equal opportunities for development for them. Since its establishment, the Commission has convened meetings many times to carry out the *2012–2016 Work Plan for the Protection of the Rights and Interests of Women and Children in the ASEAN Community*. The ASEAN community has also continued to show greater care for the disadvantaged groups and the socially marginalized groups. The 19th ASEAN Summit announced that the period of 2011–2020 was identified as the 10-year period for the handicapped in the ASEAN community. In 2010, the ASEAN community established the ASEAN Children's Forum. Regarding environmental protection, the 13th ASEAN Environmental Ministers' Meeting 2015 was held in Hanoi, which evaluated the implementation of various cooperation arrangements in the ASEAN's

[24]Luo Youngkun, The Process, Driving Factors and Prospects for the Construction of the ASEAN Community, *Guo Ji Yan Jiu Can Kao*, 2016(2), p. 6.

[25]ASEAN Secretariat. Mid-Term Review of the ASEAN Socio-Cultural Community Blueprint (2009–2015), Jakarta: ASEAN Secretariat, February 2014, p. 16.

environmental field since the 12th meeting in 2012, and put forward the suggestions and measures for the ASEAN countries' cooperation on the environment after the construction of the community. The *Declaration on Institutionalizing the Resilience of the ASEAN Group and Its Communities and Peoples to Disasters and Climate Change*, signed during the 26th ASEAN Summit, is of a guiding significance for promoting the coordinated sustainable development of the region.

IV. Abstract Goals Versus Concrete Means: The Progressive Construction of the ASEAN Community

According to the above analysis, the goals to be achieved in the construction of the ASEAN Community represent a relatively abstract state of integration; however, in practice, the ASEAN community has to depict these goals through the implementation of concrete measures. This is the reason why the construction of the ASEAN political and security community, the economic community and the sociocultural community is promoted by refining the construction into a series of specific construction goals. The strategy of using concrete progress to depict the abstract goals of the community determines that the construction of the ASEAN Community is progressive. Furthermore, many goals determined by the ASEAN for the community are progressive to a certain extent; for example, tariff reduction, the proportion of products included in the tariff reduction, the elimination of the internal developmental gap are progressive goals, and these factors reflect progressiveness in the construction of the community. Moreover, the construction of the ASEAN Community also faces some other difficulties, such as the economic and social developmental gap among member countries, as well as religious and cultural differences. Overcoming these difficulties entails long-term efforts, so the construction of the ASEAN Community will be a long-term process.

1. The factors leading to a long-term process of constructing a community

First, the ASEAN countries, except Thailand, were colonies of Western powers during the Second World War; these emerging countries have a stronger appeal for sovereignty. With long-term cooperation, the ASEAN way — one of its characteristics is non-interference in internal affairs — has taken shape, thus when the construction of the political and security community involves the issue of sovereignty, the ASEAN cannot make a substantive breakthrough. This also causes the following situation: the ASEAN's multilateral security cooperation is mainly based on a security dialogue and cooperation forum; it is difficult to develop a common security policy.[26] For example, the ASEAN group expressed no opinions on Thailand's military coup d'etat in 2006, suggesting that this cooperation characteristic of the ASEAN restricts, to a certain extent, the level which the ASEAN political and security community can reach.

Second, the ASEAN countries have adopted different industrialization paths due to historical experiences. Member countries are extremely unbalanced in economic foundation and economic level and so there is a huge gap among member countries. According to the data from the World Bank, the highest per capita GDP in ASEAN member countries in 2013 occurred in Singapore and reached USD 55,182, while the lowest one occurred in Cambodia and was USD 1,007. The per capita GDP gap was about 55 times, much higher than 15 times within the EU and five times within the North American Free Trade Area. The differences in the level of economic development among member countries have exerted a great negative impact on realizing the goal of the ASEAN's integration.

At present, the implementation of the final action plan for the ASEAN Economic Community will be subject to great challenges, involving the protection of intellectual property trade, non-tariff barriers to trade, free movement of labor and unified quality standards for the ASEAN's products. The disagreements in these in-depth issues among various countries will exert an important impact on future negotiations. In fact, although many types of tariffs have been reduced substantially, the enterprises in various countries still face difficulties due to non-tariff barriers. Moreover, the ASEAN countries are different in their level of infrastructures, thus increasing the costs for cross-border freight transportation and the weakening

[26]Ma Ying, The Evolution and Prospect of the ASEAN's Security Strategy, *International Studies*, 2008(2), pp. 60–64.

of the driving forces for member countries to deepen their economic cooperation.

Finally, the construction of the ASEAN Community is carried out under a mode of top-down recognition and promotion, the ASEAN people have less knowledge of the community and many enterprises and individuals do not know the benefits that the establishment of the community will bring to them.[27] According to a survey conducted by the Vietnam Chamber of Commerce & Industry, 80% of Vietnamese enterprises knew little about the economic community, and only 10% said that they had prepared for addressing its establishment.[28] The efforts made by the ASEAN so far in social publicity of the community and citizen education are less than those made by the EU when that single market was established.

2. The ASEAN: stage goals are set to address the progressive construction of the community

As early as 2013, the ASEAN started to plan the post-2015 construction of the community. The 23rd ASEAN Summit and the 25th ASEAN Summit separately issued the Bandar Seri Begawan Declaration and the Naypyidaw Declaration on the ASEAN Community's Post-2015 Vision. During the 27th ASEAN Summit, the ASEAN's leaders signed and adopted the *Kuala Lumpur Declaration on ASEAN 2025: Forging Ahead Together*; this declaration presents the developmental roadmap for the ASEAN group in the next 10 years and aims at building a peaceful and stable community with unity and solidarity as well as shared prosperity, building a law-abiding, people-oriented community with strong cohesion on the basis of the goals and principles specified in the ASEAN Charter, enhancing the ASEAN's capability for coping with challenges and safeguarding its core role in East Asian cooperation. In order to chime in with the vision plan for the ASEAN Community at the next stage, the ASEAN's leaders also announced that the ASEAN community

---

[27] Zhang Yunling, How to Understand the ASEAN — The Principle of Inclusiveness and the Successful Experience of the ASEAN, *Journal of Contemporary Asia-Pacific Studies*, 2015(1), pp.4-20.

[28] Luan He, New Breakthroughs Are Sought in the Construction of the ASEAN Economic Community, *China Trade News*, February 4, 2016, Page 2.

would improve their operating procedure, strengthen internal collaboration and enhance their ability to execute systems, so as to improve the working efficiency of bodies within the ASEAN group and reinforce the role of the ASEAN Secretariat.

In the meantime, recognizing the negative impact of the huge gap among member countries with respect to the construction of the community, the Ad Hoc Group for the Initiative of ASEAN's Integration is working with various countries to develop the Phase III Work Plan for the Initiative of ASEAN's Integration ("IAI Work Plan III"). The ASEAN's future cooperation in narrowing the developmental gap will focus on five priorities: grain and agriculture, trade facilitation, the development of micro, small and medium-sized enterprises, education, health and welfare.[29]

Regarding economic cooperation with foreign countries, the ASEAN community has stepped up efforts to conclude negotiations involving the RCEP.

According to the plan for the vision of post-2015 construction of the ASEAN Community, by 2025, the ASEAN will have become an inclusive political and security community with solidarity and self-improvement; an ASEAN Economic Community which features close connection, high competitiveness, active innovation and will have become part of an international economic integration; an ASEAN Sociocultural Community which extensively attracts people and brings tangible benefits to people. It will also be an inclusive and active community with sustainable development and self-improvement.

V. Conclusions

According to the analysis in this paper, the announcement, made 12 years ago, that the ASEAN Community had been established was only a new starting point in the long-term construction of the ASEAN Community. The goals are abstract and the means are concrete, so the construction of the ASEAN Community will certainly be a process. In the meantime, the realization of

[29] ASEAN Countries Agreed upon the Strategic Priorities in Narrowing the Developmental Gap, see http://zh.vietnamplus.vn/东盟各国就缩小发展差距的战略优先达成一致/49529.vnp, accessed on 2016-07-21.

some goals which need to be achieved with respect to the community is a huge challenge for the ASEAN, a diversified organization. For the ASEAN, which always upholds the principle of coordination, this means that the construction of a community is a long-term process. Nevertheless, as shown by the course of the construction of the ASEAN Community, the ASEAN group is maintaining internal solidarity in the process and is gradually moving towards becoming a community.

Chapter 23

Myanmar's General Election and Its Impact on China–Myanmar Relations

Huang Ai'lian*

Myanmar's 2015 general election, which drew wide attention, came to a conclusion; Myanmar's National League for Democracy gained a complete victory in this general election. According to the results announced by the Myanmar Federal Election Commission, the National League for Democracy obtained 886 seats, 255 seats at the House of Representatives and 135 seats at the House of Nationalities — both houses constitute the Assembly of the Union — and 496 seats at local assemblies, ranking it the No. 1 Party. This means that the National League for Democracy gained the power to form a new government, Myanmar will enter the era of the National League for Democracy in the future and Myanmar's diplomacy under democracy will present new characteristics. How the China–Myanmar relations will develop in the era of the National League for Democracy has become another focus for the attention of the outside world.

* Huang Ai'lian, Director, Professor at the Myanmar Institute of the China–ASEAN Research Institute of Guangxi University.

I. Analysis of Myanmar's 2015 General Election

1. Background of the General Election

a. *Various parties contended with each other on the issue of constitutional amendments*

At present, the amendment to the *Constitution of the Republic of the Union of Myanmar* is the uppermost focus in this general election; this has a vital bearing on the eligibility of Aung San Suu Kyi, the leader of the National League for Democracy, which has been out of power, for joining the presidential election. According to Clause 59 of the *Constitution of the Republic of the Union of Myanmar* promulgated in 2008, the person whose child or children is or are the citizen(s) of a foreign country shall not run for presidency. Both children of Aung San Suu Kyi are citizens of the UK; this means that she fails to comply with the clause concerning the qualifications of the President in the *Constitution of the Republic of the Union of Myanmar*. How Aung San Suu Kyi, as the leader of the National League for Democracy, can realize the leadership over the country is a tough issue. Therefore, since Aung San Suu Kyi appeared on Myanmar's political stage, she and the National League for Democracy have never given up their efforts to exert pressure on the government with respect to a constitutional amendment. Since 2012, she and the National League for Democracy have contended with the Union Solidarity and Development Party, the military and other forces for several rounds. Subject to the pressure from Aung San Suu Kyi, the National League for Democracy and their supporters, the Government of the Union Solidarity and Development Party seemingly expressed their willingness to discuss the issue of a constitutional amendment. For example, the session of the Central Committee of the Union Solidarity and Development Party adopted the recommendations concerning a constitutional amendment in December 2013, and President Thein Sein expressed the support for a constitutional amendment at the broadcast speech for the first time in January 2014. However, the Union Solidarity and Development Party has a profound military background, its fundamental position is the same as that of the military. In the past 2 years, the proposals for a constitutional amendment have often been thwarted due to obstruction from the powerful military, while the Union Solidarity and Development Party have often taken an ambiguous attitude amidst the contention between the two sides.

b. *Myanmar has been in a crucial period of democratization*

As of 2011, when the ruling by the military government ended, Myanmar started a preliminary exploration of democratization. For many years, certain achievements have been made in reforming the political system, relaxing control over the public opinion of the media and safeguarding the rights and interests of the citizens. Regarding the reform of the political system, the Government of the Union Solidarity and Development Party has been committed to rectifying the bureaucratic organizations arising in the period of the military government on the one hand; on the other hand, it has amended laws to recognize the legal statuses of the opposition parties including the National League for Democracy and the 88 Generation Students Group. Regarding the public opinion of the social media, the Union Solidarity and Development Party has gradually relaxed publication and cyber censorship; so far, 26 private daily newspapers have been permitted to publish their issues. The Assembly of the Union of Myanmar adopted the new radio and television law in August 2015, giving the green light to run private television stations. Moreover, progress has also been made accordingly in safeguarding the basic rights and interests of Burmese citizens, such as establishing the Myanmar National Human Rights Commission consisting of retired officials and scholars, and publishing draft bills of the Commission on official media. Based on the above achievements, this general election will undoubtedly exert a crucial impact on the direction of the development of Myanmar's democratization in the future.

c. *Opening-up has made Myanmar's economic development enter a fast track*

Myanmar was economically backward for a long time. In 1987, Myanmar was identified by the United Nations as one of the least developed countries in the world. This dilemma was largely caused by the following factors: Myanmar's economic policies lagged far behind during the ruling of the military government, and Myanmar was subject to many sanctions imposed by Western countries. As these factors existed, the channels for introducing foreign capital were narrow, a number of industrial fields which urgently needed to be developed lacked necessary support, including capital, technology and human resources.

Since the Government of the Union Solidarity and Development Party came into power in 2010, Myanmar's opening-up has been promoted noticeably, thus extensively attracting capital from various countries to cultivate Myanmar's industrial foundation. In 2012, Myanmar revised the *Foreign Investment Law*, further widening the scope of providing access to foreign capital, especially attaching importance to guiding capital to agriculture, tourism, manufacturing industries and other areas relating to the people's livelihood. Furthermore, Myanmar has also actively participated in various regional frameworks for trade cooperation; for example, Myanmar has, in conjunction with other ASEAN countries, joined the China–ASEAN Free Trade Area (CAFTA). Thanks to close investment and trade cooperation, Myanmar has witnessed rapid economic growth in recent years. In the fiscal year 2014–2015 (April 1, 2014–March 31, 2015), Myanmar's foreign trade totaled USD 29,157 million, up 16.8%.[1] Foreign investments in Myanmar totaled USD 8,011 million in this fiscal year, up 100%.[2] This provides an excellent economic environment for Myanmar's 2015 general election.

d. *Tension has tended to ease on the issue of armed ethnic groups*

The issue of armed ethnic groups in northern Myanmar has always been the focus of attention from various parties in Myanmar; it is also one of the greatest barriers to Myanmar's national unity and democratic transformation. Beginning in January 2015, military conflicts escalated again between Myanmar's governmental army and the armed ethnic groups in northern Myanmar, including the Kachin Independence Army and the Myanmar National Democratic Alliance Army, while the Government of the National League for Democracy contended with armed ethnic groups over the 2015 general election. Both sides hoped to enhance their bargaining chip in peace negotiations before the general election by demonstrating respective military strength. After a number of conflicts and consultations, on October 15, 2015, witnessed by the representatives of various countries, the signing ceremony of

---

[1] *Source*: The Central Statistical Organization of Myanmar, https://www.csostat.gov.mm/s1.3MA02.htm.

[2] https://www.csostat.gov.mm/s5.2MA0201.htm.

Myanmar's national ceasefire agreement was held in Naypyidaw; this marked substantive historic progress made in Myanmar's peace process. Only eight out of 15 armed groups across the country signed the agreement in this ceremony, the relatively powerful armed groups, including Wa State, Karen and Kokang, did not attend this ceremony, but the signing of Myanmar's national ceasefire agreement created a stable environment for Myanmar's general election.[3] Moreover, the National League for Democracy invited a large number of minority nationals, as its members, to participate in the election in the constituencies inhabited by the minority nationals; to a certain degree, this also helped the National League for Democracy build closer connections with the armed ethnic groups.

2. The characteristics of the general election and analysis of the causes for the victory of the National League for Democracy in the general election

a. *Main characteristics of this general election*

Myanmar's 2015 general election presents distinctive characteristics and surpasses the previous general elections in many respects. The time of this general election is the most regular since Myanmar gained independence in 1948, with 91 participating political parties, more than 6,000 parliamentary candidates and more than 10,000 domestic and foreign observers, numbers that are several times those in the previous general election. Among the characteristics of this general election, the one which most deserves attention from the outside world is that 80% of the Burmese people voted, suggesting that the people from various sectors of the society were active in voting. In fact, the Burmese people's enthusiasm for this general election was kindled before the formal polling day. On November 1, barely a week earlier, more than 50,000 Burmese people attended the campaign rally held by the National League for Democracy.

[3] Foreign Media: Myanmar Signed the National Ceasefire Agreement, But It Was Not National and There Was No Ceasefire, www.ifeng.com, http://news.ifeng.com/a/20151018/45501585_0.shtml.

b. *Multiple factors helped the National League for Democracy win this general election*

Myanmar's 2015 general election with the participation of the highest proportion of the population was concluded with the victory of the National League for Democracy. The victory resulted from multiple factors and also showed the contest, between the two parties, for gaining popular support. On the one hand, the failure of the Union Solidarity and Development Party came from its negative image among the Burmese people, which stemmed from its nepotism with the former military government. Many core members of the Government of the Union Solidarity and Development Party had a strong military background and developed close ties with the former military government. However, the ruling of the former military government begot much discontent among the Burmese people; this became a great burden after the Union Solidarity and Development Party came into power. About 60% of the Burmese population is an agricultural population. Thus, after the Union Solidarity and Development Party came into power, it attached great importance to addressing the issues regarding the livelihood of the population represented by the issues of agriculture, rural areas, and rural people, and hoped to funnel benefits to farmers so as to highlight its difference from the former military government characterized by autarchy, corruption, low efficiency and bureaucratization. However, this strategy, in the end, failed to reverse the situation in this general election; this is because the overall negative image of the Union Solidarity and Development Party among the Burmese people had been deep-rooted and the Union Solidarity and Development Party was considered as the continuity of the former military government.

On the other hand, Aung San Suu Kyi and the National League for Democracy gained popular support thanks to their image of democratization, and this largely covered the disadvantage of the National League for Democracy — lack of experience in governing. This image of democratization was first embodied in the personal charisma of Aung San Suu Kyi. Aung San Suu Kyi is the daughter of General Aung San, the leader of the Burmese movement for independence, and she opposed the military government for a long time and established the relationship of a natural "alliance" with the Burmese people. As from 2010 when Aung San Suu Kyi was released, she frequently carried out various political activities, gaining a large number of supporters among the people. After the National League for Democracy was established in 1988, besides Aung San Suu Kyi, many members of the National League for Democracy participated in the campaign against the military government; for example, Win Tin, one of the founders of the National League for Democracy, was imprisoned for a long time due to his publicity efforts against the government. Therefore, the National League for Democracy, which opposed the military government, naturally cultivated a broad base among the masses. In this general election, Burmese voters generally believed that Aung San Suu Kyi and the National League for Democracy were closer to the people, so they very much hoped that the National League for Democracy would be able to lead Myanmar to further improve the people's livelihood and the process of democratization in Myanmar.

Furthermore, after Myanmar was opened to the outside world in 2011, it engaged in close cooperation and exchange with more Western countries, the Burmese people had more opportunities for maintaining contacts with inbound tourists from Western countries and foreigners permanently resident in Myanmar, thus the mindsets of the people from various classes of the society changed unconsciously. These changes were first reflected in the Burmese people's lifestyle, and then changes also took place in deep-set philosophies, such as cultural values, the social system, ideology and developmental mode. In particular, at present, many people belonging to Myanmar's emerging elite class have started to accept Western democratic thought, while the awareness of the ordinary people for expressing political appeals has also improved significantly. In the meantime, Western countries also actively infiltrated ideas into various classes of Myanmar; for example, in the past 20 or more years, the governments and NGOs of Western countries, led by the USA, developed a number of Burmese elites who align their sentiments and positions with Western countries and believe in Western values, and they also set up many NGOs in Myanmar through these elites. These NGOs in Myanmar demonstrated their influence mainly by conducting ability training, holding workshops and releasing relevant research reports.[4] Therefore, Aung San Suu Kyi, hailed by Western countries as a fighter for democracy,

[4]Western Countries Vigorously Exported Soft Power to Myanmar for Influencing and Controlling Myanmar's Developments, http://www.globalview.cn/html/global/info_2574.html.

has enjoyed extraordinarily high appeal among Burmese elites, thus significantly increasing the degree of support for her participation in the election.

II. The New Outlook on Maintaining a Balance among the Great Powers under the Leadership of the National League for Democracy

1. The formation of the strategy of maintaining a balance among great powers

Neutralism was originally the traditional philosophy in Myanmar's diplomatic policy. In 1955, Myanmar and the Indonesian Government jointly initiated and held the famous Asian–African Bandung Conference, laying a foundation for carrying out an international non-aligned movement; this also was the embryonic form of Myanmar's diplomacy of maintaining a balance among the great powers. As the Burmese military government, which came into power through a coup d'état in 1988, was subject to sanctions imposed by Western countries, it had to develop the relations with China to stabilize its domestic situation. However, the policy of the Burmese military government towards China was not unchanged in the period of its governance from 1988 to 2010, during which its diplomatic strategy experienced a process of adjustment, balancing and rebalancing, and it was always fine-tuned in light of Myanmar's national interests at different stages; this period can be regarded as the period of experimenting with Myanmar's diplomacy of maintaining a balance among the great powers. From 1992 to 1997, with the gradual consolidation of the political power of the military government, Myanmar sought to improve the relations with various countries in the region, and its diplomatic strategy preliminarily tended to be diversified; in particular, it strengthened its relations with ASEAN countries and India. As of 1997, China and Myanmar showed disagreements over some projects, but Myanmar still failed to overcome diplomatic and economic developmental dilemmas after it joined the ASEAN, so Myanmar had to predominantly side with China. In particular, from 2003 to 2010, Western countries intensified their sanctions against Myanmar and China–Myanmar economic and trade ties reached an unprecedented level.

After the Union Solidarity and Development Party, with its military background, came into power in 2011, amicable cooperation generally continued to be maintained between China and Myanmar, but Myanmar's diplomatic strategy apparently broke away from unilateral dependence upon China, its strategic line of thought of keeping a balance among the great powers preliminarily took shape. A number of incidents — including the shelving of the Myitsone Power Station Project, obstruction to Letpadaung Copper Mine Project and the cancellation of the China–Myanmar high-speed railway project — arose due to this strategic line of thought adopted by the Union Solidarity and Development Party. To a certain extent, the Government of the Union Solidarity and Development Party had no choice but to adopt the diplomatic strategy of keeping a balance among the great powers. The Union Solidarity and Development Party had close ties with the former military government, so after it came into power, it deliberately disagreed with China on some issues in order to remove the negative impact of the military government. In fact, the line of thought of keeping a balance among the great powers or equidistant diplomacy in Myanmar's diversified diplomatic strategy was not absolute, China had a special status in it; in other words, it was a China-centered diversified strategy. From another perspective, the Government of the Union Solidarity and Development Party still attached great importance to China in the diplomatic field, the leaders of both sides basically maintained the fine tradition of frequent reciprocal visits, and both countries had clearly moved to develop a partnership of comprehensive strategic cooperation.

2. The core of the outlook of the National League for Democracy on maintaining a balance among great powers: Pragmatic and flexible

The Government of the National League for Democracy, which will hold power after this general election, will continue to adopt the diplomatic strategy of maintaining a balance among the great powers established in the period of the Union Solidarity and Development Party, but the specific manner of implementing that strategy will obviously differ from that of the Union Solidarity and Development Party. Myanmar's diplomacy of maintaining a balance among the great powers in the era of the National League for Democracy will prominently present the following characteristics: pragmatism and flexibility.

These characteristics mainly come from the behavioral style of Aung San Suu Kyi and the long-time identity of the National League for Democracy as a party that has been outside of the circle of power. On the one hand, Aung San Suu Kyi takes a friendly and pragmatic attitude towards China. Considering that Aung San Suu Kyi enjoys high prestige and wields a huge influence within the National League for Democracy, an analysis of her comments on China–Myanmar relations reveals the National League for Democracy's position on China. In November 2010, on the day following the removal of her house arrest, she stated, "China is a very important neighbor of Myanmar, Myanmar should not consider China as a foe".[5] Aung San Suu Kyi also stressed on many occasions, "China and Myanmar are neighbors, and neighbors cannot be chosen". She once suggested that as long as it was open and transparent, the Myitsone Power Station Project and the high-speed railway project which had been halted could be restarted. In response to many problems with the Letpadaung Copper Mine Project based on a joint venture between China and Myanmar, the Investigation Committee led by Aung San Suu Kyi presented an objective and pertinent evaluation in its investigation report released in March 2013, which stated that the project can continue to be executed after rectification. Moreover, Aung San Suu Kyi also praised the Belt and Road Initiative put forward by China and hoped that the Belt and Road Initiative could achieve the outcomes beneficial for various parties. On the other hand, since its establishment, the National League for Democracy has always been active among the people as a party that is outside the circle of power in Myanmar, it has gained a deeper understanding of the actual livelihood demands of the Burmese people, so it will give more considerations to the actual interests of the people when developing a relevant diplomatic policy. Furthermore, the policy, led by the National League for Democracy, of keeping a balance among the great powers will constantly change in light of targets in due time. Specifically, at present, the members and team of the National League for Democracy have gotten old,

[5] Liu Wu, The Impact of Myanmar's Political Development on China–Myanmar Relations, *Indian Ocean Economic and Political Review*, 2015(2), pp. 20–33.

there are no other prominent core figures except Aung San Suu Kyi, and the National League for Democracy has no sufficient governance experience since it has been outside the circle of power for a long time. The above obstacles require the National League for Democracy to be flexible in foreign contacts; in particular, it is necessary for it to flexibly adjust its policy towards China in light of the real situation, so that the Government of the National League for Democracy can gain support from China on many issues.

III. Overview of the Relations between China and the National League for Democracy

Aung San Suu Kyi, the leader of the National League for Democracy, has a profound relationship with China. Her father, General Aung San, once prepared Myanmar's independence movement in Xiamen, China. Her mother Khin Kyi was an old friend of China; when Soong Ching-ling visited Myanmar, Khin Kyi once accompanied Soong Ching-ling during the whole process; she met with Chinese Premier Zhou Enlai when Zhou Enlai visited Myanmar, and she visited China. The family of Aung San Suu Kyi has also collected some gifts from Chinese Premier Zhou Enlai.

In 1990, Aung San Suu Kyi and the National League for Democracy won the general election; the then Chinese ambassador to Myanmar was one of the first people to send a telegraph of congratulations to her. At that time, the military government refused to accept the election results, and also did not adopt the suggestion, reported to be put forward by China, about the relations between the National League for Democracy and the military government. However, during the 20-year period of governance by the military government in Myanmar, given the sensitivity of the military government, the Chinese Government reduced the engagement with Aung San Suu Kyi and the National League for Democracy to the lowest level. Chinese diplomats, government officials, scholars and the business circle almost had no ties with the National League for Democracy.[6]

---

[6] Sun Yun, China–Myanmar Relations: Does the Governance by the National League for Democracy Mark a New Era?, *Asia Times*, December 10, 2015.

After the new government of Myanmar came into power in 2011, China gradually increased its engagements with Aung San Suu Kyi and the National League for Democracy. As of 2011, three Chinese ambassadors to Myanmar, including Li Junhua, Yang Houlan and Hong Liang, regularly met with Aung San Suu Kyi. In 2013, four groups of the National League for Democracy visited China. In 2014, the National League for Democracy more frequently sent delegations to China, Aung San Suu Kyi sent her private representative to Xiamen to find traces of her father, while U Thein Lwin, a member of the Central Committee of the National League for Democracy, visited Yunnan University. In June 2015, thanks to a number of factors, Aung San Suu Kyi led a delegation to pay a five-day official visit to China for the first time, and met with General Secretary Xi Jinping. Aung San Suu Kyi stated, "the National League for Democracy attaches importance to the amicable relations between China and Myanmar, and admires the tremendous developmental achievements made by China led by the Communist Party of China, and the National League for Democracy hopes that this visit can deepen the relations between the two parties and promote the development of the friendly relationship between the people of the two countries". This visit filled the gaps in Aung San Suu Kyi's diplomatic policy and China's policy toward Myanmar. Overall, there is a long history of engagement between China and the National League for Democracy; the personal friendship between Chinese leaders and the leaders of the National League for Democracy, the political contacts between the Chinese Government and the National League for Democracy all show that China and the National League for Democracy have attached great importance to each other, and that bilateral relations have been good and generally stable.

IV. The National League for Democracy's Future Policy toward China and Its Impact

1. The overall keynote of its policy towards China will be consistent

After the National League for Democracy comes into power, internally, Myanmar will continue its process of democratization; externally, Myanmar will continue carrying out the diplomatic strategy of maintaining a balance among the great powers. However, considering that China and Myanmar are neighbors and that China enjoys enormous influence, the National League for Democracy will naturally not ignore the importance of China–Myanmar relations; generally, it will be friendly to China. In November 2015, during an interview with the journalist from the Xinhua News Agency, Aung San Suu Kyi, the General Secretary of the National League for Democracy, stated that Myanmar would continue carrying out the diplomatic policy of being friendly to all countries, attach greater importance to the relations with its neighboring countries and continue pursuing a friendly foreign policy towards China.[7] Furthermore, Aung San Suu Kyi has reached the consensus on cooperation in a smooth transition with the current President of Myanmar Thein Sein, the Speaker of the House of Representatives of Myanmar, Shwe Mann, and the Commander-in-Chief of the Myanmar Armed Forces, Min Aung Hlaing. This indicates that the National League for Democracy might not immediately make a drastic change in Myanmar's domestic and foreign policies. Therefore, the National League for Democracy will basically continue the general keynote of the Union Solidarity and Development Party's policy towards China during the initial stage of the governance by the National League for Democracy.

From the perspective of geopolitics and economic dependence, the National League for Democracy must deal with the issues concerning China in a pragmatic way, and Myanmar's elites have reached a consensus that Myanmar cannot adopt too aggressive a policy towards China. In the meantime, it is impossible that USA will fully lift the sanctions against Myanmar in the near future, and even some people in the US political circle believe that USA should intensify the sanctions against Myanmar, so USA's future policy towards Myanmar remains uncertain. For this consideration, after the National League for Democracy comes into power, it will continue ensuring that China–Myanmar relations are stable and developing so as to prevent risks in Myanmar's diplomatic relations with USA. Moreover, capital from Western countries, including Japan and South Korea, did not massively enter Myanmar after 2011. In Myanmar, infrastructure is relatively out-dated,

[7]The General Secretary of the National League for Democracy of Myanmar Stated that Myanmar Would Continue Upholding the Friendly Foreign Policy towards China, http://news.xinhuanet.com/photo/2015-11/18/c_128442046.htm.

domestic nationalism and populism are on the rise, government efficiency is low and corruption is still relatively rampant, policies are not transparent, so foreign investors will exercise prudence and take a wait-and-see attitude in the future though the number of foreign investors entering Myanmar will increase to a certain extent. Myanmar will still highly depend on Chinese capital in the future, which also largely requires the National League for Democracy to mitigate the volatility of its policy towards China.

2. The policy towards China will be more objective and rational

As Myanmar depended excessively on China during the period of the military government, after the Union Solidarity and Development Party with a military background came into power in 2011, the Union Solidarity and Development Party catered to the demands of anti-China forces on some issues in order to seek support from the people. Unlike the Union Solidarity and Development Party, the National League for Democracy has enjoyed popular support from the beginning of its governance, and so there are more conditions for it to renew the relations with China. Therefore, relatively speaking, the National League for Democracy is in a more favorable position, it can conduct an objective evaluation according to specific advantages to develop the corresponding policy towards China; it is well-positioned to act with less burden, rationally deal with China and engage in cooperation with China in light of the actual conditions without historical or affective burden. Therefore, Aung San Suu Kyi and the National League for Democracy give first priority to Myanmar's national interests, they do not necessarily obey Western countries, including USA, and in every way they will comprehensively weigh the advantages and disadvantages and then make objective and rational decisions.

Moreover, there is a very large space for China–Myanmar cooperation. The economic construction and effective improvement of the people's livelihood are the factors determining the status of the National League for Democracy in Myanmar's politics in the future, thus it is impossible for the new government of Myanmar to refuse to cooperate with China on economic matters. In the future, besides continuing to focus bilateral cooperation on agriculture, human resources, natural resource development and infrastructure construction, China and Myanmar will also strengthen their cooperation on trade, investments, energy and on other issues. In particular, thanks to its unique geographical location, Myanmar will serve as the energy channel for China and the important route for the importation of commodities to and exportation of commodities from southwest China, thus China–Myanmar cooperation will develop rapidly regarding railways, highways and waterways. Although the Myitsone Power Station Project has been put aside, there is still some space for China and Myanmar to rapidly push forward their cooperation in the fields of oil, gas, hydropower and other energy sources.[8]

3. The making of the policy towards China will take into account the say of the people more

In the process of democratization, in recent years, Myanmar's policies have increasingly focused on the people's livelihood; Myanmar has placed increasing emphasis on the industries which can apparently stimulate employment, such as agriculture, manufacturing and tourism. Aung San Suu Kyi and the National League for Democracy have always been close to the people, Aung San Suu Kyi has been hailed by Western countries, including USA, as the model of democratic movement. After the National League for Democracy takes over power, it will naturally proceed more from the perspective of the people's livelihood in considering its foreign investment policy, and will value the say of the people in the economic, political and cultural fields; for example, at present, China's investments in Myanmar are concentrated in such industries as energy and mining, and Chinese investors have received much criticism due to the problems relating to resource consumption, environmental pollution and relocation of residents. In the meantime, particular Chinese enterprises have often been criticized by Myanmar's public opinion due to their less open and transparent operations in Myanmar. The obstructions to the Letpadaung Copper Mine Project, the Myitsone Power Station Project and the high-speed railway project have been considered to be associated with the increased say of the Burmese people to a certain degree. In the

[8] Li Chenyang, China–Myanmar Relations after the 2010 General Election: Challenges and Prospects, *Peace and Development*, 2012(2), pp. 29–37.

future, the National League for Democracy will pay more attention to the say of the Burmese people when engaging in investment project cooperation with China; in particular, as the emerging forces in Myanmar's transition, the NGOs will participate more in establishing the country's policy towards China regarding the introduction of investments.

V. The Suggestions for China's Policy towards Myanmar in the Era of the National League for Democracy

1. China should uphold its principles and firmly safeguard its legitimate interests in Myanmar

China and Myanmar have always been friendly neighbors; in particular, since the establishment of diplomatic relations between China and Myanmar, both countries have jointly advocated a diplomatic policy of the Five Principles of Peaceful Coexistence, which has been highly commended by the rest of the world. As both countries have jointly observed this norm for several decades, the friendly relations between China and Myanmar have survived many setbacks. Given the changes arising out of the general election in Myanmar at present, it is more necessary for China to uphold this norm when dealing with Myanmar and refrain from interfering in its internal affairs, and to actively promote Myanmar's stability and development. In the regular press conference held by the Ministry of Foreign Affairs of China on November 19, Chinese Foreign Ministry spokesman, Hong Lei, said, "China will always uphold its friendly policy towards Myanmar, and actively engage with various friendly parties of Myanmar, including the National League for Democracy". While being friendly to Myanmar as a whole, China should also realize that some anti-China forces still exist in Myanmar, while Western countries, including USA, may also further take advantage of the National League for Democracy to contain China after the National League for Democracy takes power. Therefore, the Chinese Government should convey, through various channels, to the Government of the National League for Democracy, China's determination to safeguard its legitimate interests in Myanmar, especially ensuring that the large projects in which the Chinese have invested in Myanmar are carried out smoothly.

2. China should seek trust from the people and take the initiative in the relations with Myanmar in the new period

No matter who will serve as the new President of Myanmar in 2016, the National League for Democracy will lead Myanmar's domestic and foreign affairs in the next 5 years. Therefore, China should not take a wait-and-see attitude towards Myanmar's political situation; instead, China should actively take actions to make a good start in China–Myanmar relations in the new period, especially seeking breakthroughs in China's investment dilemma in Myanmar. For China's investments in Myanmar, after the general election, Aung San Suu Kyi stated, "In order to make China's investments more successful in Myanmar, the most important factor is the acceptance by our people, the most needed work lies in seeking trust from the people". Therefore, China should understand the wishes of the National League for Democracy to respond more to the people and accept the new political reality in Myanmar. The NGOs are becoming increasingly strong in Myanmar, so the Chinese Government should also encourage domestic NGOs to actively get involved in Myanmar's cooperation, publicize the positive benefits from cooperation projects to the local people. The Chinese-funded enterprises should adapt to the new social developments in Myanmar, seek to change China's image demonized at the non-governmental level in Myanmar to a certain extent, and change from a previous emphasis on dealing with the government to a balance between the governmental and non-governmental levels.

3. China should make full preparations to maintain the relations with other political forces in Myanmar

The National League for Democracy won the general election and will govern Myanmar in the next 5 years, but the Union Solidarity and Development Party, the military and other political forces still exert an influence in Myanmar. At present, the military's influence still permeates various aspects of the political life in Myanmar. The contradictions between Aung San Suu Kyi, the National League for Democracy and the military have not yet been completely eliminated. Aung San Suu Kyi once said that the next President of Myanmar cannot have a military background, and she would extend this requisite beyond the President. This remark triggered discontent among some people in the Union Solidarity and Development Party and the military. These contradictions cause great uncertainties in the future political situation in Myanmar, and it is possible that the Union Solidarity and Development Party might come into power again. Therefore, it is necessary for China to maintain good relations with all political parties. China once overwhelmingly supported a certain political force, making China pay a heavy price, thus it is less likely that this will occur again.

4. China should build bridges and respect Myanmar's traditional social culture

China and Myanmar are neighbors, geographically adjacent and are akin in cultural roots, but there are great cultural differences between Myanmar and China in many respects; in particular, religion plays an important role in the life of the Burmese people. As Myanmar has reached a higher level of economic development and openness, the Burmese people have gradually boosted their self-confidence and self-respect in Burmese traditional culture, many Burmese people now believe that Myanmar should exert the influence of Burmese culture abroad. The Chinese Government should increase the opportunities for engaging in cultural exchanges between the people of the two countries, and enhance their mutual understanding; for example, China and Myanmar can regularly carry out the activities relating to the year of cultural exchanges with each other. Besides improving China's image in Myanmar, bilateral cultural exchanges should also embody China's respect for the unique Burmese culture. Moreover, Chinese enterprises investing in Myanmar should respect Myanmar's local customs during the construction of the projects. Myanmar is a devout Buddhist country, 90% of the Burmese people believe in Buddhism; Myanmar has a history of believing in Buddhism that goes back more than 1,000 years, and so Buddhist thought has been deeply rooted in various classes of the Burmese society and various aspects of Myanmar's social life.

VI. Conclusions

After Myanmar's general election, the changes in Myanmar's domestic politics and the improvement of the relations between Western countries and

Myanmar pose objective challenges to China–Myanmar relations, especially the relations between China and the National League for Democracy. However, geopolitical and geo-economic factors still exist between China and Myanmar, the inertia of all-round cooperation between the two countries in the past several decades will not vanish all at once. As the winner in the general election, the National League for Democracy will continue to cooperate with China in the political, economic and social fields, and this comprehensive strategic cooperative partnership will be further improved. The adjustment of the US policy towards Myanmar and the changes in Myanmar's politics will not fundamentally change China–Myanmar relations, but the days when China prevails among many great powers in the relations with Myanmar have ended, and Myanmar will naturally have more initiative in China–Myanmar relations. Although the diversity in Myanmar's foreign relations does not exert a great negative impact on China, China really needs to seriously consider the drawbacks in the relations with Myanmar, solve the problems regarding its cooperation on economics and trade with Myanmar and improve China's image in Myanmar. Only in this way can the sustainable development of China–Myanmar relations be guaranteed.

Chapter 24

Report on the Bangkok Bombing in 2015

Yue Han*

During the two days of August 17–18, 2015, bombs exploded at the Erawan Shrine in the center of Bangkok City, Sathorn Pier and other places in Thailand; foreigners, including Chinese tourists, suffered heavy causalities in the bombings. These attacks left 23 people dead[1] and 123 injured. After Thai police conducted a three-week investigation, two suspects directly involved in these attacks were arrested, and these attacks were identified by the Government of Thailand as the revenge on the Government of Thailand by human smuggling groups.

I. Overview of the Bombing

1. Twenty-four hours after the bombing

At 7:07 p.m. on August 17, 2015, an approximately 3 kg TNT explosive detonated before the Erawan Shrine at the Ratchaprasong intersection in the

---

*Yue Han, special commentator at the Thailand Institute of the China–ASEAN Research Institute of Guangxi University, chief editor of www.taiguo.com.

[1]Thailand 9 people, Chinese Mainland 5, Hong Kong 2, Malaysia 5, Indonesia 1 and Singapore 1.

center of Bangkok; as a result, the surrounding areas in a circumference of 100 m were affected, the balustrade on one side of the Erawan Shrine, venerated by Chinese tourists, was destroyed, and tourists and citizens suffered heavy casualties. This city, immersed in the atmosphere of Mother's Day just one day before, was suddenly rocked by an unprecedented disaster.

Immediately after the information on the scene was delivered first time through an online platform, local Thai media and international news agencies responded. The BBC, Reuters, CCTV and other media released the initial on-the-spot reports to the rest of the world.

At 7:40 p.m., the police cleared the surrounding commercial shopping centers and prohibited outsiders from entering the site. Many onlookers stood beside the scene, media rushed to the hospitals which had received the casualties. Later, overseas Chinese language and culture media in Thailand sent journalists to hospitals and the scene. *Sing Sian Yer Pao Daily News* reported that hospitals had received a large number of Chinese tourists, and Chinese interpreters were urgently needed for assistance; it also collected the list of casualties and contacted the separated family members.

At 8:00 p.m., the government released the first information on the casualties and confirmed that 15 people were dead and more than 100 people were injured.

At 9:00 p.m., the deputy spokesperson of the Royal Thai Police said that the police discovered the unexploded explosives in the surrounding areas and conducted a search and check. In the meantime, various kinds of contradictory information, difficult to be confirmed, were available online, false information — such as "serial explosions", "classes were suspended throughout the city" and "10 transportation hubs were identified as dangerous areas" — went viral online. Afterwards, the government denied the rumors.

At 9:12 p.m., the Thai police first released the list of confirmed victims, including 1 Thai, 1 Filipino and 2 Chinese.

At 10:00 p.m., the Ministry of Education of Thailand announced that classes were to be suspended throughout Bangkok City on the 18th day.

At 1:00 a.m. on the 18th day: the Thai police corrected and supplemented the list of victims, and confirmed that 19 people were dead and 117 injured, two seriously wounded Chinese tourists were dead, thus the combined number of Chinese tourists who were dead increased to 4, including 2 from the

Chinese Mainland and 2 from Hong Kong. In an interview, the Thai police chief announced that the police had completely taken over the case, and that he had also gone to the hospitals to visit the injured. After 0:00 midnight, the bomb squad of the Thai police temporarily withdrew from the scene, and the scene was cordoned off. The police expert said that on-the-spot explosives were "inconsistent" with the usual practice of the highly suspected Islamic separatists in the southern area.

After the bombing, the global media shifted their attention to the culprit behind the bombing. The police exercised consistent caution about the progress in the case, while senior leaders of the military government of Thailand made various contradictory speculations and suggestions. The Defense Minister of Thailand, Prawit Wongsuwan, incredibly claimed that this incident was not a terrorist attack and was not relevant to politics. When answering questions from journalists on the 18th day, the Prime Minister of Thailand, General Prayuth Chan-ocha, stated that the police had known the background of the suspect and "basically confirmed" that the suspect was the anti-government organization in the northeastern area. As the northeastern area was the stronghold of the Red Shirts controlled by Thaksin Shinawatra, Prayuth Chan-ocha's remark was directed at Thaksin Shinawatra's group.

In the evening, former Prime Minister Thaksin Shinawatra tweeted, "I was in Berlin when the incident occurred, I was shocked and felt frustrated upon learning about the Bangkok bombing, I hereby express sincere condolences to the families of the victims and the wounded. I hope that relevant departments can work with domestic and foreign experts and scholars in relevant fields to investigate the perpetrators and manipulators, so as to bring to justice the criminals as early as possible." Former Prime Minister, Yingluck Shinawatra, strongly condemned the attackers. The Deputy Prime Minister and Defense Minister, Prawit Wongsuwan, expressed sincere condolences to the victims, but he also stated that it was too early to identify the incident as a politically motivated one or as a terrorist attack.

After investigating the camera footage from the CCTV on the scene, the Thai police found that a man was seriously suspected of having committed the crime. At 9:00 on the 18th day, the police released a picture of the suspect from the surveillance video, while the sketch was drawn by the police according to the on-the-spot surveillance video. According to the police, the surveillance video showed that this man had sat on a bench for a while on the scene, and then laid down a backpack before leaving, while a CCTV camera from another perspective indicated that after leaving, this man stood in the distance, took out a mobile phone to dial, and then quickly ran away from the scene; later, the bomb exploded — at this point, there were speculations that the people from northeastern Thailand or white Arabs had committed the crime, so the case became more complicated and confusing.

On the morning of the 18th day, in response to the previous information that the bombing might be relevant to Thailand's repatriation of human smugglers, the Chief of the Royal Thai Police, Somyot Poompanmuang, said in an interview that at present, there was no evidence showing it was associated with human smugglers and that they cannot conclude that this incident was directed at the Chinese because the casualties included people from many other countries, including Thailand, in addition to Chinese.

At noon of the 18th day, the death toll had reached 20.

The Prime Minister of India, Narendra Modi, also strongly condemned these attacks. The US Embassy in Thailand issued a travel warning and called upon the US citizens to take care and keep away from the area where this incident occurred. The Chinese Embassy in Thailand specially warned the Chinese citizens planning to visit Thailand and those in Thailand to strengthen their awareness, traveling in a safe way and rationally planning the traveling routes. The Hong Kong Special Administrative Region also immediately increased the level of travel warning regarding Bangkok to "red" and called upon citizens to avoid non-essential travel to Bangkok, and kept the level of travel warning for the rest of Thailand at "yellow". At noon on the same day, traffic resumed at the bombing scene.

At 1:30 p.m. on the 18th day, a bombing occurred near Sathorn Pier in Bangkok. According to an eyewitness, someone stood on the overpass connecting Saphan Taksin with BTS and threw a bomb, but the bomb fell into the river after touching a pillar of the bridge and exploded in the water, causing no casualties, producing light effects on the ships moored alongside the pier. As shown by the on-the-spot surveillance video, at 7:20 p.m. on the 17th day, a 170-cm tall man between the ages of 35 and 40, wearing a long-sleeved blue shirt, suspiciously appeared near the overpass connecting Sathorn Pier with BTS Saphan Taksin.[2]

2. Detection

After the bombing, the police criticized the Bangkok Municipal Government for shoddiness or the malfunctioning of surveillance cameras installed near the Erawan Shrine, which gave the investigators very limited clues regarding the suspect. Following an arduous three-day search, the police made the first breakthrough and preliminarily inquired of a tuk-tuk driver who had delivered the suspect to the front of the Erawan Shrine. According to the driver, the suspect was a foreigner, he got in the vehicle at the Hualampong Railway Station and got out in front of the Erawan Shrine, with a car fare of 200 Thai baht. The police also investigated two other suspected accomplices shown in the surveillance video, among whom one man went home after inquiry and another man was a Chinese tourist who returned to China.

Another taxi driver who drove the suspect, as shown in the surveillance video, provided a more important clue to the police. According to the taxi driver, he drove the man from Rama 4 Road to Hualampong Railway Station in Bangkok. The Taxi driver said, "The suspect spoke Thai but had a foreign accent, I think he wasn't Thai, he and the man in the video were the same person." Thus, the police identified the scope of the areas where the suspect may have lived for a long time and appeared.

On August 22, the spokesperson of the Royal Thai Police said that the police sketch of the suspect had been delivered to 190 countries for seeking help from other countries.

According to the investigation group, in 2011, there were foreigners teaching how to assemble TNT explosives in Thailand. On August 25, the Thai investigation group conducted a DNA test on the 20 baht banknote paid to the taxi driver by the suspect. According to the investigation on various aspects, the investigation group preliminarily confirmed that these serial

[2]Yue Han, 20h Snapshot after Bangkok Bombing, *Sing Sian Yer Pao Daily News*, August 18, 2015, http://www.wx135.com/articles/20150818/55d3447c-9b80-44e2-9397-0e8102734e20.html.

explosions were organized actions, there was a mastermind and accomplices, while the mastermind was most likely a foreigner stealing into Thailand.

3. Preliminary outcome

During the second week after this incident, the police narrowed the scope of investigation according to the clues at hand. The police screened 17 stowaways who had escaped from prison and 20 Turks who had entered Thailand before the bombing. In the meantime, with the help of mobile technology, the police conducted a mobile phone data investigation, the largest one in history, so that the police found out and arrested one key suspect involved in the bombing. The police investigated phone calls and focused on three Turkish phone numbers whose international roaming had been activated and which were used near the bombing scene, the first suspect was finally captured.

On the afternoon of August 29, the police arrested the first suspect Adem Karadag at an apartment in Nong Chok District, Bangkok, and the police held a press conference. The spokesperson of the National Council for Peace and Order said that the suspect was a foreigner with an unidentified nationality, but it was initially determined that the suspect was associated with both explosions in Bangkok because more than 250 forged Turkish passports and many raw materials for explosives had been discovered at the same time.

On the evening of August 29, the Chief of the Royal Thai Police, Somyot Poompanmuang, gave an interview with respect to the arrested suspect involved in the Bangkok bombing, and he said the police had obtained a lot of information on suspects, they could not release their list right then, but the police can confirm that more than 10 people, including those who were still in Thailand and had exited Thailand, had been involved in the bombing. There was a doubt that the Bangkok bombing was the "revenge action" taken by criminal gangs.

On the afternoon of August 30, according to Bangkok Business News Online, the spokesperson of the Royal Thai Police said that relevant personnel of Turkish Embassy in Thailand investigated the arrested suspect and then concluded that the suspect arrested by the police was not Turkish. Moreover, the spokesperson of the Royal Thai Police pointed out before the

Agence France Presse that they believed that the recently arrested suspect came from a human trafficking ring dedicated to obtaining forged certificates for illegal immigrants. These serial explosions represented a revenge on Thailand's crackdown on human traffickers. The Prime Minister of Thailand, Prayuth Chan-ocha, stated that the police had a great deal of information on suspects, but currently it was necessary to carefully weigh and study this information. When asked about whether the arrested suspect was associated with the organizations which helped human smuggling, Prayuth Chan-ocha said that he was.

On August 31, the Commander in Chief and Assistant Defense Minister, General Udomdej Sitabutr, said that the arrested suspect involved in the Bangkok bombing confessed to have had 2–3 accomplices. Moreover, according to the spokesperson of the Royal Thai Police, the police had searched a suspicious apartment in the Minburi District, Bangkok, on August 30, and found that bomb-making materials also existed, thus the police applied to the court for the arrest of two suspects who might be involved in the bombing, of whom one was the owner of the apartment, a Thai citizen aged 26 and another one was a man with an unidentified name and nationality.

At 5:00 p.m. on August 31, JS100 reported that when the police investigated the home of this wanted Thai female citizen, her family members said that she had gone to Turkey.

On September 1, her parents said that their daughter had resided in Turkey for a long time, they were surprised at her daughter suddenly becoming a suspect, and this woman claimed that she was innocent. According to the Bangkok Post, the two wanted people did not escape to Turkey; instead, they hid in Cambodia. Although she claimed that she would "contact the police", so far, the woman who claimed to be innocent was still unavailable.

4. "The water had subsided, but the rocks still did not emerge"

On September 1, the Prime Minister, Prayuth Chan-ocha, confirmed that another suspect involved in the Bangkok bombing had been arrested in Sa Kaeo. The suspect was a foreign citizen; when the suspect prepared to escape from Sa Kaeo to other countries, the suspect was arrested by the Thai security department and sent by military helicopter to Bangkok for interrogation.

On September 2, the deputy spokesperson of the Government of Thailand, Werachon Sukhonhapatipak, made a remark on the progress of the police investigation by saying that as diplomacy was involved, the police and the Ministry of Foreign Affairs were working together to confirm whether the passports of the suspects were genuine, so that at the moment, the nationality of the suspect could not be made public. The Chief of the Royal Thai Police, Somyot Poompanmuang, confirmed that there were Thai citizens assisting the criminals in the bombing, and stressed that the police did not rule out any doubt, and that he believed that it was not caused by international terrorist groups. Upon an application filed by the police, Minburi Court approved and issued arrest warrants for three accomplices in the Rachaprasong and Sathorn Pier explosions.

While pursuing and capturing suspects, the officers with malpractice accusations were removed from the police. Some suspects confessed that they had used false passports and were released by Sa Kaeo Immigration Office after paying about 20,000 Thai baht as bribe money, so the Chief of the Royal Thai Police, Somyot Poompanmuang, issued an order on the evening of the 31st day to transfer more than 20 police officers of the Sa Kaeo Immigration Office to other posts. Minburi Criminal Court also approved the order for listing as wanted the husband, Emrah Davutoglu, of the female suspect Wanna Suansan because he illegally possessed explosives.

A relevant investigation identified the second arrested suspect as Yusufu Mieraili, who was arrested in Sa Kaeo on September 1. An analysis showed that the fingerprint of Yusufu Mieraili was the same as that on the container with explosives discovered by the police at an apartment on August 29. The spokesperson of the Thai police stated that there was evidence that this man was involved in the bomb attack and he may have carried the explosives to the scene.

With the DNA analysis, the Thai police found that Yusufu Mieraili's DNA was inconsistent with that on the 20 baht banknote and the backpack with explosives, so he was not the bomber dressed in yellow, but the police still believed that the suspect was part of the bomb assembling gang. According to the BBC, the Thai police said that both arrested suspects in the Bangkok bombing were not the mastermind, and that therefore, the most important suspect was still at large.

On September 5, the spokesperson of the Royal Thai Police said that the police had interrogated the first arrested suspect, Adem Karadag, involved in the Bangkok bombing, that he had provided information about another suspect, and that at present, the police had issued an order for the arrest of the 10th suspect involved in the bombing; he said that the suspect was a foreigner; furthermore, Adem Karadag's passport had been delivered to the Turkish Embassy for investigation.

On the afternoon of September 7, the Deputy Chief of the Royal Thai Police said that the investigators responsible for tracking the case of the Bangkok bombing found the whereabouts of the man dressed in yellow, who was the prime culprit of the bombing, in southern Thailand; now the police had sent investigators to the area.

Moreover, during interrogation on the same day, Yusufu Mieraili admitted that he was associated with the bombing and carried bombs to the man dressed in yellow, and detonated the bombs.

The Chief of the Royal Thai Police, Somyot Poompanmuang, stated that during the interrogation by the police, Yusufu Mieraili's confession was quite complete and tallied with the evidence, so the police knew about the other suspects involved in the bombing. According to Somyot Poompanmuang, Yusufu Mieraili may have lived with the first arrested suspect Adem Karadag in the same room; they used the knowledge acquired at university to assemble the bombs, but they did not know who the mastermind was, they only knew the payer, the situation behind the bombing was fairly complicated.

On the morning of September 9, the spokesperson of the Royal Thai Police and the police led Yusufu Mieraili, a criminal from the gang involved in the Bangkok bombing, to the Rachaprasong area in the center of Bangkok, to the Hualampong Railway Station and other areas in a simulation of the bombing. Yusufu Mieraili was also led to the apartment in Nong Chok to simulate the bombing event.[3]

5. Aftermath

On February 16, 2016, two suspects involved in the Bangkok bombing, Adem Karadag and Yusufu Mieraili, stood trial at the Thailand Military Tribunal.[4]

---

[3]Yue Han, The Three-week Investigation of August 17 Bangkok Bombing, *Sing Sian Yer Pao Daily News*, September 10, 2015, http://blog.sina.cn/dpool/blog/s/blog_c11c62120102vqre.html?md=gd.

[4]As the Thai military controls the government, all cases with great impact are heard at the Military Tribunal.

As reported by the *Bangkok Post* on the 16th day, they were charged with eight crimes, including murder and illegal immigration. According to the Agence France Presse, both suspects overthrew the previous confession and refused to admit their involvement in the bombing on the 16th day.

According to the Agence France Presse, previously the Thai police stated that the suspects had confessed and admitted to having committed the crimes. When Adem Karadag was arrested at an apartment, many tools for making bombs and a number of forged Turkish passports were discovered. Afterwards, he admitted that he was once instigated to carry bombs. However, during the court hearing on the 16th day, both suspects refused to accept the charges relating to the bombing, while Adem Karadag admitted illegal immigration. He said that he had entered Thailand via Laos 4 days after the bombing by bribing immigration inspectors.

When the two suspects appeared at the Military Tribunal for the first time in November 2015, they refused to defend themselves for the reason that no interpreter was available on the spot. According to *the Bangkok Post*, the defense lawyer for the suspect Adem Karadag said that previously Adem Karadag had pleaded guilty "under torture", three weeks after Adem Karadag was arrested in late September last year, he was maltreated and forced to admit that he was the man dressed in yellow with a backpack shown in the surveillance video and who had placed bombs near the Erawan Shrine.[5]

II. The Government's Position — the Background of Changing the Investigation Direction Several Times

After the Bangkok bombing, the Prime Minister of Thailand, Prayuth Chan-ocha, described the bombing as the deadliest attack in history in Thailand; he said, "The small bombing may be only noise, but it was directed at the life of the innocent, and aimed at destroying our economy and tourism industry". Without stating the subject in this remark, the Government of Thailand hoped to focus the investigation of the "troublemaker" on Thaksin

[5]Dong Xue, The Suspects Involved in the Bangkok Bombing Withdrew Confessions at the Military Tribunal, the Police Is Still Pursuing Other Suspects, www.huanqiu.com, February 17, 2016, http://news.xinhuanet.com/thailand/2016-02/17/c_128728043.htm.

Shinawatra. After the case finally became clear, as it involved diplomatic disputes with foreign countries, the Government of Thailand downplayed it.

After the bombing occurred, the "alternate suspects" — the radicals in the Red Shirts, Muslims in the three provinces of southern Thailand, overseas terrorists, stowaways recently suspected again and again — became the focus of suspicion and also the targets concealed by Thailand as much as possible. On the evening of August 17, the Deputy Prime Minister and Defense Minister, Prawit Wongsuwan, first made a remark; he strangely stated that the Bangkok incident was not a terrorist attack and not relevant to politics. The US position was similar to Prawit Wongsuwan's remark; the US held that it was too early to identify this incident as a terrorist attack. Prawit Wongsuwan's remark meant that "it is inappropriate to immediately, arbitrarily link this incident to any terrorist organization" rather than "it was not a terrorist attack".

After the bombing, the radical members of the Red Shirts who have taken frequent actions recently, the Islamic separatists who often ambushed the military and teachers beside roads in southern Thailand, were the first to become suspects. The Thai military always primarily conciliates rather than sieges the Islamic separatists, it has suspended military suppression on them, and it has, through the Government of Malaysia — sharing the same culture and origin with the Islamic separatists — as the intermediary, actively engaged in negotiations with the mainstream factions of the separatists in southern Thailand. If the Islamic separatists became the chief culprit, the policy of holding the "southern peace talks" would fail to a certain extent, the promising peace process in southern Thailand would come to naught, the military would change the policy from "conciliating" to "appeasing" and the peace talk route persistently adopted since the Government of Yingluck Shinawatra would become the target of public criticism.

Therefore, in fact, the military did not hope that this incident was linked to the Islamic separatists. In the initial investigation, the Thai police quickly concluded that the Bangkok bombing was inconsistent with the practice of the Islamic separatists and that it was impossible to state that it was associated with the affairs of southern Thailand, thus it is not difficult to understand that the Thai police urgently took the initiative to whitewash the separatists in southern Thailand.

For the Red Shirts, USA has been the supporter of Thaksin Shinawatra and Yingluck Shinawatra, and has long criticized the military for suppressing the Shinawatra family, so USA naturally did not hope that the Government of Thailand would rashly accuse the Red Shirts. The military government of Thailand was divided over Thaksin Shinawatra. The "hawks" in the military government, including Prayuth Chan-ocha, showed no mercy towards Thaksin Shinawatra and the Red Shirts, but the "doves" did not agree to treat Thaksin Shinawatra ruthlessly.

The Defense Minister Prawit Wongsuwan, who first made a remark about the bombing, had personal friendship with the Thaksin family, he acted as the envoy in negotiation between the military government and Thaksin Shinawatra many times, and strove to make both sides reach reconciliation — at least temporary reconciliation. Therefore, Prawit Wongsuwan was unwilling to, at the beginning, drive Thaksin Shinawatra to a dead end, and so his position that this incident was not a terrorist attack was nothing but an expression which left room for giving another explanation.

Early on the morning of August 18, the Prime Minister of Thailand, General Prayuth Chan-ocha, declared his position for the first time. After stating, with justice before journalists, that the objective of the criminal was to crumple Thailand's economy, he revealed that the police had "basically ascertained" the identity of the suspect involved in the bombing, and claimed that the suspect was most likely from the anti-government group from northeastern Thailand — the people who know a little about the "color map" of Thailand understand that the Isaan region in northeastern Thailand has long been the die-hard ticket bunker of Thaksin Shinawatra and the core stronghold of the Red Shirts. In the political context of Thailand, "from northeastern Thailand" was almost equal to direct accusation against the Thaksin faction.

However, although the Government of Prayuth Chan-ocha hoped to put the blame on the Thaksin group, the result of subsequent investigations ran counter to the military's calculation, after the Turkish far-right Xinjiang separatist organization was basically identified as the suspect, the Government of Thailand was forced to change countermeasure.

As the police did not crack the case in the end, the Government of Thailand elected to further downplay it; the only change after the bombing has occurred in border control, entry and exit administration. In the future, on more sufficient security grounds, the Government of Thailand will further tighten control over entry and exit, and will take stricter measures to prevent, block and dispel external stowaways.

At the diplomatic level, the Government of Thailand will mitigate the impact of this incident, and repair the fence to seriously deal with penetration.

Chapter 25

Political Crisis and Trends in Malaysia

Lu Xiaoxiao*

After the Malaysian website *Sarawak Report* and the US newspaper *New York Times* first reported severe debt and corruption problems at the Malaysian national investment fund 1MDB (1MDB) early this year, the 1MDB case continued to ferment. After the US newspaper the *Wall Street Journal* reported on July 3 that an entity related to 1MDB had remitted nearly USD 700 million to the private bank account of the Prime Minister of Malaysia, Najib Razak, the 1MDB case reached the boiling point and became the important focus of Malaysia throughout 2015. Since the case broke out, domestic and foreign media, the opposition parties and the former Prime Minister have criticized, and all across the country people changed their opinion about, Najib Razak, exerting a continuous impact on the political life of the Prime Minister. Worse, Malaysia subsequently fell into an economic plight across the board as a result of the political chaos, the governing party, the United Malays National Organization, faced an unprecedented political crisis. This 1MDB scandal appeared to epitomize the internal and external pressure on Prime Minister Najib Razak in the past 2 years, but fundamentally, it revealed the long-standing problems in Malaysia's political system

* Lu Xiaoxiao, Research Assistant at the Malaysia Institute of the China–ASEAN Research Institute of Guangxi University.

and social contradictions. It may exert an inestimable impact on the current strife among political parties in Malaysia and the future political trends of the whole of Malaysia.

I. Direct Cause: 1MDB's Debts and Corruption Scandal

Since its inception, 1MDB has been shrouded in mystery. It surged in 5-year development, it is not easy to analyze its development, and it is also difficult to evaluate its gain and loss. It was finally sieged by social pressure in 2015 due to its investments, debts and corruption, fully triggering an outburst in Malaysia's political situation, which remained fragile for a long time. The 1MDB scandal not only raised concerns among the Malaysian people, but also became the commanding height for which domestic politicians vied.

1. Establishment: It vowed solemnly to honor the "One Malaysia" commitment

The sovereign wealth fund Terengganu Investment Authority, established in 2008, was the predecessor of 1MDB. The fund once acquired at premium the assets of a Malaysian company and made donations to a charity organization led by Najib Razak so as to indirectly solicit votes for Najib Razak in the 2008 general election. Upon taking office in 2009, Najib Razak, who was successfully elected Prime Minister, used the concept of "One Malaysia" to officially turn the sovereign wealth fund 1MDB into one wholly owned by the government, with a view to helping Malaysia develop the industries of energy, real estate, tourism, agriculture and other new industries, while he served as Chairman of 1MDB's board of directors, and repeatedly claimed that 1MDB would boost Malaysia's economic development by attracting foreign investments, so as to realize the ambition, set by him when he ran for Prime Minister, that wealth can be equally distributed in One Malaysia, regardless of race and ethnic origin. 1MDB also thus enjoyed many conveniences provided by the Government of Najib Razak and was granted the privilege of developing most prime lots of the government.

2. Development: It deviated from the original aspiration by borrowing and spending money

However, patronage from the government did not deliver substantive performance to 1MDB; instead, 1MDB became debt-ridden — with the help of Goldman Sachs, the fledgling 1MDB raised USD 6.5 billion through bond issuance, and it used part of the funds so raised to purchase power plants, while the use and whereabouts of the remaining funds cannot be traced. 1MDB raised USD 3 billion through the issuance of a bond two months before the 2013 general election, and it stated that the funds would be used to develop the financial center project in Kuala Lumpur, the capital of Malaysia; however, afterwards, the project was shelved, and the use of the funds was also unknown. In 2014, the cumulative debts of 1MDB approached 36.25 billion ringgits. In late 2015, 1MDB postponed repayment of 2 billion ringgits in loans from Maybank and the RHB Bank at least two times. While 1MDB became debt-ridden, it extravagantly spent money in the political field. After interviewing the politicians from the governing coalition and former government employees and consulting relevant documents of 1MDB, the *Wall Street Journal* found that the unreported political expenditure worth billions of US dollars heavily depended on 1MDB — in early 2010, 1 Malaysia Charity, established with the approval of Najib Razak, allocated USD 140 million to people-benefiting projects, including hospitals, schools and low-cost housing, with a view to increasing the possibility that the United Malays National Organization would achieve victory. In July 2010, during his visit to Sarawak, Najib Razak earmarked USD 540,000 to fund the construction of houses for local aboriginal tribes, so as to seek support from voters in Sarawak, especially aboriginal tribes; given the 2013 general election, 1MDB established Ihsa Perdana, nominally responsible for executing 1MDB's projects relating to corporate social responsibility, in 2011; however, in fact, this company served as a secret channel for transferring funds to politicians, and enjoyed the privilege of not providing financial statements. According to the investigative documents from the Government of Malaysia, the transferred funds relating to the election campaign amounted to hundreds of millions of USD at the end of the 2013 general election.

3. Outburst of the case: Long-term accumulation led to "fatal explosion"

As 1MDB's debts snowballed, Anwar Ibrahim first required in 2011, in the capacity of the leader of the party out of power in the parliament, the Public Accounts Committee of the parliament to investigate 1MDB Petro Saudi Limited jointly operated by 1MDB and PetroSaudi International, and he castigated 1MDB for incurring massive debts. In 2014, the National Publicity Secretary of the Democratic Action Party Tony Pua Kiam Wee and the Secretary of the People's Justice Party Rafizi Ramli officially, openly questioned 1MDB's management, and made public its financial frauds. In March 2015, the UK newspaper the *Sunday Times* and the *Sarawak Report* reported, "after investigation of thousands of the details and emails about 1MDB's transactions, it has been found that 1MDB is being caught in a great debt hole of USD 11 billion", stirring a public outcry in Malaysia. The former Prime Minister Mahathir Mohamad immediately criticized Najib Razak for failure to explain 1MDB's fund flow and the complicated relationship with Najib Razak, and required Najib Razak to step down at once. With the simmering debt scandal at 1MDB, the Prime Minister Najib Razak, who concurrently served as Chairman of 1MDB's board of directors, was finally found to be involved in the scandal. On July 3, 2015, the *Wall Street Journal* quoted bank statements and documents to detail an accusation that a huge sum of money, USD 700 million, suspected of coming from 1MDB was remitted to the private bank account of Prime Minister Najib Razak. Almost in the meantime, Najib Razak's wife Datin Seri Rosmah Mansor was reported to have made luxury consumption overseas, the media also revealed that a man remitted 2 million ringgits, divided into several portions, to her account at Affin Bank. After this information was exposed, a great repercussion was triggered among the parties in and out of power and the people in Malaysia, the image of the Prime Minister Najib Razak and his future political life were severely affected.

4. Aftermath: The whole country denounced the Prime Minister, while the Prime Minister toughly sought self-protection

Huge debts, a corruption scandal and luxury consumption caused strong dissatisfaction among the officials within the United Malays National Organization;

furthermore, the above phenomena also led to the following reactions: the long-standing hatred of Najib Razak among the opposition factions was ignited; the then Deputy Prime Minister Muhyiddin Yassin immediately urged Najib Razak to explain the charge involving the flow of USD 700 million into his private account, and called upon relevant law enforcement agencies of Malaysia, including the Malaysian Anti-Corruption Commission, Bank Negara Malaysia, the Royal Malaysia Police, the Attorney General's Office, to work together to thoroughly investigate this case; the leaders of the opposition parties called upon the authorities to order the Malaysian Anti-Corruption Commission to freeze Najib Razak's private bank account for investigation, and required Najib Razak to take the blame and resign; NGOs required Najib Razak to produce evidence involving the charges to give an explanation before the people, and called for suspending the Prime Minister from his post to receive an investigation; former Chairman of Bersih 2.0 Ambiga Sreenevasan also supported the dismissal of Prime Minister Najib Razak from his post, and called for carrying out the general election to correct this chaos. Najib Razak, beleaguered by the public opinion storm, took a series of drastic measures to toughly fight back — reshuffling the cabinet, disturbing the investigation, rectifying media and suppressing the dissidents. First, he dismissed and replaced officials, reshuffled the cabinet — on July 28, Najib Razak announced the dismissal and replacement of Muhyiddin Yassin, and suspended Abdul Gani Patail, the Attorney General of Malaysia responsible for investigating the 1MDB case, from his post which he was not informed; moreover, several cabinet ministers and deputy ministers, who did not clearly side with Najib Razak's camp in the 1MDB case, were also dismissed from their posts, and several important officials of the cabinet, who got to the root of the 1MDB case, were transferred to other posts. Second, personnel changes led to the suspension of investigation into the 1MDB case — Najib Razak quickly appointed four members of the Public Accounts Committee, who were investigating 1MDB, to the cabinet, and he temporarily canceled the extraordinary session of the parliament designed to appoint the new Chairman of the Public Accounts Committee; this meant that the investigation into the 1MDB case could not be normally carried out in a short time.[1]

[1]Li Huimin, Malaysian Cabinet Was Reshuffled, the Deputy Prime Minister Was Dismissed and Replaced, http://www.bbc.com/zhongwen/simp/world/2015/07/150728_malaysian_government_naiib.

Third, Najib Razak settled accounts with the media — on July 20, the Malaysia National News Agency and the Multimedia Commission sealed up the website *Sarawak Report*, which was the first to expose the 1MDB scandal, upon the charges of presenting improper content and violating national laws; on July 24, the Ministry of Home Affairs criticized *The Edge Weekly* and *The Edge Financial Daily* for the reason that their reports on 1MDB might cause public opinion panic and might threaten public security and national interests, and it decided to revoke their publishing permits for three months; on August 18, Ku Seman Ku Hussain, the Editor of the *Utusan Malaysia*, saw the cancellation of the special column for writing articles criticizing the incident of USD 700 million; the Government of Malaysia also planned to revise the *Communications and Media Act* to control online media and deal with the people who abuse the Internet. Najib Razak tried various means to suppress dissidents — the parliamentary member of the Democratic Action Party, Tony Pua Kiam Wee, and the parliament member of the People's Justice Party, Rafizi Ramli, and the Executive Chairman of The Edge Media Group, Tong Kooi Ong, who got to the bottom of the 1MDB case, were prohibited from leaving the country by the Immigration Department; after the Malaysian Anti-Corruption Commission arrested and detained the people involved in the case, the police summoned the senior officials of the Malaysian Anti-Corruption Commission for the reason of "assisting the investigation into disclosure of 1MDB documents".

The Prime Minister Najib Razak finally had the opportunity to relax for a while through tough measures. In early August 2015, there was good news from the authorities — the Malaysian Anti-Corruption Commission claimed that the USD 700 million flowing into Najib Razak's private bank account was a political contribution rather than the money from 1MDB; this explanation separated Najib Razak from 1MDB, so Najib Razak expressed with satisfaction the willingness to set up the Political Contribution Information Committee for controlling political contributions, and creatively proposed to make laws to disclose the sources of political contributions. On August 17, 2015, the Kuantan UMNO division chief, Datuk Seri Wan Adnan Wan Mamat, further clarified the political contribution received by Najib Razak; he stated that the USD 700 million had been donated by Saudi Arabia for supporting Malaysia's efforts in combating the terrorist organization of the Islamic State, while Deputy Prime Minister Ahmad Zahid Hamidi also confirmed that this political contribution had come from the Middle East because he read relevant documents and also met with the chief investment officer of the donator and the family financial fund trustor. Several days later, when meeting with the representatives of 145 UMNO divisions at the congress of Kuantan UMNO division's women's group, youth group and female youth group, Najib Razak admitted, "The USD 700 million was in fact remitted to my personal account, but like other things I have done, I received this political contribution for the sake of the party's interests rather than personal gains, and the Malaysian Anti-Corruption Commission has also confirmed that I have not violated laws; I am willing to do my best for the party, the people and Malaysia's future, I hope that this topic ends here".

With a series of counterattacks and official explanations, Najib Razak, who was in a precarious situation, seemed to be cleared of wrongdoing. However, in late August 2015, the "Bersih 4.0 Rally", which required Najib Razak to step down due to a financial scandal, was held in Kuala Lumpur, Kota Kinabalu and Kuching, while former Prime Minister Mahathir Mohamad, reputed as the evergreen in Asia's political circle, also appeared in the procession and called for overthrowing Najib Razak by the power of the people. In the meantime, the opposition parties publicly expressed strong views: the parliamentary member of the People's Justice Party, Rafizi Ramli, said, "The Malaysian Anti-Corruption Commission's clarification does not clarify it, the source and use of contribution is unconvincing and cannot restore the public's trust in the Prime Minister"; the leader of the Democratic Action Party, Lim Kit Siang, said, "Only when the Prime Minister proves before the people and the world that he is innocent can he lead Malaysia". With frequent criticism from the previous leaders, denouncement from the dismissed officials, the rise of anti-Najib Razak forces within the United Malays National Organisation, the hatred from the opposition parties and dissatisfaction from the people, a more powerful anti-Najib Razak force was stirring an overwhelming political tsunami against the Government of Najib Razak, political turbulence aimed at making it necessary for Najib Razak to step down had unfolded.[2]

[2]Xu Liping, Malaysia Initiated a Political Wave against Najib Razak, *World Affairs Press*, 2015(18).

II. Catalyst: Financial Turmoil Amidst Economic Downturn

The 1MDB scandal caused an uproar within Malaysia, but the politics itself was not the great weakness, while the economy was the most important trump card for safeguarding national stability. After Malaysia gained independence, it was one of the countries with the best economic performance in East Asia and Southeast Asia. In the 1970s, Malaysia utilized inexpensive labor resources to attract foreign capital and technologies to develop the labor-intensive industries, thus Malaysia rapidly became industrialized. As early as 1977, Malaysia's per capita GNI reached USD 1,030, making Malaysia one of the middle-income countries. In 1995, Malaysia's per capita GNI hit USD 4,010, Malaysia reached an economic level above average. However, in the late 1990s, as structural imbalance in income distribution, fragile financial system and other drawbacks loomed large, Malaysia's economy started to slow down; Malaysia's economic growth rate was only 2.07% during the period 1998–2010; although the Government of Malaysia adjusted the economic structure in the early 21st century, only a slight effect was produced. In particular, in 2015, with the global economic slowdown, the decline in the prices of bulk commodities in the world, the adoption of a consumption tax, and the impact of domestic and international factors, including the 1MDB scandal, Malaysia's economy extremely stagnated, and the year 2015 saw the worst economic performance in recent years.

1. The impact of external factors

a. *The inevitable effects from the global economic slowdown*

In early 2015, the World Bank (WB) made the judgment of economic development that China would slow down again, Europe would not recover and Russia would be on a continuing decline, and it predicted that the strong recovery of USA, as an engine, would not be sufficient to boost global economic development, thus the expectation about global economic growth in 2015 was reduced, while Malaysia, an outward-looking economy, would also not be free from impact. Against the background of a global economic slowdown, Malaysia was subject to the most obvious impact from the US as the spearhead of the world's economy and China as Malaysia's largest trading partner: As of the first quarter of 2015, the appreciation of the US dollar tended to be increasingly apparent and there was enhanced expectation that the Federal Reserve would raise interest rates, suggesting a strong return of the USD; this exerted a certain positive impact on Malaysia's exports; however, like many other exporting countries, Malaysia not only competed with the markets with exports to USA, but it also struggled to depreciate the domestic currency, thus foreign capital withdrew from Malaysia, and Malaysia faced the risk of exposure; in the meantime, China, a large country in the region, experienced a sharp economic slowdown in 2015, so Malaysia was faced with an increasingly severe overseas environment.

b. *Great impact from the fall in bulk commodities including oil and gas*

Malaysia ranks Nos. 29 and 14 in the world in oil and gas output, respectively, it is the second largest liquefied natural gas exporter in the world and the second largest oil and gas producer in Southeast Asia, thus the oil and gas industry is the pillar industry in Malaysia's national economy. With industrial and agricultural raw materials, including palm oil and soybeans, available in Malaysia, Malaysia's exportation of bulk commodities accounted for 35% of its total exports, the income from that area made up 30% of Malaysia's fiscal revenue. However, the era of high oil prices, arising out of the Iraq War in 2003, no longer brought brilliance after the global financial crisis in 2008 and the adoption of loose monetary policy by the Federal Reserve in 2009, accompanied by a full continued fall in international bulk commodities; in July 2015, the bulk commodities were extremely weak around the world, with the price of crude oil plunging by more than 20%; this exerted a huge negative impact on Malaysia's economy, the ringgit exchange rate was thus subject to pressure from depreciation.

2. The impact from internal factors

a. *The dilemma caused by the introduction of consumption tax*

A sharp decrease in the oil-related tax revenue greatly restricted the government from distributing "generous gifts" to the contractors of the United Malays National Organization; this aroused, to a certain extent, the anti-government sentiment among some groups within the United Malays National Organization; for the ordinary people, the decrease in oil revenue for the government meant that the services supplied by the government decreased and more taxes were levied. Unsurprisingly, on April 1, 2015, the Government of Malaysia adopted a consumption tax at a rate of 6% to replace the original business tax (10%) and service tax (6%); the introduction of the consumption tax affected the retail sector, including groceries, drugs, entertainment and food, and directly drove up the prices of goods and services, and increased the economic burden on the ordinary people, especially the middle-low income groups; as a result, the purchasing power of Malaysian households declined and the income disparity problem became increasingly acute in the Malaysian society. In other words, after the consumption tax policy was introduced, the disposable income of each household decreased, so consumption expenditures certainly shrank; in particular, the low-income families eligible for applying for BR1M financial assistance, which made up more than 60%, in Malaysia were financially overburdened, while the revenue obtained from corporate taxation by the government decreased accordingly, and this scenario epitomized the economic downturn precisely; this sowed the seeds of a crisis in the political circle.

b. *Chain reactions from the* 1MDB *scandal*

In 2015, Malaysia's economic performance was quite unsatisfactory, while the 1MDB scandal added more difficulties and worsened the economy, the performance on various indicators was not good: regarding the exchange rate, from early January to late August 2015, the Malaysian currency ringgit declined against the USD for 10 consecutive weeks, the exchange rate reached the lowest level in 17 years, the cumulative decline in the past 12 months exceeded 25%, and it was the currency with the worst performance in Asia in the same period; regarding the stock market, in the last week of August, the stock index on the Malaysia Stock Exchange fell by 8.5%, and touched the lowest level since 2012; concerning treasury bonds, although the rating agency believed that Malaysia's debts were safe, the prices of government bonds remained low; in July, overseas investors reduced the holding of Malaysia's treasury bonds to USD 51 billion, the lowest level since

August 2012, and the 10-year treasury bonds saw the greatest decline in two months. Malaysia's exchange, stock and bond markets showed an emergency across the board, exacerbating panic within the market, and international investors were withdrawing capital at the fastest pace ever. According to statistical data, in the first three weeks of August, there was a net outflow of nearly USD 786 million in foreign capital, almost half of the net outflow of foreign capital in 2014; as of August 15, the foreign exchange reserve of Malaysia's central bank decreased to USD 94.5 billion, lower than USD 100 billion for the first time since 2010 and a record low in 6 years; Malaysia's debts denominated in foreign currencies exceeded USD 130 billion. The depreciation of the ringgit certainly raised the prices of import commodities; even though the prices of foreign commodities had declined, the depreciation of the ringgit would increase the prices of commodities, there were all-round increases in the prices of goods, while wages stagnated, so the Malaysian people bore more pressure on their lives in addition to the pressure from consumption tax.

In response to such a bad economic situation, the Government of Malaysia invited the senior leaders of many domestic and foreign financial institutions and related companies to study the measures for addressing Malaysia's economic situation — Prime Minister Najib Razak stressed that Malaysia would not once again carry out the capital control or fixed exchange rate system; the authorities announced the establishment of the Ad Hoc Economic Committee — chaired by the Minister in the Prime Minister's Department, Abdul Wahid Omar, and consisting of nine members including enterprise representatives, financial professionals and academic experts — responsible for assisting the government in stabilizing national economic fundamentals and financial and capital markets, and improving the people's lives; the Ad Hoc Economic Committee would continue to operate and pay attention to economic issues on attracting domestic and foreign investments, stabilizing the national economy, controlling inflation and ensuring resource supply; furthermore, the government also urged a number of Malaysia's government-linked enterprises operating overseas to sell their assets and reduce outward foreign investments to repatriate funds, so as to assist the government in stabilizing the ringgit. Amidst public denunciation arising out of the political scandal, all-out efforts were made to address economic issues, suggesting that what the Government of Malaysia was facing was not merely a political or economic issue.[3]

III. Where to Go: Intricate Political Situation in Malaysia

In any part of the world, politics is always closely correlated to the economy — the decline of the political system and institution often causes economic contradictions, while economic and financial factors can also intensify the political conflicts among the governing elites, and there is no exception for Malaysia.[4] In recent years, Malaysia's political circle has always been controlled by the United Malays National Organization, but internally this party has not been as calm as common people think. In 2015, the 1MDB scandal made the Government of Najib Razak the focus of public attention. Given all political and economic factors, and a series of problems caused by Najib Razak's involvement in corruption, at present, the governing status of the United Malays National Organization in Malaysia's political circle has become precarious, and the opposition factions have stepped up efforts to overthrow Najib Razak in order to save Malaysia. The contradictions within the governing party have become acute, and there is strong strife among the parties that are out of power, making it difficult to predict the direction of Malaysia's political situation and complicating the same.

In the short term, it is difficult to rock the long-standing governing status of the United Malays National Organization; this is because the mindset that "Malaysians are the United Malays National Organization, and vice versa" has been deeply rooted among the people; the United Malays National Organization managed to get more than 70% of the votes in the previous general elections. This fully proves that the United Malays National Organization is the core and pillar of Malaysia's governing coalition. However, from the long-term perspective, the problems in the United Malays National Organization have become increasingly severe, the 1MDB corruption case

---

[3]Zhang Qianye, Chain Reactions from Malaysia's Political Turbulence, *South Reviews*, 2015(15).

[4]Zhang Yun, The Situation of Political Parties and Their Trends in Malaysia, *Southeast Asian Studies*, 2001(2), p. 28.

and the corruption scandal concerning Najib Razak have caused a drastic decline in the status of the United Malays National Organization among the Malaysian people; political strongmen have exerted pressure again and again, Najib Razak has reshuffled the cabinet in order to maintain stability and the United Malays National Organization has faced internal and external problems; in the 2013 general election, the Pakatan Rakyat (People's Alliance), supported by 80% of the Chinese in Malaysia, failed, the National Front was criticized for fraud, and the Chinese complained: where to go for Malaysia's democracy; racial problem loomed large; on March 8, 2014, after Malaysia Airlines Flight 370 disappeared, Malaysia released inaccurate information many times, the country was criticized for concealing the truth of this incident, and it was condemned by the international community. The national will led by the United Malays National Organization has run counter to the pursuit of democracy and equality by various races and classes in Malaysia; the governance capacity of the United Malays National Organization has been questioned by the people from various sectors. Now the Government of Najib Razak has neither political aspirations nor political capital to carry out in-depth and meaningful structural reform, it may become worse before the situation improves; this winter may be the coldest winter which the United Malays National Organization needs to survive.

IV. China's Position: Addressing Changes with the Fundamental Principle

For a long time, China–Malaysia relations have been the bilateral relations characterized by interdependence and win–win cooperation. On May 31, 1974, Malaysia and China established diplomatic relations. Malaysia is the first ASEAN country to establish diplomatic relations with China and to promote an ASEAN–China dialogue. Malaysia has always upheld China's standpoint that territorial disputes should be settled in a peaceful way. Malaysia has denied the China Threat Theory in international conferences on many occasions. With the China–Malaysia partnership, the two countries share the same standpoints; more importantly, bilateral trade and exchanges have served as the bond. According to relevant data, in 2015, China–Malaysia trade reached 97.36 billion yuan, Malaysia was the sixth largest trading partner of China in the world, and China continued to be Malaysia's largest trading partner, the largest source of imports and the second largest export destination for Malaysia. Malaysia was also China's largest trading partner in the ASEAN community, Malaysia–China trade accounted for 20.6% of China–ASEAN trade, China–Malaysia trade continued to play the leading role in ASEAN countries. In 2010, Malaysians visited China 1,245,200 person-times, while the Chinese visited Malaysia 1,033,700 person-times. China has become one of the main sources of overseas visitors for Malaysia.

The China–Malaysia comprehensive strategic partnership is based on bilateral needs, a common will of the leaders and people of the two sides as well as the choice of a historical trend. No matter how turbulent Malaysia's political situation is, Malaysia needs China, a reliable trading partner, to revitalize its declining economy. For China, as the Belt and Road Initiative and the task of building the Asian Infrastructure Investment Bank have been put forward, the efforts to increase China's say in the ASEAN community needs support from the authorities of various countries, while Malaysia enjoys the Strait of Malacca and Kuantan Port and is the coveted strategic route for the Maritime Silk Road put forward by China, so Malaysia plays a very important role in the strategic deployment for the Belt and Road.

Therefore, Malaysia's political turmoil will not exert a substantive impact on China–Malaysia relations; both the National Front and the People's Alliance need China, while China also needs Malaysia. When dealing with the two sides, China should fully observe the Five Principles of Peaceful Coexistence and fully keep neutral even though one side is the United Malays National Organization, which exercises absolute control over Malaysia and leads the general situation, another side is the People's Alliance supported by 80% of the Chinese in Malaysia. China cannot excessively align itself with either side, otherwise, the image of China as a large country will be damaged in the international community, and China will attend to one side but lose another side, so pursuing the middle of the road and coping with changes maintaining its fundamental principle is the best way for China to address China–Malaysia relations.

Chapter 26

The Challenges for Singapore in the Post-Lee Kuan Yew Era

Chen Caijian and Yi Yin*

I. Background

Singapore is a city-state. It covers an area of 719.1 km^2. As of November 2015, its permanent resident population was 5,535,000. In the 25 years from 1965 when Singapore gained independence to 1990, Lee Kuan Yew served as the Prime Minister; afterwards, he served as the Minister Mentor until May 2011. During his governance, Lee Kuan Yew successfully developed Singapore into one of the most developed countries in Asia in three decades. From 2011 to 2015, when Lee Kuan Yew passed away, he held no post, but thanks to his high prestige in Singapore, his governance philosophy and economic, diplomatic, social and other policies were retained. When Lee Kuan Yew passed away, the people had a terrible doubt: Will Singapore change in the post-Lee Kuan Yew era? If it changes, what will be the direction of that change? What challenges will Singapore have? This paper will discuss these hot issues.

* Chen Caijian, Deputy Director, Associate Research Fellow at the Singapore Institute of the China–ASEAN Research Institute of Guangxi University; Yi Yin, Research Assistant at the Singapore Institute of the China–ASEAN Research Institute of Guangxi University.

II. Overview of Singapore in the Era of Lee Kuan Yew

1. Politics

Since its independence, Singapore has been governed by the People's Action Party founded by Lee Kuan Yew. Singapore practices the centralization of authority characterized by top-down meritocracy. Although the Government of Singapore has a very high status in the country, it is clean and honest in the eyes of the people from the rest of the world. Furthermore, there is exceptional solidarity within Singaporean leadership. Decisions on matters are made through consultation, showing the style of collective leadership.

a. *Constitution*

The Constitution of Singapore is the supreme law of the Republic of Singapore. It stipulates the basic principles and framework for executive, legislative and judicial branches. The Constitution of Singapore cannot be amended unless more than 2/3 of the members of parliament grant approval.

b. *Parliament*

The President of Singapore and the Parliament are collectively referred to as the legislative organ. The Parliament of Singapore follows the British democratic parliamentary system; the members of parliament are elected in a general election. The leader of the political party obtaining the majority of seats in the Parliament serves as the Prime Minister (PM). The Prime Minister chooses the elected parliamentary members as cabinet members to form the cabinet. The term of office of each parliament is 5 years. The next general election is held within three months after the dissolution of Parliament. Parliament performs mainly three functions: making laws, controlling the fiscal position of the country, playing the crucial and accountability role of supervising and inspecting the behavior of the governing party and the cabinet.

c. *Political party*

The governing party in Singapore is the People's Action Party founded on November 21, 1954. At the beginning, the People's Action Party was a unity of two left wings, including the pro-socialism left wing led by Lee Kuan Yew and the pro-communist left wing led by Lim Chin Siong. However, the latter soon broke away from the People's Action Party. The People's Action Party is the most successful political party with the longest history in Singapore. In Singapore, it is relatively easy to establish a political party — several people can establish a political party by establishing a party program and registering the party with the relevant department. At present, there are 43 legitimate political parties, large and small, in Singapore. Besides the People's Action Party, the large political parties include the Workers' Party, the Democratic Progressive Party and the Singapore Democratic Alliance.

d. *Parliamentary election*

The greatest characteristic of Singapore's system of general elections is that the People's Action Party in power firmly controls the electoral committee, the high court, the media and the government-sponsored institutions and influences the direction of voting through these institutions. Most importantly, the constituencies are identified under the principle of being beneficial for the governing party to obtain more votes; if in a certain constituency, the opposition parties have a great influence and are likely to obtain most of the votes in the election, the electoral committee will divide this constituency into several constituencies or merge part of this constituency with other constituencies, so as to disperse the sources of the votes for the opposition parties. The constituencies in Singapore are divided into single-member constituencies and group representation constituencies. In the single-member constituency, each party nominates a single candidate to participate in the election. A group representation constituency is equal to several single-member constituencies in terms of population and size, thus each party chooses 5–6 people to form a group as a candidate for participating in the election. If a certain opposition party is likely to obtain a simple majority in a single-member constituency with a small number of people, this single-member constituency will be merged into a large group representation constituency, so the opposition party can only obtain a minority; the possibility that this opposition party wins in a large group representation constituency will decrease greatly.

2. Economy

Singapore is characterized by a small area, a small population, a scarcity of resources and an outward-looking economy. Singapore's economy is dominated by electronic, petrochemical, financial, shipping and service industries, and it heavily depends on the international market. Over 50 years since the founding of Singapore, under the leadership of Lee Kuan Yew and the People's Action Party, Singapore made remarkable achievements in economic development, it came out in front worldwide, and even surpassed many traditional developed countries in a number of economic indicators — the GDP soared from less than USD 1 billion in 1965 to nearly USD 300 billion in 2015, an average annual growth of 12.65%; the per capita GDP surged from USD 500 in 1965 to nearly USD 53,000 in 2015, an average annual growth of 10.21%.

3. Diplomacy

In order to survive the complex international situation, Singapore must develop good diplomatic relations with large countries in the capacity of a small country. How to survive among the surrounding countries and great powers in the world and thus obtain influence was an important issue for Lee Kuan Yew. The diplomatic philosophy of developing good diplomatic relations with large countries in the capacity of a small country and maintaining a balance among the great powers is an important guiding principle in Lee Kuan Yew's diplomatic strategic thought. Lee Kuan Yew is famous for upholding the diplomacy of maintaining a balance among the great powers: First, building a nonalignment line of thought, maintaining friendly relations with USA, but refraining from establishing official ally relations with it; second, adopting a policy of neutrality in international relations, making as many friends as possible, reducing the number of hostile relationships, refraining from taking sides with one of the two opposing sides as much as possible; third, breaking the silence while refraining from taking sides, finding the appropriate issues and opportunities to express views and positions, so as to demonstrate Singapore's influence and presence. In the relations with China, Lee Kuan Yew's diplomatic philosophy of maintaining a balance among the great powers has also worked marvelously. As a Singaporean with Chinese origins, deeply influenced by Confucianism, Lee Kuan Yew was very familiar with China. In his opinion, the rise of China is irresistible, and China's national reunification is only a matter of time. In the meantime, as China became increasingly powerful, Lee Kuan Yew also pointed out that USA should continue to contain China, and warned such countries as Japan and India of raising vigilance against the rise of China. Therefore, in a sense, Lee Kuan Yew showed a dual character in diplomatically dealing with China. This mainly stems from his diplomatic philosophy of maintaining a balance among the great powers and is also associated with his ideological philosophy. In his memoir, Lee Kuan Yew said that when two elephants fought each other, the grassland would suffer; when two elephants made love, the grassland would also suffer; Singapore was the grassland between USA and China; in the past, Singapore relied on USA to survive among the Islamic countries in Southeast Asia, so he opened Singapore's port to USA for replenishing aircraft carriers; he had always sought to become the leader of the ASEAN community, but other countries did not agree with this idea since Singapore was too small; in recent years, Singapore had attached importance to economic cooperation with China, while Singapore leant towards USA in political and military cooperation.[1]

4. Population and immigration policy

Singapore has a population of more than 5 million, 77% of whom are Chinese, 14% Malayan, 8% Indian, 1% Eurasian and other nationals. In Singapore, there are official languages, including Malay, Chinese, Tamil and English. English is the official language and the language used in business. Religions mainly include Islam, Buddhism, Christianity, Hindu, Sikhism, Judaism and Zoroastrianism.

In 2013, the Government of Singapore issued the white paper on population policy, pinpointing the direction of its population development. According to the white paper, like other developed countries and territories, such as Hong Kong, Japan and Taiwan, Singapore has been continuously at low levels in population aging and fertility rate. If Singapore does not import new immigrants, its population will decrease as of 2025. As it is estimated

[1] http://www.ynpxrz.com/n300644c1416.aspx.

that its fertility rate cannot reach 2.1 in a short time, Singapore boldly proposes that it will turn 15,000–25,000 people into citizens each year and introduce 30,000 permanent residents each year — permanent residents can apply for becoming Singaporean citizens 2 years after they obtain the permanent resident status; the Government of Singapore has planned to keep their number at 500,000–600,000; the ultimate goal is to increase the population of Singapore to 6.50–6.90 million by 2030, and decrease the proportion of citizens from 62% in June 2012, to 55% in 2030. For massive population growth, the government will provide the corresponding supporting facilities, including housing and railways, to meet the citizens' needs.

III. The Challenges for Singapore in the Post-Lee Kuan Yew Era

1. Politics

a. *The stability of the political system*

Singapore's political system has enjoyed a certain level of stability in the post-Lee Kuan Yew Era. This can be analyzed according to the result of Singapore's election in 2015. The election result was unveiled on September 2. As shown by the result, the People's Action Party in power obtained nearly 70% of the votes and won the election for the first time in the post-Lee Kuan Yew Era. This means that the People's Action Party recovered the constituencies which it lost in the 2011 general election and also controlled the momentum of the opposition parties; more meaningfully, it conveys a clear signal to the outside world: although Singapore has lost Lee Kuan Yew, Singapore and its political order remain unchanged. Therefore, Singapore's political system has remained stable in the post-Lee Kuan Yew Era in the short term. The tremendous achievements made by Singapore in the economic field are associated with a high level of stability of the political system established by Singapore. The British-style democratic parliamentary system built by Singapore, the systems advocated by Singapore and deeply rooted among the people — including the founding of the country under the rule of law, multi-ethnic harmonious coexistence, ability-based appointment of the people and strong campaign against corruption — will continue to safeguard Singapore's continued development. In particular, Singapore's unique election system characterized by single-member constituencies and group representation constituencies will continue to guarantee the status of the People's Action Party as the governing party.

b. *The trend towards political diversity*

The political stability in the post-Lee Kuan Yew era is relative. The apparent stability does not cover some changes behind it. This can be seen from Singapore's 2011 general election. Although the People's Action Party obtained a majority of the parliamentary seats in the 2011 general election, the result of the general election showed some changes.

According to Table 1, the maximum number of single-member constituencies reached 12; however, when there was only one elected member of parliament, the number of members of parliament was only 12; the number of 5-person group representation constituencies was 11, equivalent to that of single-member constituencies, but the number of the elected members of parliament hit 55, almost five times that of the members of parliament in single-member constituencies. Therefore, a political party cannot win in group representation constituencies unless it is sufficiently powerful. Under this system, there was no problem for the People's Action Party to win a majority of parliamentary seats. However, as shown in Table 2, the Workers' Party — which ranked No. 2 in the percentage of votes obtained — and the National Solidarity Party — which ranked No. 3 — lagged far behind the People's Action Party, which ranked No. 1, but the percentage of votes obtained increased by 6–8% compared with the 2006 general election; the Workers' Party obtained six parliamentary seats, while the percentage of votes

Table 1. Classification of Singapore's Constituencies in the 2011 General Election

Type of constituency	Number of constituencies	Number of people
Single-member constituency	12	12
4-person group representation constituency	2	8
5-person group representation constituency	11	55
6-person group representation constituency	2	12
Total	27	87

Table 2. Distribution of Political Parties and Candidates in Singapore's 2011 General Election

Political party	Single-member constituency (person)	Group representation constituency			Election ratio (%)	Percentage of votes obtained (%)	Increase or decrease over 2006 (%)	Number of parliamentary seats obtained	Percentage of parliamentary seats obtained (%)
		4 persons	5 persons	6 persons					
People's Action Party	12	2	11	2	100	60.14	−6.46	81	93
Workers' Party	4	1	3	—	26.4	12.83	+8.15	6	7
National Solidarity Party	4	—	4	—	27.6	12.04	+6.37	—	
Democratic Party	2	1	1	—	12.6	4.83	+13.53	—	
Reform Party	—	—	11	12.6	4.28	—	—		
Peoples Party	2	—	1	—	8	3.11	+8.9	—	
Democratic Alliance	1	—	—	18	2.78	−2.46	—		

Note: The election ratio means the proportion of the seats for which the political party runs among all the seats across the country.

Source: Forecast of Singapore's General Election — Demystifying the General Trend of the Politics in the Post-Lee Kuan Yew Era, www.yan.sg, June 24, 2015.

obtained by the People's Action Party decreased by 6% points compared with the previous general election. This suggests that the voting intentions of voters became diverse, the parties out of power started to participate in and discuss political affairs, while this was impossible in the general elections in and before 2006. This also signifies that as economic prosperity, a high level of social stability and political integrity have gradually become normal in Singapore since the 1980s–1990s, the people have started to require the parliament to have "multiple voices" and question a tough stance in control, so the approval rating of the opposition parties has risen. Although there has been a sign of political diversity, the possibility of governance by the opposition parties in the future depends upon the development of the situation: First, can the opposition parties be united as one and combined according to advantages to end the situation in which single parties are weak and act in their own ways? According to the 2011 general election and two by-elections, the relatively powerful opposition parties have gradually developed their own unique characteristics, but there is a long way to go before they are combined according to their advantages. Second, even though the opposition parties are combined according to advantages, success depends upon their ability to attract a wealth of outstanding political talents to form a force capable of countering the People's Action Party. A very great problem in the opposition parties is lack of talents and failure to cultivate successors in a systematic way. Third, can the People's Action Party stay the same, avoid internal strife and prevent different factions under the political pressure? The People's Action Party is the party with the highest level of solidarity among all political parties in Singapore. This is also an important reason why it is possible for the People's Action Party to always be powerful while the opposition parties have failed to become powerful over a period of several decades. When Lee Kuan Yew was alive, different opinions, even acute contradictions, within the People's Action Party could be resolved through consultation. However, in the post-Lee Kuan Yew era, there is no authority; this shows that if the spiritual leader is not available, the ability to maintain intraparty solidarity may become problematic. In the 2016 general election, under the leadership of Lee Hsien Loong, the ability to keep solidarity within the People's Action Party was beyond doubt. However, "after Lee Hsien Loong, the People's Action Party will face increasing pressure in politics and election campaigns, two even three totally different political views may occur within the People's

Action Party and these cannot be reconciled, so it is not surprising that it will be split in the end; this may be the biggest potential challenge for the People's Action Party in the post-Lee Kuan Yew era."[2]

c. *The changes in voters' appeals*

The age structure of Singaporean voters has also changed in the post-Lee Kuan Yew era; in the past, voters were the people born in the 1940s, the 1950s and the 1960s; now, voters are dominated by the young people born in the 1970s and the 1980s. In particular, the young voters have not experienced the hardships during the initial stage of Singapore's birth after its founding and the subsequent great efforts led by Lee Kuan Yew to make Singapore one of the economically developed countries in the world. Therefore, these voters pay attention to issues different from those in the era of their predecessors and their appeals have also changed. Besides employment, livelihood welfare and other economic issues, they also pay attention to political issues, such as the issue of open civic rights. As the Prime Minister who founded the country, Lee Kuan Yew had capital to foster his own style of "strongman politics" and turn Singapore into the kingdom of Lee. Thus, Singaporeans thank Lee Kuan Yew; however, in recent years, Singaporeans have been increasingly unsatisfied with such issues as Singapore's housing, rising transportation fees, the inflow of foreign immigrants and the widening wealth gap, and the young voters have more demands for embodying their appeals in elections. With the disappearance of the "strongman politics", his political authority has faded away. Singapore, a wealthy, developed and open country, does not hope to be in the charge of a "father" who is hardworking but strict. With the enhancement of the consciousness of one's rights and the awareness of diverse cultures, Singaporeans hope to have more opportunities for expressing their appeals. Since the previous general election, the opposition parties have started to challenge the governance system characterized by one-party dominance which has been carried out since the founding of Singapore.[3]

---

[2] Where to Go for Singapore in the Post-Lee Kuan Yew Era? *The Beijing News*, March 24, 2015.
[3] Singapore Ushers in the Post-Lee Kuan Yew Era, www.cri.cn, May 26, 2011.

2. Economy

a. *The continuity of the economic policy*

In the post-Lee Kuan Yew era, Singapore's economic policy will not change and will be continued to a certain extent. The long-term governance by Lee Kuan Yew has laid an excellent legal foundation, shaped the economic market policy and built a solid industrial base, thus as long as the successors observe his policy and economically execute the rules, regulations and systems developed in the era of Lee Kuan Yew, it will be possible for Singapore to achieve long-term and stable economic development. However, some problems may arise; for example, the government's expenditure on welfare is too large and the development of the real estate market is hindered. Recently these problems have exerted increasing pressure on Singapore's economy. Once the post-Lee Kuan Yew era sees a decline in the power for controlling and solving the above problems, increases in housing prices and house rents, negative development of welfare distribution as well as a widening wealth gap, there will likely be a series of changes taking place in Singapore's economic policy.

b. *The adjustment of the economic structure*

Singapore's development is subject to natural resources. To some extent, there are no issues relating to agriculture, rural areas and farmers. In order to address the developmental issue, Singapore has built zones for industrial development to attract domestic and foreign investors, especially foreign enterprises, to massively develop industrialization; Singapore has fully leveraged its geographical advantage of a country strategically situated at the Strait of Malacca to develop such service industries as shipping, wharfside services and finance. According to estimates, the primary, secondary and tertiary industries accounted for 0.1%, 32% and 67.9% of Singapore's economic aggregate in 2015, respectively.

Thanks to the superior location at the Strait of Malacca, Singapore has become one of the busiest trade hubs in the world and controls the vital route connecting Europe, Southeast Asia with South Asia. This has also laid a good foundation for Singapore to develop a powerful industrial manufacturing industry, stimulating vigorous development of the financial and hi-tech sectors. However, industrial manufacturing has become saturated and needs to be transformed, thus Singapore's service industry has flourished in the economy.

In fact, in the view of Paul Krugman, who was awarded the Nobel Prize in Economics in 2008, Singapore's economic growth is attributable to the growth of investments from the outside world rather than the improvement of economic productive forces. In the opinion of Lee Hsien Loong, from a long-term perspective, the challenge for Singapore lies in improving its productive forces, while economic transformation is the only way out.[4] With respect to transformation, for Singapore as a country with a lack of natural resources, first, it is necessary to increase the proportion of the service industry, especially the financial sector, in the GDP, so that Singapore can continue to maintain its status of Asian financial center.[5] In reality, Singapore's economic development has always been accompanied by an increasing proportion of the financial services sector in the GDP. In order to keep sustained economic growth, the Government of Singapore has sought new growth patterns, conducted economic restructuring, worked on enhancing domestic productive forces, especially strengthening the development of the financial sector. According to www.ftchinese.com, as there is no economic hinterland, it is likely that Singapore's economic growth will need to be promoted by the development of the financial services sector, but Singapore may face challenges from Shanghai and Shenzhen, China.

Second, it is essential to carry out industrial innovation. According to economist Rajiv Biswas, if Singapore hopes to maintain the status of the country with the highest per capita GDP in Asia, it will be necessary to maintain the strong momentum of the growth of productivity in order to support a stable growth in salaries while controlling the unit labor cost. Therefore, the future success of Singapore will depend upon sustained transformation of the economy towards the high value-added industries.[6] Singapore needs more

---

[4] Vanguard in Overseas Investment, Financing and Offshore Operations: Detailed Introduction to Key Industries in Singapore, http://www.erichina.cn.

[5] The Per Capita GDP Is Too High, Singapore Needs to Make Bolder Economic Transformation, compiled by Lu Peiyi, www.cnyes.com, March 26, 2015.

[6] William Pesek, Can Singapore Continue the Miracle in the Post-Lee Kuan Yew Era?, *Bloomberg Businessweek*, August 9, 2015.

innovations and should provide financial support to various sectors — such as software, biotechnology, energy, logistics and health care — for funding the research and development of cutting-edge technologies.

3. Diplomacy

a. *The diplomatic philosophy of maintaining a balance among the great powers*

The philosophy is one of the valuable political legacies left by Lee Kuan Yew; it is applied in the whole diplomatic policy system of Singapore so that Singapore, a small country, can adeptly utilize its excellent capability; it helps Singapore win a stable environment for political and economic development. Even after Lee Kuan Yew's passing away, Singapore does not want to change this important diplomatic philosophy and its relations with the great powers will not be subject to a great impact.

(i) Singapore will continue to rely on military support from extraterritorial forces

More directly, this extraterritorial force is USA. As a small country, Singapore is inherently fragile, so it needs military protection from extraterritorial great powers and it hopes that a foreign military can be a permanent resident. Singapore believes that USA is a "well-intentioned" great power;[7] once USA is present in Southeast Asia, it can maintain the balance among various forces in the region, safeguard regional security and stability, deter Singapore's neighboring countries and mitigate the potential threats from neighboring countries to Singapore. At present, Singapore is USA's main military base in Southeast Asia. Not long ago, Singapore made an agreement with the US military for deploying the anti-submarine reconnaissance plane P-8 Poseidon in Singapore for a short period every several months. Generally, Singapore will not change its pro-American stance in the military field unless it finds a new "well-intentioned" great power.

---

[7] Evaluation and Analysis of Singapore's Foreign Policy Trends, http://cpc.people.com.cn/n/2015/0922/c191095-27618288.html.

(ii) Singapore will maintain a geographical balance among the great powers

Singapore's diplomatic philosophy of maintaining a balance among the great powers determines that it will not let its destiny be controlled by a great power, nor will Singapore side with only one of the great powers. It needs to guarantee its independence, and hopes that different extraterritorial forces will get involved in Southeast Asia and contend with each other, thus achieving a check and balance. In the post-Lee Kuan Yew era, Singapore will continue to seek a balance among USA, China, Japan and India. Singapore understands that the rise of China is inevitable; furthermore, there are close relations of cooperation on economics and trade between China and Singapore, so Singapore welcomes the rise of China. In the meantime, Singapore will also rope in USA, Japan and India to contain the ever-growing power of China. From Singapore's perspective, USA is the main force for maintaining a regional balance of power, Japan has always enjoyed traditional interests in Southeast Asia, while India shows a strong momentum of economic and military development, thus Singapore wants to rely on them to prevent China from excessively expanding its influence in Southeast Asia. In order to keep regional balance, Singapore will continue to support the US strategy of the Asia-Pacific rebalancing in a certain period of time to come, and Singapore also hopes that Japan can contend with China over Southeast Asia, while involving India in the Southeast Asian affairs to exert a geopolitical influence in the region will become an important trend. Furthermore, Australia and Southeast Asia will become closer in political and economic ties, while the cooperation in the non-traditional security fields will also be further enhanced. As Australia becomes the first comprehensive strategic partner of Singapore, in the future, it is worth observing whether Singapore will actively involve Australia in the Southeast Asian affairs.

b. *Foreign policy with neighboring countries*

Singapore is an island dominated by the people of Chinese origin in the Malay ocean. From the ethnic, religious and historical perspectives, it seeks survival in a hostile environment. Situated between Malaysia and Indonesia, Singapore must exercise prudence and attach great importance to maintaining good relations with both neighbors. Lee Kuan Yew demonstrated a strong personal style in dealing with Malaysia and Indonesia; this cannot be duplicated in the post-Lee Kuan Yew era. In the post-Lee Kuan Yew era, given two powerful neighboring countries and civilian development of the political situation in Southeast Asia, coping with changes according to the fundamental principle in handling the diplomatic relations with the neighboring countries is the best policy for Singapore.

(i) Singapore continues to be friendly with its neighboring countries and frequently exchanges visits with them

Since the Prime Minister Lee Hsien Loong established the new government and appointed Vivian Balakrishnan as the Minister of Foreign Affairs in October 2014, Vivian Balakrishnan first visited the neighboring countries in Southeast Asia, including Malaysia and Indonesia, once again highlighting the long-term close friendly relations with both countries. Singapore and its neighboring countries share relevant interests in a range of issues from water supply, cross-border haze to regional counter-terrorism. In the future, Singapore will more frequently interact with its neighboring countries in the diplomatic field, so as to expand bilateral cooperation, share information and address many outstanding issues.

(ii) Singapore continues to maintain the role of coordinator in the ASEAN community

Without the political strongman Lee Kuan Yew, Singapore's influence in the ASEAN group may decline, but its status in it will not be weakened, so its role in the most important organization in the region will not change greatly. Singapore is the most developed country in Southeast Asia. It is a small county, and will not play a decisive role in the ASEAN community, but it can continue to serve as an excellent promoter and coordinator. The ASEAN Economic Community (AEC), established in late 2015, is very beneficial to Singapore, a country which is undergoing economic transformation; from the long-term perspective, the AEC can benefit Singapore's economic growth. On the issue of the South China Sea which affects ASEAN–China relations, Singapore will play an effective role of coordinator, it will not side with either side; instead, it will actively stimulate the stakeholders to establish the *Code of Conduct in the South China Sea* as early as possible. As a small country vulnerable to the external environment, Singapore needs a stable ASEAN community for guaranteeing a peaceful regional environment.

c. *Securing a position in the international arena*

Singapore's diplomatic policy fundamentally consists of addressing Singapore's fragility, but it cannot be ignored that Singapore actively seeks to become part of the international community. Lee Kuan Yew promoted the Brand of Singapore to the world and turned Singapore into the venue of international conferences — conferences covering political, military, economic, trade and other fields, thus greatly enhancing the popularity of Singapore in the international community and demonstrating its diplomatic influence. According to the current Prime Minister, Lee Hsien Loong, Singapore does not accept the predestination that a small country has no diplomacy and hopes to defend and promote national interests through diplomacy[8]; Singapore actively engages in international cooperation in addressing climate change and countering terrorism and other fields, building up Singapore's status in the international arena. Without Lee Kuan Yew, a diplomatic strongman, Singapore needs to consider how to continue adeptly coping with the increasingly complex regional environment and international landscape by continuously leveraging its influence in the future.

4. Population and immigration policy

Since the 21st century, Singapore has seen a fertility rate lower than 1.4 and has entered an aging society. In 2015, the proportion of the elderly above 65 years old increased to 13.1%. Considering the domestic shortage of human resources, the Government of Singapore carried out the open and loose immigrant labor and immigration policy in the past, but the white paper on population issued by the government in 2013 stirred a great uproar in Singapore; the most controversial issue was that the ratio of citizen population

[8]The Prime Minister Lee Hsien Loong: Singapore Does Not Accept the Predestination that a Small Country Has No Diplomacy, Singapore Defends and Promotes National Interests through Diplomacy, http://www.zaobao.com/special/outline/story20151128-553996.

to non-citizen population[9] may reach 55:45 by 2030, thus Singaporean citizens have been extremely dissatisfied with the influx of a population from the outside. Subject to pressure, in recent years, the Government of Singapore has implemented a tight policy regarding external population and immigrant labor, it has transformed the economy, reduced the dependence upon external labor and only introduced high-caliber talents. In 2015, Singapore's overall population growth rate dropped to a record low in 10–20 years and was only 1.2%; this is mainly because the growth of the external population decreased greatly in the same period. At present, Singapore is undergoing painful economic transformation, and the slowdown of immigrant labor influx may adversely affect its economic growth. In the next step, the Government of Singapore needs to address the issue on how to strike a balance between Singaporeans and the external population and reach a new consensus on new immigrants.

IV. China and Singapore in the Post-Lee Kuan Yew Era

Since China and Singapore established diplomatic relations 25 years ago, both countries have frequently exchanged visits, and leapfrog development has been made in bilateral relations. Chinese President Xi Jinping described China and Singapore as intimate and special partners. Lee Kuan Yew, the Prime Minister who founded Singapore, visited China more than 30 times, he laid the foundation for and promoted bilateral relations. Under the new background that both countries have decided to establish a comprehensive cooperative partnership in sync with the times, bilateral relations will reach a new height.

1. Political trends

a. *The mutual political trust between the two sides has been increasingly enhanced*

As shown by the history of China–Singapore contacts, the senior leaders of Singapore, from the Prime Minister to ministers, basically visited China once a year, while Chinese leaders were often invited to visit Singapore for political

---

[9] [Singapore] John WONG, ZHAO Litao, *Singapore's Social Development in Transition*, (Singapore) World Scientific Publishing, 2013, pp. 63–69, 99–105.

consultation. In November 2015, Xi Jinping visited Singapore in the capacity of top Chinese leader for the first time, and historically met with Taiwan's leader Ma Ying-jeou, highlighting the mutual trust between the two sides. After Xi Jinping visited Singapore, bilateral relations were upgraded to a comprehensive partnership, laying the foundation for both sides to go beyond respective developmental difficulties and the regional geopolitical dilemma.

b. *The diplomatic cooperation has tended to be pragmatic*

Singapore will serve as the coordinator in the China–ASEAN dialogue in the 3 years following August 2015. Given the close partnership between Singapore and China, China is full of expectations about Singapore's efforts in promoting China–ASEAN relations. In particular, as the issue of the South China Sea has frequently affected the cooperation between China and the ASEAN community as a whole, Singapore, which has pledged not to side with either side, can play a bigger role as the coordinator, easing the tension over the South China Sea and thus making China–ASEAN relations more solid.

c. *Possible problems in the future*

As USA is aware that the continued rise of China is inevitable, it has actively gotten involved in the Southeast Asian affairs, with an attempt to confront China and challenge China's geopolitical role in the region. Singapore, which leans towards the US militarily and China economically, is able to maintain a balance, but it is also possible that Singapore will be forced to clearly express its position; this will pose potential threats to the amicable relations between China and Singapore. Moreover, being rooted in Southeast Asia, Singapore attaches great importance to the regional organization of ASEAN, so China–Singapore relations will be inevitably affected by the development of the relations between China and the entire Southeast Asian area, the ASEAN community.

2. Economic cooperation

a. *The intergovernmental cooperation projects have flourished*

Both the governments of China and Singapore have engaged in cooperation on intergovernmental industrial parks since the 1990s, the two sides have built Suzhou Industrial Park and Tianjin Eco-city. In November 2015, the two countries reached an agreement on the third intergovernmental cooperation project between the two sides — The China–Singapore (Chongqing) Demonstration Initiative on Strategic Connectivity. This project is being carried out in coordination with the Belt and Road Initiative, it can push forward the development of the western region and inland areas of China, and also produce effects on simulating the development of the Yangtze River Economic Zone.

b. *Financial cooperation has been expanded continuously*

Singapore officially launched the cross-border RMB trade settlement service in 2009. In 2015, the two sides agreed to extend the pilot cross-border RMB service, which originally only covered the Suzhou Industrial Park and Tianjin Eco-city, to all of Suzhou City and the Tianjin Municipality; afterwards, the two sides decided to extend it to the China–Singapore Chongqing Cooperation Project. Such rapid development has indicated that China and Singapore will further achieve connectivity in the financial market, creating a huge developmental space for the enterprises and financial institutions of both countries.

c. *Great achievements can be made in new projects*

From the Belt and Road to the Asian Infrastructure Investment Bank, the future cooperation between Singapore and China can be expected. As a country along the 21st Century Maritime Silk Road, Singapore will be remarkable in status and role. Thanks to the geographical advantages due to an excellent natural harbor, as the logistics center, communication center and aviation center in the world, Singapore can provide full services for the 21st Century Maritime Silk Road. Furthermore, Singapore is also a founding member of the Asian Infrastructure Investment Bank. As the country with the highest level of development in Southeast Asia, Singapore enjoys a robust infrastructure ecosystem; Singapore's financial institutions have undertaken 70% of the infrastructure and financial projects in Southeast Asia. Thus, Singapore's experience can produce a good demonstration effect on the development of the Asian Infrastructure Investment Bank.

3. People-to-people exchanges

Singapore, a country dominated by the people of Chinese origin, has natural cultural ties with China; there is a huge space for people-to-people exchanges between the two countries. At present, tens of thousands of Chinese students receive education in Singapore, and this figure still increases year by year, while more than 5,000 Singaporeans study in China. Both countries will continuously introduce new cooperation modes in the educational field, thus boosting China–ASEAN educational exchanges and cooperation. Moreover, currently, China is the largest source of tourism as foreign exchange and the second largest tourist source for Singapore. As Singapore has gradually relaxed control over visas for Chinese citizens, more Chinese tourists will visit Singapore, promoting people-to-people exchanges between the two countries. The Singapore China Cultural Centre, officially inaugurated in November 2015, serves as an important means for promoting China–Singapore cultural cooperation, thus opening a new chapter for people-to-people exchanges between the two countries. It can be predicted that people-to-people exchanges between the countries will become normal.

Chapter 27

A Review of the Exportation of China's High-Speed Railway to Southeast Asia

Fang Jingjing*

The development of Asia's high-speed railway started in Japan. As Taiwan and South Korea have followed in Japan's footsteps to complete the construction of a high-speed railway, and China has built a network of high-speed railways across the country, the Asian high-speed railway market has entered the stage of fierce competition, two-power competition has just begun as China promotes high-speed railways in Southeast Asia. In order to vie for the market, it is essential for China, as an up-rising star, to conduct diplomatic mediation in this period. In recent years, the media have never stopped liking "high-speed railway diplomacy" in China; even in the eyes of foreign media, China has sought to use tactics. The exportation of China's high-speed railway to Southeast Asia may be a great event, but it is also easy to underestimate its difficulties. In fact, so far, China has only inked a deal on the exportation of a high-speed railway as a whole — the Jakarta–Bandung High-speed Railway Project. The railway projects based on cooperation between China and other Southeast Asian countries are not really high-speed rail projects; the railways

*Fang Jingjing, Research Assistant at the Laos Institute of the China–ASEAN Research Institute of Guangxi University.

under construction or to be built under the existing agreements are basically the medium-speed railways below 200 km/h. However, the construction of these transnational railways has initiated the exportation of high-speed railway as a whole, and also means that it is not impossible to export China's high-speed railway to Southeast Asia and build a trans-Asian high-speed railway network.

I. The Progress in the Exportation of China's High-speed Railway to Southeast Asia

The initiative and vision of China–Southeast Asia cooperation in railway construction has not been put forward only recently; the initiative of the Trans-Asian Railway had appeared earlier in the media, even the railway roadmap was once posted on media websites, but substantive progress was not really made until China put forward regional common development plans, such as the construction of the Belt and Road and the China–ASEAN Community with a Common Destiny. In 2015, progress was achieved in the planning of the Belt and Road put forward by China, a good start was made in exporting China's high-speed railway to Southeast Asia, but China faced fierce competition and hardship in this process.

1. The achievements in the exportation of China's high-speed railway to Southeast Asia

As China strives to promote high-speed rail projects in Southeast Asia, the Chinese Government has impressed the world as a vigorous supporter and promoter of China's high-speed railway, but only a small number of projects have been ultimately carried out; this may be associated with the short period of China's high-speed rail development, the supporting facilities along the industrial chain and maturity, or national diplomacy, policy and strategy. The first project of exporting high-speed railways as a whole — the Jakarta–Bandung High-speed Railway Project — marks the initiation of the export of China's high-speed railway or is a demonstration project, and China was subject to much disturbance in an effort to bid for the project. For the Singapore–Kuala Lumpur High-speed Railway Project, whose bidding will kick off soon, the media comments show that China is very likely to ultimately win the bidding, but it is difficult to measure that possibility of winning.

The Jakarta–Bandung High-speed Railway Project suffered setbacks. As early as 2011, Japan started to follow up the project and conduct a feasibility study, while China got involved in the project later. Originally, Japan was determined to win the bidding for the Jakarta–Bandung High-speed Railway Project, but Japan finally failed after competing with China in bidding for several months. It was not easy for China to ultimately win the bidding. China succeeded in the bidding just because China hit the key points which Indonesia had grappled with for a long time with respect to high-speed railway construction. After Joko served as the President of Indonesia, he honored the commitment to improving domestic infrastructure, but the issues concerning funds necessary for the high-speed railway project became an obstacle. China's final plan for the high-speed railway was that the price was lower than that set by Japan, and China did not require Indonesia to provide a governmental budget and a sovereign guarantee for the high-speed railway project. As China responded to the needs, it ultimately won the order involving cooperation in Indonesia's high-speed railway project.

The bidding is about to kick off with regard to the Singapore–Kuala Lumpur High-speed Railway Project connecting Singapore with Malaysia, and China will get caught up in the fierce competition with Japan. Japan responds through a consortium composed of enterprises, government support and the superior technical advantage relating to high-speed railways, while China does not retreat and still mainly promotes the advantages in project financing planning; China cooperated with Malaysian enterprises early on, paving the way for the bidding relating to the Singapore–Kuala Lumpur High-speed Railway Project. Besides the capital and technical advantages, China is responsible for nearly 80% of the existing railway projects in Malaysia; the recent example is the double-track electric train railway from Gemas to Johor Bahru, which was built by China Railway Corporation. However, there is uncertainty as to whether the Singapore section of the Singapore–Kuala Lumpur High-speed Railway Project will also be awarded to China. This is because Singapore's leadership generally shows prudence and concern. This will not be a smooth negotiation process (see Table 1).

Table 1. Chronicle of Events Involving the Exportation of China's High-speed Railway to Southeast Asia

	Events
Jakarta–Bandung High-speed Railway Project	In 2011, Japan spent USD 15 million to conduct a feasibility study of the Jakarta–Bandung High-speed Railway Project. In 2014, during the Beijing APEC Meeting, Xi Jinping met with the President of Indonesia Joko, the two sides focused on discussing infrastructure construction. In March 2015, the President of Indonesia Joko visited China, and the two sides signed the *Memorandum of Understanding between China and Indonesia on Cooperation on the Jakarta-Bandung High-speed Railway Project*. In April 2015, Chinese President Xi Jinping visited Indonesia, and the two sides signed the *Framework Arrangements for the Jakarta–Bandung High-speed Railway Project*. In July 2015, Japanese Prime Minister Shinzo Abe sent special envoy Hiroto Izumi to deliver the high-speed railway construction plans developed by Japan. In August, Chinese President Xi Jinping sent a special envoy, the Chairman of National Development and Reform Commission, Xu Shaoshi, to deliver the plan for the project developed by China. In October 2015, in the briefing held on October 1, the Minister of State-Owned Businesses of Indonesia Rini Soemarno said that Japan's plan was vetoed because it did not meet Indonesia's requirement of "not occupying a state budget and using a state guarantee". China's plan became the only choice for Indonesia. On October 16, 2015, the China Railway Corporation was awarded the Jakarta–Bandung High-speed Railway Project, making it the first project for all-round exportation of China's high-speed railway as an entire unit. In January 2016, the ground-breaking ceremony of the Jakarta–Bandung High-speed Railway Project was held. On March 16, 2016, the joint venture of the Jakarta–Bandung High-speed Railway Project signed a concession agreement with the Ministry of Transportation of Indonesia, suggesting that the important legal guarantee had been obtained for full construction of the Jakarta–Bandung High-speed Railway Project.

Table 1. (*Continued*)

	Events
Singapore–Malaysia (Singapore–Kuala Lumpur High-speed Railway Project)	On February 19, 2013, the Prime Minister of Malaysia, Najib Razak, met with the Prime Minister of Singapore, Lee Hsien Loong, the two sides announced that both countries had agreed to build a high-speed railway from Kuala Lumpur to Singapore, and that it was scheduled to be put into operation by 2020.
	On May 13, 2015, the deal on the terminal station of the Singapore–Kuala Lumpur high-speed railway, with a full length of 350 km, was basically finalized.
	In September 2015, the Ministry of Finance of Malaysia announced that the MyHSR Corp had been established.
	On October 7, 2015, the official website of the Public Land Transportation Commission of Malaysia released the Request for Expressions of Interest concerning the Singapore–Kuala Lumpur High-speed Railway Project jointly issued by the Public Land Transportation Commission of Malaysia and the Land Transportation Authority of Singapore, the preliminary work on the bidding of the Singapore–Kuala Lumpur High-speed Railway Project was initiated.
	On November 23, 2015, Chinese Premier Li Keqiang met with the Prime Minister of Malaysia, Najib Razak. The two sides actively discussed their cooperation on the construction of the Singapore–Kuala Lumpur high-speed railway, the railway construction in southern Malaysia and the China Malaysia Port Alliance.
	In December 2015, Tan Sri Syed Hamid Albar, Chairman of the Public Land Transportation Commission of Malaysia, said that the authority had invited 14 enterprises, including the China Railway Corporation, to discuss the Singapore–Kuala Lumpur High-speed Railway Project and offer relevant suggestions.

Source: The author's research.

2. The achievements in promoting China's cross-border railway

The year 2015 witnessed great achievements in exporting China's railway to Southeast Asia. In 2015, the foundation stone-laying ceremony was held with respect to the China–Laos Railway whose negotiation had lasted for 5 years, and the launching ceremony for the railway project based on cooperation between China and Thailand was held at the same time, suggesting the entry into the practice stage involving the railway line planned by China to connect Thailand, Malaysia and Singapore by means of the China–Laos Railway. In early November 2015, Chinese President Xi Jinping paid the first state visit to Vietnam, the two sides reached a series of agreements, including the agreements under which China and Vietnam will initiate the feasibility study of the Lào Cai Railway Project from Hanoi to the border, and the railway will be extended to Haiphong, the third largest city in Vietnam.

The substantive progress made in the cross-border railway lines between China and Southeast Asian countries was steadier than the progress on the exportation of China's high-speed railway to Southeast Asia, but such steadiness was achieved at the price of the suspension of the China–Myanmar Railway during its early stage. Originally, the Kyaukpyu–Kunming Railway between China and Myanmar advanced earlier than the China–Laos Railway and the China–Thailand Railway, but Myanmar's civic organizations and the residents in the areas along the Kyaukpyu–Kunming Railway lodged protests against the Government of Myanmar on many occasions, they claimed that the railway project would exert a negative impact on localities, and as a result, China suspended the railway project. Afterwards, in an effort to promote the China–Laos Railway, China became more cautious in the resettlement of the immigrants along the railway and the survey report on the surrounding environment of the railway. At present, relevant work is proceeding smoothly (see Table 2).

The cross-border railway which has been put into operation is mainly the cross-border railway from Kunming to Hekou, but the cross-border railway only links the areas within China to the border with Vietnam, and it does not go deep into Vietnam. The agreement on the Hanoi–Lào Cai–Haiphong Railway Project, reached during Chinese President Xi Jinping's visit to Vietnam in late 2015, covers the section, within Vietnam, of the China–Vietnam cross-border railway. Therefore, with respect to the originally planned international great corridor connecting China with

Table 2. The Chronicle of Events Involving the Exportation of China's High-speed Railway to Southeast China

	Events
The China–Thailand Railway	In April 2012, the Chinese Government and the Thai Government signed a memorandum of understanding on cooperation in railway development. China started to carry out the technical training relating to the high-speed railway among Thai working personnel, and the two sides jointly completed the feasibility study of the high-speed rails from Bangkok to Chiengmai and from Bangkok to Nong Khai.
	In October, 2013, China and Thailand signed the *Memorandum of Understanding between the Chinese Government and the Thai Government on the Intergovernmental Cooperation Projects Regarding the Development of Thailand's Railway Infrastructure and Thailand's Agricultural Product Exchange*; afterwards, they were put aside due to the coup d'état in Thailand.
	On June 9, 2014, the National Council for Peace and Order of Thailand, chaired by the military leader Prayuth Chan-ocha, decided to re-evaluate a number of large infrastructure construction projects, including China's "rice for high-speed railway".
	On December 19, 2014, Chinese Premier Li Keqiang met with the Prime Minister of Thailand, Prayuth Chan-ocha. After meeting, they jointly witnessed the signing of the *Memorandum of Understanding on Cooperation on the China–Thailand Railway.*
	On June 26, 2015, the Deputy Prime Minister of Thailand, Pridiyathorn Devakula, said that the high-speed railway plan for the China–Thailand Railway would be abandoned, and both sides would jointly build the 873 km medium-speed railway (express railway) at the designing speed of 160–180 km/h from Bangkok to Nong Khai.
	On December 3, 2015, the Chinese Government and the Thai Government signed the intergovernmental framework agreement on China–Thailand railway cooperation. The China–Thailand railway cooperation project is an 867 km double-track railway at a speed of about 180 km/h, including four lines: Bangkok–Kaeng Khoi, Kaeng Khoi–Map Ta Phut, Kaeng Khoi–Nakhon Ratchasima, and Nakhon Ratchasima–Nong Khai.

(*Continued*)

Table 2. (*Continued*)

	Events
	On December 19, 2015, the launching ceremony of the China–Thailand railway cooperation project was held at Chiang Rak Noi Railway Station in Ayutthaya Province, Thailand.
	On March 25, 2016, the Thai Government decided to only build the Bangkok–Nakhon Ratchasima section with the design speed increased to 250 km/h, and raise funds by itself, no longer seeking loans from China, with technology, signaling system and trains from China, raw materials, equipment, labor and subcontractors from Thailand.
The China–Laos Railway	On October 4, 2010, China and Laos signed the *Memorandum of Understanding on Railway Cooperation* and the *Meeting Minutes on Further Implementing* the *Memorandum of Understanding on Cooperation,* defining the China–Laos railway project.
	On December 23, 2010, the Tenth Session of the Sixth National Assembly of Laos ratified the plan for building a high-speed railway from China to Laos.
	On April 8, 2014, during the Boao Forum for Asia, the Prime Minister of Laos, Thongsing Thammavong, and Chinese Premier Li Keqiang jointly announced that the negotiation concerning the China–Laos intergovernmental railway agreement was initiated with a focus on pushing forward the China–Laos Railway.
	On August 31, 2015, construction was officially started at Yuxi, Yunnan Province, China, with respect to a section — the construction of which was scheduled to have started earlier — of the Yuxi-Mohan railway line, suggesting the official start of construction on the section within China of the China–Laos cross-border railway.
	On December 2, 2015, construction was started on the China-Laos Railway during the 40th anniversary of the founding of Laos. The Chairman of the Standing Committee of the National People's Congress of China, Zhang Dejiang, and the President of Laos, Choummaly Sayasone, attended the foundation stone-laying ceremony of the China–Laos Railway.
The Hanoi–Lào Cai–Haiphong Railway	On November 5, 2015, Chinese President Xi Jinping paid the first state visit to Vietnam. During this visit, the two sides reached an agreement on supporting and assisting the feasibility study of the Hanoi–Lào Cai–Haiphong Railway Project.

Source: The author's research.

Southeast Asia — the eastern, middle and western lines,[1] substantive progress has been made on the middle line and the eastern line, while temporarily no progress has been made in the section, within Myanmar, of the China–Myanmar cross-border railway. However, although the railway section, within Myanmar, of the western line along the Southeast Asia Great Corridor has been temporarily put aside, construction has never been stopped on the section, within China, of the China–Myanmar Railway. On December 6, 2015, construction was started on the Dali–Lincang Railway, an important project along the Bangladesh–China–Myanmar–India Economic Corridor to be built under the national *Medium and Long-term Railway Plan*. On January 24, 2016, construction was fully started on the Nujiang Bridge, a specially long-span bridge, the control project at the Daili–Ruili section of the China–Myanmar international railway.

The initiative and expectation of building railways and the golden corridor between China and Southeast Asian countries, and the Trans-Asian Railway network date back to the 1990s instead of 1–2 years ago, but they were postponed for various reasons. In 2010, the China–ASEAN Free Trade Area (CAFTA) was completed. It is now more urgent to plan and build the railway network connecting China with Southeast Asia. The completion of the above cross-border railway lines will be beneficial to strengthening the exchange of materials among Southeast Asian countries, accelerating the development of the Mekong River Basin, enhancing the connection between China and Southeast Asia and connecting two vast markets — China and the ASEAN community. The railway projects, which are of great significance and involve many countries, entail complicated international cooperation and international negotiations, so the almost perfect "Golden Corridor" connecting China with Southeast Asia remains at the initial stage.

[1] According to relevant plan, the middle line is an international railway channel from Kunming to Singapore, which starts from Kunming–Yuxi South Station, passes Simao, Jinghong, Shangyong, leaves China's territory at Mohan Port to enter Lao's territory; the west line starts from Guangtong, connects Dali Railway Station, passes Baoshan and leaves China's territory at Ruili to enter Kyaukpyu, Myanmar, finally reaching Singapore; the east line is an international railway channel from Kunming to Singapore, which starts at Kunming, extends southward, connects up with the Vietnam Railway at Hekou Port.

II. The Dilemmas in the Exportation of China's High-speed Railway to Southeast Asia

As China has been growing in the maturity of its high-speed railway technology and operational mileage, the countries around the world have turned their attention to China's high-speed railway and the high-speed railway orders obtained by China. The neighboring countries in Southeast Asia have focused their attention on China's high-speed railway at the same time, but whether the high-speed railway project orders can be carried out is another matter. Unlike a general railway, a high-speed railway involves high cost and high requirements for technical transformation. The vision of exporting China's high-speed railway to Southeast Asia is beautiful, but there are many dilemmas. First, one of these dilemmas is cost and an operational dilemma caused by high speed, so a number of economically underdeveloped countries in Southeast Asia cannot bear it and have to choose a general railway; second, the media have exaggerated such strategic planning as "high-speed rail diplomacy"; originally, Southeast Asian countries were concerned that China's dominance would suppress Southeast Asia; at this point, China is striving to promote its high-speed railway which cannot make profits in a short time; China also holds high the banner of solving financing difficulties, and this causes doubts among many conspiracy theorists; third, while pushing forward high-speed railway projects in Southeast Asia, China also provides supporting funds. It is difficult to assess whether this thoughtful marketing strategy and China's good faith can exert a positive impact.

1. The dilemma regarding high speed

According to international standards, a high-speed railway refers to the railway system whose speed exceeds 250 km/h if it is newly built or 200 km/h if it is renovated. Few railway projects based on cooperation between China and Southeast Asian countries can reach this standard, only the above-mentioned Jakarta–Bandung Project and the Singapore–Kuala Lumpur Project can be considered real high-speed railway projects, while other railway projects, including the China–Vietnam, the China–Laos and the China–Myanmar railway projects, have a design speed below 200 km/h. When the China–Thailand Railway was initiated in late 2015, the original plan was that the general railway below 200 km/h would be built, but the Thai Government changed its mind in late March 2016, and decided to first build the Bangkok–Nakhon Ratchasima railway section and put aside the other two sections; and it increased the speed for the Bangkok–Nakhon Ratchasima section to 250 km/h, almost the speed of a high-speed railway.

Changing the railway plan from a high-speed railway to a medium-speed or express railway is not an intentional act of countries. The economic strength imposes great constraints on many economically undeveloped countries in Southeast Asia, so they refrain from choosing a high-speed railway, which is a luxury, for economic considerations, and they have to turn to general necessities. The Southeast Asian countries are generally underdeveloped in infrastructure, so it is essential for them to build railways, but the building of a high-speed railway depends upon economic strength. Therefore, China's high-speed railway has been promoted to Southeast Asia in a wonderful way, but China's efforts are hindered by the high price of a high-speed railway. In reality, this goes beyond subjective factors and is not a totally bad thing. As China's high-speed railway shakes the Southeast Asian countries thanks to advanced technology, the Southeast Asian countries at a certain level of strength will choose the most cutting-edge technology, and the best evidence is Thailand, which changed its mind to choose a high-speed railway. Thailand is willing to reduce the construction of railway lines in order to build a section of high-speed railway, indicating that the Southeast Asian countries yearn for modernizing and upgrading their infrastructure; this may present an important prompt for China as it endeavors to promote its high-speed railway in Southeast Asia.

2. The dilemma in the government's intention and popular will

The Southeast Asian countries which have signed railway cooperation agreements with China show many uncertainties from planning to implementation. The greatest uncertainties are the government's intention and popular will, while the strife among great powers in Southeast Asia has also brought many troubles.

For the railway cooperation projects promoted by the Chinese Government in Southeast Asia, the two sides had good intentions at the initial stage; however, after consultations and negotiations, great powers with ill intentions stepped in, and as a result, many projects saw no progress for a long time. These changes in the international environment and the shift of the intentions in the senior leaders of the Southeast Asian countries have become the highly uncontrollable factors for China as it promotes its high-speed railway.

For example, the Kyaukpyu–Kunming Railway Project between China and Myanmar was made public in 2010, but no progress was made in the following 3 years; in March 2014, Japan announced that it would donate 7.8 billion yen (about 472 million yuan) to Myanmar for helping Myanmar build such infrastructure as a railway, and Japan meddled in Myanmar's railway construction; in May 2014, the Government of Myanmar announced that the China–Myanmar railway project could not be carried out because it was not approved by the people, putting the project completely aside. The Northern Luzon Railway Project in the Philippines, undertaken by a Chinese enterprise, was terminated. As early as 2003, the China National Machinery Industry Corporation and the Philippines officially signed the business contract on the Northern Luzon Railway Project in Manila. In 2006, it was reported that construction had officially started on Section One, Phase I, of the Northern Luzon Railway Project in the Philippines. The project was put aside in 2009; in 2012, the Government of the Philippines announced that the project had been terminated and the loans relating to the project from China were returned. In December 2015, Japan announced that it had signed a loan agreement worth USD 2 billion (about 12.7 billion yuan) with the Philippines with a view to building a passenger railway, so Japan entered the Philippines' railway construction field.

What China learns from the suspension of preliminary projects is that changes may occur with time. However, as China promoted railway cooperation in the later period, it lost no time in holding the launching ceremony, changes still cannot be prevented. For example, China and Thailand signed the *Memorandum of Understanding on Railway Cooperation* in December 2014, the launching ceremony was held 1 year later. However, the Thai Government changed its mind just two months after the launching ceremony. In fact, construction should have been started earlier on the China–Thailand railway cooperation, but construction was postponed again and again, and several rounds of negotiations between the two sides, designed to finalize the construction plan, failed.

After changes happened, the practical problems concerning the relations between China and Southeast Asian countries surfaced. The media made speculations: Are the relations between China and Southeast Asian countries firm and healthy as generally claimed? In the final analysis, exporting China's high-speed railway to Southeast Asia is a process of breaking away from the diplomatic and political dilemmas between China and Southeast Asian countries. In this process, China's speed, efficiency and technology are only catalysts, while the decisive factors are the government's intention and popular will in Southeast Asian countries.

3. The dilemma in brand and financing

The Southeast Asian countries engaging in cooperation with China on high-speed rail construction are mostly attracted by China's great capital strength, financing convenience and high-speed railway prices which are lower than those set by Japan, while the promotion of China's high-speed railway technology brand does not make China's advantages recognized as expected. For example, during the early stage of expected railway cooperation between China and Thailand, the Ministry of Transportation of Thailand and the Chinese side jointly held several road shows in 4–5 provinces along the proposed railway; however, so far, only the people in Nakhon Ratchasima Province are optimistic about China's railway technology.

The formidable competitor for China's high-speed railway in Southeast Asia is Japan's Shinkansen. Japan has carefully operated Shinkansen's brand and technology for several decades, making Shinkansen deeply rooted among the people, so it will take time for China to obtain the high-speed railway orders from the Southeast Asian countries. The strong advantage from China's combination of high-speed railway projects and financing cannot result in a unique monopolistic advantage; on the contrary, China provides financing convenience, but Japan enjoys the advantage of a low interest rate. In late 2015, in the bidding for the Bombay–Ahmedabad high-speed railway project in India, Japan utilized the preferential loan policy to prevail over China and ultimately won the order. As indicated, as China promotes the high-speed railway in Southeast Asia, it is difficult to win in the protracted war merely relying on financing convenience and price advantage. Furthermore, China's combination of high-speed railway projects and financing is a good thing, but whether the Southeast Asian countries will accept China's solution is another matter. In most cases in which China finances railway construction in Southeast Asia, joint ventures were established for joint construction, and China also participates in railway operations.

Will the Southeast Asian countries worry that the mode of joint venue plus joint operations violates their "right of way"? Regarding China–Thailand railway construction, Thailand finally decided to raise funds by itself, one view held that Thailand was unwilling to let China get involved in its domestic railway operations, while another view held that Thailand believed that the loan interest rate provided by China to Thailand was too high compared with the financing for Indonesia's high-speed railway project. Regardless of the reasons, this is a dilemma amidst the advantage from China's combination with financing, the advantage becomes a bargaining chip for the Southeast Asian countries, running counter to China's original idea of financing railway construction. Moreover, as China vigorously promotes high-speed railway projects, it is also necessary for China to evaluate financing risks. Although the exportation of China's high-speed railway focuses on a future long-term plan, it is essential to consider the risk of capital recovery.

III. The Outlook for the Exportation of China's High-speed Railway to Southeast Asia

China's high-speed railway technology results from introduction, assimilation and re-innovation. China successively learnt from Sweden, Canada, Germany, France and Japan. After introducing technology, China renovated it and developed the proprietary intellectual property rights of the high-speed railway, so China can export its high-speed railway to other countries without restrictions. It is worth noting that when China introduced high-speed railway technology, it intentionally fostered a domestic high-speed railway industrial chain; China required that all the components necessary for a high-speed railway manufactured by China must be made in China, even if the components temporarily cannot be made in China and must be purchased from foreign countries, foreign companies cannot be included in the procurement list unless they established joint ventures with domestic enterprises. Such a hard-and-fast requirement and measure has enabled many domestic manufacturers to rapidly upgrade their technologies and has improved the whole high-speed railway industrial chain. At present, the overall design of China's high-speed railway is conducted by Chinese rolling stock manufacturers, and its final assembly and commissioning are also carried out by domestic rolling stock manufacturers. All this is the embodiment of China's excellent high-speed railway technology.

China has made great progress in its high-speed railway technology, and comes out in front in the design speed and operational mileage of high-speed railways; China is not inferior to Japan, Germany and France in these respects. In China, like such programs as aerospace activities and lunar exploration, the high-speed railway is regarded as a national scientific and technological program of innovation. Thanks to China's vigorous technical support, excellent high-speed railway operational planning and rich experience, China is sufficient to meet the high-speed railway construction needs of the Trans-Asian Railway line; this is undoubtedly true. Furthermore, there is a complete high-speed railway industrial chain in China, so China can provide one-package service as China contracts for building high-speed railway projects in Southeast Asia. Compared with the mere exportation of technology and subsequent subcontracting of other works, China's solution is more able to fill the gap in financial resources and technical workers in the Southeast Asian countries.

From another perspective, the Asian Infrastructure Investment Bank (AIIB) — China plays the leading role in its establishment — focuses on supporting infrastructure construction and also works on promoting connectivity in Asia; it will serve as the vigorous financial support for exporting China's high-speed railway to Southeast Asia. Large railway transportation projects have always faced the struggle to strike a balance between business interests and social benefits; for example, the Southeast Asian countries adopt the internationally-accepted Public–Private Partnership (PPP) mode; the large projects involving a long period of time and uncertainties in investment returns are less attractive to commercial banks but are suitable for the AIIB, and sovereign wealth funds for participation. Therefore, from the long-term perspective, as the financial support for infrastructure construction, the AIIB will gradually perform its great functions and will help export China's high-speed railway to Southeast Asia.

Part 5

A Short Review of Country-Specific Research on the ASEAN Community in 2015

Part 5

Chapter 28
An Analysis of the Kra Canal Plan

Liu Xinyuan*

The Kra Canal Plan is a canalization plan developed by the Thai Government. The core of the plan is that an artificial canal, connecting the Gulf of Thailand with the Andaman Sea, is dug at Thailand's Isthmus of Kra. Geographically, the proposed canal is situated in the hinterland of southern Thailand; it connects the Indochina Peninsula on the north, the Malay Peninsula on the south, faces the Gulf of Thailand on the east and the Andaman Sea on the west. Upon completion, the canal will offer a new waterway connecting the Indian Ocean with the Pacific Ocean, and it will play an important role in waterway transportation. Thus the plan for digging such an extremely valuable artificial canal has still not been abandoned though it dates back 100 years; meanwhile, controversies have never stopped.

I. The Origin and Development of the Kra Canal Plan

In the history of Thailand, there were not a few developmental plans for utilizing the natural conditions of the Isthmus of Kra to dig artificial canals like the Kra Canal Plan. These plans were very bold, but they got nowhere for various reasons. However, in the 21st century with a high scientific,

---

* Liu Xinyuan, Research Assistant at the Thailand Institute of the China–ASEAN Research Institute of Guangxi University.

technological and production level, when the Kra Canal Plan is once again mentioned by Western media, it creates a great sensation.

1. The origin of the Kra Canal Plan

Historically, during the period of Emperor Wanli (1573–1620) in the Ming Dynasty, Thai King Naresuan in the Ayutthaya Dynasty envisioned an artificial canal connecting the Indian Ocean with the Pacific Ocean in southern Thailand.[1] Unfortunately, the technical conditions at that time could not turn his idea into reality. In A.D. 1677, when King Narai, called the King of the Siamese Ayutthaya Kingdom, reigned, based on conducting a feasibility study of the canal project, the French engineer de Lamar systematically put forward, for the first time, a complete plan for digging a canal at the Isthmus of Kra.[2] In the Bangkok Dynasty, Thai King Rama V once again envisioned an artificial waterway connecting the Pacific Ocean with the Indian Ocean. In order to realize this idea, Thai King Rama V once visited European countries with the hope of adopting the advanced technology of European countries to turn his great idea into reality. However, the ensuing world war made Chulalongkorn (Rama V)'s efforts fruitless.

2. The development of the Kra Canal Plan

After the Second World War, Thailand ushered in a golden age of economic development. With the rapid development of the national economy, the Thai Government showed strong interest in the Kra Canal Plan, PTT Public Company Limited once carried out a feasibility study of the plan, but the Thai National Security Council held that the implementation of the plan would adversely affect Thailand's national security and forcibly suspended the plan. In the 1970s, the economic and political contacts became increasingly close between Thailand and USA, the US enterprise TAMS and the US Lawrence Livermore National Laboratory (LLNL) also cooperated on

[1] Ling Shuo, Behind the "Mist" at Thailand's Isthmus of Kra: It Is Not Easy to Dig a Canal, Xinhuanet, May 22, 2015.

[2] Sun Haiyong, The Kra Canal Plan: Challenges, Significance and China's Strategic Choice, *Pacific Journal*, 2014(7).

planning a rational canal channel route for the Kra Canal Plan. During the 1980s, the Thai Government and the US Government cooperated to conduct a profound feasibility study of the Kra Canal Plan, and some experts even proposed digging a canal by means of nuclear explosions for a peaceful purpose.[3] However, that discussion did not ultimately give rise to a canal. As Thailand's political circle became turbulent due to frequent coup d'états, the Thai Government's attention to the Kra Canal Plan decreased greatly. The Thai Government did not anchor its hope on digging a canal to revitalize Thailand's economy until the economic crisis in the period 1997–1998. Unfortunately, afterwards, coup d'états still occurred frequently in Thailand's political circle, so the implementation of the Kra Canal Plan was postponed indefinitely.

II. The Significance of the Implementation of the Kra Canal Plan

Being strategically located, the Kra Canal, once dug and put into operation, will exert an inestimable impact on Thailand, on Asia and even on the whole world. Specifically, the importance of carrying out the Kra Canal Plan is mainly reflected in the following aspects:

1. At the economic level: multiple parties will obtain benefits

The Kra Canal is likely to attract widespread attention because it can connect the Indian Ocean with the Pacific Ocean and serve as another shipping channel connecting both oceans in addition to the Strait of Malacca. It will provide a new shipping channel to about 520,000 vessels currently passing through the Strait of Malacca. Once the canal is dug, these vessels can change their course to the canal for shortening by a great distance compared with other straits; the canal can help greatly reduce both shipping time and operating costs (as shown in Table 1). As for the host country of the canal, the Thai Government will collect a "canal toll" from the vessels passing through the canal according

[3]Meghan Rouillard and Asuka Saito, Building the Kra Canal and Southeast Asian Development. Executive Intelligence Review, October 11, 2013, p. 20.

Table 1. The Impact of the Kra Canal on Shipping

Name of shipping route	Distance saved (km)	Time saved (day)
The Strait of Malacca	1200–1400	1–3
The Sunda Strait	2500–3000	4–5
The Lombok Strait	3000–3500	5–7

Source: The author's research.

to a certain standard. Although a single "canal toll" is not high, as indicated by rough estimates from the media, even if it is expected that only 300–400 vessels pass through the canal each day,[4] the income from the "canal toll" is considerable. From this perspective, the canal is very important for the host country, vessels and for the development of the ocean shipping industry in the countries along the Indian Ocean and the Pacific Ocean.

2. Energy security in East Asia can be guaranteed

In recent years, the crude oil imported to East Asia mainly came from the Middle East and Africa and was transported mainly through the Strait of Malacca. The Strait of Malacca is extremely important for the energy security in the East Asian countries. As estimated by BP, from 2011 to 2030, the global energy demand will soar by 36%, and 93% of the newly increased energy demand will come from non-OECD countries; by 2030, oil and gas will account for 53% of global energy consumption. At present, the Strait of Malacca is the second largest seaway following the Strait of Dover. According to incomplete statistics, about 70,000 vessels pass through the Strait of Malacca each year. Since the beginning of the 21st century, the academic circle has paid increasing attention to the Malacca Dilemma, while the Malacca Dilemma is caused by the following factors: First, the transportation capacity of the Strait of Malacca is close to saturation, the channel conditions restrict the tonnage and number of vessels; second, piracy, terrorist activities and accidents may lead to the interruption of shipping in the Strait of Malacca. Given these factors, the Kra Canal can further diversify the channels for

[4]Ling Shuo, Five Questions about Thailand's Canal, *Hainan Daily*, May 23, 2015.

importing energy to East Asia, it is conducive to guaranteeing energy security in East Asia, and it can play a crucial role in economic growth and economic security in the East Asian countries.

3. At a military level: the strategies of multiple countries will change

After the Second World War, tremendous changes took place on the world's political and military landscape; the standoff between the East and the West existed for a long time. Although global economic integration has, to a certain extent, eased the tension between the countries in the East and the West, the important channels connecting the Indian Ocean with the Pacific Ocean, mainly the Strait of Malacca, remain the focus of attention from various countries, and many countries, led by USA, have deployed military forces near the Strait of Malacca. Once the Kra Canal is put into operation, it will be as strategically important as the Strait of Malacca from a military perspective as it will play an important role in connecting the Indian Ocean with the Pacific Ocean.[5] The countries led by USA will certainly adjust their military deployment, and this will trigger chain reactions, thus many countries will adjust their military policies toward Southeast Asia accordingly.

III. Main Challenges for the Kra Canal Plan

Considering that the Kra Canal Plan has suffered many setbacks, its development is tortuous and it is still at the stage of theoretical planning; the efforts to promote the Kra Canal Plan are still subject to many grave challenges. Specifically, these challenges are mainly embodied in the following aspects:

1. Pressure of huge capital

In early 2003, the Thai Government authorized a Hong Kong-based specialized company to conduct a feasibility study of the Kra Canal Plan. The company

[5]Wang Qun, Jiang Li, An Analysis of the Security Issue at the Strait of Malacca, *Marine Information*, 2014(2).

concluded that the cost for completing the whole Kra Canal Plan would hit USD 25 billion, and the construction period would be 10–15 years. Thirteen years have gone by since the plan was introduced and the technology for digging the canal has improved greatly, but the overall cost for digging the canal has surged. In such an economic environment, the management of the construction of such a gigantic artificial project will require more funds than expected. The investment funds on an unclear scale will exert a heavy fiscal burden on the Thai Government.

2. The turbulent political situation in Thailand

In the late 20th century and early 21st century, the Thai Government planned to promote the Kra Canal Plan. However, afterwards, frequent coups d'état changed the political landscape in Thailand, thus aborting the Kra Canal Plan. Moreover, although Thailand is a Buddhist country, about 5% of Thailand's population are Muslim, and more than 65% of the Muslim population is concentrated in the Pattani area in southern Thailand.[6] The cultural difference caused by a difference in faith has made a certain impact on the political stability in southern Thailand. Fundamentally, the implementation of the Kra Canal Plan must be based on consensus and support from the Muslim communities in southern Thailand, but the Muslim communities in southern Thailand have no consensus on this issue, so it is difficult to address it.

3. Complicated pressure from the outside world

The importance of the Strait of Malacca for the Asia-Pacific region is self-evident. As the Kra Canal has not yet been dug, the US Pivot to the Asia-Pacific strategy focuses on the Strait of Malacca, making it difficult to overcome the Malacca Dilemma at present. The Kra Canal is considered by many countries as the best way to tackle the Malacca Dilemma.[7] Once the

---

[6]Gong Haoqun, The Dilemmas in National and Ethnic Integration: Fission in the Malay Muslim Society in Southern Thailand since the 20th Century, *Southeast Asian Studies*, 2011(3).

[7]Li Ying, Why Is Thailand's Kra Canal Project Mysterious? www.cankaoxiaoxi.com, May 25, 2015.

Kra Canal is available, it will undoubtedly replace the Strait of Malacca to become the new strategically important place in the Asia-Pacific region. USA certainly hopes to exert its influence on the host country of the Kra Canal. Likewise, once the Kra Canal is completed, in order to ensure that the Strait of Malacca — the marine lifeline — is smooth, Japan will also exert its political influence on the host country of the Kra Canal which is as important as the Strait of Malacca. India, which is implementing the Look East Strategy, also plans to expand its naval base in the Andaman Islands, so as to enhance India's influence on the security of the sea areas near the Strait of Malacca. These countries are trying to exert their influence on the host country of the Kra Canal. If the Thai Government fails to properly handle the relations with any of these countries, the implementation of the Kra Canal Plan will be affected.

Chapter 29

The Dollarization of the Cambodian Currency: Process, Causes, Advantages and Disadvantages

Li Xiongshi*

Since 1992, the US dollar has gradually replaced Cambodia's domestic currency, the riel, to become the largest currency in use and circulation in Cambodia, making Cambodia one of the typical countries with a currency dollarization in today's world. Since then, more than 20 years have elapsed. The dollarization of the Cambodian currency stemmed from a special historical background and practical considerations. Currency dollarization is a double-edged sword for Cambodia's economy; it has brought advantages and disadvantages. In recent years, the Government of Cambodia has gradually realized that currency dollarization is not a long-term strategy for the development of Cambodia's economy. Currency dollarization at that time was based on the reality that advantages outweighed disadvantages, but now the actual situation is totally different: For the Government of Cambodia which is committed to developing domestic economy and restoring the financial system, currency dollarization has greatly hindered the economy.

* Li Xiongshi, Full-time Assistant at the Data Center of the China–SEAN Research Institute of Guangxi University, Research Assistant at the Cambodia Institute of the China–ASEAN Research Institute of Guangxi University.

In response to dilemmas, the Government of Cambodia has started to make some de-dollarization efforts, which have produced some effects; the people's confidence in the domestic currency, the riel, has been gradually enhanced. According to the latest data released by the National Bank of Cambodia, since 2015, the riel has gradually appreciated, reflecting an increasing confidence of the international community in the riel. Of course, Cambodia cannot achieve de-dollarization in a short time. Shaking the status of the US dollar in Cambodia's economic life is a systematic and complex task. This chapter is designed to present the process of the dollarization of the Cambodian currency and analyze the causes, advantages and disadvantages.

I. The Process of the Dollarization of the Cambodian Currency

Currency dollarization means that the residents of a country hold a considerable part of foreign currency assets in their assets. Currency dollarization mainly occurred in the period of the 1970s–1990s. In this regard, there are three phenomena: Currency dollarization occurred in Latin American countries in the period of the 1970s–1980s; it appeared in the Soviet Union and eastern European countries in the period from the early 1980s–1990s; and it occurred in some small emerging open economies. As a typical country with currency dollarization, Cambodia was part of the third phenomenon. In every part of Cambodia, the US dollar can be found; the US dollar has replaced the domestic currency, the riel, to become a common currency and one that is widely accepted by the people in Cambodia. For a long period of time, the wages for workers, even civil servants, were paid in US dollars, while the riel was only used on some "small occasions", such as making change for buying something.

As the foreign currency in Cambodia was basically the US dollar, the degree of currency dollarization was calculated by the foreign currency deposit divided by M2. As shown in Figure 1, as of 1993, currency dollarization has shown a long-term upward trend in Cambodia. In 1995, the degree of currency dollarization in Cambodia exceeded 50%; afterwards, it was not lower than that level. It showed an obvious short-time decline during the Asian financial crisis in 1998, but it basically grew in other years; in particular, in recent years, the degree of currency dollarization has stood at about 80%. Even though the Government of Cambodia has taken some measures

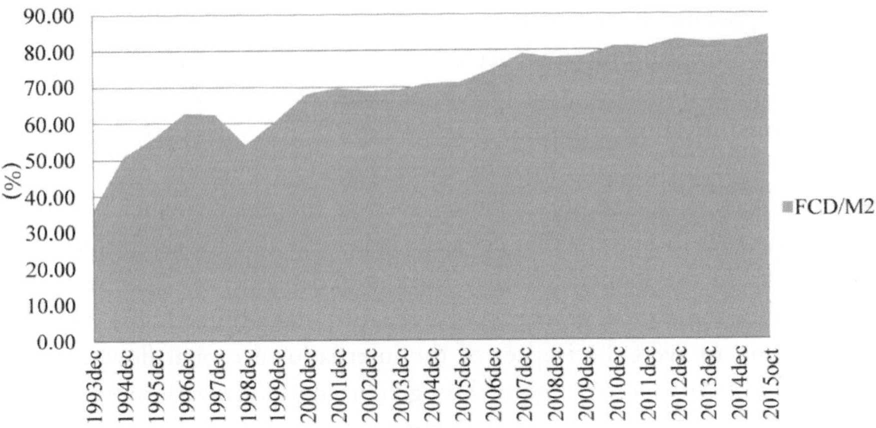

Figure 1. The Degree of Currency Dollarization in Cambodia

Source: Selected Issue: dollarization Issue: Advantages, disadvantages and ways forward, April 2015, World Bank; Economic and monetary statistics, National Bank of Cambodia.

to promote the use and circulation of the domestic currency, the riel, the status of the US dollar remains unshakable.

II. The Causes for Currency Dollarization in Cambodia

The dollarization of the Cambodian currency resulted from a special historical background and practical considerations. Overall, it can be analyzed from the perspectives of the international background and Cambodia's real situation:

1. From the perspective of the international background

In the 1990s, with the deepening economic globalization, an increasingly large and rapid flow of international capital, the greatest external impact on or threat to the small, weak economies, especially the emerging open market economies, shifted from the original fluctuation of import and export prices to the flow of international capital; the sudden change in the direction and quantity of the international capital flow greatly disrupted their economies. The direct consequence was that a country under a floating exchange rate system did not necessarily gain independence on monetary policy (according to the Impossible Trinity Theory, a country under the floating exchange rate system can gain independence on monetary policy by allowing the free flow of capital and a free float of the exchange rate); in other words, when international investors withdraw massive capital from these economies, the economies under the pure floating exchange rate system are likely to face the risk of an exchange rate collapse (such as the Asian financial crisis in 1997); in order to prevent that collapse, it is inevitable for the interest rate to increase, so the monetary policy loses its independence. Against such a background, some small emerging open-market economies choose currency dollarization to avert the impact of the international capital flow, namely, currency independence is forgone through currency dollarization, so that the currency value becomes stable and capital flows freely almost "forever". In the 1990s, the countries which adopted the policy of currency dollarization were not rare; for example, Argentina, Turkey, Israel and Poland had different degrees of currency dollarization. Against such an international background, there were references for currency dollarization, and currency dollarization was a natural choice for Cambodia, a small emerging open economy.

2. From Cambodia's perspective

The currency dollarization in Cambodia resulted from a series of historical events. These events dented the trust of Cambodian people in the ability of the government to stabilize the value of their domestic currency, the riel, and finally the people lost confidence altogether; this was the most fundamental cause for currency dollarization in Cambodia. As early as the period of the Khmer Republic during the years 1970–1975, a certain quantity of US dollars were circulating in Cambodia, but the domestic currency, the riel, remained the main currency. During the years 1975–1979, the Khmer Rouge was in power, Cambodia's financial system was systematically damaged, even the National Bank of Cambodia was destroyed, so that trade was dominated by barter trade; rice or gold once served as the universal equivalent in the later period of the Khmer Rouge regime. In 1980, Cambodia's central bank — the People's Bank of Cambodia — was re-established, the riel once again became the legal tender in Cambodia; the People's Bank of Cambodia played multiple roles at that time, including monetary authority, government cash machine and the only commercial bank service institution (providing such services as deposits, loans and a payment tool). Under the then centralization of authority, Cambodia practiced a planned economy; although foreign currencies, including the US dollar and the Thai baht, were restricted by the government from being used, with the concerns about the political system and the security situation at that time, the people's confidence in the riel was still at a low level; Cambodian people still generally held the US dollar and the Thai baht, especially gold, as the tools for the preservation of value. In the late 1980s, Cambodia started to transform from a planned economy to a market economy, it carried out reform and opening-up, and both politically and economically leant towards the West. The US dollar massively flowed into Cambodia, initiating the process of currency dollarization. During the years 1991–1992, the United Nations Transitional Authority in Cambodia (UNTAC) was established and USD 1.7 billion were injected, thus the US dollar poured into Cambodia and started to be used as the medium of exchange and the charge unit together with the domestic currency, it served as a reserve currency together with the domestic currency. In that period, Cambodia was economically underdeveloped, causing an insufficiency of taxes; moreover, the fiscal policy was inefficient and there was no international aid, so the government deficit was high; the government forced the central bank to issue more riel, and this measure directly led to a rapid depreciation of the riel, finally an alarming inflation occurred, dealing a massive blow to the people's confidence in their domestic currency. In 1992, inflation was controlled in Cambodia, the purchasing power of the riel had been battered, and as a result, the US dollar was widely used, like other areas with a high inflation rate in the world, dollarization rapidly spread in Cambodia. During the years 1997–1998, the Asian financial crisis broke out, Cambodia's economy reached a high degree of currency dollarization and thus obtained benefits, the impact of the financial crisis on Cambodia was mitigated, and the status of the US dollar was further consolidated.

III. The Advantages and Disadvantages of Currency Dollarization in Cambodia

According to the above causes for currency dollarization in Cambodia, the dollarization was a process of weighing advantages and disadvantages. The US dollar is a double-edged sword for Cambodia's economy. It has brought gains and caused losses to Cambodia's economy and society. In the following part, we analyze the advantages and disadvantages of currency dollarization in Cambodia:

1. Advantages

First, currency dollarization has created good policy conditions for Cambodia's economic development in the past 20 years, thus bolstering its economic development during those years. Currency dollarization brought about strict financial discipline and contained Cambodia's impulse of banknote printing — this behavior caused an inflationary spiral in Cambodia in the 1980s and the early 1990s. Currency dollarization linked the riel to the US dollar, ensuring price stability and providing a good environment for a healthy economic development.

Second, currency dollarization eliminated exchange rate risks. That elimination had two advantages: (1) reducing the transaction costs in Cambodia's foreign trade — transaction costs include service charges for currency exchange and the obstructions to trade opportunities caused by exchange rate risk — and boosting Cambodia's exports; (2) helping Cambodia attract more capital and achieve a high level of opening up, developing Cambodia into a country with free trade and investment, enabling it to better participate in the international division of labor.

Finally, currency dollarization enhanced Cambodia's ability to withstand the external impact from the liquidity shortage of the US dollar. There were many US dollars in circulation in Cambodia; they were able to cover the deficit in Cambodia's financial sector in case of US dollar shortage and serve as a foreign exchange reserve.

2. Disadvantages

First, currency dollarization deprived Cambodia of the independence of its monetary policy. In particular, it made the central bank no longer capable of serving as the lender of the last resort, so Cambodia's central bank could not take active and well-targeted measures to cope with the economic cycle and external impact, such as adopting the expansionary monetary policy to address unemployment and utilizing exchange rate tools to keep an international balance of payment for a certain period of time and sharpen the competitiveness of domestic products.

Second, currency dollarization incurred a coinage tax loss to the Government of Cambodia. The coinage tax is a kind of revenue and comes from the book value of currency in circulation minus its production cost. According to rough estimates, the coinage tax loss incurred to the Government of Cambodia was USD 1–2 billion.

Third, most bulk commodities and oil on the international market were denominated in and settled by the US dollar, so the prices of bulk commodities and oil rose on the international market; it was very easy to import an inflation impact into Cambodia through the US dollar.

Finally, currency dollarization may also cause Cambodia to be disadvantaged in international trade competition. In the early stage, USA was the main export market for Cambodia, currency dollarization removed the exchange rate risks for both sides, so Cambodia enjoyed advantages in its exportation to USA, the amount of Cambodia's exports grew, and the exportation of ready-made garments had a high status in its economic development. However, as the export destinations for Cambodia became diverse and the status of the US market declined, currency dollarization reduced the export competitiveness of Cambodian products in other areas.

IV. Conclusions

Currency dollarization was a choice which Cambodia was forced to make in its special historical period. At present, the Government of Cambodia has realized the necessity for de-dollarization and has taken some measures to increase the needs for using its domestic currency, the riel; this is undoubtedly of important significance for the long-term healthy development of Cambodia's economy in the future. The author, however, holds that de-dollarization is a long-term complicated and systematic task and entails long-term planning; de-dollarization cannot be sought in a too hasty way and should be pursued gradually. On the one hand, currently the US dollar still makes many contributions to Cambodia's economic development; if Cambodia rashly introduces some de-dollarization measures, they may trigger fluctuation in economic development, thus the introduction of relevant measures should take into account the market response and the degree of acceptance by the people; on the other hand, the growth of economic strength is the source of confidence for any national currency, and the process of de-dollarization should be supported by continuous economic development and improvement in Cambodia. For Cambodia, only when the economy develops healthily can a sufficient policy space be created for de-dollarization. Long-term benign economic development requires long-term planning, prevention of short-sighted behavior and steady and solid improvement. Therefore, Cambodia needs to gradually carry out the de-dollarization policy amidst long-term healthy economic development; in the meantime, proper de-dollarization is also conducive to further developing Cambodia's economy.

Chapter 30

A Brief Analysis of Aung San Suu Kyi's Ice-Breaking Trip to China

Yu. Guan Yudong*

On June 10, 2015, at the invitation of the International Department of the Central Committee of the Communist Party of China, Aung San Suu Kyi, the leader of the National League for Democracy — the largest opposition party in Myanmar, made a 5-year ice-breaking trip to China. She visited Beijing, Shanghai and Kunming, arousing great enthusiasm for Myanmar in China. Aung San Suu Kyi's visit to China drew widespread attention from the media because she was an important figure in Myanmar's political circle. She visited China during the sensitive and subtle period of China–Myanmar relations. The Western media held that her visit to China was a pragmatic choice made in response to Myanmar's presidential election in November. The Burmese media paid more attention to economic development and believed that her visit to China would bring more economic interests to Myanmar.

* Yu. Guan Yudong, Research Assistant at the Myanmar Institute of the China–ASEAN Research Institute of Guangxi University.

I. Aung San Suu Kyi's Visit to China: A Good Thing Did Not Come Easily

The Chinese Government has long engaged with Aung San Suu Kyi. During the years 1988–1989, the then Chinese ambassador to Myanmar, Cheng Ruisheng, met with Aung San Suu Kyi on many occasions, laying a solid foundation for the later engagement between China and Aung San Suu Kyi and the National League for Democracy.[1] The National League for Democracy, led by Aung San Suu Kyi, achieved a landslide victory in Myanmar's first general election in 1990; however, the Burmese military government did not recognize the election result, refused to hand over the political power, and declared that the National League for Democracy was an illegal organization; Aung San Suu Kyi was put under long-term house arrest. In the subsequent 20 years, Aung San Suu Kyi was intermittently put under house arrest by the military government for 15 years. The engagement between China and the National League for Democracy of Aung San Suu Kyi was interrupted; Aung San Suu Kyi was not allowed to visit China.

After Aung San Suu Kyi was released in November, 2010, she stepped into politics again and frequently appeared in the international arena. She visited USA, Europe, Japan and India and received a high level of courteous reception, but she was not allowed to visit China, Myanmar's most important neighbor. For her, this was an unfavorable political regret for consolidating her influence in Myanmar. Whether Aung San Suu Kyi could visit China and when she would visit China became an important issue in the international public opinion.[2] She expressed the willingness to visit China on many public occasions, China also conveyed an active signal of welcoming her visit, but the plan for her visit to China was postponed for various reasons. Aung San Suu Kyi originally planned to visit China in December, 2014, but her plan was delayed due to her diplomatic status. In June 2015, she ultimately successfully visited China.

[1]Li Chenyang, An Analysis of Aung San Suu Kyi's Visit to China, *World Affairs*, 2015(13), p. 26.

[2]Jia Xiudong, A Visit with Win–win Outcome for China and Myanmar, *People's Daily Online*, June 15, 2015, http:// www.people.com.cn.

II. An Analysis of China's Invitation to Aung San Suu Kyi to Visit China

1. China attached great importance to Aung San Suu Kyi's visit to China

When Aung San Suu Kyi was in Beijing, she met with the General Secretary of the Communist Party of China, Chinese President Xi Jinping; the two sides held talks on the issues concerning China and Myanmar, and the development of the relations between the two parties. Vice Chairman of the National Committee of the Chinese People's Political Consultative Conference, the Minister of the International Department of the Central Committee of the Communist Party of China, Wang Jiarui, State Councilor Yang Jiechi, Vice chairman of the Standing Committee of the National People's Congress, Chairman of the All-China Women's Federation Shen Yueyue met with her.[3] When Aung San Suu Kyi was in Shanghai, Han Zheng, a member of the Political Bureau of the Central Committee of the Communist Party of China, the Secretary of the Shanghai Municipal Party Committee met with her.[4] As mentioned before, China attached great importance to Aung San Suu Kyi's visit to China. However, some domestic media reported that China gave an exceptionally courteous reception to Aung San Suu Kyi; the Chinese ambassador to Myanmar broke diplomatic practices to bid farewell to her at the airport. The report was untrue. Chinese ambassador Yang Houlan greeted important political figures of Myanmar, who were returning to Myanmar after visiting China. On many occasions he bid farewell to important political figures of Myanmar, who departed for China, more than once; for example, on November 7, 2014, he bid farewell to the President of Myanmar Thein Sein, who departed for China to attend the Dialogue on Strengthening Connectivity Partnership, at the Naypyidaw International Airport.[5] On November 9, 2014, the President of Myanmar, Thein Sein, returned to Naypyidaw after attending the Dialogue on Strengthening the Connectivity Partnership in Beijing, and the Chinese ambassador Yang

[3]June 10, 2015, http://www.xinhuanet.com.

[4]June 13, 2015, http://www.xinhuanet.com.

[5]November 8, 2014, http://www.fmprc.gov.cn.

Houlan greeted him at the Naypyidaw International Airport.[6] On April 25, 2015, when the President of the Union Solidarity and Development Party, Thura Shwe Mann, departed for China, the Chinese ambassador, Yang Houlan, bid farewell to him at the airport.[7]

2. China did not intentionally choose the time of inviting Aung San Suu Kyi to visit China

As China had invited Aung San Suu Kyi to visit China, China needed to communicate with the Government of Myanmar and also arrange the appropriate time for Chinese President Xi Jinping and Aung San Suu Kyi's meeting; the preparatory work took a certain period of time. Furthermore, China had long planned the invitation of Aung San Suu Kyi to visit China, the invitation was absolutely not associated with the situation in northern Myanmar and the military exercise conducted by the Chinese People's Liberation Army at the China–Myanmar border on June 2. The media intensely analyzed Aung San Suu Kyi's visit to China, but their analyses were assumptions, including the following: "China intentionally invited the leader of the opposition party Aung San Suu Kyi to visit China during the sensitive period of China–Myanmar relations; this invitation was a further response to the incident in which the Burmese military dropped bombs onto China's territory. In doing so, China exerted pressure on the Burmese authorities and sent an unusual warning to the Government of Myanmar: China will make great adjustments regarding its policy toward Myanmar."

III. Aung San Suu Kyi's Visit to China: A Pragmatic Action

Myanmar's general election was held in November 2015. Although Aung San Suu Kyi had no opportunity to be elected as the President of Myanmar, the National League for Democracy, led by her, won the general election, and faced a number of pressing political issues, including Myanmar's process of democratization, the domestic economic development, the conflicts between

---

[6]November 11, 2014, http://www.fmprc.gov.cn.

[7]April 25, 2015, http://www.xinhuanet.com.

the government troops and armed ethnic groups, religious and ethnic conflicts.[8] The National League for Democracy lacks governance experience, and Myanmar's economic foundation is weak. Maintaining good relations with China, the neighboring giant, can improve the influence of the National League for Democracy in Myanmar, and actively promote constitutional amendments strongly demanded by the National League for Democracy and its participation in the general election; this would be beneficial for the National League for Democracy to come into power, even govern Myanmar for a long time. As China is Myanmar's largest trading partner and source of investment, China's assistance and investments are indispensable for Myanmar's economic development. Aung San Suu Kyi, an influential politician, is keenly aware of the special connection between China and Myanmar. As mentioned by Aung San Suu Kyi when meeting with Chinese President Xi Jinping, China and Myanmar are neighbors. As neighbors cannot be chosen, it is crucial to be committed to developing friendly relations between the two countries. Aung San Suu Kyi's visit to China can help the National League for Democracy gain more popularity in the general election and lay the foundation for future governance by the National League for Democracy; this visit can prove that she is able to engage in cooperation with Myanmar's most important neighbor and she has the governance capacity for dealing with domestic and diplomatic affairs, thus this visit can help her obtain more extensive support; this visit is really pragmatic. This visit is the forward-looking deployment made by her for the period following Myanmar's 2015 general election; this visit also marks the change of her status from a democratic fighter to a realist politician.

IV. The Far-reaching Significance of China's Invitation to Aung San Suu Kyi to Visit China

1. It is conducive to fostering the new diplomatic image of China

China's invitation to Aung San Suu Kyi, the democratic goddess, to visit China has broken Western media's speculations about whether China would really

[8]Zhang Yanli, Chen Zeran, Aung San Suu Kyi Paid her First Visit to China: The Politically Pragmatic Democratic Goddess, June 19, 2015, http://www.caijing.com.cn.

invite Aung San Suu Kyi and about China–Myanmar relations; this invitation has also demonstrated China's new posture of policy toward Myanmar to the whole world. This invitation has also indicated that China attaches importance to the National League for Democracy led by her, China's engagement with it can help the parties out of power in Myanmar understand China in a deeper and objective way, and it will be conducive to consolidating the foundation for public opinion regarding China–Myanmar relations. Western countries have always criticized China for engaging only with the failed states that find it difficult to integrate themselves into the international community; this invitation has rendered Western media speechless. In the meantime, with this invitation, other countries in the region can also become aware that China's diplomatic policy towards Southeast Asia is becoming more open and inclusive; this will be beneficial to China in fostering the new diplomatic image in the region and promoting China's engagement with the countries in the region.[9]

2. This invitation safeguards China's economic interests in Myanmar

In recent years, China has suffered many setbacks when investing in Myanmar. The Letpadaung Copper Mine Project has not gone well, the Myitsone Power Station Project has been suspended, and the China–Myanmar Railway Plan has gotten nowhere. China's investments have faced unprecedented challenges in Myanmar. One of the causes is that Chinese enterprises have not understood the social changes and the people's appeals in Myanmar and have placed excessive emphasis on "the upper class". Aung San Suu Kyi has Western values, but she is not a pro-Western politician; she is a mature, pragmatic politician. On the issue of the Letpadaung Copper Mine, she voiced a rational opinion: "If Myanmar unilaterally tears up the project contracts which have been signed with foreign companies and are being executed, Myanmar will lose its international reputation". China's invitation to Aung San Suu Kyi to visit China has strengthened its engagement with the

[9]Aung San Suu Kyi's Visit to China Is Beneficial to China in Developing the Relations with Myanmar and the Countries in the Region, People's Daily Online, June 10, 2015, http://www.people.com.cn.

opposition party in Myanmar; it can help more Burmese people understand China and boost China's credibility; it can also actively guide Burmese people to view China–Myanmar economic cooperation in an impartial and rational way; it is conducive to making sure that China's investments in Myanmar go smoothly and better safeguarding China's economic interests in Myanmar.

V. Aung San Suu Kyi's Visit to China is a Successful Ice-breaking Trip

Although the two sides have different political philosophies, they can, based on common interests, fairly and rationally view the other side's historical status and achievements, pragmatically discover and seek the foundation and possibility of cooperation, inherit and carry forward the history of amicable relations between the two countries, and manage and eliminate irrational and staged unstable factors; this should be the goal pursued by both China and Aung San Suu Kyi. Aung San Suu Kyi is one of the most influential politicians in Myanmar and the irreplaceable figure in Myanmar's political process. The National League for Democracy, led by her, is the largest opposition party in Myanmar, while China is Myanmar's most important neighboring country, so both Aung San Suu Kyi and China need to establish ties with each other, and prove and demonstrate that the other side is the reliable partner in bilateral relations. Taking the initiative to invite Aung San Suu Kyi and the delegation of the National League for Democracy is an important measure for pushing forward the inter-party exchange between the Communist Party of China and the National League for Democracy and the relations between the two countries in sync with the times; it reflects China's attention to Myanmar's situation and China's sincerity in engaging with different groups and political parties in Myanmar, including the parties in power and out of power. China hopes that Aung San Suu Kyi's visit to China can further boost communication and understanding between China and Myanmar, help the people of both countries enhance their mutual trust and dispel doubts; this visit can mitigate the misunderstanding between the people of the two countries, promote the Paukphaw friendship between the people of the two countries and let Burmese friends really feel that China supports Myanmar's democratic transformation and economic development, so as to deepen the China–Myanmar friendship, push forward the mutual political trust and friendly cooperative partnership between the two countries as well as deliver win–win outcomes. Aung San Suu Kyi wants to show through this visit that she is China's friend and supports China–Myanmar relations. The National League for Democracy, led by her, will take a pragmatic policy towards China. Moreover, obtaining support through diplomatic activities to increase the possibility that the National League for Democracy wins the general election is also an important objective of her visit to China.

VI. Conclusions

Myanmar is undergoing a democratic transformation and is in a fast diversified political process, so the main actors in China–Myanmar relations have transformed from the government to multiple actors including the government, the military, the parliament, the political parties in power and out of power, NGOs, the media and the people, so China–Myanmar relations have entered a new stage. Building the relations with a more solid foundation of public opinion between China and Myanmar on the basis of mutual respect exerts a great and far-reaching impact on Myanmar's political transformation. Aung San Suu Kyi's visit to China can transform and develop China–Myanmar relations from the previous single intergovernmental exchange to more emphasis on the people-to-people diplomatic mode; this visit will certainly become the model for deepening bilateral cooperation. However, one visit paid by Aung San Suu Kyi cannot solve all of the problems in China–Myanmar relations. Only when the governments, political parties and NGOs of both countries engage in an all-round exchange, maintain amicable relations and establish a profound friendship, can China–Myanmar relations withstand the test of political changes and develop normally.

Chapter 31

The Impact of the Issue of the South China Sea on China–Vietnam Economic Relations

Sun Shuo*

In 2016, the long-standing maritime territorial disputes between China and Vietnam may escalate again. In January, as China and Vietnam accused each other of violating their sovereignty over the oil-rich South China Sea, the tension between the two countries intensified to a certain extent. The spokesperson for the Ministry of Foreign Affairs of Vietnam stated that on January 16, 2016, China moved the HY-981 drilling platform to the area about 21.4 sea miles east of the presumable medium line of the basic boundary between China and Vietnam, this area was an area where Vietnam's central continental shelf and the continental shelf of China's Hainan Island overlapped and also an area where the boundary between the two sides had not yet been identified. He required China to refrain from conducting drilling activities in this area of the water and withdraw from the area. When answering questions

* Sun Shuo, Doctor of Economics at the China–ASEAN Research Institute of Guangxi University. This paper is jointly funded by a special research project of the China–ASEAN Collaborative Innovation Center for Regional Development and the Cheung Kong Scholars and Innovation Team Development Program initiated by the Ministry of Education (contract number: CW201603).

in the regular press conference on January 20, 2016, the spokesperson for the Ministry of Foreign Affairs of China, Hong Lei, affirmed that the drilling platform operated inside China's undisputed area of water. He hoped that Vietnam would be able to view this matter calmly.

I. The Causes

In 2014, China moved the drilling platform to the same water area over which Vietnam claimed sovereignty, triggering a two-month standoff between the two countries at sea, and anti-China demonstrations broke out in Vietnam on many occasions, leaving at least 16 people dead.[1] After the battle of the Xisha Islands between China and Vietnam in 1974, the Xisha Islands were basically under China's actual control, the 981 drilling platform was only 17 sea miles away from Zhongjian Island and fell within the nine-dotted line identified by China. The drilling platform of the China National Offshore Oil Corporation conducted drilling in the Xisha Area, arousing a strong reaction from Vietnam; this was closely associated with Vietnam's current economic development. So far, Vietnam has basically inherited the typical East Asian Development Mode — the growth of the export-oriented manufacturing industry (plus rice, coffee and other agricultural products), while the development of offshore oil and gas resources has brought to Vietnam massive US dollar assets much-needed for expanding its scale of production. In the past almost 10 years, the output value from the development of offshore oil and gas resources has accounted for about 1/3 of Vietnam's GDP.

The 981 drilling platform marked the beginning of China's development of deep-sea oil and gas resources and of China's intensified effective control over the South China Sea; this posed a big challenge to Vietnam, a country relying on the oil and gas resources in the South China Sea. Vietnam possesses 29 islands and reefs in the South China Sea, and even the oil and gas resources exploited by Vietnam are exported to China. After the standoff between China and the Philippines over Huangyan Island in 2012, Vietnam called for making the code of conduct concerning the South China sea on many international occasions, and multilateralized the issue of the South China Sea.

[1] Report from Reuters on May 15, 2014.

In 2013, Chinese Premier Li Keqiang visited Vietnam, the two sides agreed to establish the Working Group for Consultation on Maritime Joint Development, so the outside world had good expectations about the disputes between China and Vietnam over the South China Sea, but the Working Group made little progress. With the standoff between China and Vietnam at sea in 2014, the mechanism of consultation on joint development has gradually become ineffective. Given the overall situation of the South China Sea, the contradictions between China and Vietnam might likely be the acutest.

II. The Impact of Maritime Conflicts on the Economy of the Two Countries

Although Vietnam holds that China has become aggressive in the South China Sea, its reaction may ease due to the fact that the Chinese Government has an enormous influence on Vietnam's economy. Great changes took place in Vietnam in 30 years of reform. Vietnam has undergone a gradual transformation, made great progress in reforming its economy from a planned one to a market one, and achieved a certain degree of success in undertaking international industrial transfer. Now, Vietnam has become a vibrant emerging country. Although China and Vietnam have territorial disputes and once took hostile actions against each other, the economic relations between the two countries have been very close. At present, China is Vietnam's largest source of imports and its fourth largest export market, and Vietnam is China's second largest trading partner in the ASEAN community, only second to Malaysia. According to the statistical data from China, the bilateral trade was USD 95,819 million in 2015, up 14.6%, accounting for 2.4% of China's foreign trade, up 1.4 percentage points compared with that of 5 years ago. China's exports to Vietnam were USD 66.1 billion, up 3.8%, while China's imports from Vietnam were USD 29.7 billion, up 49.1%. Currently, China ranks No. 9 among the countries and territories making direct investments in Vietnam. China's investments in Vietnam are conducive to addressing the employment issue in Vietnam, improving Vietnam's production chain and promoting Vietnam's industrialization. However, such economic relations have been unbalanced: Vietnam's trade deficit with China was USD 36.4 billion in 2015, down USD 7.4 billion over 2014.[2] Vietnam exported crude oil, rubber, marine products and other bulk commodities, and it also imported mechanical equipment, chemical products, electronic products and other finished products from China.

With Vietnam's industrialization, Vietnam's demand for infrastructure investment has been very brisk. Take electric power infrastructure as an example: with rapid economic growth, Vietnam's electric power consumption has grown by about 10% each year. At present, the power generation in Vietnam cannot meet such electric power demand, and a number of provinces in northern Vietnam have imported electric power from China. According to the state-owned electric power monopoly enterprise Electricity of Vietnam, the electric power imported from China accounts for 6% of Vietnam's total electric power supply. In the energy field, Vietnam will need to invest USD 8 billion each year by 2020.[3]

As the electricity prices set by the Government of Vietnam are much lower than those in the neighboring countries of Cambodia, China and Laos, it is very difficult for most foreign investors to find profitable electric power projects in Vietnam. However, the China Development Bank (CDB) and the China Export–Import Bank have offered a huge sum of concessional loans for the new power stations in Vietnam. In return, Dongfang Electric, Harbin Power Equipment and Shanghai Electric and other large Chinese energy enterprises have been awarded lucrative electric power equipment supply contracts by Vietnam, and have built power stations in various parts of Vietnam. For a long time, the energy enterprises in USA, Europe, Japan and South Korea have shown a strong interest in Vietnam's underdeveloped electric power industry; however, these enterprises cannot compete with Chinese enterprises because Chinese enterprises can provide lower quotations and readily available concessional loans compared with the energy enterprises in the above countries.

However, since anti-China riots broke out in Vietnam in May 2014, Chinese banks have frozen the line of credit for many Engineering, Procurement and Construction (EPC) contracts in Vietnam, thus paralyzing a large number of projects and forcing some projects to be reorganized.

---

[2]The report from the Vietnam News Agency on March 9, 2015.

[3]The report from VietNamNet Bridge on February 27, 2016.

Therefore, Vietnam is seeking to diversify its investment partners and energy mix. The electric power agreements concluded or announced by Vietnam in 2015 cover not only the companies from Japan and South Korea, but also the companies from Thailand, Malaysia, India and Russia. In the meantime, Vietnam has restored its negotiations with Exxon Mobil with respect to the construction of land-based natural gas power stations. Furthermore, Vietnam has also planned to build nuclear power stations in the long term by attracting the companies from Western countries, Russia, Japan and South Korea. However, although Vietnam may successfully diversify its key investment relations, the relations between Vietnam and the neighboring country to the north cannot be completely replaced.

In the country famous for cheap labor and a vast market with more than 90 million consumers, Chinese enterprises are also building long-term interests. Vietnam enjoys an excellent geographical location, ample labor sources, low prices; it also benefits from a series of free trade agreements. In 2015, Vietnam concluded two important free trade agreements — the *EU–Vietnam Free Trade Agreement* with the EU and the *Trans-Pacific Partnership Agreement* (TPP) with USA, and the number of countries recognizing the full market economy status of Vietnam rose to 56. As Chinese exportation manufacturers have struggled to cope with weak demand and rising wages, more and more Chinese manufacturers have turned to Vietnam, a place of manufacturing at lower prices. In the meantime, the TPP has provided international capital with another investee which can replace the Chinese Mainland; it may give birth to an investment paradise geographically close to China for rapidly absorbing international capital from China; it may also squeeze China out of the overseas market because the US and European enterprises have shifted their global focus to the TPP and the TIPP. As reported, some far-sighted enterprises, including Chinese enterprises, have moved factories to TPP member countries, such as Vietnam. According to a 2015 survey report released by the Standard Chartered on the enterprises in the Pearl River Delta, 36% of the enterprises under survey in the Pearl River Delta which planned to shift their capacity for manufacturing production to foreign countries planned to move to Vietnam, 11% higher than those planning to move to Cambodia which ranked No. 2.

The East Asian region has gradually become a uniform market, except for North Korea, and it has seen a very high degree of interdependence regarding industrial connections. Although China–Vietnam relations have often become strained, industrial cooperation has never stopped; Vietnam has disputes with China over the South China Sea, but its importations heavily rely on China; in particular, against the general background of industrial transfer, it is very difficult for Vietnam to economically decouple itself from China. Moreover, economic growth has always been the bright spot in East Asia, while China has shown the willingness to rebuild the East Asian network of economic cooperation; the long-range plans, including the Asian Infrastructure Investment Bank and the 21st Century Maritime Silk Road, will bring dividends to Vietnam.

III. Prospects and Challenges

Since the new Government of Vietnam took office, Vietnam has been endeavoring to seek a balance; the new leader will not drastically adjust the policy direction, regardless of the political camp. The political observers generally believe that there are different views on the policy towards China within the Communist Party of Vietnam, but their common purpose lies in safeguarding national interests. All of the important figures within the party in Vietnam tend to agree with the necessity for reform, they are just unable to reach a consensus on the pace and scale of that reform. How to manage China–Vietnam relations will be the top priority in Vietnam's political circle. In the opinion of analysts, significant changes will not take place in Vietnam's positions on major issues, such as the sovereignty disputes with China over the South China Sea and a series of trade agreement negotiations.

Both China and Vietnam are socialist countries, and the two countries share the same official ideology; however, given the historical and realistic feuds between China and Vietnam, the Government of Vietnam has always been consciously instilling into the people's mind the consciousness of exercising vigilance regarding China. Few people are really pro-Chinese in the leadership of the Communist Party of Vietnam. Unlike the Communist Party of China, since the era of Ho Chi Minh, the Communist Party of Vietnam has been divided into the Southern Group and the Northern Group, and there are different views on China between the two groups. The Northern Group advocates strengthened connections with China, while the Southern Group holds that Vietnam should get close to USA and Europe.

However, not all of the people in the Northern Group are pro-Chinese. Obviously, it is too simple an approach to distinguish them from a pro-Chinese or pro-American perspective. The current General Secretary of the Communist Party of Vietnam, Nguyen Phu Trong, adopts the diplomatic line of thought of keeping a balance among the great powers. On the one hand, he is committed to friendly relations between China and Vietnam, he has visited China six times; in 2015, he exchanged visits with Xi Jinping; however, in 2015, he also visited Japan and unprecedentedly visited USA. In 2013, he also visited India. Recently, India and Vietnam have planned to build a satellite tracking and data reception center in Ho Chi Minh City, helping intensify the monitoring of the South China Sea. Therefore, both pro-Chinese and pro-American people act for the sake of Vietnam's national interests.

Vietnam is keen on moving among China, USA and other great powers, it upholds the strategy of "counteracting" to seek gains from multiple sides by keeping a balance among the great powers. The tension between China and Vietnam is unfavorable for regional economic growth, especially affecting regional investments and the business environment. High geopolitical risks and regional tensions may further hinder China's investments in Vietnam.

The anti-China demonstrations in Vietnam in 2014 also sent a warning to the Chinese people that dealing with the other side in an unduly unilateral way cannot bring about a relationship with the surrounding areas that is characterized by amity, sincerity, mutual benefit and inclusiveness, and China should address the issue of the South China Sea in a realistic way in the diplomatic field. We cannot overestimate the economic and trade influence of and underestimate the complexity within Vietnam. The trade in which excessive benefits are surrendered to the other side may make a small country obedient for a short time, but it cannot result in long-term sincere cooperation. The document *Vision and Actions on Jointly Building the Silk Road Economic Belt and the 21st Century Maritime Silk Road*, released by China, stresses the realization of shared growth through consultation and collaboration, and the connection of the developmental strategies of the countries along the routes, with a view to making the countries along the routes realize that the Belt and Road presents opportunities for them rather than posing risks to them. However, the economy and security are two different matters, especially in the disputes involving national territory and maritime rights and interests.

Chapter 32

Is Laos' Heavy Economic Dependence on China Real?

Fang Jingjing*

As reported by www.cankaoxiaoxi.com on April 25, 2015, the US media claimed that with the expansion of investment and trade, China's influence in Laos had kept growing. Some international bodies warned that Laos' financial dependence on China had become unhealthy. In the view of analysts, Laos is seeking support from Vietnam and Western countries to counteract China's influence.[1] Carl Thayer, a defense analyst at the University of New South Wales, Australia, said that the Belt and Road Initiative marked further extension of China's influence, especially to the ASEAN countries, particularly Thailand, Myanmar and Cambodia. Surat Horachaikul, Deputy Dean of Chulalongkorn University's Faculty of Political Science, pointed out that China took Laos as the key step for expanding its regional influence. He said, "Among all of the countries involved in projects, Laos is subject to the greatest risk of being led by China." "Fiscal austerity endangers Laos. Laos' macroeconomic condition is not good, thus Laos must rely on China, while China seizes the opportunity to offer more loans to Laos and carry

* Fang Jingjing, Research Assistant at the Laos Institute of the China–ASEAN Research Institute of Guangxi University.

[1] The US Media: As Laos Economically Relies on China, It Seeks Support from the Western Countries to Keep Balance, *Reference News*, April 25, 2015.

out more projects for Laos, so Laos must guard against China." Martin Stuart-Fox, an emeritus professor of history at the University of Queensland, said, "As China's economic influence is on the rise, its political clout grows. The Chinese people are determined to exert at least as much influence as Vietnam."

I. The Key Points of the Foreign Media's Views

The foreign media has claimed more than once that China has tried to influence and lead Laos through massive direct investments. The website www.cankaoxiaoxi.com reported the views of the Japanese media on March 14, 2012; according to the Japanese media, as Laos organized the Asia Europe Meeting, almost all of the related projects, including the Laos International Convention Center, hotels and airport expansions, were carried out by Chinese-funded enterprises. For Laos, a country with an urgent need for developing resources and building infrastructure, although Chinese capital was attractive, massive influx of labor had severely affected the Laotian society. In the meantime, the increase of RMB settlement was also one of the causes for Laos' adjustment of its policy for dependence on China. *Nikon Keizai Shimbun* pointed out that more and more Laotian people were concerned with excessive dependence on China in the economic field; the Prime Minister of Laos, Thongsing Thammavong, expressed expectations about Japanese enterprises and suggested vigilance against China's power.

The views of the Japanese media at that time were the same as that of the US media at present. In recent years, foreign media frequently warned that Laos depended on China; for example, in December 2014, the German media reported a list of countries dependent on China, prepared by German economists according to the data from IMF, and all of the countries included in the list saw their respective exportations to China accounting for 15% of their respective total exports, and Laos was among these countries. Not all of these countries were poverty-stricken developing countries. Many emerging countries and developed countries also needed China; for example, Japan (18.5%), New Zealand (22.6%), South Korea (25.5%) and Australia (36.2%) were included in the list.

No matter whether foreign media were neutral or showed obvious political prejudice in terms of evaluating such "dependence", it cannot be denied that China's utilization of its economic prowess really exerted an enormous influence. However, whether that influence has become unhealthy for the recipient country needs to be proved by concrete data and examples.

II. Is Laos' Heavy Economic Dependence on China Real?

Has Laos' economic dependence on China become abnormal? In the following, we analyze Laos' dependence on China from the perspectives of its dependence on foreign trade and its dependence on foreign investments.

1. Dependence on foreign trade

Dependence on foreign trade is often used to measure the extent to which the economy of a country is dependent on a foreign market, while dependence on foreign trade with a single country reflects that country's dependence on the market of a single country. As shown in Tables 1 and 2, Laos was relatively dependent on the markets within the ASEAN community, and Laos has had frequent trade contacts with Thailand. As indicated, with respect to its dependence on foreign trade, Laos was relatively dependent on the markets within the ASEAN community, especially Thailand, while this situation will not change greatly in a short time due to its geographical location and consumption habits.

Table 1. The Proportion of Laos' Import Trade with Countries (Unit: %)

	2007	2008	2009	2010	2011	2012	2013
Within the ASEAN community	80.04	85.51	—	85.59	70.1	60.3	75.93
Thailand	70.57	68.19	—	75.59	60.1	41.8	—
Vietnam	4.96	6.34	—	7.09	9.3	17.5	—
Outside the ASEAN community	19.2	14.17	—	14.14	26.9	38.9	24.07
China	4.98	7.79	—	9.7	17.3	21.6	—
27 EU countries	4.31	1.37	—	0.73	2.9	10.9	—
Japan	0.18	0.37	—	0.39	1.8	2.4	—
The Republic of Korea	2.71	2.81	—	1.87	2.4	1.9	—

Source: Laos Statistical Yearbook, Lao Statistics Bureau; ASEAN Statistical Yearbook 2014.

Table 2. The Proportion of Laos' Export Trade with Countries (Unit: %)

	2007	2008	2009	2010	2011	2012	2013
Within the ASEAN community	79.13	73.01	80.62	74.1	55	67.2	47.6
Thailand	55.35	59.6	69.13	71.4	44.6	54.3	—
Vietnam	10.75	13.37	11.42	2.58	10.1	12.6	—
Outside the ASEAN community	20.29	13.07	—	14.24	42.5	32.1	52.4
Australia	11.91	12.48	19.38	5.79	26.6	20.5	—
China	0.66	1.85	0.23	4.62	4	6.4	—
27 EU countries	2.62	1.81	6.17	3.16	7.2	2.8	—
Japan	—	0.29	0.75	—	2.7	2.3	—

Furthermore, even though the trade between Laos and China has gradually expanded, this is just because Laos needs more diverse markets to transfer its economic market risks, not because China subjectively wants to lead Laos. In short, Laos' economic scale is small, economic diversification is a daunting task, thus as Laos carries out economic reform, it needs to maintain close trade contacts with some countries; it does not matter whether one of these countries is Thailand or China, Laos certainly proceeds from its national interests.

Moreover, from China's perspective, the country with the heaviest dependence on trade with China was Mongolia — 93% of the commodities exported from Mongolia were purchased by Chinese People — followed by Turkmenistan, Myanmar and Laos, whose exports to China accounted for 68.8%, 41.4% and 35.2% of their total exports, respectively. Myanmar mainly exported oil to China, while Turkmenistan exported natural gas to China and Laos exported various raw materials, such as minerals and timber, to China.[2] From the perspective of the appropriateness of the dependence on foreign trade, as of 2014, Laos' dependence on the Chinese export market did not exceed 50%, which is sufficient to prove that although currently China exerts a great trade influence on Laos, it has not yet reached the extent that China leads Laos.

[2] [Germany] Christopher Sackman, 40 Countries Are Dependent on China, the List Is Becoming Longer, *Global Times*, December 13, 2014.

2. The dependence on direct investment

Recently, foreign media have always targeted the superior proportion of China's direct investments in Laos; in particular, the huge investment debt behind the China–Laos Railway Project has become the key point in the incident. As reported by the Voice of America on April 24, 2014, China became the main investor in Laos, with total investments exceeding USD 5 billion and projects involving mining, resources, hydropower stations and agriculture.

According to Table 3, from 1989 to 2015, China's cumulative investments in Laos accounted for only 22% of the total foreign investments

Table 3. The Statistics on Investments in Laos: Cumulative Value of Investment Projects by Country (1989–2015)

	Country	Number of investment projects	Total investments (USD)	Proportion of cumulative investments (%)
1	Laos*	2561	6,252,316,159	25.54
2	China	834	5,484,429,971	22.41
3	Thailand	748	4,491,684,613	18.35
4	Vietnam	417	3,574,681,539	14.61
5	The Republic of Korea	291	751,072,139	3.1
6	France	223	490,626,243	2
7	The USA	114	149,800,113	0.6
8	Malaysia	103	812,558,773	3.32
9	Japan	102	438,267,441	1.79
10	Australia	87	127,652,812	0.52
11	Singapore	79	187,761,475	0.767
…	…	…	…	—
Total**		6015	24,476,953,967	—

*represents including 100% domestic investment projects and the domestic investment share in joint ventures.

**represents the number of projects in the table may be larger than the total number of investment projects in Laos because the investors of some projects include multiple countries.

Note: Including 100% domestic investment projects and the domestic investment share in joint ventures; the number of projects in the table may be larger than the total number of investment projects in Laos because the investors of some projects include multiple countries.

Source: The official website of the Ministry of Planning and Investment of Laos.

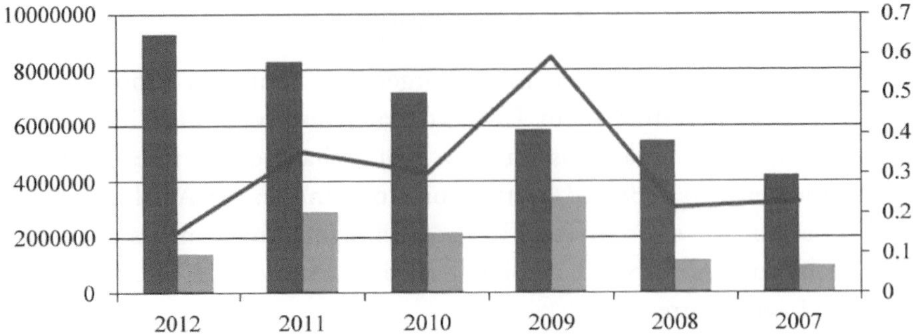

Figure 1. Laos' Dependence on Foreign Trade, 2007–2012 (Unit: 1,000 USD)
Source: Laos Statistical Yearbook, Lao Statistics Bureau.

received by Laos, followed by the investments from Thailand and Vietnam; China did not have any specially obvious advantages. Like the results shown by the above trade data, the direct investments in Laos were not completely dependent on China and were divided among China, Thailand and Vietnam.

Laos suffers a capital shortage, thus the country has always been active in attracting foreign investments; does this mean that foreign investments exert a great and decisive impact on Laos' economic development? As shown by the trend of change of Laos' dependence on foreign investments in Figure 1, foreign investments were really important for Laos' economic reform and development, but their impact was not as great as we imagine. The flow of foreign investments attracted by Laos accounted for less than 30% of Laos' GDP each year from 2007 to 2012; this means that without foreign investments, Laos' economic development speed would be relatively low, but Laos' economy would not become stagnant. This suggests that even if China invested in many projects in Laos, China had not developed the absolute leading advantage in Laos; besides, other countries, including Thailand, Vietnam and Japan, also actively participated in project bidding in Laos.

III. Why Were There Negative Views on China?

In the author's opinion, the international public opinion involved complicated national interests. With relevant data as evidence, we express the following views by merely focusing on the above trade and investment issues.

First, this time the US media only chose the views, not in favor of China, of the scholars from various countries and even presented relevant views out of context. These scholars came from Thailand and Australia. Why did the scholars from Thailand and Australia express views on these issues? According to the above trade and investment data, with increasing economic contacts between China and Laos, the market shares of Thailand and Australia shrank to some extent, while USA had never had a place in the Laotian market. Therefore, from the perspective of trade, the cause for expressing negative views on China may be that China's expanded trade influence in Laos squeezed the market shares of Thailand and Australia in Laos. For China's investments subject to repeated negative views, a large number of projects in Laos were undertaken by Chinese-funded enterprises, the project funds involved may also have been provided by Chinese financial institutions; this offered excellent choices for Laos. Other countries had concerns regarding China because the market shares available for them had decreased.

Secondly, it might make other countries worry as China progressed really fast and expanded its influence on the economy of its neighboring countries. According to the short-term data collected in this paper, China's trade with and investments in Laos grew rapidly over a period of several years; initially China's economic influence was slight; later it became enormous, this process only took a very short time to happen. The "China Speed" became a fact before other countries had fully adapted to and accepted it. From this perspective, it is not surprising that China's improved influence in Laos has disoriented other countries.

Chapter 33
Lee Kuan Yew and China

He Zheng*

In the wee hours of March 23, 2015, the Prime Minister's Office in Singapore released a message that former Prime Minister Lee Kuan Yew had passed away at the age of 91. This message stunned the world; it made the headlines around the world, drawing worldwide attention. The passing of the giant in Singapore's political circle exerted a far-reaching impact on the world's landscape.

I. Profile of Lee Kuan Yew

In Singapore, the world-famous garden city state, Lee Kuan Yew is known to all. As the founding Prime Minister of Singapore, former Minister Mentor of Singapore and one of the founding fathers of Singapore, Lee Kuan Yew served as the Prime Minister for 32 years, and he is one of the highly influential figures in Singapore's political circle. During his governance, Singapore's per capita GDP soared from USD 516.29 in 1965 when Singapore was founded to USD 52,888 in 2015,[1] an astonishing increase of nearly 102 times in more than 40 years, creating an economic miracle. As the founder of modern

* He Zheng, Director, Senior Economist at the Laos Institute of the China–ASEAN Research Institute of Guangxi University.

[1] Wind Economic Database (EBD).

Singapore, he is hailed by Singaporeans as the father of Singapore, and is widely respected and revered. On May 14, 2011, he announced that he had resigned from Singapore's cabinet; this marked the end of an era, but Singapore remained under the strong influence of Lee Kuan Yew; his political influence goes far beyond Singapore, a small country; he was a sharp-eyed observer, a highly respected politician and thinker on the Asian stage. The important political figures of many countries in the world greatly welcomed his visits, and were eager to obtain his political insights and pertinent advice.

Lee Kuan Yew was born in Singapore on September 16, 1923. His ancestral home was Dangxi Town, Dabu County, Guangdong Province, China. He graduated from Singapore Raffles College. During the period of 1940–1950, he studied at the London School of Economics and Political Science, the University of Cambridge and the Middle Temple. He was called to the Bar at the Middle Temple in 1950. In November 1954, he participated in establishing the People's Action Party of Singapore and served as the Secretary General. In 1955, he was elected the member of the Legislative Assembly (renamed the Parliament in December 1965). In June 1959, he became the first Prime Minister of the Singapore Autonomous Government. On August 9, 1965, Singapore separated itself from the Federation of Malaysia and became a republic. Lee Kuan Yew served as the Prime Minister of the republic until November 27, 1990. He served as the Senior Minister of the Prime Minister's Office from September 1991. On October 5, 1994, he was elected the Honorary Chairman of the newly formed International Confucian Association. He served as Minister Mentor (the Prime Minister's Office) from January 1997 and he was reappointed Minister Mentor again in November 2001. Lee Kuan Yew received an English education from childhood, he also assiduously learnt Chinese and China's Minnan dialect; in particular, he liked learning and reciting Chinese four-character idioms, so he was an expert in China. He is the father of Lee Hsien Loong, the current Prime Minister of Singapore, and he had a profound relationship with China.

II. Lee Kuan Yew's Contributions to Promoting China–Singapore Relations

Lee Kuan Yew, who passed away at the age of 91, was our respected elder; he was experienced in the international political arena. He visited China

33 times. He was the foreign leader who visited China most frequently during his term of office. Lee Kuan Yew attached great importance to and was committed to developing amicable relations with China, and he was an old friend of China's. He made outstanding contributions to pushing forward China–Singapore relations.

1. The new book *One Man's View of the World* fully reflects the great attention to China

In August 2014, the launching ceremony of Lee Kuan Yew's *One Man's View of the World* was held at the Istana. During the launching ceremony, Lee Kuan Yew, at the age of 90, said that this book, with more than 400 pages of words and pictures, presented his political career and experience of more than 50 years. This book expounds China in the first chapter, showing the importance attached by him to China. As stated in this book, China has a 5,000-year-old culture and history, it is believed that only when the central authorities become powerful can a country be safe; it is absolutely impossible for China to develop into a democratic country under the Western concept, China will carefully and gradually carry out reform in its own way.

Regarding foreign policy, in the opinion of Lee Kuan Yew, China will continue to become stronger and enhance its influence in a low-profile way, but China will flex its power when necessary.[2] In his view, internally, the main obstacle to China's realization of national rejuvenation comes from its culture and language and its failure to attract and assimilate other countries' talents; China will face challenges in governance in the future.

Concerning the rise of China, undoubtedly, Lee Kuan Yew gained a greater understanding than the observers or analysts outside China. Will China challenge the status of USA to become an Asian power? Will China become a world power? Most decision-makers and experts have given unclear answers to these important questions, while Lee Kuan Yew categorically responded, "Yes. The Chinese people's sense of national mission about rejuvenation generates a powerful force; China has the strength to become a world power. China hopes that the world can accept what it was rather than

[2] Lee Kuan Yew: It Is Believed That China Will Rise Peacefully, But China Will Flex Its Power. http://gx.people.com.cn/n/2013/0808/c229256-19259424.html.

accept it as the dependency of the Western society." All of these judgments made by Lee Kuan Yew seem to be happening around us. Lee Kuan Yew impressed the people with his keen insight and excellent judgment.

2. Lee Kuan Yew's contributions to promoting the establishment of diplomatic relations between China and Singapore and economic development

In fact, Lee Kuan Yew's attitudes towards China changed many times. In the initial stage after Singapore gained independence, the surrounding countries were hostile to and guarded against the neighboring country dominated by the people of Chinese origin; they worried that it was the Trojan Horse implanted in Southeast Asia. At that time, Singapore, very friendly to USA, assumed an anti-China and anti-communist attitude; in Lee Kuan Yew's books and speeches, he expressed high vigilance against China. Changes took place as of the 1970s; in particular, as Sino-Soviet relations broke down, Lee Kuan Yew started to hope that China, an ever-developing country, could play a bigger role in Asia. Later, Singapore voted for resumption of China's status as a permanent member of the UN Security Council, and supported the establishment of diplomatic relations between China and USA. The Minister of Foreign Affairs of Singapore and Lee Kuan Yew visited China on many occasions. A series of moves rapidly melted the ice in China–Singapore relations. It should be noted that the leaders of the two countries started engagement with each other as of 1976, but China and Singapore did not officially establish diplomatic relations until 1990.

Although the two countries established diplomatic relations late, bilateral relations developed very rapidly. The two countries carried out a landmark cooperation project — the establishment of the Suzhou Industrial Park, the first transnational hi-tech industrial park in China. As early as 1994, Suzhou Industrial Park, based on cooperation between China and Singapore, was officially established. In the following decade, the park's economic aggregate reached the level of the entire Suzhou City before its development, equivalent to the creation of another Suzhou in a decade, while the driving force for the establishment of the park came precisely from Lee Kuan Yew. In around 1993, Lee Kuan Yew visited Suzhou twice, ultimately resulting in the establishment of the industrial park. Furthermore, Lee Kuan Yew visited China on many occasions. In May 2005, he was awarded an honorary doctorate degree by Fudan University during his visit to China. In August 2008, Lee Kuan Yew attended the opening ceremony of the 29th Olympic Games and relevant activities in China.

China and Singapore maintained a close cooperative partnership for a long time. In more than 20 years since China and Singapore established diplomatic relations, bilateral relations developed constantly, bilateral trade surged from USD 2.83 billion in 1990 to USD 79.57 billion in 2015, China became Singapore's largest trading partner, while Singapore became China's second trading partner in the ASEAN community.[3] Singapore has served as the "bridgehead" for connection between China and the ASEAN countries. Interestingly, Lee Kuan Yew, always an anti-communist, maintained a good personal relationship with Deng Xiaoping; he expressed admiration for Deng Xiaoping on many occasions. During the southern tour in 1992, Deng Xiaoping vowed to learn from and surpass Singapore, stimulating many Chinese delegations to visit Singapore for observation and study, thus accelerating the development of bilateral relations.

3. Lee Kuan Yew's contributions to the relations across the Taiwan Straits — Bringing about the Wang Koo Talks

With respect to the Taiwan issue, Lee Kuan Yew firmly upheld "One China". In 1992, Lee Kuan Yew volunteered to make arrangements, the then Chinese President Yang Shangkun invited him to send a message that the two sides across the Taiwan Straits could first attempt to develop the economy, and Lee Kuan Yew served as the special envoy for sending that message; afterwards, the Wang Koo Talks, which pioneered the exchanges across the Taiwan Straits, were ultimately held in Singapore. The relations between the two sides across the Taiwan Straits developed by leaps and bounds, thus promoting the exchanges of mail correspondence, trading, air and shipping services, and exchanges and cooperation in other fields between the two sides across the Taiwan Straits.

---

[3] The Department of Asian Affairs, the Ministry of Commerce of China. http://yzs.mofcom.gov.cn/article/t/201602/20160201252478.shtml.

III. Lee Kuan Yew's Diplomatic Strategy: Work with USA to Contain China

Singapore is a small country with a shortage of resources. To seek space for survival for Singapore in the complex environment of various countries around the world, Lee Kuan Yew actually endeavored to keep a balance among the great powers in the diplomatic field, with efforts to vigorously seek support from USA while not offending China. From the perspective of security, however, it was very difficult to keep a balance between USA and China as put forward by Lee Kuan Yew; subject to external pressure, Singapore has been forced to choose either China or USA; as a matter of fact, Singapore has taken actions to support USA's presence in Asia; the Singapore Changi Air Base has become the only permanent US military base in Southeast Asia.[4]

IV. Conclusions

The year 2015 marked the 25th anniversary of the establishment of diplomatic relations between China and Singapore and also the 50th anniversary of the founding of Singapore. Singapore is the coordinator in China–ASEAN relations. China–Singapore relations will advance to a new historical starting point in promoting the construction of the 21st Century Maritime Silk Road and the milestone upgrading of the China–ASEAN Free Trade Area (CAFTA). Although Lee Kuan Yew, a great political thinker with sagacity, has left us, he will be deeply remembered by later generations for his great contributions to China–Singapore relations.

---

[4] Why Does Lee Kuan Yew Please the US and Restrain China, *Global Times*, November 4, 2009.

Chapter 34

The Jakarta–Bandung High-Speed Railway Project in Indonesia — Battles between China and Japan

Wen Jianchun*

After several setbacks, the Jakarta–Bandung High-speed Railway Project in Indonesia was finally settled. After several rounds of pitched battles between China and Japan, China ultimately triumphed. On October 16, 2015, the China Railway Corporation signed an agreement with four Indonesian state-owned enterprises in Jakarta, the capital of Indonesia, under which a joint venture would be established. This indicated that Chinese enterprises had officially won the Jakarta–Bandung High-speed Railway Project. It is the first high-speed railway project in Indonesia; it is about 142 km long (originally it was 150 km, later the length of the route was shortened) and costs USD 5,135 million (about 33,199 million yuan); its maximum design speed is 300 km/h. Its construction began in January 2016. It is scheduled to be completed and open to traffic on May 31, 2019.[1]

* Wen Jianchun, Research Assistant at the Indonesia Institute of the China–ASEAN Research Institute of Guangxi University.

[1] Wikipedia, https://en.wikipedia.org/wiki/High-speed-rail-in-Indonesia.

I. A Review of Pitched Battles

1. The first stage: Japan planned to win Indonesia's high-speed railway project

For a long time, Japan deliberated on the plan to export its Shinkansen technology to Indonesia. In November 2008, Japan demonstrated its Shinkansen technology before an Indonesian audience during the Indonesia–Japan Friendship Festival. In 2009, the feasibility study of Indonesia's high-speed railway project, funded by the Japanese Government, kicked off. The high-speed railway spans the Java Island from Jakarta to Surabaya. Its speed reaches 300 km/h, it is 730 km long. The Japan International Cooperation Agency (JICA) tracked the Jakarta–Bandung High-speed Railway Project; it conducted the preliminary study as of 2012 and completed the feasibility study in 2014.

After this idea had been in the planning for several years, a new proposal appeared and sought to carry out the high-speed railway project by stages, with the first stage from Jakarta to Bandung at the full length of 150 km and a travel time of 35 min (currently, the conventional train takes 3 h). Japan, a country reputed as a world-class rolling stock manufacturer, seemed to be bound to win the project. However, as President Joko took office in October 2014, this situation changed. The Joko Government basically stopped the preparatory work for the high-speed railway project on the grounds that its cost was too high and infrastructure construction was needed more urgently in the remote underdeveloped islands outside the Java Island.

2. The second stage: China got involved in the project, initiating the battles between China and Japan

Japan's leading role in the high-speed railway project always seemed to be unshakable until April 2015, when China participated in bargaining together with Japan. Not long ago, President Joko met with Japanese Prime Minister Shinzo Abe in March 2015, and Indonesia obtained the loan support from Japan with respect to Jakarta's urban railway network; however, Japan went nowhere in the Jakarta–Bandung High-speed Railway Project. In March, President Joko visited China, Chinese President Xi Jinping openly announced

China's support for Indonesia's high-speed railway project; the governments of the two countries signed the *Memorandum of Understanding between China and Indonesia on Cooperation in the Jakarta–Bandung High-speed Railway Project*. In April, Chinese President Xi Jinping visited Indonesia, the two sides signed the *Framework Arrangements for Cooperation in the Jakarta–Bandung High-speed Railway Project*. Thus, China officially got involved in Indonesia's high-speed railway project.[2]

3. The third stage: The battles around the high-speed railway project became fierce

From July to August, 2015, China and Japan sent special envoys to Indonesia for communication on this matter several times. In July, the Indonesian Government officially announced that Indonesia planned to build a high-speed railway from the capital, Jakarta, to Bandung.

In early July, a special Japanese envoy visited Indonesia and put forward the optimized plan for the construction of a high-speed railway, presented a number of favorable conditions including a shorter period of construction, a lower interest rate and looser loan conditions, and stressed efforts to push forward infrastructure construction projects including the Jakarta–Bandung High-speed Railway Project.

In August, a special Chinese envoy visited Indonesia and presented China's feasibility study report to President Joko, giving detailed descriptions about China's scheme.

On August 12, the President of Indonesia announced a cabinet reshuffling, the pro-Japanese minister Rachmat Gobel was replaced, the Japanese media believed that this move would exert a negative impact on Japan in the battle for Indonesian's high-speed railway project. On August 26, Japan once again sent a special envoy to Indonesia; this time Japan further optimized its scheme and reduced the ratio of a sovereign guarantee in loans and pledged to assist the development and construction in eastern Indonesia.

On August 28 and 31, the Chinese Ambassador to Indonesia met with the senior officials in charge of the Jakarta–Bandung High-speed Railway

[2] Behind the High-speed Railway Project in Indonesia, What is the 'Big Move'?, http://opinion.huanqiu.com/1152/2016-03/8732962.html.

Project, and stated that China had only one scheme for the Jakarta–Bandung High-speed Railway Project and the scheme was the most suitable and catered most to Indonesia's needs. China also displayed China's high-speed railway technology at the Senayan Shopping Center in Jakarta. At this stage, China and Japan lobbied many times and engaged in fierce competition. The two sides demonstrated a high level of courage and confidence in this competition, far beyond the economic scope. In fact, this competition was only the tip of the iceberg in Asia amidst the efforts made by both Asian great powers in seeking greater strategic influence in the Asia-Pacific region.

4. The fourth stage: Brief suspension

In early September, as the people expected that President Joko would announce the winner of the bidding for the first high-speed railway project, the Indonesian Government surprisingly announced the cancellation of that project on September 3 on the grounds that they hoped to replace it by the railway with a lower speed and a lower price.

On the next day, the Indonesian Government announced that the schemes of both China and Japan had been returned. After the cancellation was announced, China once again engaged with Indonesia with respect to the project, while Japan took no action.

5. The fifth stage: China surpassed Japan to win

In mid-September, China pledged to fully satisfy the requirements of the Indonesian Government, and presented a proposal in which Indonesia was not required to bear the subsequent fiscal burden or debt guarantee for the project. After several months of bidding and revision, talks between senior government officials and a brief suspension of the bidding on the project, later in September, Indonesia chose China's USD 5 billion scheme. In the competition on the financing scheme, China ultimately defeated Japan. The Chief Cabinet Secretary of Japan, Yoshihide Suga, said that Indonesia's move was very difficult to understand and extremely regrettable, and that the situation was very sad.

On October 16, the China Railway Corporation signed an agreement with four Indonesian state-owned enterprises in Jakarta, the capital of Indonesia, under which a joint venture would be established, suggesting that Chinese enterprises had officially won the Jakarta–Bandung High-speed Railway Project.[3]

6. The sixth stage: Setbacks after the commencement of the construction and harvest

On January 21, 2016, the construction of the Jakarta–Bandung High-speed Railway Project was officially started, and the groundbreaking ceremony of the project was held in Bandung Barat. However, several days later, on January 29, the project was suspended. The Ministry of Transportation of Indonesia stated that the joint venture for undertaking the project had not yet provided relevant documents involving the development design, the engineering diagram and field data, and some documents were in Chinese, so the Indonesian Government could not evaluate the project, so the construction permit and the concession agreement had not yet been issued. Moreover, the Transportation Minister of Indonesia, Ignasius Jonan, added that the negotiations involving the project were still underway with respect to a series of sensitive issues; for example, problems that occurred in the project construction, and the Indonesian Government would not bear the heavy burden.

In March, the builder of the Jakarta–Bandung High-speed Railway Project obtained the "construction certificate concerning the 5 km section of the Jakarta–Bandung High-speed Railway Project in the Halim Area of Jakarta" issued by the Ministry of Transportation of Indonesia; a relevant agreement required construction to be completed within 3 years after the issuance of the construction permit.[4] In the meantime, the joint venture for undertaking the project was granted 50-year concessions.

II. Why Was is Possible for China to Win?

1. The most crucial points

China pledged neither to use Indonesia's national budget nor require Indonesia to provide a governmental guarantee. As Indonesia briefly canceled

---

[3] Chinese Enterprises Won the Jakarta-Bandung High-speed Rail Project, http://news.ifeng.com/a/20151017/45337523_0.shtml.

[4] The 5 km Section of the Jakarta-Bandung High-speed Railway Project in the Halim Area Will First Be Built, Xinhuanet. http://news.xinhuanet.com/world/2016-03/18/c_128811393.htm.

the plan for the high-speed railway project, President Joko presented three requirements: First, Indonesia hoped to realize the high-speed railway project under the enterprise-to-enterprise rather than government-to-government business cooperation mode; second, the project did not occupy any part of the national budget; finally, the government was not required to provide a guarantee. This suggested that the Indonesian Government was unwilling to fund the project and could not provide a fund guarantee for the costly project. China expressed understanding of the above requirements and was aware that there was an urgent need for Indonesia to develop infrastructures, but Indonesia temporarily lacked funds. Thus, China made an active response accordingly and adjusted its scheme, while the new scheme became the only scheme which reached Indonesia's criteria. Japan did not make any response. Japan held that the high-speed railway project was subject to risks and should be conditional upon the Indonesian government's guarantee, putting Japan in a disadvantaged position.

2. Construction period

According to Japan's scheme, the construction of the high-speed railway project would begin in 2018 and would be completed by 2021; therefore, the construction period would be 4 years. According to China's scheme, the construction of the high-speed railway project would begin in September, 2015 (subsequently adjusted to November 2015) and it would be completed and open to traffic by 2019, the construction period would be about 3 years. In this regard, the Chief Cabinet Secretary of Japan, Yoshihide Suga, said that it was impossible to complete the Jakarta–Bandung High-speed Railway Project within 3 years as pledged by China, so this was an impossible task. The Chinese Ambassador to Indonesia, Xie Feng, replied that it was more valuable because it was difficult, that it was really not an easy thing, but that China had created not a few impossible miracles in the high-speed railway field, so we should believe in the "China Speed" in the field of high-speed railways.

3. Project cost

On the construction cost, China's high-speed rail would cost about USD 30 million/km, lower than the cost of a foreign high-speed railway (USD

50 million/km). Regarding the terms of the loan, the term of the loan under both China's and Japan's scheme is 40 years, including a 10-year extension and grace period; with respect to the interest rate, the financing condition provided by Japan is an annual 0.1% in yen, while the interest provided by China is an annual 2% in USD, so Japan gained the upper hand in this regard. However, Japan upheld the conventional yen lending mode, while China adopted the lending mode which combines the RMB with the USD, and the joint venture mode under which a consortium established together with Indonesian enterprises would be responsible for building and operating the project. This showed that China's scheme was more flexible.

4. Route development mode

According to China's scheme, 30% of the profits come from the development along the route, which is combined with the real estate and the commercial sector; with this developmental mode there can be substantially increased project returns compared with the single railway mode. Japan's scheme did not provide a specific estimation in this respect. Furthermore, under China's scheme, the high-speed railway project would stimulate the development of a range of industries, including metallurgical, manufacturing and electric power industries, along the route, it would likely increase job opportunities while improving infrastructures. Thus, China's scheme greatly prevailed over Japan's scheme regarding the operational mode, project construction and stimulation of employment.

5. Technology and experience

China's high-speed railway reaches the highest degree of modernization and can adapt to multiple geomorphic and weather conditions, China has built the only tropical high-speed railway in the world — the Eastern Hainan Railway; this is of great referential significance for Indonesia's high-speed railway project in the tropical zone.

III. The Risks Which China Should Guard Against

For the Jakarta–Bandung High-speed Railway Project, initially, China "snatched food from the jaws of a tiger", overcame various obstacles, and finally achieved success with its unique mode; in this process, China suffered many setbacks. As the project is gradually carried out, China should prudently guard against risks. In the opinion of the author, the project mainly involves the following risks:

1. The risks amidst the absence of a governmental guarantee

The unique cooperation mode — absence of a governmental guarantee — is the key to China's success in the project and also highly controversial. The Jakarta–Bandung High-speed Railway has an enormous economic value; however, if the project goes under poor operations in the future, it will be difficult for China to seek a fund guarantee.

2. The risks amidst the strife among political parties in Indonesia

During the period of President Susilo Bambang Yudhoyono, the government and construction enterprise came to an understanding and agreed to build the Sunda Strait Bridge, a bridge connecting the Java Island in western Indonesia with the Island of Sumatra. However, after President Joko took office in 2014, the Indonesian Government opposed the construction of the bridge on the grounds that the project was not consistent with the developmental vision of turning Indonesia into a Global Maritime Axis, so the project was shelved. Now the incumbent President Joko expresses support for the Jakarta–Bandung High-speed Railway Project, but the shelving of the Sunda Strait Bridge adds political risks for the ultimate completion of the project.

3. The land development risk due to Indonesia's private land ownership

The construction of the high-speed rail project cannot bypass the difficulties in obtaining extensive land, while Indonesia practices private land ownership, thus as the project is carried out, the construction enterprise may need to take a lot of time or money to consult with local people; this will increase the cost of the project to a certain extent.

Overall, as an infrastructure project which draws attention of the whole ASEAN community, the Jakarta–Bandung High-speed Railway Project is beset with many difficulties, but opportunities and challenges, risks and benefits coexist.

IV. The Great Significance of China's Victory

The year 2015 marked the 65th anniversary of the establishment of diplomatic relations between China and Indonesia, and bilateral relations are ushering in the best period in history. As mentioned by Chinese Ambassador Xie Feng, the Jakarta–Bandung High-speed Railway Project is so far the largest cooperation project between China and Indonesia, it is the flagship and landmark project in China–Indonesia strategic cooperation in the new period; it is a milestone for both countries.

For China, the Jakarta–Bandung High-speed Railway Project results in exporting China's high-speed railway as a whole in an all-round way, from technical standards, survey and design, engineering construction, equipment manufacturing to material supply, operational management and talent training.[5] The Jakarta–Bandung High-speed Railway Project will help realize the vision of the Belt and Road put forward by China and make a solid step forward in infrastructure connectivity. Subsequently, the invitation for bids involving the Singapore–Malaysia high-speed railway connecting Singapore with Kuala Lumpur, the capital of Malaysia, will be carried out soon, and Chinese and Japanese enterprises have expressed the willingness to bid for the project. The battles between China and Japan in high-speed railway projects in Southeast Asia will continue. The subsequent progress deserves our attention.

---

[5] With USD 5.1 Billion Order at Hand, China Will Extend Its Stunning High-speed Rail around the Globe, www.sohu.com. http://mt.sohu.com/20160320/n441239234.shtml.

Chapter 35

The Opportunities and Challenges for the Development of Chinese-Funded Enterprises in Brunei

Wang Yong*

An important objective of the Belt and Road Initiative put forward by China is to create a good external environment for Chinese enterprises to go global. The countries along the Belt and Road greatly differ from China in their environments for enterprise development. How to actively adapt to and integrate themselves into the environment of the countries where investments are made is a great issue for Chinese enterprises as they go global. Brunei covers a small area and has a small population with a less diversified economic structure; it is a Malay Islamic monarchy, and is typical among the countries along the Belt and Road. This paper focuses on analyzing the opportunities and challenges for the development of Chinese-funded enterprises in Brunei, and offers countermeasures and suggestions on how Chinese-funded enterprises better take root and flourish in Brunei, so as to provide reference for Chinese enterprises to go global under the Belt and Road Initiative in a better way.

*Wang Yong, Research Assistant at the Brunei Institute of the China–ASEAN Research Institute of Guangxi University.

I. The Opportunities for the Development of Chinese-funded Enterprises in Brunei

1. The political and social environment is stable and harmonious

A stable and harmonious political and social environment is the prerequisite for and foundation of the development of Chinese-funded enterprises in Brunei. Brunei is hailed as the Abode of Peace. The Sultan's Government has vigorously carried out the policy of malayanization, islamization and monarchy, and has continuously consolidated and expanded the governing foundation of the royal family, so the political situation in Brunei is very stable. The monarchy can bring about effective control over Brunei, a small country with a small population; it makes sure that government decrees and directives can be smoothly transmitted from higher levels to lower levels and can be executed; it can also prevent the governing policies from easily changing under the multi-party system due to the change of the governing party, so as to guarantee the stability and continuity of Brunei's economic and social development policies. It is beneficial for Chinese-funded enterprises to have stable policy expectations and mitigate policy risks caused by incomplete information. Moreover, in Brunei, there is a beautiful and harmonious social environment, the Bruneian people are courteous and friendly, indigenous Malays and the people of Chinese origin get on well with each other, no anti-China demonstrations or Chinese exclusion incidents occur, creating a loose and good social environment for the development of Chinese-funded enterprises in Brunei.

2. Brunei enjoys the conditions of an excellent location

First, the geographical location is superior. Brunei is situated in the northwestern part of Kalimantan Island, faces the South China Sea on the north with China on the opposite side, and borders the Sarawak State on the east, south and west; it is the economic center in the East ASEAN Growth Area and also an important node of the 21st Century Maritime Silk Road. Second, natural resources are abundant. Brunei abounds in oil and gas; it is the third largest oil-producing country in Southeast Asia and the fourth

Table 1. The Main Strategic Cooperation Agreements Signed by Brunei (2014)

Strategic cooperation agreement	Total population (100 million)	GDP (one trillion USD)
The ASEAN Economic Community	5.62	2.52
ASEAN–New Zealand	5.67	2.72
ASEAN–Australia–New Zealand	5.9	4.18
ASEAN–China	19.26	12.87
ASEAN–South Korea	6.13	3.93
ASEAN–Japan	6.89	7.12
ASEAN–India	18.57	4.57
Trans-Pacific Partnership Agreement (TPP)	8.1	28.07
Regional Comprehensive Economic Partnership (RCEP)	34.27	22.59

Source: The World Bank Database.

largest liquefied natural gas exporter. Furthermore, marine, forest and natural tourist resources are also relatively abundant. Third, transportation is convenient. Brunei is the shipping center in the East ASEAN Growth Area, marine transportation is very convenient; marine transportation provides Brunei with access to the main markets in the world along the Maritime Silk Road, and Brunei is witnessing the gradual formation of an integrated transportation system covering sea, land and air transportation. Fourth, it connects vast markets. Brunei has a population of 420,000, its domestic market is limited, but Brunei gets access to very vast markets by having signed strategic cooperation agreements with the main international partners (see Table 1); these factors are beneficial for Chinese-funded enterprises to develop processing trade and entrepôt trade — sourcing raw materials from and marketing products to the world market — in Brunei.

3. Brunei's economic diversification strategy entails a huge demand for foreign capital

Brunei features a less diversified economic structure, and oil and gas industries are the absolute pillars of Brunei's national economy. In the first three quarters of 2015, their output value accounted for 43.9% of the GDP, their export accounted for 93.04% of total exports. As oil and gas resources are nonrenewable resources, the world's economy is weak, shale gas is massively developed and exploited, and the international crude oil prices are on the decline; Brunei's economy is deeply affected by the fluctuation of the international crude oil prices. In order to break away from the constraints from the less diversified economic structure and maintain long-term steady economic growth, the Government of Brunei actively explores and implements the economic diversification strategy, encourages deep processing of products, processing of halal food, development of medical services and health care, information communications, logistics storage and transportation and supporting industries (chain). However, Brunei's industrial base is weak, the supporting industrial sectors are not complete, there is a shortage of industrial talents and the development and management experience is insufficient, so it is difficult for Brunei to achieve economic diversification by relying on its own strength; Brunei must introduce foreign capital and cultivate local industrial technical personnel through foreign capital, thus ultimately achieving localized operations. In this regard, the Government of Brunei is mainly planning for 10 industrial parks (see Table 2) to attract foreign investments. Brunei's economic diversification strategy, which involves a huge demand for foreign capital, offers great opportunities and space for the development of Chinese-funded enterprises.

4. Brunei's investment policies are preferential and convenient

Brunei provides foreign investors with extremely preferential and convenient policies and conditions. On taxation, in Brunei, there are no individual income taxes, business taxes, payroll taxes, capital gains taxes or manufacturing taxes; corporate income tax is relatively low (18.5%), and the taxation policies for the enterprises granted with the pioneer industry certificate are particularly preferential (see Table 3). As the industrial system is not complete, many industries in Brunei need to be cultivated and developed, and it is easy for Chinese-funded enterprises to obtain a pioneer certificate. Regarding government subsidies, the Government of Brunei encourages foreign enterprises to carry out design, research and development, employ and train local people in Brunei, and thus specially establishes the research subsidy and training subsidy funds. Regarding the investment and production costs, in Brunei, the industrial electricity price is only 0.09 Brunei ringgits/kW/h, the diesel price is 0.5 Brunei ringgits/L, the average land lease price

Table 2. Brunei's Main Industrial Parks

No.	Name of industrial park	Planning area (hectare)	Main uses
1	Pulau Muara Besar	955	Oil and gas downstream industries, shipbuilding and repair base
2	Sungai Liang Industrial Park	271	Oil and gas downstream industries, high-tech industry
3	Salambigar Industrial Park	121	Food, pharmaceutical processing industries
4	Digital junction	15	High-tech information services, data and disaster recovery center
5	Telisai Industrial Park	2808	Deep-sea farming processing, pharmaceutical planting and processing
6	Bukit Panggal Industrial Park	50	Energy-intensive manufacturing industry
7	Lou Malpass Industrial Park	25	Agriculture and processing
8	Anggerek Desa Technology Park	30	Hi-tech research and development center
9	Bio innovation corridor	500	Halal and agriculture-related industries
10	Seria Industrial Park	83	Crude oil and gas industries

Source: Brunei Economic Development Board (BEDB).

Table 3. Tax Holidays for the Pioneer Industries in Brunei (as of the Production Date)

Registered capital	Tax holiday
500,000–2.5 million Brunei Ringgit	5 years
Above 2.50 million	8 years
Within hi-tech parks	11 years
Extension of tax holiday	3 times a year, not longer than 11 years in total
(Industrial parks) extension of tax holiday	5 times a year, not longer than 20 years in total

Source: Brunei Economic Development Board (BEDB).

in industrial parks is USD 2.12/m^3/year, Chinese-funded enterprises enjoy obvious competitive advantages in development thanks to low investment and production costs. Furthermore, the Government of Brunei has also specially established the Brunei Economic Development Board, which, under the direct leadership of the Sultan, provides foreign investors with one-stop services, assists and supports the smooth operation of investment projects in Brunei; it offers convenience for Chinese-funded enterprises to carry on business in Brunei.

5. The friendly exchanges between China and Brunei have become increasingly close

The friendly bilateral exchanges provide a strong guarantee for the development of Chinese-funded enterprises in Brunei. Since China and Brunei officially established diplomatic relations in 1991, bilateral relations have developed steadily. The mutual political trust has improved continuously, the senior leaders have engaged in close exchanges, a strategic bilateral partnership has also been established, the two countries have cooperated better on many regional and international issues; in particular, on the issue of the South China Sea, they have reached a consensus on resolutely safeguarding the peace and stability of the South China Sea. Bilateral economic and trade cooperation has become increasingly stronger. Bilateral trade soared from USD 13.11 million in 1991 to USD 1.51 billion in 2015, an increase of 115.18 times. The two sides have also made great progress in cooperation and exchange in such fields as mutual investments, contractual labor services, construction of infrastructures and tourism. Bilateral social and cultural exchanges have also been intensified constantly. Thanks to the friendly exchanges between the two countries, it is easier for Chinese-funded enterprises to be recognized and supported by local people in Brunei, and it is convenient for enterprises to smoothly carry on business.

II. The Challenges for the Development of Chinese-funded Enterprises in Brunei

1. The government is inefficient in administrative examination and approval, the decision-making mechanism is inflexible

The Government of Brunei is relatively inefficient in administrative examination and approval, as it is bogged down in red tape. The process from project initiation to official operations is subject to a series of administrative examination and approval formalities, and the Government of Brunei lacks relevant industrial standards, some of the governmental staff seek comfort, and are unwilling to and do not dare to take the initiative in assuming responsibilities, so project examination and approval is severely delayed. Moreover, Brunei is not flexible in the decision-making mechanism for economic development. Although the Brunei Economic Development Board has been established to provide foreign investors with one-stop service, assist and support the operation of investment projects, it only serves as the messenger between Brunei's government departments and foreign enterprises, and does not have the *de facto* administrative examination and approval power relating to project operations; it is impossible to eliminate the inefficiency in administrative examination and approval of the projects. Thus, the expected operation dates of most projects carried out by Chinese-funded enterprises have been postponed or their construction periods have been extended, so the actual operating costs are much higher than the budget costs.

2. The industrial system is not complete, relevant supporting facilities for industries are less available

Brunei's industrial system is not complete, the oil and gas industry is dominant, while the developmental foundation for other industries is very weak, most industries need to start from scratch, and relevant supporting facilities for industries are extremely scarce. Most raw materials, mechanical parts and electronic components necessary for production performed by Chinese-funded enterprises in Brunei need to be imported. In order to ensure smooth and orderly production at enterprises, it is necessary to increase the inventory, so inventory cost is on the rise. Chinese-funded enterprises are not able to enjoy an economy of scale, an economy of scope or the effect of a home market resulting from industrial clusters and complete supporting facilities for industries, therefore making it inconvenient for production operation at enterprises and increasing production costs.

3. There is a shortage of local labor, the access for foreign labor has been tightened

As the population is only 420,000 in Brunei, the total quantity of local labor is very small and there is a structural problem in local labor. At present, 60%

of the Bruneian people work in government departments or state-owned institutions, and small and medium-sized enterprises or foreign enterprises are not popular among Bruneian people. Moreover, as a high social welfare policy has been introduced, some people become lazy and less aggressive. In Brunei, dirty, laborious and unskilled work is carried out mainly by foreign workers, and foreign workers make up a large proportion of all of the employed people. In order to prevent excessive foreign workers from affecting local employment and to increase the employment of local residents, the Government of Brunei has decided to reduce worker quota. In the meantime, the obtaining of work permits for foreign workers is subject to strict examination and red tape; in practice, work permits are granted on a case-by-case basis, and it generally takes three months or more to obtain quota after filing out the relevant application.[1] This poses challenges to Chinese-funded enterprises with respect to production and employment in Brunei.

4. Chinese-funded enterprises have not yet fully integrated themselves into the Bruneian society, they engage in fierce competition with Western multinational corporations

As Chinese-funded enterprises initiated their investments in Brunei relatively late, they are at a lower level of international operations compared with the mature Western multinational corporations; besides their gap in core competitiveness including technology, capital and management, Chinese-funded enterprises have often incurred vicious incidents, such as labor disputes, cutthroat competition, dishonest operations and destruction of the local environment. Chinese-funded enterprises do not adapt to international competition rules and find it hard to integrate themselves into the Bruneian society, as evidenced by the following aspects: First, they lack research and recognition of Bruneian Malay and Islamic cultures, it is difficult for them to integrate themselves into Bruneian Malay mainstream society; second, they are less enthusiastic about the social programs for public good in Brunei; third, they do not attach importance to publicity, their brand awareness is poor, their business relies too heavily on local partners; fourth, they lack a

[1] Brunei Tightens the Access Policy for Foreign Workers. http://brunei.caexpo.com/zcfx_wl/zcdx/2014/05/29/3623684.html.

strategic line of thought and long-term considerations, with shortsighted decision-making qualities and behaviors.[2] Therefore, local people accept and recognize Chinese-funded enterprises less and they favor Western multinational corporations in project bidding; in many cases, Chinese-funded enterprises respond to bidding with lowest cost but finally fail in the bidding; Chinese-funded enterprises are often in the subordinate position of subcontractors in project contracting.

III. The Suggestions on the Development and Growth of Chinese-funded Enterprises in Brunei

1. Chinese-funded enterprises should increase their level of international operations

The international operation of Chinese-funded enterprises is the essential requirement of taking root in Brunei. First, they should attach great importance to enterprise innovation, make bold changes, constantly carry out institutional, technical and management innovations, they should fully leverage their comparative advantages and continuously enhance their core competitiveness; second, they should train more personnel, and vigorously cultivate the inter-disciplinary talents who cater to the needs of internationalization; they should actively carry out the strategy of localizing employees, turning local people into talents skillful in business, technology and management; finally, they should strictly observe Brunei's laws and regulations and international competition rules, abandon the bad habits of addressing interpersonal relationship and acting through improper channels in handling matters, they should act in accordance with laws and regulations and keep production operations on the right track.

2. They should strengthen cooperation with local enterprises in Brunei

Cooperating with local enterprises is the essential condition for Chinese-funded enterprises to perform localized operations in Brunei. Chinese-funded

---

[2] Huang Hongtao, As Chinese Enterprises Go Global, They Should Integrate Themselves into the Local Society, *International Business Daily*, July 25, 2006.

enterprises should attach importance to cooperating with local enterprises and helping local enterprises operate and develop. They should support local enterprises in undertaking business at various links including research, development and design, production, circulation and sales, thus improving the technical management and competitiveness of local enterprises. They should establish a good relationship with local chambers of commerce, associations, manufacturers and consumers; they should set up an effective mechanism of communication and coordination, and actively make themselves become part of Brunei's economic diversification strategy.

3. They should enhance integration into local society

Respecting local culture and achieving integration into the local society constitutes the important foundation for the development and growth of Chinese-funded enterprises. On the one hand, as the Bruneian society has its special characteristics, maintaining close connection with the upper class and mainstream of the Bruneian society is particularly important for Chinese-funded enterprises to carry on business, Chinese-funded enterprises can keep and develop a good working relationship and personal relationship with the royal family and the Government of Brunei by exchanging visits between senior government officials, inviting enterprises to visit and actively participating in major activities. On the other hand, Chinese-funded enterprises should actively participate in various recreational, sports and festival activities, and properly provide financial aid and support. In the meantime, they should actively participate in the social programs for the public good in Brunei to win recognition by local residents, and to expand the popularity and influence of Chinese-funded enterprises in Brunei.

Chapter 36

The 2015 APEC Leaders' Meeting and China–Philippines Relations

Cai Qi*

During the two days of November 18–19, 2015, the 23rd APEC Leaders' Meeting was held in Manila, the Philippines. The Philippines once again held the APEC Meeting after nearly 20 years since it held that Meeting in 1996 during the period of President Fidel Valdez Ramos. In fact, the Government of Benigno Aquino III paid particular attention to the APEC Meeting.

I. The Background of the Philippines' Holding of the APEC Leaders' Meeting

The 2015 APEC Leaders' Meeting was considered to be held in an eventful year. On the one hand, a Russian passenger plane was destroyed by terrorists in Egypt and terrorist attacks, which shocked the world, occurred in Paris, France, ahead of the meeting; as an important global leaders' meeting, the APEC Leaders' Meeting incorporated counter-terrorism as the focus which could not be ignored. On the other hand, the Philippines pledged not to

* Cai Qi, Research Assistant at the Philippines Institute of the China–ASEAN Research Institute of Guangxi University.

put the issue of the South China Sea on the agenda of the APEC Leaders' Meeting, an economic and trade forum, but USA repeatedly stressed that it would discuss the issue of the South China Sea during the APEC Leaders' Meeting, and the issue of the South China sea drew widespread attention. A number of signs showed that the APEC Leaders' Meeting was not merely a regional economic and trade forum, but it involved a political factor and internationalized regional issues.

Within the Philippines, the APEC Leaders' Meeting was highly controversial. As the 2016 general election in the Philippines drew near, the APEC Leaders' Meeting became the last large show arranged by President Benigno Aquino III within his term of office. Many flights were canceled at the Manila International Airport, many roads in urban areas were closed to traffic, government institutions and schools had a four-day holiday to alleviate the pressure of urban traffic. Therefore, some people believed that the expense of the great meeting would overwhelm the fragile fiscal system of the Philippines, and the people's requirement for tax reduction was not satisfied; the people complained that the APEC Leaders' Meeting would affect their work and lives; many reports questioned the government's ability to hold the APEC Leaders' Meeting.

II. The Achievements Made in the APEC Leaders' Meeting in the Philippines

The Philippines spent 10 billion pesos on the APEC Leaders' Meeting and thus Philippine taxpayers lodged many complaints, but the Government of Benigno Aquino III obtained great benefits due to the APEC Leaders' Meeting. According to Chinese Commercial News, during the APEC Leaders' Meeting, the Government of Benigno Aquino III signed a number of agreements with many countries, covering the economic, security, educational and other fields (see Table 1). Regarding the objectives of the above signing, one view held that as the holding of the APEC Leaders' Meeting was costly, the Government of Benigno Aquino III had to make some "achievements" in order to silence the critics in the Philippines' political circle; another view held that some agreements signed by the Philippines were designed to counter China, the agreements or commitments between

Table 1. The Achievements Made During the 2015 APEC Leaders' Meeting in the Philippines

The Philippines and the USA	Barack Obama reaffirmed the United States' resolve to defend the Philippines, and expressed support for the Philippines' appeals for the South China Sea; Barack Obama announced that USA would provide two US ships to the Philippines for improving the Philippines' capability for patrolling the sea.
The Philippines and Japan	The two countries signed the agreements on strengthening bilateral cooperation on national defense, social security and railway projects.*
The Philippines and Russia	The two countries reached an agreement on the establishment of the Philippines–Russia Trade and Economic Committee, and signed a memorandum on cracking down on new psychotropic drugs.
The Philippines and Vietnam	The two countries signed a declaration on the establishment of a strategic partnership, and exchanged the revised 2010 Philippines–Vietnam memorandum agreement on the supply of Vietnam's rice to the Philippines.
The Philippines and Chile	The two countries signed a letter of intent on studying the interests in the free trade agreement between the two countries and a memorandum of understanding on disaster reduction risk management.
The Philippines and South Korea	The President of South Korea, Park Geun-hye, expressed support for the Philippines' military modernization act.
The Philippines and Australia	The two countries signed a joint declaration on the Philippines–Australia comprehensive partnership, and a memorandum of understanding on cooperation in vocational and technical education.
The Philippines and Papua New Guinea	The two countries reaffirmed their efforts at strengthening their commitment to cooperation starting from 1975, and at developing policy consultation, health and medical tourism, investment promotion and capacity building.
The Philippines and Mexico	The two countries signed an agreement on the avoidance of double taxation and tax evasion, and a memorandum of understanding on cracking down on the trafficking of narcotics, psychotropic drugs, similar drugs and toxic chemicals, as well as a memorandum of understanding between the Philippines and Mexico on cooperation on tourism.

(*Continued*)

Table 1. (*Continued*)

The Philippines and Canada	The Prime Minister of Canada undertook to support the Philippines in joining the TPP.
The Philippines and Columbia	The two countries discussed the possibility of expanding their cooperation on energy and gas resources.

Notes: *The railway project was originally assisted by China in construction in 2005, but currently it is frozen, Japan will offer loans to the Philippines for supporting the construction of the railway.
Source: *Chinese Commercial News*. The List of Agreements and Commitments between the Philippines and Other Countries, *Chinese Commercial News*, November 20, 2015, http://www.shangbao.com.ph/fgyw/2015/11-20/45628.shtml.

the Philippines and USA, Japan, Vietnam, South Korea and Australia involved national defense, even the agreements between the Philippines and USA, while those with Japan also involved the issue of the South China Sea; the Philippines also signed a strategic partnership agreement with Vietnam, a country also laying claim to the South China Sea. As indicated, the Philippines were establishing the strategic encirclement ring against China.

III. China–Philippines Relations during the APEC Leaders' Meeting

1. The Philippines hoped that China would be able to attend the APEC Leaders' Meeting

Before the APEC Leaders' Meeting, the result of the arbitration case against China, concerning the disputes over the South China Sea, brought to the United Nations by the Philippines was announced, showing that the ad hoc arbitration tribunal of the United Nations had the jurisdiction over the case and China excessively laid claim to the South China Sea. As the arbitration result was announced, the Philippines welcomed the arbitration result on the one hand and worried that its relations with China would worsen on the other. In particular, as the 2016 general election of the Philippines approached, the policy adopted by the Government of Benigno Aquino III needed to take into account more the candidate from the Liberal Party Mar Roxas, taking an undue tough stance against China, which went against the Philippines' situation during the next step. In 2016, the Philippines' vice presidential candidate, senator Bongbong Marcos, pointed out that President Benigno Aquino III needed to rely on APEC to get along well with Xi Jinping. Being aware of the situation, President Benigno Aquino III continuously expressed goodwill on the issue of Xi Jinping's visit to the Philippines and emphasized that the issue of the South China Sea would not be discussed during the APEC Leaders' Meeting. Ultimately, Chinese President Xi Jinping confirmed on November 9 that he would attend the APEC Leaders' Meeting. In particular, as the President of Russia Vladimir Putin and the President of Indonesia Joko were absent from the APEC Leaders' Meeting in Manila, and the media read too much into their absence, the arrival of Chinese President Xi Jinping greatly relieved the Government of The Philippines. On November 10, 2015, Chinese Foreign Minister Wang Yi paid a lightning visit to the Philippines for arranging Xi Jinping's visit to the Philippines, he met with President Benigno Aquino III, which was deemed as a sign that China–Philippines relations had improved to some extent.

The media also anticipated Xi Jinping's attendance at the APEC Leaders' Meeting, but the media were divided over whether the APEC Leaders' Meeting should involve the issue of the South China Sea. The *Philippine Daily Inquirer* commented that the APEC Leaders' Meeting was an economic forum for promoting free trade and sustainable development in the Asia-Pacific region, and expected Chinese President Xi Jinping to attend the APEC Leaders' Meeting.[1] In an article in the *Manila Standard Today*, Victor Avecilla believed that Xi Jinping's visit to the Philippines presented a good opportunity for the Philippines, but President Benigno Aquino III pledged not to discuss the issue of the South China Sea and gave up the opportunity of negotiating with China through the APEC Leaders' Meeting. The article held that the Department of National Defense of the

[1]The Philippines Pledges to Not Discuss the Issue of the South China Sea during the APEC Leaders' Meeting, and Will Arrange the Chinese Side to Deliver a Keynote Speech. http://www.hqrw.com.cn/2015/1110/40331.shtml.

Philippines was nothing but a corrupt hollow institution and the Philippines cannot rely on its own strength to counter China, so the Philippines had no choice but to seek support from the international community; as Benigno Aquino III sat close to Xi Jinping during the APEC Leaders' Meeting, it was the best opportunity for obtaining a commitment face-to-face.[2] However, anyhow, Xi Jinping's attendance at the APEC Leaders' Meeting was a good thing for various sectors of the Philippines. Even the anti-China group in the Philippines "gave face" very much. According to the Chinese Commercial News, an important member of the anti-China group in the Philippines, former National Security Advisor Roilo Golez, said that all of the visitors were guests and pledged not to carry out demonstrations during the meeting.

2. The US interference and the dual character of the Philippines

The Philippines promised that as the APEC Leaders' Meeting was an economic and trade forum, its agenda did not cover the issue of the South China Sea, but USA, an ally of the Philippines, stated outright that the US would discuss the issue of the South China Sea during the APEC Leaders' Meeting, while the Philippines stated that the Philippines cannot prohibit member countries from discussing the issue of the South China Sea. During the APEC Leaders' Meeting, the issue of the South China Sea was not involved, but Barack Obama embarked on the Philippines' warship to express support for the Philippines' claims over the South China Sea, Japan vowed to provide military support to the Philippines and the Philippines signed a series of agreements concerned, undoubtedly, these moves put the issue of the South China Sea on the table. In the author's opinion, as recently the Philippines has become increasingly close to Vietnam in dealing with China, the Philippines shows a dual character. On the one hand, the Philippines upholds a tough stance on military issues, including the issue

[2]Victor Avecilla. Aquino goofs up again, this time on Apec, http://manilastandardtoday.com/opinion/columns/hail-to-the-chair-by-victor-avecilla/191872/aquino-goofs-up-again-this-time-on-apec.html.

of the South China Sea, and builds the image of a small and weak country. In this regard, the Philippines' media have acted in a very prominent way on the issue of the South China Sea; they always report that China "bullies" the Philippines. On the other hand, on the political and economic fronts, the Philippines hopes to maintain amicable relations with China so as to obtain more support and help.

3. The achievements made by Xi Jinping's attendance at the APEC Leaders' Meeting

The exchanges between Chinese and Philippine leaders during the APEC Leaders' Meeting revealed great disagreements between the two countries. Although the Philippines hoped that the APEC Leaders' Meeting might help break the ice between China and the Philippines, in reality, the interaction between Chinese and Philippine leaders was limited.

Nevertheless, in the view of the author, Xi Jinping's attendance at the APEC Leaders' Meeting in Manila gained fruitful achievements. First, Chinese President Xi Jinping showcased the image of China as a responsible great power to the Asian-Pacific nations, and even to the world, China did not take an attitude of exclusion towards the APEC Leaders' Meeting held by the Philippines due to the issue of the South China Sea between China and the Philippines; instead, China actively participated in the meeting and demonstrated the look of a great power. Led and driven by the Chinese Government, the people from various sectors in China actively participated in the APEC Leaders' Meeting, giving advice and suggestions on global development. Second, during the APEC Leaders' Meeting, Chinese President Xi Jinping delivered a speech "Giving Full Play to the Leading Role of the Asia-Pacific in Addressing the World Economic Challenges", expounding China's viewpoints and approach concerning global economic growth, demonstrating China's confidence, pinpointing the direction for regional, even global, economic and trade cooperation, expressing the view that as long as positions were upheld in China–Philippines relations, relevant issues can be ultimately addressed in a proper way. Third, the ice in China–Philippines relations was broken to some extent through the APEC Leaders' Meeting, fostering a good atmosphere for further improving bilateral relations.

IV. The Countermeasures for China–Philippines Relations in the Next Step from the Perspective of the APEC Leaders' Meeting

1. China should break the encirclement ring against China

How can it be broken? The author holds that China should take the following actions. First, China should break the alliance with the surrounding countries against China. The countries having territorial disputes with China, including the Philippines, Vietnam, Japan, even India, should come together because the extraterritorial forces act as a go-between and these countries hope to enhance their strength by forging an alliance. However, all of these countries have close economic and trade ties with China; for some small countries, a stable and peaceful economic environment is the important guarantee for development, and worsening relations with China will, in the end, harm their own interests. China can focus on some countries to make breakthroughs, gradually break the encirclement ring against China and improve the surrounding environment. Second, China should build an image of China as a responsible great power in order to enhance mutual political trust. A lack of trust in China and the fear that the rise of China will harm their own interests results in some countries coming together. China has conveyed to the world the message that the rise of China is a peaceful rise. Regarding future development, China should let the world understand China, while to this end, China should build an image of a responsible great power. In practice, China should make the surrounding countries believe that China is responsible, thus dispelling their doubts about China.

2. China should flexibly cope with the situation where the Philippines often changes its promises

The democratic system and open public opinion in the Philippines determine that the Philippines frequently changes its promises on many issues, and that even such change has become an important diplomatic means for the Philippines. In this regard, following the developments in the Philippines' public opinion and making flexible responses to the Philippines' changes is the key. Most importantly, China must deepen its understanding of the

Philippines; only when China understands the Philippines can China better deal with that country. The first step for gaining an understanding lies in strengthening communications with the Philippines, really experiencing and understanding the Philippines.

3. The people-to-people exchanges should be enhanced to ease the tension between the two countries

As shown by the exchanges between the leaders of both countries during the APEC Leaders' Meeting, it is difficult to break the ice in intergovernmental cooperation in a short time; only enabling people-to-people exchanges to enhance intergovernmental exchange is feasible. It is necessary to mobilize the Chinese organizations in the Philippines — including the Federation of Filipino–Chinese Chambers of Commerce and Industry, the Federation of the Filipino–Chinese Association of the Philippines, the Philippine Chinese Chamber of Commerce and Industry, and Filipino–Chinese Amity Club — to enhance communication and mutual understanding between China and the Philippines, to reach consensuses, and gradually remove the Philippines' attitude of exclusion towards China, thus creating the conditions for resuming official exchanges between China and the Philippines; only in this way can China–Philippines relations be improved fundamentally.

Part 6
The Chronicle of Events

Chapter 37

The Chronicle of Events in China–ASEAN Cooperation in 2015

Luo Chuanyu*

January

- **22nd:** In 2014, Taiwan's exports to the ASEAN community amounted to USD 59,281 million, showing the trend of a slowdown.
- **25th:** The 5th informal meeting of the secretariat of the China–ASEAN Center, the Japan–ASEAN Center, the South Korea–ASEAN Center was held in Naypyidaw, Myanmar.
- **29th:** The Secretary of Foreign Affairs of the Philippines, Albert del Rosario, openly required, for the first time, the ASEAN countries to "express positions" on China's land reclamation in the South China Sea, and "warned" that China's actions would eventually "pose threats" to the Southeast Asian countries.

February

- **9th:** The 7th round of negotiations involving the Regional Comprehensive Economic Partnership (RCEP) was held in Bangkok, Thailand.

* Luo Chuanyu, Assistant to the Director of the China–ASEAN Research Institute of Guangxi University, Director of the Public Opinion Monitoring Center, Associate Professor, Doctor of Laws. Cooperator: Zhao Hui, research assistant at the China–ASEAN Research Institute.

March

- **2nd:** The Director of the ASEAN Harmonised Tariff Nomenclature (AHTN) under *the Framework Agreement on Comprehensive Economic Cooperation between the Association of Southeast Asian Nations and the People's Republic of China* came into effect.
- **6th:** The 1st Lancang–Mekong River Dialogue and Cooperation Senior Officials' Meeting was held in Beijing, China.
- **11th:** The ASEAN Secretary General Le Luong Minh previously stated that China's position of the nine-dotted line in the South China Sea was illegitimate; the Ministry of Foreign Affairs of China responded that the ASEAN community would abide by the ASEAN community's neutral position on the issue of the South China Sea.

April

- 10th: The 16th meeting of the China–ASEAN Joint Cooperation Committee was held in Indonesia.
- 27th: The 26th ASEAN Summit was held in Kuala Lumpur, Malaysia, in which China's island and reef project in the South China Sea became the focus. The Prime Minister of Singapore, Lee Hsien Loong, discussed the situation of the South China Sea for the first time during the summit.
- 31st: As of this day, ten ASEAN countries became the official prospective founding members of the Asian Infrastructure Investment Bank.

May

- 1st: The ASEAN community, China, Japan and South Korea (10+3) Finance Ministers' Meeting was held in Baku, the capital of Azerbaijan.
- 14th: The 6th informal meeting of the secretariat of the China–ASEAN Center, the Japan–ASEAN Center, the South Korea–ASEAN Center was held in Jakarta, Indonesia.
- 26th: The 2nd China–ASEAN People-to-people High-level Dialogue was held in Nusa Dua, Indonesia.
- 29th: The 14th Shangri-La Dialogue was inaugurated in Singapore.

June

- 18th: The new Chinese Ambassador to the ASEAN, Xu Bu, officially submitted a letter of appointment to the ASEAN Secretary General, Le Luong Minh, in Jakarta, Indonesia.

July

- 11th: The five-person arbitration panel established by the International Tribunal for the Law of the Sea under the United Nations listened to the appeals expressed by the delegation of the Philippines.
- 21st: The US Center for Strategic and International Studies (CSIS) held the 5th seminar on the issue of the South China Sea.
- 28th: The 9th ASEAN–China Forum on Social Development and Poverty Reduction was held in Vientiane, Laos.
- 29th: The 9th Senior Officials' Meeting on the Issue of the South China Sea was held in Tianjin, China.
- 6th: The 48th ASEAN Foreign Ministers' Meeting, the ASEAN community and China, Japan, South Korea Foreign Ministers' Meeting, and the East Asia Summit Foreign Ministers' Meeting were held in Kuala Lumpur, Malaysia.
- 23rd: The 21st Japan–ASEAN Economic Ministers' Meeting, the 18th ASEAN "10+3" Economic Ministers' Meeting were held in Kuala Lumpur, Malaysia.

September

- 1st: Chinese Ambassador to the ASEAN, Xu Bu, attended the large picture show commemorating the 70th anniversary of the victory of the War of the Chinese People's Resistance against Japanese Aggression, Indonesia's independence and the victory of the World Anti-fascist War.
- 12th: The cooperation agreement on the China–ASEAN (Nanning) Currency Index was signed in Nanning, Guangxi.
- 16th: The launching ceremony of the *Annual Report on the Development of China–ASEAN Cooperation (2014–2015)* was held in Nanning, Guangxi.
- 17th: The 1st China–ASEAN Forum on the Handicapped was inaugurated in Nanning, Guangxi.

- 18th: The 12th China–ASEAN Expo, the China–ASEAN Business and Investment Summit were inaugurated in Nanning, Guangxi.
- 18th: The 12th China–ASEAN Expo Trade Facilitation & High-level Seminar on the 20th Anniversary of the Establishment of the WTO was held in Nanning, Guangxi.
- 19th: The launching ceremony of the China–ASEAN Cross-border E-commerce Platform was held in Nanning, Guangxi, the leaders of the chambers of commerce and industry from the ASEAN countries and the China Council for the Promotion of International Trade signed the *Memorandum of Cooperation in the China–ASEAN Cross-border E-commerce Platform*.
- 20th: The China–ASEAN Mayors' Forum 2015 was inaugurated in Nanning, Guangxi.
- 6th: The High-level Forum on the ASEAN Economic Community and the China–ASEAN Cooperation in Production Capacity was held in Jakarta, Indonesia.

October

- 5th–7th: The ASEAN community and China, Japan, South Korea Energy Senior Officials' Meeting and the 33rd ASEAN Energy Ministerial Meeting were held in Kuala Lumpur, Malaysia.
- 14th–16th: The Asian Political Parties' Special Conference on the Silk Road was held in Beijing, China.
- 16th–17th: The China–ASEAN Defense Ministers' Informal Meeting was held in Beijing, which was the first meeting of that kind held in China.
- 20th: China and the ASEAN countries held the 10th Senior Officials' Meeting on the Implementation of the *Declaration on the Conduct of Parties in the South China Sea*, the 15th Meeting of the Joint Working Group was held on a back-to-back basis.
- 20th: The "10+3" Science and Technology Ministers' Meeting was held in Daejeon Metropolitan City, South Korea.
- 20th: The "10+3" Tourism Youth Summit was held in Cebu, the Philippines.
- 23rd: The China–ASEAN Law Enforcement and Security Cooperation Ministerial Dialogue was held in Beijing, China.

- 26th–31st: The 14th "10+3" Environment Ministers' Meeting was held in Hanoi, Vietnam.

November

- 3rd–5th: The 3rd ASEAN Defense Ministers' Meeting was held in Kuala Lumpur, Malaysia.
- 4th: The 10th ASEAN–China People's Friendship Meeting was held in Bandar Seri Begawan, Brunei.
- 5th–6th: The 14th ASEAN–China Transport Ministers' Meeting was held in Malaysia.
- 6th: The Minister of National Development Planning of Indonesia, Sofyan Djalil, said that Indonesia had prepared a series of blue books on infrastructure construction plans, and planned to apply for USD 38 billion loans from the Asian Infrastructure Investment Bank.
- 7th: The 14th Asian Art Festival and the 2nd Maritime Silk Road International Arts Festival were inaugurated in Quanzhou City, Fujian Province, China.
- 11th: The 5th Meeting of the China–ASEAN Inter-bank Association Executive Committee and Academic Seminar were held.
- 12th: The 1st Foreign Ministers' Meeting on Lancang-Mekong Cooperation was held in Jinghong, Yunnan Province, China and the Lancang-Mekong cooperation mechanism was officially established.
- 14th: The 32nd Meeting of the Asian Bankers Association was held in Taipei, Taiwan, China.
- 16th: The 5th East Asia Ocean Conference jointly held by the Partnerships in Environmental Management for the Seas of East Asia (PEMSEA) and its member countries was inaugurated in Da Nang City, Vietnam.
- 18th–19th: The 23rd APEC Leaders' Meeting was held in Manila, the Philippines.
- 20th–31st: The football clubs from the ASEAN countries took part in an international football match held in Kunming City, Yunnan Province.
- 21st: The 27th ASEAN Summit was inaugurated in Kuala Lumpur.
- 22nd: The Chinese Government and 10 ASEAN countries signed the *Protocol to Amend the Framework Agreement on Comprehensive*

Economic Cooperation and Certain Agreements Thereunder between the Association of Southeast Asian Nations (ASEAN) and the People's Republic of China in Kuala Lumpur, Malaysia; the China–ASEAN Free Trade Area (CAFTA) was officially upgraded.

- 23rd: The China Construction Bank (Asia) successfully issued the world's first 21st Century Maritime Silk Road RMB bond at the Kuala Lumpur Stock Exchange, Malaysia; the 1 billion yuan bond was the first RMB bond in the history of Malaysia.
- 25th: The 9th China–ASEAN Procurators-General Conference was inaugurated in Nanning, Guangxi.

December

- 2nd: The meeting of the 5th Board of Governors of the China–ASEAN Center was held in Kunming, China.
- 14th: The 2nd ASEAN Development Forum was held in Hong Kong, China.

Chapter 38

The Chronicle of Events in China's Cooperation with ASEAN Countries in 2015

The Chronicle of Events in China–Thailand Cooperation in 2015

Yue Guining[1]

January

- **4th:** The Prime Minister of Thailand, Prayuth Chan-ocha, met with the visiting President of the Chinese Academy of Sciences, Bai Chunli.
- **12th:** The first Alumni Association of the Confucius Institute in Thailand — the Alumni Association of the Confucius Institute at BSRU — was established in Bangkok.
- **17th:** The launching ceremony of the Thailand–China Talent Exchange Association — the Thailand–China Talent Exchange Information Online — was held at the China Cultural Center in Bangkok, Thailand.

[1]Yue Guining, Director of the Thailand Institute of the China–ASEAN Research Institute of Guangxi University. Cooperator: Liu Xinyuan, Research Assistant at the Thailand Institute of the China–ASEAN Research Institute of Guangxi University.

February

- **5th:** Meng Jianzhu visited Thailand and met with the Prime Minister of Thailand, Prayuth Chan-ocha, the Deputy Prime Minister and Defense Minister Prawit Wongsuwan, the two countries signed the document on cooperation in law enforcement and security.
- **6th:** Chinese Defense Minister Chang Wanquan paid a two-day visit to Thailand.
- **9th–13th:** The three-training-ship fleet of the Royal Thai Navy arrived at Zhanjiang to pay a four-day visit to the South China Sea Fleet.

March

- **11th:** The 1st meeting of the Thailand–China Joint Committee on Agricultural Trade was held.
- **11th–12th:** The 3rd meeting on the Thailand–China railway cooperation plan was held, and a formal contract was signed.
- **17th:** The 2015 Wuhan-Thailand Series Exchange Activities were launched, and a number of memoranda on economic and trade cooperation were signed.
- **19th:** The Deputy Chief of the Joint Staff of the People's Liberation Army, Qi Jianguo, met with the counter-terrorism delegation led by the Commander of the Counter-terrorism Center at the Supreme Command of the Thai Armed Forces.
- **20th:** Thailand's Buddhist circle respectfully greeted the relics of the eminent centenarian monk, Benhuan, from China.
- **23rd:** Meng Jianzhu and Guo Shengkun met with the delegation led by the Secretary-General of the National Security Council of Thailand.
- **24th:** The President of the National Assembly of Thailand Pornpetch Wichitcholchai, held talks with Zhang Dejiang in Beijing; on the next day, he met with Li Yuanchao.
- **30th:** The China Study-Abroad Centre (CASC), the Thai Pan Pacific Trade Association and 19 well-known Chinese universities jointly held the first "examination concerning a scholarship for studying in China" in Thailand.

- **30th:** Chengdu and Chiang Mai Province, Thailand officially established sister-city ties.

April

- **1st:** A delegation led by the Culture Minister of Thailand, Vira Rojpojchanarat, visited China.
- **2nd:** The China–ASEAN Expo Thailand Exhibition was inaugurated in Bangkok; Peng Qinghua, the Secretary of the Party Committee of the Guangxi Zhuang Autonomous Region, met with the Prime Minister of Thailand, Prayuth Chan-ocha.
- **3rd–6th:** At the invitation of China, Thai King's Princess, Maha Chakri Sirindhorn, visited China; she met with Li Yuanchao, Yu Zhengsheng and Liu Yandong.
- **8th:** The Chinese State Councilor and Defense Minister, Chang Wanquan, held talks with the Deputy Prime Minister of Thailand and Defense Minister, Prawit Wongsuwan. On the next day, Chinese Vice Premier Zhang Gaoli met with Prawit Wongsuwan.
- **14th:** China invested 10 billion yuan in the wastewater recycling project at the rubber park in Thailand.
- **22nd:** The Industrial and Commercial Bank of China (Thailand) Co., Ltd. officially launched the RMB clearing bank service.
- **27th:** Thai KASIKORNBANK, Alipay and King Power Group signed an agreement to jointly launch a duty-free commodities online shopping service.

May

- **8th:** The Prime Minister of Thailand Prayuth Chan-ocha met with the Secretary of the Secretariat of the CPC Central Committee, State Councilor Yang Jing.
- **21st:** The opening ceremony of China–Fujian Week & Zhangzhou Industrial Project Promotion Fair were held in Bangkok.
- **29th:** The 2015 China-ASEAN Expo Culture Exhibition was inaugurated in Nanning, Guangxi.

- **29th:** Fuzhou Kaiyuan Temple and Chulalongkorn University Thailand held the ceremony of signing a memorandum on the joint construction of the Mahayana Research Center.
- **30th:** The Year of Thailand·China (Shandong) Culture 2015 was inaugurated in Bangkok.

June

- **10th:** The Interior Minister led the delegation of provincial governors to attend the 7th Economic Corridor Ministerial Meeting and Local Provincial Governors' Meeting held in Yunnan Province.
- **11th:** The 7th Greater Mekong Subregion (GMS) Economic Corridor Forum was held in Kunming.
- **12th:** The 3rd China–Southeast Asia Expo was inaugurated in Kunming.
- **15th:** Harbin Engineering University and Kasetsart University, Walailak University signed a memorandum of cooperation.
- **20th:** The 2015 Sichuan Tourism Promotion Fair was successfully held in Bangkok.
- **24th:** The 1st Confucius Institute for the Maritime Silk Road in the world was officially established at Dhurakij Pundit University.

July

- **10th:** Bangkok and Shenzhen signed a memorandum of cooperation on sister cities and established sister-city ties.
- **17th:** *China–ASEAN Panorama* (China) and *ASEAN Business* (Thailand) signed a cooperation agreement in Bangkok.
- **18th:** The activity commemorating the 40th anniversary of the establishment of diplomatic relations between China and Thailand kicked off at the China Cultural Center in Bangkok.
- **21st–24th:** The Chairman of the Chinese People's Political Consultative Conference, Yu Zhengsheng, visited Thailand and met with Princess Maha Chakri Sirindhorn, the President of the National Assembly of Thailand, Pornpetch Wichitcholchai, the President of the Privy Council, Prem Tinsulanonda, and the Prime Minister of Thailand, Prayuth Chan-ocha.

August

- **6th:** The Confucius Classroom at Chongfah Sinseung Wanich Bamrung School in Chiang Mai was inaugurated.
- **6th–8th:** The Transportation Minister of Thailand visited China.
- **9th:** The 12th Chinese Bridge–Baoshiwang Cup was held in Bangkok, Thailand.
- **25th:** The China–Thailand Business Forum was held in Bangkok, Thailand.

September

- **2nd–5th:** The Deputy Prime Minister and Defense Minister, Prawit Wongsuwan, attended the series activities commemorating the 70th anniversary of the victory of the War of the Chinese People's Resistance against Japanese Aggression.
- **12th:** The 14th Confucius Institute was established at Assumption University, Thailand.
- **16th:** City Airways and Commercial Aircraft Corporation of China Ltd., ICBC Leasing signed a memorandum of understanding on cooperation in the purchase/leasing of ten C919 large passenger aircraft and 10 ARJ21-700 aircraft.
- **18th:** The Chinese Calligraphy and Painting Charity Show Party Celebrating the 40th Anniversary of the Establishment of Diplomatic Relations between China and Thailand and the 60th Birthday of Her Royal Highness, Princess Maha Chakri Sirindhorn was held in Bangkok.
- **29th:** Thailand became the 52nd signatory of the Asian Infrastructure Investment Bank.

October

- **1st:** Thailand Airport Express purchased seven trains (28 carriages in total) from the China CNR Corporation.
- **3rd:** The 5th Yunnan–Thailand (North) Cooperation Working Group Meeting was held in Kunming.
- **7th:** The Foreign Minister of Thailand, Don Pramudwinai, attended the activity celebrating the 40th Anniversary of the Establishment of Diplomatic Relations Between China and Thailand in China.

- **15th–18th:** The Deputy Prime Minister and Defense Minister, Prawit Wongsuwan, attended the China-ASEAN Defense Ministers' Informal Meeting, and the 6th Xiangshan Forum.

November

- **5th:** The government delegations of Dalian, Shanghai, Shandong, Guangzhou, Wuhan and Beijing attended the Meeting on Strengthening Sister-City Cooperation and Exchanges in Bangkok.
- **10th:** Thailand and China jointly established the Thailand–China Institute of Science and Technology focusing on the high-speed railway system courses.
- **12th–30th:** The air forces of China and Thailand conducted Yingji — 2015 joint training at Korat Air Force Base.
- **13th:** The Year of Thailand–China (Shandong) Culture 2015 kicked off in Bangkok, and the Sino-Thai International Rubber College was inaugurated.
- **17th:** The Thai cabinet approved the draft cooperation framework on the Thailand–China (Quasi) High-speed Railway Development Project.

December

- **3rd:** China and Thailand signed the framework document on intergovernmental railway cooperation between China and Thailand.
- **3rd:** COFCO and the Department of Foreign Trade under the Ministry of Commerce of Thailand signed an importation contract for 1 million tons of Thai rice.
- **16th–20th:** The Chinese State Council Wang Yong visited Thailand and met with the Prime Minister of Thailand, Prayuth Chan-ocha.
- **17th:** The pilot areas for the RMB Qualified Foreign Institutional Investor (RQFII) were extended to Thailand, with the pilot investment quota being 50 billion yuan.
- **17th:** The 2015 China–Thailand Business Forum was held in Bangkok, the 4th meeting of the China–Thailand Joint Committee on Economics and Trade Cooperation was held, the two sides signed an agreement on quarantine and inspection of the rice imported from Thailand to China.

- **19th:** The groundbreaking ceremony of the China–Thailand Railway Cooperation Project was held at Chiang Rak Noi Railway Station, Bang Pa-in County, Phra Nakhon Si Ayutthaya.

The Chronicle of Events in China–Vietnam Cooperation in 2015

Jin Dan[2]

January

- **3rd:** The ceremony celebrating the 2nd anniversary of the establishment of the Vietnam–Macao Friendship Association was held in Macao.
- **6th:** The Government of Vietnam issued the implementation regulations for the use of a hotline in case of an emergency in marine fishery activities between China and Vietnam.
- **16th:** The Vietnam Union of Friendship Organizations and the China–Vietnam Friendship Association held the ceremony commemorating the 65th anniversary of the establishment of diplomatic relations between China and Vietnam in Hanoi.

February

- **10th:** The Ministry of Industry and Trade of Vietnam issued the Circular No. 1093 and approved the plan of the year 2025 for the construction of a China–Vietnam border warehouse towards the year 2035.
- **11th:** The General Secretary of the Communist Party of Vietnam, Nguyen Phu Trong, communicated with the General Secretary of the Communist Party of China, Xi Jinping, by phone with respect to the 65th anniversary of the establishment of diplomatic relations between China and Vietnam.

---

[2]Jin Dan, Director of the Vietnam Institute of the China–ASEAN Research Institute of Guangxi University.

- **12th:** The Secretary of the Party Committee of Hanoi City, Phạm Quang Nghị, met with the Chinese Ambassador to Vietnam, Hong Xiaoyong.

March

- **14th:** The leaders of the Binh Lieu District of Quảng Ninh Province and Fangchenggang City of Guangxi held talks, the two sides agreed to launch the construction project of Dang Mo Bridge at Dang Mo-Tongzhong Port as early as possible, providing convenience for border trade between the two countries.
- **13th–15th:** The China–Vietnam Working Group for Consultation on Maritime Cooperation and Joint Development held the fourth round of consultations in Da Nang, Vietnam.
- **15th:** The bridge approach of the Beilun River No. 2 Bridge connecting Mong Cai City, Vietnam with Dongxing City, China broke ground.
- **27th:** The international academic seminar on "The New Stage of China–Vietnam Cooperative Relations" was held in Hanoi.

April

- **2nd:** The Chinese Ambassador to Vietnam, Hong Xiaoyong, and the Vietnamese delegation paid tribute to Chinese martyrs who sacrificed their lives in Vietnam's war of resistance against US aggression at a martyrs cemetery in Thai Nguyen, Vietnam.
- **7th–10th:** At the invitation of Chinese President Xi Jinping, the General Secretary of the Communist Party of Vietnam, Nguyen Phu Trong, paid an official visit to China.
- **9th:** The Minister of Planning and Investment of Vietnam, Bui Quang Vinh, met with the Chairman of the National Development and Reform Commission, Xu Shaoshi, the two sides signed a memorandum of understanding on the establishment of the working group for infrastructure cooperation.
- **16th:** The Defense Minister of Vietnam, Phung Quang Thanh, met with Chinese Public Security Minister, Guo Shengkun, the two sides signed an agreement on the three-level border defense cooperation mechanism between China and Vietnam.

- **22nd–25th:** China and Vietnam held the fifth round of negotiations involving the *Treaty on Free Navigation in the Beilun Estuary Area*, the two sides agreed on the contents of a draft treaty and sought to sign it as early as possible.
- **24th:** China and Vietnam conducted the 10th joint fishery patrol in Beibu Gulf.
- **25th:** The Working Committee between four border provinces of Vietnam, including Quang Ninh and Lang son, and Guangxi, China held their 7th meeting.
- **27th:** The Voice of Vietnam and China National Radio signed a memorandum of cooperation.
- **30th:** Wei Chaoan, the Deputy Secretary of the Party Committee of the Guangxi Zhuang Autonomous Region, visited Binh Dinh Province, Vietnam, and said that Guangxi and Binh Dinh Province should establish amicable relations.

May

- **13th:** The Prime Minister of Vietnam Nguyen Tan Dung met with the delegation of the Yunnan Provincial Government.
- **14th:** The Vice Minister of Public Security of Vietnam, Thượng tướng To Lam, met with the delegation of the Guard Bureau under the Ministry of Public Security of China, which had paid a working visit to Vietnam.
- **15th:** The Defense Minister of Vietnam, Phung Quang Thanh, and Chinese Defense Minister Chang Wanquan co-chaired the 2nd symposium on amicable border defense between China and Vietnam.
- **16th:** The People's Republic of China issued the annual ban on fishing in the South China Sea, the Vietnamese authority raised objection and claimed that China's move was null and void.
- **16th:** The border forces of China and Vietnam conducted a joint patrol in Lao Cai Province on Vietnam's northern border.
- **18th:** The 2nd activity of friendly exchanges in border defense between China and Vietnam was conducted in Yunnan Province, Vietnam.

- **20th:** The Ministry of Agriculture and Rural Development and the Ministry of Agriculture of China signed a memorandum on agricultural cooperation.
- **25th:** The People's Committee of Lao Cai Province, Vietnam and Honghe Autonomous Prefecture, Yunnan Province, China held talks on speeding up the construction of the Lao Cai-Honghe Cross-border Economic Cooperation Zone.
- **26th:** Lao Cai Provincial Library, Vietnam exchanged 100 books with Minzu Library in Hekou County, Honghe Autonomous Prefecture, Yunnan Province.

June

- **6th:** The China–Vietnam Working Group for Sea Areas Outside the Mouth of Beibu Gulf held the 7th consultation in Hanoi, reaching a consensus on demarcation and cooperative development of the less sensitive sea areas.
- **10th:** The Customs Office of Lang son Province, Vietnam and Nanning Customs Office held the 2nd talks in 2015.
- **12th:** The Deputy Prime Minister of Vietnam, Hoang Trung Hai, attended the 3rd China-Southeast Asia Expo held in Yunnan Province.
- **15th:** The Guangxi Public Security and Border Defense Corps and the border defense forces of four provinces of Vietnam, including Quang Ninh and Lang Son, jointly held the meeting on jointly building friendly stations (teams) and villages as well as a safe border.
- **17th–19th:** The Deputy Prime Minister and Foreign Minister of Vietnam, Pham Binh Minh, attended the 8th meeting of the Steering Committee for China–Vietnam Bilateral Cooperation held in China.
- **24th:** The Deputy Head of the General Political Department of the Vietnam People's Army met with the Political Commissar of the PLA Xi'an Political Academy.
- **29th:** The Deputy Minister of Publicity of Vietnam met with the delegation of China's Xinhua News Agency.
- **29th:** The Governor of the State Bank of Vietnam, Nguyen Van Binh, and other founding members of the Asian Infrastructure

Investment Bank signed the "basic law" of the Asian Infrastructure Investment Bank in Beijing.

July

- **7th:** The Minister of Industry and Trade of Vietnam, Tran Tuan Anh, attended the Vietnam-China (Guangdong) Rice and Agricultural Products Fair held in Guangzhou, China.
- **18th:** The General Secretary of the Communist Party of Vietnam, Nguyen Phu Trong, met with Chinese Vice Premier, Zhang Gaoli, stressing that China and Vietnam should strengthen pragmatic and effective exchanges and cooperation in various fields.
- **18th:** The President of the Vietnam Union of Friendship Organizations, Vu Xuan Hong, granted the souvenir medal "Peace and Friendship for Various Ethnic Groups" to Li Xiaolin, the Chairperson of the Chinese People's Association for Friendship with Foreign Countries.

August

- **2nd:** China and Vietnam held the fourth round of negotiations on the *Treaty of Joint Development and Protection of Tourism Resources in the Ban Gioc Waterfall Area* in Beijing, China.
- **11th:** The Defense Minister of Vietnam, Phung Quang Thanh, met with the delegation of the Ministry of Defense of China.
- **12th:** Vietnam and China signed the agreement on inland water transportation.
- **13th:** The Vietnam Chamber of Commerce and Industry and the Hubei Chapter of the China Association of International Trade was held during the 2015 China (Hubei)–Vietnam Economic and Trade Fair.
- **19th:** The border defense force of Mong Cai International Port, Vietnam and Dongxing Border Inspection Station, China held the launching ceremony of the China–Vietnam joint efforts in increasing the level of border inspection service between China and Vietnam.
- **25th–27th:** The China–Vietnam Working Group for Consultation on Maritime Cooperation and Joint Development held the fifth round of negotiations in Dalian City.

September

- **3rd:** The President of Vietnam, Trương Tan Sang, attended the meeting commemorating the 70th anniversary of the victory of the War of the Chinese People's Resistance against Japanese Aggression and the victory of the World Anti-fascist War.
- **11th:** The Ministry of Information and Communications of Vietnam and the State Post Bureau of China signed a memorandum of understanding on cooperation in the postal field.
- **18th:** Chinese Vice Premier, Zhang Gaoli, and the Deputy Prime Minister of Vietnam, Nguyen Xuan Phuc, attended the opening ceremony of the 12th China–ASEAN Expo & Business and Investment Summit.

October

- **14th–18th:** The Defense Minister of Vietnam, Phung Quang Thanh, attended the China-ASEAN ("10+1") Defense Ministers' Informal Meeting & the 6th Xiangshan Forum held in Beijing.
- **19th:** The Prime Minister of Vietnam, Nguyen Tan Dung, met with the delegation led by Chinese State Security Minister Geng Huichang at the Government Headquarters.
- **20th:** The Deputy Minister of Industry and Commerce of Vietnam, Nguyen Cam Tu, attended the 9th meeting of the China–Vietnam Economic and Trade Cooperation Committee in Beijing.
- **23rd:** The General Secretary of the Communist Party of Vietnam, Nguyen Phu Trong, met with the Minister of the International Department of the Central Committee of the Communist Party of China, Wang Jiarui.

November

- **4th:** The Deputy Prime Minister of Vietnam, Nguyen Xuan Phuc, met with Peng Qinghua, the Secretary of the Party Committee of the Guangxi Zhuang Autonomous Region, at the Government Headquarters.
- **5th–6th:** The General Secretary the CPC Central Committee, Chinese President Xi Jinping paid a state visit to Vietnam.

- **5th:** The Bank for Investment and Development of Vietnam and the China Development Bank signed a 5-year loan contract worth USD 200 million.
- **6th:** The General Secretary the CPC Central Committee, Chinese President Xi Jinping, attended the 10th Session of the 13th National Assembly of Vietnam, and delivered a speech.
- **12th:** The Deputy Prime Minister and Foreign Minister of Vietnam, Pham Binh Minh, attended the 1st Lancang–Mekong Cooperation Foreign Ministers' Meeting in Jinghong, Yunnan Province, China.
- **12th–17th:** The 15th China–Vietnam International Trade Fair 2015 was held in Lao Cai Province, Vietnam.
- **24th:** The Vietnam Chamber of Commerce and Industry, the Hanoi Center for Investment, the Trade and Tourism Promotion and the China–ASEAN Center jointly held the China–Vietnam Agricultural Products Trade and Investment Fair in Hanoi.
- **25th:** The Deputy Defense Minister of Vietnam, Nguyen Chi Vinh, met with the delegation of Yunnan Provincial Military Region led by the Commander of Yunnan Provincial Military Region, Yang Guangyue.

December

- **6th:** Phạm Quang Nghị, a member of the Political Bureau of the Central Committee of the Communist Party of Vietnam, met with the Secretary of the Party Committee of Gansu Province, Wang Sanyun.
- **13th:** Vietnam required Taiwan to immediately stop the act of seriously violating Vietnam's territorial sovereignty.
- **17th:** The Deputy Prime Minister and Foreign Minister of Vietnam, Pham Binh Minh, met with the delegation led by the Executive Vice Chairman of Guangxi People's Government, Tang Renjian.
- **23rd:** The Chairman of the National Assembly of Vietnam, Nguyen Sinh Hung, arrived at Beijing for a 5-day official friendly visit to China.

The Chronicle of Events in China–Myanmar Cooperation in 2015

Huang Ailian[3]

January

- **4th:** Chinese Ambassador to Myanmar Yang Houlan attended the 67th Myanmar Independence Day Military Parade and Reception in Naypyidaw, Myanmar.
- **8th:** The iron tower at Yunnan (Menglong)–Myanmar (eastern Shan State) 110 kV transmission and transformation project carried out by Yunnan International Co., Ltd. of the China Southern Power Grid passed acceptance inspection.
- **27th:** Yunnan University and the University of Foreign Languages, Mandalay signed, in Mandalay, Myanmar, a cooperation agreement on the joint running of the first Confucius Institute in Myanmar.
- **28th:** The China–Myanmar crude oil pipeline project was put into trial operation, the Port of Maday Island from which the project starts was officially put into service.

February

- **2nd:** COFCO and the Myanmar Rice Association reached a consensus on the type and quantity of rice exported from Myanmar to China as well as the export mode, and signed a memorandum.
- **6th:** The Yunnan Branch of the China Construction Bank and the Myanmar Cooperative Bank signed an agreement on cross-border settlements.
- **12th:** China and Myanmar launched the Shanghai-Rangoon direct sea transportation business, greatly shortening the time for transferring from Chinese ports to Rangoon.

---

[3]Huang Ailian, Director of the Myanmar Institute of the China-ASEAN Research Institute of Guangxi University. Cooperator: Wang Kezhen, Master Degree Candidate at the Business School of Guangxi University.

March

- **13th:** The Burmese military airplane crossed the boundary illegally and dropped bombs onto Lincang City, Yunnan Province, causing the death of four civilians and injuring nine.
- **20th–21st:** CITIC Group conducted the first training under the Rural Public Welfare Fund Program at Kyaukpyu Town, Rakhine State, Myanmar.
- **25th:** The delegation of state-owned enterprises from Tianjin and the Union of Myanmar Federation of Chambers of Commerce and Industry held a meeting in Naypyidaw, Myanmar, and the two sides signed 16 memoranda.

April

- **7th:** All of the four distribution stations along the China–Myanmar gas pipeline built by PetroChina (Myanmar section) were put into operation.
- **22nd:** Chinese President Xi Jinping met with the President of Myanmar, Thein Sein, in Jakarta, the capital of Indonesia, and the two sides held consultations on the issues concerning the Belt and Road.
- **27th:** Chinese President Xi Jinping met with the delegation of the Union Solidarity and Development Party led by Shwe Mann, the Chairman of the Union Solidarity and Development Party, the Speaker of the Assembly of the Union and the Speaker of the House of Representatives of Myanmar.

May

- **1st:** China National Machinery Import and Export Corp. and the Ministry of Rail Transportation of Myanmar signed a locomotive purchase agreement worth USD 11 million in Naypyidaw, Myanmar.
- **19th:** The Vice Minister of the International Department of the Central Committee of the Communist Party of China, Chen Fengxiang, met with the Commander-in-Chief of the Myanmar Armed Forces, Min Aung Hlaing, and the two sides discussed the

issues concerning the border between their countries and efforts to promote bilateral relations.

- **27th:** The Burmese omnimedia platform of the website www.china.com was officially launched, covering news, films, China Today, E-magazine and Made in China.

June

- **8th:** The Chinese Embassy in Myanmar and the Ministry of Foreign Affairs of Myanmar jointly held the reception celebrating the 65th anniversary of the establishment of diplomatic relations between China and Myanmar.
- **10th:** The Myanmar Investment Environment & the China–Myanmar Cultural Industry Road Show was held at the Embassy of Myanmar in China.
- **10th–14th:** The delegation of the National League for Democracy led by the National League for Democracy visited China, met with Chinese leaders, including Xi Jinping and Li Keqiang.
- **29th:** The delegation of the China–Myanmar Friendship Association visited Luoyang, Henan for enhancing bilateral cooperation in the religious field.

July

- **11th:** The China–Myanmar Agricultural Technology and New Energy Technology Matchmaking Meeting was officially inaugurated in Rangoon, Myanmar.
- **19th:** Myanmar sent a delegation for the first time to Shanghai to attend the 11th Shanghai International Youth Interactive Friendship Camp.
- **20th–24th:** The 3rd China–Myanmar Business Forum was held in Rangoon, Myanmar.
- **29th:** The Chinese Ambassador to the Republic of the Union of Myanmar was replaced, Hong Liang succeeded Yang Houlan to serve as Chinese Ambassador to Myanmar.
- **30th:** The President of Myanmar, Thein Sein, signed an order of general amnesty for immediately releasing 155 Chinese lumberjacks given a sentence by a Burmese court.

August

- **3rd–7th:** China Blue Sky Rescue went to the flood-stricken areas of Sittwe City in Rakhine State, Myanmar to provide disaster relief, and offered emergency material assistance worth 10 million yuan to Myanmar.
- **10th:** Chinese Ambassador to Myanmar Hong Liang and a delegation met with the Vice President of Myanmar, U Nyan Tun, in Naypyidaw, Myanmar, and the two sides discussed the matters concerning disaster relief, rebuilding, bilateral economic, trade and cultural cooperation.
- **22nd:** The 2015 China Book Fair & the China–Myanmar Intertranslation and Publication Forum were inaugurated in Mandalay, Myanmar.

September

- **4th:** Xi Jinping met with the President of Myanmar, Thein Sein, who attended the activity, conducted in China, commemorating the 70th anniversary of the victory of the War of the Chinese People's Resistance against Japanese Aggression and the victory of the World Anti-fascist War.
- **17th:** Chinese Vice Premier Zhang Gaoli met with the Vice President of Myanmar, Sai Mauk Kham, who attended the 12th China-ASEAN Business and Investment Summit in Nanning.
- **20th:** The inaugural meeting of the Zhejiang Chamber of Commerce in Myanmar was held in Rangoon, Myanmar.
- **28th:** The 3rd China (Yunnan)–Myanmar Cooperation Forum was held in Kunming, Yunnan Province, and the two sides signed the *Minutes of the 3rd China (Yunnan)–Myanmar Cooperation Forum.*

October

- **14th:** The Chinese Teaching Class specially designed by the FuQing Confucius Class in Mandalay, Myanmar for the University of Mandalay was launched, and Chinese teaching entered Myanmar's comprehensive university for the first time.
- **16th:** The Chinese State Councilor and Defense Minister, Chang Wanquan, met with the Defense Minister of Myanmar, Sein Win,

who was attending the China–ASEAN Defense Ministers' Informal Meeting and Xiangshan Forum in Beijing.

- **20th–21st:** The President of the China–Myanmar Friendship Association, Geng Zhiyuan, visited the areas hit worst by floods in Irrawaddy Province, Myanmar.
- **30th:** The delegation of the China–ASEAN Research Institute of Guangxi University visited the Ministry of Commerce, the Ministry of Hotels and Tourism of Myanmar, and the two sides held talks on China–Myanmar economic, trade and tourism cooperation under the Belt and Road Initiative.

November

- **11th:** Chinese Foreign Minister, Wang Yi, met with the Foreign Minister of Myanmar, Wunna Maung Lwin, who was attending the 1st Foreign Ministers' Meeting on Lancang–Mekong Cooperation in Jinghong, Yunnan Province, and the two sides discussed the issues concerning Lancang–Mekong cooperation.
- **13th:** The Yunnan Zhonglu International Travel Agency of China Yunnan Press Media (Group) and Myanmar's iHome Group Of Companies signed a cooperation agreement on tourism industry projects.
- **21st–22nd:** The academic seminar on educational and cultural exchanges celebrating the 65th anniversary of the establishment of diplomatic relations between China and Myanmar was held in Mandalay, Myanmar.

December

- **5th:** Chinese Deputy Foreign Minister and the special envoy of the Chinese Government, Liu Zhenmin, met with Aung San Suu Kyi in Naypyidaw, Myanmar, and the two sides discussed the issues concerning the relations between China and Myanmar.
- **11th:** The 13th China–Myanmar Bilateral Meeting on Drug Control Cooperation was held in Kunming, Yunnan Province, the drug control departments of the two sides agreed to improve the situation of drugs in both countries and in the region and consolidate the drug control cooperation relations between the two countries.

- **15th:** The 15th China–Myanmar Border Economic and Trade Fair was held in Ruili, Yunnan Province; it had 459 booths, several hundred merchants from both countries participated in the exhibition.
- **30th:** China CITIC Group was granted the right to develop the deepwater port and industrial zone projects in the Myanmar Kyaukpyu Special Economic Zone.
- **30th:** China and Myanmar signed economic and technical cooperation agreements in Naypyidaw, Myanmar; China would provide assistance to Myanmar in various social and economic development programs, including post-flood rebuilding, national health and the drug program.

The Chronicle of Events in China–Malaysia Cooperation in 2015

Lu Xiaoxiao[4]

January

- **1st:** Four Chinese universities, which are Peking University, Tsinghua University, Fudan University and Shanghai Jiaotong University, carried out enrollment work in Malaysia.
- **13th:** The first batch of materials offered by China to assist Malaysia in combating the floods arrived at Kuala Lumpur.
- **15th:** The Chinese Embassy in Malaysia promoted the development of local Chinese language and culture education, and planned to invite local teachers to visit China, as well as stimulating Chinese teachers to engage in volunteer exchanges in Malaysia.
- **20th:** The Guangxi Beibu Gulf International Group completed the plan for acquiring 40% equity in the Port of Kuantan; the Port of Kuantan innovation project was initiated.

[4]Lu Xiaoxiao, Research Assistant at the Malaysia Institute of the China–ASEAN Research Institute of Guangxi University.

February

- **10th:** The Prime Minister of Malaysia Najib Razak met with Meng Jianzhu, a member of the Political Bureau of the Central Committee of the Communist Party of China and the Secretary of the Political and Judiciary Commission.
- **27th:** Malaysian Foreign Minister Anifah Aman met with Chinese Foreign Minister Wang Yi in New York, the two sides discussed the issues concerning the deepening of China–Malaysia cooperation and China–ASEAN relations of cooperation as well as other respects.

March

- **4th:** The Ministry of International Trade and Industry of Malaysia expressed the desire to establish China's Economic Strategy Committee.
- **27th:** The China Construction Bank planned to set up eight overseas branches, with the Southeast Asian branches targeting Malaysia.
- **27th–29th:** The Prime Minister of Malaysia Najib Razak arrived at Haikou to attend the 2015 Boao Forum for Asia, he stated that Malaysia would like to establish visa processing centers in Nanning and Xi'an, China.
- **29th:** The 2nd Malaysia–Hong Kong, China RMB Offshore Service Sector Dialogue was held in Johor Bahru.

April

- **10th:** The Chief Minister of Malacca State Idris Haron led a state delegation to visit Guangzhou and Zhuhai in Guangdong Province.
- **12th:** Malaysia and China signed a memorandum of understanding on recognition of liberal arts-related academic achievements under Malaysia's educational diploma.
- **19th:** The Chinese Ambassador to Malaysia Huang Huikang stated that China would like to provide the 3-year multiple-entry visa convenience for the people engaged in commercial activities or tourists who frequently travel between China and Malaysia.

May

- **8th:** Chinese Premier Li Keqiang met with the President of the Upper House of the Parliament of Malaysia, Abu Zahar Ujang.
- **13th:** The Haoyue Group in Jilin Province, China planned to establish a halal product logistics production base in Malacca.
- **17th:** China announced that the number of Malaysian universities and colleges recognized by China was increased to 76.

June

- **1st:** The Minister of Agriculture and Agro-based Industry of Malaysia stated that Malaysia would establish agricultural supermarkets in six Chinese cities.
- **9th:** Malaysia planned to work with China to build a Malaysia–China Building Material Industrial Park, helping Chinese building material enterprises to develop in the ASEAN market.
- **11th:** Malaysia and Taiwan decided to establish the Malaysia–Taiwan Economic Cooperation Committee.
- **30th:** China and Malaysia discussed the signing of the bilateral free trade area agreement.

July

- **1st:** Two Malaysian companies and the Taiwan Institute for Information Industry signed a cooperation treaty for introducing advanced big data analysis and computing techniques from Taiwan.
- **6th:** The State Administration for Quality Supervision and Inspection and Quarantine of China went to Malaysia for inspecting the specification and quality of yellow pears and jackfruit; both fruits were expected to enter the Chinese market as from the next year.
- **12th:** China established an overseas railway equipment manufacturing center in Batu Gajah, Perak State, Malaysia.
- **13th:** The Minister of Transportation of Malaysia, Liow Tiong Lai, led a delegation to attend "The Belt and Road" China–Malaysia Business Dialogue.
- **17th:** The Malaysian Consulate General in Nanning, Guangzhou was officially put into service.

- **30th–31st:** The Prime Minister of Malaysia, Najib Razak, and Chinese Vice Premier, Liu Yandong, held talks on the issues concerning bilateral trade, economics, national defense, tourism and other fields.

August

- **3rd:** Malacca State and Guangdong Province, China established sister province ties.

September

- **14th:** The Malaysian Government announced that Malaysia had adopted the visa-free policy for Chinese group visitors from October 1 to March 31, 2016.
- **17th:** China and Malaysia conducted the "Peace Friendship 2015" joint exercise in the Strait of Malacca and adjacent sea areas.
- **18th:** Tanjung Offshore Services SdnBhd (TOS) and Yantai Jereh Petroleum Equipment & Technologies Co., Ltd.– which is the largest private listed company in China's oil service field and a subsidiary of the Jereh Group – signed a cooperation agreement.
- **19th:** Malaysia's Proton and China's Geely Auto Group discussed the possibility of the joint manufacturing of ASEAN Automobiles and the joint development of the ASEAN automobile market.
- **20th:** The Malaysia External Trade Development Corporation and China's Alibaba cooperated to expand the online trade program.
- **20th:** The Guangdong Provincial Government and Malacca State signed seven cooperation agreements regarding the economic, developmental, medical and other fields.
- **22nd:** The 12th China–ASEAN Expo witnessed the participation of 149 Malaysian enterprises at the exhibition, involving the food, medical, educational and other fields.
- **22nd:** The GB Asiatic Venture, the China Machinery Engineering Corporation, the Archetype Group & Louis Berger Collaboration signed four memoranda of cooperation with a total development cost of 6.3 billion ringgit.

- **27th:** The Ministry of Transportation of Malaysia planned to forge an alliance with Chinese ports and strengthen port cooperation between the two countries.
- **30th:** The Federation of Chinese Physicians and Acupuncturists Associations of the Malaysia and Guangxi University of Chinese Medicine signed a cooperation agreement on traditional Chinese medicine.

October

- **23rd:** The Vice Minister of Home Affairs of Malaysia met with Chinese State Councilor and Public Security Minister, Guo Shengkun.
- **24th:** The "Increasing the Trade and Investment Between Malaysia, the ASEAN community and China & Opening Shandong's Economic, Trade and Investment Gateway" Roundtable Conference, held by the China–ASEAN Business Association, made great break-throughs and reached consensuses.
- **26th:** China announced that Air China's direct flight between Beijing and Kuala Lumpur had been resumed.

November

- **5th:** The Chinese State Councilor and Defense Minister, Chang Wanquan, held talks with the Minister of Defense of Malaysia, Hishammuddin Hussein, in Kuala Lumpur.
- **6th:** A consortium consisting of the China Railway Group Limited, the China Railway Construction Corporation and China Communications Construction was expected to be awarded Malaysia's railway project worth 9.3 billion ringgit.
- **14th:** Malaysia's Port Swettenham and the Port of Shenzhen, China established sister port ties.
- **19th:** The Minister of Transportation of Malaysia, Liow Tiong Lai, pointed out that the Malaysian Government was working on establishing a port alliance of the countries along the Belt and Road, with a view to fully implementing the Belt and Road Initiative.

- **21st:** Malaysia agreed to permit the People's Liberation Army Navy to use the Port of Kota Kinabalu.
- **23rd:** The Prime Minister of Malaysia, Najib Razak, met with Chinese President Xi Jinping during the 23rd APEC Leaders' Meeting.
- **23rd:** The "Melaka Gateway" Mega Development Plan, reported by the Chief Minister of Malacca State Idris Haron, was supported by China.
- **23rd–25th:** Chinese Premier Li Keqiang visited Malaysia, focusing on economic and trade cooperation.
- **24th–25th:** The China General Nuclear Power Corporation allocated USD 2.3 billion to purchasing the electric power assets under 1MDB and would undertake all of the debts of Edra Global Energy Bhd.

December

- **1st:** The China–ASEAN Business Association (Malaysia) and the People's Government of Dezhou City, Shandong Province, China signed a strategic cooperation agreement.
- **2nd:** According to the survey on the countries most dependent on China in the world posted on the website of US Forbes magazine, Malaysia's exports to the Chinese Mainland accounted for 12% of the total exports, ranking it No. 8.
- **12th:** The China High-speed Railway Exhibition, sponsored by the China Railway Corporation, was inaugurated in Kuala Lumpur; the Malaysian Government announced that the double-track railway project worth about 7,130 million ringgit from Gemas in Negeri Sembilan to Johor Bahru in Johor would be built by the China Railway Corporation.
- **26th:** The Malaysia National Information Technology Research and Development Center, the Shanghai Changda Investment Management Co., Ltd. and the Malaysia Softegic Systems Management Sdn Bhd signed a tripartite memorandum, *China–Malaysia Open Innovation Platform*.

The Chronicle of Events in China–Singapore Cooperation in 2015

Yi Yin[5]

January

- **14th:** The tugboat Wan Shen Zhou 67 sank in the area of water near Jingjiang City, Taizhou, Jiangsu Province, China, China and Singapore worked closely to search for and rescue the sunken tugboat.

February

- **1st:** The Ministerial Joint Committee for the third intergovernmental cooperation project between Singapore and China led a delegation of nearly 100 people to visit three candidate cities including Chongqing, Chengdu and Xi'an.
- **4th:** The Standard Chartered Bank of Singapore extended a 50 million yuan cross-border RMB loan to a company in the Sino-Singapore Tianjin Eco-City, it became the first non-Chinese bank which offered such a kind of loans to the Sino-Singapore Tianjin Eco-City.
- **22nd:** The Centre for Remote Imaging, Sensing and Processing of the National University of Singapore and the China Center for Resources Satellite Data and Application signed a cooperation agreement, with a view to sharing satellite data.
- **22nd:** The Embassy of Singapore in China held the "Singapore–China Cooperation for 25 Years" photo contest.

March

- **7th:** The Mayor of New Taipei City, Taiwan, Eric Chu, visited Singapore and met with the Prime Minister, Lee Hsien Loong.

---

[5]Yi Yin, Research Assistant at the Singapore Institute of the China–ASEAN Research Institute of Guangxi University. Cooperator: Shi Yirong, Research Assistant at the China-ASEAN Research Institute of Guangxi University.

- **29th:** Chinese Vice President Li Yuanchao, as the special envoy of Chinese President Xi Jinping, attended the funeral of former Prime Minister of Singapore Mr. Lee Kuan Yew.
- **30th:** Singapore's Pacific Integrated Logistics and the Management Committee of the Nantong Coastal Park, China held a signing ceremony for a 12-year cooperation project.

April

- **7th–12th:** The Deputy Prime Minister of Singapore, Teo Chee Hean, led a delegation to pay a six-day visit to China.
- **7th:** Singapore officially donated 3.71 million yuan to the earthquake-stricken Ludian Area in Yunnan Province, China, and built three school houses for 1,200 primary school students.
- **13th:** The Prime Minister of Singapore, Lee Hsien Loong, met with the Secretary of the Party Committee of Shaanxi Province, Zhao Zhengyong.
- **20th:** The Singapore–Sichuan Trade and Investment Committee held the 16th meeting at the Singapore EXPO Convention & Exhibition Centre.
- **29th:** The Singapore Branch of the Bank of China would like to offer cross-border RMB loans in China's three free trade areas, including Tianjin, Guangdong and Fujian.

May

- **6th:** The personnel of Singapore Customs detained about 700 fake ladyross-border RMB loans in China's three free trade Tanjong Pagar Distripark.
- **7th:** The Suzhou Branch of the OCBC BANK (China) was inaugurated at the Suzhou Industrial Park.
- **9th:** Li Huabo, a highly corrupt inferior officer in Jiangxi Province, was repatriated to China after absconding to Singapore for 4 years.
- **12th–14th:** The Mayor of Shanghai, Yang Xiong, led a delegation to visit Singapore, and met with the Prime Minister of Singapore, Lee Hsien Loong.
- **15th:** The Immigration and Checkpoints Authority of Singapore announced that as from June 1, Singapore would issue a multiple

journey-visa (MJV) to Chinese citizens for a maximum period of ten years, while visa fees and application procedures remained unchanged.
- **20th:** The Chinese Navy's missile destroyer "Yulin" appeared at the Singapore Defense Expo.
- **19th:** China and Singapore signed a memorandum for promoting cooperation on trademark registration.

June

- **8th:** China Life Insurance officially set up branches in Singapore, entering the overseas market outside the Greater China Region for the first time.
- **8th:** The 2015 China–Singapore Business Forum was held at the Tan Kah Kee Auditorium of the Singapore Chinese Chamber of Commerce.
- **9th:** The Qingdao Municipal Government, the DBS Bank and the OCBC Bank initiated comprehensive strategic cooperation and signed a number of key projects.
- **9th–11th:** At the invitation of the Ministry of Trade and Industry of Singapore, the Governor of Shandong Province, Guo Shuqing, visited Singapore.
- **10th:** The Guangxi Beibu Gulf International Port Group worked with the Port of Singapore Authority (PSA) and the Pacific International Lines (PIL) to establish the Guangxi Beibu Gulf-PSA International Container Terminal Co., Ltd.
- **15th:** The Chinese Ambassador to Singapore, Chen Xiaodong, took office; he is the 10th Chinese Ambassador to Singapore.
- **18th:** The China (Jiangxi)–Singapore Economic and Trade Cooperation Fair was held in Singapore.
- **26th:** The Singapore Branch of the Bank of China issued 500 million Singapore dollar "The Belt and Road" unsecured bonds.
- **29th:** At the invitation of Chinese President Xi Jinping, the President of Singapore, Tan Keng Yam, paid a six-day state visit to China.

July

- **8th:** The Chinese e-commerce giant Alibaba allocated 187.1 million yuan to acquire an additional 5% equity at Singapore Post, making the equity held by Alibaba soar to 14.51%.

- **20th–21st:** The 6th Future China Global Forum, sponsored by Business China, was held at the Shangri-La Hotel in Singapore.
- **27th:** The Singapore Business Federation held the first Singapore Regional Business Forum for discussing the impact of the 21st Century Maritime Silk Road on regional business and the business opportunities brought by it.

August

- **3rd:** Chinese Foreign Minister Wang Yi met with Singaporean Foreign Minister Vivian Balakrishnan in Singapore.
- **4th:** The Industrial and Commercial Bank of China (Singapore) launched the 24-h RMB clearing service.
- **5th:** Singapore replaced Thailand to serve as the coordinator of China–ASEAN relations.
- **6th:** The International Enterprise Singapore announced cooperation with China's Tmall.
- **14th:** A briefing was held on the "Singapore–Shandong as the Partners on the Belt and Road" policy.
- **19th:** Alibaba Cloud established a data center and its international business headquarters in Singapore.

September

- **8th:** Singapore launched the Unionpay Quick Pass service.
- **9th:** The Singapore Chinese Chamber of Commerce visited www.99114.com to explore the new line of thought regarding e-commerce.
- **18th:** The China–Indo-China Peninsula International Economic Corridor Cooperation and Development Roundtable Conference was held in Nanning.
- **19th:** The China–ASEAN Technology Matchmaking Fair Singapore/South Korea Matchmaking Session was held in Nanning, Guangxi.

October

- **3rd:** The Chinese and Singaporean leaders exchanged congratulatory messages for celebrating the 25th anniversary of the establishment of diplomatic relations.

- **9th:** The Emeritus Senior Minister of Singapore, Goh Chok Tong, attended the Working Meeting of the Boao Forum for Asia Board of Directors in Hangzhou, and met with the Secretary of the Party Committee of Zhejiang Province, Xia Baolong.
- **12th–14th:** Chinese Vice Premier Zhang Gaoli visited Singapore and he and the Deputy Prime Minister of Singapore, Teo Chee Hean, co-chaired the 12th meeting of the China-Singapore Joint Committee on Bilateral Cooperation, the 17th China–Singapore Joint Steering Council Meeting for Suzhou Industrial Park and the 8th China–Singapore Joint Steering Council Meeting for Tianjin Eco-City.
- **13th:** The Singapore Monetary Authority stated that China and Singapore had agreed to extend pilot cross-border RMB service to Suzhou City and to the Tianjin Municipality.
- **16th:** The Defense Minister of Singapore Dr NG Eng Hen attended the China–ASEAN Defense Ministers' Informal Meeting.
- **21st:** The Singapore Tourism Board and Chinese online tourism service companies www.alitrip.com and www.tuniu.com, and www.dianping.com and www.mafengwo.cn signed memoranda of understanding on cooperation.
- **31st:** At the invitation of the organizer, The Emeritus Senior Minister of Singapore, Goh Chok Tong, delivered a keynote speech during the 21st Century Maritime Silk Road Expo Forum in Guangzhou.

November

- **6th:** Chinese passport holders who satisfy conditions can enjoy faster customs clearance service provided by Singapore.
- **6th–7th:** Chinese President Xi Jinping paid a two-day state visit to Singapore. This was the first time that Xi Jinping has paid an official visit to Singapore in the capacity of Chinese President.
- **7th:** During his visit to Singapore, Chinese President Xi Jinping held historic talks with Taiwan's leader, Ma Ying-jeou.
- **9th:** Singapore and China deepened their cross-border financial and monetary cooperation.

December

- **1st:** The Singapore Monetary Authority stated that after the IMF incorporated the RMB into its Special Drawing Rights Basket, it would be committed to cooperating with China on increasing the use of RMB in Singapore and Southeast Asia.

The Chronicle of Events in China–The Philippines Cooperation in 2015

Wang Xinyuan[6]

January

- **24th:** The Secretary of Foreign Affairs of the Philippines, Albert del Rosario, stated that the Philippines had attempted to normalize China–The Philippines relations.

February

- **14th:** President Benigno Aquino III delivered a congratulatory message for celebrating the Chinese New Year.

March

- **3rd:** The Department of Foreign Affairs of the Philippines and the National Commission for Culture and the Arts jointly held The Philippine Traditional Festival Photo Show & the Launching Ceremony of the Activity Celebrating the 40th Anniversary of the Establishment of Diplomatic Relations between China and the Philippines.
- **8th:** The Embassy of the Philippines in China and the China Branch of the National Arnis Association of The Philippines held a Seminar on Philippine Arnis Stick: a Bridge for Enhancing Friendship and Understanding.
- **15th:** The 30 MW photovoltaic power station on an island of the Philippines, built by the Chinese company NARI Technology Co., Ltd., was smoothly put under grid-connected operations.

---

[6]Wang Xinyuan, Research Assistant at the China-ASEAN Research Institute of Guangxi University.

- **19th:** The Philippines Business Bank stated that it would take RMB as the foreign currency only second to the USD for real-time domestic clearing.

April

- **1st:** The China Root-finding Tour 2015 — The Philippine Overseas Chinese Students Summer Camp for Learning Chinese was launched in Jimei.
- **5th:** The Chinese Ambassador to the Philippines, Zhao Jianhua, paid tribute to Chinese martyrs who had sacrificed their lives in the Philippine war of resistance against Japanese aggression at the Manila Chinese Cemetery.
- **15th:** The Xiamen Municipal Bureau of Commerce stated that the Philippines was one of the nine key countries under the action plan of Xiamen City for carrying out the Belt and Road Initiative.
- **15th:** The Vice President of the Philippines, Jejomar Binay, said that if he was elected President of the Philippines, he would promote bilateral negotiations between China and the Philippines on the issue of the South China Sea.
- **24th:** The Vice President of the Philippines, Jejomar Binay, said that the Philippines and China should jointly develop oil and gas in the disputed areas in the South China Sea.

May

- **6th:** The Coast Guard of the Philippines started discussing the possibility of conducting joint exercises with China.
- **13th:** The Vice President of the Philippines, Jejomar Binay, stated that the claims to the sovereignty over the South China Sea should not harm relations between China and the Philippines.

June

- **4th:** A poll showed that 55% of Filipinos believed that the Philippines should address the disputes with China through diplomacy rather than arbitration.
- **8th:** The Presidential Palace of the Philippines stated that the Philippines only had disagreements with Chinese leaders over

territorial disputes, but did not have enmity towards the Chinese people.

- **9th:** The Embassy of the Philippines in China and the Chinese People's Association for Friendship with Foreign Countries jointly held the reception celebrating the 40th anniversary of the establishment of diplomatic relations between China and the Philippines.
- **12th:** The Chinese Ambassador to the Philippines, Zhao Jianhua, attended the reception celebrating Philippine Independence Day.
- **23rd:** The Rizal Center under the theme of Filipino art, culture and language was inaugurated within the Embassy of the Philippines in China, which is located in Beijing.
- **23rd:** At the invitation of the organizer, the Chinese Ambassador to the Philippines, Zhao Jianhua, attended the inaugural ceremony of new memorial archway at Chinatown in Manila, and delivered a speech.
- **24th:** The Confucius Institute of the Angeles University Foundation in the Philippines held the activity celebrating the 5th anniversary of its establishment.
- **26th:** The Chinese Embassy in the Philippines and the Chinese communities in the Philippines jointly held "The History of Blood — the Crimes of Japanese Militarism in the Asia-Pacific Region" Photo Show.
- **28th:** The Chinese Embassy in the Philippines held the reception celebrating Chinese Army Day.

July

- **7th:** Philippine Jollibee Foods Corporation stated that it would set up at least 1,400 Dunkin' Donuts outlets in China within 20 years.
- **9th:** The Haier Group launched AQUA home appliances in the Philippines.
- **17th:** The Macau Red Cross donated computers and communication equipment worth 10.10 million pesos to the schools in the areas hit by Typhoon Haiyan.
- **17th–21st:** The Philippine Chinese Table Tennis Federation and the affiliated Competitive Sports School of the Capital University

of Physical Education and Sports signed a letter of intent on cooperation.

- **26th:** Huaqiao University held the graduation ceremony of the 10th Chinese Class for Foreign Government Officials, in which the certificate of completion was granted to five Philippine students.
- **29th:** The Northeast No.1 Electric Power Construction Co., Ltd. of the China Energy Engineering Group and PCPC signed a contract on the operation maintenance of a coal-fired power plant.

August

- **6th:** A China–Philippines friendship table tennis competition was inaugurated in Beijing.
- **6th:** The Chinese Embassy in the Philippines donated 1,844 books to the National Library of the Philippines.
- **10th:** The Philippine SM Group planned to develop four new integrated commercial and residential real estate projects in China.
- **15th:** The Chinese Embassy in the Philippines and more than 200 Chinese communities in the Philippines held a meeting commemorating the 70th anniversary of the victory of the War of the Chinese People's Resistance against Japanese Aggression and the victory of the World Anti-fascist War.
- **15th:** The prototype train made for the Metro Rail Transit Line 3 by CNR Dalian Locomotive & Rolling Stock Co., Ltd. arrived at Manila.
- **15th:** The Presidential Palace of the Philippines stated that maritime disputes should not affect the trade and diplomatic relations between China and the Philippines.
- **25th:** The State Council Information Office of China announced that China had invited five overseas Chinese in the Philippines to mount the Tian'anmen Gate Tower to watch the military parade commemorating the victory of the War of the Chinese People's Resistance against Japanese Aggression held on September 3, 2015.
- **27th:** The Manila Municipal Government commemorated the Hong Kong victims in the Manila hostage crisis.

September

- **3rd:** The Mayor of Manila, Joseph Ejercito Estrada, and the Philippine Ambassador to China, Erlinda Basilio, attended China's military parade, Joseph Ejercito Estrada met with Chinese Vice President Li Yuanchao.
- **5th:** The Chairman of the Financial Supervisory Commission of Taiwan, Tseng Ming-chung, visited the Philippines.
- **12th:** The Chinese Ambassador to the Philippines, Zhao Jianhua, provided scholarships to 10 students in the areas hit by Typhoon Haiyan and 45 other students from different areas of the Philippines.
- **18th:** The Deputy Secretary of Trade and Industry of the Philippines attended the 12th China–ASEAN Expo, the China–ASEAN Business and Investment Summit.
- **19th:** Guigang City, Guangxi and Zamboanga City, the Philippines held the ceremony of signing a letter of intent on the establishment of sister city ties.
- **20th:** The Vice Chairman of the People's Political Consultative Conference of Guangxi, Liu Zhiyong, attended the Philippines' national investment fair and delivered a speech.
- **28th:** The Chinese Embassy in the Philippines held a reception celebrating the 66th anniversary of the founding of the People's Republic of China.
- **24th:** The Secretary of Commerce and Economic Development of Hong Kong, Gregory So Kam-leung, attended a seminar under the theme of "Hong Kong - Enjoying Favorable Location, Seizing the Opportunities", held in Manila, to introduce the business opportunities in Hong Kong to Philippine enterprises.

October

- **1st:** Various groups from Chinese communities in the Philippines jointly celebrated the 66th anniversary of the founding of the People's Republic of China.
- **12th:** The Confucius Institute at the University of the Philippines was inaugurated.

- **13th:** The Chinese Ambassador to the Philippines, Zhao Jianhua, donated 1.54 million pesos to the victims hit by Typhoon Haiyan.
- **27th–28th:** The Chinese Ambassador to the Philippines, Zhao Jianhua, visited temporary sites for resettlement of victims hit by Typhoon Haiyan.

November

- **5th:** China and the Philippines signed the 2015–2018 execution plan for cultural exchanges between China and the Philippines.
- **5th:** Taiwan and the Philippines signed the *Agreement on Taiwan–Philippines Cooperation in Law Enforcement on Fishery Matters.*
- **9th:** Haier expressed its plan for turning the Philippines into a strategic market for sales in Japan and the ASEAN community.
- **10th:** The Chinese and Philippine foreign ministers held talks in Manila.
- **11th:** The President of the Philippines, Benigno Aquino III, met with Chinese Foreign Minister, Wang Yi.
- **11th:** Senator Bongbong Marcos stated that President Benigno Aquino III should mend the relations with China.
- **17th:** Chinese President Xi Jinping arrived at Manila for attending the 23rd APEC Leaders' Meeting.
- **19th:** Chinese President Xi Jinping delivered a speech in Manila, stating that he believed that China–Philippines relations would ultimately return to normal.

December

- **2nd:** The central bank of the Philippines stated that it considered increasing the holding of RMB assets.
- **7th:** The central bank of the Philippines stated that it was studying the suggestion from the banking sector concerning the establishment peso-RMB direct exchange arrangements.
- **9th–10th:** Francis Chua, a well-known overseas Chinese in the Philippines, was invited to attend the first Silk Road International Investment Forum & the Inauguration Ceremony of the Silk

Road Chamber of International Commerce, and he was appointed the Vice Chairman of the Silk Road Chamber of International Commerce.

- **10th:** The Confucius Institute at the Ateneo De Manila University, the Philippines donated bilingual books and Chinese traditional games to the Philippine General Hospital.
- **14th:** The "Tasting Philippine Delicious Foods" Philippine gourmet festival activity, held by the Embassy of the Philippines in China, was inaugurated in Xi'an.
- **16th:** The Chinese Embassy in the Philippines held a media reception in Makati.
- **21st:** Philippine Ambassador to China, Erlinda Basilio, stated that China and the Philippines should strengthen their cooperation on tourism.
- **31st:** The representative of the Government of the Philippines signed the *Agreement on the Asian Infrastructure Investment Bank* in Beijing.

The Chronicle of Events in China–Laos Cooperation in 2015

Wang Hui[7]

January

- **8th:** Yunnan Aluminium Co., Ltd. proposed to acquire 51% of the equity in an aluminum firm in Laos.
- **8th:** The China Embassy in Laos granted a Chinese Ambassador Scholarship.
- **10th:** The Phase II project of the Sanjiang International Shopping Mall, the largest Chinese-funded shopping mall in Laos, was launched.

February

- **6th:** The Nam Theun No. 2 Dam integrated irrigation project in Laos, built based on assistance from China, was completed and handed over.

[7]Wang Hui, Research Assistant at the Laos Institute of the China-ASEAN Research Institute of Guangxi University.

- **9th:** The Deputy Director of the China National Tourism Administration, Wu Wenxue, and the Minister of Information, Culture and Tourism of Laos, Bosengkham Vongdara, held talks in Vientiane.

March

- **20th:** China handed over population census assistance materials to Laos.
- **30th:** The Ministry of Public Security of Laos cooperated with Huawei to issue the new electronic ID card.

April

- **2nd:** China donated assistance materials worth more than USD 108 million to the unexploded bomb victims in Laos.
- **9th:** The Deputy Administrator of the Civil Aviation Administration of China, Li Jian, led a delegation to visit Laos, and the civil aviation administrations of both countries amended and signed a memorandum of understanding.
- **20th:** The Vice Chairman of the Central Military Commission of China, Xu Qiliang, led a delegation to visit Laos.
- **21st:** The Minister of Publicity under the Central Committee of the Communist Party of China, Liu Qibao, met with the delegation of the Lao People's Revolutionary Party led by the General Secretary of the Central Committee of the Lao People's Revolutionary Party.
- **22nd:** The gas station built by Chinese enterprises in Houayxay, Laos was open for business.
- **25th:** The Chinese Theater jointly run by the media of both countries was launched in Vientiane.
- **30th:** The Government of Laos granted a First Class Development medal to the Chinese Government.

May

- **8th:** The Yunnan Provincial Energy Investment Group signed the joint venture framework agreement on a project in Laos.
- **11th–15th:** The China–Laos Joint Committee on the Boundary held their 8th meeting in Vientiane, Laos.

- **26th:** The Deputy Minister of the International Department of the Central Committee of the Communist Party of China, Liu Hongcai, led a delegation to visit Laos.
- **28th:** The China–Laos Mixed Committee on Economic and Trade Cooperation held their 7th meeting in Vientiane.
- **29th:** The "Approaching Laos" investment and trade fair was held in Chongqing.

June

- **12th:** The Prime Minister of Laos, Thongsing Thammavong, attended the 3rd China-Southeast Asia Expo & the 23rd China Kunming Import & Export Fair in China.
- **14th:** The delegation of "China·Fujian Week" visited Laos to engage in an exchange.
- **15th:** The Chinese Deputy Minister, Liu Zhenmin, met with the Director of the General Office of the Ministry of Foreign Affairs of Laos, Kanpau Intawan.
- **19th:** The China Poly Group and the Government of Laos signed the joint venture agreement on a pyrophyllite project.
- **26th:** The Lao–China Joint Investment Co., Ltd. and the Vietnam National Petroleum Group signed the land transfer agreement on the Laos National Oil Reserve Depot.
- **26th–29th:** At the invitation of Laos, Chinese Deputy Minister Liu Zhenmin visited Laos.

July

- **1st:** The Chairman of the Chinese People's Political Consultative Conference, Yu Zhengsheng, met with the Executive Vice President of the Central Committee of the Lao Front for National Construction.
- **8th:** The Vice Chairman of the Central Military Commission of China, Xu Qiliang, and the Chinese Defense Minister, Chang Wanquan, met with the Defense Minister of Laos, Sengnuon Saynhalat.

- **13th:** The Export–Import Bank of China offered the first loan to the Yunnan Copper Group with respect to the international resort hotel project in Luang Prabang, Laos.
- **14th:** The Chinese Embassy in Laos donated medical materials to the Medical Rehabilitation Center under the Ministry of Health of Laos.
- **16th:** The China–Laos Information Platform for the medical and health service community of five provinces in northern Laos was launched in Louang Namtha Province, Laos.
- **21st:** Wang Jiarui, the Vice Chairman of the Chinese People's Political Consultative Conference and the Minister of the International Department of the Central Committee of the Communist Party of China, met with the delegation of the Commission for External Relations of the Central Committee of the Lao People's Revolutionary Party.
- **21st:** The Hebei Construction & Investment Group signed the H.La–Nge hydropower station project in Xekong Province, Laos.
- **28th:** The Defense Minister of Laos, Sengnuon Saynhalat, attended the reception celebrating the 88th anniversary of the founding of the Chinese army held at the Chinese Embassy in Laos.
- **29th:** China Eastern Airlines launched the Kunming–Xishuangbanna–(Laos) Luang Prabang air route.
- **29th:** The Lao Chinese Chamber of Commerce was established in Vientiane.

August

- **4th:** Chinese Foreign Minister, Wang Yi, met with the Deputy Prime Minister and Foreign Minister of Laos, Thongloun Sisoulith, in Kuala Lumpur, Malaysia.
- **14th:** The Laos–China Technical Research Center was officially inaugurated in Laos.
- **13th:** China donated 100 million Kip to the victims in the flood-stricken areas in Laos.
- **19th:** Lao cinemas concurrently introduced Chinese films for the first time.

- **25th:** China Unionpay worked with BCEL to issue the first aviation co-branded credit card.
- **27th:** The Yunnan Quality Supervision Bureau and the Yunnan Construction Engineering Group signed a cooperation agreement on Laos' testing center project.
- **31st:** Chinese President Xi Jinping met with the President of the People's Democratic Republic of Laos, Choummaly Sayasone, in Beijing, and the governments of the two countries signed the *Overall Plan for Joint Construction of the China-Laos Mohan–Boten Economic Cooperation Zone.*

September

- **1st:** Li Keqiang met with the President of the People's Democratic Republic of Laos, Choummaly Sayasone, in Beijing.
- **2nd:** The President of the People's Democratic Republic of Laos, Choummaly Sayasone, attended the LAOSAT-1 satellite delivery ceremony and wrote an inscription for the satellite.
- **3rd:** The President of the People's Democratic Republic of Laos, Choummaly Sayasone, attended the meeting commemorating the 70th anniversary of the victory of the War of the Chinese People's Resistance against Japanese Aggression and the victory of the World Anti-fascist War.
- **9th:** Mohan Sub-center of the Pan-Asian Service Center of the Agricultural Bank of China successfully handled the first individual Lao Kip foreign exchange purchasing and remittance service.
- **13th:** The China National Internet Information Office and the Ministry of Post and Telecommunications of Laos signed the *Memorandum of Understanding on Cyberspace Cooperation and Development.*
- **13th–16th:** The Vice Chairman of the Standing Committee of the National People's Congress, Ai Li Geng·Yi Ming Ba Hai, led a delegation to visit Laos.
- **17th–18th:** The Asian Development Bank held a seminar on the preparation of the *China* (*Xishuangbanna*)*–Laos* (*Namtha*) *Regional Plan* in Vientiane.

- **18th:** The Deputy Prime Minister of Laos, Somsavat Lengsavad, attended the opening ceremony of the 12th China–ASEAN Expo and delivered a speech.
- **18th:** Chongzuo City, Guangxi and Thakhek City, Khammouane Province, Laos established international sister city ties.
- **20th–26th:** The General Administration of Quality Supervision of China conducted a pre-inspection of the rice to be exported from Laos to China.
- **27th:** The 230 kW power grid EPC project in northern Laos, built by the China Southern Power Grid, was successfully put into operation.
- **28th:** The artistic performance celebrating the 66th anniversary of the establishment of the founding of the People's Republic of China was held at the Lao National Culture Hall in Vientiane.

October

- **2nd:** The Nam Ngiep No. 2 Hydropower Project, built by the China Three Gorges Corporation, was put into operation.
- **14th:** Liu Yunshan, a member of the Standing Committee of the Political Bureau of the CPC Central Committee, met with the President of the National Assembly of Laos, Pany Yathotu, in Beijing.
- **15th:** The Nanjing Federation of Industry and Commerce and the Lao National Chamber of Commerce and Industry established a friendly cooperative relationship.
- **16th:** The Chinese Ambassador to the ASEAN community, Xu Bu, met with the Deputy Prime Minister and Foreign Minister of Laos, Thongloun Sisoulith, in Vientiane.
- **17th:** The lecture "The Belt and Road Strategy" of "Discover China" was held at the National University of Laos.
- **19th:** Wang Jiarui, the Vice Chairman of the Chinese People's Political Consultative Conference and the Minister of the International Department of the Central Committee of the Communist Party of China, met with Sounthone Xayachack, the Chairman of the Commission for External Relations of the Central Committee of the Lao People's Revolutionary Party.

- **19th–21st:** The Working Group for Yunnan, China–Northern Laos Cooperation held the 7th meeting in VangVieng, Laos, and reached several consensuses.
- **21st:** The Chinese "Ambassador Study Room" was inaugurated at primary and middle schools in Vientiane, Laos.
- **23rd:** The Chinese Public Security Minister, Guo Shengkun, met with the Lao Public Security Minister in Beijing.
- **30th:** Chinese and Lao enterprises signed a stockholders agreement and initiated commercial operations of the LAOSAT-1 satellite project.
- **30th:** The Ningxia Folk Custom Exhibition was held at the Lao National Culture Hall in Vientiane.

November

- **11th:** The Laos Nam Ngum No.3 Hydropower Station, to be built by a subsidiary of the Power Construction Corporation of China, broke ground.
- **12th:** The Deputy Prime Minister and Foreign Minister of Laos, Thongloun Sisoulith, attended the 1st Foreign Ministers' Meeting on Lancang–Mekong Cooperation in China.
- **13th:** The governments of the two countries signed an intergovernmental railway cooperation agreement in Beijing, suggesting that the China–Laos railway project had entered the stage of execution.
- **14th:** The Houay Lamphan Gnai Hydropower Station in Laos, built by the China Gezhouba Group Corporation, was completed and delivered.
- **18th:** The Lao Fujian Chamber of Commerce was established in the Ton Pheung District, Laos.
- **19th:** The Center for Chinese Studies at the National University of Laos was officially established.
- **21st:** The LAOSAT-1 communications satellite was successfully launched at the Xichang Satellite Launch Center.
- **24th:** Yunnan State Farms Rubber Investment Co., Ltd. was established in Vientiane.
- **27th:** The Lao ATM Pool Switch (LAPS), donated by China, was launched in Vientiane.
- **29th:** The first power grid cooperation project for the Belt and Road was put into operation in Luang Prabang, Laos.

- **30th:** The Lao national bank card payment system, jointly built by China Unionpay, the China Development Bank and the central bank of Laos, was officially launched.

December

- **1st:** China Radio International and Lao News Agency signed a cooperation agreement.
- **1st:** The Chairman of the Standing Committee of the National People's Congress, Zhang Dejiang, led a delegation to attend the celebration of the 40th anniversary of the founding of Laos, and delivered an autographed letter written by Chinese President Xi Jinping to the President of the People's Democratic Republic of Laos, Choummaly Sayasone.
- **2nd:** The groundbreaking ceremony of the China–Laos railway project was held in Vientiane, Laos.
- **7th–8th:** A seminar on the development of Laos' vocational education was held in Vientiane, and relevant departments reached the preliminary consensus on the construction of the China–Laos Friendship Vocational Technical School.
- **9th:** The Laos HongSha coal-fired power station, built by China National Electric Engineering Corporation, was officially put into operation.
- **10th:** Laos exported the first batch of rice to China.
- **10th:** The Ningxia Painting and Calligraphy Academy held a work exhibition at the China Culture Center in Laos.
- **11th:** Chengdu and Luang Prabang Province, Laos established a friendly cooperative relationship.
- **21st:** The Laos–China Bank, a joint venture between China and Laos, became the correspondent bank for the financing project of the World Bank for promoting the development of small and medium-sized enterprises in Laos.
- **21st:** China Electric Power Equipment and Technology Co., Ltd. and Electricitt du Laos signed the EPC contract on the Vientiane ring network power transmission and transformation project.
- **23rd:** *China–Yunnan*, a special issue jointly run by Yunnan Daily and Vientiane Times, was first published in Vientiane.

The Chronicle of Events in China–Brunei Cooperation in 2015

Wang Yong[8]

January

- **22nd:** The China Railway Construction Corporation Limited visited the Ministry of development of Brunei.
- **26th:** The Chinese Ambassador to Brunei, Yang Jian, presented her credentials to Brunei Sultan Hassanal Bolkiah.

February

- **19th:** Brunei launched the direct tourist charter flight service from Xiamen to Brunei; this is the first direct charter flight route from the Chinese Mainland to Brunei.
- **27th:** Chinese smartphone manufacturer Vivo carried out promotional activities in Brunei, officially entering the Bruneian market.
- **28th:** 14 students from the Universiti Brunei Darussalam were funded by the Zhejiang Hengyi Group to study at Zhejiang University.

March

- **5th:** The Chinese Government provided four full scholarship quotas to Bruneian students for the school year 2015–2016.
- **23rd:** A special exhibition, jointly held by the Quanzhou Overseas Transportation History Museum and the Brunei Darussalam Maritime Museum, was inaugurated in Brunei.
- **25th:** Chiwan Base B, in conjunction with Singaporean enterprises, bid for Brunei's international oil and gas service base project.
- **27th:** The 2015 Chinese Culture Land Brunei Camp — sponsored by the Overseas Chinese Affairs Office of the State Council and organized by the Overseas Chinese Affairs Office of Guangdong Province, the Foreign and Overseas Chinese Affairs Bureau of

[8]Wang Yong, Research Assistant at the Brunei Institute of the China-ASEAN Research Institute of Guangxi University. Cooperator: Tian Ruifan, research assistant at the China-ASEAN Research Institute of Guangxi University.

Huizhou City, Guangdong Province and the Brunei Chung Hwa Middle School — was held at Brunei Chung Hwa Middle School.

- **28th:** The China Harbour Engineering Company (CHEC) successfully obtained the contract for the Muara Bridge Project.
- **30th:** Peng Qinghua, the Secretary of the Party Committee of the Guangxi Zhuang Autonomous Region, led a delegation to visit Brunei to promote the construction of the Brunei–Guangxi Economic Corridor.
- **30th:** A 12-person delegation of Huizhou City, Guangdong Province paid a friendly visit to a well-known overseas Chinese society in Bandar Seri Begawan, Brunei.

April

- **20th:** The Chinese Embassy in Brunei planned to carry out publicity activities designed to attract more Bruneian students to apply for the scholarships of Chinese universities and colleges.
- **22nd:** The Chinese Ambassador to Brunei, Yang Jian, held a press conference on *Vision and Actions on Jointly Building the Silk Road Economic Belt and the 21st Century Maritime Silk Road* at the residence of the Chinese Embassy.
- **23rd:** China and Brunei would like to establish three industrial parks in southern Guangxi, with a view to promoting trade and investment between the two countries through the Brunei–Guangxi Economic Corridor.
- **28th:** The Mayor of Yulin City, Guangxi Su Haitang, met with a delegation led by He Rongyao, an advisor to the Government of Brunei.
- **29th:** The Chinese Ambassador to Brunei, Yang Jian, gave an exclusive interview to the journalist of the Xinhua News Agency on China–ASEAN relations, setting high expectations about future bilateral cooperation.

May

- **4th–5th:** The Honorary President of the Pacific Economic Cooperation Council, Huang Mengfu, met with the Second Minister of Foreign Affairs and Trade of Brunei, Lin Yucheng, and exchanged views with the representatives of Chinese-funded enterprises in Brunei.

- **6th:** A delegation from Dalian City, China visited the representatives of Chinese businessmen in Brunei, discussing some issues on promoting bilateral economic and trade cooperation and investments.
- **10th:** The Deputy President of the Fuzhou Association in Brunei, Dr. Liu Shiquan, led a 36-person delegation to Fuzhou to attend the Representative Congress of the World Federation of Fuzhou Association LTD.
- **17th:** Hengyi Industrial Co., Ltd. and the Brunei Economic Development Board jointly conducted the fourth stakeholder contact dialogue to report on the progress of the project and its impact on the surrounding communities.

June

- **26th:** Beijing Sesame World Technology Co., Ltd. worked on building the first Southeast Asian base in Brunei.
- **29th:** The Second Finance Minister, Pehin Dato Rahman, attended the signing ceremony of the Asian Infrastructure Investment Bank.

July

- **3rd:** The first group of 13 students from Universiti Brunei Darussalam, financially assisted by the Zhejiang Hengyi Group, attended the graduation ceremony, and they smoothly finished their studies in China.
- **7th:** Guo Zhijie, the Activity Director of the Seri Mulia Sarjana School, visited the Guangzhou Chanwu Center, China to receive lion dancing and martial arts training.
- **15th:** Chinese President Xi Jinping sent a letter to congratulate Brunei Sultan Hassanal Bolkiah on his 69th birthday.
- **21st:** The press corps of Hainan Daily, China visited the Hainan Association in Brunei.
- **27th:** The Chinese Ambassador to Brunei, Yang Jian, issued a letter of admission to Bruneian students who had been granted a scholarship by the Chinese Government.

August

- **2nd–4th:** The Secretary of the Party Committee of Hainan Province, Luo Baoming, visited Brunei.
- **2nd:** The Brunei Martial Arts Team participated in the 8th Asian Youth Martial Arts Championship in Xilinhot, Inner Mongolia.
- **15th:** Brunei Sultan Hassanal Bolkiah sent a condolence message to Chinese President Xi Jinping and Chinese Premier Li Keqiang for the serious fire accident in Tianjin.
- **18th:** The President of the Fuzhou Association in Brunei, Chen Jiaxing, held a banquet for a delegation of the Department of Commerce of Fujian Province.
- **22nd:** Royal Brunei Airlines planned to engage in code sharing cooperation with China Eastern Airlines.
- **29th:** China's import and export trade with Brunei totaled US $867 million from January to July 2015, down 8.25%.

September

- **2nd:** Huawei Brunei held a dinner party for the returned students participating in Huawei's Future Seed program.
- **12th:** The joint venture between the China State Construction Engineering Corporation and Brunei's Ocean Quarry & Construction Sdn Bhd was awarded the contract for the construction of the viaduct and highway project on the Temburong section of the Temburong cross-sea bridge.
- **16th:** The Minister of Industry and Primary Resources of Brunei, Pehin Dato Awang Haji Yahya, left for Nanning, Guangxi, China, and attended the 12th China–ASEAN Expo.
- **17th:** The Chinese Ambassador to Brunei, Yang Jian, went to University of Brunei Darussalam to meet with the second group of 10 young volunteers from China to assist Brunei.
- **20th:** The Deputy Executive Secretary of the Ministry of Communications of Brunei and the Chairman of Guangxi Beibu Gulf International Port Group, Zhou Xiaoxi, signed the *Letter of Intent on Cooperation between the Government of Brunei Darussalam and the Guangxi Beibu Gulf International Port Group*.

- **20th:** The Ministry of Industry and Primary Resources of Brunei held a seminar on the promotion of Brunei at the Nanning International Convention and Exhibition Center, promoting Brunei's investment projects, tourism resources and Halal certification, introducing the Brunei–Guangxi Economic Corridor and the Brunei Biological Innovation Corridor.

October

- **1st:** The Brunei Sultan sent a congratulatory message to Chinese President Xi Jinping and Chinese Premier Li Keqiang on the 66th anniversary of the founding of the People's Republic of China.
- **10th:** China's import and export trade with Brunei from January to August, 2015 decreased by 2.9%, with exports increasing by 9.2%.
- **19th:** The Minister of Energy of Brunei said that Brunei welcomed China to continue participating in the support for the ASEAN community and its multilateral defense initiative, and extended thanks to China for its contributions to regional security.
- **20th:** The Chinese Ambassador to Brunei Yang Jian inspected the first industrial investment project of Chinese enterprises in Brunei – the construction site of the Huludao Steel Pipe Plant.
- **27th:** China's exports to Brunei from January to September 2015 increased by 3.09%, while imports decreased by 68.04%.

November

- **4th:** The 10th China–ASEAN People and People's Friendship Meeting was held in Bandar Seri Begawan.
- **23rd:** During the 18th ASEAN-China Summit, the Sultan praised Chinese Premier Li Keqiang for his view on promoting the strategic partnership between the ASEAN community, Brunei and China.
- **24th–25th:** The Attorney General of Brunei attended the 9th China–ASEAN Procurators-General Conference in Nanning, China.
- **29th:** Four officials of the Brunei History Centre left for Nanjing and Guangzhou to get an in-depth understanding of the commercial and trade ties between ancient Brunei and China and their historical process.

December

- **3rd:** A delegation of students from Tai Ji Class at Wushu Federation of Brunei Darussalam left for Liuzhou, Guangxi to participate in the 3rd China-ASEAN Martial Arts Festival Shadowboxing Competition.
- **14th:** 26 students from the Huizhou Zhonghua Middle School, China took part in the 4th Southeast Asia Overseas Chinese Juvenile Student Camping Activity.
- **16th:** Bruneian singer Dayang Sri Nazrina sang at the China-ASEAN Friendly Concert in Beijing.
- **17th:** Ma Kaixian, the Vice Chairman of the People's Political Consultative Conference of Yunnan Province, China and a member of the China National Steering Committee for Islamic Teaching Affairs led a 16-person commercial delegation to visit Brunei.

The Chronicle of Events in China–Cambodia Cooperation in 2015

Zhang Tianlu[9]

January

- **13th:** The counselor at the Chinese Embassy, Li Zhigong, met with the Khmer-Chinese Association in the Kingdom of Cambodia.
- **16th:** The Chinese Government donated 200 ambulances to the Ministry of Health of Cambodia.
- **26th:** The Ministry of the Post and Telecommunications of Cambodia and the Ministry of Industry and Information Technology of China signed a cooperation agreement on information and communication technology.

[9]Zhang Tianlu, graduate student at the Business School of Guangxi University. Cooperator: Shi Kehan, graduate student at the Business School of Guangxi University.

February

- **4th:** The Prime Minister of Cambodia, Hun Sen, met with Edmund Ho Hau Wah, the Vice Chairman of the Chinese People's Political Consultative Conference and former Chief Executive of the Macao Special Administrative Region in Siem Reap.
- **9th:** The Governor of Siem Reap, Khim Bunsongs allotted the ambulances donated by the Chinese Government to various counties.
- **11th:** The Chinese Embassy in Cambodia held a reception celebrating the New Year 2015.
- **11th:** Chinese Deputy Foreign Minister Liu Zhenmin met with a delegation led by the Chairman of the Commission of Diplomatic and International Cooperation and Media News at the Parliament of Cambodia, which was visiting China.

March

- **4th:** The first Vice-President of Cambodia's National Assembly, Kem Sokha, met with the Chinese Ambassador to Cambodia, Bu Jianguo.
- **10th:** The Cambodian Khmer International Media Group sent a powerful press corps to cover Two Sessions held in China.
- **22nd:** A youth delegation sent by the Central Committee of the Cambodian People's Party (CPP) visited China.
- **23rd:** The ceremony in which the Ministry of Culture of China donated cultural apparatuses to Cambodia was held.
- **25th:** The Tourism Minister of Cambodia, Thong Khon, visited the Chinese Embassy and pledged to provide Chinese tourists with higher quality services.

April

- **3rd:** The Northeast Representative Office of China's Economic and Trade Promotion Council of the Cambodia International Chamber of Commerce was inaugurated in the Liaotong Economic and Technological Development Zone, China.
- **7th:** The Vice Chairman of the Cambodian Rice Alliance said that future rice exportations would focus on the Chinese market.
- **8th:** The China Alumni Association in Cambodia was established in Phnom Penh.

- **14th:** The Minister of Agriculture, Forestry and Fisheries of Cambodia said that Cambodia planned to export corn, soybeans, mangoes, bananas and other agricultural products to China.
- **18th:** The Prime Minister of Cambodia, Hun Sen, met with the Chinese State Councilor and Public Security Minister, Guo Shengkun, in Phnom Penh.
- **21st:** Chinese Vice President Li Yuanchao met with the President of the Funcinpec Party of Cambodia, Norodom Ranariddh.
- **24th:** Lurui Co., Ltd., an enterprise in Shandong, China, built a modern agricultural industrial park in Cambodia.

May

- **2nd:** The Phnom Penh Municipal Government purchased 100 buses from China, which would be used to expand the bus lines in Phnom Penh.
- **4th:** The groundbreaking ceremony of the Highway 55 Project in Cambodia, to be built with concessional loans from China, was held in Pursat Province.
- **18th:** The former Prime Minister of Cambodia, Nhek Bun Chhay, attended the 9th Expo of Central China.
- **25th:** The Chinese Government donated 44 military vehicles and other military equipment to Cambodia.
- **25th:** The China–Fujian Week & the Industrial Project Promotion Fair were held in Phnom Penh, Cambodia.
- **25th:** The Prime Minister of Cambodia, Hun Sen, met with Chinese Deputy Commerce Minister Gao Yan in Phnom Penh.
- **26th:** The Commissioner of the National Health and Family Planning Commission of China, Li Bin, met with the Minister of Health of Cambodia, Mam Bunheng, in Beijing.
- **26th:** The Deputy Prime Minister of Cambodia met with Zhang Gaoli, a member of the Standing Committee of the Political Bureau of the CPC Central Committee and Chinese Vice Premier.

June

- **2nd:** The opening ceremony of Highway 41 in Cambodia, built with concessional loans from the Chinese Government, was held.

- **15th:** The handover ceremony in which the Chinese Government donated 200 medical ultrasonic apparatuses to the Ministry of Health of Cambodia was held.
- **23rd:** Chinese Deputy Foreign Minister Liu Zhenmin met with the President of the Union of Youth Federation of Cambodia.

July

- **2nd:** General Tea Banh, the Deputy Prime Minister and Defense Minister of Cambodia, visited the Chinese Embassy in China.
- **10th:** The Chinese Chamber of Commerce in Cambodia held the ceremony for the establishment of the 7th board of directors and the director inauguration ceremony in Phnom Penh.
- **14th:** The Ministry of Foreign Affairs of Cambodia conducted the handover activity in which the Chinese Embassy donated four vehicles and 45 smartphones.
- **15th:** Two Cambodian young people won the championship in the 2015 China Skills Competition.
- **16th:** A new teaching building, whose construction was assisted by China, at a middle school in Cambodia was officially put into use.
- **16th:** The Chairman of the National Anti-corruption Commission of Cambodia met with a delegation led by Yang Xiaodu, the Secretary of the Party Committee of the Central Commission for Discipline Inspection and the Ministry of Supervision of China.
- **20th:** Qin Jun, the Mayor of Xiangyang City, Hubei Province, China, met with Sok An, the Deputy Prime Minister of Cambodia and the Minister for the Office of the Council of Ministers.
- **21st:** Hor Namhong, the Deputy Prime Minister of Cambodia and the Minister of Foreign Affairs and International Cooperation, met with the new Chinese Ambassador to the ASEAN, Xu Bu, in Phnom Penh.

August

- **2nd:** he Governor of Siem Reap, Khim Bunsong, led a delegation, in conjunction with the representatives of the Zhejiang Chamber of Commerce, to visit China.

- **3rd:** Sok An, the Deputy Prime Minister of Cambodia and the Minister for the Office of the Council of Ministers, attended the China–ASEAN Educational Exchange Week Activity.
- **4th:** Hor Namhong, the Deputy Prime Minister of Cambodia and the Minister of Foreign Affairs and International Cooperation, met with Chinese Foreign Minister Wang Yi in Kuala Lumpur, Malaysia.
- **7th:** Sun Jianguo, the Deputy Chief of the Joint Staff of the Chinese People's Liberation Army, met with the Deputy Commander in Chief of the Royal Cambodian Army in Beijing.
- **31st:** The King of Cambodia, Norodom Sihamoni, visited China and met with Chinese President Xi Jinping.

September

- **3rd:** The King of Cambodia, Norodom Sihamoni, attended the military parade commemorating the 70th anniversary of the victory of the War of the Chinese People's Resistance against Japanese Aggression.
- **17th:** The President of the National Assembly of Cambodia, Heng Samrin, met with the Vice Chairman of the Standing Committee of the National People's Congress, Ai Li Geng–Yi Ming Ba Hai.
- **19th:** Wang Qinmin, the Vice Chairman of the Chinese People's Political Consultative Conference and the Chairman of the All-China Federation of Industry and Commerce visited the Sihanoukville Special Economic Zone in Cambodia.
- **19th:** The ceremony of cerebrating the 15th anniversary of the establishment of the Cambodia–China Friendship Association was held in Phnom Penh.
- **26th:** The launching ceremony of the China–ASEAN 2015 International Auto Rally was held in Phnom Penh, Cambodia.
- **29th:** The Chinese Ambassador to Cambodia, Bu Jianguo, held the National Day reception celebrating the 66th anniversary of the founding of the People's Republic of China.

October

- **1st:** The public schools for oversea Chinese in a Cambodian city celebrated the 66th anniversary of the founding of the People's Republic of China.

- **6th:** The Prime Minister of Cambodia, Hun Sen, met with Xu Dazhe, the Deputy Minister of Industry and Information Technology of China and the Director of the State Administration for Science, Technology and Industry for National Defense of China in Phnom Penh.
- **17th:** A series of meetings, which the Prime Minister of Cambodia Hun Sen and his wife Bun Rany attended in Macao and Beijing, came to a successful conclusion.
- **20th:** A delegation led by the President of the Police Academy of Cambodia visited the Yunnan Police Officers Academy, China.
- **20th:** The Ministry of Tourism of Cambodia actively carried out the *Strategy for Attracting Chinese Tourists*.
- **22nd:** The Deputy Prime Minister and the Minister of the Interior of Cambodia led a delegation to visit China.
- **26th:** The Maritime Silk Road China–Cambodia Forum was held in Phnom Penh.

November

- **1st:** The first library in Kampong Speu Province, whose construction was assisted by the Chinese Government, broke ground.
- **2nd:** Construction was officially started on Highway 1577 in Battambang Province, whose construction was assisted by the Chinese Government.
- **3rd:** The Chinese Embassy in Cambodia donated 100 computers to the General Department of Immigration of Cambodia.
- **6th:** Tea Banh, the Deputy Prime Minister and Defense Minister of Cambodia, held talks with the State Councilor and Defense Minister, Chang Wanquan, in Phnom Penh.
- **10th:** The General Department of Immigration of Cambodia cooperated with the Ministry of Public Security of China to repatriate 168 Chinese suspected of committing telecommunications fraud.
- **17th:** Cambodia applied to China for US $300 million in concessional loans so as to promote the development of the rice production fields in Cambodia.
- **21st:** The Prime Minister of Cambodia, Hun Sen, attended the 18th ASEAN-China ("10+1") Leaders' Meeting.

December

- **17th:** The ceremony of the official handover and commissioning of medical materials and equipment donated by the Ministry of Defense of China to the General Hospital of the Royal Cambodian Army.
- **20th:** The Chinese Government donated 200 bicycles to 22 middle schools in Kampong Speu Province.
- **21st:** Sok An, the Deputy Prime Minister of Cambodia and the Minister for the Office of the Council of Ministers, praised the Belt and Road Initiative put forward by China.
- **24th:** The ceremony of the handover of the materials donated by China to the Mine Action Center of Cambodia and the ASEAN community was held.
- **26th:** The 2015 evening party of the China Alumni Association in Cambodia was held in Phnom Penh.
- **31st:** The office building of Cambodia's Senate, whose construction was assisted by the Chinese Government, broke ground.

The Chronicle of Events in China–Indonesia Cooperation in 2015

Wei Baoyi[10]

January

- **1st:** The China-Indonesia New Silk Road Committee was established.
- **12th:** China's Virtue Dragon Nickel Industry Co., Ltd. would like to build a nickel smelting plant in the Konawe Industrial Zone in Sulawesi Tenggara, Indonesia.
- **27th:** Chinese Premier Li Keqiang met with the special envoy of the President of Indonesia and the Coordinating Minister for Economic Affairs of Indonesia, Sofyan Djalil, stating that China was willing to assist Indonesia in carrying out the construction of infrastructures.

[10]Zhang Tianlu, Deputy Director of the Indonesia Institute of the China-ASEAN Research Institute of Guangxi University.

February

- **2nd:** General Motors confirmed that it would cooperate with SAIC General Motors to build a factory in Indonesia.
- **3rd:** President Joko met with Chinese special envoy Meng Jianzhu, and the two sides discussed the issues concerning the rule of law and anti-corruption cooperation.
- **9th:** The Confucius Institute at the University of Al Azhar Indonesia and the Language Center of the Headquarters of the Indonesian National Police officially launched the 7th teaching cooperation.
- **14th:** The Ministry of Defense of China donated Chinese education facilities to the Ministry of Defense of Indonesia.
- **21st:** Indonesia initiated the Route of Zheng He's Travelling to the West.

March

- **10th:** China supported Indonesia's maritime construction and provided US $40 billion to the Maritime Silk Road Fund.
- **20th:** The Bank of China would like to offer about 20 trillion rupiah low-interest loans to Indonesian small and medium-sized enterprises.
- **26th:** Chinese President Xi Jinping held talks with President Joko, and the two sides decided to establish a vice-premier-level people-to-people exchange mechanism and develop a future five-year action plan.
- **27th:** President Joko and the Chinese Premier jointly attended the China–Indonesia Economic Cooperation Forum.

April

- **4th:** Indonesia and China discussed an agreement on the exchange of the Komodo dragon and the Chinese giant panda.
- **22nd:** The People's Republic of China and the Republic of Indonesia issued a joint press communiqué.
- **24th:** China Minsheng Investment Co., Ltd. planned to invest US $1.6 billion in building a steel plant in Indonesia.

May

- **1st:** China's Midea Group set up plants in Indonesia.
- **4th:** The Indonesia Takalar coal-fired steam power plant project to be built by China officially broke ground.

- **19th:** The Ministry of Communication and Information Technology of Indonesia and Huawei Technologies Investment Co., Ltd. signed a memorandum of understanding on cooperation on the ICT innovation center.
- **21st:** ICBC Indonesia and Sahabat Sampoerna signed a memorandum of understanding on cooperation in loans for micro, small and medium-sized enterprises.
- **27th:** Chinese Vice Premier Liu Yandong visited Indonesia, stressing that the China–Indonesia people-to-people exchange mechanism was a great event in the history of the two countries.
- **27th:** Chinese Vice Premier Liu Yandong left for Jakarta to attend the launching ceremony of the China–Indonesia radio and television cooperation, and announced the launch of the Chinese TV program H1-1NDO.

June

- **4th:** The Financial Services Authority of Indonesia and the China Banking Regulatory Commission signed an agreement on strengthening information sharing and cooperation supervision.
- **12th:** Indonesia announced the adoption of the free-visa policy for the tourists from the Chinese Mainland for a stay of a maximum of 30 days.
- **23rd:** Chinese President Xi Jinping communicated with President Joko by phone.

July

- **6th:** he Chinese Ambassador to Indonesia, Xie Feng, donated 100 million rupiah to the Islamic boarding schools under the Nadhaltul Ulama.

August

- **12th:** China's Gree Electric Appliances (Indonesia) was open for business.

September

- **12th:** The missile destroyer Yucheng of the Chinese Navy left for Indonesia to participate in the international fleet review activity celebrating the 70th anniversary of Indonesia's independence.

- **15th:** The Ministry of Public Works and Housing of Indonesia and a contractor consortium consisting of Chinese enterprises and Indonesian state-owned construction enterprises signed a contract on a 10.1-km highway which would connect West Java with Central Java and which is worth 3.48 trillion rupiah.
- **16th:** Yinhua TV, dominated by the Chinese language, was established.
- **16th:** The China Development Bank offered US $3 billion in a loan to three state-owned banks in Indonesia.
- **16th:** ICBC Indonesia and Bank Tabungan Negara (BTN) signed a memorandum of understanding on cooperation on the "1 million homes" housing program.
- **22nd:** The ICBC (Asia), ICBC Indonesia and the Indonesia Eximbank signed a loan agreement on USD 500 million in working capital.
- **29th:** The China Civil Engineering Construction Corporation and the Directorate General of Railways under the Ministry of Transportation of Indonesia signed a US $226 million contract on the Phase II project of Indonesia's railway material purchase.

October

- **9th:** China helped Indonesia cope with forest fires.
- **11th:** China's US $3 billion loan shook the market, the 1 USD: 13,407 rupiah exchange rate was expected to decline.
- **12th:** The ceremony of naming and inaugurating Rumah Soekarno (Indonesia–China Cooperation Center) was held in Shenzhen, China.
- **16th:** A consortium of Chinese enterprises led by the China Railway Corporation and a consortium of Indonesian state-owned enterprises led by WIKA signed a joint venture agreement on the Jakarta–Bandung High-speed Railway.
- **26th:** The issue of cracking down on human trafficking was included in the draft of extending the memorandum of understanding on cooperation between Indonesian and Chinese police.
- **28th:** China Minsheng Investment Co., Ltd. (CMI) decided to invest US $5 billion to build an industrial park on West Java Island.

November

- **2nd:** The first BOO project carried out by Shanghai Electric Power Construction Co., Ltd. of the Power Construction Corporation of China — the 2 × 167 MW unit project in Medan, Indonesia broke ground.
- **10th:** SINOSTEEL MECC, a wholly-owned subsidiary of SINOSTEEL, and Indonesia's PT CPS Indonesia Medan signed an EPC contract on a municipal waste incineration power plant in Medan, Indonesia, which is worth about US $175 million.
- **12th:** The China Shenhua Group won the bidding for Indonesia's power plant project under the BOO mode.
- **12th:** The Export-Import Bank of China offered a 10 trillion rupiah loan in advance, boosting the construction of four highways in Indonesia on schedule.
- **13th:** RMB settlement was made within Indonesia–China trade as from 2016.
- **17th:** Indonesia and China agreed to increase the amount of the bilateral currency swap agreement from US $15 billion to US $20 billion.
- **18th:** The first China–Indonesia national sand table exercise of maritime search and rescue was conducted in Haikou, Hainan.
- **23rd:** The first flagship store of the Chinese company Lenovo in Indonesia was open for business.

December

- **7th:** The Export–Import Bank of China extended the first US $288.9 million loan to Indonesia for supporting the construction of two toll highways.
- **11th:** The Shanghai Commercial & Savings Bank, Ltd. officially entered Indonesia and set up the Jakarta Office.
- **16th:** Antam and Inalum chose the Aluminum Corporation of China as the partner for developing an aluminum ingot smelting plant in Mempawah, West Kalimantan, with the joint venture scale of US $1.8 billion.
- **17th:** The aquaculture, cassava planting and processing project in Pulau Bangka, jointly promoted by INDUK KUD and China, was launched at Pangkal Pinang in Kepulauan Bangka Belitung, Indonesia.

- **18th:** Chinese steel entrepreneur Dai Guofang invested 6 billion yuan in building a plant in Indonesia.
- **20th:** Hefei launched a direct flight to Bali, Indonesia for the first time.
- **21st:** The Chinese company Skyworth acquired one of Toshiba's TV set factories in Indonesia.
- **28th:** The Indonesian language accounts of the Xinhua News Agency on overseas social media platforms Facebook and Twitter were officially launched.

Appendix: Statistical Data

Table A.1. The Territory, Population and Economic Scale of China and 10 ASEAN Countries in 2014

			GDP		Per capita GDP	
Country	Area (km^2)	Population (10,000)	Current USD (USD 100 million)	On PPP basis (100 million international dollar)	Current USD (USD)	On PPP basis (international dollar)
Brunei	5,270	41.74	171.05	297.12	40,979.6	67,912
Cambodia	176,520	1,532.81	167.78	500.10	1,094.6	3,113
Indonesia	1,811,570	25,445.48	8,885.38	26,761.09	3,491.9	10,033
Laos	230,800	668.93	119.97	355.93	1,793.5	5,076
Malaysia	328,550	2,990.20	3,381.04	7,666.45	11,307.1	24,460
Myanmar	653,080	5,343.72	643.30	—	1,203.8	—
The Philippines	298,170	9,913.87	2,847.77	2,872.5	2,872.5	6,649
Singapore	707	546.97	3,078.60	4,526.91	56,284.3	78,958
Thailand	510,890	6,772.60	4,048.24	10,656.73	5,977.4	15,012
Vietnam	310,070	9,072.89	1,862.05	5,107.15	2,052.3	5,370
ASEAN	4,325,627	62,329.21	25,205.18	—	127,057.0	—
China	9,388,211	135,070	103,548.32	180,170.73	7,590.0	12,599

Note: PPP-based GDP refers to GDP in international dollar based on the PPP rate.

Source: The World Bank.

Table A.2. Per capita GDP in 10 ASEAN Countries, 2007–2014 (Unit: USD)

Country	2007	2008	2009	2010	2011	2012	2013	2014
Brunei	32,707.7	37,798.4	27,726.5	31,453.2	41,787.0	41,807.7	39,151.2	40,979.6
Cambodia	629.3	742.9	735.4	782.7	879.2	946.5	1,024.6	1,094.6
Indonesia	1,860.6	2,167.9	2,262.7	3,125.2	3,647.6	3,700.5	3,623.5	3,491.9
Laos	711.0	900.5	948.0	1,147.1	1,301.0	1,445.9	1,701.0	1,793.5
Malaysia	7,240.7	8,486.6	7,312.0	9,069.0	10,427.8	10,834.7	10,973.7	11,307.1
Myanmar	333.0*	436.0*	538.0*	706.0*	869.0*	1,421.5	1,107.0	1,203.8
The Philippines	1,678.9	1,929.1	1,836.9	2,145.2	2,371.9	2,604.7	2,787.0	2,872.5
Singapore	39,223.6	39,721.0	38,577.6	46,569.7	53,121.4	54,576.8	55,980.2	56,284.3
Thailand	3,962.8	4,384.8	4,231.1	5,111.9	5,539.5	5,917.9	6,229.2	5,977.4
Vietnam	919.2	1,164.6	1,232.4	1,333.6	3,800.5	1,754.5	1,907.6	2,052.3
ASEAN	88,933.8	97,295.8	84,862.6	100,737.6	122,875.9	125,010.7	124,485.0	127,057.0
China	2,673.3	3,441.2	3,800.5	3,800.5	5,574.2	6,264.6	6,264.6	7,590.0

Note: Data come from *ASEAN Statistical Yearbook 2013*.

Source: Data come from the World Bank.

Table A.3. The Changes in the Structure of the Primary, Secondary and Tertiary Industries in China and 10 ASEAN Countries, 2005–2013 (Unit: %)

	Agricultural sector			Industrial sector			Service sector		
Country	2005	2010	2013	2005	2010	2013	2005	2010	2013
Brunei	1.3	1.1	1.3	61.2	52.5	51.0	37.5	46.3	47.8
Cambodia	31	29.4	26.0	28.3	28.6	32.2	40.7	42.0	41.9
Indonesia	14.5	13.2	12.3	44.1	41.1	39.9	41.4	45.7	47.8
Laos	45	31.6	—	29.6	27.7	—	25.5	40.7	—
Malaysia	8.4	7.7	7.2	44.3	38.6	36.9	47.3	53.8	55.9
Myanmar	—	39.9	—	—	22.6	—	—	37.5	—
The Philippines	19.1	11.6	10.4	32.8	32.6	32.8	48.1	55.8	56.8
Singapore	0.1	0.0	0.0	32.6	33.6	28.0	67.3	66.3	71.9
Thailand	9	8.3	8.3	46.9	48.7	46.0	44	43.0	45.8
Vietnam	19.6	16.5	17.6	40.2	41.9	38.6	40.3	41.6	43.9
ASEAN	11.7	9.6	9.4	46.9	46.2	43.7	41.4	44.2	46.9

Sources: The data on the ASEAN countries come from *ASEAN Statistical Yearbook 2012* and *ASEAN Statistical Yearbook 2014*, while that on China are based on the data from the National Bureau of Statistics.

Table A.4. The Development of the Agricultural Sector in 10 ASEAN Countries in 2012 and 2013 (Unit: %)

	The proportion in GDP*		Employment proportion		Export proportion		Import proportion	
Country	2012	2013	2012	2013	2012	2013	2012	2013
Brunei	1.3	1.3	—	—	0.05	0.16	11.95	15.17
Cambodia	25.0	—	—	—	3.00	4.52	6.95	6.25
Indonesia	12.5	12.3	35.9	34.8	17.13	17.4	8.55	8.97
Laos	26.9	—	—	—	18.77	21.14	6.68	4.98
Malaysia	7.3	7.2	12.6	12.7	12.02	10.54	8.50	7.67
Myanmar	34.9	—	—	—	35.35	29.60	8.53	8.54
The Philippines	11.1	10.4	32.3	—	9.27	10.92	10.95	10.82
Singapore	0.0	0.0	—	—	2.21	3.37	3.37	3.55
Thailand	8.4	8.3	38.9	36.2	14.02	5.23	5.23	5.27
Vietnam	15.8	17.6	—	—	14.59	8.05	8.05	7.98

*The proportion in GDP is based on constant price.

Source: *ASEAN Statistical Yearbook 2014*.

Table A.5. The Development of the Industrial Sector in 10 ASEAN Countries in 2012 and 2013 (Unit: %)

	The proportion in GDP*		Employment proportion		Export proportion		Import proportion	
Country	2012	2013	2012	2013	2012	2013	2012	2013
Brunei	51.0	51.0	—	—	5.5	3.1	77.2	74.8
Cambodia	29.7	—	—	—	96.9	95.4	75.9	81.8
Indonesia	40.3	39.9	13.9	13.3	46.8	47.8	67.2	65.0
Laos	28.3	—	—	—	68.1	53.0	67.4	75.1
Malaysia	36.8	36.9	17.5	16.8	66.6	66.2	75.9	74.8
Myanmar	27.4	—	—	—	40.4	28.6	66.9	73.7
The Philippines	32.0	32.8	8.3	—	86.0	80.7	65.3	66.3
Singapore	32.1	28.0	14.1	13.6	71.0	72.0	61.9	63.1
Thailand	47.1	46.0	14.7	16.2	79.0	79.8	75.2	74.2
Vietnam	41.6	38.6	—	—	73.4	77.3	80.7	82.3

*The proportion in GDP is based on constant price.

Source: *ASEAN Statistical Yearbook 2014*.

Table A.6. Total Import and Export Trade in 10 ASEAN Countries, 1950–2015 (Unit: Million USD)

Year	1950	1955	1960	1965	1970	1975	1980	1985
Brunei	87	129	100	101	179	1,322	5,153	3,587
Cambodia	57	86	165	208	93	65	196	140
Indonesia	1,240	1,576	1,415	1,403	2,110	11,872	32,743	28,852
Laos	2	20	20	34	121	57	120	247
Malaysia	1,542	1,639	2,097	2,332	3,088	7,409	23,724	27,569
Myanmar	230	407	486	472	263	368	834	592
The Philippines	707	1,008	1,339	1,592	2,277	6,050	14,032	10,062
Singapore	2,075	2,363	2,469	2,224	4,015	13,509	43,383	49,097
Thailand	513	673	858	1,364	2,009	5,488	15,719	16,363
Vietnam	163	332	326	229	381	1,331	1,652	2,555
Total	6,616	8,233	9,275	9,959	14,536	47,471	137,556	139,064

Year	1990	1995	2000	2005	2010	2013	2014	2015
Brunei	3,214	4,493	5,010	7,740	11,445	15,060	14,108	9,185
Cambodia	250	2,042	3,328	7,019	11,934	22,300	24,360	26,360
Indonesia	47,512	86,047	108,998	162,721	293,397	370,638	354,472	292,977
Laos	264	900	865	1,435	3,806	5,284	6,933	6,200
Malaysia	58,710	151,606	180,192	255,950	363,234	434,290	442,778	375,830
Myanmar	595	2,186	3,991	5,684	13,421	23,276	27,257	21,870
The Philippines	21,121	45,843	75,105	90,742	109,964	121,795	129,819	128,568
Singapore	113,629	242,775	272,349	429,696	662,658	783,266	776,034	647,251
Thailand	56,113	127,225	130,981	229,114	376,227	479,253	455,272	417,029
Vietnam	5,156	13,604	30,121	69,203	157,076	264,066	298,066	328,210
Total	306,564	676,721	810,940	1,259,304	2,003,162	2,519,228	2,529,099	2,253,480

Source: Total Merchandise Trade in Statistical Database on the official website of the WTO.

Table A.7. The Ranking of the ASEAN Countries Among Countries Around the World in Trade in Goods and Services in 2014 and 2015 (Unit: 100 million USD, %)

Item	World ranking	Exporting country	Amount	Proportion	World ranking	Exporting country	Amount	Proportion
Trade in goods		2014				2015		
	14	Singapore	4,100	2.2	15	Singapore	3,660	1.9
	23	Malaysia	2,340	1.2	24	Thailand	2,280	1.2
	24	Thailand	2,280	1.2	26	Malaysia	2,090	1.1
	28	Indonesia	1,760	0.9	28	Indonesia	1,780	0.9
	32	Vietnam	1,500	0.8	32	Vietnam	1,490	0.8
					44	The Philippines	680	0.4
	Total		11,980	6.3			Total	11,980
Trade in services	9	Singapore	1,400	2.8	10	Singapore	1,410	3.0
	24	Thailand	550	1.1	28	Thailand	530	1.1
	31	Malaysia	390	0.8	30	Malaysia	450	0.9
	37	The Philippines	250	0.5	32	Indonesia	330	0.7
	39	Indonesia	23	0.5				
	Total		2,613	5.7			Total	2,720

Note: The table only covers the ASEAN countries among the top 50 countries around the world in import and export trade in goods and the top 40 countries around the world in import and export trade in services.
Source: WTO International Trade Statistics 2015.

Table A.8. The ASEAN's Top 10 Trading Partners/Territories in 2014 (Unit: Million USD, %)

Trading partner	Export		Import		Import and export	
	Amount	Proportion	Amount	Proportion	Amount	Proportion
ASEAN	329,642.08	25.5	278,564.88	22.5	608,207.0	24.1
China	150,406.55	11.6	216,119.36	17.5	366,525.9	14.5
European	132,483.98	10.3	115,823.62	9.4	248,307.6	9.8
U.S.A	122,374.70	9.5	90,053.87	7.3	212,428.6	8.4
Japan	120,224.15	9.3	108,817.69	8.8	229,041.8	9.1
The	51,624.21	4.0	79,814.82	6.5	131,439.0	5.2
India	43,325.81	3.4	24,381.97	2.0	67,707.8	2.7
New	6,381.07	0.5	4,326.48	0.3	10,707.5	0.4
Pakistan	5,667.06	0.4	1,031.18	0.1	6,698.2	0.3
Russia	5,414.83	0.4	22,542.9	1.4	22,542.9	0.9
Subtotal	1,020,359.0	79.0	1,987,134.5	78.2	1,987,134.5	78.6
Other	272,040.8	21.0	541,481.4	21.8	541,481.4	21.4
Total	1,292,399.8	100.0	2,528,615.9	100.0	2,528,615.9	100.0

Source: ASEAN Merchandise Trade Statistical Database.

Table A.9. The Changes in the Trade Within and Outside ASEAN, 1994–2014 (Unit: 100 million USD)

	Trade within ASEAN		Trade outside ASEAN		ASEAN's total trade	
Year	Export	Import	Export	Import	Export	Import
1994	585.72	469.12	1,881.93	2,203.30	2,467.65	2,672.42
1995	701.79	536.02	2,265.18	2,649.53	2,966.97	3,185.55
1996	809.74	642.11	2,423.88	2,863.95	3,233.61	3,506.06
1997	853.52	646.21	2,573.18	2,913.51	3,426.70	3,559.72
1998	693.13	516.05	2,473.38	2,078.52	3,166.51	2,594.57
1999	749.04	577.71	2,669.08	2,235.75	3,418.12	2,813.46
2000	933.80	734.66	3,167.61	2,723.91	4,101.41	3,458.57
2001	826.81	676.40	2,876.75	2,494.89	3,703.56	3,206.35
2002	867.07	732.02	2,971.48	2,549.11	3,838.54	3,299.63
2003	1,003.19	758.80	3,307.15	2,840.10	4,367.82	3,636.56
2004	1,200.69	1,017.97	4,055.67	3,581.48	5,517.39	4,921.86
2005	1,638.63	1,410.31	4,842.85	4,357.12	6,481.48	5,767.43
2006	1,891.77	1,635.95	5,615.31	4,905.03	7,507.08	6,540.98
2007	2,173.34	1,845.86	6,424.70	5,663.98	8,598.04	7,509.84
2008	2,424.60	2,155.80	6,366.82	6,156.39	8,791.43	8,312.29
2009	1,995.87	1,766.20	6,109.02	5,497.34	8,104.89	7,263.54
2010	2,679.81	2,518.24	8,029.60	7,229.66	10,709.41	9,747.90
2011	3,275.31	2,707.10	9,147.54	8,755.95	12,422.86	11,463.05
2012	3,238.55	2,781.93	9,307.26	9,436.54	12,545.81	12,218.47
2013	3,303.79	2,782.53	9,406.94	9,622.23	12,710.73	12,404.76
2014	3,296.42	2,785.65	9,627.58	9,576.51	12,924.00	12,362.16

Source: ASEAN Merchandise Trade Statistical Database.

Table A.10. The Top 10 Goods in the Import and Export Trade of 10 ASEAN Countries and their Proportions, 2012–2013 (Unit: %)

	2012		2013	
Export	Chapter 85 motor, electrical, audio video equipment and their parts and accessories	20.7	Chapter 85 motor, electrical, audio video equipments and their parts and accessories	21.8
	Chapter 27 mineral fuel, mineral oil and their products; asphalt, etc.	18.1	Chapter 27 mineral fuel, mineral oil and their products; asphalt, etc.	17.3
	Chapter 84 nuclear reactor, boiler, mechanical appliances and parts	11.0	Chapter 84 nuclear reactor, boiler, mechanical appliances and parts	10.9
	Chapter 15 animal and plant oil, grease and wax; refined edible fat and oil	3.5	Chapter 87 vehicles and their parts and accessories, except railway rolling stock	3.2
	Chapter 40 rubber and its products	3.4	Chapter 40 rubber and its products	3.1
	Chapter 87 vehicles and their parts and accessories, except railway rolling stock	3.2	Chapter 39 plastics and their products	3.1
	Chapter 39 plastics and their products	3.0	Chapter 15 animal and plant oil, grease and wax; refined edible fat and oil	3.0
	Chapter 29 organic chemicals	2.9	Chapter 90 optical, photographic, medical and other equipments, parts and accessories	2.6
	Chapter 90 optical, photographic, medical and other equipments, parts and accessories	2.5	Chapter 29 organic chemicals	2.6
	Chapter 71 jewelry, precious metals and products; imitation jewelry; coin	2.3	Chapter 71 jewelry, precious metals and products; imitation jewelry; coin	2.1

(*Continued*)

Table A.10. (*Continued*)

	2012		2013	
Import	Chapter 27 mineral fuel, mineral oil and their products; asphalt, etc.	22.3	Chapter 27 mineral fuel, mineral oil and their products; asphalt, etc.	22.1
	Chapter 85 motor, electrical, audio video equipments and their parts and accessories	19.4	Chapter 85 motor, electrical, audio video equipments and their parts and accessories	20.1
	Chapter 84 nuclear reactor, boiler, mechanical appliances and parts	13.2	Chapter 84 nuclear reactor, boiler, mechanical appliances and parts	12.6
	Chapter 72 iron and steel	3.6	Chapter 72 iron and steel	3.5
	Chapter 87 vehicles and their parts and accessories, except railway rolling stock	3.6	Chapter 39 plastics and their products	3.3
	Chapter 39 plastics and their products	3.2	Chapter 87 vehicles and their parts and accessories, except railway rolling stock	3.3
	Chapter 71 jewelry, precious metals and products; imitation jewelry; coin	2.4	Chapter 71 jewelry, precious metals and products; imitation jewelry; coin	2.7
	Chapter 90 optical, photographic, medical and other equipments, parts and accessories	2.2	Chapter 90 optical, photographic, medical and other equipments, parts and accessories	2.2
	Chapter 29 organic chemicals	2.1	Chapter 29 organic chemicals	2.1
	Chapter 73 steel products	2.0	Chapter 73 steel products	2.0

Note: Based on the goods with double-digit international customs HS code.
Source: *ASEAN Statistical Yearbook 2014*.

Table A.11. Customs Statistics on China's Total Import and Export Trade in Goods with the ASEAN Countries, 2013–2015 (Unit: 100 million USD)

	2013			2014			2015		
Country	Total	Export	Import	Total	Export	Import	Total	Export	Import
ASEAN	4,436.11	2,440.70	1,995.41	4,801.25	2,717.92	2,083.32	4,721.6	2,774.86	1,946.77
Brunei	17.94	17.04	0.9	19.36	17.47	1.90	15.1	14.09	0.97
Myanmar	101.50	73.40	8.1	249.73	93.70	156.03	152.8	96.55	56.25
Cambodia	37.72	34.11	3.62	37.57	32.75	4.83	44.3	37.65	6.67
Indonesia	683.55	369.32	314.22	635.86	390.62	245.25	542.3	343.42	198.88
Laos	27.41	17.20	10.21	36.14	18.43	17.72	27.8	12.27	15.54
Malaysia	1,060.75	459.33	601.43	1,019.75	462.79	556.97	972.9	439.90	533.00
The Philippines	380.66	198.35	182.3	444.43	234.59	209.83	456.5	266.73	189.76
Singapore	759.14	458.64	300.5	796.48	488.46	308.02	795.7	520.08	275.56
Thailand	712.61	327.38	385.23	726.75	343.02	383.73	794.6	382.93	371.70
Vietnam	654.82	485.93	168.9	835.16	636.11	199.05	959.7	661.24	298.42

Source: The website of the Department of Asian Affairs, the Ministry of Commerce of China.

Table A.12. Customs Statistics on the Import and Export Trade in Goods between the Provinces, Autonomous Regions and Municipalities in Chinese Mainland and the ASEAN Countries, 2010–2015 (Unit: 10,000 USD)

	2010				2011		
	Import	Export	Import and export		Import	Export	Import and export
Beijing	450,650	297,370	748,020	Beijing	439,719	279,379	719,098
Tianjin	446,309	322,843	769,151	Tianjin	606,131	439,873	1,046,003
Hebei	102,684	269,094	371,779	Hebei	166,499	380,568	547,067
Shanxi	25,233	33,908	59,141	Shanxi	20,893	45,094	65,988
Inner	6,738	34,485	41,223	Inner	10,457	53,219	63,676
Liaoning	276,959	624,067	901,026	Liaoning	270,014	639,288	909,302
Jilin	17,103	35,625	52,728	Jilin	39,658	33,209	72,867
Heilongjiang	9,400	29,151	38,551	Heilongjiang	14,567	51,800	66,367
Shanghai	2,564,642	1,760,566	4,325,207	Shanghai	3,355,077	1,964,858	5,319,935
Jiangsu	2,890,994	2,284,259	5,175,253	Jiangsu	3,406,850	2,794,084	6,200,934
Zhejiang	682,844	1,381,041	2,063,885	Zhejiang	905,025	1,735,910	2,640,935
Anhui	59,358	95,955	155,313	Anhui	90,168	153,863	244,031
Fujian	545,385	727,908	1,273,293	Fujian	772,931	937,028	1,709,960
Jiangxi	47,620	178,146	225,766	Jiangxi	62,832	185,750	248,582
Shandong	1,386,074	893,596	2,279,670	Shandong	1,968,217	1,185,715	3,153,933

Henan	64,432	170,600	235,032	Henan	106,533	214,283	320,816
Hubei	71,072	190,608	261,680	Hubei	94,051	257,721	351,772
Hunan	15,367	117,995	133,362	Hunan	22,679	155,788	178,467
Guangdong	5,060,282	3,545,368	8,605,649	Guangdong	5,720,937	4,404,287	10,125,224
Guangxi	246,419	131,629	378,049	Guangxi	419,679	207,910	627,589
Hainan	72,249	63,955	136,204	Hainan	107,293	28,340	135,633
Chongqing	44,634	108,205	152,839	Chongqing	219,870	205,676	425,546
Sichuan	80,028	154,628	234,656	Sichuan	123,067	193,452	316,518
Guizhou	32,627	32,530	65,157	Guizhou	44,348	51,945	96,293
Yunnan	146,005	207,646	353,651	Yunnan	217,854	259,474	477,328
Tibet	34	3	37	Tibet	5	27	32
Shaanxi	87,945	84,330	172,275	Shaanxi	63,751	92,545	156,296
Gansu	2,640	12,126	38,530	Gansu	17,279	15,240	32,519
Qinghai	17	736	904	Qinghai	1,310	1,392	2,702
Ningxia	8,246	12,790	21,036	Ningxia	11,416	16,633	28,049
Xinjiang	2,166	14,818	16,984	Xinjiang	2,700	22,708	25,408
Total	15,470,072	13,815,981	29,286,054	Total	19,301,809	17,007,061	36,308,870

(Continued)

Table A.12. (*Continued*)

	2012				2013		
	Import	Export	Import and export		Import	Export	Import and export
Beijing	439,033	342,949	781,982	Beijing	412,817	346,776	759,593
Tianjin	665,132	589,394	1,254,525	Tianjin	774,341	691,390	1,465,730
Hebei	160,447	479,673	640,120	Hebei	185,196	593,756	778,952
Shanxi	31,823	64,857	96,680	Shanxi	23,190	64,211	87,400
Inner	7,693	67,199	74,891	Inner	7,877	70,451	78,328
Liaoning	324,587	721,775	1,046,361	Liaoning	371,672	941,793	1,313,465
Jilin	38,046	39,923	77,969	Jilin	32,057	53,152	85,208
Heilongjiang	9,980	47,377	57,356	Heilongjiang	11,019	83,099	94,118
Shanghai	3,618,885	1,968,248	5,587,133	Shanghai	3,224,585	2,017,121	5,241,706
Jiangsu	3,146,851	3,166,359	6,313,210	Jiangsu	2,733,435	3,348,069	6,081,504
Zhejiang	955,020	1,929,853	2,884,873	Zhejiang	1,048,166	2,270,543	3,318,709
Anhui	65,151	229,821	294,972	Anhui	118,183	272,566	390,749
Fujian	829,124	1,163,785	1,992,909	Fujian	835,038	1,270,166	2,105,204
Jiangxi	57,176	239,742	296,919	Jiangxi	70,762	345,740	416,502
Shandong	1,856,952	1,238,040	3,094,992	Shandong	1,762,718	1,467,854	3,230,572
Henan	251,816	254,227	506,043	Henan	251,354	312,696	564,049

Hubei	105,271	239,417	344,687	Hubei	121,020	369,108	490,128
Hunan	27,293	185,702	212,995	Hunan	26,565	177,123	203,689
Guangdong	5,488,489	5,887,542	11,376,031	Guangdong	5,957,490	7,706,453	13,663,943
Guangxi	323,150	229,859	553,009	Guangxi	340,507	250,470	590,977
Hainan	138,089	57,702	195,791	Hainan	198,716	86,787	285,503
Chongqing	480,506	376,851	857,357	Chongqing	595,856	398,271	994,126
Sichuan	198,751	394,822	593,573	Sichuan	330,057	513,311	843,368
Guizhou	24,002	64,497	88,499	Guizhou	24,610	69,427	94,037
Yunnan	248,297	255,288	503,586	Yunnan	373,364	469,246	842,610
Tibet	1,210	5,584	6,794	Tibet	408	2,070	2,478
Shaanxi	70,064	114,621	184,685	Shaanxi	81,288	132,394	213,682
Gansu	8,644	23,126	31,770	Gansu	20,544	23,805	44,349
Qinghai	4,634	3,952	8,587	Qinghai	8,059	1,712	9,771
Ningxia	6,924	17,166	24,090	Ningxia	9,460	20,538	29,998
Xinjiang	6,121	26,108	32,228	Xinjiang	5,475	33,885	39,360
Total	19,589,161	20,425,458	40,014,619	Total	19,955,829	24,403,982	44,359,811

(*Continued*)

Table A.12. (*Continued*)

	2014				2015		
	Import	Export	Import and export		Import	Export	Import and export
Beijing	424,010	318,939	742,948	Beijing	420,873	307,475	728,347
Tianjin	744,546	794,652	1,539,198	Tianjin	569,690	840,432	1,410,122
Hebei	98,923	848,448	947,372	Hebei	70,451	840,381	910,832
Shanxi	58,288	74,125	132,413	Shanxi	58,135	80,003	138,138
Inner	9,504	114,919	124,423	Inner	18,831	105,956	124,787
Liaoning	315,440	1,004,866	1,320,306	Liaoning	246,504	1,021,944	1,268,448
Jilin	33,439	81,020	114,460	Jilin	34,472	61,161	95,633
Heilongjiang	6,979	83,062	90,040	Heilongjiang	5,934	38,759	44,693
Shanghai	3,032,155	2,147,382	5,179,537	Shanghai	3,090,959	2,000,639	5,091,598
Jiangsu	2,881,626	3,511,915	6,393,540	Jiangsu	2,737,075	3,661,996	6,399,071
Zhejiang	930,809	2,344,508	3,275,318	Zhejiang	831,391	2,446,936	3,278,327
Anhui	155,446	290,227	445,673	Anhui	179,045	304,535	483,580
Fujian	832,386	1,306,365	2,138,751	Fujian	778,599	1,296,789	2,075,388
Jiangxi	77,876	387,690	465,566	Jiangxi	98,044	453,383	551,427
Shandong	1,640,840	1,650,690	3,291,530	Shandong	1,536,231	1,671,815	3,208,047
Henan	251,444	358,469	609,913	Henan	244,638	427,052	671,691

Hubei	168,198	329,662	497,860	Hubei	253,919	332,723	586,643
Hunan	79,603	245,676	325,279	Hunan	53,186	291,455	344,641
Guangdong	6,413,987	8,802,135	15,216,122	Guangdong	5,746,541	9,148,989	14,895,531
Guangxi	318,458	467,258	785,715	Guangxi	958,483	443,745	1,402,228
Hainan	170,267	130,040	300,307	Hainan	161,670	189,184	350,854
Chongqing	1,094,060	422,562	1,516,623	Chongqing	527,460	428,207	955,666
Sichuan	432,656	488,568	921,224	Sichuan	230,808	426,640	657,448
Guizhou	17,059	79,443	96,502	Guizhou	15,403	111,270	126,673
Yunnan	514,242	606,731	1,120,973	Yunnan	488,027	572,170	1,060,197
Tibet	470	743	1,213	Tibet	22	605	627
Shaanxi	87,929	140,029	227,957	Shaanxi	69,422	160,768	230,190
Gansu	22,074	60,766	82,840	Gansu	29,219	25,343	54,562
Qinghai	4,510	5,245	9,755	Qinghai	3,500	3,677	7,176
Ningxia	8,285	42,295	50,581	Ningxia	6,143	21,502	27,645
Xinjiang	5,376	43,916	49,292	Xinjiang	3,063	33,473	36,536
Total	20,830,885	27,182,346	48,013,231	Total	19,467,742	27,749,006	47,216,748

Source: National Customs Information Center. The provinces, autonomous regions and municipalities are arranged in the order of customs codes.

Table A.13. Statistics on the Ranking of the Provinces, Autonomous Regions and Municipalities in Chinese Mainland in Trade with the ASEAN, 2011–2015 (Top 15)

Ranking	2011	2012	2013	2014	2015
1	Guangdong	Guangdong	Guangdong	Guangdong	Guangdong
2	Jiangsu	Jiangsu	Jiangsu	Jiangsu	Jiangsu
3	Shanghai	Shanghai	Shanghai	Shanghai	Shanghai
4	Shandong	Shandong	Zhejiang	Shandong	Zhejiang
5	Zhejiang	Zhejiang	Shandong	Zhejiang	Shandong
6	Fujian	Fujian	Fujian	Fujian	Fujian
7	Tianjin	Tianjin	Tianjin	Tianjin	Tianjin
8	Liaoning	Liaoning	Liaoning	Chongqing	Guangxi
9	Beijing	Chongqing	Chongqing	Liaoning	Liaoning
10	Guangxi	Beijing	Sichuan	Yunnan	Yunnan
11	Hebei	Hebei	Yunnan	Hebei	Chongqing
12	Yunnan	Sichuan	Hebei	Sichuan	Hebei
13	Chongqing	Guangxi	Beijing	Guangxi	Beijing
14	Hubei	Henan	Guangxi	Beijing	Henan
15	Henan	Yunnan	Henan	Henan	Sichuan

Source: National Customs Information Center.

Table A.14. Top 10 Goods in the Import and Export Trade between the ASEAN and China and their Proportions, 2012–2013

	2012		2013	
Export	Chapter 85 motor, electrical, audio video equipments and their parts and accessories	25.3	Chapter 85 motor, electrical, audio video equipments and their parts and accessories	25.8
	Chapter 27 mineral fuel, mineral oil and their products; asphalt, etc.	15.2	Chapter 27 mineral fuel, mineral oil and their products; asphalt, etc.	13.9
	Chapter 84 nuclear reactor, boiler, mechanical appliances and parts	11.4	Chapter 84 nuclear reactor, boiler, mechanical appliances and parts	9.0
	Chapter 40 rubber and its products	8.7	Chapter 40 rubber and its products	8.0
	Chapter 39 plastics and their products	5.9	Chapter 39 plastics and their products	6.1

(*Continued*)

Table A.14. (*Continued*)

	2012		2013	
	Chapter 29 organic chemicals	5.2	Chapter 29 organic chemicals	5.4
	Chapter 15 animal and plant oil, grease and wax; refined edible fat and oil	5.1	Chapter 15 animal and plant oil, grease and wax; refined edible fat and oil	3.7
	Chapter 26 ore sand, slag and ash	2.6	Chapter 26 ore sand, slag and ash	3.6
	Chapter 90 optical, photographic, medical and other equipments, parts and accessories	1.9	Chapter 90 optical, photographic, medical and other equipments, parts and accessories	2.2
	Chapter 44 wood and wood products; charcoal	1.8	Chapter 44 wood and wood products; charcoal	2.2
Import	Chapter 85 motor, electrical, audio video equipments and their parts and accessories	30.2	Chapter 85 motor, electrical, audio video equipments and their parts and accessories	31.5
	Chapter 84 nuclear reactor, boiler, mechanical appliances and parts	21.0	Chapter 84 nuclear reactor, boiler, mechanical appliances and parts	19.5
	Chapter 72 iron and steel	4.7	Chapter 72 iron and steel	4.9
	Chapter 73 steel products	3.5	Chapter 27 mineral fuel, mineral oil and their products; asphalt, etc.	4.1
	Chapter 27 mineral fuel, mineral oil and their products; asphalt, etc.	3.2	Chapter 73 steel products	3.2
	Chapter 39 plastics and their products	2.7	Chapter 39 plastics and their products	2.9
	Chapter 29 organic chemicals	2.1	Chapter 29 organic chemicals	2.1
	Chapter 90 optical, photographic, medical and other equipments, parts and accessories	1.9	Chapter 87 vehicles and their parts and accessories, except railway rolling stock	1.9
	Chapter 87 vehicles and their parts and accessories, except railway rolling stock	1.8	Chapter 90 optical, photographic, medical and other equipments, parts and accessories	1.8
	Chapter 55 chemical fiber short fiber	1.5	Chapter 76 aluminum and its products	1.3

Note: Based on the goods with double-digit international customs HS code.
Source: *ASEAN Statistical Yearbook 2014*.

Table A.15. FDI Inflow to China and 10 ASEAN Countries, 1990–2014 (Unit: Million USD)

Year	1990	1995	2000	2005	2010	2011	2012	2013	2014
Brunei	7.0	582.8	549.6	289.5	625.7	1,208.3	864.8	895.0	567.9
Cambodia	—	150.7	148.5	381.2	782.6	814.5	1,446.5	1,396.0	1,730.4
Indonesia	1,092.0	4,419.0	-4,550.0	8,336.0	13,770.6	19,241.3	19,138.0	18,444.0	22,579.6
Laos	6.0	95.1	33.9	27.7	278.8	300.8	294.4	296.0	720.8
Malaysia	2,611.0	5,815.0	3,787.6	4,065.3	9,060.0	12,197.6	10,073.9	12,305.7	10,799.2
Myanmar	225.1	317.6	208.0	234.9	1,284.6	2,200.0	2,243.0	2,621.0	946.2
The Philippines	550.0	1,459.0	2,240.0	1,664.0	1,070.4	2,007.2	3,215.4	3,859.8	6,200.5
Singapore	5,574.7	11,942.8	15,515.3	18,090.3	55,075.8	50,367.7	61,159.4	63,772.3	67,523.0
Thailand	2,575.0	2,070.0	3,410.1	8,066.6	9,146.8	3,709.6	10,705.3	12,945.6	12,565.7
Vietnam	180.0	1,780.4	1,289.0	1,954.0	8,000.0	7,519.0	8,368.0	8,900.0	9,200.0
ASEAN	12,820.8	28,632.4	22,632.1	43,109.4	99,095.2	99,565.9	117,508.7	125,435.4	132,867.2
China	3,487.1	37,520.5	40,714.8	72,406.0	114,734.0	123,985.0	121,080.0	123,911.0	128,500.0

Source: Table 1 in The World Investment Report 2014. http://unctad.org/en/Pages/DIAE/World%20Investment%20Report/Annex-Tables.aspx.

Table A.16. The Stock of FDI Inflow to China and 10 ASEAN Countries, 1990–2014 (Unit: Million USD)

Year	1990	1995	2000	2005	2010	2011	2012	2013	2014
Brunei	33.1	641.8	3,867.6	9,222.7	11,244.0	12,452.3	13,317.1	14,212.1	6,218.9
Cambodia	37.7	355.9	1,579.9	2,471.0	5,958.4	6,556.3	8,002.8	9,398.8	13,035.0
Indonesia	8,732.5	20,626.5	25,060.5	41,187.0	160,735.1	184,804.0	211,900.0	230,344.0	253,081.7
Laos	12.6	211.5	588.3	680.8	1,887.7	2,188.5	2,482.9	2,778.9	3,630.4
Malaysia	10,318.0	28,730.6	52,747.5	44,459.5	101,620.1	115,064.0	132,399.7	144,705.4	133,767.2
Myanmar	281.1	1,209.7	3,211.0	4,686.0	8,751.5	9,667.2	11,910.2	14,171.0	17,651.9
The	3,267.9	6,729.9	13,762.0	14,978.0	25,896.0	25,479.8	28,687.5	32,547.2	57,093.0
Singapore	30,468.0	65,644.2	110,570.3	237,009.4	622,507.2	673,033.4	796,559.1	837,652.3	912,355.4
Thailand	8,242.2	17,684.4	31,118.0	62,832.6	142,498.2	159,342.7	185,688.8	185,463.1	199,310.9
Vietnam	242.9	5,743.3	14,739.3	22,453.3	56,915.0	64,434.0	72,802.0	81,702.0	90,991.3
ASEAN	61,636.1	147,577.8	257,244.4	439,980.4	1,138,013.2	1,253,022.3	1,463,750.0	1,552,974.8	1,687,452.1
China	20,690.6	101,098.0	193,348.0	272,094.0	587,817.0	711,802.0	832,882.0	956,793.0	1,085,293.0

Source: Table 3 in the World Investment Report 2014. http://unctad.org/en/Pages/DIAE/World%20Investment%20Report/Annex-Tables.aspx.

Table A.17. Top 10 Sources of FDI for the ASEAN, 2013–2015 (Unit: Million USD, %)

	2013		2014		2015	
Source	Amount	Proportion	Amount	Proportion	Amount	Proportion
ASEAN	19,562.2	15.7	22,265.8	17.1	21,938.5	18.4
European	24,511.3	19.6	25,028.5	19.2	19,640.3	16.4
Japan	24,750.2	19.8	15,698.7	12.1	17,324.2	14.5
U.S.A	7,157.2	5.7	14,571.7	11.2	12,184.5	10.2
China	6,426.2	5.1	7,016.4	5.4	8,161.2	6.8
The	4,303.3	3.4	5,744.1	4.4	5,668.9	4.7
Australia	2,587.7	2.1	6,267.6	4.8	5,176.9	4.3
Hong Kong, China	5,251.2	4.2	9,812.8	7.5	3,440.2	2.9
Taiwan, China	1,381.8	1.1	3,257.9	2.5	2,645.8	2.2
New	335.9	0.3	549.9	0.4	2,241.1	1.9
Subtotal	96,267.1	77.1	11,0213.5	84.7	98,421.7	82.4
Other	28,597.4	22.9	19,835.5	15.3	20,990.7	17.6
Total	124,864.5	100.0	130,049.0	100.0	119,412.4	100.0

Source: ASEAN Foreign Direct Investment Statistics Database.

Table A.18. FDI Flow from China to 10 ASEAN Countries, 2006–2013 (Unit: Million USD)

Year	2006	2007	2008	2009	2010	2011	2012	2013	Total
Brunei	4.76	17	0	0	0.01	0	0	0	22
Cambodia	130	165	77	97	127	180	368	287	1,430
Indonesia	124	117	531	359	354	215	335	591	2,625
Laos	5	2	43	36	46	278	0	0	410
Malaysia	-7	70	57	-121	-6	-15	34	133	144
Myanmar	2	349	349	371	1,521	671	482	793	4,537
The Philippines	2.3	-0.1	-0.2	-3.3	0.2	-4	-2	6	-1
Singapore	1,582	1,087	-172	1,090	1,190	5,856	3,409	5,407	19,449
Thailand	26	73	8	25	707	295	561	479	2,174
Vietnam	89	250	53	112	115	383	190	948	2,140
ASEAN	1,958	2,130	947	1,965	4,052	7,858	5,377	8,644	32,930

Source: *ASEAN Statistical Yearbook 2014*, p. 142.

Table A.19. CPI in China and the ASEAN Countries, 2006–2014 (2010 = 100)

Year	2006	2007	2008	2009	2010	2011	2012	2013	2014
Brunei	95.7	96.6	98.6	99.6	100.0	102.0	102.5	102.9	102.7
Cambodia	71.9	77.4	96.8	96.2	100.0	105.5	108.6	111.8	116.1
Indonesia	77.7	82.7	90.7	95.1	100.0	105.4	109.9	116.9	124.4
Laos	83.8	87.6	94.3	94.4	100.0	107.6	112.2	119.3	124.2
Malaysia	90.9	92.7	97.7	98.3	100.0	103.2	104.9	107.1	110.5
Myanmar	53.4	72.2	91.5	92.8	100.0	105.0	106.6	112.4	118.6
The Philippines	83.0	85.4	92.4	96.3	100.0	104.6	108.0	111.2	115.8
Singapore	88.9	90.8	96.7	97.3	100.0	105.3	110.0	112.6	113.8
Thailand	90.6	92.6	97.7	96.8	100.0	103.8	106.9	109.3	111.3
Vietnam	64.4	69.7	85.8	91.9	100.0	118.7	129.5	138.0	143.6
China	87.9	92.1	97.5	96.8	100.0	105.4	108.2	111.1	113.2

Source: The World Bank.

Table A.20. HDI in China and the ASEAN Countries, 1990–2014

Year	1990	2000	2010	2011	2012	2013	2014
Brunei	0.782	0.819	0.843	0.847	0.852	0.852	0.856
Cambodia	0.364	0.419	0.536	0.541	0.546	0.550	0.555
Indonesia	0.531	0.606	0.665	0.671	0.678	0.681	0.684
Laos	0.397	0.462	0.539	0.552	0.562	0.570	0.575
Malaysia	0.641	0.723	0.769	0.772	0.774	0.777	0.779
Myanmar	0.352	0.425	0.520	0.524	0.528	0.531	0.536
The Philippines	0.586	0.623	0.654	0.653	0.657	0.664	0.668
Singapore	0.718	0.819	0.897	0.903	0.905	0.909	0.912
Thailand	0.572	0.648	0.716	0.721	0.723	0.724	0.726
Vietnam	0.475	0.575	0.653	0.657	0.660	0.663	0.666
China	0.501	0.588	0.699	0.707	0.718	0.723	0.727

Note: HDI is based on such important indicators as life expectancy, degree of education and per capita GDP (PPP). In 2013, among 187 countries and territories around the world in HDI, Brunei ranked 31st, Cambodia 143rd, Indonesia 110th, Laos 141st, Malaysia 62nd, Myanmar 148th, the Philippines 115th, Singapore 11th, Thailand 93rd, Vietnam 116th and China 90th.
Source: International Human Development Indicators, http://hdr.undp.org/en/composite/trends.

Index

L

M

N